The Rough Guide to

Peru

There are more than one hundred and fifty Rough Guide titles
covering destinations from Amsterdam to Zimbabwe

Forthcoming titles include
Argentina • Croatia • Ecuador • Southeast Asia

Rough Guide Reference Series
Classical Music • Country Music • Drum 'n' Bass • English Football
European Football • House • The Internet • Jazz • Music USA • Opera
Reggae • Rock Music • Techno • Unexplained Phenomena • World Music

Rough Guide Phrasebooks
Czech • Dutch • Egyptian Arabic • European Languages • French • German
Greek • Hindi & Urdu • Hungarian • Indonesian • Italian • Japanese
Mandarin Chinese • Mexican Spanish • Polish • Portuguese • Russian
Spanish • Swahili • Thai • Turkish • Vietnamese

Rough Guides on the Internet
www.roughguides.com

ROUGH GUIDE CREDITS

Text editor: Geoff Howard
Series editor: Mark Ellingham
Editorial: Martin Dunford, Jonathan Buckley, Jo Mead, Kate Berens, Amanda Tomlin, Ann-Marie Shaw, Paul Gray, Helena Smith, Judith Bamber, Orla Duane, Olivia Eccleshall, Ruth Blackmore, Sophie Martin, Claire Saunders, Gavin Thomas, Alexander Mark Rogers, Polly Thomas, Joe Staines, Lisa Nellis, Andrew Tomičić, Claire Fogg, Richard Lim, Duncan Clark, Peter Buckley (UK); Andrew Rosenberg, Mary Beth Maioli, Don Bapst, Stephen Timblin (US)
Production: Susanne Hillen, Andy Hilliard, Link Hall, Helen Ostick, Julia Bovis, Michelle Draycott,

Katie Pringle, Robert Evers, Niamh Hatton, Mike Hancock, Robert McKinlay
Cartography: Melissa Baker, Maxine Repath, Nichola Goodliffe, Ed Wright
Picture research: Louise Boulton, Sharon Martins
Online editors: Kelly Cross (US)
Finance: John Fisher, Gary Singh, Edward Downey, Mark Hall, Tim Bill
Marketing & Publicity: Richard Trillo, Niki Smith, David Wearn, Jemima Broadbridge, Chloë Roberts (UK); Jean-Marie Kelly, Myra Campolo, Simon Carloss (US)
Administration: Tania Hummel, Charlotte Marriott, Demelza Dallow

ACKNOWLEDGEMENTS

Dilwyn Jenkins would like to thank the following for additional accounts, research and other vital support: John Forrest; Geoff Howard; Kate Berens; John Fisher; Carlos Montenegro; Hector Vega; Graham Preston; Maureen Llewllwyn-Jones; Ignacio and Miranda; Antonio Montenegro; Benjamin and Vera; Peter Frost; Juan Maldonado; Peter Schneider; Wendy Weeks; Marcia Walker; Lieve Coppin; Pablo Rey de Castro; Mirko Fontana Piskulich; Gringo Bill; Rocío Valcárcel; Paul Wright; Jamie Read; Peter Jenson; Julio; Tino; Beder Chavez; Barry and Charo Walker; Lourdes Perez Wicht; Miriam

Galloso; Viviana Diaz; Andres Guiulfo Pons; Viado Soto; Rafael Belmonte (Peru Expeditions); Alberto Cafferata (Pony Expeditions); Juan Carlos Santoyo; and last but certainly not least, my family, who shared the travel and research experience for this edition – Claire, Tess, Bethan, Max and Teilo Jenkins.

The editor would like to thank Elaine Pollard for proofreading; Katie Pringle for smooth typesetting; Melissa Baker and Maxine Repath for cartography; and Kate Berens for last-minute help.

PUBLISHING INFORMATION

This fourth edition published June 2000 by Rough Guides Ltd, 62–70 Shorts Gardens, London, WC2H 9AB.
Distributed by the Penguin Group:
Penguin Books Ltd, 27 Wrights Lane, London W8 5TZ
Penguin Putnam, Inc. 375 Hudson Street, NY 10014, USA
Penguin Books Australia Ltd, 487 Maroondah Highway, PO Box 257, Ringwood, Victoria 3134, Australia
Penguin Books Canada Ltd, 10 Alcorn Avenue, Toronto, Ontario, Canada M4V 1E4
Penguin Books (NZ) Ltd, 182–190 Wairau Road, Auckland 10, New Zealand
Typeset in Linotron Univers and Century Old Style to an original design by Andrew Oliver.
Printed in England by Clays Ltd, St Ives PLC
Illustrations in Part One and Part Three by Edward Briant.

Illustrations on p.1 by Dilwyn Jenkins and p.415 by Henry Iles.
© Dilwyn Jenkins 2000
No part of this book may be reproduced in any form without permission from the publisher except for the quotation of brief passages in reviews.
512pp – Includes index
A catalogue record for this book is available from the British Library
ISBN 1-85828-536-4

The publishers and authors have done their best to ensure the accuracy and currency of all the information in *The Rough Guide to Peru*, however, they can accept no responsibility for any loss, injury, or inconvenience sustained by any traveller as a result of information or advice contained in the guide.

The Rough Guide to

Peru

written and researched by

Dilwyn Jenkins

ROUGH
GUIDES

THE ROUGH GUIDES

TRAVEL GUIDES • PHRASEBOOKS • MUSIC AND REFERENCE GUIDES

 We set out to do something different when the first Rough Guide was published in 1982. Mark Ellingham, just out of university, was travelling in Greece. He brought along the popular guides of the day, but found they were all lacking in some way. They were either strong on ruins and museums but went on for pages without mentioning a beach or taverna. Or they were so conscious of the need to save money that they lost sight of Greece's cultural and historical significance. Also, none of the books told him anything about Greece's contemporary life – its politics, its culture, its people, and how they lived.

So with no job in prospect, Mark decided to write his own guidebook, one which aimed to provide practical information that was second to none, detailing the best beaches and the hottest clubs and restaurants, while also giving hard-hitting accounts of every sight, both famous and obscure, and providing up-to-the-minute information on contemporary culture. It was a guide that encouraged independent travellers to find the best of Greece, and was a great success, getting shortlisted for the Thomas Cook travel guide award,

and encouraging Mark, along with three friends, to expand the series.

The Rough Guide list grew rapidly and the letters flooded in, indicating a much broader readership than had been anticipated, but one which uniformly appreciated the Rough Guide mix of practical detail and humour, irreverence and enthusiasm. Things haven't changed. The same four friends who began the series are still the caretakers of the Rough Guide mission today: to provide the most reliable, up-to-date and entertaining information to independent-minded travellers of all ages, on all budgets.

We now publish more than 150 titles and have offices in London and New York. The travel guides are written and researched by a dedicated team of more than 100 authors, based in Britain, Europe, the USA and Australia. We have also created a unique series of phrasebooks to accompany the travel series, along with an acclaimed series of music guides, and a best-selling pocket guide to the Internet and World Wide Web. We also publish comprehensive travel information on our Web site:

www.roughguides.com

HELP US UPDATE

We've gone to a lot of effort to ensure that the fourth edition of The Rough Guide to Peru is accurate and up-to-date. However, things change – places get "discovered", opening hours are notoriously fickle, restaurants and rooms raise prices or lower standards. If you feel we've got it wrong or left something out, we'd like to know, and if you can remember the address, the price, the time, the phone number, so much the better.

We'll credit all contributions, and send a copy of the next edition (or any other Rough Guide if you prefer) for the best letters. Please mark letters: "Rough Guide Peru Update" and send to:
Rough Guides, 62–70 Shorts Gardens, London WC2H 9AB, or Rough Guides, 4th Floor, 345 Hudson St, New York, NY 10014.
Or send email to: mail@roughguides.co.uk
Online updates about this book can be found on Rough Guides' Web site at www.roughguides.com

THE AUTHOR

Dilwyn Jenkins first travelled to Peru at the age of 18 and has continued to explore the country most years since 1976. He graduated in social anthropology from Cambridge a few years later, worked as a journalist and teacher in South America, and has led expeditions to and made films with indigenous groups in the Peruvian Amazon. Dilwyn also co-writes *The Rough Guide to Brazil*, is a rainforest development consultant and writes endless articles focussing mainly on travel, environmental issues or indigenous affairs. During the 1980s he also led his own tours of Peru. In the 1990s he worked to raise funds and develop projects for Peruvian Non Governmental Organizations to provide legal and practical support to Ashaninka indigenous people. These days he lives with his wife and four children on a smallholding in Wales, where he is director of a company that implements renewable energy projects across the world.

READERS' LETTERS

Thanks to all the readers who took the trouble to write in with their comments on the previous edition (apologies for any omissions or misspellings):

Gina Ambrosini and Martin Kala; Nik Anthony; Michelle Armstrong; Linda Bamford; Mr P. Bear and the Brown family; Rafael Belmonte; Joseph Bowbeer; Maison Bush; Alberto Cafferata; Simon Calder; Peter Cole and Liz Griggs; Tom Crow; Olivia Duncan; Jane Eberhart; P.J. Ellis; Michael Fardell; Bruno Fontaine; R.A. Horne; Trev Johnson and Fiona McPalin; Barb Dumas; Geronimo Madrid; Barry Masters; Paul Meredith; Posie Millet; Elizabeth Pech, Nick Preljlik; Eleanor Rumbal; Judith Samson; Matthew Schwartzberg; Stephen Scott; Vanessa Smith Holburn; Helena Tompkins; B.L. Underwood; Wendy Von Beek; John Wilkinson; T.J. Winnifrith; and Justin Zaman.

CONTENTS

Introduction x

• CHAPTER 3: THE SOUTH   173–244

• CHAPTER 4: ANCASH AND HUÁNUCO   245–283

• CHAPTER 5: TRUJILLO AND THE NORTH   284–356

• CHAPTER 6: THE JUNGLE   357–413

PART THREE CONTEXTS 415

LIST OF MAPS

MAP SYMBOLS

═══	Highway	⁖	Ruins
══	Major road	▮	Fort
──	Minor road	⊻	Viewpoint
═ ═ ═	Dirt track	◖	Cave
─ ─ ─	Path	⌃⌃	Mountain range
▬▬	Railway	▲	Mountain peak
─ ─	Ferry route	ⓘ	Information centre
▬▪▬▪▬	International border	⊠	Post office
─ ─ ─	Chapter division boundary	ℂ	Telephone
────	River	🅢	Bank
✕	Airport	Ⓗ	Hospital
◎	Hotel/Restaurant	★	Public transport stop
⚠	Campsite	▮	Building
◆	Ancient site/Point of interest	✚	Church
⸸	Church (regional maps)	▨	National Park/Reserve
♦	Museum	▨	Park
🏛	Monument		

INTRODUCTION

T he land of gold and of the sun-worshipping Incas, Peru was sixteenth-century Europe's major source of treasure, and once the home of the largest empire in the world. Since then the riches of the Incas have fuelled the European imagination, although in many ways the country's real appeal lies in the sheer beauty of its various landscapes, the abundance of its wildlife, and the strong and colourful character of the people – newly recovered after a period of political upheaval, from the 1980s until the early 1990s, that was as bloody and unpredictable as any during the country's history.

Above all, Peru is the most varied and exciting of all the South American nations. Most people visualize the country as mountainous, and are aware of the great Inca relics, but many are unaware of the splendour of the immense **desert coastline** and the vast tracts of **tropical rainforest**. Dividing these contrasting environments, chain after chain of breathtaking peaks, **the Andes**, over seven thousand metres high and four hundred kilometres wide in places, ripple the entire length of the nation. So distinct are these three regions that it is very difficult to generalize about the country, but one thing for sure is that Peru offers a unique opportunity to experience an incredibly wide range of spectacular scenery, a wealth of heritage, and a vibrant living culture.

The Incas and their native allies were unable to resist the mounted and fire-armed conquerors, and following the Spanish Conquest in the sixteenth century the colony developed by exploiting its Inca treasures, vast mineral deposits and the essentially slave labour which the colonists extracted from the indigenous people. After achieving independence from the Spanish in the early nineteenth century, Peru became a republic in traditional South American style, and although it is still very much dominated by the Spanish and *mestizo* descendants of Pizarro, some ten million Peruvians (more than half the population) are of pure Indian blood. In the country, native life can have changed little in the last four centuries. However, "progress" is gradually transforming much of Peru – already the cities wear a distinctly Western aspect, and roads and tracks now connect almost every corner of the Republic with the industrial *urbanizaciones* that dominate the few fertile valleys along the coast. Only the Amazon jungle – nearly two-thirds of Peru's landmass but with a mere fraction of its population – remains beyond its reach, and even here oil and lumber companies, cattle ranchers, cocaine producers and settlers, are taking an increasing toll.

Always an exciting place to visit, and frantic as it sometimes appears on the surface, the laid-back calmness of the Peruvian temperament continues to underpin life even in the cities. Lima may operate at a terrifying pace at times – the traffic, the money-grabbers, the political situation – but there always seems to be time to talk, for a *ceviche*, another drink . . . It's a country where the resourceful and open traveller can break through complex barriers of class, race, and language far more easily than most of its inhabitants can; and also one in which the limousines and villas of the elite remain little more than a thin veneer on a nation whose roots lie firmly, and increasingly consciously, in its ethnic traditions and the earth itself.

Where to go
With each region offering so many different attractions, it's hard to generalize about the places you should visit first: the specific attractions of each part of Peru are discussed in greater detail in the chapter introductions. Apart from the ostensibly unat-

tractive capital, **Lima**, where you may well arrive, **Cusco** is perhaps the most obvious place to start. It's a beautiful and bustling colonial city, the ancient heart of the Inca Empire, surrounded by some of the most spectacular mountain landscapes and palatial ruins in Peru and magnificent hiking country. Yet along the coast, too, there are fascinating archeological sites – the bizarre **Nazca Lines** south of Lima, the great adobe cities and ceremonial centres of **Chan Chan**, **Túcume** and **Batan Grande** in the north – and a rich crop of sea life, most accessible around the **Paracas National Park**. The coastal towns, almost all of them with superb beaches, also offer nightlife and great food. For mountains and long-distance treks there are the stunning glacial lakes, snowy peaks and little-known ruins of the sierra north of Lima, above all around **Huaraz, Cajamarca and Chachapoyas**. If it's wildlife you're interested in, there's plenty to see almost everywhere. The **jungle**, however, provides startling opportunities for close and exotic encounters. From the comfort of tourist lodges in **Iquitos** to exciting river excursions around the **Manu** reserved areas or **Puerto Maldonado**, the fauna and flora of the world's largest tropical forest can be experienced first-hand perhaps more easily than in any other quarter of the Amazon.

When to go
Picking the **best time to visit** Peru's various regions is complicated by the country's physical characteristics. Summer along the **desert coast** more or less fits the expected image of the southern hemisphere – extremely hot and sunny between December and March (especially in the north), cooler and with a frequent hazy mist between April and November. Sometimes though, in the polluted environs of **Lima**, the coastal winter can get cold enough to require a sweater. Swimming is possible all year round, though the water itself (thanks to the Humboldt Current) is cool-to-cold at the best of times, except for the most northern beaches. To swim or surf for any length of time south of **Máncora**, you'd need to follow local custom and wear a wetsuit. Apart from the occasional shower over Lima it hardly ever rains in the desert. The freak exception, every ten years or so, is when the shift in ocean currents of **El Niño** causes torrential downpours, devastating crops, roads and communities all down the coast. It last broke in 1998, and previous to that in 1983, both times bringing with it the devastation to crops, bridges and any houses constructed in or too close to apparently dry river beds.

In **the Andes**, the seasons are more clearly marked, with heavy rains from December to March and a relatively dry period from June to September, when, although it can be cold at night, it is certainly the best time for **trekking** and most outward-bound activities. Some of the mountain rivers go up a few levels for **rafting and canoeing** in the rainy season, but anyone serious about this should contact the experts in the field for advice on planning an itinerary. And of course, there are always a few sunny weeks in the rainy season and wet ones in the dry. A similar pattern dominates much of **the jungle**, though rainfall here is heavier and more frequent, and it's hot and humid all year round. The lowland rainforest areas around Iquitos have a fairly consistent pattern of rain and sun all year, but they are affected by rising or dropping water levels, according to the rainy season or dry season in the mountains where the headwaters starts. This means that water levels are higher between December and January, which offers distinct advantages for spotting wildlife and access by canoe to remote creeks.

At the risk of over-generalizing then, the coast should be visited around January while it's hot, and the mountains and jungles are at their best after the rains, from May until September, except for the Iquitos region. Since this is unlikely to be possible on a single trip, there's little point in worrying about it – the country's attractions are invariably enough to override the need for guarantees of good weather.

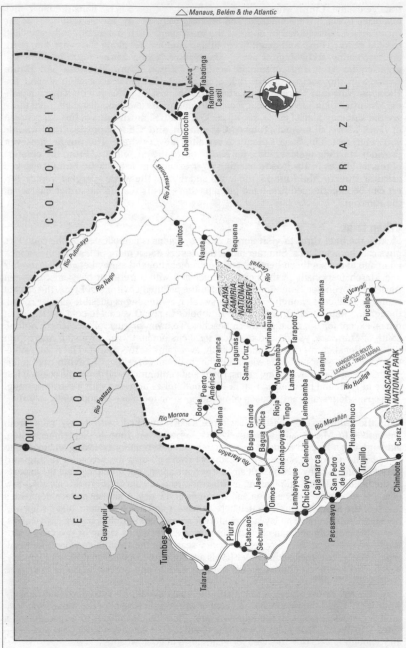

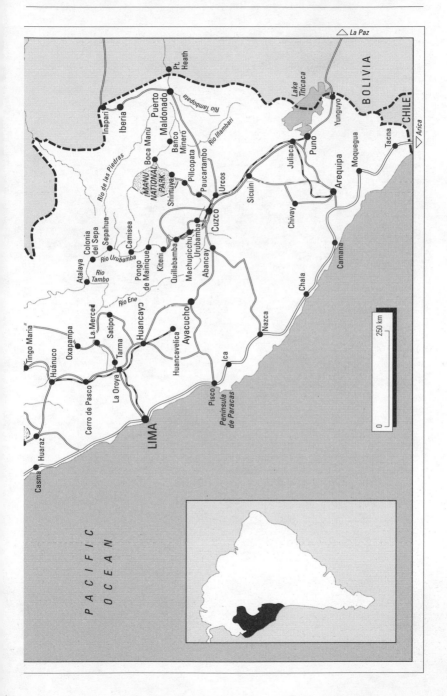

BASICS

GETTING THERE FROM NORTH AMERICA

Most flights from North America to Lima go via Miami. Although prices vary depending on the time of year, and the type of ticket, the main operators seem to hold fares fairly steady. High season is usually mid-December to mid-January and July to mid-August; low season is mid-January to June and mid-August to mid-December.

SHOPPING FOR TICKETS

Barring special offers, the cheapest of the airlines' published fares is usually an **Apex** ticket, although this will carry certain restrictions: you have to book – and pay – at least 21 days before departure, spend at least seven days abroad (maximum stay 3 months), and you tend to get penalized if you change your schedule. Some airlines also issue **Special Apex** tickets to people younger than 24, often extending the maximum stay to a year. Many airlines offer youth or student fares to **under-25s**; a passport or driving licence is sufficient proof of age, though these tickets are subject to availability and can have eccentric booking conditions. It's worth remembering that most cheap return fares involve spending at least one Saturday night away and that many will only give a percentage refund if you need to cancel or alter your journey, so make sure you check the restrictions carefully before buying a ticket.

You can normally cut costs further by going through a **specialist flight agent** – either a **consolidator**, who buys up blocks of tickets from

the airlines and sells them at a discount, or a **discount agent**, who in addition to dealing with discounted flights may also offer special student and youth fares and a range of other travel-related services such as insurance, car rental, tours and the like. Bear in mind, though, that penalties for changing your plans can be stiff.

FLIGHTS FROM THE US

With the exception of Continental's daily non-stop service from Newark to Lima (low season $770; high season $820), all flights to Peru from the US go **via Miami**. Most of the airlines can book connecting flights to Miami from a range of cities throughout the US, and, strangely, fares from New York (via Miami) cost no more than fares from Miami. For example, American's flights **from Miami** to Lima start at around $710 (low season) and rise to $810 in high season, while its twice-daily service **from New York** (via Miami) starts at $770 (low season). Its flights **from Chicago** start at around $950, while flights **from Los Angeles** begin at around $880; both go via Miami. The Peruvian airline Lan Peru offers similar deals, flying daily from Miami to Lima with low-season fares starting at $499 and high season at around $599. There are currently no **flight passes** available, but it's always worth checking.

FLIGHTS FROM CANADA

All **flights from Canada** also go **via Miami,** unless you connect with Continental's flight from Newark (see above). Air Canada can book you all the way through, but there are no great deals to be had, except occasionally through discount travel agents. Flying **from Toronto or Montreal** to Miami with Air Canada, then on to Lima with a US or Peruvian airline (see above for details) will cost from CDN$1400.

PACKAGES AND SPECIALIZED TOURS

There are a huge variety of **tours and packages** on offer from the US to Peru, starting from around $500 for a two- to three-day package and ranging up to $3000–4000. Many of the tours involve some sort of **adventure** element, be it trekking the Inca Trail, whitewater rafting or wildlife photo safaris in the Amazonian jungle. You'll also find a number of packages which include Peru on their itineraries, as part of a longer South American tour.

OVERLAND TO PERU

Although it's virtually impossible to travel overland because of the **Darien Gap** – a section of Panamanian jungle that's uncrossed by road or rail – a few hardy souls manage to jeep, hike, sail or even cycle the swampy route. Bear in mind, though, that a few would-be explorers have met bad ends at the hands of drug smugglers in this area, and the Peruvian consulate strongly advises against attempting the journey.

There are ways, however, to avoid the dangerous Darien Gap, the shortest route being via **San Andres Island** or **Panama City** to mainland Colombia. San Andres is a useful anomaly on international air routes: it's a bit of Colombian territory in the Caribbean just east of Nicaragua, and is served by almost every national airline hereabouts at least daily. Although San Andres is quite remote from Colombian centres – 1600km from Cali, for example – the fact that the onward flight is a domestic one keeps something of a ceiling on fares. Alternatively, you can take a **ferry** or short flight directly from Panama to **Barranquilla** or Cartagena in Colombia. Allow a minimum of a week to travel overland the final 1800km from the Colombian Caribbean coast to the Peruvian frontier.

There are also a number of overland routes from other South American countries. **From Brazil**, you can take the boat ride up the Amazon from Manaus to Iquitos – this is a ten-day ride which,

---

AIRLINES IN NORTH AMERICA

Air Canada ☎1-800/663-3721 in BC; ☎1-800/542-8940 in Alberta, Saskatchewan and Manitoba; ☎1-800/268-7240 in eastern Canada; *www.aircanada.com*

American Airlines ☎1-800/433-7300, *www.aa.com*

Continental ☎1-800/231-0856, *www.flycontinental.com*

Lan Peru ☎1-800/735-5590, *www.lanperu.com*

United Airlines ☎1-800/538-2929, *www.ual.com*

NORTH AMERICAN DISCOUNT AGENTS AND TRAVEL CLUBS

Air Brokers International, 323 Geary Street, Suite 411, San Francisco, CA 94102 (☎1-800/883-3273 or ☎415/397-1383, *www.airbrokers.com*). Consolidator and specialist in round-the-world tickets.

Air Courier Association, 15000 W. Sixth Avenue Golden, CO 80401 (☎303/278-8810, *www.aircourier.org*). Courier flight broker.

Council Travel, 205 E 42nd Street, New York, NY 10017 (☎212/822-2700 or ☎608/256-5551) and branches in many other US cities. Student/budget travel agency.

Educational Travel Center, 438 N Frances Street, Madison, WI 53703 (☎1-800/747-5551 or ☎608/256-5551, *edtrav.com*). Student/youth and consolidator fares.

Moment's Notice, 7301 New Utrecht Ave, Brooklyn, NY 11204 (☎718/234-6295 or ☎888/241-3366, *moments-notice.com*). Discount travel club.

Now Voyager, 74 Varick Street, Suite 307, New York, NY 10013 (☎212/431-1616, *www.nowvoyager.com*). Courier flight broker and consolidator.

Skylink, 265 Madison Ave, fifth floor, New York, NY 10016 (☎1-800/AIR-ONLY or ☎212/599-0430) with branches in Chicago, Los Angeles, Toronto, and Washington DC. Consolidator.

STA Travel, 10 Downing Street, New York, NY 10014 (☎1-800/777-0112 or ☎212/627-3111, *www.sta-travel.com*), and other branches in the Los Angeles, San Francisco and Boston areas. Worldwide discount travel firm specializing in student/youth fares; also student IDs, travel insurance, car rental etc.

TFI Tours International, 34 W 32nd Street, New York, NY 10001 (☎1-800/745-8000 or ☎212/736-1140), and other offices in Las Vegas and Miami. Consolidator.

Travel CUTS, 187 College Street, Toronto, ON M5T 1P7 (☎416/979-2406, *travelcuts.com*), and other branches all over Canada. Organization specializing in student fares, IDs and other travel services.

Worldtek Travel, 111 Water Street, New Haven, CT 06511 (☎1-800/243-1723 or ☎203/772-0470; *www.worldtek.com*). Discount travel agency for worldwide travel.

Andina Tours and Travel, 9805 NE 116th Street, Suite 7225, Kirkland, WA 98043-4248 (☎206/820-9966). Customized tours to Peru, including airfare, transfers, accommodation, meals and excursions.

Brazil Nuts, 1150 Post Road, Fairfield, CT 06430 (☎1-800/553-9959 or ☎203/259-7900, www.brazilnuts.com). Specializes in tours to Brazil, but can also do tailor-made add-ons in Peru.

eXito, 5699 Miles Avenue, Oakland, CA 94618 (☎1-800/655-4053, fax 510-655-4566, exito@ wonderlink.com). Latin American specialists in cut-rate fares, student tickets, year-long tickets, land packages and tours, with savings of up to 40% off regular fares. Good for travel advice.

Himalayan Travel, 110 Prospect Street, Stamford, CT 06901 (☎1-800/225-2380). A variety of tours – the 15-day "Inca Empire" package includes La Paz, Lima, Cusco, hiking the Inca Trail, Puno, Lake Titicaca and a hydrofoil back to La Paz, for $1195.

Holbrook Travel, 3540 NW 13th Street, Gainsville, FL 32609 (☎1-800/451-7111 or ☎352/377-7111, www.holbrooktravel.com). All-inclusive natural history and cultural tours, for 7 or 12 days, with certified local guides or US experts.

Journeys, 107 April Drive, Ann Arbor, Michigan 48103 (☎1-800/255-8735 or ☎734/665-4407, www.journeys-intl.com). A variety of packages, including an 8-day Sacred Valley Exploration, with hiking, nature watch and rafting in Cusco, Urubamba, Pisac and Machu Picchu for $1445, excluding airfare.

Latour, 630 Third Avenue, New York, NY 10017 (☎1-800/825-0825 or ☎212-370-4007). Specializes in 2- and 3-night packages in Cusco, with an excursion to Machu Picchu, starting at $515.

Latin American Reservation Centre, 902 Valentina Drive, Dundee, FL 33838 (☎1-800/327-3573 or ☎863/439-2118). Puts together individual itineraries, based on personal interests.

Nature Expeditions International, 7860 Peters Road, Suite F-103, Plantation, FL 33324 (☎1-800/869-0639 or ☎954/693-8852, fax 954/0693-8854, Natur@aol.com, www.naturexp.com). Pioneers in wildlife, natural history and cultural expeditions, NEI

specialize in creating distinctive itineraries, led by expert guides, arranging tours to Cusco, Machu Picchu and the Amazon rainforest, by land or on a cruise.

Overseas Adventure Travel, 625 Mt Auburn Street, Cambridge, MA 02138 (☎1-800/221-0814, www.oatravel.com). A variety of tours, including the 15-day "Four Worlds of the Andes" package, with stops in La Paz, Cusco, Lima, Machu Picchu, Lake Titicaca and the Amazon, for $2598 including airfare from Miami.

Peru Tourist Centre, 130 W 42nd Street, Suite 401, New York, NY 10036 (☎212/398-6555). Doesn't sell its own packages, but works with many different tour operators to provide information about a wide range of holidays.

University Research Expeditions Program, 2223 Fulton Street, Desk H22, Berkeley, CA 94720-7050 (☎530/753-0692, www.urep.ucdavis.edu). Offers research trips to lay travellers, on subjects such as exploring the origins of the Andes, and excavating the prehistoric villages of Lake Titicaca; prices start from $1085.

Safaricentre, 3201 North Sepuneda Blvd, Manhattan Beach, CA 90266 (☎1-800/223-6046 or ☎310/546-4411, www.safaricentre.com). Land-only packages, including a classic Cusco, and Machu Picchu trip for $860 and a 5-day Inca Trail trek for $725.

Sunny Land Tours, 166 Main Street, Hackensack, NJ 07601 (☎201/487-2150 or ☎800/783-7839, sunnylandtours.com). Offers an 11-day Inca Trail trek, including 5 days' walking, one day whitewater rafting and city tours of Lima, Cusco and Pisac for about $2000.

Voyagers International, PO Box 915, Ithaca, NY 14851 (☎ 1-800/633-0299). Nature, cultural and photography trips for 12 to 21 days, including visits to Machu Picchu, Cusco, Arequipa, Tambopata and Colca Canyon; prices start at $2500 without airfare.

Wilderness Travel, 1102 Ninth Street, CA 94710 (☎1-800/368-2794 or ☎510/548-0420). A variety of programmes in Peru, from 9-day hotel-based holidays to 24-day camping and trekking trips, some of which include Bolivia in the itinerary, plus Inca trail tours culminating in the June solstice Inti Raymi festival in Cusco. Prices range from $1595 to $3295 excluding airfares.

if you're prepared for a few discomforts (such as unexciting food and frequently overcrowded boats), can prove to be a memorable experience. Take a hammock and plenty of reading material. From Brazil's western Amazon department of Río Acre, there is a relatively simple entry by bus along jungle roads to Puerto Maldonado in southeast Peru; from here you can go by road or fly to Cusco and on to Lima.

A more commonly followed overland route arrives in southern Peru **from Bolivia**. The trip simply requires catching a bus, either direct or in stages, from La Paz across the *altiplano* to Copacabana on Lake Titicaca and on to Puno or even straight to Cusco (see Chapter Three, p.241, for details). **From Chile** it's also an easy bus ride, across the southern border from Arica to Tacna, which has good connections with Lima and

Arequipa. **From Ecuador**, there are two routes, the most popular being a scenic coastal route, starting by road from Huaquillas, crossing the border at Aguas Verdes then a short bus or taxi ride on to Tumbes, from where there are daily buses and flights to Chiclayo, Trujillo and Lima. An alternative crossing, also by a rather scenic road, comes into Peru from Macára in Ecuador over the frontier to La Tina, from where there are daily buses to Sullana on the coast. An almost unused but eminently practical route, enters Peru **from Colombia** by river or air at Leticia, at the three-way frontier where Peru, Brazil and Colombia touch. From Leticia there are speedboats up the Río Amazonas more or less daily to Iquitos, and light aircraft which leave from just across the river at the Peruvian port of Santa Rosa, a couple of times a week for Iquitos (see Chapter 6, pp.412 & 413 for details).

GETTING THERE FROM BRITAIN

The most common way to get from Britain to Peru is to fly into Lima. High season for flights is December, July and August; low season is September to November and January to June.

FLIGHTS FROM BRITAIN

There are no **direct flights** from Britain to Peru, and getting there always involves a stopover and more often than not a change of planes either in

Europe or America. From Heathrow you can expect the journey to take anything between 16 and 22 hours, depending on the routing and stopovers. The permutations are endless, but the most common routes are via Amsterdam on KLM, via Madrid on Iberia, via Frankfurt on Lufthansa or via Caracas on Viasa. There are also, of course, innumerable flights via the States – all of which involve changing planes in Miami, except the Continental flight, which offers excellent value (as low as £400 out of season) and follows some unusual routings including Gatwick to Houston/Houston to Lima with no overnight stay and less than two hours between connections; Contintental also offer occasional routings via New York and Miami.

Fares vary almost as much as routings, and you'd be well advised to go to a specialist to check out what's on offer – there's also a wide range of limitations on the tickets (fixed-date returns within 3 months, yearly returns, Apex, etc), and options such as "open-jaw" flights (flying into Lima and home from Rio, for example). Having established the going rate, you can always check these prices against those on offer at bucket shops and other travel agents. Fares from London start at around

£520 in the low season (£650 in high season) for a fixed-date return within three months; if you hunt around, however, you may be able to get a return ticket for as low as £480 in April or May.

Some of the best **specialist operators**, like Journey Latin America, are listed here, but it's also worth checking through the classified ads in magazines and newspapers, where the cheapest of flights sometimes crop up. The best deals can usually be found advertised in the London listings magazines like *Time Out* and *City Limits* or in any of the national papers, particularly the Sundays. Children under 12 can sometimes get half fare, while students, school children, and anyone under 26, may be eligible for special fares – contact STA or Campus Travel for details.

It's best to avoid buying international air tickets in Peru, where prices are inflated by a high tax (and are not cheap to begin with). If you're uncertain of your return date, it will probably still work out cheaper to pay the extra for an open-ended return than to buy a single back from Peru.

AIRLINES IN BRITAIN

Continental ☎0800/776464.
Iberia ☎020/7830-0011.
KLM ☎08705/074 074.

Lufthansa ☎0345/737747.
Viasa contact Iberia for details.

FLIGHT AGENTS IN BRITAIN

Journey Latin America, 12–13 Heathfield Terrace, London W4 4JE (☎020/8747 3108, *sales@journeylatinamerica.co.uk*). Good fares and adept at multiple stops, stopovers, open jaws etc. Also offers package tours, see below.

STA Travel, 86 Old Brompton Road, London SW7 3LH; 117 Euston Road, London NW1 2SX; 38 Store Street, London WC1E 7BZ; 11 Goodge Street, London W1P 1FE (Europe ☎020/7361 6161, worldwide ☎020/7361 6262); 38 North Street, Brighton (☎01273/728 282); 25 Queens Road, Bristol BS8 1QE (☎0117/929 4399); 38 Sidney Street, Cambridge CB2 3HX (☎01223/366 966); 75 Deansgate, Manchester M3 2BW (☎0161/834 0668); 88 Vicar Lane, Leeds LS1 7JH (☎0113/244 9212); 78 Bold Street, Liverpool L1 4HR (☎0151/707 1123); 9 Street Mary's Place, Newcastle-upon-Tyne NE1 7PG (☎0191/233 2111); 36 George Street, Oxford OX1 2OJ (☎01865/792 800); 27 Forrest Road, Edinburgh (☎0131/226 7747); 184 Byres Road, Glasgow G1 1JH (☎0141/338 6000); 30 Upper Kirkgate, Aberdeen (☎0122/465 8222); *www.statravel.co.uk*; and branches on university campuses in London, Birmingham, Bristol, Canterbury, Cardiff, Coventry, Durham, Glasgow, Leeds, Loughborough, Nottingham, Sheffield and Warwick. Worldwide specialists in low-cost flights and tours for students and under-26s, though other customers welcome.

Steamond Travel, 23 Eccleston Street, London SW1 (☎020/7730-8646). Flights with most main carriers, including KLM, Iberia, American Airlines and Varig (for routes via Brazil and Rio de Janeiro).

The Travel Bug, 125 Gloucester Road, London, SW7 4SF (☎020/7835-2000); 597 Cheetham Hill Road, Manchester M8 5EJ (☎0161/721-4000); *www.flynow.com*. Large range of discounted tickets.

Usit Campus, national call centre ☎0870/240-1010, *www.usitcampus.co.uk*; 52 Grosvenor Gardens, London SW1W 0AG (Europe ☎020/7730-3402, North America ☎020/7730-2101, world-wide ☎020/7730-8111); 541 Bristol Road, Selly Oak, Birmingham B29 6AU (☎0121/414-1848); 61 Ditchling Road, Brighton BN1 4SD (☎01273/570226); 37–39 Queen's Road, Clifton, Bristol BS8 1QE (☎0117/929-2494); 5 Emmanuel Street, Cambridge CB1 1NE (☎01223/324283); 53 Forest Road, Edinburgh EH1 2QP (☎0131/225-6111, telesales 668-3303); 122 George Street, Glasgow G1 1RF (☎0141/553-1818); 166 Deansgate, Manchester M3 3FE (☎0161/833-2046, telesales 273-1721), 105–106 Street Aldates, Oxford OX1 1DO (☎01865/242 067). Student/youth travel specialists, with branches also in YHA shops and on university campuses all over Britain.

Wexas International, 45–49 Brompton Road, Knightsbridge, London SW3 1DE (☎020/7589-3315, fax 7589-8418, *mship@wexas.com*). The World Expeditionary Association, a well-established travel club, offers flights at reduced prices for members.

PACKAGES AND SPECIALIZED TOURS

Adventure tours are often good value, though they can be limiting – you'll see only what's in the itinerary – but they do provide a considerable degree of comfort and peace of mind. Always check in advance about what's included – many only provide guides, planning and in-country transport costs, others may have their own vehicles and camping equipment. Other **specialist companies** organize **treks** and **overland travel**, often based around some special interest, such as the rainforest, native culture or Inca sites, offering a far better opportunity to get to know the country. Some of the best of these operators are listed

SPECIALIST TOUR OPERATORS

Encounter Overland, 267 Old Brompton Road, London SW5 9JA (☎020/7370-6845). Operates longhaul overland group trips around South America, which spend at least a couple of weeks visiting Peru's major sites. Good value and good fun.

Exodus Expeditions, 9 Weir Road, London SW12 0LT (☎020/8675-5550, brochure requests ☎020/8673-08590, *sales@exodustravels.co.uk*). Well-organized truck tours, such as the 24-day Inca Royal Highway, in addition to some excellent treks in various regions of Peru at different levels of difficulty. Good value.

Explore Worldwide, 1 Frederick Street, Aldershot, Hants GU11 1LQ (☎01252/760000, *www.explore.co.uk*). Operates 3 tours in Peru, 2 of which include a visit to Bolivia. The tours are mainly walking holidays with a tour leader and the prices, which are very reasonable, include a return flight from the UK.

Guerba Expeditions, Wessex House, 40 Station Road, Westbury, Wiltshire, BA13 3JN (☎01373/826611, fax 858351). Runs 1- to 3-week tours, mainly using local transport and staying in small family-run hotels. Some trips include trekking and camping with Spanish-speaking tour leaders and local guides. Also has an extensive Amazon programme visiting the jungle of Madre de Dios via Puerto Maldonado, as well as treks offering whitewater rafting.

Journey Latin America (see box on previous page for address). Experienced tour operator using well-informed Spanish-speaking tour guides to accompany small groups, mostly on local transport. Operates a number of tours, some of which include Peru as part of a larger itinerary, and most of which have an option for doing the Inca Trail. Very good value.

Reef and Rainforest Tours, 1 The Plains, Totnes, Devon TQ9 5DR (☎01803/866965, fax 865916). Specializes in 14-day tours to the Manu Biosphere Reserve in the Amazon, involving several nights in the rainforest. The tours are very good for wildlife and well organized, but quite expensive.

Thomas Cook Holidays, PO Box 5, 12 Coningsby Road, Peterborough PE3 8XP (☎01733/330200). These are the most expensive of the tours to Peru, but offer the best quality travel and accommodation facilities.

Trailfinders, 1 Threadneedle Street, London EC2R 8JX (☎020/7628-7628); 42–50 Earls Court Road, London W8 6FT (☎020/7938-3366); 194 Kensington High Street, London, W8 7RG (☎020/7938-3939); 215 Kensington High Street, London W6 6BD (☎020/7937-5400); 58 Deansgate, Manchester M3 2FF (☎0161/839 6969); 254–284 Sauchiehall Street, Glasgow G2 3EH (☎0141/353 2224); 22–24 The Priory Queensway, Birmingham B4 6BS (☎0121/236 1234); 48 Corn Street, Bristol BS1 1HQ (☎0117/929 9000); *www.trailfinders.co.uk*. One of the best-informed and most efficient agents for independent travellers; they produce a very useful quarterly magazine worth scrutinising for round-the-world routes (for a free copy call ☎020/7938-3366).

Travelbag Adventures, 15 Turk Street, Alton Hampshire, GU34 1AG; ☎01420/541007, fax 541022, *info@travelbag-adventures.co.uk*, *www.travelbag-adventures.co.uk*; direct bookings on ☎01420/541007, *sales@travelbag-adventures.co.uk*). Three-week or longer tours incorporating the Inca Trail and Lake Titicaca; also on offer are shorter tours that don't involve trekking.

The Adventure Travel Centre, 131–135 Earls Court Road, London SW5 9RH (☎020/7370-4555). From 15- to 105-day tours, most including some time in Bolivia. They have their own expedition vehicles and tend to choose mid-range hotels.

Trips Worldwide, 9 Byron Place, Clifton, Bristol BS8 1JT (☎0117/987-2626; fax 987-2627). A wide range of other tours.

BY SEA

There are various options now having been slow to reappear after the economic doldrums of the late 1980s, mainly with a handful of freighters who cross the Atlantic. They can be booked through one of a few specialized agencies. The cargo-carrying Polish Ocean Line takes passengers from **Hamburg to Lima**, sometimes via Felixstowe, but it's a long four-week trip costing in the region of £2000. Pricier, the Panamanian shipping company Promotora de Navigacion sails regularly from Vancouver, Seattle and Los Angeles, but you have to book your own flights to the US. Either option is likely to cost considerably more than simply taking a plane. Contact Hamburg-Sud, Hamburg, Germany (fax 49/40-37052420) and the Strand Cruise Centre, Charing Cross Shopping Concourse, The Strand, London WC2N 4HZ (☎020/7836-6363; fax 7497-0078), for further information on both the above services.

GETTING THERE FROM AUSTRALIA & NEW ZEALAND

FLIGHTS FROM AUSTRALIA AND NEW ZEALAND

Only two flight seasons operate with trips to South America. **High season** runs from December to February, and **low season** is the rest of year. With some airlines, there is no season variation – the price changes according to the length of your time away.

Currently the **cheapest return scheduled fare to Lima** is with Aerolineas Argentinas, who fly twice weekly from Sydney in low season and

Scheduled flights to Peru from this part of the world to Lima are rather limited and tend to involve changing planes somewhere in the Pacific or Los Angeles. High season is December to February; low season is the rest of the year, but prices also vary depending on how long you stay (between a minimum of 21 days and a maximum of a year). There is no Peruvian Tourist Office as such in Australia or New Zealand, but Destination Travel, 34A Main Street, Croydon, Victoria (☎03/9725-4655), can provide information about all aspects of travel to South America.

AIRLINES IN AUSTRALIA AND NEW ZEALAND

Aerolineas Argentinas, Level 2, 580 George Street, Sydney (☎02/9283-3660, *www.aerolineas.com.au*); Fifth Floor, ASB Centre, 135 Albert Street, Auckland (☎09/379-3675, *www.aerolineas.co.nz*).

Air New Zealand 139 Queen Street, Auckland (☎0800/737000 or ☎09/357-3000); 5 Elizabeth Street, Sydney (☎13/2476); *www.airnz.co.nz*.

Lan Chile Airlines, 64 York Street, Sydney (☎02/9244-2333); Level 3, 87 Queen Street, Auckland (☎09/309-8673); *www.lanchile.cl*.

Qantas, 70 Hunter Street, Sydney (☎13/1313); 154 Queen Street, Auckland (☎09/357-8900 or ☎0800/808767); *www.qantas.com.au*.

United Airlines, 10 Barrack Street, Sydney (☎131 777); 5–7 City Road Auckland (☎09/379 3800); *www.ual.com*.

FLIGHT AGENTS AND TOUR OPERATORS

Adventure Travel Company, 64 Parnell Road, Parnell, Auckland (☎09/379-9755, *advakl@hot.co.nz*); First Floor, Lambton Square, Lambton Quay, Wellington (☎04/494-7180, *advwlg@hot.co.nz*); 60 Oxford Street, Christchurch (☎03/379 7134; *advchc@hot.co.nz*)

Anywhere Travel, 345 Anzac Parade, Kingsford, Sydney (☎02/9663-0411, *anywhere@ozemail.com.au*).

Budget Travel 16 Fort Street, Auckland; other branches around the city (☎09/366-0061, toll-free ☎0800/80040); *www.budgettravel.co.nz*.

Destinations Unlimited Seventh Floor FAI Building 220 Queen Street Auckland (☎09/373-4033); 13 Clyde Road Browns Bay Auckland (☎09/478-5042); *www.travel-nz.com*.

Flight Centre Australia: branches nationwide (☎13/1600 for your nearest office). New Zealand: National Bank Towers, 205–225 Queen Street, Auckland (☎0800/354448); plus branches nationwide; *www.flightcentre.com*.

Harvey World Travel, 631 Princes Highway, Kogarah, Sydney (☎02/9567-6099 or ☎13/2757); *www.harveyworld.com.au*. Branches nationwide.

National World Travel, Level One, 1 McLaren Street, North Sydney (☎13/1435; *www.natworldtravel.com.au*).

Northern Gateway, 22 Cavenagh Street, Darwin (☎08/8941-1394).

Passport Travel, Suite 11, 401 Street Kilda Road, Melbourne (☎03/9867-3888 or ☎1800/337031, fax 03/9867-1055, *www.travelcentre.com.au*)

STA Travel Australia: 256 Flinders Street, Melbourne (☎03/9654-7266); 855 George Street, Sydney (☎02/9212-1255 or toll-free ☎1800/637444); other offices in state capitals and major universities (☎1300/360960 or *www.statravelaus.com.au* for details). New

Zealand: Travellers' Centre, 10 High Street, Auckland (☎09/309-0458); 90 Cashel Street, Christchurch (☎03/379-9098); 130 Cuba Street, Wellington (☎04/385-0561); other offices in Dunedin, Palmerston North, Hamilton and major universities (*www.statravel.co.nz* for details).

Thomas Cook Australia: 257 Collins Street, Melbourne (☎03/9282-0222 or ☎13/1771); 175 Pitt Street, Sydney (☎02/9231-2877 or ☎1800/801002); branches in other state capitals. New Zealand: 159 Queen Street, Auckland (☎09/379-3924 or ☎0800/353535).

Topdeck Travel, 65 Glenfell Street, Adelaide (☎08/8232 7222).

Trailfinders, 8 Spring Street, Sydney (☎02/9247-7666, *www.trailfinders.com.au*).

Travel.com, 80 Clarence Street, Sydney (☎02/9290-1500, *www.travel.com.au*).

Tymtro Travel, 428 George Street, Sydney (☎02/9223-2211).

USIT Beyond, corner of Shortland Street and Jean Batten Place, Auckland (☎09/379-4224); plus offices in Hamilton, Palmeston North, Wellington and Christchurch; *www.usitbeyond.co.nz*.

UTAG Travel, 122 Walker Street, North Sydney (☎02/9956-8399 or ☎13/1398); plus agencies throughout Australia; *www.utag.com.au*.

YHA Travel Centres 38 Stuart Street, Adelaide (☎08/8231-5583); 154 Roma Street, Brisbane (☎07/3236-1680); 191 Dryandra Street, O'Connor, Canberra (☎02/6248-0177); 69a Mitchell Street, Darwin (☎08/8981-2560); 28 Criterion Street, Hobart (☎03/6234-9617); 83 Hardware Lane, Melbourne (☎03/9670-9611); 236 William Street, Northbridge, Perth (☎08/9227-5122); 422 Kent Street, Sydney (☎02/9261-1111); *www.yha.com.au*.

---

three times a week in high season via Auckland and Buenos Aires, with connecting flights to Lima. Fares start at A$1900/NZ$1900 rising to around A$2600/NZ$2600 in high season. Air New Zealand fly to LA (from A$1450/NZ$1600, depending on length of stay and date of departure) from Australia and New Zealand, but have no connections to Peru. Quantas have four flights a week from Sydney and Auckland (two code-

sharing) to Buenos Aires, with connecting flights to Lima; prices start at A$1900/A$2500 from Sydney and NZ$1900/NZ$2500 from Auckland. Lan Chile offer three flights a week in high season (two in low season) from Sydney via Auckland to Lima; their cheapest tickets are 45-day returns at A$2200/2500, NZ$2150/2350. Daily flights from Sydney, Melbourne or Auckland to LA with a connecting flight to Lima. United Airlines, who fly

SPECIALIST AGENTS

Adventure Associates 197 Oxford Street, Bondi Junction, Sydney (☎02/9389-7466 or ☎1800/222141, *www.adventureassociates.com*). Tours to South America, Mexico & Antarctica. City and day tours and a selection of archeological/natural history tours from Lima.

Adventure World, 73 Walker Street, North Sydney (☎02/9956-7766 or ☎1800/221931, *www.adventureworld.com.au*); plus branches in Brisbane and Perth; 101 Great South Road, Remuera, Auckland (☎09/524-5118, *www.adventureworld.co.nz*).

Austral Tours, 118 Queen Street, Melbourne (☎03/9600-1733 or ☎1800/620822, *www.australtours.com*). Long-established South American specialist.

Australian Andean Adventures, Shop P33, Imperial Arcade, Pitt Street, Sydney (☎02/923-1889). Can organize South American trekking expeditions.

Contours, Level One, 84 Williams Street, Melbourne. (☎03/9670-6900). They are able to arrange special interest tours for the independent traveller.

Inca Tours 3 Margaret Street, Wyong, NSW (☎02/4351-2133 or ☎1800/024955, fax 02/4351-2526, *www.southamerica.com.au*). Established South American specialist offering a variety of tours, from backpacker to upmarket, groups to tailor-made holidays.

Peregrine Second Floor, 258 Lonsdale Street, Melbourne (☎03/9662-2700, fax 9662-2422, *travelcentre@peregrine.net.au*); First Floor, 132 Wickham Street, Fortitude Valley Brisbane (☎07/3854-1022, fax 3854-1079, *peregrin@eis.net.au*); First Floor, 192 Rundle Street, Adelaide (☎08/8223-5905, fax 8223-5347, *peretrav@camtech.net.au*); First Floor, 862 Hay Street, Perth (☎08/9321-1259, fax 9481-7375, *peregrinewa@tpg.com.au*); Fifth Floor, 38 York Street, Sydney (☎02/9290-2770, 9290-2155); *www.peregrine.net.au*. See Adventure World (above) for their agent in New Zealand. Offers a 16-day Inca Highland Trek from Lima, exploring La Paz and Lake Titicaca before setting out on a horse-trek through the Andes to Machu Picchu.

South American Adventures, 169 Unley Road, Unley, Adelaide (☎08/8272-2010). Experienced agents in travel around Peru. They can arrange tours or independent travel packages.

Panorama/South American Travel Centre, 69 Liverpool Street, Sydney (☎02/9264-6397; *panorama@wr.com.au*). Travel agent specializing in tours to South America and Peru.

South America Travel Centre, 104 Hardware Street, Melbourne (☎1800/655-051 or ☎03/9642-5353); Specialize in organizing trips for independent travellers.

South American Travel Services, Level One, 293 Queen Street, Brisbane (☎07/3002-7171, fax 3229-3334, *travel@travelconnexions.com.au*). Offers a good range of tours to Peru and South America.

World Expeditions Third Floor, 441 Kent Street, Sydney (☎02/9264 3366, fax 9261-1974, *enquiries@worldexpeditions.com.au*); Shop 2, 36 Agnes Street, Fortitude Valley Brisbane (☎07/3216-0823, fax 3216-0827, *adventure@worldexpeditions.com.au*); First Floor, 393 Little Bourke Street, Melbourne (☎03/9670-8400, fax 9670-7474, *travel@worldexpeditions.com.au*); 21 Remuera Road, Newmarket, Auckland (☎09/522-9161, fax 522-9162; *enquiries@worldexpeditions.co.nz*); *www.worldexpeditions.com.au*. Long-established adventure tour specialist, with regular free slide shows and talks on Peru.

Wiltrans, 189 Kent Street, Sydney (☎02/9255-0899). Cruises, with shore excursions, along the coast of Peru and other South American countries.

daily from Melbourne via Sydney, Auckland and Los Angeles (stopovers in the US available) have fares that start at A$2320/NZ$2700 for a maximum stay of 45 days and range up to A$3920/NZ$4600 for a six-month return in high season, with connecting flights to Lima.

Round-the-world (RTW) tickets including Peru can work out very good value. Aerolineas Argentinas, in combination with other airlines, allow you to stop up to four places in South America from A$3200/NZ$3200.

All the Peruvian domestic airlines offering **flight passes** went bust in the late 1990s, and airline companies are in a state of flux in Peru. As new ones arrive and competition for passengers increases, passes are likely to become available again, and it's worth checking with your travel agent or with the major airlines on arrival in Peru.

RED TAPE AND VISAS

EU, US, Canadian, Australian and New Zealand citizens can all currently stay in Peru as tourists for up to ninety days without a visa. However, the situation does change periodically, so always check with your local Peruvian embassy some weeks before departure.

All nationalities, however, need a **tourist or embarkation card** *(tarjeta de embarque)* to enter Peru, issued at the frontiers or on the plane before landing in Lima. Tourist cards are usually valid for between sixty to ninety days – only sixty for US citizens. In theory you have to show an outbound ticket (by air or bus) before you'll be given a card, but this isn't always checked. For your own safety and freedom of movement a copy of the tourist card must be kept on you, with your passport, at all times – particularly when travelling away from the main towns.

Should you want to **extend your visa** (between 30 and 60 days), there are two basic options: either cross one of the borders and get a new tourist card when you come back in; or go through the bureaucratic rigmarole at a Migraciones office – easiest in Lima, but expect it to take the best part of a day, and arrive before 8.30am to be at the front of the queue. It costs $20 for the *recibo de pago*, plus a further $7 for the Migraciones forms, and you may also be asked to provide evidence of a valid exit ticket from Peru. Migraciones is also the place to sort out new visas if you've **lost your passport** (having visited your embassy first) and to get passports re-stamped.

PERUVIAN EMBASSIES AND CONSULATES

Australia

40 Brisbane Ave, Barton, Canberra (☎02/6273-8752, fax 6273-8754).

36 Main Street, Croydon, Melbourne (☎03/9725-4908).

Level Three, 30 Clarence Steet, Sydney (☎02/9262-6464, fax 9290-2939).

Canada

130 Albert Street, Suite 901, Ottawa, Ontario K1P 5G4 (☎613/238-1777).

10 Mary Street, Suite 301, Toronto M4Y 1P9 (☎416/963-9696).

New Zealand

Level Eight, Cigna House, 40 Mercer Street, Wellington (☎04/499-8087, fax 499-8057).

199–209 Great North Road, Grey Lynn, Auckland (☎09/376-9400).

United Kingdom

52 Sloane Street, London SW1X 9SP (☎020/7235-1917).

USA

180 N Michigan Ave, Suite 1830, Chicago, IL 6-601 (☎312/853-6170).

5177 Richmond Ave, Suite 695, Houston, Texas 77056 (☎713/355-9517)

3460 Wilshire Blvd, Suite 1005, Los Angeles 90010 (☎213/252-5910).

444 Brickell Ave, Suite M135, Miami 33131 (☎305/374-1305).

100 Hamilton Plaza, Twelfth Floor, Paterson, New Jersey 07505 (☎973/278-3324)

215 Lexington Ave, Twenty First floor, New York, NY 10016 (☎212/481-7410).

870 Market Street, Suite 579, San Francisco, CA 94102 (☎415/362-5185).

1700 Massachusetts Ave NW, Washington DC 20036 (☎202/462-1084).

Student visas (which last 12 months) are best organized as far in advance as possible through the British Embassy in Peru, the Peruvian Embassy and the relevant educational institution. **Business visas** only become necessary if you are to be paid by a Peruvian organisation, in which case get your Peruvian employers to do this for you. Having a business visa means that you are eligible for taxation under Peruvian law and will not be allowed to leave the country until this has been accounted for, which entails obtaining a letter from SUNAT (the Peruvian State Taxation Agency) stating that all outstanding taxes have been settled.

COSTS, MONEY AND BANKS

During the late 1980s Peru's rate of inflation was running at thousands of percent, but President Fujimori's economic shock tactics of the early 1990s brought it fairly tightly under control, so that by 1999 it was below the four percent mark. Devaluation is a regular occurrence, however, and in 1986 the whole currency was changed from the sol (Spanish for sun) to the inti (Quechua for sun) and in the process three zeros were removed – one inti was worth 1000 sols. The inti has since been replaced by the nuevo sol, still called a simple sol on the streets, and whose symbol is S/.

Despite being closely tied to the US dollar, the value of the nuevo sol still varies from day to day, so we have quoted prices throughout this book in US dollars, against which costs have so far remained relatively stable. At the time of going to press, the exchange rate for the nuevo sol was roughly S/3.5=$1, S/2.3=CDN$1 S/5.8=£1, S/2.3=A$1 and S/1.7=NZ$1.

COSTS

Peru is certainly a much cheaper place to visit than Europe or the US, but how much so will depend on where you are and when. As a general rule low-budget travellers should – with care – be able to get by on around $10–20 per person per day. If you intend staying in mid-range hotels, eating in reasonable restaurants and taking the odd taxi, $40 a day should be adequate, while $60 a day will allow you to stay in some comfort and sample some of Peru's best cuisine.

In most places in Peru, a good **meal** can still be found for under $3, **transport** is very reasonable, a comfortable double **room** costs from $10–35 a night, and **camping** is usually free. Expect to pay a little more than usual in the larger towns and cities, and also in the jungle, as many supplies have to be imported by truck from other regions. In the villages and rural towns, on the other hand, things come cheaper – and by roughing it in the countryside, and buying food from local villages or the nearest market, you can live well on next to nothing.

In the more popular parts of Peru, costs vary considerably with the seasons. Cusco, for instance, has its best weather from June to August, when many of its hotel prices go up by around 25–50 percent. The same thing happens at fiesta times – although on such occasions you're unlikely to resent it too much. As always, if you're travelling alone you'll end up spending considerably more than you would in a group of two or more people. It's also worth taking along an international **student card**, if you have one, for the occasional reduction (up to 50 percent in some museums).

TRAVELLER'S CHEQUES, CASH AND CREDIT CARDS

For safety's sake the bulk of your money should be carried as **traveller's cheques** – preferably of two different types, as rumoured forgeries make individual brands difficult to exchange, from time to time. American Express is probably the best bet since it has its own offices in Lima and Cusco, is widely recognized by *casas de cambio*, hotels, travel agents and is exchangeable in Peru's most efficient bank, the Banco de Credito. American Express also offers an efficient poste restante service. Master Card traveller's cheques (such as those issued by Thomas Cook and HSBC) are exchangeable for nuevo soles in the Banco Wiese and Banco Latino.

US dollars (preferably cash) are by far the best currency to carry in Peru – anything else will almost certainly prove hard to get rid of outside Lima, and the dollar exchange rate is the one most keenly followed. **Pounds sterling** cash, or even as traveller's cheques, really aren't worth carrying; you often get a very poor exchange rate. Damaged dollar notes will not generally be accepted anywhere, but the same isn't true of nuevo soles.

Credit cards are accepted in the more expensive restaurants and hotels of large cities throughout Peru, such as Lima, Arequipa, Trujillo and Cusco, and increasingly even in smaller places (especially Visa) such as Puerto Maldonado, Huaraz and Iquitos, as well as for car rental. The better known ones (including Mastercard, Visa, Diners Club and Citicorp) can also be used with larger travel companies, but not to pay for bus or train journeys, or at cheaper hotels or restaurants. American Express cards are not that widely accepted. **Local currency** can be

withdrawn from ATMs at a number of banks, including Interbanc (Visa), Banco Latino (Mastercard and Cirrus), Banco de Wiese (Amex, Citicorp, Diners Club International and Mastercard) and Banco de Credito (Visa), and Unicard (Plus). Be careful using the ATMs, though, they have become a target for muggings. These banks will also advance cash on these cards for a small fee – the amount varies considerably, so check beforehand.

Getting **change** from your nuevo soles is almost always a problem. Large denominations should be avoided; you'll find them more difficult to change anywhere in South America. It's particularly hard to change the larger notes in jungle towns, and even in Cusco and Lima shopkeepers and waiters are often reluctant to accept them; if they do, they'll end up running around trying to find small change, which is a time consuming drag for both parties. It's best to break up large notes at every opportunity – in major shops, bars and post offices. If you hang on to the smaller nuevo soles notes you'll have few difficulties in even the remotest villages.

BANKS, CASAS DE CAMBIO AND THE BLACK MARKET

Bank opening hours vary enormously from region to region and from bank to bank, but as a general rule most open weekdays from 9am until 5pm and in Lima, in particular, many of them close for the afternoon at about 1pm from January to March; the Banco de Credito has some branches which open on Saturday mornings, but this isn't the norm. It's also the most efficient bank, with fast service, a ticket system, and videos to keep you amused should there be queues. The Banco de la Nación is the one that officially deals with foreign currency, but it's the least efficient of them all. Most banks will change dollar traveller's cheques and there are often relatively shorter lines at the Banco Continental and Banco Latin. Interbanc and Citibank tend to have air-conditioned offices and quite an efficient service. Try to avoid going to the bank on Friday afternoons, and it's generally better to arrive first thing in the morning. As the rate of exchange varies daily, you're better off changing a little at a time, although there's an enormous amount of paperwork involved in even the simplest transactions – some places fill out several copies of each form – which takes a good deal of time. You'll always need to show your passport.

CREDIT CARD COMPANIES IN PERU

Visa, Avenida 28 de Julio 873, 3rd floor, Miraflores, Lima (☎01/242-2975, toll-free ☎0800/15555)

Mastercard ☎01/222-4242, toll-free ☎0800/40190.

American Express, Belen 1040, Lima Centro (☎01/330-4485, 330-4482 or 330-4484, toll-free ☎001/800-8602908)

Diners Club International, Avenida Canaval y Moreyra 535, San Isidro, Lima (☎01/221-2050 or 442-5433).

Peruvian **hotels** tend to offer the same rate of exchange as the banks, though they may fix their own rate, which is usually slightly worse and averages some five percent below the black market rate. For convenience there's a lot to be said for the **casas de cambio** which can be found in just about any town on the tourist circuit. They are open all day, are rarely crowded, and the rate of exchange is often better than or the same as the banks'. Rates on the streets tend to drop during fiesta and holiday times, so change enough beforehand to see you through.

The very best exchange rates are found on the street in what is loosely called the *mercado negro* or **black market**. In Peru the difference is never as dramatic as it is in some other South American countries, but it is possible to gain between five and fifteen percent over the official rate. "Black market" is a rather nebulous term, encompassing any buyer from the official **cambistas** who wear authorization badges from the local municipalities, to hotel clerks and waiters. Official *cambistas* usually offer the best rates of all and can be spotted in the commercial or tourist centre of any large town, generally around the corners by the main city banks, and, rather less official ones at all border crossings.

It is not illegal to buy nuevo soles from street dealers, but if you do exchange on the black market, count your change very carefully and have someone watch your back if you're changing a large amount of money. Theft of signed or unsigned traveller's cheques, sometimes under threat of violence, is always a slight risk, particularly in Lima: when changing money on the street, play it safe – and never hand over your cheques until given the cash. Going into unfamiliar buildings (with hidden back staircases) "to negotiate" is also *not* advisable. Watch out, too, for forgeries, which are generally pretty crude.

EMERGENCY CASH

If you're in a large city in Peru, probably the quickest method of getting **emergency cash** is to use your credit card to withdraw money from the ATMs of major banks, or get a cash advance on your credit card. Otherwise, you can get a **direct transfer** from an account back home to an affiliated branch of the better Peruvian banks, like Banco del Credito (check with your bank in advance for details). The money is best transferred and picked up in dollars; if you ask for a swiftcode transfer it usually takes five working days. In Lima, Western Union can facilitate more or less immediate money transfers (see Listings for Lima, p.86)

INSURANCE

If you fall ill, the bills can mount up rapidly, so some form of insurance – preferably including air evacuation in the event of serious emergency – is essential. Even with insurance most Peruvian clinics will insist on cash up front except in really serious hospital cases, so some emergency cash is a good idea. Keep all receipts and official papers, so that you can make a claim when you get back home.

NORTH AMERICAN COVER

Canadians are usually covered for medical mishaps overseas by their provincial health plans, while holders of official **student/teacher/youth cards** are entitled to accident coverage and hospital in-patient benefits. **Students** will often find that their student health cover extends during the vacations and for one term beyond the date of last enrolment, while **homeowners' or renters'** insurance often covers theft or loss of documents, money and valuables while overseas, though conditions and maximum amounts vary.

After exhausting the possibilities above, you might want to contact a specialist **travel insurance** company; your travel agent can usually recommend one, or see the box overleaf. Policies are comprehensive, but maximum payouts tend to be

TRAVEL INSURANCE COMPANIES IN NORTH AMERICA

Access America, PO Box 90310, Richmond, VA 23230 (☎1-800/284-8300, *www.accessamerica.com*).

Carefree Travel Insurance, PO Box 310, 120 Mineola Blvd, Mineola, NY 11501 (☎1-800/323-3149).

International Student Insurance Service (ISIS) – sold by STA Travel (see p.4).

Travel Guard, 1145 Clark Street, Stevens Point, WI 54481 (☎1-800/826-1300, *www.noelgroup.com*).

Travel Insurance Services, 2930 Camino Diablo, Suite 300, Walnut Creek, CA 94596 (☎1-800/937-1387, *www.travelinsure.com*).

meagre. Most North American travel policies apply only to items lost, stolen or damaged while in the custody of an identifiable, responsible third party – hotel porter or airline, say, or luggage consignment. Premiums vary, so shop around. The **best deals** are usually through student/youth travel agencies – ISIS policies, for example, cost around $35 for a week depending on coverage; $55 for eight to fifteen days; $115 for a month; and up to $730 for a year. If you're planning to do any "dangerous sports", figure on a surcharge of 20–50 percent.

BRITISH COVER

Most travel agents and tour operators will offer you **insurance** policies when you book your flight or holiday. These are usually reasonable value, though as ever, you should check the small print. If you feel the cover is inadequate, or want to compare prices, any travel agent, insurance broker or bank should be able to help. If you have a good "all risks" **home insurance policy** it may well cover your possessions against loss or theft when overseas, and many **private medical schemes** also cover you when abroad – make sure you know the procedure and the helpline number.

For Peru, Journey Latin America (see p.7) has one of the most – if not *the* most – comprehensive deals around, covering you for up to £2,500,000 in medical expenses, £2,000,000 in personal liability, and baggage up to £1250.

Prices start at £40 for eight days, £85 for 45 days, £153 for three months, and then £37 for each subsequent month. Slightly cheaper is the ISIS policy, available from branches of STA (see p.7), which costs £35 for a month's cover. Other good, reasonably priced policies are issued by Endsleigh Insurance, Cranfield House, 97–107 Southampton Row, London WC1B 4AG (☎020/7436 4451); Frizzell, Frizzell House, County Gates, Bournemouth, Dorset BH1 2NF (☎01202/292333); Columbus Direct Insurance, 17 Devonshire Square, London EC2M 4SQ (☎020/7375 0011, *www.columbusdirect.co.uk*), who offer a very good-value annual multi-trip policy for £125; and Wexas (see p.7).

AUSTRALIAN AND NEW ZEALAND COVER

Comprehensive travel insurance to cover medical expenses and loss or theft of bags or cash is available from most travel agents or direct from insurance companies, for periods ranging from a few days to a year or even longer. Most policies are similar in premium and coverage. A typical policy covering medical costs, lost baggage and personal liability for the Americas, including Peru, starts at about A$120/NZ$140 for two weeks, A$190/NZ$220 for one month, A$300/NZ$375 for two months and A$390/NZ$490 for three months. These are over-the-counter prices; you could save up to 25 percent booking over the Internet. Check the policy if you intend to do any adventure sports, such as mountaineering, as you will usually need to take out extra cover for these.

AUSTRALIAN AND NEW ZEALAND INSURANCE COMPANIES

AFTA, 144 Pacific Highway, North Sydney (☎02/9956-4800)

Cover More, Level Nine, 32 Walker Street, North Sydney (02/9202-8000, *www.cover-more.com.au*)

FAI Travel Insurance, 141 Walker Street, Dandenong, Melbourne (☎03/9771-4000 or ☎1300/555018, fax 03/9771-4003); and 63 Albert Street, Auckland (☎09/300-5333, fax 307-0035).

Travel.com, 80 Clarence Street, Sydney (☎02/9290-1500, *www.travel.com.au*)

HEALTH

No inoculations are currently required for Peru, but it's a good idea to check with the embassy or a reliable travel agent before you go. Your doctor will probably advise you to have some anyway: typhoid, cholera and yellow fever shots are all sensible precautions, and it's well worth ensuring that your polio and tetanus-diphtheria boosters are still effective. Immunization against hepatitis A is also usually recommended.

Yellow fever still breaks out now and again in some of the jungle areas of Peru; it is frequently obligatory to show an inoculation certificate for yellow fever when entering the Amazon region – if you can't show proof of immunization you'll be jabbed on the spot. **Rabies** still exists and people do die from it. If you get bitten anywhere in Peru by a dog or vampire bat (only likely in some parts of the Amazon region), you should undergo a series of injections administered to the stomach (available in most Peruvian hospitals) within 24 hours. This is the only cure, unless you have been inoculated in advance with one of the new anti-rabies jabs.

Malaria is quite common in Peru these days, particularly in the Amazon regions to the east of the country. If you intend going into the jungle regions, malaria tablets should be taken – starting a few weeks before you arrive and continuing for some time after. Make sure you get these, or whatever is recommended by your doctor, before leaving home. The prophylactics most commonly recommended against Peruvian malaria tend to be a combination of Paludrin and Cholorquine tablets. Few people who have to spend a lot of time in the rainforest regions use prophylactics, preferring to treat the disease if they contract it, believing that the best prevention is to avoid getting bitten if at all possible, by wearing long sleeves, long trousers, socks, even mostquito-proof net hats, and sleeping under good mosquito netting or well-proofed quarters. There is more information on this issue in Chapter Six (p.362) or check out *www.cdc.gov/travel/regionalmalaria*.

DIARRHOEA, DYSENTERY AND GIARDIA

Diarrhoea is something everybody gets at some stage, and there's little to be done except drink a lot (but not alcohol) and bide your time. You

should also replace salts either by taking oral rehydration salts or by mixing a teaspoon of salt and eight of sugar in a litre of purified water. You can minimize the risk by being sensible about what you eat, and by not drinking tapwater anywhere. This isn't difficult, given the extreme cheapness and universal availability of soft drinks and *água mineral*, while Brazilians are great believers in herbal teas, which often help alleviate cramps.

If your diarrhoea contains blood or mucus, the cause may be dysentery or giardia. With a fever, it could well be caused by **bacillic dysentery** and may clear up without treatment. If you're sure you need it, a course of antibiotics such as tetracyclin or ampicillin (travel with a supply if you are going off the beaten track for a while) should sort you, but they also destroy "gut flora" which help protect you. Similar symptoms without fever indicate **amoebic dysentery** which is much more serious, and can damage your gut if untreated. The usual cure is a course of metronidazole (Flagyl), an antibiotic which may itself make you feel ill, and should not be taken with alcohol. Similar symptoms, plus rotten-egg belches and farts, indicate **giardia**, for which the treatment is again metronidazole. If you suspect you have any of these, seek medical help, and only start on the metronidazole (750mg three times daily for a week for adults) if there is definitely blood in your diarrhoea and it is impossible to see a doctor.

WATER AND FOOD

Water in Peru is better than it used to be, but it can still trouble non-Peruvian (and even Peruvian) stomachs, so it's a good idea to only drink **bottled water** (*água mineral*), available in various sizes, including litre and two-litre bottles from most corner shops or food stores. Stick with known brands, even if they are more expensive, and always check that the seal on the bottle is intact, since refilling with local water is not uncommon. Carbonated water is generally safer as it is more likely to be the genuine stuff. You should also clean your teeth in bottled water and avoid raw foods washed in local water.

Apart from bottled water, there are various methods of **treating water** whilst you are

MEDICAL RESOURCES FOR TRAVELLERS

NORTH AMERICA

Canadian Society for International Health, 1 Nicholas Street, Ottawa, ON K1N 7B7 (☎613/230-2654, *www.csin.org*). Distributes a free pamphlet, "Health Information for Canadian Travellers".

International Association for Medical Assistance to Travellers (IAMAT), 417 Center Street, Lewiston, NY 14092 (☎716/754-4883); 40 Regal Rd, Guelph, ON N1K 1B5 (☎519/836-0102); *www.sentex.net/~iamat*. A non-profit organization, which also has offices at 40 Regal Road, Guelph, Ontario N1K 1B5, Canada (☎519/836-0102). Can provide a list of English-speaking doctors in Peru, climate charts and leaflets on various diseases and inoculations.

International SOS Assistance, PO Box 11568, Philadelphia, PA 19116 (☎1-800/523-8930; Canada ☎1-800/363-0263; *www.intsos.com*). Members receive pre-trip medical referral info,

as well as overseas emergency services designed to complement travel insurance coverage.

Medic Alert, 2323 Colorado Ave, Turlock, CA 95381 (☎1-800/432-5378; Canada ☎1-800/668-1507; *www.medicalert.org*). Sells bracelets engraved with traveller's medical requirements in case of emergency.

Travel Medicine, 351 Pleasant Street, Suite 312, Northampton, MA 01060 (☎1-800/872-8633, *www.travelmed.com*). Sells first-aid kits, mosquito netting, water filters and other health-related travel products.

Travelers Medical Center, 31 Washington Square, New York, NY 10011 (☎212/982-1600). Consultation service on immunizations and treatment of diseases for people travelling to developing countries.

UK

British Airways Travel Clinic, 156 Regent Street, London W1 (☎020/7439-9584). Appointment-only branches at 101 Cheapside, London EC2 (☎020/7606-2977) and at the BA terminal in London's Victoria Station (020/7233-6661); other clinics throughout the country (call ☎01276/685040 for the one nearest to you or

consult *www.britishairways.com*). All these clinics sell travel-associated accessories, including mosquito nets and first-aid kits.

Hospital for Tropical Diseases Travel Clinic, second floor, Mortimer Market Centre, off Capper Street, London WC1E 6AU (☎020/7388-9600;

travelling whether your source is tap water or natural groundwater such as a river or stream. **Boiling** is the time-honoured method which will be effective in sterilizing water, although it will not remove unpleasant tastes. A minimum boiling time of five minutes (longer at higher altitudes) is sufficient to kill micro-organisms. In remote jungle areas, **sterilizing tablets** like *Potable Agua* or liquid iodine are a better idea, although they leave a rather bad taste in the mouth. Pregnant women or people with thyroid problems should consult their doctor before using iodine sterilizing tablets or iodine-based purifiers. In emergencies and remote areas in particular, always check with locals to see whether the tap water is okay (*es potable?*) before drinking it. For more information check out *www.gorge.net/ham/*.

Peruvian **food** has been frequently condemned as a health hazard, particularly during rare but recurrent cholera outbreaks. Be careful about any-

thing bought from street stalls, particularly seafood, which may not be that fresh. Salads should be avoided, especially in small settlements where they may have been washed in river water or fertilized by local sewage waters.

THE SUN

The sun can be deceptively hot, particularly on the coast or when travelling in boats on jungle rivers when the hazy weather or cool breezes can put visitors off their guard; remember, sunstroke is a reality and can make you very sick as well as burnt. Wide brimmed hats, sun screen lotions (factor 15 advisable) and staying in the shade like the locals whenever possible are all good precautions. Note that **suntan lotion** and **sunblock** are more expensive in Peru than they are at home, so take a good supply with you. If you do run out, you can buy Western brands at most *farmacias*,

Mon–Fri 9am–5pm, by appointment only). A consultation costs £15, which is waived if you have your injections here). A recorded Health Line (☎0839/337 733; 50p per min) gives hints on hygiene and illness prevention as well as listing appropriate immunizations.

Homeway Ltd, Fighting Cocks, West Amesbury, Salisbury, Wilts SP4 7BH. These are suppliers of travel medical kits.

MASTA (Medical Advisory Service for Travellers Abroad), London School of Hygiene and Tropical Medicine. Operates a pre-recorded 24-hour

Travellers' Health Line (☎0906/822-4100; 60p per min), giving written information tailored to your journey by return of post.

Nomad Pharmacy, surgeries 40 Bernard Street, London WC1, opposite Russell Square tube station; and 3-4 Turnpike Lane, London N8 (020/7833-4114 to book a vaccination appointment; Mon–Fri 9.30am–6pm). They give advice free if you go in person, or their telephone helpline is ☎0891/633414 (60p a minute). They can give information tailored to your travel needs.

AUSTRALIA AND NEW ZEALAND

Auckland Hopsital, Park Road, Grafton (☎09/379-7440).

Travel-Bug Medical and Vaccination Centre, 182 Ward Street, North Adelaide (☎08/8267-3544).

Travel Health and Vaccination Clinic, 114 Williams Street, Melbourne (☎03/9670-2020).

Traveller's Immunization Service, 303 Pacific Highway, Sydney (☎02/9416-1348).

Travellers' Medical and Vaccination Centres, ☎1300/658844 local call within Australia, or *www.tmvc.com.au* for general information on travel health and a list of the clinics and contact details for Australia and New Zealand. Australia: 27–29 Gilbert Place, Adelaide

(☎08/8212-7522); Fifth Floor, 247 Adelaide Street, Brisbane (☎07/3221-9066); Fifth Floor, 8–10 Hobart Place, City, Canberra (☎02/6257-7156); 5 Westralia Street, Darwin (☎08/8981-2907); 270 Sandy Bay Road, Sandy Bay, Hobart (☎03/6223-7577); Second Floor, 393 Little Bourke Street, Melbourne (☎03/9602-5788), Royal Melbourne Hospital, Royal Parade (☎03/9347-7132); 5 Mill Street, Perth (☎08/9321-1977); Seventh Floor, 428 George Street, Sydney (☎02/9221-7133). New Zealand: Level One, 170 Queen Street, Auckland (☎09/373-3531); 147 Armagh Street, Christchurch (☎03/379-4000); Shop 15, Grand Arcade, 14-16 Willis Street, Wellington (☎04/473-0991).

though you won't find a very wide choice, especially in the higher factors. Also make sure that you increase your water intake, in order to prevent dehydration.

ALTITUDE SICKNESS

Altitude sickness – known as *soroche* in Peru – is a common problem for visitors, especially if you are travelling quickly between the coast or jungle regions and the high Andes. The best way to prevent it is to eat light meals, drink lots of *coca* tea, and spend as long as possible acclimatizing to high altitudes (over 2500m) before carrying out any strenuous activity. Anyone who suffers from headaches or nausea should rest; more seriously, a sudden bad cough could be a sign of pulmonary edema and demands an immediate descent and medical attention – altitude sickness can kill. People often suffer from altitude sickness on

trains crossing high passes; if this happens, don't panic, just rest and stay on the train until it descends. Most trains are equipped with oxygen bags or cylinders that are brought around by the conductor for anyone in need.

INSECTS

Insects are more of an irritation than a serious problem, but on the coast, in the jungle and to a lesser extent in the mountains, the **common fly** is a definite pest. Although it can carry typhoid, there is little one can do; you might spend mealtimes successfully fighting flies from your plate but even in expensive restaurants it's difficult to regulate hygiene in the kitchens. A more obvious problem is the **mosquito**, which in some parts of the lowland jungle carries malaria. Repellents are of limited value – it's better to cover your arms, legs and feet with a good layer of clothing.

Mosquitoes tend to emerge after dark, but the daytime holds even worse biting insects in the jungle regions, among them the **Manta Blanca** (or white blanket), so called because they swarm as a blanket of tiny flying insects. They don't hurt when they bite but itch like crazy for a few days after. **Antihistamine creams** or tablets can reduce the sting or itchiness of most insect bites, but try not to scratch them, and if it gets unbearable go to the nearest *farmacia* for advice. To keep hotel rooms relatively clear, buy some of the spirals of incense-like **pyrethrin**, available cheaply everywhere.

HIV AND AIDS

HIV and **AIDS** (known as SIDA in Latin America) are a growing problem in South America, and whilst Peru does not have as bad a reputation as neighbouring Brazil, you should still take care. Although all hospitals and clinics in Peru are supposed to use only sterilized equipment, many travellers prefer to take their own sealed hypodermic syringes in case of emergencies. It goes without saying that you should take the same kind of precautions as you would in your country when having sex (see Contraception, below).

CONTRACEPTION

Condoms (*profilacticos*) are available from street vendors and some *farmacias*. However, they tend to be expensive and often poor quality (rumour has it that they are US rejects, which have been sold to a less discriminating market), so bring an adequate supply with you. **The pill** is also available from *farmacias*, officially on prescription only, but is frequently sold over the counter. You're unlikely to be able to match your brand, however, so it's far better to bring your own supply. It's worth remembering that if you suffer from

moderately severe diarrhoea on your trip the pill (or any other drug) may not be in your system long enough to take effect.

FARMACIAS

For **minor ailments** you can buy most drugs at a *farmacia* without a prescription. Antibiotics and malaria pills can be bought over the counter (it is, however, important to know the correct dosage), as can antihistamines (for bite allergies) or medication for an upset stomach (try Lomotil or Streptotriad). You can also buy Western-brand **tampons** at a *farmacia*, though they are expensive, so better to bring a good supply. For any serious illnesses, you should go to a doctor or hospital; these are detailed throughout the Guide in the relevant town Listings, or try the local phone book.

TRADITIONAL MEDICINES

Alternative medicines have a popular history going back at least two thousand years in Peru and the traditional practitioners – *herbaleros*, *hueseros* and *curanderos* – are still commonplace. **Herbaleros** sell curative plants, herbs and charms in the streets and markets of most towns. They lay out a selection of ground roots, liquid tree barks, flowers, leaves and creams – all with specific medicinal functions and sold at much lower prices than in the *farmacias*. If told the symptoms, a *herbalero* can select remedies for most minor (and apparently some major) ailments. **Hueseros** are consultants who treat diseases and injuries by bone manipulation, while **curanderos** claim diagnostic, divinatory and healing powers and have existed in Peru since pre-Inca days. For further information on alternative medicine and traditional healing, see *Ancient Wizardry in Modern Peru*, on p.439.

INFORMATION AND MAPS

in Lima (see p.86), Cusco (see p.136), and their **main office** is in the US, at 126 Indian Creek Road, Ithaca, NY 14850 (☎607/277-0488, fax 277-6122, *www.samexplo.org, explore@ samexplo.org*), plus there's a clubhouse in Ecuador at Jorge Washington 311, Quito (☎02/225228); postal address, Apartado 21-431, Eloy Alfaro, Quito, Ecuador.

A *Peru Guide* booklet is available free from hotels and travel agencies in most major cities; it has a few good city maps and gives recommendations for hotels and restaurants plus other useful information for Lima, Arequipa, Cusco, Huaraz, Chiclayo, Ica/Nasca/Paracas and Iquitos.

Peru has no official tourist offices abroad, but you can get a range of information from its embassies in Britain, Europe, North America and Australia and New Zealand. However, you'll probably find that most tour companies can supply better, more up-to-date information.

In Peru you'll find some sort of tourist office in most towns of any size, which can help with information and sometimes free local maps. Quite often, though, these are simply fronts for tour operators, and are only really worth bothering with if you have a specific question – about fiesta dates or local bus timetables, for example. The **South American Explorers' Club** is probably your best bet for getting relevant and up-to-date information both before you leave home and when you arrive in Lima. It is a non-profit-making organization founded in 1977 to support scientific and adventure expeditions and to provide services to travellers. In return for membership (from $40 a year, depending on the type of membership), you get four copies of the magazine *South American Explorer* a year, and you can use the club's facilities, which include an excellent library, access to the map collection, trip reports, listings, a postal address, storage space, discounts on maps, guidebooks, information on visas, doctors and dentists, a network of experts with specialist information, and an "emergency crash pad". They have clubhouses

MAPS

Maps of Peru fall into three basic categories. A standard **road map** should be available from good map sellers just about anywhere in the world (see box overleaf for map outlets in North America, Britain, Australia and New Zealand) or in Peru itself from street vendors or *librerías*; the Touring Y Automovil Club de Peru, Avenida Cesar Vallejo 699, Lince, Lima (☎01/440-3270) is worth visiting for its good route maps. **Departmental maps**, covering each *departmento* (Peruvian state) in greater detail, but often very out of date, are also fairly widely available. **Topographic maps** (usually 1:100,000) cover the entire coastal area and most of the mountainous region. In Lima, they can be bought from the Instituto Geográfico Nacional, Avenida Aramburu 1190, Surquillo (☎01/475-3085 or 475-3075, *postmaster@ ignperu.gob.pe*); the Servicio Aerofotografico Nacional, Las Palmas Airforce Base in Barranco (☎01/477 3682); Ingemmet, Avenida Canada, 1470, San Borja (☎01/225-3158); the Touring Y Automovil Club de Peru, Avenida Cesar Vallejo 699, Lince (☎01/440-3270); and the Sevicio Aerofotografico Nacional, Base Fap, Las Palmas (Mon–Fri 9am–5pm; ☎01/467-1341). Maps are also available at the South American Explorers' Club (see above), along with a wide variety of hiking maps and guidebooks for all the most popular hiking zones and quite a few others.

MAP OUTLETS

NORTH AMERICA

The Complete Traveler Bookstore, 199 Madison Ave, New York, NY 10016 (☎212/685-9007); 3207 Fillmore Street, San Francisco, CA 92123 (☎415/923-1511).

Forsyth Travel Library, 9154 W 57th Street, Shawnee Mission, KS 66201 (☎1-800/367-7984).

Map Link Inc, 25 E Mason Street, Santa Barbara, CA 93101 (☎805/965-4402. *www.maplink.com*).

Open Air Books and Maps, 25 Toronto Street, Toronto, ON M5R 2C1 (☎416/363-0719).

Phileas Fogg's Books & Maps, #87 Stanford Shopping Center, Palo Alto, CA 94304 (☎1-800/233-FOGG in California; ☎1-800/533-FOGG elsewhere in US).

Rand McNally,* 444 N Michigan Ave, Chicago, IL 60611 (☎312/321-1751); 150 E 52nd Street,

New York, NY 10022 (☎212/758-7488); 595 Market Street, San Francisco, CA 94105 (☎415/777-3131); 1201 Connecticut Ave NW, Washington DC 20003 (☎202/223-6751).

Sierra Club Bookstore, 730 Polk Street, San Francisco, CA 94109 (☎415/923-5500).

Traveler's Bookstore, 22 W 52nd Street, New York, NY 10019 (☎212/664-0995).

Ulysses Travel Bookshop, 4176 Street-Denis, Montréal (☎514/289-0993).

World Wide Books and Maps, 1247 Granville Street, Vancouver, BC V6Z 1G3 (☎604/687-3320).

*Rand McNally now has 24 stores across the US: call ☎1800/333-0136 ext 2111 for the location of your nearest store, or for **direct mail** maps.

UK

Daunt Books, 83 Marylebone High Street, W1M 3DE (☎020/7224-2295, fax 020/7224-6893); 193 Haverstock Hill, NW3 4QL (☎020/7794-4006).

John Smith and Sons, 57–61 St Vincent Street, Glasgow (☎0141/221-7472, fax 248-4412).

National Map Centre, 22–24 Caxton Street, SW1H 0QU (☎020/7222-2466, *www.mapsworld.com*).

Stanfords, 12–14 Long Acre, WC2E 9LP (☎020/7836-1321); at Campus Travel at 52

Grosvenor Gardens, SW1W 0AG (☎020/7730-1314); and within the British Airways offices at 156 Regent Street, W1R 5TA (☎020/7434-4744), 29 Corn Street, Bristol BS1 1HT (☎0117/929 9966). Maps by mail or phone order are available on this number and via email (*sales@stanfords.co.uk*).

The Travel Bookshop, 13–15 Blenheim Crescent, W11 2EE (☎020/7229 5260, *www.thetravelbookshop.co.uk*).

AUSTRALIA AND NEW ZEALAND

Map Land, 372 Little Bourke Street, Melbourne (☎03/9670-4383, *mapland@lexicon.net*).

The Map Shop, 16a Peel Street, Adelaide (☎08/8231-2033, *mapshop.net.au*).

Perth Map Centre, 884 Hay Street, Perth (☎09/9322-5733, *www.perthmap.co.au*).

Map World, 371 Pitt Street, Sydney (☎02/9261-3601).

Travel Bookshop, Shop 3, 175 Liverpool Street, Sydney (☎02/9261-8200).

Speciality Maps, 58 Albert Street, Auckland (☎09/307-2217).

Mapworld, 173 Gloucester Street, Christchurch (☎03/374-5399, *maps@mapworld.co.nz*, *www.mapworld.co.nz*).

Worldwide Maps and Guides, 187 George Street, Brisbane (☎07/3221-4330, *www.powerup.com.au/~wwmaps*).

WEB SITES

Peru is surprisingly switched on to electronic communications, with Internet cafés in all towns of any size and in many small, out-of-the-way places. There's a vast list of sites for the armchair enthusiast, potential visitor, or traveller in the field, and we've listed a few of the more useful ones below.

Latin American Travel Advisor, *www.amerisplan.com/lata*
Pre-trip advice and help with planning.

Machu Picchu, *www.machupicchuperu.com*
Tours, reports and listings for this popular trekking destination at the end of the Inca Trail.

PromPeru, *www.peruonline.net*
Great source of general background information,

including history, culture and activities, in English and Spanish.

Rumbos, *rumbosperu.com*
Environmental and travel magazine, loaded with practical tips on tours and background information on all the sites.

South American Explorers Club,
www.samexplo.org
The latest travel reports on Latin America.

Sustainable Sources, *www.greenbuilder.com*
Eco-travel in Latin America.

Touring y Automovil Club del Peru,
www.hys.pe/tacp
Peruvian motoring association information, in Spanish.

GETTING AROUND

Most Peruvians get around the country by bus, as these go just about everywhere and are extremely good value. However, wherever possible, visitors tend to use one of the country's trains – an experience in itself – despite being considerably slower than the equivalent bus journey. With the distances in Peru being so vast, many Peruvians and travellers are increasingly flying to their destinations, as all Peruvian cities are within a two-hour flight of Lima. Approximate journey times and frequencies of all services can be found in "Travel Details" at the end of each chapter, and

local peculiarities are detailed in the text of the Guide.

Driving around Peru is generally not a problem outside of Lima, and allows you to see some out-of-the-way places that you might otherwise miss. However, the traffic in Lima is abominable, both in terms of its recklessness and the sheer volume. Traffic jams are ubiquitous between 8 and 10am and again between 4 and 6pm every weekday, while the pollution from too many old and poorly maintained vehicles is a real health risk, particularly in Lima Centro and to a lesser extent in Arequipa.

BY BUS

Peru's **buses** are run by a variety of private companies, all of which offer remarkably low **fares**, making it possible to travel from one end of the country to the other (over 2000km) for under $30. Long-distance bus journeys cost around $1.50 per hour on the fast coastal highway, and are even cheaper on the slower mountain and jungle routes. The condition of the buses ranges from the relatively luxurious Cruz del Sur fleet that runs along the coast, to the scruffy old ex-US school-buses used on local runs throughout the country. Some of the better bus companies, such as Cruz del Sur, Ormeño and Movil, offer excellent onboard facilities including sandwich bars and video entertainment. The major companies generally offer two or three levels of service anyway, and many companies run the longer journeys by night. If you don't want to miss the scenery, you can hop relatively easily between the smaller towns, which usually works out at not much more.

As the only means of transport available to most of the population, buses run with surprising regularity, and the coastal Panamerican Highway and many of the main routes into the mountains have now been paved (one of President Fujimori's most successful construction programmes), so on such routes services are generally punctual. On some of the rougher mountainous routes, punctures, arguments over rights of way and, in the rainy season, landslides may mean you arrive several hours late.

At least one **bus depot** or **stopping area** can be found in the centre of any town. Peru is investing in a series of **terminal terrestres**, or **terra-puertos**, centralizing the departure and arrival of the manifold operators, but it's always a good idea to double-check where the bus is leaving from, since in some cities, notably Arequipa, bus offices are in different locations to the bus terminal. Lima has so many buses that the major companies are in the middle of rationalizing their own private terminals and departure points (presently incredibly complex) while the rest still cling to depots mostly in the heart of Lima Centro and traffic congestion. If you can't get to a bus depot or terminal terrestre, you can try to catch a bus from the police *control* on the edge of town, or flag one down virtually anywhere, though there's no guarantee of getting a ride or a seat. For inter-city rides, it's best to buy **tickets** in advance direct from the bus company offices; for local trips, you can buy tickets on the bus itself. On long-distance journeys, try and avoid getting seats right over the jarring wheels, especially if the bus is tackling mountain or jungle roads.

TAXIS, MOTOTAXIS AND COLECTIVOS

Taxis can be found anywhere at any time in almost every town. Any car can become a taxi simply by sticking a taxi sign up in the front window; a lot of people, especially in Lima, take advantage of this to supplement their income. Whenever you get into a taxi, always fix the **price** in advance since few of them have meters, even the really professional firms. In Lima, the minimum fare is S/3-4 – around $1 – but it's generally a bit cheaper elsewhere. Even relatively long taxi rides in Lima are likely to cost less than $10, except perhaps to and from the airport, which ranges from $15 to 25, depending on how far across the city you're going, how bad the traffic is, and how many passengers there are. Taxi drivers in Peru do not expect tips.

In many rural towns, you'll find small cars – mainly Korean Ticos and motorcycle rickshaws, known variously as **mototaxis** or **motokars**, vying for custom as taxis. The latter are always cheaper if slightly more dangerous and not that comfortable, especially if there's more than two of you or if you've got a lot of luggage.

Colectivos (shared taxis) are a very useful way of getting around that's peculiar to Peru. They connect all the coastal towns, and many of the larger centres in the mountains. Like the buses, many are ageing imports from the US – huge old Dodge Coronets with a picture of the Virgin Mary dangling from the rear-view mirror – though increasingly, fast new Japanese and Korean minibuses are running between the cities. Colectivos tend to be faster than the bus, though are often as much as twice the price. Most colectivo **cars** manage to squeeze in about six people plus the driver (3 in the front and 4 in the back), and can be found in the centre of a town or at major stopping-places along the main roads. If more than one is ready to leave it's worth bargaining a little, as the price is often negotiable. Colectivo **minibuses**, also known as **combis**, can squeeze in twice as many people, or often more.

In the cities, particularly in Lima, colectivos (especially colectivo minibuses) have an appalling reputation for **safety**. There are crashes reported in the Lima press every week, mostly caused by the highly competitive nature of the business. There are so many combis covering the same major arterial routes in Lima that they literally race each other to be the first to the next street corner. They frequently crash, turn over and knock down pedestrians. Equally dangerous is the fact that the driver is in such a hurry that he does not always wait for you to get in. If you're not careful he'll pull away while you've still got a foot on the pavement, putting you in serious danger of breaking a leg.

BY TRAIN

Peru's spectacular **train** journeys are in them-selves a major attraction, and you should aim to take at least one long-distance train during your trip, especially as the trains connect some of Peru's major tourist sights. At the time of writing, the **Central Railway**, which climbs and switch-backs its way up from Lima into the Andes as far as Huancayo on the world's highest standard-gauge tracks, is currently operational for passen-gers only on the last Sunday of the month (return-ing Monday); but this situation is likely to improve.

The **Southern Railway**, starting on the south coast at Arequipa, heads inland to Lake Titicaca before curving back towards Cusco, from where a line heads out down the magnificent Urubamba Valley, past Machu Picchu, and on into the fringes of the Amazon forest. The trains move slowly, are much more bumpy than buses, depending both on the level of track maintenance (presently poor between Cusco and Puno, for instance) and, of course, the state of the comparative road the bus is taking. Trains, however, generally allow ample time to observe what's going on outside, but you do have to keep one eye on events inside, where the carriages – often extremely crowded – are notori-ous for **petty thefts**. Wherever possible **tickets** should be bought in advance by at least a day.

Most trains in Peru offer three different class-es. **Ecomonico** is the cheapest and most basic, usually with hard seats, overcrowding and a rep-utation for pickpockets and petty thieves. **Pullman** costs substantially more, but is still cheap by European or North American standards; this has better security, is more comfortable, has waitress service and tends to be less crowded. **Inca** or **Turimso** class is pricier still, has waitress service, a bar and dining, very comfortable seats and generally has more empty seats.

BY PLANE

Some places in the jungle can only sensibly be reached by **plane** and Peru is so vast that the odd flight can save a lot of time. There are three major companies; Aero Continente, who fly to all of the main cities and many smaller destinations; TANS, the commercial arm of Peruvian Air Force; and Lan Peru, which has strong links with Lan Chile. A couple of smaller companies – Aero Condor and Aero Santander – are currently gearing up their operations. **Tickets** can be bought from travel agents or airline offices in all major towns. The most popular routes, such as Lima–Cusco cost upwards of $60 and usually need to be booked at least a few days in advance (more during the run-up to and including major fiestas). Other less busy routes tend to be less expensive.

In addition to the commercial airlines, **Grupo Ocho**, the Peruvian Air Force, carries passengers on some of its standard flights. Less regular or reliable than the commercial companies, these compensate by being very much cheaper. Check availability at the major airports, but don't be too surprised if the promised plane never materializes.

On all flights it's important to **confirm your booking** two days before departure. Flights are often cancelled or delayed, and sometimes they leave earlier than scheduled – especially in the jungle where the weather can be a problem. If a passenger hasn't shown up twenty minutes before the flight, the company can give the seat to someone on the waiting list, so it's best to be on time whether you're booked or are merely hope-ful. The luggage allowance on all internal flights is 16kg not including hand luggage.

There are also **small planes** (6- and 10-seaters) serving the jungle and certain parts of the coast. A number of small companies fly out of Jorge Chavez Airport in Lima most days (their counters are between the international check-in counters and the domestic departure area), but they have no fixed schedules and a reputation for being dangerous and poorly maintained. The jun-gle towns, such as Pucallpa, Tarapoto, Satipo and San Ramon, also tend to have small **air colecti-vo** companies operating scheduled services between larger settlements in the region, at quite reasonable rates. For an *expresso* **air taxi**, which

---

AIRLINES IN PERU

Aero Condor, Juan de Arona 781, San Isidro, Lima (☎01/442-5663).

Aero Continente, Avenida José Pardo 651, Miraflores, Lima (☎01/242-4260, fax 444-5014, *www.aerocontinente.com.pe/*).

Aero Santander, 2 de Mayo 294, Cusco (☎084/571754).

Lan Peru, Avenida Los Incas 172, eighth floor, San Isidro, Lima (☎01/221-3764, fax 421-8914, *www.lanperu.com*).

TANS, Avenida Arequipa 5200, Miraflores, Lima (☎01/445-7327 or 445-7107).

will take you to any landing strip in the country whenever you want, you'll pay over $200 an hour; this price includes the return journey, even if you just want to be dropped off.

All the Peruvian domestic airlines offering **flight passes** went bust in the late 1990s, and airline companies are in a state of flux in Peru. As new ones arrive and competition for passengers increases, passes are likely to become available again, and it's worth checking with your travel agent or with the major airlines on arrival in Peru.

BY CAR

Cars can be very handy for reaching remote rural destinations or sites, but if you are planning to explore **by car**, it's best to avoid Lima as far as possible. Driving in the capital takes a bit of getting used to, even as a passenger.

If you bring a car into Peru that is not registered there, you will need to show (and keep with you at all times) a *libreta de pago por la aduana* (proof of customs payment) normally provided by the relevant automobile association of the country you are coming from. **Spare parts**, particularly tyres, will have to be carried as will a tent, emergency water and food. The chance of **theft** is quite high – the vehicle, your baggage and accessories are all vulnerable when parked.

What few **traffic signals** there are are either completely ignored or used at the drivers' "discretion". The pace is fast and roads everywhere are in bad shape: only the Panamerican Highway, running down the coast, and a few short stretches inland, are paved. **Mechanics** are generally good and always ingenious – they have to be, due to a lack of spare parts! Also, the 95-octane **petrol** is much cleaner than the 84, though both

are cheap by European, North American or Australian and New Zealand standards. **International driving licences** are generally valid for thirty days in Peru, after which a permit is required from the Touring y Automovil Club del Peru, Cesar Vallejo 699, Lince, Lima (Mon–Fri 9am–4.45pm; ☎01/440-3270, fax 422-5947, *touring@hys.com.pe*, *www.hys.com.pe/tacp*).

CAR RENTAL

Renting a car costs much the same as in Europe and North America. The major rental firms all have offices in Lima, but outside the capital you'll generally find only local companies are represented; see the relevant Listings for details. You may find it more convenient to rent a car in advance from your own country (see below for details) – expect to pay around $US35/£21 a day, or $US200/£130 a week for the smallest car. In the jungle it's usually possible to **hire motorbikes** or **mopeds** by the hour or by the day: this is a good way of getting to know a town or to be able to shoot off into the jungle for a day.

BY BOAT

There are no coastal **boat** services in Peru, but in many areas – on **Lake Titicaca** and especially in the **jungle regions** – water is the obvious means of getting around. From Puno, on Lake Titicaca, there are currently no regular services to Bolivia by ship or hydrofoil (though check with the tour agencies in Puno), but there are plenty of smaller boats that will take visitors out to the various islands in the lake. These aren't expensive and a price can usually be negotiated down at the port.

In the jungle areas **motorized canoes** come in two basic forms: those with a large outboard motor

---

CAR RENTAL AGENCIES

UK		AUSTRALIA	
Avis	☎0990/900500	Avis	☎1800/225533
Budget	☎0800/181181	Budget	☎1300/362848
Hertz	☎0990/996699	Hertz	☎1800/550067
NORTH AMERICA		**NEW ZEALAND**	
Avis	☎1-800/331-1084	Avis	☎09/526-2847
Budget	☎1-800/527-0700	Budget	☎09/375-2222
Dollar	☎1-800/800-6000	Hertz	☎09/309-0989
Hertz	☎1-800/654-3001(US)		
	☎1-800/263-0600 (Canada)		

and those with a Briggs and Stratton *peque-peque* engine. The outboard is faster and more manoeuvrable, but it costs a lot more to run. Occasionally you can hitch a ride in one of these canoes for nothing, but this may involve waiting around for days or even weeks and, in the end, most people expect some form of payment. More practical is to **hire a canoe** along with its guide/driver for a few days. This means searching around in the port and negotiating, but you can often get a *peque-peque* canoe from around $40–50 per day, which will invariably work out cheaper than taking an organized tour, as well as giving you the choice of guide and companions. Obviously, the more people you can get together, the cheaper it will be per person.

If you're heading downstream it's often possible in the last resort to buy, borrow or even make a **balsa raft**. Most of the indigenous population still travel this way so it's sometimes possible to hitch a lift, or to buy one of their rafts. Riding with someone who's going your way is probably better, since rafting can be dangerous if you don't know the river well; for more details see p.365.

ON FOOT

Even if you've no intention of doing any serious **hiking**, there's a good deal of walking involved in checking out many of the most enjoyable Peruvian attractions. Climbing from Cusco up to the fortress of Sacsayhuaman, for example, or wandering around at Machu Picchu, involves more than an average Sunday afternoon stroll. Bearing in mind the rugged terrain throughout Peru, the absolute minimum footwear is a strong pair of running shoes. Much better is a pair of hiking boots with good ankle support.

Hiking – whether in the desert, mountains or jungle – can be an enormously rewarding experience, but you should go properly equipped and bear in mind a few of the **potential hazards**. Never stray too far without food and water, something warm and something waterproof to wear. The weather is renowned for its dramatic changeability, especially in **the mountains**, where there is always the additional danger of *soroche* (altitude sickness – see p.19). In **the jungle** the biggest danger is getting lost. If this happens, the best thing to do is follow a water course down to the main stream, and stick to this until you reach a settlement or get picked up by a passing canoe. If you get caught out in the forest at night, build a leafy shelter and make a fire or try sleeping in a tree.

In the mountains it's often a good idea to hire a **pack animal** to carry your gear. **Llamas** can only carry about 25–30kg and move slowly, a **burro** (donkey) carries around 80kg, and a **mule** – the most common and best pack animal – will shift 150kg with relative ease. Mules can be hired from upwards of $5 a day, and they normally come with an *arriero*, a muleteer who'll double as a guide. It is also possible to hire mules or horses for **riding** but this costs a little more. With a guide and beast of burden it's quite simple to reach even the most remote valleys, ruins and mountain passes, travelling in much the same way as Pizarro and his men over four hundred years ago.

HITCHING

Hitching in Peru usually means catching a ride with a truck driver, who will almost always expect payment. With most **trucks** you won't have to pay before setting off, but you should always agree a sum before getting in as there are stories of drivers stopping in the middle of nowhere and demanding unreasonably high sums (from foreigners and Peruvians alike) before going any further. Trucks can be flagged down anywhere but there is greater choice around markets, and at police *controls* or petrol stations on the outskirts of towns. Trucks tend to be the only form of public transport in some less accessible regions, travelling the roads that buses won't touch and serving remote communities, so you may end up having to sit on top of a pile of potatoes or bananas.

Hitchhiking in **private cars** is not recommended, and, in any case, it's very rare that one will stop to pick you up, though some travellers have had lifts of over 1000km this way.

ORGANIZED TOURS

There are hundreds of **travel agents** and **tour operators** in Peru, and reps hunt out customers at bus terminals, train stations and in city centres. While they can be expensive, organized excursions can be a quick and relatively effortless way to see some of the popular attractions and the more remote sites, while a prearranged trek, like the Inca Trail, can take much of the worry out of camping preparations and ensure that you get decent campsites, a sound meal and help with carrying your equipment in what can be difficult walking conditions (mainly due to the high altitude).

Many **adventure tour companies** offer excellent and increasingly exciting packages and itineraries – ranging from mountain biking, whitewater rafting, jungle photo-safaris, mountain trekking and climbing, to more comfortable and gentler city and countryside tours. Tours cost $25–60 a day and, in Cusco and Huaraz in particular, there's an enormous selection of operators to choose from. **Cusco** is a pretty good base for hiking, whitewater rafting, canoeing, horse-riding or going on an expedition into the Amazonian jungle with an adventure tour company (see p.137 & p.377); **Arequipa** offers superb hiking and the surrounding area boasts two of the deepest canyons on the planet, all

serviced by tour companies (see p.215); **Huaraz** is a good base for trekking and mountaineering; **Iquitos**, on the Amazon river, is one of the best places for adventure trips into the jungle and has a reasonable range of tour operators (see p.408). Several of these companies have branches in Lima, if you want to book a tour in advance; see Lima Listings on p.86. For up-to-the-minute information and recommendations, contact the Asociacion Peruana de Operadores de Turismo, Bajada Balta 169, Dpto 203, Miraflores (☎01/446-0422, *apotur@amauta.rcp.net.pe*) or the Asociacion Peruana de Tursimo de Aventura y Ecoturismo, Santander 170, Miraflores (☎01/221-4283).

ACCOMMODATION

Peru has the typical range of Latin American accommodation, from top-class international hotels at prices to compare with any Western capital down to basic rooms or shared dorms in hostals, which are unaffiliated to Hostelling International. The biggest development over the last 10 years has been

the rise of the mid-range option, reflecting the growth of both domestic and international tourism. Camping is frequently possible, sometimes free and perfectly acceptable in most rural parts of Peru, though there are very few formal campsites.

Accommodation denominations of *hotel*, *hostal*, *residencial*, *pension* or *hospedaje* are almost meaningless in terms of what you'll find inside. Virtually all upmarket accommodation will call itself a **hotel** or, in the countryside regions, a **posada**. In the jungle, **tambo lodges** can be anything from quite luxurious to an open sided, palm-thatched hut with space for slinging a hammock. Technically speaking, somewhere that calls itself a **pension** or **residencial** ought to specialize in longer term accommodation, and while they may well offer discounts for stays of a week or more, they are just as geared up for short stays.

There's no standard or widely used rating system, so, apart from the information given in this

---

ACCOMMODATION PRICE CODES

Unless otherwise indicated, **accommodation** in this book is coded according to the categories below, based on the price of a double room in high season.

① under $5	③ $10–20	⑤ $30–40	⑦ $50–70
② $5–10	④ $20–30	⑥ $40–50	⑧ over $70

book, the only way to tell whether a place is suitable or not is to walk in and take a look around – the proprietors won't mind this, and you'll soon get used to spotting places with promise. A handy phrase is "*Quisiera ver un cuarto (con cama matrimonial)*" ("I'd like to see a (double) room").

HOTELS

The **cheaper hotels** are generally old – sometimes beautifully so, converted from colonial mansions with rooms grouped around a courtyard – and tend to be within a few blocks of a town's central plaza, general market, or bus or train station. At the cheapest end of the scale, which can be fairly basic with shared rooms and a communal bathroom, you can usually find a bed for between $5 and $10, and occasionally even less. For a few dollars more you can find a good, clean single or double room with bath in a **mid-range hotel**, generally for somewhere between $15 and $45. A little haggling is often worth a try, and if you find one room too pricey, another, perhaps identical, can often be found for less, the phrase "*Tiene un cuarto más barato?*" ("Do you have a cheaper room?") is useful. Savings can invariably be made, too, by sharing rooms – many have two, three, even four or five beds. A double-bedded room (*con cama matrimonial*) is usually cheaper than one with two beds (*con dos camas*).

The privatized chain of formerly state-run hotels – *Hotels de Turistas* – has been carved up and the hotels sold off to a number of entrepreneurs. The hotels can be found in all the larger Peruvian resorts as well as some surprisingly offbeat ones, often being the only place around with a swimming pool and generally among the flashiest places in town. Since privatization they have lost their corporate chain image and are increasingly being known by new names, though taxi drivers will still recognize them as *Hotel de Turistas*. They still tend to be among the best **upmarket accommodation** options in all towns outside of Lima. Out of season some of these can be relatively inexpensive (from around $15–20 per person), and if you like the look of a place it's often worth asking. Note that all luxury hotels in Peru charge eighteen percent **tax** and often ten percent **service** on top of this again; always check beforehand whether the quoted price includes these extras.

One point of caution – it's not advisable to pay tour or travel agents in one city for accommoda-

SOME ACCOMMODATION TERMS	
Ventilador	Desk fan or ceiling fan
Aire-acondicionado	Air-conditioned
Baño colectivo /compartido	Shared bath
Agua caliente	Hot water
Agua fría	Cold water
Cama matrimonial	Double bed
Sencillo	Single bed
Cuarto simple	Single room
Impuestos	Taxes
Hora de salida	Check-out time (usually between 12.30 and 2pm)

tion required in the next town. By all means ask agents to make reservations but do not ask them to send payments; it is always simpler and safer to do that yourself.

YOUTH HOSTELS

There are currently 28 **youth hostels** (*hostals*) spread throughout Peru. They are not the standardized institution found in Europe, but they are relatively cheap and reliable; expect to pay $4–10 for a bed, though you may pay slightly more in Lima. All hostels are theoretically open 24 hours a day and most have cheap cafeterias attached. Many of the hostels don't check that you are a member, but if you want to be on the safe side, you can join up at the Associación Peruana de Albergues Turísticos Juveniles, Casimiro Ulloa 328, San Antonio, Miraflores, Lima 18 (☎01/446-5488, fax 444-8187, *hostel@cosapidata.com.pe*). You can get a full list of all the country's hostels here, and they can also make advance bookings for you.

CAMPING

Camping is possible almost everywhere in Peru, and it's rarely difficult to find space for a tent. Camping is free since there are only one or two organized campsites in the whole country. It's also the most satisfactory way of seeing Peru, as some of the country's most fantastic places are well off the beaten track: with a tent – or a hammock – it's possible to go all over without worrying if you'll make it to a *hostal*.

It's usually okay to set up camp in fields or forest beyond the outskirts of settlements, but ask

permission and advice from the nearest farm or house first. Apart from a few restricted areas, Peru's enormous sandy coastline is open territory, the real problem not being so much where to camp as how to get there; some of the most stunning areas are very remote. The same can be said of both the mountains and the jungle – camp anywhere, but ask first, if you can find anyone to ask.

There have been reports of tourists being attacked and robbed while camping in fairly **remote areas**. This is still rare, though, and some reports suggest that the robberies have been carried out by other foreign tourists, rather than Peruvian thieves. But whoever the culprits are, it does happen, particularly along such popular routes as the Inca Trail. Travelling with someone else or in groups is always a good idea, but even on your own there are a few basic precautions that you can take: let someone know where you intend to go; be respectful, and try to commu-nicate with any locals you may meet or be camping near; and be careful who you make friends with en route.

Camping equipment is difficult to find in Peru and relatively expensive. One or two places sell, rent or buy secondhand gear, mainly in Cusco, Arequipa and Huaraz, and there are some reasonably good, if quite expensive shops in Lima. It's also worth checking the noticeboards in the popular traveller's hotels and bars for equipment that is no longer needed or for people wanting trekking companions – something you might find useful to do yourself to cut down on baggage, or by hawking it around the rental shops. Camping Gaz butane canisters are available from most of the above places and from some *ferreterías* (hard-ware stores) in the major resorts. A couple of essential things you'll need when camping in Peru are a mosquito net and repellent, and some sort of water treatment system (see p.17)

EATING AND DRINKING

As with almost every activity, the style and pattern of eating and drinking varies consid-erably between the three main regions of Peru. Depending on the very different ingre-dients available locally, food in each area is essentially a mestizo creation, combining indigenous Indian cooking with four hun-dred years of European – mostly Spanish – influence.

Guinea pig (cuy) is the traditional dish most associated with Peru, and indeed, you can find it in many parts of the country, but especially in the mountain regions, where it is likely to be roasted in an oven and served with chips. In the past twenty years, with the wave of North American interests in the country, fast food has become commonplace. You'll find *Kentucky Fried Chicken* in Lima; and hamburgers, as well as the ubiqui-tous pizza, which the Peruvians have adopted with enthusiasm, are more readily available than the traditional guinea pig.

SNACKS AND LIGHT MEALS

All over Peru, but particularly in the large towns and cities, you'll find a good variety of traditional **fast foods and snacks** such as *salchipapas* (fries with sliced sausage covered in various sauces), *anticuchos* (a shish kebab made from marinated lamb or beef heart) and *empanadas* (meat- or cheese-filled pies). These are all sold on street corners until late at night. Even in the villages you'll find cafés and restaurants which double as bars, staying open all day and serving anything from coffee with bread to steak and fries or lobster. The most popular **sweets** in Peru are made from either *manjar blanco* (sweetened condensed milk) or fresh fruits.

In general, the **market** is always a good place to head for – you can buy food ready to eat on the spot or to take away and prepare, and the range and prices are better than in any shop. Most food prices are fixed, but the vendor may throw in an orange, a bit of garlic, or some coriander leaves for good measure. Markets are the best places to stock up for a trek, for a picnic, or if you just want to eat cheaply. Smoked meat, which can be sliced up and used like salami, is normally a good buy.

RESTAURANTS

All larger towns in Peru have a fair choice of **restaurants**, most of which offer a varied menu. Among them there's usually a few *chifa* (**Chinese**) places, and nowadays a fair number of **vegetarian** restaurants too. Most restaurants in the larger towns stay open seven days a week from around 11am until 11pm, though in smaller settlements they may close one day a week, usually Sunday. Often they will offer a *cena*, or **set menu**, from morning through to lunchtime and another in the evening. Ranging in price from $1 to $3, these most commonly consist of three courses: soup, a main dish, and a cup of tea or coffee to follow. Every town, too, seems now to have at least one restaurant that specializes in *pollos a la brasa* – spit-roasted chickens. **Tipping** in budget or average restaurants is normal, though not obligatory and you should rarely expect to give more than about $0.5. In fancier places you may well find a **service charge** of ten percent as well as a **tax** of eighteen percent added to the bill, and in restaurants and peñas where there's live music or performances the **cover charge** can go up to $5. Even without performance, cover charges of around $1 are sometimes levied in the flashier restaurants in major town centres.

Along the coast, not surprisingly, **seafood** is the speciality. The Humboldt Current keeps the Pacific Ocean off Peru extremely rich in plankton and other microscopic life forms, which attract a wide variety of fish. *Ceviche* is the classic Peruvian seafood dish and has been eaten by locals for over two thousand years. It consists of fish, shrimp, scallops or squid, or a mixture of all four, marinated in lime juice and chilli peppers, then served "raw" with corn and sweet potato and onions. You can find it, along with fried fish and fish soups, in most restaurants along the coast for around $2. *Escabeche* is another tasty fish-based appetizer, this time incorporating peppers and finely chopped onions. The coast is also an excellent place for eating scallops – known here as *conchitas* – which grow particularly well close to the Peruvian shoreline. *Conchitas negras* (black scallops) are a delicacy in the northern tip of Peru. Excellent **salads** are also widely available, such as *huevos a la rusa* (egg salad), *palta rellena* (stuffed avocado), or a straight tomato salad, while *papas a la Huancaina* (a cold appetizer of potatoes covered in a spicy light cheese sauce) is great too.

Mountain food is more basic – a staple of potatoes and rice with the meat stretched as far as it will go. *Lomo saltado*, or diced prime beef sautéed with onions and peppers, is served anywhere at any time, accompanied by rice and a few french fries. A delicious snack from street vendors and cafés is *papa rellena*, a potato stuffed with vegetables and fried. **Trout** is also widely available, as are cheese, ham and egg sandwiches. *Chicha*, a **corn beer** drunk throughout the *sierra* region and on the coast in rural areas, is very cheap with a pleasantly tangy taste. Another Peruvian speciality is the **Pachamanca**, a roast prepared mainly in the mountains but also on the coast by digging a large hole, filling it with stones and lighting a fire over them, then using the hot stones to cook a wide variety of tasty meats and vegetables.

In the **jungle**, the food is different. **Bananas** and **plantains** figure highly, along with *yuca* (a manioc rather like a yam), rice and plenty of fish. There is **meat** as well, mostly chicken supplemented occasionally by **game** – deer, wild pig, or even monkey. Every settlement big enough to get on the map has its own bar or café, but in remote areas it's a matter of eating what's available and drinking coffee or bottled drinks if you don't relish the home-made *masato* (cassava beer).

DRINKING

Beers, **wines** and **spirits** are served in almost every bar, café or restaurant at any time, but there is a deposit on taking beer bottles out (canned beer is one of the worst inventions to hit Peru this century – some of the finest beaches are littered with empty cans).

FOOD AND DRINK

BASICS

Arroz	Rice	*fritos*	fried	*Miel*	Honey
Avena	Oats (porridge)	*duros*	hard boiled	*Mostaza*	Mustard
Galletas	Biscuits	*pasados*	lightly boiled	*Pan (integral)*	Bread (brown)
Harina	Flour	*revueltos*	scrambled	*picante de. . .*	spicy dish of . . .
Huevos	Eggs	*Mermelada*	Jam	*Queso*	Cheese

SOUP (SOPAS) AND STARTERS

Caldo	Broth	*Huevos a la rusa*	Egg salad
Caldo de gallina	Chicken broth	*Palta*	Avocado
Causa	Mashed potatoes and shrimp	*Palta rellena*	Stuffed avocado
		Papa rellena	Stuffed fried potato
Conchas a la parmesana	Scallops with parmesan	*Sopa a la criolla*	Noodles, vegetables and meat

SEAFOOD (MARISCOS) AND FISH (PESCADO)

Calamares	Squid	*Langosta*	Lobster
Camarones	Shrimp	*Langostino a lo macho*	Crayfish in spicy shellfish sauce
Cangrejo	Crab		
Ceviche	Marinated seafood	*Lenguado*	Sole
Chaufa de mariscos	Chinese rice with seafood	*Paiche*	Large jungle river fish
Cojinova		*Tiradito*	*ceviche* without onion or sweet potato
Corvina	Sea bass		
Erizo	Sea urchin	*Tollo*	Small shark
Jalea	Large dish of fish with onion	*Zungarro*	Large jungle fish

MEAT (CARNES)

Adobo	Meat/fish in mild chilli sauce	*Higado*	Liver
Aji de galina	Chicken in chilli sauce	*Jamon*	Ham
Anticuchos	Skewered heart (usually lamb)	*Lechon*	Pork
		Lomo asado	Roast beef
Bifstek (bistek)	Steak	*Lomo saltado*	Sautéed beef
Cabrito	Goat	*Mollejitos*	Gizzard
Carne a lo pobre	Steak, fries, egg and banana	*Pachamanca*	Meat and vegetables, cooked over hot buried stones
Carne de res	Beef		
Carapulcra	Pork, chicken and potato casserole	*Parillada*	Grilled meat
		Pato	Duck
Chicharrones	Deep-fried pork skins	*Pollo (a la brasa)*	Chicken (spit-roasted)
Conejo	Rabbit	*Pavo*	Turkey
Cordero	Lamb	*Tocino*	Bacon
Cuy	Guinea pig (a traditional dish)	*Venado*	Venison
Estofado	Stewed meat (usually served with rice)		

VEGETABLES (LEGUMBRES) AND SIDE DISHES

Aji	Chilli	*Lechuga*	Lettuce
Camote	Sweet potato	*Papa rellena*	Fried potato balls, stuffed with
Cebolla	Onion		olives, egg and mincemeat
Choclo	Corn on the cob	*Tallarines*	Spaghetti noodles
Fideos	Noodles	*Tomates*	Tomatoes
Frijoles	Beans	*Yuca*	Manioc (like a yam)
Hongos	Mushrooms	*a la Huancaina*	in spicy cheese sauce

FRUIT

Chirimoya	Custard apple (green and fleshy outside, tastes like strawberries and cream)	*Maracuya*	Passion fruit
		Palta	Avocado
		Piña	Pineapple
Lucuma	Small nutty fruit (used in ice creams and cakes)	*Tuna*	Pear-like cactus fruit (refreshing but full of hard little seeds)

SWEETS (DULCES)

Barquillo	Ice cream cone	*Manjar blanco*	Sweetened condensed milk
Flan	Créme caramel	*Mazamorra morada*	Fruit/maize jelly
Helado	Ice cream	*Panqueques*	Pancakes
Keke	Cake	*Picarones*	Doughnuts with syrup

SNACKS (BOCADILLOS)

Castanas	Brazil nuts	*Sandwich de lechon*	Pork salad sandwich
Chifles	Fried banana slices	*Tamale*	Maize flour roll stuffed
Empanada	Meat or cheese pie		with olives, egg, meat
Hamburguesa	Hamburger		and vegetables
Salchipapas	Potatoes, sliced frankfurter sausage and condiments	*Tortilla*	Omelette cum pancake
		Tostados	Toast
Sandwich de butifara	Ham and onion sandwich		

FRUIT JUICES (JUGOS)

Especial	Fruit, milk, sometimes beer	*Papaya*	Papaya
Fresa	Strawberry	*Piña*	Pineapple
Higo	Fig	*Platano*	Banana
Manzana	Apple	*Surtido*	Mixed
Melon	Melon	*Toronja*	Grapefruit
Naranja	Orange	*Zanahoria*	Carrot

BEVERAGES (BEBIDAS)

Agua	Water	*Limonada*	Real lemonade
Agua Mineral	Mineral water	*Masato*	Fermented manioc beer
Algarrobina	Algarroba-fruit drink	*Pisco*	White grape brandy
Cafe	Coffee	*Ponche*	Punch
Cerveza	Beer	*Ron*	Rum
Chicha de jora	Fermented maize beer	*Te*	Tea
Chicha morada	Maize soft drink	*con leche*	with milk
Chilcano de pisco	Pisco with lemonade	*de anis*	aniseed tea
Chopp	Draught beer	*de limon*	lemon tea
Cuba libre	Rum and coke	*hierba luisa*	lemon grass tea
Gaseosa	Soft carbonated drink	*manzanilla*	camomile tea
Leche	Milk		

Most **Peruvian beer** – except for *cerveza malta* (black malt beer) – is bottled lager almost exclusively brewed to five percent, and extremely good. In Lima the two main beers are *Cristal* and *Pilsen. Cuzqueña* (from Cusco) is one of the best and by far the most popular at the moment, but not universally available; you won't find it on the coast in Trujillo, for example, where they drink *Trujillana*, nor are you likely to encounter it in every bar in Arequipa where, not surprisingly perhaps, they prefer to drink *Arequipeña* beer. You can usually buy *Cuzqueña* in Lima though. **Soft drinks** range from mineral water, through the ubiquitous *Coca Cola* and *Fanta*, to home-produced novelties like the gold-coloured *Inca Cola*, with rather a homemade taste, and the red, extremely sweet *Cola Inglesa*. **Fruit juices** (*jugos*), most commonly papaya or orange, are prepared fresh in most places, and you can get **coffee** and a wide variety of herb and leaf **teas** almost anywhere. Surprisingly, for a good coffee-growing country, the coffee in cafés and restaurants leaves much to be desired, commonly prepared from either *café pasado* (previously passed or percolated coffee mixed with hot water to serve) or simple

powdered Nescafé. You have to search out the odd café, which you'll find in most larger towns, which prepares good fresh *espresso, cappuccino* or filtered coffee.

Peru has been producing **wine** (*vino*) for over four hundred years, but with one or two exceptions it is not that good. Among the better ones are *Vista Alegre* (*tipo familiar*) – not entirely reliable but only around $1 a bottle – and *Tacama Gran Vino Blanco Reserva Especial,* about $7 or $8 a bottle. A good Argentinian or Chilean wine will cost from $10 upwards.

As for **spirits,** Peru's main claim to fame is *Pisco*. This is a white grape brandy with a unique, powerful and very palatable flavour – the closest equivalent elsewhere is probably tequila. Almost anything else is available as an import – Scotch whisky is cheaper here than in the UK – but beware of the really cheap imitations which can remove the roof of your mouth with ease. The jungle regions produce *cashassa*, a sugar-cane rum also called *aguardiente*, which has a distinctive taste and is occasionally mixed with different herbs, some medicinal. Whilst it goes down easily, it's incredibly strong stuff and leaves you with a very sore head the next morning.

COMMUNICATIONS – POST, PHONES AND MEDIA

The Peruvian postal service is reasonably efficient, if slightly irregular. Letters from Europe and the US generally take around one or two weeks – occasionally less –

while outbound letters to Europe or the US seem to take between ten days and three weeks. Stamps for airmail letters to the UK, the US, and to Australia and New Zealand all cost around $1.

Be aware that **parcels** are particularly vulnerable to being opened en route – in either direction – and expensive souvenirs can't be sure of leaving the building where you mail them. Likewise, Peruvian postal workers are liable to "check" incoming parcels which contain cassettes or interesting foods.

POSTE RESTANTE

You can have mail sent to you **poste restante** care of any main post office (Correo Central), and, on the whole, the system tends to work quite smoothly. Have letters addressed: full name (last name in capitals), Poste Restante, Lista de

Correos, Correo Central, city or town, Peru. To pick up mail you'll need your passport, and you may have to get the files for the initials of all your names (including Ms, Mr, etc) checked. Rather quirkily, letters are sometimes filed separately by sex, too – in which case it's worth getting both piles checked. Some post offices let you look through the pile, others won't let you anywhere near the letters until they've found one that fits your name exactly.

An alternative to the official *lista* is to use the **American Express** mail collection service. Their main offices in Peru are in Lima, c/o Lima Tours, Belén 1040, near Plaza San Martin (☎01/424-7560 or 424-5110, fax 330-4488, *inbound@ limatours.com.pe*) and in Cusco, c/o Lima Tours,

Avenida Machu Picchu D-6, Urb. Manuel Prado (☎084/228431 or 235241). Officially, American Express charges for this service unless you have one of their cards or use their traveller's cheques, though they rarely seem to. The **South American Explorers' Club** (see p.21) offers members a postal address service.

TELEPHONES

With a little patience you can make **international calls** from just about any town in the country. In recent years the telephone system has dramatically improved, partly due to being taken over by a Spanish telephone company and partly because of modernization and an increasing use of satellites.

TELEPHONE CODES AND USEFUL NUMBERS

TO PHONE ABROAD FROM PERU

Dial the country code (given below) + area code (minus initial zero) + number

Australia 0061	Ireland 00353	UK 0044
Canada 001	New Zealand 0064	USA 001

TO PHONE PERU FROM ABROAD

Dial the international access code (see below) + 51 (country code) + area code (minus intitial zero; see below) + number.

International access code

Australia 0011	Ireland 00	UK 00
Canada 001	New Zealand 00	USA 001

Peruvian town and city codes

Arequipa 054	Iquitos 094	Pisco 034
Ayacucho 064	Jaen 074	Piura 074
Cajamarca 044	Jauja 064	Pucallpa 064
Cusco 084	Juliaca 054	Puerto Maldonado 084
Chiclayo 074	La Merced 064	Puno 054
Chimbote 044	La Oroya 064	Quillabamba 084
Chincha 034	Lambayeque 074	Tacna 054
Huancavelica 064	Lima 01	Tarapoto 094
Huancayo 064	Moquegua 054	Tarma 064
Huanuco 064	Moyobamba 094	Trujillo 044
Huaraz 044	Nasca 034	Tumbes 074
Ica 034	Pisac 084	

USEFUL TELEPHONE NUMBERS

Directory enquiries 103	Operator 100
Emergency services 105	International operator 108

All Peruvian towns have a **Teléfonica del Peru** office, which offers an operator service; give the receptionist your destination number and they will allocate you to a numbered phone booth when your call is put through (you pay afterwards). These offices also have have phones taking cards (see below). In Lima, the central Teléfonica del Peru office (see p.86) is often crowded, so a better option is to phone from your hotel or from the street **telephone kiosks**.

All phone kiosks are operated by coins or *tarjetas telefonicas* – **phone cards** – which are available in a variety of denominations, and nuevo sol coins. You can buy phone cards from corner shops, *farmacias* or on the street from cigarette stalls in the centres of most towns and cities. There are currently two phone outfits, Telefonica del Peru and Telepoint, each of whom produce their own cards for use in their phones only.

You should be able to make direct, international calls without much problem from anywhere in Peru, but if you need to contact the **international operator**, dial ☎108. **Collect calls** are known either simply as *collect* or *al cobro revertido* and are fairly straightforward. Calls are cheaper at night. Most shops, restaurants or corner shops in Peru have a phone available for public use, which you can use for calls within Peru only.

THE MEDIA

There are many poor-quality newspapers and magazines available on the streets of Lima and throughout the rest of Peru. Many of the newspapers stick mainly to sex and sport, while magazines tend to focus on terror and violence and the frequent deaths caused by major traffic accidents. The two most established (and establishment) **daily newspapers** are *El Comercio* and *Expreso*; the latter devoting vast amounts of space to anti-Communist propaganda. *El Comercio* (*www.elcomercio.com.pe/*) is much more balanced but still tends to toe the political party of the day's line. *El Comercio's* daily *Seccion C* also has the most comprehensive cultural listings of any paper – good for just about everything going on in Lima. In addition, there's the sensationalist tabloid *La Republica*, which takes a middle-of-the-road to liberal approach to politics; and *Cambio* provides interesting tabloid reading. One of the better weekly **magazines** is the fairly liberal *Caretas*, generally offering mildly critical support to whichever government happens to be in power. There's one environmental and travel magazine – *Rumbos* – which publishes articles in both Spanish and English and has excellent photographic features.

The Cusco-based weekly, *New World News*, is an excellent **English-language newspaper**, available weekly across Peru in the major cities. It reports on issues relevant to tourism plus news around South America and world issues. The business weekly *Lima Herald*, also in English, can be bought in Lima Centro and sporadically in Cusco. For more serious, in-depth coverage, the monthly *Andean Report*, is particularly good on Peruvian and Andean political and economic issues.

International newspapers are fairly hard to come by; your best bet for **English papers** is to go to the Embassy in Lima, which has a selection of one- to two-week old papers, such as *The Times* and *Independent* for reference only. **US papers** are easier to find; the bookstalls around Plaza San Martin in Lima Centro and those along Avenida Larco and Diagonal in Miraflores sell the *Miami Herald*, the *Herald Tribune*, *Newsweek* and *Time* magazine, but even these are likely to be four or five days old. If you're not moving around too much, consider having *The Guardian Weekly*, which has comprehensive international coverage, sent to you poste restante.

Peruvians watch a lot of **television** – mostly soccer and soap operas, though TV is also a main source of news. Many programmes come from Mexico, Brazil and the US (*The Flintstones* and *Bewitched* are perennial favourites), with occasional eccentric selections from elsewhere and a growing presence of manga-style cartoons. There are nine main terrestial channels, of which channels 7 and 13 show marginally better quality programmes. Panamericana is Peru's top station, but all the channels are crammed with adverts.

Cable and, even more so, **satellite channels** are increasingly forming an important part of Peru's media. Partly due to the fact that it can be received in even the remotest of settlements and partly because it is beyond the control of any government or other censorship, satellite TV appears set to dominate the media scene and the world view of the nation's youth.

If you have a **radio** you can pick up the BBC World Service at most hours of the day – frequencies shift around on the 19m, 25m and 49m short-wave bands; for a schedule of programmes, contact the British Council in Lima (see p.84). The

Voice of America is also constantly available on short wave. The radio station Sol Armonia is dedicated to classical music on FM89. Also, the RPP (Radio Programmes del Peru) on FM 89.7 has 24-hour bulletins

Alternatively, you can tune in to an incredible mess of **Peruvian stations**, nearly all of which are music and advertisement based. International pop, salsa and other Latin pop can be picked up most times of day and night all along the FM wave band, while traditional Peruvian and Andean folk music can usually be found all over the AM dial. Radio Miraflores (96FM) is one of the best, playing mainly disco and new US/British rock, though also with a good jazz programme on Sunday evenings and an excellent news summary every morning from 7 to 9am. Radio Cien (100FM) has the occasional programme in English (on Sunday mornings, for example).

THE INTERNET

Peru has good **Internet** connections, with cyber cafés and Internet cabins in the most unlikely of small towns breaking down barriers of distance more effectively than the telephone ever did. Lima and Cusco have abundant Internet facilities, closely followed by Arequipa, Huaraz, Puno, Iquitos and Trujillo; beyond that it gets a little patchy, but the odd public access office or café does exist and many hotels now offer access too. The general rate is $1.20–1.75 an hour, though thity- and fifteen-minutes options are often available. One of the most widespread and professional **service providers** in Peru is RCP (Red Cientifica Peruana; *webmaster@rcp.net.pe*), who have a Lima office, as well as one in Cusco where they offer inexpensive computer-to-telephone international calls.

CRIME AND PERSONAL SAFETY

The biggest problem for travellers in Peru is, without a doubt, thieves, for which the country has one of the worst reputations in South America – on one particular train journey (the Arequipa–Puno night service) many tourists have been robbed over the years. As far as violent attacks go, you're probably safer in Peru than in New York, Sydney or London. And as for terrorism – as the South American Explorers' Club once described it – "the visitor, when considering his safety, would be better off concentrating on how to avoid being run over in the crazed Lima traffic".

THEFT

The dangers of **pickpockets and robberies** cannot be over emphasized, though the situation does seem to have improved since the dark days of the late 1980s. Without encouraging a permanent state of paranoia and constant watchfulness in busy public situations, common sense and general alertness are recommended. The South American Explorers' Club (see p.21) can give you the low-down on the latest thieving practices, some of which have developed over the years into quite elaborate and skilful techniques.

Generally speaking, **thieves** (*ladrones*) work in teams of often smartly dressed young men and women, in crowded markets, bus depots and train stations, targeting anyone who looks like they've got money. One of them will distract your attention (an old woman falling over in front of you or someone splattering an ice cream down your jacket) while another picks your pocket, cuts open your bag with a razor, or simply runs off with it. Peruvians and tourists alike have even had earrings ripped out on the street. Bank **ATMs** are a target for muggers in cities, particularly after dark, so visit them with a friend or two during daylight hours or make sure there's a policeman within visual contact. **Armed mugging** does happen in Lima, and it's best not to resist, and "strangle mugging" has been a bit of a problem in Cusco and Arequipa, usually involving night attacks when the perpetrator tries to make the victim unconscious by strangulation. Again, be careful not to walk down badly lit streets alone in the early hours. **Theft from cars** and even more so, theft of car parts, is rife in Peru, particularly in Lima. Also, in some of the more popular hotels in the large cities, especially Lima, bandits masquerading as policemen break into rooms and steal the guests' most valuable possessions while holding the hotel staff at gun point. Objects left on restaurant floors in busy parts of town, or in unlocked hotel rooms, are obviously liable to take a walk.

You'd need to spend the whole time visibly guarding your luggage to be sure of keeping hold of it; even then, though, a determined team of thieves will stand a chance. However, a few simple **precautions** can make life a lot easier. The most important is to keep your ticket, passport (and tourist card), money and traveller's cheques on your person at all times (under your pillow while sleeping and on your person when washing in communal hotel bathrooms). **Money belts** are a good idea for traveller's cheques and tickets, or a holder for your passport and money can be hung either under a shirt, or from a belt under trousers or skirts. A **false pocket**, secured by safety pins to the inside of trousers, skirts or shirts also makes it harder for thieves or muggers to find your cash reserve (and is easy to transfer between items of clothing). Some people go as far as lining their bags with chicken wire (called *maya* in Peru) to make them knife-proof, and wrapping wire around camera straps for the same reason (putting their necks in danger to save their cameras).

The only certain course is to **insure** your gear and cash before you go (see p.15). Take refundable traveller's cheques, register your passport at your embassy in Lima on arrival (this doesn't take long and can save days should you lose yours), and keep your eyes open at all times. If you do get ripped off, report it to the tourist police in larger towns (see opposite), or the local police in more remote places, and ask them for a certified

denuncia – this can take a couple of days. Many insurance companies will require a copy of the police *denuncia* in order to reimburse you, though some only require proof of your whereabouts at the time of the incident (for example a hotel bill or a tour company letter or report). Check with your insurance company before leaving for Peru as to what their requirements are.

TERRORISM

Terrorism is much less of a problem in Peru these days than it was in the 1980s and 1990s. You can get up-to-date information on the situation in each region from the South American Explorers' Club (see p.21), Peruvian Embassies abroad (see p.12) or your embassy in Lima (see p.85). There are two main **terrorist groups** active in Peru – the Sendero Luminoso (the Shining Path) and Tupac Amaru (MRTA).

The **Sendero Luminoso** sprang from rural Quechua dissidents and educated middle classes originally operating mainly in the central highlands and Lima. These days their influence has waned enormously and, apart from the occasional car bomb in Lima, their paramilitary activities are by and large restricted to certain areas of the jungle and to a lesser extent the remote areas of the central highland region. They have a reputation for ruthless and violent tactics, sweeping away all left-wing and popular resistance to their aims and methods by the rule of the gun. When their leader Guzman was captured in 1992, the movement began to fade fast, and with the capture of their number two Feliciano, in 1999, it appears for now that their activities are limited almost exclusively to narco-terrorism (cocaine producing and smuggling) in the **Alto Huallaga** valley. This area – basically the region and road between Tingo Maria and Tarapoto – should still be avoided at all costs. It's often difficult to distinguish between drug trafficking and terrorism in certain places, and much of the coca-growing area of the eastern Andes and western Amazon is beyond the law.

The **Tupac Amaru**, on the other hand, have a slightly more populist image, focusing on military or political targets. They rose to prominence at Christmas 1996 when they took hostages at the Japanese Embassy in Lima, but this ended fatally for the terrorists and took the wind out of their sails quite severely. Incidents these days are very rare; they might still stop the odd bus in remote jungle areas, but they're more likely to ask for a "voluntary" contribution than execute the passengers on political grounds. So far, although tourists have been killed, neither group has resorted to taking foreigners hostage and tourists are not considered political targets. Keep to the beaten track, keep yourself well informed, travel in the daytime, and you should be safe. For more background on this, see Contexts, pp.431–433.

THE POLICE

Most of your contact with the **police** will, with any luck, be at frontiers and controls. Depending on your personal appearance and the prevailing political climate the police at these posts (*Guardia Nacional* and *Aduanas*) may want to search your luggage. This happens rarely, but when it does it can be very thorough. Occasionally, you may have to get off buses and register documents at the police *controls* which regulate the traffic of goods and people from one *departmento* of Peru to another; these are usually situated on the outskirts of large towns on the main roads, but you sometimes come across a *control* in the middle of nowhere. Always stop, and be scrupulously polite – even if it seems that they're trying to make things difficult for you.

In general the police rarely bother travellers but there are certain sore points. The possession of (let alone trafficking in) either soft or hard **drugs** (basically grass or cocaine) is considered an extremely serious offence in Peru – usually leading to at least a ten-year jail sentence. There are many foreigners languishing in Peruvian jails, some of whom have been waiting two years for a trial – there is no bail for serious charges. If you want to visit one of them you can get details from your embassy.

Drugs apart, the police tend to follow the media in suspecting all foreigners of being **political subversives** and even gun-runners or terrorists; it's more than a little unwise to carry any Maoist or radical literature. If you find yourself in a tight spot, don't make a statement before seeing someone from your embassy, and don't say anything without the services of a reliable translator. It's not unusual to be given the opportunity to pay a **bribe** to the police (or any other official for that matter), even if you've done nothing wrong. You'll have to weigh up this situation as it arises – but remember, in South America bribery is seen as an age-old custom, very much part of the culture rather than a nasty form of corruption, and it can work to the advantage of both parties, however irritating it might seem. It's also worth noting that all police are armed with either a revolver or a submachine gun and will shoot at anyone who runs.

THE TOURIST POLICE

If you're unlucky enough to have anything stolen, your first port of call should be the **tourist police** (*policia de turismo*). Bear in mind that the police in popular tourist spots, such as Cusco, have become much stricter about investigating reported thefts, after a spate of false claims by dishonest tourists. This means that genuine victims may be grilled more severely than expected, and the police may even come and search your hotel room for the "stolen" items. However, provided your claim is genuine, you should stick to your guns and make sure you get a written report. Peru's **headquarters** for the tourist police is in Lima at the Museo de La Nacion, Javier Prado Este 2465, 5th floor (☎01/225-8699, 437-8171 or 435-1342).

If you feel you've been ripped off or are unhappy about your treatment by a tour agent, hotel,

---

TOURIST PROTECTION SERVICE

OFFICES

Arequipa Indecopi, Calle Moral 316.

Cusco Indecopi, Portal de Carrizos 250, Plaza de Armas.

Lima Indecopi, Calle de La Prosa 138, San Borja (*tour@indecopi.gob.pe*).

Trujillo Indecopi, Independencia 630, Casona Ganoza Chopitea.

HOTLINE NUMBERS

National toll-free ☎0800/44040 or 42579
Arequipa ☎054/212054
Cusco ☎ & fax 084/252974
Iquitos ☎094/233409
Lima ☎01/224-7888
Piura ☎074/332609
Puno ☎054/366138
Trujillo ☎044/204146

restaurant, transport company, customs, immigration or even the police, you can call the 24-hour **Tourist Protection Service** hotline (Servicio de Protecion al Turista, also known as INDECOPI); see the box on the previous page for numbers to call. Staff are trained to handle complaints in English and Spanish. If an immediate solution is not possible, the the service claims to follow up disputes by filing a formal complaint with the relevant authorities.

TRAVELLING WITH CHILDREN

South Americans hold the family unit in high regard and children are central to this, but outlined below are some pointers to help prepare for a family visit to Peru.

Consult your doctor before leaving home regarding **health issues**. Sunscreen is an important consideration, as are sun-hats (cheap and readily available in Peru) and even a parasol for the really small. Conversely, it can get cold at night in the Andes, so take plenty of warm clothing. In the mountains, the altitude doesn't seem to cause children as many problems as it does their elders, but they shouldn't walk too hard above 2000m without full acclimatization. In Lima, where the water is just about good enough to clean your teeth but not to drink, the issues for local children are mainly bronchial or asthmatic, with humid weather and high pollution levels causing many long-lasting chest ailments. This shouldn't be a problem for any visiting children unless they already have difficulties. The major risk around the regions is a bad stomach and **diarrhoea** from water or food. The best way to avoid and treat this is outlined on p.17; the only difference where children are concerned, particularly those under ten, is that you should be more ready to act sooner, particularly with rehydration salts. In the jungle, the same precautions for adults apply to children (see p.362).

The **food and drink** in Peru is varied enough to appeal to most kids. Pizzas are available almost everywhere, as are good fish, red meats, fried chicken, french fries, corn-on-the-cob and nutritious soups, and vitamin supplements are always a good idea. There's also a wide range of **soft drinks**, from the ubiquitous Coca Cola and Sprite to Inka Cola. Some recognizable commercial **baby food** (and nappy brands) are available in all large supermarkets. **Restaurants** in Peru cater well to children and some offer smaller, cheaper portions; if they don't publicize it, it's worth asking.

Like restaurants, **hotels** are used to handling kids. They will sometimes offer discounts, especially if children share rooms or beds. The lower to mid-range options are the most flexible in this regard, but even the expensive ones can be helpful. Many, hostals included, have collective rooms, large enough for families to share, at reasonable rates.

Prices can often be cheaper for children. Tours to attractions can occasionally be negotiated on a family rate basis and entry to sites is often half price or less (and always free for infants). Children under ten generally get half fare on local (but not inter-regional) buses, while trains and boats generally charge full fare if a seat is required. Infants who don't need a seat often travel free on all transport except planes, when you pay around ten percent of the fare.

Travelling around the country is perhaps the most difficult activity. Bus and train journeys are generally long (12 hours or more). Crossing international borders is a potential hassle; although Peru officially accepts children under sixteen on their parents' **passports**, it is a good idea for them to have their own to minimize problems.

WOMEN TRAVELLERS

So many limitations are imposed on women's freedom to travel together or alone that any advice or warning seems merely to reinforce the situation. However, machismo is well ingrained in the Peruvian male mentality, particularly in the towns, and female foreigners are almost universally seen as liberated and therefore sexually available. Having said that, in most public places and in genuine friendly contact situations women travelling on their own tend to get the "pobrecita" ("poor little thing") treatment because they are alone, without family or a man.

HARASSMENT AND SAFETY

On the whole, the situations you'll encounter are more annoying than dangerous, with frequent comments such as *que guapa* ("how pretty"), intrusive and prolonged stares, plus whistling and hissing in the **cities**. Worse still are the occasional rude comments and groping, particularly in crowded situations such as on buses or trains. Blonde and fair-skinned women are likely to suffer much more of this behaviour than darker, Latin-looking women. Mostly these are situations you'd deal with routinely at home – as Limeña women do here in the capital – but they can, understandably and rightly, seem threatening without a clear understanding of Peruvian

Spanish and slang. To avoid getting caught up in something you can't control, any provocation is best ignored. In a public situation, however, any real harassment is often best dealt with by loudly drawing attention to the miscreant. Bear in mind that sexual assault in Peru is a rare thing; it is mostly just a matter of macho bravado, and rarely anything more serious.

In the predominantly Indian, **remote areas** there is less of an overt problem, though this is surprisingly where physical assaults are more likely to take place. They are not common, however – you're probably safer hiking in the Andes than walking at night in most British or North American inner-cities. Two obvious, but enduring, pieces of advice are to travel with friends (being on your own makes you most vulnerable), and if you're camping, to be quite open about it. As ever, making yourself known to locals gives a kind of acceptance and insurance, and it may even lead to the offer of a room – Peruvians, particularly those in rural areas, can be incredibly kind and hospitable. It's also sensible to check with the South American Explorers' Club, particularly in Cusco, for information on the latest trouble spots.

THE FEMINIST MOVEMENT

Though a growing force, **feminism** is still relatively new to Peru, and essentially urban. However, there are two major feminist groups: Flora Tristan, Avenida Arenales 601, Lima, which is allied to the United Left and whose basic tenet is "first socialism, then the feminist revolution"; and the less radical Peru Mujer, though neither of these are likely to be of enormous interest to travellers.

Peru's one **feminist magazine**, *Mujeres y Sociedad* (*Women and Society*), is published quarterly. For other literature and advice, try Flora Tristan, the Libreria de la Mujer bookshop in Avenida Arenales, Lima; or the Women's Centre, Quilca, Lima, which is run by nuns. The **Peruvian Women's Association** (Association Peru Mujer) can be contacted at Leon Velarde 1275, Lima (☎01/422-3655, 441-5187 or 471-1524).

OPENING HOURS, PUBLIC HOLIDAYS AND FESTIVALS

Public holidays, Carnival and local fiestas are all big events in Peru, celebrated with an openness and a great gusto that gives them enormous appeal for visitors. The main national holidays take place over Easter, Christmas and during the month of October, in that order of importance. Be aware, though, that during public holidays, Carnival and even the many local fiestas everything shuts down: banks, post offices, information offices, tourist sites and museums. It is worth planning a little in advance to make sure that you don't get caught out.

OPENING HOURS

Most **shops** and **services** in Peru open Monday to Saturday 9am–5pm or 6pm. Many are open on Sunday as well, if for more limited hours. Peru's more important **ancient sites** and ruins usually have opening hours that coincide with daylight – from around 7am until 5pm or 6pm daily. Smaller sites are rarely fenced off, and are nearly always accessible 24 hours a day for moonlit strolls. For larger sites, you normally pay a small admission fee to the local guardian – who may then walk round with you, pointing out features of interest. Only Machu Picchu charges more than a few dollars' entrance fee – this is one site where you may find it worth presenting an ISIC or FIYTO student card (which generally gets you in for half-price).

Of Peru's **museums**, some belong to the state, others to institutions, and a few to individuals.

Most charge a small admission fee and open Monday to Saturday 9am–noon and 3–6pm.

Churches open in the mornings for mass (usually around 6am), after which the smaller ones close. Those which are most interesting to tourists, however, tend to stay open all day, while others open again in the afternoon from 3 to 6pm. Very occasionally there's an admission charge to churches, and more regularly to monasteries (*monasterios*). Try to be aware of the strength of religious belief in Peru, particularly in the Andes, where churches have a rather heavy, sad atmosphere. You can enter and quietly look around all churches, but in the Andes especially you should refrain from taking photographs.

FIESTAS, FESTIVALS AND PUBLIC HOLIDAYS

Peruvians love any excuse for a celebration and the country enjoys a huge number of religious ceremonies, festivals and local events. Cusco, in particular, is a great place for both Christian celebrations and for Inca festivals like Inti Raymi in June. In October, Lima, and especially its suburb of La Victoria, takes centre stage, with processions dedicated to Our Lord of Miracles, in memory of the ever-present earthquake danger. **Carnival** time (generally late Feb) is lively almost everywhere in the country, with *fiestas* held every Sunday – a wholesale licence to throw water at everyone and generally go crazy. It's worth noting that most hotel prices go up significantly at *fiesta* times and bus and air transport can be fully booked days in advance.

In addition to the major regional and national celebrations, nearly every community has its own saint or patron figure to worship at town or **village fiestas**. These celebrations often mean a great deal to local people, and can be much more fun to visit than the larger countrywide activities. Processions, music, dancing in costumes, and eating and drinking form a natural part of these parties. In some cases the villagers will enact symbolic dramas with Indians dressed up as Spanish colonists, wearing hideous blue-eyed masks with long hairy beards. In the hills around towns like Huaraz and Cusco, especially, it's quite

MAJOR FESTIVALS AND PUBLIC HOLIDAYS

JANUARY

1 New Year's Day.

FEBRUARY

2 Candlemas
Folklore music and dancing throughout Peru, but especially lively in Puno at the Fiesta de la Virgen de la Candelaria, and in the mountain regions.
Carnival
Wildly celebrated immediately prior to Lent, throughout the whole country.

MARCH/APRIL

Easter Semana Santa (Holy Week)
Superb processions all over Peru (the best are in Cusco and Ayacucho), with the biggest being on Good Friday and in the evening on Easter Saturday, which is a public holiday.

MAY

1 Labour Day.

2–3 Fiesta de la Cruz (Festival of the Cross)
Celebrated all over Peru in commemoration of ancient Peruvian agro-astronomical rituals and the Catholic annual cycle.

JUNE

Beginning of the month Corpus Christi
This takes places exactly nine weeks after Maundy Thursday, and usually falls in the first half of June. It's much celebrated, with fascinating processions and feasting all over Peru, but is particularly lively in Cusco.

24 Inti Raymi
Cusco's main Inca festival (see p.107 for details).

29 Street Peter's Day
A public holiday all over Peru, but mainly celebrated with *fiestas* in all the fishing villages along the coast.

JULY

15–17 Virgen de Carmen
Dance and music festivals at Pisac and Paucartambo (see p.161 for details).

28–29 National Independence Day
Public holiday with military and school processions.

AUGUST

13–19 Arequipa Week
Processions, firework displays, plenty of folklore dancing and craft markets take place throughout Peru's second city.

30 Santa Rosa de Lima
Public holiday.

SEPTEMBER

End of the month Festival of Spring
Trujillo festival involving dancing, especially the local Marinera dance and popular Peruvian waltzes (see p.295 for details).

OCTOBER

8 Public holiday to commemorate the Battle of Angamos.

18–28 Lord of Miracles
Festival featuring large and solemn processions (the main ones take place on October 18, 19 and 28); many women wear purple for the whole month, particularly in Lima, where bullfights and other celebrations continue throughout the month.

NOVEMBER

1–30 International Bullfighting Competitions These take place throughout the month, and are particularly spectacular at the Plaza de Acho in Lima.

1–7 Puno Festival
One of the mainstays of Andean culture, celebrating the founding of the Puno by the Spanish Conquistadores and also the founding of the Inca Empire by the legendary Manco Capac and his sister Mama Ocllo who are said to have emerged from Lake Titicaca. The fifth is marked by vigorous colourful community dancing.

1 Fiesta de Todos los Santos (All Saints Day)
Public holiday.

2 Diá de los Muertos (All Souls Day)
A festive remembrance of dead friends and relatives taken very seriously by most Peruvians and a popular time for baptisms and roast pork meals.

12–28 Pacific Fair
One of the largest international trade fairs in South America – a huge, biannual event, which takes place on a permanent site on Avenida La Marina between Callao and Lima Centro.

DECEMBER

8 Feast of the Immaculate Conception
Public holiday.

25 Christmas Day.

common to stumble into a village *fiesta*, with its explosion of human energy and noise, bright colours, and a mixture of pagan and Catholic symbolism.

However, such celebrations are very much local affairs, and while the occasional traveller will almost certainly be welcomed with great warmth, none of these remote communities would want to be invaded by tourists waving cameras and expecting to be feasted for free. The dates given on the previous page are therefore only for established events which are already on the tourist map, and for those that take place all over the country. For full details of celebrations in the Cusco region – one of the best places to catch a *fiesta* – see p.106.

In many coastal and mountain haciendas (estates), **bullfights** are often held at *fiesta* times. In a less organized way they happen at many of the village *fiestas*, too – often with the bull being left to run through the village until it's eventually caught and mutilated by one of the men. This is not just a sad sight, it can also be dangerous for you, as an unsuspecting tourist, if you happen to wander into an apparently evacuated village. The Lima bullfights in October, in contrast, are a very serious business; even Hemingway was impressed.

NATIONAL PARKS AND RESERVES

Almost ten percent of Peru is incorporated into some form of protected area, including seven national parks, eight national reserves, seven national sanctuaries, three historical sanctuaries, five reserved zones, six buffer forests, two hunting reserves, and an assortment of communal reserves and national forests.

The largest of these protected areas is the **National Reserve of Pacaya-Samiria**, an incredible tropical forest region in northern Peru covering some 2,080,000 hectares. This is closely followed in size by the **Manu National Park and Biosphere Reserve**, another vast and stunning jungle area of about 1,532,806 hectares, and the **Tambopata-Candamo Reserved Zone and Bahuaja-Sonone National Park**, again, an Amazon area, over 1,478,942 hectares in extent, with possibly the richest flora and fauna of any region on the planet. Smaller but just as fascinating to visit are the **Huascaran National Park** in the high Andes near Huaraz, a popular trekking and climbing region some 340,000 hectares in area, and the lesser visited **National Reserve of Pampa Galeras**, close to Nasca, which was established mainly to protect the dwindling but precious herds of *vicuña*, the smallest and most beautiful member of the South American cameloid family.

Bear in mind that the parks and reserves are enormous zones, within which there is hardly any attempt to control or organize nature. The term "park" probably conveys the wrong impression about these huge, virtually untouched areas, which were designated by the National System for Conservation Units (SNCU), with the aim of combining conservation, research and, in some cases (such as the Inca Trail; see p.149), recreational tourism. In December 1992, the Peruvian National Trust Fund for Parks and Protected Areas (PROFONANPE) was established as a trust fund managed by the private sector to provide funding for Peru's main protected areas. It has assistance from the Peruvian government, national and international non-governmental organizations, the World Bank Global Environment facility and the United Nations Environment Program.

VISITING THE PARKS

There's usually a small charge **to visit** the national parks or nature reserves. Sometimes, as at the Huascaran National Park, this is a daily rate; at others, like the Paracas Reserve on the coast south of Pisco, you pay a fixed sum to enter. If the park is in a particularly remote area, which most of them are, permission may also be needed – either from the National Institute of Culture, by the Museo de La Nacion at Avenida Javier Prado Este 2465, San Borja (☎01/476-9873) who are responsible for all matters of cultural heritage, and/or the Instituto Nacional de Recursos

Naturales, Calle Diecisiete 355, Urbino El Palomar, San Isidro (☎01/224-3298, 224-2858) who cover permits and queries relating to all Peru's protected sites and natural resources. For more details check with the South American Explorers' Club in Lima (see p.21) or at the local tourist office.

GEOGRAPHY, CLIMATE AND SEASONS

Peru is one of the larger South American countries – some ten times the size of England – covering an area of 1,285,000 square kilometres and with a population of over 26 million. Around seventy percent of its inhabitants live in cities, which are mainly located along the coast and limited almost exclusively to half a dozen thin but relatively fertile river valleys running into the Pacific.

Peru is unique in possessing such a wide variety of **ecosystems** ranging from the dryest hot desert in the Americas, to the high Andean peaks (over 7600m above sea level); from a two-thousand-kilometre-long belt of cloud forest, rich in flora and fauna, to a vast area of lowland Amazon jungle, covering about half the country. The three main zones of Peru are known as **La Costa** (the coast), **La Sierra** (the mountains) and **La Selva** (the jungle). Within a matter of hours, you can leave the scorching desert coastline with some of the Pacific Ocean's best fishing, cross the world's highest tropical mountain range – the Andes – and plunge down into our planet's biggest tropical rainforest.

The unusual **weather conditions** in Peru are created mainly by two major offshore ocean currents – the cold Humbolt Current coming up from Chile and the Antarctic, which meets the warm, tropical **El Niño** current coming down from the Pacific along the Ecuadorian coast. The Humbolt is largely responsible for the dry desert coastline of Peru and Northern Chile, sending Pacific clouds up into the Andes where they precipitate as rain. Traditional Peruvian wisdom says that it only really rains on the Peruvian coast about once every twenty years or so, when the El Niño current pushes further down the coast, warming the seas and causing disruptive rains in the desert. These rains bring devastating floods to towns and settlements poorly prepared for tor-

rential downpours and often inhabited by migrants from the mountains. However, the rains also bring the desert into bloom as all the wild flower seeds, preserved by the drought conditions, suddenly burst into life. Over the last few years, the Peruvian weather has been rather unsettled and El Niño has been acting even more unpredictably than usual, possibly as a result of global warming. However, it still rarely rains on the coast, although the Lima region does experience substantial smog, coastal fogs or mists and even drizzle, particularly between the months of May and November.

The climate in the Sierra and Selva regions can be fairly clearly divided into a **wet season** (Oct–April) and a **dry season** (May–Sept). There is, of course, some rain during the dry season, but it is much heavier and much more frequent in the wet season, when travel becomes much harder: roads are often impassable, flights are frequently cancelled or delayed due to poor conditions, and landslides affect trains and bus routes alike. Trekking in the mountains and canoeing on the Andean or jungle rivers are also much less enjoyable during the wet season than at other times of year. Equally frustrating – especially if you've travelled halfway across the world to be here – is the fact that some of the stupendous views, particularly those around Cusco and in the Cordillera Blanca, are often obscured by clouds at this time of year. If you want to visit several different regions of Peru, then your best bet is to travel round in the middle of the dry season between June and September.

Again, weather conditions have been quite unsettled in these regions over the last ten years or so, with the Altiplano zone, around Puno, being affected by serious **droughts**, which have left the water level of Lake Titicaca at its lowest for years.

CINEMA

South America is seen by film distributors as part of the American market, so new films from the US arrive quickly in Lima, where they're shown cheaply and in the original language (usually but not necessarily English) with Spanish subtitles. European movies are also regularly screened, especially in Lima (again in the original language), but the sound is often turned down low or so distorted that it is difficult to understand.

THE PERUVIAN FILM INDUSTRY

Peru really started making its own **films** in the late 1970s, when various producers and directors got together and, with the help of distributors, managed to set up a domestically oriented production industry. Getting it off the ground required some unusual steps, one of which made it obligatory to distribute and show all Peruvian-made films for eighteen months after release. This means that a short (15–20min) film is often shown before the full-length feature. The bureaucracy involved in getting films to the screen has ensured that a lot of them are thematically (and ideologically) unsound as well as often pretty poor technically. In recent years a few cinema clubs have sprung up around Lima, giving audiences a chance to become more critical and to see less commercially oriented films.

Two promising young Peruvian directors are **Francisco Lombardi** and **Chicho Duran**, who have both made interesting feature films dealing with important sociological and political issues. Well worth seeing if you get the chance are *Maruja en el Infierno*, by Lombardi and *Ojos de Perro* and *Malabrigo*, and most recently, *Coraje*, about the life of Moyano, all by Duran. Lombardi's film, *La Boca del Lobo* (*The Mouth of the Wolf*), is an interesting Spanish co-production attempting, without taking sides, to deal with the brutality and ideology surrounding terrorism in Peru and his *No Se Lo Digas a Nadie* is also very good. Also worth looking out for is Chico Duran's powerful film *Alias la Gringa* – the true story of a Peruvian bankrobber. Nicknamed *La Gringa* because of his blonde hair and blue eyes, he was a member of the first gang of bankrobbers in Peru to use machine guns, and was arrested and imprisoned for seventeen years. The film deals principally with his real-life experiences in a Peruvian jail.

Another new director worth looking out for is **Cusi Barrios**, whose first feature film, *La Capyura del Siglo* (*The Capture of the Century*), deals with the capture of Abimael Guzman, leader of the Shining Path, and has been critically acclaimed throughout Peru.

DIRECTORY

ADDRESSES These are frequently written with just the street name and number: for example, Pizarro 135. Officially, though, they're usually prefixed by Calle, Jirón (street) or Avenida. The first digit of any street number (or sometimes the first two digits) represents the block number within the street as a whole. Note too that many of the major streets in Lima and also in Cusco have two names – in Lima this is a relic of the military governments of the 1970s, in Cusco it's more to do with a revival of the Inca past.

ADVENTURE ACTIVITIES Peru has many adventure activites to offer, and we've listed them throughout the Guide where relevant. For general information of mountaineering and winter sports contact: Federacion Peruana de Andinismo y Desportes de Invierno, block 3 of Jose Diaz, Lima Centro (☎01/424-0063); Casa de Guias, Parque Ginebra 28-G; Club de Montañismo Américo Tordoya, Tarapacá 384, Lima (☎01/460-6101 or 431-1305); Club de Andinismo de la Univeridad de Lima, Avenida Javier Prado Este, Lima 33 (☎01/437-6767, extension 30775); Club Andino Peruano, Avenida Dos de Mayo 1545, Oficina 216, Lima 27.

ARTESANIA Traditional craft goods from most regions of Peru can be found in markets and shops in Lima. Woollen and alpaca products, though, are usually cheaper and often better quality in the *sierra* – particularly in Cusco, Juliaca and Puno; carved gourds are imported from around Huancayo, while the best places to buy ceramic replicas are Trujillo, Huaraz, Ica and

Nasca. Jungle crafts are best from Pucallpa and Iquitos.

BARGAINING In markets and with taxi drivers (before getting in), you are generally expected to bargain. It's also sometimes possible to haggle over the price of hotel rooms, especially if you're travelling in a group. Food and shop prices, however, tend to be fixed.

CUSTOMS Regulations stipulate that no items of archeological or historical value or interest may be removed from the country. Many of the jungle craft goods which incorporate feathers, skins or shells of rare Amazonian animals are also banned for export – it's best not to buy these if you are in any doubt about their scarcity. If you do try to export anything of archeological or biological value, and get caught, you'll have the goods confiscated at the very least, and may find yourself in a Peruvian court.

DIVING AND FISHING For information on this contact the Federacion Peruana de Caza Submarina y Actividades Acuaticas, Estadio Nacional, Lima Centro (☎01/433-6626, *didimar@mail.cosapidata.com.pe*).

ELECTRIC CURRENT 220 volt/60 cycles AC is the standard all over Peru, except in Arequipa where it is 220 volt/50 cycles. In some of Lima's better hotels you may also find 110 volt sockets to use with standard electric shavers. Don't count on any Peruvian supply being one hundred percent reliable and, particularly in cheap hostals and hotels be very wary of the wiring, especially in electric shower fittings.

FOOTBALL Peru's major sport is football and you'll find men and boys playing it in the streets of every city, town and settlement in the country down to the remotest of jungle outposts. The big teams are Cristal, Alianza and El U (for Universitario) in Lima and Ciencianco from Cusco. The "Classic" game is between Alianza, the poor man's team from La Victoria suburb of Lima, and El U, generally supported by the middle class. In recent years the sport has taken a European turn in the unruly and violent nature of its fans. This is particularly true of Lima where, in late 1995, the "Classic" had to be stopped because of stones thrown at the players by supporters. Known as *choligans* (a mixture of the English "hooligan" and the Peruvian *cholo*, which means dark-skinned Quechua-blooded Peruvian), these unruly supporters have taken to painting their faces, attacking the opposing fans and causing major riots outside the football grounds.

GAY LIFE Homosexuality is pretty much kept underground in what is still a very macho society, though in recent years Lima has seen a liberating advance and transvestites can walk the streets in relative freedom from abuse. However, there is little or no organized gay life. The Peruvian Homosexual and Lesbian Movement can be contacted at Calle Mariscal Miller 828, in Jesus Maria (☎433-5519).

INSULTS Travellers sometimes suffer insults from Peruvians who begrudge the apparent relative wealth and freedom of tourists. Remember, however, that the terms "gringo" or "mister" are not generally meant in an offensive way in Peru.

LANGUAGE LESSONS You can learn Peruvian Spanish all over Peru, but the best range of schools are in Cusco, Arequipa and Huancayo. Check the relevant Listings sections in the Guide.

LAUNDRY Most basic hotels have communal washrooms where you can do your washing; failing this, labour is so cheap that it's no real expense to get your clothes washed by the hotel or in a *lavandería* (laundry). Things tend to disappear from public washing lines so be careful where you leave clothes drying.

NATURAL DISASTERS Peru has more than its fair share of avalanches, landslides and earthquakes – and there's not a lot you can do about any of them. If you're naturally cautious you might want to register on arrival with your embassy; they like this, and it does help them in the event of a major quake (or an escalation of terrorist activity). Landslides – *huaycos* – devastate the roads and rail lines every rainy season, though alternative routes are usually found surprisingly quickly.

PHOTOGRAPHY The light in Peru is very bright, with a strong contrast between shade and sun. This can produce a nice effect and generally speaking it's easy to take good pictures. One of the more complex problems is how to take photos of people without upsetting them. You should always talk to a prospective subject first, and ask

if s/he minds if you take a quick photo (*una fotito, por favor* – "a little photo please"); most people react favourably to this approach even if all the communication is in sign language. Slide film is expensive to buy, and not readily available outside of the main cities; colour Kodac and Fuji films are widely available, but black and white film is rare. If you can bear the suspense it's best to save getting films developed until you're home – you'll probably get better results. Pre-paid slide films can't be developed in Peru.

PUNCTUALITY Whilst buses, trains or planes won't wait a minute beyond their scheduled departure time, people almost expect friends to be an hour or more late for an appointment (don't arrange to meet a Peruvian on the street – make it a bar or café). Peruvians stipulate that an engagement is *a la hora inglesa* ("by English time") if they genuinely want people to arrive on time, or, more realistically, within half an hour of the time they fix.

TIME Peru keeps the same hours as Eastern Standard Time, which is (generally) five hours behind GMT.

WORK Your only real chance of earning money in Peru is teaching English in Lima, or with luck in Arequipa or Cusco. Given the state of the economy there's little prospect in other fields, though in the more remote parts of the country it may sometimes be possible to find board and lodging in return for a little building work or general labouring. This is simply a question of keeping your eyes open and making personal contacts. There is an enormous amount of bureaucracy involved if you want to work (or live) officially in Peru. For biology, geography or environmental science graduates there's a chance of free board and lodging and maybe a small salary if you're willing to work very hard for at least three months as a tour guide in a jungle lodge, under the Resident Naturalist schemes. Several lodges along the Río Tambopata offer such schemes and other research opportunities. For more details, write to the lodges directly; for independent advice contact the Tambopata Reserve Society (TreeS), 64 Belsize Park, London, NW3 4EH, UK. Arrangements need to be made at least six months in advance.

PART TWO

THE

GUIDE

COLOMBIA

ECUADOR

CHAPTER 6
THE JUNGLE

CHAPTER 5
TRUJILLO AND
THE NORTH

BRAZIL

CHAPTER 4
ANCASH AND
HUANUCO

CHAPTER 1
LIMA AND
AROUND

PACIFIC

OCEAN

CHAPTER 2
CUSCO AND
AROUND

BOLIVIA

CHAPTER 3
THE SOUTH

N

CHILE

CHAPTER ONE

LIMA AND AROUND

O nce reputed to be the most beautiful city in Spanish America, **Lima** today retains some of its charm, despite its rather shapeless expanse of modern suburbs and dusty *pueblos jovenes* shanty towns that run for many miles in each direction along the Panamerican Highway. Long established as Peru's seat of government, the city is home to more than eight million people, over half of whom live in relative poverty without decent water supplies, sewage or electricity. This is not to say you can't enjoy the place – Limeños are generally very open, and their way of life is distinctive and compelling – but it's important not to come here with false expectations. There is still a certain elegance to the old colonial centre, and the city hosts a string of excellent and important museums, but Lima is not exotic, though the central areas have been cleaned up in recent years – streets swarm with orange-uniformed sweepers – and are packed with colonial relics and twenty-first century features. The pollution and the ever-increasing traffic remain, though environmental awareness is rising fast.

The area immediately **around Lima** offers plenty of reasons to delay your progress on towards Arequipa or Cusco. Within an hour or so's bus ride south is the coastline, often deserted, lined by a series of attractive beaches. Above them the imposing fortress-temple complex of **Pachacamac** sits on a sandstone cliff, near the edge of the ocean. In the neighbouring Rimac Valley you can visit the pre-Inca sites of **Puruchuco** and **Cajamarquilla**, and, in the foothills above Lima, intriguingly eroded rock outcrops and megalithic monuments surround the natural amphitheatre of **Marcahuasi**.

Further afield, high up in the Andes, lies the quaint mountain town of **Huancavelica** and the pleasant provincial capital of **Huancayo**, which is connected to Lima by El Tren de la Sierra, the highest rail line in the world, which has happily restarted regular if infrequent passenger services. Just over the Andes, you'll find the high Amazon rainforest, the *ceja de selva*, which you can explore from bases such as the strikingly situated **Tarma**, hidden among towering limestone crags, or the small tropical towns of **San Ramon** and **La Merced**, at the gateway to the forest. If you're adventurous, you can complete a circuit through the mountains from Huancayo through **Satipo**, firmly located on the wild jungle frontier, then back to Lima via Tarma. Alternatively, you can travel south beyond Huancayo towards Ayachuco and Cusco, a popular if arduous highland trail, frequented once again after being abandoned between 1985 and 1994 due to guerrilla activity.

ACCOMMODATION PRICE CODES

Unless otherwise indicated, **accommodation** in this book is coded according to the categories below, based on the price of a double room in high season.

① under $5   ③ $10–20   ⑤ $30–40   ⑦ $50–70
② $5–10   ④ $20–30   ⑥ $40–50   ⑧ over $70

LIMA

LIMA is a boisterous, macho city, relaxed and laid-back, yet having an underlying energy, with money and expensive cars ruling the roost – you can buy anything in Lima if you have the cash, particularly in **Lima Centro**, the colonial zone of the city. The city's population has increased dramatically in the last thirty years, swollen with people arriving from the high Andes to make camp in the shanty towns that line the highways. The main plazas, once attractive meeting places, are now thick with pickpockets, exhaust fumes and, not infrequently, riot police. The **climate** in Lima seems to set the mood: in the height of summer (Dec–March) it buzzes with energy and excitement, though during the winter months (June–Sept) a low mist descends over the arid valley in which the city sits, forming a solid grey blanket from the beaches almost up to Chosica in the foothills of the Andes – a phenomenon undoubtedly made worse by traffic-related air pollution.

Lima is brimful of culture and heritage, though it's not obvious at first. On a strictly guidebook level, there are the **museums** (the best of which are excellent and should definitely be visited before setting off for Machu Picchu or any of Peru's other great Inca ruins), the Spanish **churches** in the centre, and some distinguished **mansions** in the wealthy suburbs of Barranco and Miraflores. But in their own way, too, there's a powerful atmosphere in the *pueblos jovenes*, where Peru's landless peasants have made their homes. In addition, Lima's noisy, fast-moving frenetic craziness is mellowed by the presence of the sea and beaches. The mix of lifestyles and peoples is a fascinating world of its own: from the snappy, sassy, cocaine influenced *criolla* style – all big, fast American cars, cruising the broad main streets – to the easy-going, happy-go-lucky attitude that can seem a godsend when you're trying to get through some bureaucratic hassle. And, as anyone who stays here more than a week or so finds, Limeño hospitality and kindness are almost boundless once you've established an initial rapport.

Some history

Even if you don't have the time or the inclination to search out and savour the delights and agonies of Lima, it is possible to get a good feel for the place in only a few days. Out at Ancón, now a popular beach resort just north of Lima, an important **pre-Inca** burial site shows signs of occupation – including pottery, textiles, and the oldest-known archer's bow in the entire Americas – from at least three thousand years ago. Although certainly one of the most populous valleys, the Rimac area first showed indications of true urbanization around 1200 AD with the appearance of a strong, independent culture – the **Cuismancu State** – in many ways parallel to, though not as large as, the contemporary Chimu Empire which bordered it to the north. Cajamarquilla, a huge, somewhat crowded, adobe city-complex associated with the Cuismancu, now rests peacefully under the desert sun only a few kilometres beyond Lima's outer suburbs. Dating from the same era, but some 30km south of the modern city, is the Temple of Pachacamac. For hundreds of years, until ransacked by the conquistadores, this shrine attracted thousands of pilgrims from all over Peru, the Incas being the last in a series of groups to adopt Pachacamac as one of their own major *huacas*.

When the Spanish first arrived here the valley was dominated by three important **Inca**-controlled urban complexes: Carabayllo to the north near Chillón; Maranga, now partly destroyed by the Avenida La Marina, between the modern city and the Port of Callao; and Surco, now a suburb within the confines of greater Lima but where, until the mid-seventeenth century, the adobe houses of ancient chiefs lay empty yet painted in a variety of colourful images.

Francisco Pizarro founded **Spanish Lima**, "City of the Kings", in 1535, only two years after the invasion. Evidently recommended by mountain Indians as a site for a potential capital, it proved essentially a good choice, offering a natural harbour nearby, a large well-watered river valley, and relatively easy access up into the Andes. By the 1550s the town had grown up around a large plaza with wide streets leading through a fine collection of mansions, all elegantly adorned by wooden terraces, and well-stocked shops run by wealthy merchants. Since the very beginning, Spanish Lima has been different from the more popular image of Peru: it looks out, away from the Andes and the past, towards the Pacific for contact with the world beyond.

Lima rapidly developed into the capital of a Spanish viceroyalty which encompassed not only Peru but also Ecuador, Bolivia and Chile. The University of San Marcos, founded in 1551, is the oldest on the continent, and Lima housed the headquarters of the Inquisition from 1570 until 1813. It remained the most important, the richest, and – hardly credible today – the most alluring city in South America, until the early nineteenth century.

Perhaps the most prosperous era for Lima was the **seventeenth century**. By 1610 its population had reached a manageable 26,000, made up of 40 percent blacks (mostly slaves), 38 percent Spanish, no more than 8 percent pure Indian, another 8 percent (of unspecified ethnic origin) living under religious orders, and less than 6 percent of mixed blood – now probably the largest proportion of inhabitants. The centre of Lima was crowded with shops and stalls selling silks and fancy furniture from as far afield as China. Even these days it's not hard to imagine what Lima must have been like, as a substantial section of the colonial city is still preserved – many of its streets, set in large regular blocks, are overhung by ornate wooden balconies, and elaborate Baroque facades bring some of the older churches to life, regardless of the din and hassle of modern city living. Rimac, a suburb just over the river from the Plaza Mayor, and the port area of Callao, grew up as satellite settlements – initially catering for the very rich, though they are now predominantly "slum" sectors.

The **eighteenth century**, a period of relative stagnation for Lima, was dramatically punctuated by the tremendous earthquake of 1746, which left only twenty houses standing in the whole city and killed some five thousand residents – nearly ten percent of the population. From 1761 to 1776 Lima and Peru were governed by Viceroy Amat, who, although more renowned for his relationship with the famous Peruvian actress La Perricholi, is also remembered as the instigator of Lima's rebirth. Under him the city lost its cloistered atmosphere, opening out with broad avenues, striking gardens, Rococo mansions and palatial salons. Influenced by the Bourbons, Amat's designs for the city's architecture arrived hand in hand with other transatlantic reverberations of the Enlightenment.

In the **nineteenth century** Lima expanded still further to the east and south. The suburbs of Barrios Altos and La Victoria were poor from the start; above the beaches at Magdalena, Miraflores and Barranco, the wealthy developed new enclaves of their own. These were originally separated from the centre by several kilometres of farmland, at that time still studded with fabulous pre-Inca *huacas* and other adobe ruins.

It was President Leguia who, in **1919–30**, revitalized Lima by renovating the central areas. Plaza San Martin's attractive colonnades and the *Gran Hotel Bolivar* were erected, the Palacio de Gobierno was rebuilt, and the city was supplied with its first drinking-water and sewage systems. This was the signal for Lima's explosion into the modern era of ridiculously rapid growth. The three hundred thousand inhabitants of 1930 had become over three and a half million by the **mid-1970s**, and the population has more than doubled again in the last thirty years or so. Standing at more than eight million today, most of the recent growth is accounted for by massive immigration of peasants from the provinces into the *barriadas* or *pueblos jovenes* (young towns) now pressing in on the city along all of its landbound edges. Many of these migrants escaped from the theatre of civil war that raked many highland regions between the early 1980s and 1993.

Today the city is as cosmopolitan as any other in the developing world, with a thriving middle class enjoying living standards comparable to those of the West or better, and an elite riding around in chauffeur-driven cadillacs and heading to Miami for their monthly shopping. The vast majority of Lima's inhabitants, however – who form the very core and essence of the city – scrape together meagre incomes and live in poor conditions.

Arrival, information and getting around

You will either arrive in Lima **by plane**, landing at the Jorge Chavez airport, 7km northwest of the city centre, **by bus**, most of which arrive in the older, more central areas of town, or possibly **by train** from the Andes, right into the city centre. **Driving** into the city is really only for the adventurous, as the roads are highly congested with sometimes frustrating traffic levels plus a general madness of fellow drivers, which will either send you insane or turn you into an equally erratic and unpredictable road hog. Wherever you arrive, it can be a disorienting experience, as there are few landmarks to register the direction of the centre of town.

The phone code for Lima and its surrounding regions is ☎01.

By air

Coming into Lima by air over the Andes, you can usually make out the city, crowded into the mouth of a river valley with low sandy mountains closing in around its outer fringes. After landing at the modern, bustling **Jorge Chavez airport** (flight enquiries on ☎454-9570), named after an early Peruvian pilot, the quickest way to get into the city is by **taxi**, which will take around 45 minutes to Lima Centro or downtown Miraflores. Fix the price before getting in; around $20 or more is reasonable as the total price for a shared car. If you're prepared to haggle and shop around, you may get a car for $10 or less during daylight hours, particularly if you're prepared to carry your bags outside the airport gates and search for a taxi there, but take extra care around the perimeter and on the road into Lima, as there have been thefts in these areas. A cheaper and very efficient alternative is to take the **airport shuttle** (☎451-8011), which is either a minibus or a car that will take you to your hotel anywhere in Lima, though you will almost certainly have to share the service and drop off at several other hotels en route. Tickets (around $10 per person) are available from the little office immediately outside the international arrivals terminal.

If you need to **change money** at the airport, there are counters (daily 9am–6pm) located between the international and domestic flight departure areas, but you'll get better rates in the centre of Lima.

By bus

If you arrive in Lima **by bus**, you'll probably come in at one of the **bus terminals** or offices between the *Hotel Sheraton* and Parque Universitario, or in the district of La Victoria along Avenida 28 de Julio and Prolongación Huanuco. However, many operators have depots out in the suburbs, in an attempt to avoid the Lima Centro traffic jams. For full details of Lima bus companies and their terminals, see Listings, p.84; check the address to get an idea of where you'll be pulling in. Whichever terminal you arrive at, your best bet is to hail the first decent-looking **taxi** you see and fix a price – about $3 for any destination in the central area, or $5 for anywhere else in Lima.

By train

The passenger **train** from Huancayo, in the Andes, arrives right in Lima Centro at **Desamparados Railway Station**, Jirón Ancash 201, behind the Palacio de Gobierno. Services currently arrive only on the last Monday of every month at 5.15pm (plus Tues in Oct and Dec), but with the recent privatization of the line it may well operate more frequently in the near future; check with the Fertur Peru tour company (see p.86) for the latest.

Information and tours

Tourist information offices in Lima are rather dispersed and many of the commercial tour companies (see p.86) are actually better geared up for this service, notably Fertur Peru, who also offer good **city tours**, as do Lima Vision. Free weekday morning tours (free; call for details) are also offered by the municipalidad office of Informacion Turistica, Calle Los Escribanos 125, Plaza Mayor (Mon–Fri 9am–6pm & Sat 10am–6pm; ☎427-6080 or 427-4848), in **Lima Centro**, who provide good information and occasional maps. In **Miraflores** there's a small tourist information point (daily, 9am–9pm), based in the central Parque 7 de Junio; the Central de Informacion y Promocíon Turística, Avenida Larco 770 (Mon–Fri 9am–6pm; ☎446-2649, 446-3959);

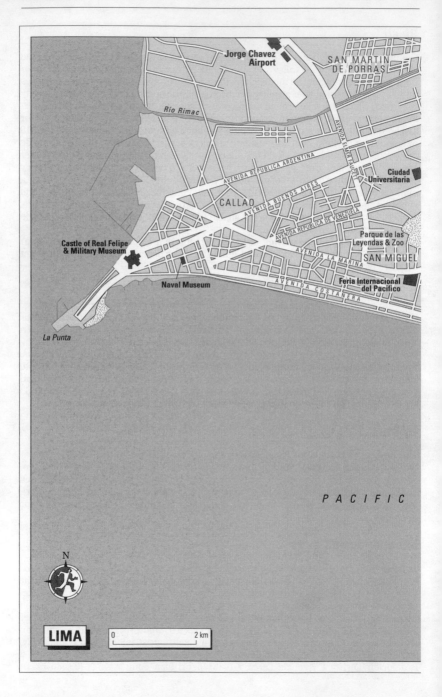

Jorge Chavez
Airport

SAN MARTIN
DE PORRAS

Río Rimac

AVENIDA ELMER FAUCETT

AVENIDA REPUBLICA ARGENTINA

Ciudad
Universitaria

CALLAO

AVENIDA BUENOS AIRES

AVENIDA REPUBLICA DE VENEZUELA

Parque de las
Leyendas & Zoo

Castle of Real Felipe
& Military Museum

AVENIDA LA MARINA

SAN MIGUEL

Naval Museum

Feria Internacional
del Pacifico

AVENIDA COSTANERA

La Punta

PACIFIC

N

LIMA

0   2 km

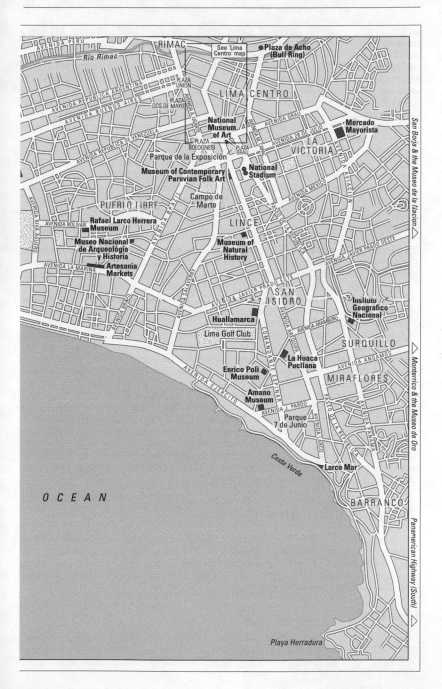

OCEAN

and El Allyu, a cultural centre at Calle San Martin 537 (☎446-0385, fax 241-7587, *webmaster@allyu-peru.org, www.allyu-peru.org*), which has a wide range of useful material. The South American Explorers' Club (see Listings, p.86) has good information, including maps, listings and travel reports, available to its members. In the last resort you might want to try **Promperu**, the official tourism arm of the Ministerio de Industria y Turismo, Calle 1, Urbino Corpac (☎427-6080), who have recently published a series of excellent information booklets and sheets covering Lima and other destinations – the problem is that they're based in the Ministery building, which is not exactly tourist-friendly as it's neither easily accessible nor strictly open to the public.

If you're planning to explore Lima in depth, you might want to get hold of the *Guía de Transportes*, a cheap **bus map** ($1.50), which you can buy from most of the stalls around Plaza San Martin and Avenida Nicolas de Pierola. The best **city map** is the pricey *Lima Guia "Inca" de Lima Metropolitan* ($13), but it is increasingly difficult to obtain; more readily available, from the stalls around Plaza San Martin and most bookshops, the *Lima Plano 2000* street map is comprehensive, but you may need a magnifying glass to read it.

City transport

It's a fairly simple matter to find your way around the rest of this huge, spread-eagled city. Almost every corner of it is linked by a regular **municipal bus service**, known to everyone as El Bussing, with flat-rate tickets (around $0.2) bought from the driver as you board. In tandem with these are the privately owned **microbuses**, older and smaller, more colourful and equally crowded, but again with flat rates (25¢). Quickest of all Lima transport, **combi colectivos** race from one street corner to another along all the major arterial city roads. You'll see "Todo Arequipa" or "Todo Benavides", for example, chalked up on their windscreens, which indicates that the colectivo runs the whole length of Avenida Arequipa or Avenida Benavides. Colectivos dash dangerously fast, frequently crashing and speeding off before their passengers have got both feet into the vehicle, and might be anything from a ramshackle Dodge Coronet to a plush fifteen-seater minibus; wave one down from any corner and pay the flat fare (around $0.4) to the driver or fare collector. You can catch colectivos or buses to most parts of the city from Avenida Abancay; for routes and destinations covered in this chapter you'll find the number or suburb name (written on the front of all buses) specified in the text. **Taxis** can be hailed on any street, and cost $2–4 to most central parts of the city. It's worth reiterating that **driving in Lima** is incredibly anarchic – it's not that fast, but it is assertive, with undertaking happening as often as overtaking and drivers, especially *taxistas*, finding gaps that don't appear to exist (one reason why there are so many damaged cars). We've recommended reliable taxi firms on p.86. If you want to **rent a car** to take out of the city, see p.85.

Accommodation

There are three main areas of Lima to stay – **Lima Centro**, which boasts hotels in just about every category imaginable, **Miraflores** (and the nearby suburbs of San Isidro, San Antonio and one or two others slightly further afield) and **Barranco**. Even more than most Peruvian cities, modern hotels in Lima tend to be very exclusive and expensive. There are no **campsites**, official or otherwise.

Lima Centro

Most travellers on a tight budget end up in one of the traditional gringo dives around the **Plaza Mayor** or the **San Francisco** church. These are mainly old buildings and tend to be full of backpackers, but they aren't necessarily the best choices in the old centre, even in their price range. If you can spend a little bit more and opt for the mid-range hotels, you'll find some interesting old buildings bursting with bygone atmosphere and style.

Budget

Hostal de los Artes, Chota 1460 (☎433-0031, *artes@telematic.com.pe*). At the southern end of Lima Centro, one block from Plaza Bolognesi, this clean, friendly place is popular with travellers. Most rooms have private bath and there's a nice patio with mosaics. Downstairs rooms are a little gloomy, but it's very good value. ①–②.

Hostal España, Jirón Azángaro 105 (☎427-9196). Rooms with or without private bath in this popular basic hostal with a nice rooftop patio and cafetería. ②.

Hostal Lima, Carabaya 147 (no phone). Basic, very cheap and leaves a lot to be desired, though it's well situated opposite the right-hand side of the Palacio de Gobierno, less than a block from the Plaza Mayor. ②.

Hostal Roma, Ica 326 (☎427-7576). A pleasant place if a bit shabby, though pretty central and with a choice of private or communal bathrooms (but only one shower for women) and a reliable luggage storage service. ③.

Hostal Samaniego, Emancipacion 184 (no phone). Small with shared rooms only, but welcoming, very clean and with access to cooking facilities. ②.

Hotel Europa, Jirón Ancash 376 (☎427-3351). One of the best-value budget pads, centrally located opposite the San Francisco church, with a lovely courtyard. Be aware, though, that it is very popular and fills up quickly. ②.

Pension Rodriguez, Avenida Nicolas de Pierola 730 (☎423-6465). Excellent value but often crowded, with shared rooms and baths. ②.

Moderate

El Balcon Dorado, Jirón Ucayali 199 (☎427-6028, 427-6029 or 922-1188, *balcondorado@hotmail.com*). Newly refurbished, this hotel now has colonial décor, a new name and a much better reputation; really well located, close to the Plaza Mayor, it's a reasonable option for this category. Private or shared bath. Price includes breakfast. ⑤.

Hostal La Estrella de Belen, Belen 1051 (☎428-6462). Very clean and pleasant rooms with private baths in a friendly hostal in the middle of Lima's busiest zone, just two blocks from the Plaza San Martin. ④.

Hostal Granada, Huancavelica 323 (☎427-9033). A welcoming place with small but tidy rooms, private baths and a welcoming atmosphere; breakfast available. ④.

Hostal Residencial Don Luis, Avenida Breña 331 (☎423-9293, fax 423-1379). Relatively close to the centre, by the Plaza Bolognesi, it can be noisy early in the morning, but it is comfortable and has a colonial feel to it. ⑤.

Hostal San Francisco, Jirón Ancash 340 (☎428-3643). Very good value but not in a particularly pleasant neighbourhood. ③.

Hostal Wircocha, Jirón Junin 284 (☎427-1178). Basic for the price but popular with travellers because of its helpful staff. ④.

Hotel La Casona, Moquegua 289 (☎427-6273, 427-6274 or 427-6275). Excellent value, with elegant, clean and spacious rooms set around an inviting colonial courtyard. The restaurant serves great-tasting and good-value set lunches in the courtyard, but take care with luggage and handbags as the courtyard opens straight onto the street. ③.

Hotel Richmond, Emancipacion 123 (☎427-9270). An interesting place in an impressive old mansion with plenty of rooms; friendly and central, overlooking the seventh block of the main shopping drag Jirón de la Union. ③.

Hotel Ritual, Jirón Ucayali 199 (☎427-6028, fax 427-6029). Right in the heart of Lima and just a block from the Plaza Mayor, this place offers comfort and safety at a reasonable price. ④.

La Posada del Parque, Velarde 60 (☎433-2412, fax 332-6927, *monden@telematic.com.peru*). In a quiet cul-de-sac in the pleasant Santa Beatrice suburb and within walking distance of Lima Centro. Friendly and comfortable, and good English is spoken. ④.

Expensive

Gran Hotel Bolivar, Jirón de la Union 958 (☎427-7672, fax 428-7674). This old, very luxurious hotel dominating the northwest corner of the Plaza San Martin has certainly seen better times and usually has more staff than guests. It's probably not worth the money to stay, but check out the cocktail lounge and restaurant, which often have live music on Sat nights. ⑧.

Hotel El Plaza, Avenida Nicolas de Pierola 850 (☎428-6270, fax 428-6274). Good value for a comfortable, central hotel, with good facilities and reasonable service. ⑥.

Lima Sheraton Hotel, Paseo de la Republica 170 (☎433-3320, fax 426-5920). A standard top-class modern international hotel – concrete, tall and blandly elegant. ⑧.

Miraflores, San Isidro, San Antonio and Barranco

Many people opt to stay further out of the city in **Miraflores**, which is close to most of Lima's nightlife, culture and commercial activity. However, most hostals start at around $20 per person and quite a few hotels go above $200. Other suburban options include **San Isidro**, **San Antonio**, and **Barranco**, which is popular as a less modern and more stylish centre.

Budget

Casa del Muchillero, Jirón Cesareo Chacallana 130a, Miraflores (☎444-9089). Located close to block 10 of José Pardo, this safe place is remarkably good value, with hot water and kitchen facilities. It's not right at the centre of Miraflores action but it's pretty close. ②.

Lima Youth Hostel, Casimiro Ulloa 328, Miraflores (☎446-5488, fax 444-8187, *hostell@mail. cosapidata.com.pe*). Unbeatable value and the best budget accommodation in Miraflores. It's located just over the Paseo de la Republica highway from Miraflores in the relatively peaceful suburb of San Antonia, in a big house with a pool. ②.

Malka Youth Hostal, Los Lirios 165, San Isidro (☎442-0165). Well located, quite comfortable and good value for this part of the city. ②.

Mochileros Backpackers, Pedro de Osma 135, Barranco (☎437-4506, *backpacker@lanet.com.pe*). One of the more popular travellers' dives, based in the lively and trendy suburb of Barranco. Good facilities, including laundry, kitchen and TV lounge. It's pretty close to the beach, clean and safe; rooms are shared but have secure lockers. They also offer bicycle rental. Discounts available to South Amerian Explorers' Club members. ③.

Moderate

B&B Hostal Tradiciones, Avenida Ricardo Palma 995 (☎445-6742, fax 446-2177, *www.taxis.com.pe/tradiciones*). Well located and in a safe environment, this reasonably priced family-run place offers cable TV, private bath, and fax and laundry services. ⑤.

Hikers Hostal, Doña Catalina 358, Los Rosales, Surco (☎271-7970, *a-mauriz@us.nety*). Located in the *segunda etapa* (second part) of Surco, level with block 38 of the Avenida Tomás Marsano, this is both comfortable and good value. Very clean and with all the services you'd expect in the mid-range. ④.

Hospedaje Yolanda, Domingo Elias 230, Miraflores (☎445-7565, *pensionyolanda@com.pe*). Very well situated just off block 47 of the Avenida Arequipa, it's close to Surquillo market and the Alliance Francaise. Comfortable and clean. ④.

Hostal Accord, Cantuarias 398 (☎444-2688). Good rooms, fair service and breakfast included, but not exceptional value. ⑤.

Hostal Carlos Tenaud, Carlos Tenaud 119 (☎421-9091). Well located, excellent value hostal, just off block 42 of Avenida Arequipa, within 15 minutes' walk of central Miraflores. ③.

Hostal El Carmelo, Bolognesi 749 (☎446-0575). Friendly, safe and popular. Clean rooms with private bath. ⑥.

Hostal El Ovalo, Avenida Jose Pardo 1110 (☎446-5549). Reasonably clean and comfortable; pretty good value for this part of town. ④.

Hostal Mami Panchita, Avenida Federico Gallesi 198 (☎263-7203, fax 263-0749, *raymi_travels@perusat.net.pe*). Very pleasant but small hostal with a shared dining room and TV lounge. They also offer an airport pickup ($15 for a group, maximum of four). Price includes breakfast.④.

Hostal Martinika, Avenida Arequipa 3701, close to the boundary of Miraflores and San Isidro (☎422-3094). Comfortable, friendly, rooms with private bath. Very reasonably priced and in an excellent location, if a little noisy in the mornings. ④.

Hotel Bellavista, 215 Jirón Bellavista 215 (☎ & fax 444-2938). A good hotel in central Miraflores, offering double rooms with bath and TV. Breakfast included. ④.

Hotel El Patio, Diez Canseco 341 (☎444-2107, fax 444-1663, *ossa@pol.com.pe*). A very agreeable and secure little place right in the heart of Miraflores; often fully booked, so reserve in advance. More expensive mini-suites and suites also available. ⑤–⑦.

Pension Jose Luis, Francisco de Paula de Ugarriza 727, Miraflores (☎444-1015, fax 446-7177, *hsjluis@telematic.edu.pe, www.telematic.edu.pe/users/hsluis*). Comfortable, modern and in a good location close to the ocean and based in a private house. It's popular with the English-speaking travelling community. ④.

Suites Eucaliptus, San Martin 511 (☎445-8594). A variety of accommodation from basic rooms up to luxurious presidential suites at a corresponding range of prices; good location and good security. ⑤–⑦.

Expensive

Boulevard, Avenida Jose Pardo 771 (☎444-6564, fax 444-6602, *boulevard@amauta.rcp.net.pe*). A full-on luxury hotel, one of the finest in the entire city. Quite well located in the hubbub of Miraflores. ⑧.

Cesar's Hotel, Avenida La Paz 463 (☎444-1212, fax 444-4444). Incredibly swish pad with a penthouse cocktail-lounge and restaurant giving spectacular views across the city; excellent service and the height of luxury. ⑧.

Colonial Inn, Comandante Espinar 310 (☎241-7471, fax 446-6662, *coloinn@telematic.edu.pe*). Great value, good service and exceptionally clean, slightly away from the fray of Miraflores. Has a lunchtime restaurant whose Belgian owner produces superb dishes. ⑥.

Embajadores Hotel, Juan Fanning 320 (☎242-9127, fax 242-9131, *htelembajadores@mixmail.com*). Part of the Best Western chain, this is well located in a quiet Miraflores area, just a few blocks from Larco Mar and the seafront. Extremely comfortable, with a gym, small rooftop pool, conference rooms, individual safes and a restaurant. ⑧.

Grand Hotel Miraflores, Avenida 28 de Julio 151 (☎447-9641). Very well priced, with friendly staff and in a good location. Has a lively disco some weekends. ⑦.

Hotel Antigua Miraflores, Avenida Grau 350, Miraflores (☎241-6116, fax 241-6115, *hantiqua@amauta.rcp.nt.pe*). Pretty central to Miraflores but in a relatively quiet spot, it has all modern conveniences but is also very stylish and elegant with gardens and balconies. Rooms in a variety of categories. ⑧.

Hostal Aleman, Avenida Arequipa 4704 (☎445-6999, fax 447-3950, *haleman@correo.dnet.com.pe*). Very good value, most rooms being spacious and well furnished; tight on security but staff are sometimes a bit unfriendly. Fairly well located within walking distance of downtown Miraflores. ⑥.

Hostal Miraflores, Avenida Petit Thouars 5444 (☎445-8745). Popular and close to most of Miraflores' shops and nightlife; good service and hard to beat for value. ⑥.

Hostal Polonia, Avenida Republica de Panama 6599 (☎446-4138, fax 446-0760). A comfortable, quiet and attractive little hotel, but a bit on the expensive side and not in a brilliant spot, though within a short taxi ride of both Miraflores and Barranco. ⑥.

Hotel Ariosto, Avenida La Paz 769 (☎444-1414). All modern comforts, good security and excellent service. ⑧.

Hotel El Marqués, Chinchon 461 (☎442-0046, fax 442-0043, *elmarques@hys.com.pe, www.elmarques.com*). Aimed at business clients, this is a very comfortable hotel with colonial-style rooms close to San Isidro commercial centre. Has meeting rooms and is pretty good value. ⑦.

Hotel El Olivar, Pancho Fierro 194, San Isidro (☎221-2121, fax 221-2141, *ventas@el-olivar.com.pe*). Modern but pleasant luxury retreat by the olive grove park of San Isidro. ⑧.

Miraflores Park Plaza, Avenida Malecon de la Reserva 1035, Miraflores (☎242-3000, fax 242-3393, *mirapph@ibm.net*). Very modern place that belongs to the exclusive Small Luxury Hotels of the World; it has great views over Miraflores, the city and the Pacific. ⑧.

Swiss Hotel Lima, Via Central 150, Centro Empresarial Real, San Isidro (☎421-9888, fax 421-4360, *peovl@ibm.net*). Luxurious with all the modern conveniences you'd expect; good for business travellers. ⑧.

The City

Laid out across a wide, flat alluvial plain, Lima fans out in long, straight streets from its heart, **Lima Centro**. The old town focuses on the colonial **Plaza Mayor** (often still called the Plaza de Armas) and the more modern **Plaza San Martin**, which are separated by some five blocks of the **Jirón de la Unión**, Lima Centro's main shopping street. At its river end, the Plaza Mayor is fronted by the Cathedral and palacio de Gobierno, while there's greater commercial activity around Plaza San Martin – money-changing facilities, large hotels and airline offices are all based here. The key to finding your way around the old part of town is to acquaint yourself with these two squares and the streets between.

From Lima Centro, the city's main avenues stretch out into the sprawling suburbs. The two principal routes are **Avenida Colonial**, heading out to the harbour area around the suburb of **Callao** and the airport, and perpendicular to this, the broad, tree-lined **Avenida Arequipa** reaching out to the old beach resort of **Barranco**. Some 7 or 8km down Avenida Arequipa, the suburb of **Miraflores** is the modern, commercial heart of Lima, where most of the city's businesses have moved during the last thirty years.

Lima Centro

Since its foundation, Lima has spread steadily out from the **Plaza Mayor** – virtually all of the Río Rimac's alluvial soils have now been built on and even the sand dunes beyond are rapidly filling up with migrant settlers. When Pizarro arrived here he found a valley dominated by some four hundred temples and palaces, most of them pre-Inca, well spread out to either side of the river; the natives were apparently peaceful, living mostly by cultivating gardens, fishing from the ocean, or catching freshwater crayfish. As usual, Pizarro's choice for the site of this new Spanish town was influenced as much by politics as it was by geography: he founded Lima on the site of an existing palace belonging to Tauri Chusko, the local chief who had little choice but to give up his residence and move away.

The Plaza Mayor

Today the heart of the old town is around the **Plaza Mayor** – until a few years ago known as the Plaza de Armas or "armed plaza" (Plaza Armada) as the early conquistadores called it. There are no remains of any Indian heritage in or around the square; standing on the site of Tauri Chusko's palace is the relatively modern Palacio Gobierno, the cathedral, which occupies occupies the site of an Inca temple once dedicated to the Puma deity, while the Municipal Building lies on what was originally an Inca envoy's mansion. The **Palacio de Gobierno** – also known as the Presidential Palace – was Pizarro's house long before the present building was conceived. It was here that he spent the last few years of his life and was assassinated in 1541. Its ground might even be considered "sacred" since as he died, his jugular severed by an assassin's rapier, he fell to the floor, drew a cross, then kissed it. The clean, almost impressive, building you can see today, however, is modern, having been completed in 1938. The **changing of the guard** takes place outside the palace (Mon–Sat at 11.45am) – it's not a particular-

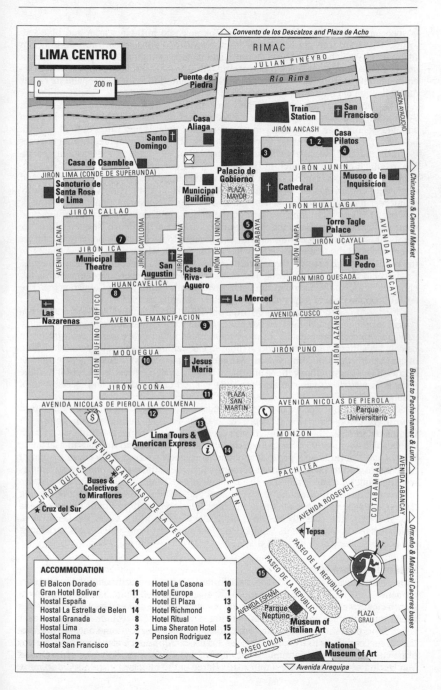

LIMA CENTRO

0   200 m

△ Convento de los Descalzos and Plaza de Acho

RIMAC

JULIAN PINEYRO

Río Rima

Puente de Piedra

Train Station

San Francisco

Casa Aliaga

JIRÓN ANCASH

Casa Pilatos

Santo Domingo

Casa de Osamblea

JIRÓN LIMA (CONDE DE SUPERUNDA)

Palacio de Gobierno

Cathedral

Museo de la Inquisición

Sanoturio de Santa Rosa de Lima

Municipal Building

PLAZA MAYOR

JIRÓN HUALLAGA

JIRÓN CALLAO

JIRÓN JUNIN

Chinatown & Central Market

JIRÓN ICA

Municipal Theatre

San Augustin

Casa de Riva-Aguero

Torre Tagle Palace

JIRÓN UCAYALI

San Pedro

HUANCAVELICA

JIRÓN MIRO QUESADA

Las Nazarenas

AVENIDA EMANCIPACION

La Merced

AVENIDA CUSCO

MOQUEGUA

JIRÓN PUNO

Jesus Maria

Buses to Pachacamac & Lurín

JIRÓN OCOÑA

PLAZA SAN MARTIN

AVENIDA NICOLAS DE PIEROLA (LA COLMENA)

AVENIDA NICOLAS DE PIEROLA

Parque Universitario

Lima Tours & American Express

MONZON

Ormeño & Mariscal Caceres buses

Buses & Colectivos to Miraflores

PACHITEA

Cruz del Sur

Tepsa

N

PASEO DE LA REPUBLICA

Museum of Italian Art

PLAZA GRAU

AVENIDA ESPAÑA

Parque Neptuno

PASEO COLÓN

National Museum of Art

▽ Avenida Arequipa

ACCOMMODATION

El Balcon Dorado	6	Hotel La Casona	10
Gran Hotel Bolivar	11	Hotel Europa	1
Hostal España	4	Hotel El Plaza	13
Hostal La Estrella de Belen	14	Hotel Richmond	9
Hostal Granada	8	Hotel Ritual	5
Hostal Lima	3	Lima Sheraton Hotel	15
Hostal Roma	7	Pension Rodriguez	12
Hostal San Francisco	2		

ly spectacular sight, though the soldiers look splendid in their scarlet and blue uniforms. There are free **guided tours** from the visitor's entrance in Jirón de la Unión (daily 10am), which last a couple of hours and include changing of the guard; to get on one you have to register in the office on the fifth floor of the building opposite the side-entrance. The tour includes the imitation Baroque interior of the palace, and its rather dull collection of colonial and reproduction furniture.

Less than 50m away, the squat and austere **Cathedral** (Mon–Sat 10am–1pm & 2–5pm; $1.50), designed by Francisco Becerra, was modelled on that of Jaén in Spain and, like Jaén, it has three aisles in a Renaissance style. When Becerra died in 1605, however, the cathedral was far from completion. The towers took another forty years to finish and, in 1746, further frustration arrived in the guise of a devastating earthquake, which destroyed much of the building; the current cathedral, which is essentially a reconstruction of Becerra's design, was rebuilt throughout the eighteenth and nineteenth centuries, then again after a further quake in 1940. However, it is primarily of interest for its **Museum of Religious Art and Treasures** (daily 10am–1pm & 2–5pm; $1.50), which contains seventeenth- and eighteenth-century paintings and some choir stalls with fine wooden carvings by Catalan artist Pedro Noguero. Its other highlight is a collection of human remains thought to be Pizarro's body (quite fitting since he placed the first stone shortly before his death), which lie in the first chapel on the right. Although gloomy, the interior retains some of its appealing Churrigueresque (highly elaborate Baroque) decor. The stalls are superb and, even more impressive, the choir was exquisitely carved in the early seventeenth century by a Catalan artist. The **Archbishop's Palace** next door was rebuilt as recently as 1924.

Directly across the square, the **Municipal Building** (Mon–Fri 9am–1pm; free) is a typical example of a half-hearted twentieth-century attempt at something neocolonial. Brilliant white on the outside, its most memorable features are permanent groups of heavily armed guards and the odd armoured car waiting conspicuously for some kind of action. Inside, the **Pinacoteca Museum** (same hours) houses a selection of Peruvian paintings, notably those of Ignacio Merino from the nineteenth century. In the library (*la biblioteca*) you can also see the city's Act of Foundation and Declaration of Independence.

Set back from one corner of the main square is the church and monastery of **Santo Domingo** (Mon–Sat 9am–12.30pm & 3–6pm, Sun & holidays 9am–1pm; $2). Completed in 1549, Santo Domingo was presented by the pope, a century or so later, with an alabaster statue of Santa Rosa de Lima. Rosa's tomb, and that of San Martin de Porres, are the building's great attractions, and much revered. Otherwise it's not of huge interest or architectural merit, although it is one of the oldest religious structures in Lima, built on a site granted to the Dominicans by Pizarro in 1535. There's a growing concentration of artesania shops around Santo Domingo area, the largest being Santo Domingo, right opposite the monastery. Nearby at the Jirón Conde de Superunda 298, you'll find the recently restored early nineteenth-century **Casa de Osambela**, which has five balconies on its façade and a look-out point from which boats arriving at the port of Callao could be spotted.

East of the Plaza Mayor

Jirón Ancash leads away from the Palacio de Gobierno towards one of Lima's most attractive churches, **San Francisco** (daily 10am–1pm & 3–6pm; $2). A large seventeenth-century construction with an engaging stone facade and towers, San Francisco's vaults and columns are elaborately decorated with *mudéjar* (Moorish-style) plaster relief. It's a majestic building that has withstood the passage of time and the devastation of successive earth tremors. The San Fransisco Monastary also contains a superb library and a room of paintings by (or finished by) Pieter Paul Rubens, Jordaens and Van Dyck. Forty-minute guided tours are offered of the monastery and its **Catacombs**

Museum (daily 9.30am–5.45pm; $1.50), both of which are worth a visit. The museum is inside the church's vast crypts, which were only discovered in 1951 and contain the skulls and bones of some seventy thousand people.

Opposite San Francisco, at Jirón Ancash 390, is **La Casa Pilatos** (Mon–Fri 11am–1.30pm; free), now the home of the Instituto Nacional de Cultura and one of several well-restored colonial mansions in Lima. Quite a simple building, and no competition for Torre Tagle (see below), it nevertheless has an attractive courtyard with an unusual stone staircase leading up from the middle of the patio.

A couple of blocks away, the **Museo de La Inquisición**, Jirón Junin 548 (Mon–Fri 9am–8pm, Sat 9am–5pm; free), faces out onto Plaza Bolivar near the Congress building. Behind a facade of Greek-style classical columns, the museum contains the original tribunal room with its beautifully carved mahogany ceiling. This was the headquarters of the Inquisition for the whole of Spanish-dominated America from 1570 until 1820, and, beneath the building, you can look round the dungeons and torture chambers, which contain a few gory, life-sized human models. The few blocks behind the museum and Avenida Abancay are taken over by the **central market** and **Chinatown**. Perhaps one of the most fascinating sectors of Lima Centro, Chinatown is now swamped by the large and colourful (if also smelly and rife with pickpockets) daily market. An ornate Chinese gateway, crossing over Jirón Huallaya, marks the site of Lima's best and cheapest *chifa* (Chinese) restaurants.

Heading from Chinatown back towards the Plaza Mayor along Ucayali, you'll pass the church of **San Pedro** (daily 7am–1pm & 6–8.30pm; free) on the corner of Jirón Azangaro. Built by the Jesuits and occupied by them until their expulsion in 1767, this richly decorated colonial temple dripping with art treasures is worth a brief look around. However, just over the road, you'll find the far more spectacular **Torre Tagle Palace**, at Ucayali 358 (Mon–Fri 9am–5pm; free), pride and joy of the old city. Now the home of Peru's Ministry for Foreign Affairs and recognizable by the security forces with machine guns on the roof and top veranda, Torre Tagle is a superb, beautifully maintained mansion built in the 1730s. It is embellished with a decorative facade and two wooden balconies, which are typical of Lima in that one is larger than the other. The porch and patio are distinctly Andalucian, although some of the intricate wood carvings on pillars and across ceilings display a native influence; the *azulejos*, or tiling, also shows a strong fusion of styles – this time a combination of Moorish and Limeño tastes. In the left-hand corner of the patio you can see a set of scales like those used to weigh merchandise during colonial times, and the house also contains a magnificent sixteenth-century carriage complete with mobile toilet. Originally, mansions such as Torre Tagle served as refuges for outlaws, the authorities being unable to enter without written and stamped permission – now anyone can go in (afternoons are the quietest times to visit).

North of the Plaza Mayor: Rimac

Heading north from the Plaza Mayor along Jirón de la Unión, you pass the **Casa Aliaga**, at no. 224, an unusual mansion occupied by the same family since 1535 and reputed to be the oldest in South America. It's one of the most elaborate mansions in the country, with sumptuous reception rooms full of Louis XIV mirrors, furniture, and doors. You need to call in advance to arrange a visit (☎427-6624; $3), or book a tour through one of the companies listed on p.86. Continuing up Jirón de la Unión, it's a short walk to the **Puente de Piedra**, the stone bridge which arches over the Río Rimac – usually no more than a miserable trickle – behind the Palacio de Gobierno. Initially a wooden construction, today's bridge was built in the seventeenth century, using egg whites to improve the consistency of its mortar. Its function was to provide a permanent link between the centre of town and the district of San Lazaro, known these days as **Rimac**, or, more popularly, as Bajo El Puente ("below the bridge"). This zone was first populated in the sixteenth century by African slaves, newly imported and awaiting purchase by big plantation owners; a few years later Rimac was beleaguered by outbreaks of leprosy. Although these days its status is much improved, Rimac is still one of the most run-down areas of Lima and can be quite an aggressive place at night – unfortunate, since some of the best *peñas* are located down here. However, a one-hour guided **tour** (Sat & Sun 10am–9pm, departing every 15min) through old Rimac and up to the top of San Cristobal departs from outside Santo Domingo monastery (see p.64) and is a good and safe way to see many of Rimac's rather run-down sites. It's best in the afternoons, when the visibility is generally better.

Rimac is also home to the **Plaza de Acho**, on Hualgayoc 332, Lima's most important bullring, which also houses the **Museo Taurino**, or Bullfight Museum (Mon–Fri 8am–3pm; $1.50), containing some original Goya engravings, several interesting paintings, and a few relics of bullfighting contests. A few blocks to the right of the bridge, you can stroll up the **Alameda de los Descalzos**, a fine tree-lined walk designed for courtship, and an afternoon meeting place for the early seventeenth-century elite. It leads past the foot of a distinctive hill, the Cerro San Cristobal, and, although in desperate need of renovation, it still possesses twelve appealing marble statues brought from Italy in 1856, each one representing a different sign of the zodiac. At the far end of the Alameda a fine, low Franciscan monastery, **El Convento de los Descalzos** (Mon–Sat 9.30am–1pm & 3–5.30pm; $1.50 including a 40min guided tour), houses a collection of colonial and Republican paintings from Peru and Ecuador, and its Chapel of El Carmen possesses a beautiful Baroque gold-leaf altar. Founded in 1592, the monastery was situated in what was then a secluded spot beyond the town, protected from earthquakes by the Cerro San Cristobal.

West of the Plaza Mayor

Two interesting sanctuaries can be found on the western edge of old Lima, along Avenida Tacna. The **Sanctuario de Santa Rosa de Lima** (daily 9.30am–12.30pm & 3.30–6.30pm; free), on the corner of Jirón Lima, is a fairly plain church named in honour of the first saint created in the Americas. The construction of Avenida Tacna destroyed a section of the already small seventeenth-century church, but in the patio next door you can visit the saint's **hermitage**, a small adobe cell, and a fascinating **Museo Etnografico**, containing crafts, tools, jewellery and weapons from jungle tribes, plus some photographs of early missionaries.

At the junction of Avenida Tacna and Huancavelica, the church of **Las Nazarenas** (daily 7am–noon & 4.30–8pm; free) is again small and outwardly undistinguished but it has an interesting history. After the severe 1655 earthquake, a mural of the crucifixion, painted by an Angolan slave on the wall of his hut, was apparently the only object left standing in the district. Its survival was deemed a miracle – the cause of popular processions ever since – and it is on this site that the church was founded. The widespread and popular processions for the Lord of Miracles, to save Lima from another earthquake, take place every autumn (Oct 18, 19, 28 & Nov 1), based around a silver litter which carries the original mural. Purple is the colour of the procession and many women in Lima wear it for the entire month.

South of the Plaza Mayor

The largest area of old Lima is the stretch between the Plaza Mayor and Plaza San Martin. Worth a quick look here is the old church of **San Augustin** (daily 8.30am–noon & 3.30–5.30pm; free), founded in 1592 and located on the corner of Ica and Camana. Although severely damaged by earthquake activity (only the small side chapel can be visited nowadays), the church retains a glorious facade, one of the most complicated examples of Churrigueresque architecture in Peru. Just over the road at Camana 459, the **Casa de Riva-Aguero** (Mon–Fri 11am–1pm & 2–8pm, Sat 9am–1pm; free) is a typical colonial house, built in the early nineteenth century and donated to the Catholic

University; its patio has been laid out as an interesting **Museuo de Arte Popular**, displaying crafts from all over Peru and contemporary paintings. The building functions as the Riva-Aguero Institute which looks after a library and historic archives.

Perhaps the most noted of all religious buildings in Lima is the **Iglesia de La Merced** (daily 7am–1pm & 4–8pm; free), just two blocks from the Plaza Mayor on the corner of Jirón de la Unión and Jirón Miro Quesada. Built on the site where the first Latin mass in Lima was celebrated, the original church was demolished in 1628 to make way for the present building. Its most elegant feature, a beautiful colonial facade, has been adapted and rebuilt several times – as have the broad columns of the nave – to protect the church against tremors. But by far the most lasting impression is made by the **Cross of the Venerable Padre Urraca**, whose miraculous silver staff is smothered by hundreds of kisses every hour and witness to the fervent prayers of a constantly shifting congregation. If you've just arrived in Lima, a few minutes by this cross will give you an insight into the depth of Peruvian belief in miraculous power. The attached **cloisters** (daily 8am–noon & 3–6pm; free) are less spectacular though they do have a historical curiosity: it was here that the Patriots of Independence declared the Virgin of La Merced their military marshal. A couple of minutes' walk further towards the Plaza San Martin, at the corner of Camana and Jirón Moquegua, stands the church of **Jesus María** (daily 7am–1pm & 3–7pm; free), home of Capuchin nuns from Madrid in the early eighteenth century. Take a look inside at its outstanding, sparkling Baroque gilt altars and pulpits.

Plaza San Martín and around

The **Plaza San Martín** is a grand, large square with fountains at its centre. It's recently been renovated and mime artists, clowns and soap box politicos frequently attract a small circle of interested faces, while shoe-shine boys and old men with box cameras on wooden legs try to win your attention. The Plaza San Martin has seen most of Lima's political rallies this century and the sight of rioting office workers and attendant police with water cannons and tear gas is still a possibility. Ideologically the Plaza San Martin represents the sophisticated, egalitarian and European intellectual liberators like San Martin himself, while remaining well and truly within the commercial world.

The wide Avenida Nicolas de Pierola (also known as La Colmena) leads off the plaza, west towards the **Plaza Dos de Mayo**, which sits on the site of an old gate dividing Lima from the road to Callao and hosts a great street market where some fascinating bargains can be found. Built to commemorate the repulse of the Spanish fleet in 1866 (Spain's last attempt to regain a foothold in South America), the plaza is probably one of the most polluted spots in Lima and is markedly busier, dirtier and less friendly than Plaza San Martin. East of Plaza San Martin, Avenida Nicolas de Pierola runs towards the **Parque Universitario**, site of South America's first university, San Marcos. Nowadays it is no longer even an important annexe for the university and the park itself is the base for numerous colectivo companies and street hawkers, and is almost permanently engulfed in crowds of cars and rushing pedestrians.

South of Plaza San Martin, Jirón Belén leads down to the Paseo de la República and the shady **Parque Neptuno**, home to the pleasant **Museum of Italian Art**, Paseo de la República 250 (Mon–Fri 9am–4pm; $1). Located inside an unusual Renaissance building, the museum exhibits contemporary Peruvian art as well as reproductions of the Italian masters and offers a very welcome respite from the hectic modern Lima outside. Just south of here at Paseo Colón 125 is the **Museo de Arte** (Tues–Sun 10am–5pm; $1.5), housed in the former International Exhibition Palace built in 1869. It contains interesting, small collections of colonial art and many fine crafts from pre-Columbian times, as well as hosting frequent temporary exhibitions of modern photography and other art forms. Film shows and lectures are also offered on some weekday evenings (for details check posters at the museum lobby). Walk 50m or so west from the museum along Paseo Colón and you'll come to the large **Parque de la**

Exposición, which stretches down to Avenida 28 de Julio. Created for the International Exhibition of 1868, the park has long been neglected and seems mainly to attract courting couples who have nowhere else to go in the evenings or on Sundays.

The suburbs

The old centre of Lima is surrounded by a number of sprawling **suburbs**, or *distritos*, which spread across the desert between the foothills of the Andes and the coast. South of Lima Centro lies the lively suburb of **Miraflores**, a slick, fast-moving and very ostentatious mini-metropolis, which has become Lima's business and shopping zone and doubles up as a popular meeting place for the wealthier sector of Lima society; a brand new clifftop development, Larco Mar has been built at the bottom of Miraflores' main street, seriously adding to this barrio's appeal. Sandwiched between Lima Centro and Miraflores is the plush suburb of **San Isidro**, boasting a golf course and surrounded by sky-scraping apartment buildings and ultramodern shopping complexes, as well as many square kilometres of simple houses looking almost pre-Inca in style. South of Miraflores begins the oceanside suburb of **Barranco**, one of the oldest and most attractive parts of the city, located above the steep sandy cliffs of the **Costa Verde**, and hosting a small but active nightlife. Southwest of Lima Centro lies the city's port area, the suburb of **Callao**, an interesting, old if rather insalubrious zone, and the peninsula of **La Punta** with its air of slightly decayed grandeur. Other than these, the main reason for venturing into Lima's suburbs is to visit some of its many and varied museums, which are scattered throughout the city's sprawl, in particular the comprehensive **Museo Nacional de Arqueología, Antropología y Historia del Peru**, the outstanding **Museo de Oro** and the modern **Museo de La Nacion**.

Miraflores

As far as Lima's inhabitants are concerned, **MIRAFLORES** is the major focus of the action and nightlife, its streets lined with cafés and the capital's flashiest shops. Although still connected to Lima Centro by the long-established Avenida Arequipa, another road – Paseo de la República (also known as the Via Expressa) – now provides the suburb with an alternative approach. The fastest way to get here is by yellow bus marked "Via Expressa" from Avenida Abancay and get off, after about 25 minutes, at the Benavides bridge. Alternatively, take a yellow bus (#2) or colectivo from the first few blocks of Avenida Garcilaso de la Vega (a continuation of Avenida Tacna) and get off at *El Haiti* café/bar, the stop just before Miraflores central park.

A good place to make for first is the **Huaca Pucllana** (Tues–Sun 10am–5pm; $1), a vast pre-Inca adobe mound which continues to dwarf most of the houses around and has a small associated site museum, craft shop and restaurant; although it may be closed for maintenance, it's still worth checking out. It's just a two-minute walk from Avenida Arequipa, on the right as you come from Lima Centro at block 44. One of a large number of *huacas* – sacred places – and palaces that formerly stretched across this part of the valley, little is known about the Pucllana, though it seems likely that it was originally named after a pre-Inca chief of the area. It has a hollow core running through its cross-section and is thought to have been constructed in the shape of an enormous frog, symbol of the rain god, who evidently spoke to priests through a tube connected to the cavern at its heart. It may well have been the mysteriously unknown oracle after which the Rimac (meaning "he who speaks") valley was named; a curious document from 1560 affirms that the "devil" spoke at this mound.

From the top of the *huaca* you can see over the office buildings and across the flat roofs of multicoloured houses in the heart of Miraflores. The suburb's central area focuses on the attractive, almost triangular **Parque 7 de Junio** (Miraflores Park) at the end of the Avenida Arequipa. The park divides into four areas of activity: at the top

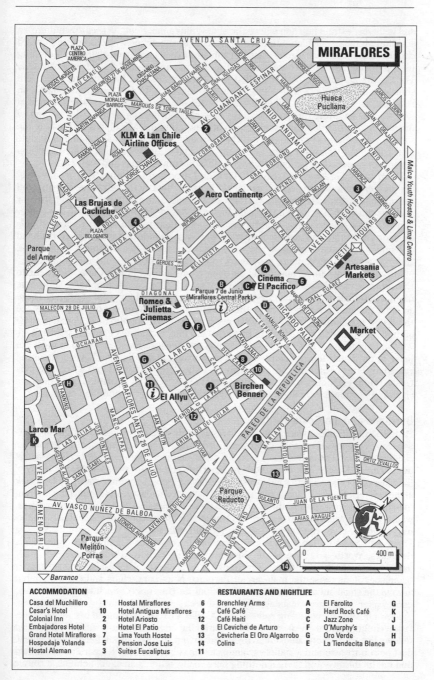

MIRAFLORES

ACCOMMODATION

Casa del Muchillero	1	Hostal Miraflores	6	
Cesar's Hotel	10	Hotel Antigua Miraflores	4	
Colonial Inn	2	Hotel Ariosto	12	
Embajadores Hotel	9	Hotel El Patio	8	
Grand Hotel Miraflores	7	Lima Youth Hostel	13	
Hospedaje Yolanda	5	Pension Jose Luis	14	
Hostal Aleman	3	Suites Eucaliptus	11	

RESTAURANTS AND NIGHTLIFE

Brenchley Arms	A	El Farolito	G	
Café Café	B	Hard Rock Café	K	
Café Haiti	C	Jazz Zone	J	
El Ceviche de Arturo	F	O'Murphy's	L	
Cevichería El Oro Algarrobo	G	Oro Verde	H	
Colina	E	La Tiendecita Blanca	D	

end is the pedestrain junction where the shoe-shiners hang out; further down there's a small amphitheatre, which often has mime acts or music; next you come to a raised circular area, which has a good craft and antiques market set up on stalls every evening (6–10pm); just down from here is a small section of gardens and a children's play area. The streets around the park are filled with flashy cafés and bars and crowded with shoppers, flower-sellers and young men washing cars. In the park, particularly on Sundays, there are artists selling their canvases – some are good, most are aimed at tourists. **Larco Mar**, the popular, flash new cliff-top development at the bottom of Avenida Larco, has done an excellent job of integrating the Miraflores park end of the suburb with what was previously a rather desolate point. Essentially a shopping zone with patios and walkways open to the sky, sea and cliffs, it's is also home to several decent bars, ice-cream parlours, eating establishments cinemas and nightclubs.

From the end of Avenida Arequipa, **Avenida Larco** and **Diagonal** both fan out along the park en route to the ocean less than 2km away. Nearby the attractive **Parque del Amor** sits on the cliff tops above the Costa Verde and celebrates the fact that for decades this area has been a favourite haunt of young lovers, particularly the poorer Limeños who have no privacy at home. A huge sculpture of a loving Andean couple clasping each other rapturously is surrounded by pairs of lovers walking hand in hand or cuddling on the cliff tops above the ocean, especially on Sunday afternoons. Unfortunately, however, there have been recent reports of night-time muggings here.

Miraflores' only important mansion open to the public is the **Casa de Ricardo Palma**, at General Suarez 189 (Mon–Fri 10am–12.30pm & 4–7pm, Sat 10am–noon; free), where Palma, probably Peru's greatest historian, lived for most of his life. There are two museums worth visiting: the **Enrico Poli Museum**, Lord Cochrane 466 (hours by appointment; ☎422-2437; $10 per person for a minimum of 5), contains some of the finest pre-Inca archeological treasures in Lima, including ceramics, gold and silver. The highlight of this private collection is the treasure found at Sepan in northern Peru, in particular four golden trumpets each over a metre long and over a thousand years old. The private **Amano Museum**, on Calle Retiro 160, off block 11 of Angamos Oeste (Mon–Fri, hours by appointment; ☎441-2909; entry by donation), also merits a visit for its fabulous exhibition of Chancay weavings, as well as bountiful ceramics.

Barranco and the Costa Verde

BARRANCO, a quieter place than Miraflores, is easily reached by taking any bus or colectivo along Diagonal. Overlooking the ocean, and scattered with old mansions as well as fascinating smaller homes, this was the capital's seaside resort during the last century and is now a kind of Limeño Left Bank, with young artists and intellectuals taking over many of the older properties. There's little to see specifically, though you may want to take a look at the cliff-top remains of a funicular rail-line, which used to carry aristocratic families from the summer resort down to the beach; also there's a pleasant, well-kept municipal park, where you can while away the afternoon beneath the trees. One block inland of the funicular, an impressive white church sits on the cliff with gardens to the front, beside the Puente de Suspiros, an attractive wooden bridge crossing a gully filled with exotic dwellings. Worth a browse is the **Museum of Electricity**, Pedro Osma 105 (daily 9am–5pm; free), which displays a wide range of early electrical appliances and generating techniques. Otherwise the main joy of Barranco is its bars, clubs and cafés clustered around the small but attractive **Plaza Municipal de Barranco**, which buzz with frenetic energy after dark whilst retaining much of the area's original charm and character.

Down beside the pounding rollers, the **COSTA VERDE**, so named because of vegetation clinging to the steep sandy cliffs, marks the edge of a continent. A bumpy road follows the shore from an exclusive yacht club and the Chorrillos fishermen's wharf, past both Barranco and Miraflores, almost to the suburb of Magdalena. The sea is cold and not too clean – and there's nothing here really, other than sand, pebbles, a couple of beach clubs, a few restaurants, and a resident surfing crowd. But Lima would seem sparse without it and swimming in the surf is as good a way as any to extend a day mooching about Barranco and Miraflores. As everywhere in Lima, however, keep a sharp eye on your clothes and valuables.

San Isidro and Lince

Unless you're shopping, or looking for a sauna or disco, there are few good reasons to stop off in **SAN ISIDRO**. One, though, might be to take a stroll through the **Bosque El Olivar**, just 150m west from block 34 of Avenida Arequipa. A charming grove first planted in 1560, it's now rather depleted in olive trees but you can still see the old press and mill-stone as well as a stage where concerts and cultural events are often held. A few blocks northwest, just off Avenida El Rosario, is an impressive reconstructed adobe *huaca*, **Huallamarca**, Nicolas de Rivera 201 (Tues–Sun 9am–2pm; free), now surrounded by wealthy suburbs. Like Pucllana, this dates from pre-Inca days and has a small site museum displaying the archeological remains of ancient Lima culture, and funerary masks and artwork found in the *huaca* – including textiles oddly reminiscent of Scottish tartans. San Isidro has just one colonial mansion worth checking out, the **Casa de la Tradición**, at Avenida Salaverry 3032 (Mon–Fri 2.30–5pm; $1.50). A rather elegant old house, it contains an interesting private collection of artefacts and pictures covering the history of Lima.

Immediately north of San Isidro is the busy, workaday suburb of **LINCE**, whose only real attraction for tourists is the little-visited, but quite fascinating, **Museum of Natural History**, Avenida Arenales 1250 (Mon–Fri 8am–1.30pm & Sat 9am–noon; $1.50). The museum presents a comprehensive overview of Peruvian wildlife and botany, with its highlight, a "sun fish", being one of only three known examples in the world. To get there take microbus #13 (red and cream) from Avenida Tacna.

Pueblo Libre

The only reason to visit the suburb of **PUEBLO LIBRE**, which lies between San Isidro and Callao, is to look round a trio of Lima's major museums. The **Museo Nacional de Arqueología, Antropología y Historia del Peru,** on Plaza Bolivar at the corner of San Martín and Antonio Pola (daily 9am–5.30pm; $1.50) posseses a varied exhibition of pre-Inca artefacts and a number of historical exhibits relating mainly to the republican period. Although there's plenty to see, much of the museum's immense collection is in storage and has been for decades, though some has shifted to the Museo de La Nacion on the other side of town (see p.73). The displays also give a detailed and accurate perspective on Peru's prehistory, a vision that comes as a surprise if you'd previously thought of Peru simply in terms of Incas and conquistadores. Divided between a number of galleries set around two colonial-style courtyards, the exhibits begin with the evolution and population of America: the earliest Peruvian pieces are stone tools some eight thousand years old. One of the finest rooms shows carved **Chavin stones** such as the magnificent Estela Raymondi, a diorite block intricately engraved with feline, serpent and falcon features, or the Tello Obelisk, a masterpiece in granite. The Manos Cruzados, or Crossed Hands stone from **Kotosh**, is also on display, evidence of a mysterious cult some five thousand years old. The **Paracas room** is rich in weavings and replete with excellent examples of deformed heads and trepanated skulls: one shows post-operative growth; in another of the cases sits a male mummy, "frozen" at the age of 30 to 35 and with fingernails still visible and with a creepy, fixed sideways glance from his misshapen head. The **Nasca room**, stuffed full of incredible ceramics, is divided according to what each pot represents – marine life, agriculture, flora, wildlife, trophy-heads, mythology, sexual and everyday life. The **Mochica** and **Chimu rooms** are also well stocked: there's one entirely devoted to music and dance, containing remarkable ceramics depicting musicians, even birds playing the drums. And, lastly, there's a room devoted to the **Incas** – a useful initial overview with impressive models of the main ruins like Machu Picchu and Tambo Colorado. To get to the museum take microbus #41 (white and blue) from the corner of Cusco and Carabaya in Lima Centro.

Integrated into the Archeological and Anthropological Museum, the **National Museum of History** (same hours and ticket), housed in an adjacent nineteenth-century mansion, is entered by the same door. It displays dazzling antique clothing, extravagant furnishings, and other period pieces complemented by early Republican paintings. The liberators San Martin and Bolivar both lived here for a while.

A fifteen-minute walk from here – north up Avenida Sucre then west along Avenida Bolivar for ten blocks – will bring you to one of the city's most unusual museums, the **Rafael Larco Herrera Museum**, Avenida Bolivar 1515 (Mon–Sat 9am–6pm; $4.50; *www.tsi.com.pe/museolarco*), which contains more than four hundred thousand excellently preserved ceramics, many of them Chiclin or Mochica pottery from around Trujillo. The museum is divided into three sections: the main museum; the warehouse museum; and the erotic art museum, which contains an intriguing selection of pre-Inca exhibits, the museum's highlight. From the centre of Lima, you can get to the museum either by bus #23 from Avenida Abancay, by green microbus #37 from Avenida Nicolas de Pierola, or on bus #41 from Avenida Emancipación or Plaza Dos de Mayo; however, it's much easier and quicker to take a taxi.

Parque de las Leyendas and the Zoo

Head west from the Larco Herrera museum to the end of Avenida Bolivar, then skirt round to the southwest of the Catholic university campus in the suburb of San Miguel, and you'll come to the **Zoo** and **Parque de las Leyendas** (daily 9am–5pm; $2, $1 for students). Located in a relatively deserted spot on the sacred site of the ancient Maranga culture, the park is laid out according to the three regions of Peru – *costa*, *sierra* and *selva*. The park and zoo has been much improved in recent years, though there's little attempt to create the appropriate habitats and the animals are caged. Nevertheless, it's a good place to get a glimpse of many of Peru's animal and bird species – condors, jaguars, sealions, snakes and pumas, king vultures, elephants, bears, and other exotica. The park makes a fine place for a picnic, and there are good *artesania* stalls just outside, selling cases of magnificent dead insects, including colourful Amazonian butterflies and tarantulas. Yellow bus #48 goes directly there from the Plaza Mayor or you can take almost any of the colectivos along Avenida La Marina or west along Avenida Javier Prado; a taxi, though easier, will cost around $3–5.

Callao and La Punta

Stuck out on a narrow, boot-shaped peninsula, Callao and La Punta (The Point) form a natural annexe to Lima, looking out towards the ocean. Originally quite separate, they were founded in 1537, and were destined to become Peru's principal treasure-fleet port before eventually being engulfed by Lima's other suburbs during the course of the twentieth century and these days it's a crumbling but attractive area.

Still the country's main commercial harbour, and one of the most modern ports in South America, **CALLAO** lies about 14km west of Lima Centro. It's easily reached on bus #25 from Plaza San Martin, which runs all the way there – and beyond to La Punta – or by taking or buses (marked "La Punta") from Avenida Arequipa west along either Avenida Angamos or Avenida Javier Prado. The suburb is none too alluring a place – its slum zones, infamous for prostitution and gangland assassins, are considered virtually no-go areas for the city's middle classes – but if you're unworried by such associations, you will find some of the best *ceviche* restaurants anywhere in the continent.

Further along, away from the rougher quarters and dominating the entire peninsula, you can see the great **Castle of Real Felipe** (Mon–Fri 9am–2pm), located on the Plaza Independencia. Built after the devastating earthquake of 1764, which washed ships ashore and killed nearly the entire population of Callao, this is a superb example of the military architecture of its age, designed in the shape of a pentagon. Although built too late to protect the Spanish treasure fleets from European pirates like Francis Drake, it was to play a critical role in the battles for independence. Its firepower repulsed both Admiral Brown (1816) and Lord Cochrane (1818), though many Royalists starved to death here when it was besieged by the Patriots in 1821, just prior to its surrender. The fort's grandeur is marred only by a number of storehouses, built during the late nineteenth century when it was used as a customs house. Inside, the **Military Museum** (Mon–Fri 9.30am–4pm; free) houses a fairly complete collection of eighteenth- and nineteenth-century arms and has various rooms dedicated to Peruvian war heroes. Also in Callao is the **Naval Museum**, Avenida Jorge Chavez 121, off Plaza Grau (Mon–Fri 9am–2pm; free), displaying the usual military paraphernalia, uniforms, paintings, photographs and replica ships.

Out at the end of the peninsula, what was once the fashionable beach resort of **LA PUNTA** is now overshadowed by the Naval College and Yacht Club. Many of its old mansions, although slowly crumbling, still remain, some of them very elegant, others extravagant monstrosities. Right at the tip, an attractive promenade offers glorious views and sunsets over the Pacific, while at the back of the strand there are some excellent restaurants serving traditional local food (many of these are difficult to find – it's best to ask locally for directions).

The Museo de La Nacion and the Museo de Oro

In the east of the city lie two of Lima's most compelling museums. The **Museo de la Nacion**, Javier Prado Este 2465 in the suburb of San Borja (Tues–Sun 9am–6pm; $1, $3 extra for exhibitions; ☎476-9875 or 476-9897), is Lima's largest modern museum and contains permanent exhibitions covering most of the important aspects of Peruvian archeology, art and culture; there's also a cafeteria (daily 10am–6pm). Exhibits are displayed mainly in vast salons and include a range of traditional, regional peasant costumes from around the country and life-sized and miniature models depicting life in pre-Conquest times. The museum can be visited by taking a colectivo along Avenida Javier Prado east from Avenida Arequipa; after ten to fifteen minutes, you'll see the vast, concrete museum on the left.

From the Museum of the Nation, walk for about five minutes or take a colectivo back along Avenida Javier Prado to the junction with Avenida Aviación, then take any bus or colectivo south to Avenida Angamos where you can catch the #72 microbus (yellow and red) or a Monterrico colectivo to the Centro Commercial shopping centre at the end of Angamos, in the well-to-do suburb of Monterrico. From here, Lima's **Museo de Oro** (daily noon–7pm; $5), Avenida Alonso de Molina 1100, is a short walk three blocks up Avenida Primavera, then two to the right along Santa Elena. Housed in a small fortress-like building set back in the shade of tall trees and owned by the high-society Mujica family, this museum is a must. Upstairs there are some fine tapestry displays, while at ground level it boasts a vast display of **arms and uniforms**, many of them incredible antiques which bring to life some of Peru's bloodier history. But it's the safe-rooms downstairs that contain the real gems. Divided into several sections, these basements are literally crammed with treasures and beautiful craft goods from **pre-Columbian** times. Most of the **gold and silver jewellery** is in the metalwork rooms, but more fascinating perhaps are the pre-Inca weapons and wooden staffs, or the astounding Nasca yellow-feathered poncho designed for a noble's child or child high-priest. One thing that generally causes a stir, too, is a skull enclosing a full set of pink quartz teeth – in the corner on the right as you enter the main room from the stairs.

The **Casa Ecologica**, which pertains to the Universidad Catolica's Group for Assistance to the Rural Sector, has an interesting green exhibit of a house with wind, solar electric, solar thermal and solar cooking facilities set in an organic garden. Based in La Molina, beyond the Museo de Oro, you need to contact Miguel Hazdich in advance to visit (☎460-2870, *grupo@pucp.edu.pe*, *www.pucp.edu.pe/~grupo*).

Eating

Among South American capitals, Lima ranks alongside Rio and Buenos Aires for its selection of **places to eat and drink**, with restaurants, bars and cafés of every type and size crowding every corner of the city, from expensive hotel dining rooms to tiny set-meal street stalls. Regardless of class or status, virtually all Limeños eat out regularly, and having a meal out usually ends up as an evening's entertainment in itself.

Cafés and snackbars

Bar/Restaurant Machu Picchu, Ancash 312. A busy place opposite San Francisco church in Lima Centro, serving inexpensive snacks; a good spot for meeting up with other travellers. Daily 8am–11pm.

Café Café, Matir Olaya 250. A groovy coffee shop playing good rock music just off Diagonal in downtown Miraflores. Daily 10am–midnight.

Café Haiti, Diagonal 160. The most popular meeting place for middle-class Limenõs, based by the Cinema El Pacifico in the heart of Miraflores; excellent snacks and drinks but expensive. Daily 8am–midnight.

Cordano, Jirón Ancash 202. Beside the Palacio de Gobierno in Lima Centro this is one of the city's last surviving traditional bar/restaurants – very good value, with old-fashioned service. Worth visiting if only to see the decaying late nineteenth- and early twentieth-century decor. Mon–Sat 8am–11pm.

Natur, Moquegua 132. A surprisingly good vegetarian restaurant and lunchtime meeting place right in the heart of Lima Centro, just a couple of blocks from the Plaza San Martin. Mon–Fri 10am–5pm.

Oro Verde, Calle Colon 569. A pleasant, traditional coffee shop attached to the Zona de Arte photographic gallery. Mon–Sat 10am–7pm.

La Tiendecita Blanca, Avenida Larco 111. Another popular meeting place, with a superb range of cakes and pastries, though they are all a bit pricey; located right on the busiest junction in Miraflores. Daily 8am–8pm.

Restaurants

Predictably, Lima boasts some of the best **restaurants** in the country, serving not only traditional Peruvian dishes, but cuisines from all parts of the world. Seafood is particularly good here, with **ceviche** – raw fish or seafood marinated in lime juice and served with onions, chillis, sweetcorn and sweet potatoes – being the speciality. Many of the more upmarket restaurants fill up very quickly, so it is advisable to reserve in advance; where this is the case we have included the phone number. All the restaurants listed below are open roughly 10.30am–11pm daily unless otherwise indicated.

Budget

Centro Naturista, Avenida Nicolas de Pierola 958. Near the Plaza San Martin, with cheap set menus from $2 and some reasonable vegetarian dishes.

Cevicheria El Oro Algarrobo, San Martin 445. A good *cevicheria* for seafood at very reasonable prices and based in one of those rare quiet streets in Miraflores.

Chifa Chun Yion, Calle Union 126 (☎477-0550). An excellent and very busy Chinese restaurant in Barranco, quite traditional with some private compartments in the back room.

Chifa Kun, San Martin 459. A good and relatively quiet Chinese restaurant, in Miraflores, just a half a block from Avenida Larco between the Park and Larco Mar.

Colina, Jirón Berlin 317. Relatively low-key but has good service, cold beers and serves passable meals and snacks; conveniently located just beyond the hustle and bustle of Miraflores' crowded main streets. Mon–Sat 11am–11pm.

El Farolito, San Martin 435 (☎445-3568). Best at lunchtimes for its full and delicious set menus, it's an inexpensive place very popular with locals in a quiet part of Miraflores.

Manna, Avenida Petit Thouars 4700. An excellent vegetarian restaurant with a pleasant atmosphere and set lunches for under $2.

Piccolo Café, Diez Canseco 126, Miraflores. A pleasant little café near the Parque 7 de Junio, serving inexpensive sandwiches, snacks and ice creams.

La Tasca, Avenida Comandante Espinar 300. Good restaurant for a lunchtime set menu ($3–5 with a choice of main course) in terms of quality and value for money; not to be missed if you're in this part of Miraflores.

Vista Alegre, 178b Bonilla. Another good vegetarian restaurant run with a lot of good heart and experience; cheap set lunch menu and great fruit salads. There may not be a sign, so it can be hard to locate.

Vrinda Vegetarian Café, Avenida Javier Prado 185. Serves good, very cheap food and has a wholefood shop attached, with excellent natural yoghurt available by the litre. Mon–Fri 10am–7pm.

Moderate

Bircher Benner, Diez Canseco 487 (☎444-5452). A mainly vegetarian restaurant and health-food shop in downtown Miraflores; relatively expensive, except for the excellent value set lunches; tasty meals and a large choice of tropical fruit juices.

El Ceviche de Arturo, Berlin 192. A centrally located lunchtime seafood restaurant in downtown Miraflores; the food is decent although by no means the best in town.

Chifa Capon, Ucayali 774. An excellent and traditional Limeñan Chinese restaurant, the best of many in this block of Chinatown, close to the centre; it offers a range of authentic *chifa* dishes, but doesn't stay open very late.

Chifa Long, Manco Capac 483, Miraflores. An inexpensive Chinese restaurant serving excellent set lunches – try the fried fish.

El Cevillano, Avenida Aviacion 3333. A relatively inexpensive but good *cevichería* serving excellent seafood dishes; rather far out, though, in the suburb of San Borja. Tues–Sun noon–5pm.

Curich, Bolognesi 753, Miraflores (☎444-5005). A few blocks from the Parque del Amor, this is a quality restaurant piano-bar and snack bar serving great *tamales* among other things.

L'Eau Vive, Ucayali 370 (☎427-5612). Opposite the Torre Tagle Palace, this very reasonably priced and interesting restaurant serves superb French food cooked by nuns; it has a set menu for lunches and evening meals and closes after a chorus of Ave Maria. Mon–Sat noon–2.45pm & 8.15–10.30pm.

Govinda Vegetarian Restaurant, Shell 634. Offers good simple fare at very reasonable prices, particularly if you go for the set menus. Run by the International Association for Krishna Consciousness, it has a pleasant, relaxed atmosphere and a health-food shop attached.

Manolo, Malecon Pardo, block 1, La Punta, Callao. A fine seafood restaurant and bar on the seafront in La Punta; a great place to eat, right on the western edge of Lima.

Meulle Viejo, Berlin 505–507. An inexpensive and pretty good seafood restaurant specializing in lunchtime *ceviches* for shop and office workers in Miraflores – try the *ceviche mixto*. Slightly off the beaten track but worth the trip.

El Otro Sitio, Calle Sucre 317, Barranco. An excellent evening restaurant serving *criolla* dishes, often accompanied by *criolla* music, in a romantic setting close to the Puente de Suspiros. Wed–Sun 8pm–midnight.

La Pergola, Boulevard San Ramon 225. Probably the best of the Italian restaurants in the "Little Italy" complex off Diagonal in Miraflores; very busy at weekends, this interesting place shares a building with the *Chemnitz video pub* and *La Glorietta Pizzeria*.

Las Trece Monedas, Jirón Ancash 536 (☎427-6547). A popular and centrally located restaurant based in one of Lima's old colonial mansions, with a very good atmosphere but relatively expensive.

Oro Verde, Colon 571. A quiet little café that specializes in coffees and set lunch menus at reasonable prices; located in the premises of a dance school, it has pleasant garden tables out the back.

La Vieja Taberna, Avenida Grau 268, Barranco (☎247-3741). A fascinating, historic place built in 1903 and the venue where the political party APRA was created. It's very stylish, with views over the plaza in Barranco and often has music in the evenings at weekends. Particularly good for tasty traditional Limeño cuisine and good value set lunches.

Expensive

Las Brujas de Cachiche, Avenida Bolognesi 460 (☎447-1883). An interestingly conceived, top-class restaurant and bar which serves mainstream Peruvian dishes as well as a range of pre-Colombian meals using only ingredients available more than 1000 years ago. Very trendy and expensive, it's dedicated to the theme of traditional healing and magic on the coast of Peru (*bruja* means "witch" and Cachiche is a small community near Ica, which is renowned for the number of witches and healers who live and work there).

Carlin, Avenida La Paz 646 (☎444-4134). Located in the flashy El Suche commercial complex in the back streets of Miraflores, this pricey restuarant serves gourmet Peruvian and international food.

La Carreta, Avenida Rivera Navarrete 740, San Isidro (☎442-2690). One of the best meat restaurants in Lima, based close to San Isidro's Centro Comercial; open til late.

Chifa Lung Fung, Avenida Republica de Panama 3165, San Isidro (☎441-8817). One of Lima's best Chinese restaurants, with wonderful gardens inside.

Club Suizo, Genaro Iglesias 550, Miraflores. Exquisite Swiss cuisine in a very pleasant environment.

Restaurant Costa Verde, Playa Barranquito (☎477-2424 or 477-5228). An exclusive restaurant serving good-quality Peruvian and international cuisine at exceptionally high prices; don't forget your credit card.

Restaurant Fuji, Avenida Paseo de la Republica 4090 (☎440-8531). A superb but expensive Japanese restaurant conveniently located in Miraflores.

Restaurante Abdala, Avenida Grau 340, Lima Centro (☎477-5577). Serves excellent Arabic, Peruvian and German dishes. Mon–Thurs & Sun 8am–midnight, Fri & Sat 8am–3am.

La Rosa Nautica, Espigon 4, Costa Verde (☎447-0057). One of Lima's more expensive seafood restaurants, based on a pier by the ocean in Miraflores, with excellent views. All major cards accepted.

El Señorio de Sulco, Malecon Cisneros 1470 (☎445-6640). Specializes in Peruvian cuisine, using the finest ingredients and preparing mainly traditional dishes in the traditional way, many cooked only in earthen pots; expensive but extremely good.

Sushi Ito, Jirón Miguel Dasso 110, San Isidro. An exclusive and excellent sushi restaurant that serves *sashami* and *maki-temaki* among other dishes.

Nightlife and entertainment

By far the best source of **information** about music, film, theatre, sporting events and exhibitions is the daily *El Comercio*. In addition, its Friday edition carries a comprehensive supplement guide to Lima's nightlife and cultural events, which is easy to understand even if your Spanish is limited. The suburb of Barranco is now the trendiest and liveliest place to hang out.

Live music and dance

All forms of **Peruvian music** can be found in Lima, some of them, like salsa and Peruvian black music, are better here than anywhere else in the country. Even Andean

---

BULLFIGHTING

Bullfighting has been a popular pastime among a relatively small, wealthy elite from the Spanish Conquest to the present day, despite 160 years of independence from Spain. Pizarro himself brought out the first *lidia* bull for fighting in Lima, and there is a great tradition between the controlling families of Peru – the same families who breed bulls on their haciendas – to hold fights in Lima during the months of October and November. They invite some of the world's best bullfighters from Spain, Mexico and Venezuela, offering them up to $25,000 for an afternoon's sport at the prestigious **Plaza de Acho** in Rimac. **Tickets** can be bought in advance from the ticket office (block 2 of Huancavelica), or on the door an hour or so before the fights, which take place most Saturday and Sunday afternoons throughout the year. The best time, however, to catch a fight is in October or November, when the international bullfighters come to the city

---

folk music is close to its best here (though Puno, Cusco and Arequipa are all contenders). As far as the **live scene** goes, the great variety of traditional and hybrid sounds is one of the most enduring reasons for visiting the capital. Unsurprisingly, things are at their liveliest on Friday and Saturday nights, particularly among the folk group *peñas* and the burgeoning *salsadromos*. Most places charge around $5–10 entrance which often includes a drink and/or a meal.

Behind the Palacio de Gobierno, on the Paseo Santo (the former Polvos Azules) there are three **open-air amphitheatres** where, every evening, live traditional music is played (usually 6–9pm, earlier at weekends). For **dance classes** and information on workshops and performances go to Danza Lima, Colon 569, Larco, in Miraflores for modern dance; for folk dancing contact El Ayllu (see Information, p.58).

Peñas

The *peñas* – some of which only open at weekends – are the surest bet for listening to authentic **Andean folk**, although some of them also specialize in Peruvian **criolla,** which brings together a unique and very vigorous blend of coastal black, Spanish influence and, to a lesser extent, Andean music. These days it's not uncommon for some of Lima's best *peñas* to feature a fusion of *criolla* and Latin jazz. Generally speaking *peñas* don't get going until after 10pm and usually the live bands play through to 3 or 4am, if not until first light.

Las Brisas del Titicaca, Jirón Wakulski 168. One of the best and cheapest of the city's *peñas*, located in Lima Centro.

La Estacion de Barranco, Avenida Pedro de Osma 112 (☎247-0344). In Barranco, just across the road from the suburb's main plaza, this established *peña* varies its flavour regularly between folklore, *criolla* and even Latin jazz at times; it has a very good atmosphere most Fridays and Saturdays.

Manos Morenas, Avenida Pedro de Osma 409. A few blocks south of the small plaza in Barranco, this club usually hosts *criolla* gigs, often with big names like Eva Ayllon and internationally renowned dance groups such as Peru Negro.

Peña La Palizada, Avenida del Ejercito 800, Miraflores. A large restaurant-cum-club, which specializes in *criolla*; very popular with Lima's middle classes.

La Peña Poggi, Luna Pizarro 587, Barranco (☎477-0878). A pleasant, initimate club, hosting most forms of live music.

Peña Sachún, Avenida del Ejercito 657, Miraflores (441-4465). Very lively and popular tourist restaurant with a good reputation for live folklore music and *criolla* dancing at weekends, usually till at least 2am.

Peña Wifala, Cailloma 633, Lima Centro. Smaller and more tourist-oriented than most of the other *peñas*, but still quite good.

Taberna 1900, Avenida Grau 268. Another popular Barranco *peña* club which can get pretty hectic at weekends and rarely finishes much before dawn; hosts both Andean folk and Peruvian black music.

Salsadromos

Lima is an excellent place for the Latin American **salsa** scene, and there are *salsadromos* scattered around many of the suburbs. Most open Friday and Saurday 10pm–3am.

Bertoloto, Avenida Malecon Bertoloto 770, San Miguel. Has spicy salsa most Fri and Sat nights.

Fiesta Latina, Federico Villareal 259, Miraflores. A lively place to get a feel for popular salsa music. Thurs–Sat 10pm–2am.

Kimbala, Avenida Republica de Panama 1401, La Victoria. A very lively nightspot, with vibrant salsa music.

Latin Brothers, José Leal 1281 (☎470-0150). A traditional seafood restaurant with background salsa music constantly blaring out; also presents salsa shows some weekends.

Muelle Uno Club, Playa Punta Roquitas (☎444-1800). Popular club on the beach below Miraflores with good salsa music at weekends.

Jazz, rock and Latin jazz

Lima is pretty hot on **jazz** and **rock** music and has several excellent **Latin jazz** bands of its own; look out in particular for Enrique Luna and Manonga Mujica.

Bar La Parada, San Martin 587, Miraflores (☎943-1211, *febril@telematic.edu.pe*). Live rock music every night, with open jam sessions on Wednesdays. Very popular.

La Casona de Barranco, Avenida Grau 329, Barranco. Very popular club with Lima's trendy under-40s and has particularly good live jazz most weekends.

El Ekeko, Avenida Grau 266, by the municipal plaza in Barranco (☎477-5823). Often has Latin jazz at weekends, though also hosts Peruvian Andean and coastal music, mainly *criolla*.

Hard Rock Café, Larco Mar, Miraflores. One of the trendiest music venues, and a good restaurant too (open for lunch); it is replete with the usual iconography.

Jazz Zone, La Paz 656, Pasaje El Suche, Miraflores (☎242-7090). Open from Tuesday to Saturday night for piped and frequently good live jazz.

Media Cuadra, San Martin, half a block from Avenida Larco. An excellent live music venue with an ever changing variety of sounds; best from Thursday to Saturday.

Medi Rock, Benavides 420, Miraflores. Hosts good live rock music at weekends; cover charge is $2.50.

10 Sesenta, Los Nardos 1060, San Isidro (☎441-0744). Club-cum-pub which serves good food and puts on live Latin jazz and *criolla* shows.

Cultural centres

Centro Cultural, Avenida Nicolas de Pierola 1222. Often presents folk music and dance, though this is more of a performance and less participatory. The centre is run by the Universitario de San Marcos, on the Parque Universitario and performances are publicized on the noticeboard at the entrance.

Centro Cultural Parra del Riego, Avenida Pedro de Osma 135. Presents Andean and *criolla* music concerts, usually Thursday to Saturday.

Centro Cultural Ricardo Palma, Avenida Larco 770, Miraflores. Often hosts excellent concerts of Andean music, but doesn't really have the same engaging, informal and participatory atmosphere of the *peñas* listed above.

Bars and clubs

Lima boasts an interesting range of exciting **clubs**, with the vast majority of its popular **bars** and discos being in the suburbs of **San Isidro** and **Miraflores**. Most open Thursday to Saturday 10pm–2am or 3am. Many clubs have a members-only policy, though if you can provide proof of tourist status, such as a passport, you usually have no problem getting in.

Bars

Bizarro, Calle Lima 417, Miraflores. An interesting little downtown pub frequented by both Limeños and gringos.

Brenchley Arms, Atahualpa 174, Miraflores. Bar trying hard to replicate a typical English pub, with a genuine dart board and English music tapes.

Dirty Nelly's Irish Pub, Pedro de Osma 135, Barranco. A livley young bar just off the plaza in Barranco.

Johann Sebastian Bar, Shell 369. A pleasant upmarket drinking dive which plays good classical music most of the time.

Juanito's, Avenida Grau 687. Probably the most traditional of Barranco's bars; facing onto the Parque Municipal, it is small and basic and offers an excellent taste of Peru as it used to be. It has no pop music and the front bar is designated for couples only during weekend evenings.

Los Olivos, Paz Soldan 225. One of the more established and traditional dives, with a posh bar that fills up with young, trendy Limeños most Thursdays, Fridays and Saturdays.

Ludwig Bar Beethoven, Avenida Grau 687. In the midst of the hectic and trendy area of Barranco this unusual bar specializes in fine classical music with a late-night cultured ambience.

O'Murphy's, Calle Schell 627, Miraflores. An Irish pub in downtown Miraflores.

Clubs

Africa, Avenida Tomas Marsano 826. Good, fun disco playing excellent international contemporary pop music.

Amadeus, Avenida Alonso de Molina 1196, Monterrico. Well-heeled trend-setting club playing solid rock and danceable pop.

Arizona Colt, beneath the cinema El Pacifico, Diagonal, Miraflores. A popular spot where tourists and Limeños mingle to the latest lightweight international pop and dance.

Faces, Centro Comercial, Camino Real, Level A 68–72. A weekend dance club that's very popular with Lima's wealthy youth.

El Grill, Barranquito Beach, Barranco. A groovy little place with a good traditional bar and disco.

Bar Kitsch, Bolognesi 243, Barranco. A mixed straight and gay crowd come here for floral wallpaper, sequined mermaids and generally kitsch décor. Plays disco and is pretty crowded at weekends. No entry fee.

Knights, Avenida Conquistadores 605, San Isidro. A lively video-pub disco that swings.

La Noche, Avenida Bolognesi 307, El Boulevard, Barranco. Right at the top end of the Boulevard, this gets really packed at weekends. Small entry fee when there's live music and free jazz sessions on Monday evening. Fine décor and arguably the top night spot in Barranco.

La Esquina del Parque, on the corner of Grau and the Boulevard, Barranco. Right by the plaza in Barranco, this is very popular with the younger Lima set; quite wild at weekends.

Mamut Club, Berlin 438, Miraflores (☎241-0460). A new, hot and huge club with a massive dance floor surrounded by bars, plus a separate bar for techno heads.

Metropolis, Avenida 2 de Mayo 1545, San Isidro. Quite an expensive restaurant cum dance club which specializes in jazz and rock; also hosts popular karaoke sessions which amply demonstrate the Peruvian love of music and singing.

Bar Quispe, Parque Raimondi, one block from Bolognesi, Barranco. Interesting photos on the walls and plays a wide range of music; peach brandy from a large vat is free to punters.

Strokers, Avenida Benevides 325, Miraflores. Low-key, traditional disco, with pool tables and bars as well as dance spaces.

Film, theatre and galleries

Going to the **cinema**, **theatre** and **exhibitions** is an important part of life in Lima. Cinema-going is a popular pastime for all Limeños, while the theatre attracts a small, select and highly cultured audience.

Cinemas

There are clusters of **cinemas** all around the Plaza San Martin, Jirón de la Unión and Avenida Nicolas de Pierola in Lima Centro, and on the fringes of the park in Miraflores. For any film that might attract relatively large crowds, it's advisable to buy tickets in advance; alternatively, be prepared to purchase them on the black market at inflated prices – queues are often long and large blocks of seats are regularly bought up by touts. The British Council often shows **English-language films**, though other cinemas show films in their original language with subtitles. For background information on the Peruvian film industry, see p.46.

ABC San Borja 1–2, Ucello 176, San Borja (☎475-3120).

Alcazar 1–4, Santa Cruz 814, Miraflores (☎422-6345).

Benavides, Avenida Benevidea 4981, Surco (☎275-4323).

British Council Cinema, Jirón Camana 787 (☎427-7927).

Cinemark Peru Jockey Plaza 12, Avenida Javier Prado 4200 (☎434-0034).

El Cine PUCP, Avenida Camino Real 1075, San Isidro (☎222-6899).

El Conquistador, Avenida España 241 (☎984-6837).

Julieta, Porta 115, Miraflores (☎444-0135).

Larco Mar 1–12, Centro Comercial Parque Salazar, Larco Mar (☎446-7336).

Lido, Jirón Moquegua 568, Lima Centro (☎442-3394).

Orrantia, Avenida Arequipa 2701, San Isidro.

El Pacifico 1–12, Avenida Jose Pardo 121, Miraflores (☎445-6990).

Roma 1–3, Emilio Fernandez 242, at the Lima Centro end of Avenida Arequipa (☎241-2956).

Romeo, Calle Porta 115, Miraflores (☎214-3524).

Theatre, ballet and classical music

Lima possesses a prolific and extremely talented **theatre** circuit, with many of its best venues based in Miraflores. In addition to the major theatres, short performances sometimes take place in theatre bars. The country's major prestige companies, however, are the **National Ballet Company** and the **National Symphony**, both based seasonally at the Teatro Municipal in downtown Lima at block 3 of Jirón Ica (☎428-2302). There are frequent performances too by international musicians and companies, often sponsored by the foreign cultural organizations, such as the Alianza Francesa, Avenida Arequipa 4595, Miraflores, the Anglo-Peruvian Cultural Association Theatre, Avenida Benavides 620, Miraflores (☎445-4326) and Instituto Cultural Peruano Norte Americano, Avenida Angamos 120, Miraflores. The British Council (see p.84) is quite active in this line, and surprisingly imaginative, while the Teatro Britanico, Bellavista 527, Miraflores (☎445-4326), puts on amateur plays in English.

Art and photographic galleries

Lima's progressive culture of **art** and **photography** is deeply rooted in the Latin American tradition, combining indigenous ethnic realism with a political edge. The city boasts a few permanent galleries, with temporary exhibitions on display in many of the main museums.

Arte y Cultura El Allyu, Avenida San Martin 537 (☎241-7587). Mostly indigenous ceramic artists. Mon–Sat 9am–6pm; free.

Centro Cultural de la Municipalidad de Miraflores, corner of Avenida Larco and Diez Canseco. Hosts a series of interesting photographic exhibitions. Daily 10am–10pm; free.

Centro Cultural de la Universidad Catolica, Avenida Camino Real 1075, San Isidro. Art gallery hosting visiting exhibitions by foreign artists. Daily 10am–10pm; free.

Corriente Alterna, Las Dalias 381, Miraflores. Often presents shows by non-Peruvian painters. Mon–Fri 10am–8pm; free.

Extramuros, Paseo de la Republica 6045. Not exclusively photographic, but frequently exhibits works by major Latin American photographers. Mon–Sat 4–9pm; free.

Forum, Avenida Larco 1150. A small but important gallery dedicated mainly to modern Peruvian art. Mon–Fri 10am–1.30pm & 5–8pm, Sat 5–9pm; free.

Galeria L'Imaginaire, Avenida Arequipa 4595, Miraflores. Usually exhibits works by Latin American painters and sculptors. Mon–Sat 5–9pm; free.

Parafernalia, Gonzales Prada 419, Surquillo. Specializes mainly in works by Peruvian artists. Mon–Fri 10am–1pm & 2–7pm, Sat 10am–2pm & 3.30–7.30pm; free.

Sala Cultural del Banco Wiese, Avenida Larco 1101. A contemporary, international art gallery in the Banco Wiese in the heart of downtown Miraflores. Mon–Sat 10am–2pm & 5–9pm; free.

Trapecio, Avenida Larco 743, Miraflores. Specializes in oils and sculpture. Mon–Sat 5–9pm; free.

Outdoor activities

For **trekking** advice and trail maps, visit the Trekking and Backpacking Club, Jirón Huascar 1152, Jesus Maria (☎423-2515), or the South American Explorers' Club (see p.86). Of the trekking companies, most run trips to the Cordillera Blanca, around the Cusco area and along the Inca Trail; the best include Expediciones Mayuc, Conquistadores 199, San Isidro (☎422-5988); Explorandes Explorandes, San Fernando 320, Miraflores (☎445-0532 or 445-8683, fax 445-4686, *postmast@explorandes.com.pe*); Peru Expeditions, Avenida 28 de Julio 569, Oficina 108, Miraflores (☎447-2057 or 953-5553); Tarpuy, Avenida Faucett 421, Oficina 201, San Miguel (☎451-1114); and Trek Andes, Avenida Benavides 212, Oficina 1203, Miraflores (☎447-8078). Peru Expeditions, Avenida Arequipa 5241–5504, Miraflores (☎447-2057, fax 445-9683, *peruexpe@amauta.rcp.net.pe*, *www.peru-expeditions.com*), offer trekking, **mountain biking** and **4x4 tours**. For **whitewater rafting**, contact Explorandes (listed above); for advice on **mountain-climbing**, Club Andino, Avenida Paseo de la República 932 (☎263-7319), is very helpful.

Shopping

Of all the Peruvian towns and cities, Lima is the most likely to have what you're looking for. For shoes and clothing it is certainly your best bet, particularly if you're on the large size or want a huge selection to choose from. The same is true of electronic goods, stationery and recorded music, though bear in mind that most Limeños who can afford it do their main shopping in Miami. Lima also has a good selection of reasonably priced arts and crafts markets and shops, which means you don't have to carry a sack full of souvenirs back from Cusco or Puno. Lima's flashiest indoor **shopping centre** is the Centro Comercial on Camino Real, near the Lima Golf Club in the heart of San Isidro. For **supermarkets** try Wongs, which you'll find across the city, notably at the San Isidro Comercial Centre, at the Ovalo Gutierrez and on Avenida Benavides in San Antonio; in downtown Miraflores, the Santa Isabela supermarket, Avenida Benavides 487, is open 24 hours.

The usual **shopping hours** are Mon–Sat 9am–6pm, though in Miraflores, the main commercial area, many shops and *artesania* markets stay open until 7 or 8pm. Some shops, but by no means all, shut for a two-hour lunch break, usually from 1 to 3pm and most shops shut on Sundays, though the *artesania* markets on Avenida La Marina and Petit Thouars tend to stay open all week until 7pm.

Arts and crafts

All types of Peruvian **artesania** are available in Lima, including woollen goods, crafts and gem stones. Some of the best in Peru are on Avenida Petit Thourars, which is home to a handful of markets between Avenida Ricardo Palma and Avenida Angamos, all well within walking distance of Miraflores centre. Artesania Gran Chimu, Avenida Petit Thouars 5495, has a wide range of jewellery and carved wooden items, as does Mercado Artesanal, also on Avenida Petit Thouars, at no. 5321. Elsewhere, Las Pallas, Cajamarca 212, Barranco (☎477-4629), around the corner from block 6 of Avenida Grau, is a fascinating and veritable museum of *artesania*, run by a British woman who has spent most of her life collecting fine works and who may be able to show you the rest of her collection (ring for an appointment). Antisuyo, Avenida Tacna 460, Miraflores (☎241-6451), sells crafts from Peru's Amazon tribes, while La Casa de Alpaca, La Paz 679, Miraflores, stocks good-quality but expensive alpaca clothing. Agua y Tierra, Diez Canseco 298 (☎444-6980) has an interesting range of ethnic and traditional healing or *curanderos's* artefacts; Collacocha, Colon 534, parallel to block 11 of Avenida Larco (☎447-4422) has a very nice, if small, collection of Andean arts and crafts; Silvana Prints, Conquistadores 915, San Isidro, produces and sells a colourful range of mainly cotton fabrics and items like cushion covers, incorporating ancient pre-Inca motifs in the design. Slightly cheaper are the *artesania* markets on blocks 9 and 10 of Avenida La Marina in Pueblo Libre and the good craft and antique market, which takes place every evening (6–9pm) in the Miraflores Park between Diagonal and Avenida Larco. Hatun Raymi Artesania Festival (July 27–Aug 13) is a great gathering of Lima based *artesania* producers; it's located on the massive esplanade of the Museo de La Nacion and entry is free.

For **jewellery**, Casa Wako, Jirón de la Unión 841, is probably the best place in Lima Centro, specializing in Peruvian designs in gold and silver at reasonable prices, while Plateria Pereda, Jirón Venecia 186a, Miraflores, stocks fine silver jewellery to suit most tastes. Nazca, Avenida La Paz 522, has a nice range, much of it in silver. For good-quality **antiques** there's Rafo, Martinez de Pinillos 1055, Barranco (☎247-0679) who have a good lunchtime restaurant too, and also Collacocha, Calle Colon 534, parallel to block 11 of Avenida Larco in Miraflores.

Books, stationery and maps

A few shops on Avenida Nicolas de Pierola stock **English-language books** (try the one at no. 689), and The Book Exchange, just around the corner at Ocoña 211, sells or swaps second-hand paperbacks. Epoca, Avenida José Pardo 399, Miraflores, has a good range of titles including many in English. The ABC Bookstores at Colmena 689, Lima Centro, and in the Todos shopping complex, San Isidro, are well supplied with all kinds of works in English, including books on Peru. On the Jirón de la Unión, the Librería Ayza usually has some interesting publications and maps, while in Miraflores the

Libreria El Pacifico, by Café Haiti, generally has a wide range of books and magazines in English. **Stationery** is available from Libreria Minerva, Larco 299, Miraflores.

The South American Explorers' Club (see p.86) operates a free book exchange for members and is also a good source of **maps**. Charts covering most of Peru in detail are available from the Instituto Geografico Nacional, Avenida Aramburu 1190, Surquillo (☎475-3085 or 475-3075, *postmaster@ignperu.qob.pe*), and from the Servicio Aerofotografico Nacional, at Las Palmas Airforce Base in Barranco (☎477-3682). Ingemmet, Avenida Canada, 1470, San Borja (☎225-3158) stock a wide range of plans, while the Touring Y Automovil Club de Peru, Avenida Cesar Vallejo 699, Lince (Mon–Fri 9am–5pm; ☎440-3270) ar good for road maps.

Food

The best place to buy **food** for a picnic is Surquillo Market (daily), a couple of blocks from Miraflores over the Avenida Angamos road bridge, on the eastern side of the Paseo de la República freeway. This colourful place is fully stocked with a wonderful variety of breads, fruits, cheeses, meats etc, though it can be a bit dodgy in terms of petty thieving, so keep your wallet and passport close. Alternatively, you could try one of the Wong Supermarkets, in San Antonio, on the corner of Avenida Republica de Panama and Avenida Benavides, or the smaller branch at Ovalo Gutierrez on the corner of Avenida Comandante Espinar and Avenida Santa Cruz; all the branches also change cash dollars. In the centre of Lima you can buy most basic foodstuffs – bread, fruit and so on – either from stalls on Avenida Emancipacion or in the central market to the east of Avenida Abancay (see p.65). The best things to buy for a tasty picnic are the delicious white *queso fresco* (cheese), avocados and pecan nuts. For **health food**, try Naturalix, Jirón Diez Canseco 440, Miraflores, or Octavios, Los Jazmines 219, Lince, which stocks a wide range of healing herbs from the Amazon and the Andes. Other good options are the Natural Co-op on Moquegua, near the corner with Torrico, and El Girasol, Camana 327, not far from the Plaza Mayor; Eco Natura, Jirón Schell 634; or Botiquin Naturista, Centro Comercial Camino del Inca, Surco, Tienda 157, upstairs.

Camping and sports equipment

Altamira, Arica 800, a block from the Ovalo Gutierrez roundabout, sells a good range of quality **camping equipment**, as do Alpaymayo, Avenida Larco 345, Miraflores. Best, Avenida Espinar 320, Mirafores, sell rucksacks, cycling equipment and surfing gear, while Todo Camping, Avenida Angamos Oeste 350, has a range of tents and other equipment. There's also the Camping Centre, Avenida Benevides 1620 (☎242-1779) in Miraflores or Sisperu, Caminos del Inca 257 (☎372-0428) in Chacarilla, and the South American Explorers' Club (see p.86) is worth trying too.

For **surfing gear** go to Best (see above), Billa Bong, Ignacio Merino 711, O'Niells, Avenida Santa Cruz 851, or Waves, Bolivar 149, all of which are in Miraflores; in Barranco there's Wayo Whilar, Avenida 28 de Julio 287. **Cycling equipment** is available from Biclas, Avenida Conquistadores 641, San Isidro (☎440-0890); Bike Mavil, Avenida Avacion 4011 (☎449-8435); Cicloroni, Calle de Las Casas, block 32 Avenida Petit Thouars, San Isidro (☎221-7643); and Will-Pro, Avenida 2 de Mayo 430, San Isidro (☎222-0289).

Photographic equipment

Photographic equipment, accessories and film developing are all a little expensive in Lima. Try Kodak Express, Avenida Larco 1005, or Lab Color Profesional, Avenida

Benevides 1171 (☎446-7421), both in Miraflores, for films and developing. Agfafoto, Diez Canseco 172, Miraflores, has films and peripherals, while Renato Service, 28 Julio 442, Miraflores, has excellent camera and video equipment. Foto Digital, Avenida larco 1005 (☎447-9398) are good for fast developing. Kodak's laboratories on Avenida Arriola, just off Javier Prado Este in La Victoria, will develop Ektachrome but not Kodachrome. For **camera repairs**, try the shop near the Camera House, Larco 1150, Oficina 39 (☎961-7590) in Miraflores.

Listings

Airlines International departure tax is $25, payable in dollars or soles at the airport before embarkation, though note that the exchange rate at the airport is poor if you pay in soles. Domestic departure tax is $3. Aero Condor, Juan de Arona 781, San Isidro (☎442-5663); Aero Continente, Avenida José Pardo 651, Miraflores (☎242-4260, fax 444-5014); American Airlines, Jirón Juan de Arona 830, fourteenth floor, San Isidro (☎442-8610); Avianca, Avenida Paz Soldan 225, Oficina C-5, Los Olivos, San Isidro (☎221-7822); British Airways, represented in Lima by Air Latin at Andalucia 174, Miraflores (☎442-6600, 422-0889 or 445-2888); Continental Airlines, Victor Andrés Belaúnde 147, Oficina 101, Edificio Real, San Isidro (☎221-4340); Iberia, Avenida Camino Real 390, Office 902, San Isidro (☎421-4616); KLM, Avenida José Pardo 805, Miraflores (☎242-1240); Lan Chile, Avenida Jose Pardo 805, fifth floor, Miraflores (☎241-5522 or 446-6995); Lan Peru, Avenida Los Incas 172, eighth floor, San Isidro (☎221-3764, fax 421-8914); Lloyd Aero Boliviano, Avenida Jose Pardo 231, first and seventh floors, Miraflores (☎241-5510); Saeta, Andalucia 174, Miraflores (☎422-1710 or 422-6600, *Airlatin@amauta.rcp.net.pe*); TANS, Avenida Arequipa 5200, Miraflores (☎445-7327 or 445-7107); Varig, Avenida Camino Real 456, Central Tower, office 803/804, San Isidro (☎442-4361).

American Express Based at Lima Tours, Belen 1040, near Plaza San Martin (Mon–Fri 9.15am–4.45pm; ☎427-6624, 426-1765 or 424-0831). Offers a poste restante service.

Anti-Rabies Centre Centro Antirabico (☎425-6313), for emergency treatment.

Banks Banco de la Nacion, Avenida Nicolas de Pierola 1065 and Avenida Abancay 491; Banco Latino, Paseo de La Republica 3505, San Isidro, which has a Mastercard ATM; Banco de Credito, Jirón Lampa 499, Avenida Larco 1099, Miraflores (well run and with small queues), and on the corner of Rivera Navarrete and Juan de Arona, San Isidro, both of which offer good rates on traveller's cheques; Banco Continental, Avenida Larco, Miraflores; Citibank, Las Begonias 441, San Isidro; Interbanc, in the Metro Supermarket, corner of Alfonso Ugarte and Venezuela, Lima Centro; and Banco Wiese, Jirón Cusco 245, Lima Centro, and Alfonso Ugarte 1292, Diagonal 176, Miraflores.

British Council Calle Alberto Lynch 110, near the Ovalo Gutierrez roundabout, San Isidro (☎470-4350); postal address PO Box 14-0114 Santa Beatriz, Lima, Peru.

Bus companies Always check which terminal your bus is departing from when you buy your ticket. El Aguilla, Jirón Galvez, La Victoria (☎424-0836), for Trujillo and Huaraz. Chanchamayo, Manco Capac 1052, La Victoria (☎470-1189), for Tarma, La Oroya, San Ramon and La Merced. Condor de Chavin, Montevideo 1039 (☎428-8122), for Callejon de Huaylas, Huarac and Chavin. Cruz del Sur have several terminals: in Lima Centro it's Jirón Quilca 531 (☎427-1311 or 423-5594) and the corner of Zavala with Montevideo (☎428-2570), for the coast, Huaraz, Huancayo, Cusco, Arequipa and Puno; for international services it's at Avenida Javier Prado at the corner with Nicoal Arriola (☎225-6200); for their Ideal service, which includes the coast, Cusco, Arequipa, Puno, Cajamarca, Huancayo and Huaraz it's Paseo de La Republica 809, La Victoria (☎332-4000). El Condor, Avenida Carlos Zavala 101, Lima Centro (☎427-0286), for Trujillo or Huancayo. Huamanga, Avenida Luna Pizarro 453, La Victoria (☎330-2206), for Ayacucho, Trujillo, Chiclayo, Moyobamba and Tarapoto. Enlaces, Avenida Paseo de La Republica 749 (☎433-3311), for Arequipa. Empresa Huaral, 131 Avenida Abancay, Lima Centro (☎428-2254), for Huaral, Ancon and Chacay. Empresa Rosario, Jirón Ayacucho 942 (☎534-2685), for Huanuco and la Union. Flores Buses, Montevideo 529, Lima Centro (☎431-0485). Hidalgo, Bolivar 1535 (☎424-0522). Leon de Huanuco, Avenida 28 de Julio, La Victoria 1520 (☎4329-0880), for Cerro de Pasco, Huanaco, Tarma and La Merced. Libertadores, Avenida Grau 491, Lima Centro (☎426-8067), for Ayacucho, Satipo, and Huanta. Lobato Buses, 28 de Julio 2101–2107, La Victoria (☎474-9411), for Tarma, La Merced and Satipo. Mariscal Caceres, Avenida 28 de Julio 2195, La Victoria (☎474-7850). Morales Moralitos, Avenida Grau 141 (☎428-6252). Movil Tours, Avenida Paseo de La Republica 646 (☎332-0024), for Huaraz, Caraz and Trujillo; head office at Jorin Montevideo 581 (☎427-5309). Oltursa, Avenida Aramburu 1160 (☎475-8559), for most coastal destinations. Ormeño, Avenida Javier Prado Este 1059 (☎472-1710), for main national and interational services, though they also pass through the central depot at Carlos Zavala 177, Lima Centro (☎427-5679): Chinchano, a subsidiary of Ormeño, serves the coast as far as Cañete, Chincha and Pisco. Peru Bus, Avenida Carlos Zavala y Loayza 221 (☎427-6310), and Avenida Circunvalacion 2534, Urbino San Luis, for the best buses for Ica. Transportes Rodriguez, Avenida Roosevelt 354 (☎428-0506), for Huaraz, Caraz and Chimbote. Tepsa, Avenida Paseo de la República 129 (☎427-5642 or 427-1233); ticket office at Jirón Lampa 1237, Lima Centro (☎427-5642). Turismo Apostolo San Pedro, Avenida Grau 711, Paruro 1457 (☎428-7810), for Huancayo and Tarma. Tours Wari, Montevideo 855 (☎426-4103), for Puno, Abancay, Nazca and Cusco (☎427-5642 or 427-1233).

Car rental Budget, Avenida Canaval y Moreyra 569, San Isidro (☎442-8703, 441-0493 or 441-9458, *vdiaz@tci.net.pe)*; Dollar, La Paz 438, Miraflores (☎444-4920; at the airport ☎452-6741); Hertz, Andres Reyes 550, second floor, San Isidro (☎442-4509, 442-4476 or 442-4475); Inka's, Jirón Canturias 160, Miraflores (☎445-5716, 447-9440, *Inkasrc@mail.cosapitdata.com.pe)*; National, Avenida España 449, Lima Centro (☎433-3750, 222-2020, *national@correo.dnet.com.pe)*.

Courier services DHL, Los Castaños 225, San Isidro (☎954-4345 or 221-2474, fax 440-5209), Las Begonias 429, San Isidro, and in Lima Tours, Belen 1040, Lima Centro and Avenida Pardo 392, Miraflores (all branches Mon–Fri 8.30am–7.30pm & Sat 9am–noon); Federal Express, Pasaje Olaya 260, Miraflores (☎242-3399; Mon–Fri 8.30am–6pm).

Dentists Dr Yolanda Montoro, Mercedes G. de Parks 314, Urbino Pando, in the *segunda etapa* (second part) of of San Miguel, close to block 22 of the Avenida La Marina (☎566-0915); or Clinica Dental Flores, Calle Centauro 177, Monterrico (☎435-2153). Your embassy can supply a list of English-speaking dentists.

Doctors Dr Aste, Antero Aspillaga 415, Oficina 101, San Isidro (☎441-7502), speaks English; Dr Alicia Garcia, Instituto de Ginecología, Avenida Monterico 1045, Surco (☎434-2650); Dr Raul Morales, Clinica Padre Luis Tezza, Avenida del Polo 570, Monterrico (☎434-6990), who speaks good English; and Dr Roberto Luna Victoria, Clinica Adventista de Miraflores, Malecon Balta 956, Miraflores (☎443-5395).

Embassies and consulates Australia, Avenida Santa Cruz 398, San Isidro (☎441-5366); Bolivia, Los Castanos 235, San Isidro (☎442-8231); Brazil, Avenida Jose Pardo 850, Miraflores (☎421-5650); Canada, Calle Libertad 130, Miraflores (☎444-4442 or 444-4015); Chile, Javier Prado Oeste 790, San Isidro (☎221-2818 or 221-2817); Ecuador, Las Palmeras 356, San Isidro (☎442-4184); Ireland, Santiago Acuña 135, Urbino La Aurora, Miraflores (☎445-6813 or 242-3849); New Zealand, see the UK; UK, Natalio Sanchez 125, Piso 11, Plaza Washington, Lima Centro (☎433-4738 or 433-8923;) USA, La Encalada, block 17, Monterrico (☎434-3000, fax 434-3037).

Exchange *Cambistas* gather on the corner of Ocoña, at the back of the *Gran Hotel Bolivar.* Alternatively, you can change cash and traveller's cheques in the smaller hostels and the many *casa de cambios* around Ocoña: Tuscon Express, Ocoña 211a; LAC Dollar, on Camana 779, second floor; and two unamed offices at Camana 814 and Camana 758, both near the corner with Ocoña. Universal Money Exchange, Avenida José Pardo 629, Oficina 16, Miraflores or Koko's Dollar, Avenida Ricardo Palma 437, Stand 21, Comercial Las Estaciones, in Miralfores, are both OK. The Wong supermarkets (see Shopping, p.83) change dollars. You can also change money at the airport, but rates are poorer than in the city centre.

Fax services Bunkers, Avenida Ricardo Palma 280 (☎953-9721, fax 241-1090); and Innova, Avenida Larco 1158, Miraflores (☎ & fax 445-9267).

Hospitals The following are all well equipped: Clinica Anglo Americana, Avenida Salazar, San Isidro (☎440-3570); Clinica Internacional, Washington 1475, Lima Centro (☎428-8060); and Clinica San Borja, Avenida del Aire 333, San Borja (☎475-3141). All have emergency departments which you can use as an outpatient, or you can phone for a house-call. For an ambulance call ☎440-0200 or 441-3141, but if you can, take a taxi – it'll be much quicker.

Internet services CyberSandeg, Jirón de La Union 853, Oficina 210, in Galerias Boza-Costado, by the Plaza Martin in Lima Centro; Dragon Fans, Tarata 230 (☎444-9325); El Allyu Cyber Café, Avenida San Martin 537, Miraflores (☎446-0385, *webmaster@allyu-peru.org, www.allyu-peru.org)*; Phantom Internet Café Bar, Avenida Diagonal 344, Miraflores (☎ & fax 242-7949, *www.phantom. com.pe)*; Plazanet, Avenida 28 de Julio 451, Miraflores (*www.plazanet.com.pe)*, which is open 24hr and has a café and TV; Red Cientifica Peruana, Augusto Tamayo 125, San Isidro (☎422-4848, *webmaster@rcp.net.pe)*; and Web-On-Line, Avenida Wilson 1160, Lima Centro (☎425-0390).

Laundry Many hotels will do this cheaply, but there are numerous *lavanderías* in most areas; the Lavanderia Saori, Grimaldi del Solar 175, Miraflores (☎444-3830; Mon–Sat 8am–7pm) is fast; LavaQueen, Avenida Larco 1158, Miraflores does washing by the kilo at reasonable prices.

Optician Avenida Jose Pardo 495, Miraflores.

Police The Tourist Police are at the Museo de La Nacion, Javier Prado Este 2465 (☎225-8699).

Postal services The main post office is at Pasaje Piura, Jirón Lima, block 1 near the Plaza Mayor (Mon–Sat 8am–8pm & Sun 8am–2pm), with other branches on Avenida Nicolas de Pierola, opposite the *Hotel Crillon* (Mon–Sat 8am–8pm, Sun 8am–noon), and in Miraflores, at Petit Thouars 5201, a block from the corner of Angamos (Mon–Fri 8am–8pm). The best bet for sending large parcels is to use KLM (see Airlines, above) who charge about $12 a kilo to Europe. Concas Travel, Alcanfores 345, Oficina 101, Miraflores (☎241-7516), can arrange larger shipments. Poste restante letters are kept for up to 3 months in the main post office (see above); address mail to Poste Restante, Correo Central, Jirón Conde de Supunda, Lima Centro, Peru. American Express (see p.84) also offer poste restante.

South American Explorers' Club The clubhouse is at Avenida Portugal 146, Breña, between avenidas Bolivia and España (☎425-0142); the postal address is Casilla 3714, Lima 100. Mon–Sat 9.30am–5pm.

Taxis and transfers Good 24hr taxi companies include: Taxi Seguro (☎275-2020); San Borja Taxis (☎476-8945, 475-5630, 225-8600); and P&P Transport Turistico (☎424-9556). For transfers, call the airport shuttle, Ricardo Palma 280 in Miraflores (☎446-9872); Calderon (☎940-7603); De Primera, an (☎475-4631); or Transporte Turistico La Inmaculada (☎917-2142, 975-8342 or 330-2195). Always agree on a price beforehand.

Telephones Phone kiosks are found all around the city. In Lima Centro the main Teléfonica del Peru office is near the corner of Wiese and Carabaya 933 (daily 8am–9pm), on Plaza San Martin.

Tourist Protection Service ☎ & fax 575-1434 ext 4141, or ☎574-8000.

Translation services Ibanez Traducciones, Miguel Dasso 126, Oficina 301, San Isidro (☎421-6526 or 421-6511, fax 441-4122).

Travel agents and tour operators For specialist outdoor activities in and around Lima, see p.81. Otherwise, the best are: Aguamarina, Avenida Sergio Bernales 465, Urbino Aurora, Miraflores (☎ & fax 241-2562 or 241-9685); Fertur Peru, Jirón Junin 211, Lima Centro (☎427-1958, fax 428-3347, *fertur@correo.dnet.com.pe*); HIRCA, Bellavista 518, Miraflores (☎241-2317 or 242-0275); Kinjyp Travel, Plaza San Martin 971 (☎427-6760); Lima Tours, Belén 1040, near Plaza San Martin (☎424-7560 or 424-5110, fax 330-4488, *inbound@limatours.com.pe*, *www.limatours.com.pe*); Marili Tours, Diez Canseco 392, Miraflores (☎444-0889, 241-0142 or 241-0384, *marili@amauta.rcp.net.pe*), who have guides and go to most of Peru, including Cusco, Madre de Dios, Puno and the Northern desert region; Overland Expeditions, Jirón Emilio Fernandez 640, Santa Beatrice (☎424-7762), who specialize in the Lachay Reserve; Panamericana de Turismo, Avenida Benavides 560-564 (☎444-1377 or 444-3250, fax 444-4665); Peruvian Life, Calle Diez Canseco 337 (☎444-8825, fax 446-3246, *peruvian@peru.itete.com.pe*); Peruvian Safaris, Avenida Inca Garcilaso de la Vega 1334 (☎431-6330); Rainforest Expeditions, Aramburu 166-4b, Miraflores (☎221-4182 or 963-8759, fax 421-8183, *Izapater@rainforest.com*, *www.perunature*.com); Raymi Travels, Avenida Federico Gallesi 198 (☎263-7203, fax 263-0749); TEBAC, Jirón Huascar 1152, Jesus Maria (☎423-2515), who specialize in trips to Marcahuasi; and Viajes Lazer, Avenida Comandante Espinar 331, Miraflores (☎447-9499, fax 447-8717).

Visas Migraciones, corner of Prolongacion Avenida España and Jirón Huaraz.

Western Union Jirón Carabaya 675, Lima Centro; Avenida Petit Thouars 3595; San Isidro (☎422-0036 or 422-9723, fax 440-7625); and Avenida Larco 826, Miraflores.

AROUND LIMA

Stretching out along the coast in both directions, the **Panamerican Highway** runs the entire 2600-kilometre length of Peru, with Lima more or less at its centre. Towns along the sometimes arid coastline immediately north and south of the capital are of minor interest to most travellers, though there are some **glorious beaches** – with next to no restrictions on beach camping – and a very impressive ruin at **Pachacamac**.

The foothills above Lima contain several places of interest, not least the animistic rock outcrops of **Marcahuasi**, a weekend trip from the city. Lima has also traditionally been the starting point for one of the world's great train journeys, climbing high up into the Andes; fortunately, passenger services are likely to start running again in the not-too-distant future. Even without the train, the high *sierra* of the Andes is only a matter of hours away by comfortable bus or slightly faster colectivo. The attractive mountain towns of **Huancay, Huancavelica** and **Tarma**, all interesting destinations in their own right, are within a day's easy travelling of the capital. From these centres it is just another few hours' steep drop down the eastern slopes of the Andes into the rainforests of the upper Amazon basin and the little-visited towns of the sweltering jungle.

The Lima Coast

Most of the better **beaches** within easy reach of Lima are to the south – beginning about 30km out at the hulking pre-Inca ruins of **Pachacamac**, a sacred citadel which still dominates this stretch of coastline. The site can easily be combined with a day at one or other of the beaches – and it's little problem to get out there from the capital. A good stopover en route to Pisco is the former plantation town and oasis of **Chincha**, a fertile coastal zone in ancient times as exemplified by the substantial number of pre-Inca sites in the region. To the north of Lima, the desert stretches up between the Pacific Ocean and the foothills of the Andes. There's not a huge amount of interest to the visitor here and very little in the way of tourist facilities, but it has a scattering of archeological sites, all of which are difficult to reach, plus – with easier access – some interesting eco-niches known as *lomas*, shrub-covered hills with their own unique climatic conditions and flora and fauna, of which the **Reserva Nacional Lomas de Lachay** is the best.

Pachacamac

PACHACAMAC (daily 9am–5pm; $2) is by far the most interesting of the Rimac Valley's ancient sites, and well worth making time for even if you're about to head out to Cusco and Machu Picchu. The entry fee for the citadel includes admission to the site museum, which merits a browse around on the way in; allow a good two hours to wander around the full extent of the ruins. **Buses** leave every two hours for Pachacamac from Avenida Abancay and around the Parque Universitario on *calles* Montevideo and Inambari in Lima Centro. Alternatively, many of the tour agencies in Lima offer half-day tours to the site (see opposite).

Pachacamac means (more or less) "the Earth's Creator", and the site was certainly occupied by 500 AD and probably for a long time before that. When other *huacas* were being constructed in the lower Rimac Valley, Pachacamac was already a temple-citadel and centre for mass pilgrimages. The god-image of Pachacamac evidently expressed his/her anger through tremors and earthquakes, and was an oracle used for important matters affecting the State: the health of the ruler, the outcome of a war, etc. Later it became one of the most famous shrines in the Inca Empire, with Pachacamac himself worshipped along with the sun. The Incas built their Sun Temple on the crest of the hill above Pachacamac's own sacred precinct. In 1533, Francisco Pizarro sent his brother Hernando to seize Pachacamac's treasure, but was disappointed by the spoils, which consisted of just a wooden idol, now shown today in the site museum. This wooden representation of Pachacamac may well have been the oracle itself: it was kept hidden inside a labyrinth and behind guarded doors – only the high priests could communicate with it face to face. When Hernando Pizarro and his troops arrived they had to pass

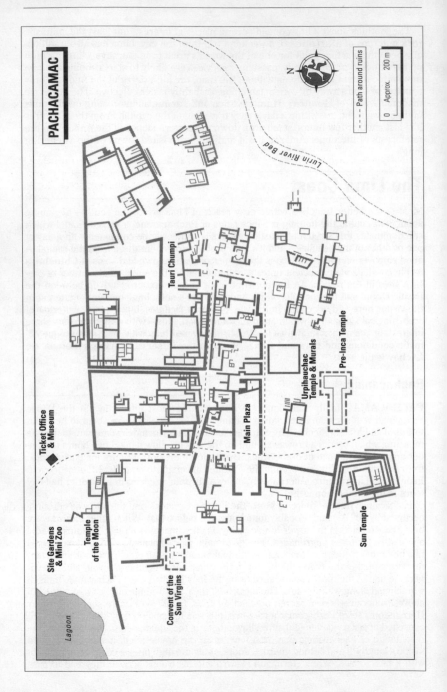

PACHACAMAC

Lagoon

Site Gardens & Mini Zoo

Temple of the Moon

Convent of the Sun Virgins

Ticket Office & Museum

Tauri Chumpi

Main Plaza

Urpihuachac Temple & Murals

Pre-Inca Temple

Sun Temple

Lurin River Bed

N

----- Path around ruins

0   Approx.   200 m

through many doors to arrive at the main idol site, which was raised up on a "snail-shaped" (or spiralling) platform, with the wooden carving stuck into the earth inside a dark room, separated from the world by a jewelled curtain.

Entering **the ruins** today, after passing the restored sectors which include the **Temple of the Moon** and the **Convent of the Sun Virgins** (or *mamaconas*), you can see the **Sun Temple** directly ahead. Constructed on the top level of a series of "pyramidical" platforms, it was built tightly onto the hill with plastered adobe bricks, its walls originally painted in gloriously bright colours. Below this is the **main plaza**, once covered with a thatched roof supported on stilts, and thought to have been the area where pilgrims assembled in adoration. The rest of the ruins, visible though barely distinguishable, were dwellings, storehouses and palaces. From the very top of the Sun Temple there's a magnificent view west beyond the Panamerican Highway to the beach (Playa San Pedro) and across the sea to a sizeable island. When viewed from the ruins, this island – clearly geologically related to the Pachacamac mound – appears like a huge whale approaching the shore.

Southern beach towns

Beyond Pachacamac lie some of Lima's most attractive beaches. Closest of these, just a couple of kilometres outside Pachacamac, is **Playa San Pedro**, a vast and usually deserted strip of sand. Constantly pounded by rollers, however, it can be quite dangerous for swimming. Much more sheltered, the bay of **El Silencio**, 6km to the south, was one of the most popular beaches in the 1980s but, suffering at the hands of bad regional planning, it has lost its edge due to the low-level pollution that occasionally appears here from new local beachside developments. Drinks and snacks are sold from hut-cafés at the back of the beach, excellent seafood restaurants sit on the cliff above, and a couple of smaller, more secluded bays lie a short drive down the coast.

At **Punta Hermosa**, about ten minutes on the bus beyond El Silencio, you come to an attractive cliff-top settlement and, down below, what's becoming Lima's leading surf resort, **Santa Maria**, a great family haunt, with plenty of hotels and a reasonable beach. Finally there's **Pucusana**, an old fishing village, gathered on the side of a small hilly peninsula, which is now perhaps the most fashionable of the beaches – a holiday resort where Limeños stay rather than just driving out for a swim. **Buses** to Pucusana travel the 65km from the corner of Jirón Montevideo and Jirón Ayacucho in Lima every two hours, passing Pachacamac, El Silencio, Punta Hermosa and Santa Maria on the way.

Continuing south, the road cruises along the coast, passing the long beach and salt-pools of **Chilca** after 5km, and the curious lion-shaped rock of **León Dormido** (Sleeping Lion) after another 15km or so. About 10km on from Chilca on the highway, where it bypasses the town of Malfa, is the **cafetería** *Dona Paulina*, a great place to sample the best *chicarones* (chunks of deep-fried pork) in the region. **Asia**, 10km down the road and spread out along it from Km 95 to 103, is essentially a small agricultural town, producing cotton, bananas and corn; the long beach here is ideal for **camping**, particularly its southern end. Some interesting archeological finds in local graveyards reveal that this site was occupied from around 2500 BC by a pre-ceramic agricultural community associated also with the earliest examples of a trophy-head cult (many of the mummies were decapitated). About 20km on from Asia is **CERRO AZUL**, located where the dual carriageway from Lima ends and becomes a single two-way road; another developing resort, particularly for surfing. The **hostals** *La Casita* (②) and *Cerro Azul* (②) offer reasonable accommodation, but fill quickly and charge more in main holiday periods. Another 8km and you come to the larger settlement of **Cañete**, an attractive town with a colonial flavour, surrounded by marigolds and cotton fields, though probably not a place you'll want to stop in, unless you happen to arrive during its annual **festival** (August 21–31), which consists of ten days of wild dancing to black Peruvian music. Chilca, Asia, Cañete and Chincha (see below) are all served from Lima by Cruz del Sur **buses** from Jirón Quilca 531, and Ormeño buses from Carlos Zavala 177, most of which continue on to Pisco, Nasca and Arequipa.

Chincha

If you feel like breaking the journey before Pisco, the best candidate is **CHINCHA**, a relatively rich oasis town that appears after a stretch of almost Saharan landscape – and a mightily impressive sand dune – at the top of the cliff. A busy little coastal centre renowned for its cheap wines and variety of **piscos**, Chincha is a strong cultural hub for black Peruvian culture, having grown up around the early colonial cotton plantations worked by slaves mainly from Guinea in Africa. One of the best places for *pisco* and local wine (*vino dulce*) is at the 100-year old **Bodega Naldo Navarro** in Sunampe, 1km north of Chincha, who offer free guided tours and samples. Several other locl *bodegas* offer similar tours. For **festivals**, the third Saturday in September is National Pisco Day when things really get lively along this section of the coast. It's also well known for its traditionally rhythmic music and annual, athletic dance festival, Verano Negro, which takes place at the end of February, while in November, the Festival de Danzas Negras is an excellent event; in both cases the celebrations are liveliest in El Carmen, 10km southeast of Chincha.

This town is also renowned for its **ruins**, with numerous *huacas* lying scattered about the oasis; it was one of the richest prior to the Conquest. Dominated in pre-Inca days by the Cuismancu (or Chincha) state, activity focused around what were probably ceremonial pyramids. One of these, the **Huaca Centinela**, sits majestically in the valley below the Chincha tableland and the ocean, around thirty minutes' walk from the *Hotel El Sausal* turning. Not far from Chincha, 40km up the Castrovireyna road which leaves the Panamerican Highway at Km 230, is another impressive Cuismancu ruin, Tambo Colorado (see p.181). In the early days of the Spanish Conquest, the conquistadores came across an Inca trading vessel, which some believe originated from the Chincha area.

Don't miss the **Hacienda San José**, Pueblo San José (daily 9am–6pm; free), 9km southeast of Chincha, in an extensive plantation, where you can see impressive Churrigueresque domed towers built in the 1680s. Its colourful history includes an owner murdered on the main steps up to the house by his black slaves. Now a semi-luxurious hotel (☎034/221458; ⑥), also bookable in Lima through Juan Fanning 328, Miraflores, Oficina 202, ☎444-5524, *hsanjose@bellnet.com.pe*). The hacienda is open to visitors to use the pool, watch local folklore shows and there are forty-five minute **tours** ($3) around the labyrinthine catacombs containing prison cells where the wilder black slaves were once shackled.

As well as the *Hacienda San José*, **accommodation** options include the flashy *Hotel El Sausal* (⑤), Km 197 Panamerican Highway, with its own pool, on the right as you come into town; the *Hostal El Sotelo* (②), one block from the plaza; the *Hotel El Valle* (④) on the main road in the centre of town; or one of the cheaper hotels along the main street (left at the fork in the road) beyond the Ormeño bus depot; the *Hotel Imperio,* on the Panamerican Highway, two blocks south of the central plaza (④), offers good rooms at reasonable prices. For **eating**, the *Palacio de Mariscos* at the *Hotel El Valle* is excellent and the restaurants *El Fogon* and *Café El Atrio* are reasonable alternatives, both on the main plaza.

North of Lima

North of Lima, the Panamerican Highway passes through the **Chillón valley**, dotted with ancient ruins, of which the most important are on the south side of the Río Chillon within 3 or 4km of the Ventanilla road. The most impressive is the 2000–3000-year-old

Temple El Paraiso, which was built by a sedentary farming community of probably no more than 1500 inhabitants and consists of three main pyramids built in rustic stones.

From here, the Panamerican Highway passes the yacht and tennis clubs that make up the fashionable beach resort of **Ancón**, about 30km from Lima, then crosses a high, often foggy, plateau from the Chillón to the **Chancay valley**. This foggy zone, still covered by sparse vegetation, was a relatively fertile *lomas* area (where plants grow from moisture in the air rather than rainwater or irrigation) in pre-Inca days and evidence of winter camps from five thousand years ago has been found. The highway bypasses the market town of Huaral and runs through **Chancay**, some 65km north of Lima, worth a visit only for its excellent cliff-top seafood restaurants, as the sea is too dangerous to swim in. Nearby the Ecotruly Ashrama, Km 63 on the Panamerican Highway, by Chacra y Mar beach (☎444-4747 or 470-8804, *isevperu@amauta.rcp.net.pe, www. vrindavan.org/trulys*) is an ashram set at the foot of desert cliffs and close to the pounding ocean. They offer guided tours of their adobe huts and organic gardens, plus yoga and meditation, hikes and workshops on ecology. Always book visits in advance.

Continuing north from Chancay, the road passes through stark desert for 20km until you reach the **Reserva Nacional Lomas de Lachay**, a protected area of unique *lomas* habitat some 5000 hectares in extent and around 600m above sea-level. The easiest way to get there is with an organized tour from Lima (Overland Expeditions are experts in the area; see p.86), but if you are doing it alone continue up the Panamerican Highway for about 6km beyond the turning for Sayan and Churin. The turn-off to the reserve is signposted at the top of a hill, but from the road it's still an hour's walk along a sandy track to the interpretive centre (daily 7am–7pm) at the entrance to the reserve. Run by the Ministry of Agriculture, the centre maintains the footpaths that thread through the reserve's beautiful scenery. Formed by granite and diorite rocky intrusions some seventy million years ago, the *lomas* – at its best between June and December when it is in full bloom – is home to more than forty types of birds including humming birds, parrots, partridges, peregrines and even condors; you also may spot various species of reptile and native deer.

A little further north of the reserve, at Km 133, a track turns off onto a small peninsula to the secluded bay of **El Paraiso** – a magical beach perfect for camping, swimming and scuba diving. Crossing more bleak sands, the Panamerican Highway next passes through **Huacho**, an unusual place with some interesting colonial architecture and a ruined church in the upper part of town. Other than turning off the Panamerican Highway to Sayan and Churin, the only town and port of Supe breaks the monotonous beauty of desert and ocean, until you reach Barrance and the labyrinthine ruins of the Fortress of Paramonga (see p.247).

Sayan and Churin

Just beyond Huacho a side road turns east into the **Huara valley** and the foothills of the Andes, to reach **SAYAN**, a small farming town where little has changed for decades (the church here has a very attractive colonial interior). An acceptable but fairly basic **place to stay** is *Hostal Tolentino*, Balta 541 (☎371018; ②), above a bakery. The **restaurant** *Jalisco*, Balta 342, serves large portions of good food – river shrimps and wine are local specialities. **Colectivos** run between Sayan and Huacho every thirty minutes.

Further up the valley lies **CHURIN**, a small thermal spar town that's very popular with Limeños during holidays. Most of the farmland on the valley floor and the Sayan to Churin road was washed away in the 1998 El Niño, and a new, rough road has been carved out between the boulders littering the valley floor. There are two **spars** in town, both fairly cool, with private and communal baths, but the El Fierro spa, ten minutes by colectivo from town, is the hottest and is reputed to be the most curative; all cost about $0.50.

There are several **buses** to and from Lima daily (a 6–7hr journey), the best being run by Transportes Estrella Polar; expect to pay around $5. There are many **places to stay**, but they all get packed out in the main holiday periods, when prices double. All the hotels are within a couple of blocks of each other in the town centre; try the *Santa Rosa* (☎373014; ⑤) and *Internacional* (☎373015; ⑤), both modern and with a range of facilities, or the *Hotel Las Termas* (☎373005; ④), which has nicer rooms and a pool. The *hostals Beatriz* (③) and *Danubio* (③) are modern, clean and friendly. Churin has many good **restaurants** and cafés, and local specialities include honey, *alfajores*, *manjar blanca* and cheeses.

An excellent day-trip from Churin can be made to more thermal baths at **Huancahuasi**. Colectivos leave from Churin church at around 8am ($3 return), returning mid-afternoon. There are two sets of hot baths at Huancahuasi (both $S0.50), and snacks such as *pachamanca* are prepared outside them. En route to Huancahuasi you'll spot a remarkable early colonial carved façade on the tiny church at Picoy.

Inland from Lima: into the foothills

There are several destinations in the **foothills of the Andes** which are within relatively easy reach of Lima. The most spectacular include the mystical plateau of **Marcahuasi**, and the impressive sites of **Puruchuco** and **Cajarmarquilla**, which are typical of ruins all over Peru and make a good introduction to the country's archeology. Both Puruchuco and Cajarmarquilla lie near the beginning of the Central Highway, the road that climbs up behind Lima towards Chosica, La Oroya and the Andes. The two sites are only 6km apart and are most easily visited on a half-day guided tour from Lima (see Listings, p.86). Alternatively, you could take a colectivo from Calle Montevideo (daily from 7am; $2) and return by waving down virtually any of the passing buses on the main Central Highway, though the Chosica to Lima bus will be the most likely to have spare seats.

Puruchuco

An eight-hundred-year-old, pre-Inca settlement, **PURUCHUCO** (daily 9am–5pm; $1.50) comprises a labyrinthine villa and a small but interesting museum containing a complete collection of artefacts and attire found at the site (all of which bears a remarkable similarity to what Amazon Indian communities still use today). The adobe structure was apparently rebuilt and adapted by the Incas shortly before the Spanish arrival: it's a fascinating ruin, superbly restored in a way which vividly captures what life was like before the Conquest. Very close by, in the Parque Fernando Carozi (ask the site guard for directions), two other ruins – **Huaquerones** and **Catalina Huaca** – are being restored, and at **Chivateros** there's a quarry apparently dating back some twelve thousand years.

Cajamarquilla

For **CAJAMARQUILLA**, the colectivo will drop you off at the refinery turn-off on the main highway, then it's about 4km, or an hour's walk, to the **ruins** (daily 9am–5pm; $1.50), which are well hidden next to an old hacienda. First occupied in the Huari era (600–1000 AD), Cajamarquilla flourished under the **Cuismancu culture**, a city-building state contemporary with the better-known Chimu in northern Peru. It was an enclosed city containing thousands of small complex dwellings clustered around a higher section, probably nobles' quarters, and numerous small plazas. The site was apparently abandoned before the Incas arrived in 1470, possibly after being devastated by an earthquake. Pottery found here in the 1960s by a group of Italian archeologists suggests habitation over 1300 years ago.

Marcahuasi and San Pedro de Casta

MARCAHUASI, standing at just over 4000m above sea level, is one of Peru's lesser-known marvels and something of a mystical enigma; it can be reached in a day from Lima and makes a fantastic weekend camping jaunt. Its main attractions are the incredible **rock formations** which, particularly by moonlight, take on weird shapes – llamas, human faces, turtles, even a hippopotamus. There's also a large clearing known locally as the amphitheatre, which hosts an incredible annual village **festival** involving three days of ceremony, music, dance and festivities on July 28–30. The easiest way to visit the site, 90km east of Lima, is with TEBAC, a Lima-based tour company (see Listings, p.86) who can also organize trips to the annual **Festival de Aventura** which takes place in Marcahuasi in early November and incorporates a combination of Latin American and rock music with outward-bound activities such as mountain biking, marathon running and motorcross. For further information on Marcahuasi contact the Oficina de Informacion San Pedro de Casta, Avenida Guzman Blanco 240, office 403, Lima (☎433-7591).

Unless you're camping, you'll have to stay in the village of **SAN PEDRO DE CASTA**, two or three hours' hard walking down the mountain. There are no direct buses from Lima to San Pedro, but if you take a bus (marked Chosica), from block 15 of Nicolas de Pierola, one block beyond the Parque Universitario, or a colectivo from Calle Montevideo, just off Avenida Abancay, in Lima Centro to Chosica, you can pick up buses and trucks to San Pedro from Parque Echinique. Empresa Santa Maria **buses** usually have signs reading "San Pedro" or "Marcahuasi", but for **trucks** it's a matter of asking all drivers where they're bound. If your bus or truck terminates at Las Cruces, you'll have half an hour's walk further to San Pedro.

In San Pedro almost everything you'll need is centred around the Plaza de Armas. The **tourist office**, Plaza de Armas (Mon–Fri 9am–6pm & Sat 9am–1pm), can arrange accommodation and even mules for the uphill climb, though note that to visit the mountain you have to register next to the *albergue municipal* and pay a small entrance fee. For **places to stay**, there's the *albergue municipal* (no phone; ②) with sixteen beds, the *Hostal Communal* (no phone; ①–②), which is really intended for large groups but may be able to accommodate individual travellers, and the *Hotel Huayrona* (no phone; ②), which is actually the schoolteacher's house but lets out rooms. *Tienda Natches* (no phone; ①), which doubles up as a tourist information centre when the official tourist office is closed, also offers cheap floor space to travellers. There are two **restaurant** cafés, but they are not always open, so take your own food.

Into the Andes

Running on the world's highest and possibly most thrilling rail lines, the **train journey** from Lima into the Andes, which stopped running in 1991, has thankfully, if fitfully, restarted. The **road journey** is almost as spectacular, offering many travellers their first sight of llamas and of Peru's indigenous Indian mountain culture. The highest pass, at some 4843m above sea level, is also some visitors' first experience of altitude sickness, *soroche*, though buses and cars do the journey much quicker than the train ever did and consequently few travellers now stay at this altitude long enough to feel its effects. It usually takes around four to five hours to reach **La Oroya** by road; nearly all of this time is spent high in the Andes as the factories and cloudy skies of Lima are swiftly left behind. From La Oroya you have the choice of turning off north and winding through 130km or so of rather desolate landscape to **Cerro de Pasco**, a bleak mining town and a possible approach to Huanuco (see p.280), Tingo Maria (see p.282) and Pucallpa (see p.392) in the Amazon jungle (all covered in Chapter Six). However, most travellers head east from La Oroya to **Tarma** and on to the jungle region of

THE ANDES RAIL LINE

The **rail line** into the Andes has had a huge impact on the region and was a major feat of engineering. For President Balta of Peru and many of his contemporaries in 1868, the iron fingers of a railway, "if attached to the hand of Lima would instantly squeeze out all the wealth of the Andes, and the whistle of the locomotives would awaken the Indian race from its centuries-old lethargy". Consequently, when the American rail line entrepreneur **Henry Meiggs** (aptly called the "Yankee Pizarro") arrived on the scene it was decided that coastal guano deposits would be sold off to finance a new rail line, one which faced technical problems (ie the Andes) never previously encountered by engineers. With timber from Oregon and the labour of thousands of Chinese workers (the basis of Peru's present Chinese communities), Meiggs finally reached La Oroya via 61 bridges, 65 tunnels and the startling 4800m pass. An extraordinary feat of engineering, it nevertheless bound Peru more closely to the New York and London banking worlds than to its own hinterland and peasant population.

Departures are from Desamparados Railway Station in Lima on the last Sunday of every month, plus Monday and Tuesday in October and December, at 7.40am, arriving in Huancayo at 6pm. The **return journey** leaves Huancayo at 7am, arriving in Lima at 5.15pm. With the recent privatization of the line, it may well operate more frequently in the near future, so it's worth checking on arrival in Lima if this trip interests you. **Tickets** ($10 on way, $20 return) are available from the office in the station (Mon–Fri 8am–4pm) or from the Lima tour operator Fertur Peru (see Listings, p.86)

Chanchamayo, or 100km or so south to **Huancayo**, through the astonishing **Jauja Valley**, which boasts beautiful scenery, striped by fabulous coloured furls of mountain.

La Oroya

LA OROYA is not a particularly inviting place, a bleak little mining town which is fiercely cold at night. If you have to **stay** overnight, try the *Hostal Inti*, Arequipa 117 (☎064/391098; ③), with hot water but shared bathrooms, or the *Hostal Chavin*, Tarma 281 (no phone; ②), also with hot water and an attached restaurant, both in the old part of town. For **food**, try the *Restaurant Punta Arenas*, Zeballos 323, which is very good for seafood and Chinese dishes, or *Restaurant La Caracocha*, Lima 168, with an excellent, inexpensive set-lunch menu. **Buses** to all destinations leave from Calle Zebollas, adjacent to the train station.

Huancayo

HUANCAYO, at 3261m, is a large commercial city and capital of the Junin Department. An important market centre thriving on agricultural produce and dealing in vast quantities of wheat, it makes a good base for exploring the Mantaro Valley and experiencing the distinct culture that it shares with Huancavelica, represented in colourful rustic costumes and dances like the Chunguinada or Huaylas. In 1999, an extensive army operation captured the leader of **Sendero Luminoso**, Oscar Ramirez Durand, who had taken over from Guzman in 1992. This essentially cleaned up the area (coincidentally at the start of the presidential electoral campaigns), and it's now much safer.

The settlement itself is very old and the cereal and textile potential of the region has long been exploited. Back in the 1460s the native Huanca tribe was conquered by the Inca Pachacuti's forces during his period of imperial expansion. Occupied by the Spanish since 1537, Huancayo remained little more than a staging point until the rail line arrived in 1909, transforming it into a city. Relatively modern, Huancayo has little of architectural or historical merit, though it's a lively place and has the extremely active weekend **Feria Dominical market** on Calle Real (best on Sun). This sells the usual fruit and vegetables, as well as a good selection of woollen and alpaca clothes and blankets, superb weavings, and some silver jewellery. It's also worth trying to coincide with the splendid **Fiesta de las Cruces** each May, when Huancayo erupts into a succession of boisterous processions, parties and festivities.

There are two main squares in Huancayo. **Plaza Constitución** is named in honour of the Liberal Constitution of Cadiz, 1812, and is where you'll find monuments in honour of Mariscal Ramon Castilla, who abolished slavery in Huancayo in 1854. The **Plaza Huamanga**, closer to the heart of the city, is the site where Huancayo was founded in 1572. Surrounded by public buildings (such as the municiplaidad) and offices, it was once home to the Feria Dominical market, which shifted some twelve blocks to Calle Real in the mid-1990s. Calle Real is also where you'll find the **Capilla La Merced** colonial church, the site for the preparation and signing of the 1839 Peruvian Constitution and now designated a historic monument. The only other significant sight within the city centre is the **Museo Salesiano**, located in the district of El Tambo, which has exhibits of local flora and fauna as well a selection of interesting rocks and minerals.

Arrival and information

There are eight daily direct **bus** services from Lima to Huancayo via Jauja; the journey costs around $5 and takes 6–8 hours. All buses arrive at their respective company offices (see Listings, p.96). For a quicker journey between Lima and Huancayo (5–6hr), you can take **colectivos** #12 and #22, which leave from Calle Loreto daily from 7am until 6pm and charge $8–10. The **train from Lima** ($10 one way, $20 return) arrives at the central station, off Calle Pachitea, a few blocks east of Plaza Constitución along Avenida Giraldez, at around 6pm on the last Sunday of every month (leaves for Lima the next day at 7am). The **train from Huancavelica** arrives at the Estacion Chilca station on Avenida Ferrocarril, at the opposite end of Calle Real from the Plaza Constitución (follow the tracks to the right when they bend). Trains to Huancavelica leave Monday–Saturday at 6.30am, 12.30pm and Sunday at 2pm. The **tourist office** (Mon–Fri 9am–6pm, Sat 9am–1pm) is inside the Casa de Artesania, just on the Plaza de la Constitución where Calle Real and Paseo La Breña meet.

Accommodation

Casa Alojamiento de Aldo y Soledad Bonilla, Huanuco 332 (☎064/232103). A friendly house with hot water and where good English is spoken. ②.

La Casa de Mi Abuela, Avenida Giraldez 724. Basic, but with good facilities including table tennis, a darts board, and an electric shower. ①.

Hostal Alpeca, Avenida Giraldez 494 (☎064/223136). New, friendly and carpeted, with TVs in most rooms. ③.

Hostal Plaza, Ancash 171 (☎064/210509). Good-value rooms with private baths; go for the rooms at the front as they have most light and the best views. ②–③.

Hostal San Martin, Ferrocarril 362. A charming little place, but no hot water; located close to the train station. ①.

Hostal Santa Felicita, Plaza de la Constitución. A very nice place and well worth the price. ③.

Hotel Baldeon, Amazonas 543 (☎064/321634). Very cheap, friendly and with use of kitchen facilities. ①.

Hotel Confort, Ancash 231 (☎064/233601). Big rooms, with or without baths; also has a car park. ②–③.

Hotel Presidente, Calle Real 1138 (☎064/231275). The height of luxury for Huancayo, clean and with good service. ④.

Huancayo Plaza Hotel, Ancash 729 (☎064/231072, fax 235211). One of the town's best hotels, with comfortable rooms, though its elegance has faded somewhat and its *pisco sour* drinks aren't what they should be. ④.

Restaurants and nightlife

It's possible to eat and drink well in any of the **restaurants** around the Plaza de la Constitución: *Olímpico*, at Avenida Giráldez 199, is especially recommended for its good regional food. Also worth trying is *Lucho Hurtado's Pizzeria*, La Cabaña 724, or, closer to the Plaza de la Constitución, the excellent *Restaurant El Padrino*, Avenida Giraldez 133, serves local dishes, including *papas a la Huancaina*, the local speciality of potatoes in a mildly spicy cheese sauce, topped with sliced egg, a black olive and some green salad.

Huancayo boasts plenty of **nightlife**: local music and dance is performed most Sundays at 3pm in the *Coliseo* on Calle Real, and there are some good *criolla* and folklore *peñas* – *Dale "U"*, on the corner of Calle Ayacucho and Huancavelica, *Algarrobo*, 13 de Noviembre, Libertad, and *Cajon*, on Calle Real, have good reputations.

Listings

Banks and exhange For traveller's cheques, the Banco de Credito, Calle Real 1039, is best. To change dollars cash, try the street *cambistas* along Calle Real, the main street.

Bicycle rental A good way to explore the local countryside; try Huancayo Tours, Calle Real 543.

Buses Antezama, Arequipa 1301, for Ayacucho and Andahuaylas; Buenaventura, Lima 180, for Lima; Central, Avenida Ferrocarril, for Chanchamayo and Tarma; Cruz del Sur, Ayacucho 287, for Lima; Etusca, Puno 220, for Lima; Expresso Molina, Angaraes 334, for Ayacucho and Andahuaylas; Hidalgo, Loreto 350, for Lima and Huancavelica; Hualtapallana, Calixto 450, for Lima; Oriental, Ferrocarril 146, for Cerro de Pasco, Huanuco and Pucallpa; Ormeño, Paseo la Breña 218, for Lima; San Juan, Quito 136, for Chanchamayo and Tarma; San Pablo, Ancash 1248, for Huancavelica; Transel, Avenida Giraldez 247, for Ayacucho and Andahuaylas; Transfano, opposite Molina, for Ayacucho and Andahuaylas; Transportes Salazar, Giraldez 245, for Cerro de Pasco, Huanuco and Pucallpa; Turismo Mariscal Caceres, Calle Real, between Angaraes and Tarapaca, for Lima.

Hospital Calle Independencia.

Post office Plaza Huamaumarca. Mon–Sat 8am–7pm.

Spanish lessons Andes Spanish Insitute, Calle Guideo 509, San Carlos, Huancayo (☎064/232157, 212827 or 234068, *andespa@hotmail.com*), offer students Spanish lessons at various levels and include accommodation, usually based in local homes with local families.

Telephones The Telefónica Peru office is on Plaza Huamanga.

Tour operators and guides Turismo Huancayo, Calle Real 517 (☎064/233351) offers tours throughout the region. Lucho Hurtado, Apartado Postal 510, Huancayo (☎&fax064/222395, *incas+lucho@hys.com.pe*) is a good guide.

Around Huancayo

Using Huancayo as a base you can make a number of excursions into the Jauja Valley. The **Convent of Santa Rosa de Ocopa** (Mon & Wed–Sun 9am–noon & 3–6pm; $1.2), about forty minutes or 30km out of town, is easily reached by taking a microbus from outside the Church of Immaculate Conception to the village of Concepcion, where another bus covers the last 5km to the monastery. Founded in 1724, and taking some twenty years to build, the church was the centre of the Franciscan mission into the Amazon, until their work was halted by the Wars of Independence, after which the mission villages in the jungle disintegrated and most of the natives returned to the forest. The cloisters are more interesting than the church, though both are set in a pleasant and peaceful environment, and there's an excellent library with chronicles from the sixteenth century onwards, plus a **Museum of Natural History and Ethnology** containing lots of stuffed animals and native artefacts from the jungle. You can also stay at the convent **guesthouse** (①). A trip out here can be conveniently combined with a visit to the nearby village of **San Jerónimo**, about 12km away, thirty-minutes by car, from the convent and well known for its Wednesday market of fine silver jewellery; a 45-minute walk from San Jerónimo brings you to **Huaylas**, where high-quality woollen goods are cheap, because you buy directly from the maker.

Another good day-trip (30min by frequent bus from the Church of Immaculate Conception in Huancayo's Plaza de la Constitución) is to the local villages of **Cochas Chicas** and **Cochas Grandes**, whose speciality is crafted, carved gourds. Strangely, Cochas Grandes is the smaller of the two villages and you have to ask around if you want to buy gourds here. You can buy straight from co-operatives or from individual artisans; expect to pay anything from $3 up to $150 for the finer gourds, and if you are ordering some to be made, you'll have to pay half the money in advance.

Some 12km west of Huancayo ($10 by taxi) near the present-day pueblo of **Huari**, stand the **Huari-Huilca ruins**, the sacred complex of the Huanca tribe which dominated this region for over two hundred years before the arrival of the Incas. The distinct style the ruins display went unrecognized until 1964 when local villagers rediscovered the site under their fields. At the site is a small museum (daily 8am–6pm; $1) showing collections of ceramic fragments, bones and stone weapons.

Jauja

Forty kilometres from Huancayo, on the road to La Oroya, is **JAUJA**, a little colonial town which was the capital of Peru before the founding of Lima. Surrounded by some gorgeous countryside, Jauja is a pleasant place, whose past is reflected in its unspoiled architecture, with many buildings painted light blue. You can rent boats ($2 for an hour) on the nearby **Laguna de Paca**, and row out to its island, though the lake is rumoured to house a mermaid which lures men to their deaths. The shoreline is lined with cafés where decent trout meals can be bought, and, on weekends, *pachamanca* are served.

Buses and **combis** leave every hour from the market in Huancayo – the combi marked *izquierda* goes via the small towns in the valley, while the *derecha* combi is more direct, though both take around an hour. Empresa San Juan buses to Jauja leave from Calle Quito 136 in Huancayo, and Turismo Central buses leave from Avenida Ferrocarril. For the return journey to Huancayo, both buses and combis leave from the Jauja's Puente Ricardo Palma, or you can catch a through-bus from Lima to Huancayo, with Mariscal Caceres, Cruz del Sur or Sudamericano, which stop two or three times daily in Jauja's Plaza de Armas. Local transport is mostly by **motorcycle rickshaw**.

If you fancy **staying** in Jauja, one of the best options is *Cabezon's Hostal*, Ayacucho 1027 (☎362206; ②), with shared bathrooms; the cheapest place in town is the *Hostal Francisco Pizarro*, Bolognesi (①) opposite the market; and beside the lake there's the

---

ANDES TRAVEL WARNING

Travelling through the Andes **at night** doesn't seem to be a problem these days. However, general advice is to travel by day if possible, particularly in the Chanchamayo region (especially between La Merced and Satipo, where MRTA guerrillas are still partially active), and to be on the safe side, in the central highlands between Huancayo, Huancavelica, Ayacucho, Abancay and Andahuaylas on the overland route to Cusco. There is presently no direct public transport between Huancavelica and Ayacucho, and although it is possible to hitch rides on trucks, these are more at risk of being stopped and robbed at gunpoint during night journeys.

recently privatized *Hotel de Turistas* (④), which is clean, comfortable and good value. As far as **food** goes there's not much choice unless you love chicken and chips, but the *Marychris*, Jirón Bolivar 1166, serves excellent lunches, and the *Ganso de Oro*, Palma 249, is also worth trying.

Huancavelica

The remote **HUANCAVELICA**, at 3680m, is a surprisingly pure Indian town in spite of a long colonial history and a fairly impressive array of Spanish-style architecture. The weight of its past, however, lies heavily on its shoulders. After mercury deposits were discovered here in 1563, the town began producing ore for the silver mines of Peru – replacing expensive imports previously used in the mining process. In just over a hundred years so many Indian labourers had died of mercury poisoning that the pits could hardly keep going: after the generations of locals bound to serve by the *mitayo* system of virtual slavery had been literally used up and thrown away, the salaries required to attract new workers made many of the mines unprofitable. Today the mines are working again and the ore is taken by truck to Pisco on the coast.

Huancavelica's main sights, around the main **Plaza de Armas**, are the **Cathedral**, with its fine altar, and a handful of churches; two of them – **San Francisco** and **Santo Domingo** – are connected to the cathedral by an underground passage. The town also boasts a small **Regional Museum**, on the corner of *calles* Muñoz and Arequipa (Mon–Sat 9am–5.30pm; $0.8), containing archeological exhibits and dispays on pre-Inca Andean cultures. These apart, there's not a lot of interest, except the Sunday **market**, which sells local food, jungle fruits, and carved gourds. A couple of pleasant **walks** from town are to the natural **hot springs** on the hill north of the river, and to visit the **weaving co-op**, 4km away at Totoral.

Practicalities

There's not a wide choice of **accommodation** available in town – the best is the comfortable *Hotel Presidente*, Plaza de Armas (☎064/952760; ③–④), which has both private and communal bathrooms; *Hostal Camacho*, Carabaya 481 (①), is excellent value, with communal bathrooms and hot water most mornings; *Hotel Savoy*, Muñoz 296 (①), is basic; while *Hostal Tahuantinsuyo*, on the corner of Muñoz and Carabay (②), is dingy but has hot water most mornings. Reasonable **food** is available from *Mochica Sachun*, Toledo 303, which does a great set lunch for $1; *Paquirri* on Arequipa serves good local dishes and the *Restaurant Olla* on Avenida Gamarra dishes up reasonably priced international and Peruvian meals in a pleasant atmosphere. The best place for chicken and fries is *Polleria Joy*, on Calle M. Segura. The **Banco de Credito**, **post office** and **telephone office** are all along Toledo.

Two types of **train** travel from Huancavelica through beautiful countryside to Huancayo. The Train Extra, a local slow train, leaves Monday to Saturday at 12.30pm, costs $1.20 in first class, $3 in the buffet wagon and takes four hours and thirty minutes, while the Train Expresso leaves Monday to Saturday at 6.30am and Sunday at 2pm, costs much the same and takes four hours. The easiest way to get to Lima **by bus** is via Huancayo. Empresa Huancavelica and Empresa Hidalgo buses leave from Muñoz blocks 4 and 5 and San Pablo buses from the corner of *calles* O'Donovan and Prada for the 5–6 hour journey as far as Huancayo along very bad roads.

Tarma and the High Jungle

The region around **Tarma**, east of the rail junction at La Oroya, is one of Peru's most beautiful corners, the mountains stretching down from high, craggy limestone

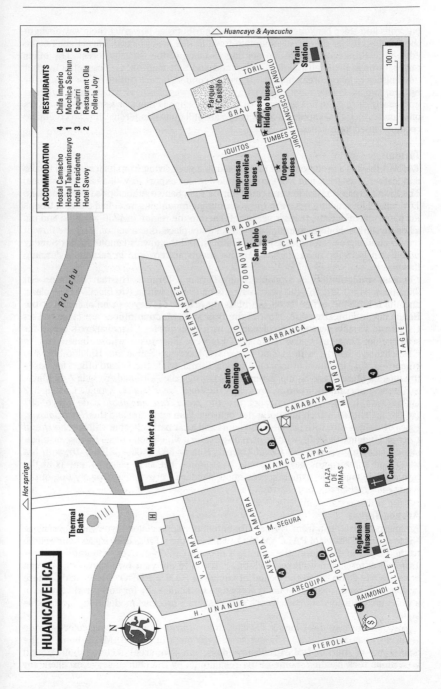

HUANCAVELICA

△ Huancayo & Ayacucho

ACCOMMODATION
Hostal Camacho 4
Hostal Tahuantinsuyo 1
Hotel Presidente 3
Hotel Savoy 2

RESTAURANTS
Chifa Imperio B
Mochica Sachun E
Paquirri C
Restaurant Olla A
Polleria Joy D

Train Station

Empressa Hidalgo buses

Empressa Huancavelica buses

Oropesa buses

San Pablo buses

Parque M. Castillo

Santo Domingo

Market Area

Thermal Baths

△ Hot springs

Rio Ichu

Regional Museum

Cathedral

PLAZA DE ARMAS

N

100 m

TORIL
GRAU
IQUITOS
TUMBES
JIRON FRANCISCO DE ANGULO
PRADA
O'DONOVAN
CHAVEZ
HERNANDEZ
V. TOLEDO
BARRANCA
M. MUNOZ
TAGLE
CARABAYA
MANCO CAPAC
M. SEGURA
AVENIDA GAMARRA
V. GARMA
H. UNANUE
AREQUIPA
V. TOLEDO
RAIMONDI
CALLE ARICA
PIEROLA

outcrops into steep canyons forged by Amazon tributaries powering their way down to the Atlantic. By far the nicest mountain town in this part of Peru, Tarma sits on the edge of the Andes almost within spitting distance of the Amazon forest. The other major towns in the High Jungle, **La Merced** and **San Ramon**, are less attractive but good places to take a break in some degree of comfort before setting off for **Pozuzo** or **Satipo**, two of Peru's most interesting jungle towns, both of which have suffered immensely during the last ten years of civil war. Satipo is more or less open to visitors once more, though **Oxapampa** and Pozuzo are still quite dangerous and can't really be recommended for tourism.

Tarma

TARMA itself is a pretty colonial town, making a good living from its traditional textile and leather industries, and from growing flowers for export as well as for its own use. The town's greatest claim to fame came during Juan Santos Atahualpa's rebellion in the 1740s and 1750s: taking refuge in the surrounding mountains he defied Spanish troops for more than a decade, though peace returned to the region in 1756 when he and his allies mysteriously disappeared. Today it's a quiet place, disturbed only by the flow of trucks climbing up towards the jungle foothills, and the town's famous Easter Sunday procession from the main plaza, when the streets are covered in carpets of dazzling flowers.

    Tourist information is available from Turismo Tarama, Huaraz 537 (Mon–Sat 9am–6pm; ☎064/321286); the **post office** is on Callao, within two blocks of the plaza; and the **telephone office** is on the Plaza de Armas. **Money** can be changed at the Banco de Credito, Lima 407. Most of the **bus** and **colectivo** offices are clustered on Calloa and Castilla near the petrol station, with Transportes Chanchapayo's office, for services to Lima, at Callao 1002 and Empresa San Juan, whose buses run to Chanchamayo hourly, at Jirón 2 de Mayo 316. Expresso Satipo and Hidalgo buses to Huancayo and Lima have offices on Avenida Tarma, while the Lobato office, for buses to Lima, La Merced and Satipo, is on the corner of Calle Arica and Avenida 2 de Mayo.

    The best **accommodation** in town is at the *Hotel Los Portales,* Avenida Castilla 512 (☎064/321411; ⑤); slightly cheaper are the *Hotel Internacional*, 2 de Mayo 307 (☎064/321830; ④), which has hot water between 6pm and 8am, and the *Hotel Galaxia*, Plaza de Armas (③), with private bathrooms and a car park; cheaper still are the *Hostal Central*, Huanuco 614 (②), with its own observatory which non-guests can use on clear-skied Friday nights, and the *Hostal Bolivar*, Huaraz 389 (☎064/321060; ②), with hot water and some rooms having private bathrooms. The best place **to eat** is at the *Señorial*, Huanuco 138, which serves good standard Peruvian fare; or try one of the many *chifa* restaurants or *pollerias*.

Around Tarma

An interesting day-trip from Tarma – though better appreciated if you camp overnight – is to the rural village of **PALCAMAYO** (90min by bus). From here it's an hour's climb to the **Caves of Huagapo**, the country's deepest explored caves, accessible for over 1km with a torch and waterproof clothing. If you've got your own transport, you can continue the 20km on to the beautiful village of **SAN PEDRO DE CAJAS**, where craftspeople produce superb quality weavings. Coincidentally (or not) the village lies in a valley neatly divided into patchwork field-systems – an exact model of the local textile style.

    Also within easy day-tripping distance from Tarma – just a short colectivo ride (expect to pay about $0.40) – is the small settlement of **ACOBAMBA**, home of the **Sanctuary of the Lord of Muruhuay** (daily 7am–7pm; free), a church built around a religious rock painting. Some of the restaurants by the church serve excellent *cuy* (guinea pig) and *pachamanca*, and next to the sanctuary you'll see a biplane set up on the hill.

San Ramon and La Merced

The twin towns of **San Ramon** and **La Merced** (80km and 90km respectively from Tarma), in the breathtaking **Chanchamayo Valley**, mark the real beginning of the **jungle** directly east of Lima. Both are well served by **buses** at least daily from Lima, and in the other direction buses and colectivos to and from Satipo and Oxapampa/Pozuzo. They leave more or less constantly from the **Terminal Terrestre** in La Merced, where it's just a matter of checking out which bus, combi or car is going where, and when.

Well-established settler towns, both on the Río Tulumayo, San Ramon and La Merced are separated by only 10km of road, some 2500m below Tarma, and are surrounded by exciting hiking country. Getting there from La Oroya, the road winds down in ridiculously precipitous curves, keeping tight to the sides of the **Rio Palca canyon**, at present used for generating hydroelectric power. Originally a forest zone inhabited only by Campa-Ashaninka Indians, this century has seen much of the best land cleared by invading missionaries, rubber and timber companies and, more recently, waves of settlers from the Jauja Valley.

The smaller of the two towns, **SAN RAMON** is probably the nicer place to break your journey. One of the best **hostals** is the *Hotel Conquistador*, at Progreso 298 (☎064/331157, fax 331771; ③), or there's *Progresso* (②), also on Calle Progresso, which is reasonably priced though pretty basic. The main reason for travellers to stop off here is for a taster of the *ceja de selva*, the cloud forest zone along the western edge of the Amazon. If you've got the money, you can head deeper into the lower Amazon basin by taking one of the daily **air taxis** to the jungle towns of Satipo, Atalaya or Pucallpa from the airstrip on the small plateau above town. The valley around San Ramon is rich in tropical fruit plantations and productive *chacras* (gardens), much of whose produce is transported over the Andes by road to Lima.

The market town of **LA MERCED** some 10km further down the attractive valley is larger and busier than San Ramon, with more than twelve thousand inhabitants, a thriving market, and several hectic restaurants and bars crowded around the Plaza de Armas. The *Hostal Rey* on Calle Junin (④) is the best place **to stay**, while the *Hotel Mercedes*, on Jirón Tarma (②) one and a half blocks from the plaza, is basic but friendly.

Satipo

SATIPO, accessible by a three- to four-hour bus ride east from La Merced, is a real jungle frontier town, where the indigenous Ashaninka Indians come to buy supplies and trade. Developing around the rubber extraction industry some eighty years ago, it now serves as an economic and social centre for a widely scattered population of over forty thousand colonists, offering them tools, food supplies, medical facilities, banks and even a cinema. With the surfacing of the road all the way from Lima, a veritable flat carpet unfurling through the jungle valleys, many more colonists have moved into the region, but the rate of development is putting significant pressure on the last surviving groups of traditional forest dwellers, mainly the Ashaninka tribe, who have mostly taken up plots of land and begun to compete with colonists or moved into one of the ever-shrinking zones out of permanent contact with the rest of Peru. You'll see them in town, unmistakable in their reddish-brown or cream *cushma* robes. Satipo is the most southern large town on the jungle-bound Carretera Marginal, but the road is continuing further and should soon reach Puerto Ocopa – a passable dirt track already does, and buses travel along it – from where it's possible to get river boats down the Rio Tambo to Atalaya.

An ideal town in which to get kitted out for a jungle expedition, or merely to sample the delights of the *selva* for a day or two, Satipo possesses an interesting daily **market**, at its best at weekends, an **airstrip**, and sits in the middle of a beautiful landscape; a fascinating walk is to follow the path from the other side of the suspension bridge to one of the plantations beyond town. Further afield, local colectivos go to the end of the Carretera Marginal into relatively new settled areas such as that around **San Martin de Pangoa** – a frontier settlement that is frequently attacked by armed bandits or terrorists who live on coca plantations in the forest (hence the sandbags lined up outside the police stations).

Satipo's best **accommodation** is at the *Hotel Majestic,* on the central plaza (③), with deliciously cool rooms, though the *Hostal Palmero* (①) is significantly cheaper and neither place has hot water. Other basic accommodation is available around the market area and along the road to the airstrip. For **eating**, the *Café Yoly,* between the plaza and the market is great for coffee, snacks and breakfasts, while the *Restaurant Turistico Oasis,* Jirón Junin 628, has a wide range of jungle cuisine available in a large, ethnically decorated place where you can also buy local crafts, mainly of Ashaninka origin. Nearby there are **petroglyphs** and **waterfalls** on the Río Mazamari (ask at the *Restauarant Oasis* for details) which is also a popular fishing spot.

Instead of retracing your steps back via La Merced and San Ramon, you can follow a breathtaking direct road to **Huancayo** – Los Andes buses do the twelve-hour journey daily (May–Oct). For the adventurous, a flight to **Atalaya** (see p.392), deep in the jungle, is an exciting excursion, though this is way off the tourist trail and any potential visitors should be warned that facilities are few and it's real jungle frontier stuff. Two commercial air-taxi companies fly most days, or on demand if you can pay the $400 per hour air taxi rate, to both Sepahua and Atalaya.

Oxapampa and Pozuzo

Pretty well off the beaten track, some 78km by road north of La Merced, lies the small settlement of **OXAPAMPA**, dependent for its survival on timber and coffee. Most of the forest immediately around the town has been cleared for cattle grazing, coffee plantations and timber, and the indigenous **Amuesha Indians**, disgruntled at being pushed off their land, are battling hard on local, national and international levels for their land rights. Strongly influenced in architecture, blood and temperament by the nearby Germanic settlement of Pozuzo, this is actually quite a pleasant frontier town in its own way, with a surprisingly good **place to stay**, the *Hotel El Rey* (③). However, visits to Oxapampa and Pozuzo (see below) are not recommended for tourists; the South American Explorers' Club in Lima (see p.86) should have the very latest on the situation, or contact your embassy.

POZUZO, a weird combination of European rusticism and native Peruvian culture, is all that's left of a unique eighteenth-century project to open up the Amazon using European peasants as settlers. Some 80km down the valley from Oxapampa, along a very rough road that crosses over two dozen rivers and streams, its wooded chalets with sloping Tyrolean roofs have endured ever since the first Austrian and German colonists arrived in the 1850s. As part of the grand plan to establish settlements deep in the jungle – brainchild of President Ramon Castilla's economic adviser, a German aristocrat – eighty families left Europe in 1857; seven emigrants died at sea and six more were killed by an avalanche, which caused another fifty to turn back only 35km from here. Many of this unusual town's present inhabitants still speak German, eat *schitellsuppe* and dance the polka. The *Hostal Tyrol* (④) and *Hotel Maldonado* (②) are the best **places to stay**. **Trucks** for Pozuzo leave every couple of days from opposite the *Hotel Bolivar* in Oxapampa.

travel details

Buses and colectivos

Huancayo to: Ayacucho (3 daily; 16–22hr); Cerro de Pasco (1 daily; 6hr); Huancavelica (2 daily; 4–5hr); Lima (10 daily; 6–8hr); Tarma (6 daily; 3–4hr).

Huancavelica to: Huancayo (2 daily; 4–5hr).

La Merced to: Oxapampa/Pozuzo (4 daily; 6–12hr); Satipo (12 daily; 3–4hr).

Lima to: Arequipa (12 daily; 13–16hr); Chincha (8 daily; 3hr); Cusco (6 daily, some change in Arequipa; 30–40hr); Huacho (12 daily; 2–3hr); Huancayo (10 daily; 6–8hr); Huaraz (10 daily; 9–10hr); La Merced (6 daily; 9hr); Pisco (8 daily; 3hr–3hr 30min); Nasca (6 daily; 6hr); Satipo (2 daily; 12–16hr); Tacna (6 daily; 20–22hr); Tarma (8 daily; 6–7hr); Trujillo (10 daily; 8–9hr).

Tarma to: La Merced (8 daily; 2–3hr); Lima (8 daily; 5–6hr).

Trains

Huancayo to: Huancavelica (Mon–Sat 2 daily, Sun 1 daily; 6–8hr).

Flights

Lima to: Arequipa (2 daily; 1hr 20min); Chiclayo (3 daily; 1hr 40min); Cusco (4 daily; 1hr); Huanuco (1 daily; 1hr); Iquitos (2 daily; 1hr 45min); Juliaca for Puno (2 daily; 2hr); Piura (2 daily; 1hr 30min); Pucallpa (2 daily; 1hr); Rioja/Moyabamba (5 weekly; 1hr 30min); Tacna (2 daily; 2hr 30min); Tarapoto (4 weekly; 1hr); Trujillo (3 daily; 45min); Yurimagus (4 weekly; 2hr).

San Ramon to: Pucallpa (1 weekly; 1hr); Satipo (2 weekly; 30min).

Satipo to: Atalaya (1 weekly; 30min); Pucallpa (1 fortnightly; 45min); San Ramon (2 weekly; 30min),

CHAPTER TWO

CUSCO AND AROUND

K nown to the Incas as the "navel of the world", **CUSCO** is an exciting and colourful city, built by the Spanish on the sumptuous and solid remains of Inca temples and palaces, and as rich in human activity today as it must have been at the height of the empire. Enclosed between high hills and dominated in equal degree by the imposing ceremonial centre and fortress of **Sacsayhuaman** and the white Christ figure, it's one of South America's biggest tourist destinations, with its thriving culture, substantial Inca ruins and architectural treasures from the colonial era attracting visitors from every corner of the world. Yet despite its massive pull, this welcoming city remains relatively unspoiled and gives you the opportunity to meet native **Quechua Indians**, who make up most of the of 300,000 people living here. Facilities are good, and its whitewashed streets and red-tiled roofs are home to a wealth of traditional culture, lively nightlife and a seemingly endless variety of museums, walks and tours.

Once you've acclimatized – and the altitude here, averaging 3500m, has to be treated with respect – there are dozens of enticing destinations within easy reach. For most people, the **Sacred Valley** of the Río Urubamba is the obvious first choice, with the citadel of **Machu Picchu** as the ultimate goal, and with hordes of other ruins – **Pisac** and **Ollantaytambo** in particular – amid glorious Andean panoramas on the way. The mountainous region around Cusco boasts some of the country's finest trekking, and beyond the **Inca Trail** to Machu Picchu are hundreds of lesser known, virtually unbeaten paths into the mountains, including the **Salcantay** and **Ausungate** treks, which begin less than a day's train ride northwest and a bus ride south of Cusco respectively. Further afield you can explore the lowland **Amazon rainforest** in Madre de Dios, such as the Tambopata and Candamo Reserved Zone, or the slightly nearer Manu Reserved Zone (all covered in Chapter Six), among the most accessible and bio-diverse wildernesses on Earth.

South of Cusco lie more Inca and pre-Inca sites at **Tipón** and **Pikillacta**, nearly as spectacular as those in the Sacred Valley yet far less visited. Travelling south from these, the highly scenic **train journey** to Puno and Lake Titicaca passes through scenery as dramatic as any in the country. To the west is the Andean region around **Ayacucho**, with its traditional villages and beautiful colonial churches, off-limits in the late 1980s and early 1990s due to the terrorist activities of the Sendero Luminoso guerrillas, but now very much open again to travellers.

As the imperial capital during Inca times, Cusco was the most important place of pilgrimage in South America, and it still is today. During Easter, June and Christmas, the city centre becomes the focus for relentless *fiestas* and carnivals as extravagant processions bring together a vibrant blend of pagan pre-Colombian and Catholic colonial cultures. Hundreds (and during festivals, thousands) of tourists arrive and leave daily, often filling every plane, bus and train, so it's important to book onward tickets a good few days before you intend travelling. The **best time to visit** the area around Cusco is during the dry season (May–Sept), when it's warm with clear skies during the day but relatively cold at night. During the wet season (Oct–April) it rarely rains every day or all week, but when it does, downpours are heavy.

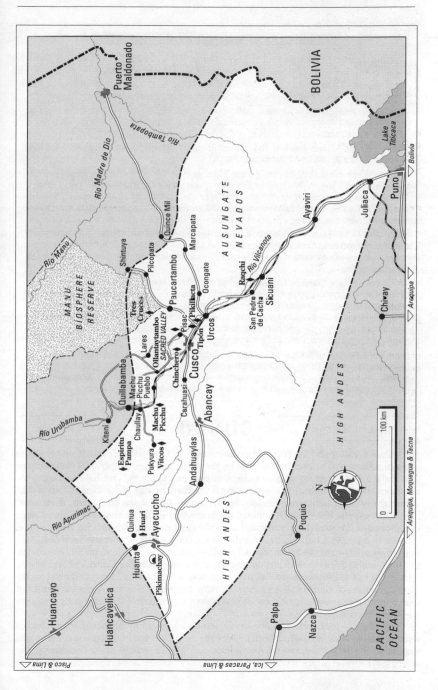

Around Jan 20 Adoracion de Los Reyes (Adoration of the Kings). Ornate and elaborate processions leave from San Blas church and parade through Cusco.

Last week of Jan Pera Chapch'y (Festival of the Pear). A harvest festival in San Sebastian, 4km southeast of Cusco, with lively street stalls and processions.

February Festividad Carnavales. Folk dancing and traditional food in the streets of Coya, Pisac and Calca; each village celebrates in a different week of the month (check with the tourist office).

First week of March Festival de Durasno (Festival of the Peach). Food stalls and folk dancing in Yanahuara and Urubamba.

Easter Week Semana Santa. On Easter Monday there's a particularly splendid procession through Cusco, with a rich and evocative mix of Indian and Catholic iconography. The following Thursday a second procession celebrates the city's patron saint, El Señor de los Temblores (Lord of Earthquakes), and on Easter Friday, street stalls sell twelve different traditional dishes.

May 2–3 Cruz Velacuy, or Fiesta de las Cruces (Festival of the Cross). All church and sanctuary crosses in Cusco and the provinces are veiled for a day, followed by traditional festivities with dancing and feasting in most communities. Particularly splendid in Ollantaytambo.

Weekend before Corpus Christi Qoyllur Riti (Snow Star, or ice festival). Held on the full-moon weekend prior to Corpus Christi in an isolated valley at the foot of a glacier, opposite the sacred mountain of Ausungate, this is one of the most exciting festivals in the Americas. You'll need to camp, and at around 15000ft it's only for the adventurous; some tour operators do go there, but it's primarily a Quechua Indian festival, with villagers arriving in their thousands in the weeks running up to it.

Corpus Christi A procession of saints' effigies through the streets of Cusco. The festival was imposed by the Spanish to replace the Inca tradition of parading ancestral mummies, but even now the local *mayordomos* (ritual community leaders, a position that rotates, mainly among the men) throw parties and feasts combining elements of reli-

CUSCO

The **Cusco Valley** and the **Incas** are synonymous in most people's minds, but the area was populated well before they arrived on the scene and they simply built their empire on the toil and ingenuity of generations of previous cultures. The **Killki** culture, for instance, whose members learned to work the hard diorite and andesite stones that abound here and, although primarily agriculturists, built stone structures, dominated the scene around 700–800 AD. Some of these structures still survive, while others were incorporated into later Inca constructions – the sun temple of Koricancha, for example, seems to have been built on the foundations a Killki sun temple. Early Inca pots, too, are stylistically close to Killki-produced items, while classical Inca pots demonstrate strong similarities to ceramics produced around 1000 AD by the **Lucre** culture, whose main site was at Choquepugio, 35km from modern Cusco. The Lucre also used significant amounts of diorite stone in their constructions and, like the Incas later, utilized such boulders in multi-angular, earthquake-proof formations. Later Inca pottery shows a strong **Wari** influence.

According to Inca legend, however, Cusco was founded by **Manco Capac** and his sister Mama Occlo around 1200 AD. Over the next two hundred years the valley was home to the Inca tribe, one of many localized warlike groups then dominating the Peruvian *sierra*. A series of chiefs led the tribe after Manco Capac, the eighth one being

giosity with outright hedonism. Calle Saphi is filled with stalls selling traditional food such as cooked guinea pig, and for the following eight days the effigies are left inside the Cathedral, after which they are taken back to their respective churches, accompanied by musicians, dancers and exploding fire-crackers.

Second week of June Cusqueña International Beer and Music Festival. Lively, week-long festival in Cusco, hosting fairly big Latin pop and jazz names, at its best from Thursday to Sunday.

June 16–22 Traditional folk festivals in Raqchi and Sicuani.

June 20–30 Fiesta de Huancaro. An agricultural show packed with locals and good fun, based in Huancaro sector of Cusco ($1 taxi ride from Plaza de Armas, or go down Avenida Sol and turn right at the roundabout before the airport).

Last week in June Cusco Carnival, or Cusco Week. Daily processions in the Plaza de Armas by army, school and civil defence groups and folk dancers, plus lively music on the streets throughout the day and night, peaking with Inti Raymi.

June 24 Inti Raymi. Popular, commercial fiesta re-enacting the Inca Festival of the Sun in the grounds of Sacsayhuaman. Many Peruvians and gringos come to Cusco just for this event.

July 15–17 Virgen de Carmen. Dance and music festival celebrated all over the highlands, but at its best in Paucartambo.

July 28 Peruvian Independence Day. Festivities nationwide, not least in Cusco.

Sept 14–18 Señor de Huanca. Music, dancing, pilgrimages and processions take place all over the region but especially lively in Calca, with a fair in the Sacred Valley.

Sept 25 to early Oct Semana Turistica (Tourist Week). Conferences and street processions in Cusco, but all rather fake and touristy.

First week of Dec Yawar Fiesta. A vibrant, uncommercial *corrida de toros* (bullfight) at the end of the week in Paruro, Cotabambas and Chumbivilcas. A condor, captured by hand, is tied to the back of a bull that battles to the death.

Dec 24 Santuranticuy. Traditional fair of *artesania*, including hand-made, wooden toys in Cusco.

Viracocha Inca, but it wasn't until Viracocha's son **Pachacuti** assumed power in 1438 that Cusco became the centre of an expanding empire. As Pachacuti pushed the frontier of Inca territory outwards, so he also master-minded the design of imperial Cusco, canalizing the Saphi and the Tullumayo, two rivers that ran down the valley, and building the centre of the city between them. Cusco's city plan was conceived in the form of a puma, a sacred animal: **Sacsayhuaman**, an important ritual centre that doubled up as a fortified area for the town's people to retreat to when threatened, is the jagged, tooth-packed head; **Pumacchupan**, the sacred cat's tail, lies at the point where the city's two main rivers merge; while between these two sites lies **Koricancha**, the Temple of the Sun, reproductive centre of the Inca universe, the loins of this sacred beast. The heart of the puma, was **Huacapata**, a ceremonial square approximating in both size and position to the modern Plaza de Armas. Four main roads radiated from the square, one to each corner of the empire. Pachacuti's palace was built on one corner of Huacapata, while his grandson, Huayna Capac, situated his palace in the opposite corner, next to the cloisters of the Temple of the Sun Virgins. The overall achievement was remarkable, a planned city without rival at the centre of a huge empire, and in building their capital the Incas endowed Cusco with some of its finest structures. All important buildings were constructed from hard volcanic rock and streets ran straight and narrow, with stone channels to drain off the heavy rains.

By the time the Spanish arrived, Cusco was a thriving capital. Nobles and conquered chieftains lived within the body of the puma, servants and artisans on the outskirts, while subjects from all over the empire made regular official pilgrimages. Of all the Inca rulers only Atahualpa, the last, never actually resided in Cusco, and even he was en route to there when the conquistadores captured him at Cajamarca. In his place, **Francisco Pizarro** eventually reached the native capital on November 15, 1533. The Spaniards were astonished: the city's beauty surpassed anything they had seen before in the New World, the stonework was better than any in Spain and precious metals were used in a sacred context throughout the city, though most of all in Koricancha. As usual, they lost no time in plundering its fantastic wealth.

The Spanish city, divided up among 88 of Pizarro's men who chose to remain as settlers, was officially founded by Pizarro on March 23, 1534. **Manco Inca** was set up as a puppet ruler, governing from a new palace on the hill just below Sacsayhuaman.

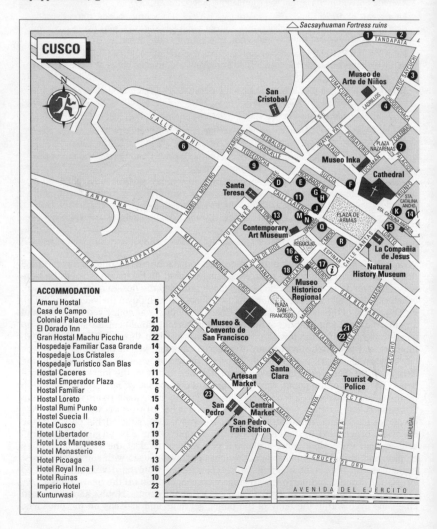

ACCOMMODATION	
Amaru Hostal	5
Casa de Campo	1
Colonial Palace Hostal	21
El Dorado Inn	20
Gran Hostal Machu Picchu	22
Hospedaje Familiar Casa Grande	14
Hospedaje Los Cristales	3
Hospedaje Turistico San Blas	8
Hostal Caceres	11
Hostal Emperador Plaza	12
Hostal Familiar	6
Hostal Loreto	15
Hostal Rumi Punko	4
Hostel Suecia II	9
Hotel Cusco	17
Hotel Libertador	19
Hotel Los Marqueses	18
Hotel Monasterio	7
Hotel Picoaga	13
Hotel Royal Inca I	16
Hotel Ruinas	10
Imperio Hotel	23
Kunturwasi	2

Within a year, power struggles between the colonists – two of whom were Pizarro's sons – had reached the point of open violence, though serious trouble was averted when their main rival, Almagro, departed to head an expedition to Chile. With him out of the way, Juan and Gonzalo Pizarro were free to abuse the Inca and his subjects, which eventually provoked Manco to open resistance. In 1536 he fled to Yucay, in the Sacred Valley, to gather forces for the Great Rebellion.

Within days the two hundred Spanish defenders, with only eighty horses, were surrounded in Cusco by over one hundred thousand rebel Inca warriors. On May 6, Manco's men attacked, setting fires among the dry thatched roofs and laying siege to the city for the following week. Finally, the Spaniards, still besieged in Huacapata, led a desperate attempt on horseback to break out, riding up to counterattack the Inca base

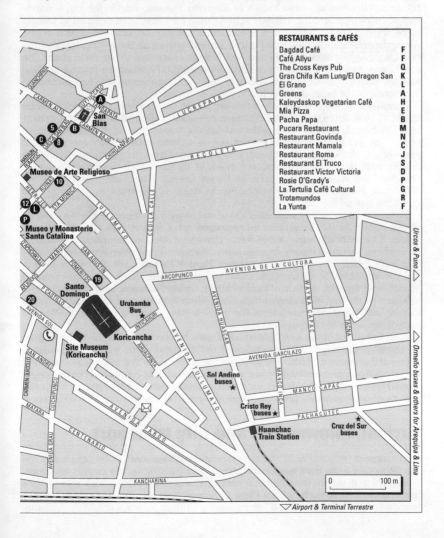

RESTAURANTS & CAFÉS

Bagdad Café	F
Café Allyu	F
The Cross Keys Pub	Q
Gran Chifa Kam Lung/El Dragon San	K
El Grano	L
Greens	A
Kaleydaskop Vegetarian Café	H
Mia Pizza	E
Pacha Papa	B
Pucara Restaurant	M
Restaurant Govinda	N
Restaurant Mamala	C
Restaurant Roma	J
Restaurant El Truco	S
Restaurant Victor Victoria	D
Rosie O'Grady's	P
La Tertulia Café Cultural	G
Trotamundos	R
La Yunta	F

in Sacsayhuaman, during which battle Juan Pizarro was fatally wounded. Incredibly, after a few days of desperate fighting, the Spanish defeated the native stronghold, putting some 1500 warriors to the sword as they took it – one of the most important battles in the conquest of Peru, for if the Incas had won, they would have regained control of all Peru except Lima.

Cusco never again came under such serious threat from its indigenous population, but its battles were far from over. By the end of the rains the following year, the small Spanish stronghold was still awaiting reinforcements: Pizarro's men were on their way up from the coast, while Almagro, returning from Chile, was at Urcos, only 35km to the south. Unsure of his loyalties and the cause of the Inca insurrection, Almagro tried to befriend Manco but the emperor chose to retreat into a remote mountain refuge at **Vilcabamba** – now known as **Espiritu Pampa**, deep in the jungle northeast of Cusco. Almagro immediately seized Cusco for himself and defeated a Pizarrist force arriving from Lima. For a few months the city became the centre of the Almagrist rebels until Francisco Pizarro himself arrived on the scene, defeated the rebel force on the edge of town and had Almagro garrotted in the main plaza. The rebel Incas, meanwhile, held out in Vilcabamba until 1572, when the Spanish colonial viceroy, Toledo, captured Tupac Aymaru – one of Manco's sons who had succeeded as emperor – and beheaded him in the Plaza de Armas.

From then on the city was left in relative peace, ravaged only by the great earthquake of 1650. After this dramatic tremor, remarkably illustrated on a huge canvas in the cathedral, **Bishop Mollinedo** was largely responsible for the reconstruction of the city, and his influence is also closely associated with Cusco's most creative years of art. The **Cusqueña school**, which emerged from his patronage, flourished for the next two hundred years, and much of its finer work, produced by native Quechua and *mestizo* artists such as Diego Quispe Tito, Juan Espinosa de los Monteros, Fabian Ruiz and Antonio Sinchi Roca, is exhibited in museums and churches around the city.

Today Cusco possesses an identity above and beyond the legacy left in the andesite stones carved by the Incas. Like its renowned art, Cusco is dark, yet vibrant with colour. It's a politically active, left-of-centre city where street demonstrations organized by teachers, lecturers, miners or some other beleagured profession are commonplace. The leading light of Cusco's left, ex-mayor **Daniel Estrada**, left the city in 1996 to become a member of Congress in Lima, taking with him much of Cusco's political vigour. However, with the help of local architect, **Guido Gallegos**, he left behind a visual legacy for the city, in its elegant Inca-like modern fountains and statues, such as the Condor and Pachacutec monuments and the new plaza in San Blas, mostly built in the early 1990s under his auspices.

With the arrival of the new millennium, Cusco has become something of a magnet for mystics expecting it to be re-vindicated as "the navel of the world", the umbilical centre of Pachamama, Mother Earth, hence the mystic tours that are now available and the rituals that have been taking place at many of the ancient ceremonial centres in and around Cusco over the last few years. The community spirit remains strong, if diverse, and street demonstrations protesting against council policies are a regular occurrence.

Arrival, information and city transport

Cusco **airport** (☎222611 or 222601 for information) is 4km south of the city centre. You can either take a taxi from outside the arrivals hall ($3–5 to the city centre) or a colectivo combi from outside the airport car park (frequent departures), which goes to Plaza San Francisco via Avenida Sol and Plaza de Armas. Note that the airport is full of tour touts, who should be avoided. If you're coming in from Juliaca, Puno or Arequipa by

The phone code for Cusco and the surrounding region is ☎084.

train, you'll arrive at the Huanchac **train station** in the southeast of the city; you can hail a taxi on the street outside (around $1 to the centre), or turn left out of the station and walk about a hundred metres to Avenida Sol, from where you can either catch the airport colectivo detailed above, or walk the eight or nine blocks up a gentle hill to the Plaza de Armas, from where it's easy to get your bearings.

Apart from Cruz del Sur, who have their own independent depot at Avenida Pachacutec, a few blocks east of Huanchaq railway station and Avenida Sol, **inter-regional and international buses** (see Listings, p.135, for details) arrive and depart from the rather scruffy Terminal Terrestre, southeast of the centre, close to the Pachacutec monument and roundabout (*ovalo*) and roughly halfway between the Plaza de Armas and the airport. Taxis from here to the city centre cost $1–2, or you can walk to the Pachacutec *ovalo* and catch a colectivo uphill to either the Plaza San Franciso or the Plaza de Armas; otherwise, it's about a half-hour walk. **Regional buses** from the Sicuani, Urcos and Paucartambo areas stop around blocks 15 and 16 of Avenida de la Cultura, from where it's a bit of a hike, so you'll almost certainly want to take a taxi ($1–2) or bus or combi colectivo ($0.3) to the centre. Almost all Sacred Valley buses come and go from *avenidas* Tullomayo or Huascar, which run parallel to each other and are also close to Huanchaq but are nearer to the centre (or a $1 taxi ride).

Information

The main **tourist office**, at Portal Mantas 188 (Mon–Sat 9am–noon & 3–6pm; ☎223701 & 263176), a short block from the Plaza de Armas, is run by the Regional Tourism Directorate. They sell the Cusco Tourist Ticket (see box overleaf) and have maps and brochures and can answer most enquiries, though they don't speak much English. Information is also available from a booth at the airport (open to meet morning flights); at Terminal Terrestre bus terminal, though this is rather dominated by one tour company; and the Instituto Nacional de Cultura office (Mon–Fri 9am–4pm) on the corner of Garcilaso, next to the Museo Regional Histórico. However, the best sources are often the **tour agents** around the Plaza de Armas or along *calles* Plateros and Procuradores (see p.137), running uphill from the plaza. They provide leaflets promoting their own tours, but many also offer idiosyncratic plans of the city and simple maps of the Sacred Valley and nearby regions. The bi-weekly English-language *New World News*, available from bookshops and on the streets, has good local information.

CRIME IN CUSCO

Cusco police have made a real effort to clean up the city's poor reputation for pickpocketing, bag snatching and street muggings. However, in recent years there have been reports of "strangle muggings", wherein tourists are jumped and strangled to the point of fainting before being robbed. Although rare, it's best to avoid walking along empty streets late at night, especially if alone. The police claim that robberies are virtually nonexistent around the Plaza de Armas or Avenida Sol, but accept that incidents are still possible in the Central Market area. The train stations tend to be well policed by private security, and inside the railway compounds problems are almost unkown. If you are unlucky enough to have anything stolen, report it to the **Tourist Police**, and if you have problems getting them to believe you, call the **Tourist Protection Service** (see Listings, p.136, for contact details for both), or contact your consulate.

THE CUSCO TOURIST TICKET

The **Cusco Tourist Ticket** ($10) is a vital purchase for most visitors. It's the only key to many of the city's main attractions and includes useful maps of the region and the city, plus it gives opening times. It's theoretically available from all of the sites on the ticket, but in practice only from those in Cusco itself, plus Sacsayhuaman, the Oficina Boleta Turistico, on the corner of Garcilaso and Heladeros (Mon–Fri 7.45am–6pm, Sat 8.30am–1pm), or from the main Tourist Information Office (see previous page); the ticket lasts for ten days only, but you can usually extend your ticket for free at the last two offices without much hassle.

City transport

Cusco's centre is small enough to **walk** around. **Taxis** can be waved down on any street, particularly on the Plaza de Armas, Avendia Sol and around the market end of Plaza San Francisco; rides within Cusco cost under $1 or $2–3 for trips to the suburbs or up to Sacsayhuaman and Quenko (some *taxistas* may prefer to charge $5 and wait for you, in which case give them half in advance and the remainder at the end of the journey). The city **bus** network is incredibly complicated to fathom, though it's cheap enough and fast, but it's largely unregulated, with minibuses chalking up their destinations in the front windscreens. More useful are the **colectivos** that run up and down Avenida Sol every couple of minutes, many of them starting from Plaza San Francisco, during daylight hours, stopping at street corners if they have any seats left; these charge a flat fare (about $0.2) and can be hailed on virtually any corner along the route For **private minibuses** (with driver) around the region, try Cultura Verde (☎270292), or if you fancy driving yourself, **car rental** is available at Auto Andes (☎247241). The **bicycle rental** offered by Bicy Centro Atoq, Calle Saphi 674 (☎236324), is good value and the standard of maintenance is high; expect to pay around $5 an hour to $30 a day (best booked in advance).

Accommodation

Much of the city's budget **accommodation** is in the zone to the north of the Plaza de Armas along *calles* Plateros, Procuradores and Saphi, but there are relatively inexpensive and reasonable mid-range hostals and hotels in most corners of the city. *Calles* Procuradores and Plateros are particularly noisy at night; more peaceful locations, though slightly pricier, are further up Calle Saphi, around Plaza Regocijo, towards San Blas and, if you are prepared to walk a little, along Choquechaca and Tandapata, further up the hill from the centre. The San Pedro region around the Central Market is cheap but pretty down-at-heel, rife with pickpockets and quite dangerous at night. As well as a wide range in prices and comfort levels, there's also a broad variety of architectural environments to choose from.

ACCOMMODATION PRICE CODES

Unless otherwise indicated, **accommodation** in this book is coded according to the categories below, based on the price of a double room in high season.

① under $5	③ $10–20	⑤ $30–40	⑦ $50–70
② $5–10	④ $20–30	⑥ $40–50	⑧ over $70

Budget

Casa Campesina, Avenida Tullumayo 274 (no tel). About four blocks from the Plaza de Armas, this basic but friendly and very clean hostal is part of a Non Governmental Organization that works with Andean peasant communities of the region. All profits are reinvested in development projects. ②.

Gran Hostal Machu Picchu, Calle Quera 282 (☎231111). About two blocks from the Plaza de Armas, this friendly, family place is hard to beat for atmosphere and value in one package, Rooms (with or without bath) are set around a colonial courtyard. ③.

Hospedaje Los Cristales, Carmen Alto 294 (☎244037, fax 221353). A pleasant family-run hostal on the edge of the pleasant San Blas area, this place has a good hot-water system, a laundry, family rooms and a comfortable lounge. Rooms come with or without private bath. ②–③.

Hospedaje Familiar Casa Grande, Santa Catalina Ancha 353 (☎264156, fax 243784). Large and very central, this has an open courtyard, some newly furbished rooms as well as more basic ones. With or without bathrooms. ②–③.

Hospedaje Osiris 616, Atoqsaykuchi 616 (☎234572). A family-run ramshackle and rustic place with occasional hot water. English, French and Spanish are spoken, plus they have a fax service, a noticeboard and offer the use of a kitchen. They also run tours. ②.

Hostal Caceres, Calle Plateros 368 (☎232616 or 228012). A popular travellers' hangout, half a block from the Plaza de Armas. It's got a courtyard and is within a stone's throw of most of Cusco's best bars and cafés. Rooms are basic and you have to ask for hot water. ②.

Hostal Colonial, Matará 288 (☎231811 or 247046). Pretty basic, but clean and with pleasant service. Many of its rooms are based around an airy courtyard in an old colonial building. Bathrooms are communal. ①.

Hostal Familiar, Calle Saphi 661 (☎239353). Quiet, safe and one of Cusco's best budget options (it's best to reserve in advance). Rooms are spartan but cool, clean and nicely furnished, with or without private bath (in which case showers are communal) and there's usually hot water in the mornings. Good breakfasts are served in the café, plus there's a free safety deposit box, a cheap left-luggage system and a laundry service. ②–③.

Hostal Rumi Punko, Choquechaca 339 (☎221102). A friendly family establishment on an old Inca temple site and in one of Cusco's nicest streets. The rooms have private hot showers, are stylish for the price, plus there's access to kitchens, a patio, a *comedor* and a small sitting room with a fireplace. Best booked in advance in high season. Price includes breakfast. ③–④.

Hostal Suecia II, Tecqusecocha 465 (☎239757). A popular backpacker place set around a covered courtyard, this is comfortable, pretty safe and very good value. Rooms are with or without private bath. ②–③.

Hostal Tumi, Siete Cuartones 245 (☎244413). Just off Plateros and a little way up from Iglesia Santa Teresa, this friendly place is popular with young travellers, quite central, has a nice courtyard, plain bedrooms, shared bathrooms, access to a kitchen and a noticeboard. ②.

Imperio Hotel, Calle Chaparro (☎228981). A family-run hostal in a rather dodgy part of town near the Central Market and right by San Pedro Station, but with water all day, exceptionally clean, friendly and undoubtedly good value. ②.

Kunturwasi, Tandapata 352a (☎227570). Excellent value, safe and popular, this friendly and smart place offers private baths, kitchen facilities and a small library. High up above the city centre, it's a bit of a hike, which can be testing on arrival from sea-level. ③.

Pakcha Real Hostal Familiar, Tandapata 300, San Blas (☎237484). An excellent family-run hostal in the attractive San Blas suberb, four steep blocks from Plaza de Armas. This pleasant, good-value modern home has a shared kitchen, a TV room and patio, constant hot water and reasonable security. Rooms are with or without bath. ③–④.

Moderate

Amaru Hostal, Cuesta San Blas 541 (☎ & fax 225933, *amaru@telser.com.pe*). There's a pleasant colonial feel here, with a lovely garden patio and another out back with views over town. There are laundry, safety deposit and left-luggage facilities, plus bottled oxygen for those in need. Good rooms, with or without private bath. ③.

Casa de Campo, Tandapata 296–298 (☎244404, fax 243069, *paula96@telser.com.pe*). Attractive rooms and cabins with great views over the city and a large patio, best booked in advance. Its quiet, pleasant location on the upper edge of Cusco is dauntingly high for your first couple of days, so take a taxi to avoid exhaustion or altitude sickness. They offer combined accommodation language-school courses with the AMAUTA language school (see Listings, p.136). Ten-percent discount to holders of the *Rough Guide Peru* and members of the South American Explorers' Club. ⑤.

Colonial Palace Hostal, Calle Quera 270 (☎232151, fax 232329). An attractive colonial building with pleasant courtyards and clean, comfortable rooms, but rather pricey. Hot water guaranteed 5am–1pm and 5.30–10pm, and other facilities include a restaurant, grocery and *artesanía*. All rooms have private bath. ⑥.

Hostal Emperador Plaza, Santa Catalina Ancha 377 (☎227412 or 261733, fax 263581, *emperador@blockbuster.com.pe* or *emperador@nexoperu.com*). Comfortable and central but modernized and rather faceless, though with 24hr hot water, bath and cable TV in all rooms. Rates include breakfast. ⑥.

Hostal Loreto, Calle Loreto 115 (☎226352). An interesting old place on the corner of an Inca stone-lined alleyway connecting Plaza de Armas with Koricancha. The best rooms incorporate the original Inca masonry of the Temple of the Virgins of the Sun, and all have private bath and hot water. Prices vary according to the room you choose and the number of people in it. ④.

Hotel Los Marqueses, Calle Garcilasco 256 (☎232512, fax 227028). This attractive and very stylish seventeenth-century mansion has one of the prettiest colonial courtyards in Cusco. Good value and there's a laundry service, but book in advance. ⑤.

Hospedaje Turistico San Blas, Cuesta San Blas 326 (☎ & fax 225781, *sanblascusco@yahoo.com*). Located in the quiet and attractive artisan suburb of San Blas, this friendly and warm place features a glass-covered courtyard. Most rooms have private bath and a safe deposit is available. They also organize tours to the Inca Trail and do river rafting on the Vilcanota. A good lower mid-range option. ③.

Expensive

El Dorado Inn, Avenida Sol 395 (☎231232 or 233112, fax 240993, *doratur@mail.cosapidata.com.p*). A classic four-star Latin-style hotel. Rooms are spotless and the service is good, but the location – less than two blocks from the Plaza de Armas – can be a bit noisy. ⑧.

Hacienda Hotel Incatambo, San Cristobal, 2km along the *carretera* to Sacsayhuaman (☎221918 or 222045). A beautiful hacienda converted into a hotel, close to Sacsayhauman and sharing some of the same magnificent views over the Cusco Valley and down to the city. Rooms are luxurious and many are set around a stunning colonial courtyard. Horse-riding is offered on their ample estate. ⑦.

Hostal Cahuide, Calle Saphi 845 (☎222771, fax 222361, *hotelcahuide@mixmail.com*). A few blocks uphill from the Plaza de Armas, beneath the woods below Sacsayhuaman. A bit pricey but better value in low season, it's pleasant with clean, modern rooms and a message board. ⑦.

Hotel Cusco, Heladeros 150 (☎224821, 221811 or 222961, fax 222832). Well-established and central, with a popular restaurant and bar, plus conference rooms. It's slightly down-at-heel these days but still has comfortable rooms with bath, TV and telephone. ⑦.

Hotel Libertador, Plazoleta Santo Domingo 259 (☎231961, fax 233152). One of the most luxurious hotels in Peru, set in a thoroughly modernized old mansion close to Koricancha, just a few blocks from the Plaza de Armas. ⑧.

Hotel Monasterio, Calle Palacio 136, Plazoleta Nazarenas (☎241777 fax 237111, *reserlima@peruhotel.com*). Cusco's latest luxurious establishment, at over $200 for a double. It's a rather fantastic place, set around massive sixteenth-century monastery cloisters. There are tables in the courtyard where you can sip drinks and eat delicious food from the plush bar and restaurants. ⑧.

Hotel Picoaga, Santa Teresa 334 (☎221269 or 227691, fax 221246, *picoaga@correo.dnet.compe*; in Lima ☎01/465-0689, fax 429-1134). A first-class hotel in one of Cusco's finest colonial mansions, centred around a beautiful, traditional courtyard close to the heart of the city. Service is excellent, and there's a large bar and restaurant. ⑧.

Hotel Royal Inca I, Plaza Regocijo 299 (☎231067 or 222284, fax 234221). A fairly luxurious hotel (which has a more expensive sister hotel – *Royal Inca II* – more or less next door) with a sauna and massage rooms. Very popular with upmarket package travellers. ⑧.

Hotel Ruinas, Ruinas 472 (☎260644 or 245920, fax 236291, *ruinas@mail-interplace.com.pe*). A very comfortable option with superb rooms, many with views from private balconies down to Ausungate. Exceptionally clean, with fridge bars and safes in each room; there's also a fine lobby, restaurant and bar, and email and fax facilities. ⑧.

The city centre

Despite the seemingly complex street structure, it doesn't take long to get to grips with Cusco. The city divides roughly into several main zones based on various squares, temples or churches, with the **Plaza de Armas** at its heart. The broad **Avenida Sol** runs southeast from the corner of the plaza by the university and Iglesia de La Compañía towards the Inca sun temple at **Koricancha**, Huanchaq train station and on to the airport in the south. Running southwest from the top of Avenida Sol, Calle Mantas leads uphill past **Plaza San Francisco** and the Iglesia di Santa Clara, then on towards the Central Market and San Pedro train station. Just one block west of the central plaza lies **Plaza Regocijo** and from the northeast corner of Plaza de Armas, Calle Triunfo leads uphill through some classic Inca stone-walled alleys towards the artisan *barrio* of **San Blas**, passing near **Plaza Nazarenas**, northeast of the centre. Calle Plateros heads northwest from Plaza de Armas, leading to Calle Saphi and Calle Suecia, both of which run uphill through quaint streets and on towards Sacsayhuaman Fortress above the city.

Each of these zones is within easy walking distance of the Plaza de Armas and their main features can be covered easily in half a day, allowing for a little extra time for browsing in the bars and shops en route. It's probably better to split your time into two or three half-day sessions in order to get the best out of the city and allow time for exploring some of the museums and archeological complexes in some depth. As you wander around, you'll notice how many of the important Spanish buildings were constructed on top of Inca palaces and temples, often incorporating the exquisitely constructed walls and doorways into the lower parts of churches and colonial structures. The closer you are to the Plaza de Armas, the more obvious this becomes.

Around the Plaza de Armas

Cusco's ancient and modern centre, the **Plaza de Armas** corresponds roughly to the ceremonial *huacapata*, the Inca's ancient central plaza, and is the obvious place to get your bearings. With the unmistakable ruined fortress of **Sacsayhuaman** towering above, you can always find your way back to the plaza simply by locating Sacsayhuaman or, at night, the illuminated white figure of Christ that stands beside the fortress on the horizon. The plaza is always busy, its northern and western sides filled with shops and restaurants. The **Portal de Panes** is a covered cloister pavement hosting processions of boys trying hard to sell postards, and waiters and waitresses competing for custom, trying to drag passing tourists into their particular dive. The stalls and shoe-shine boys who used to compete in the same arena have now had their activities restricted by the *concejo* to the hinterland of backstreets emanating from the plaza, particularly the zone facing onto the Plaza Regocijo, behind the Plaza de Armas. The Portal de Panes used to be part of the palace of Pachacuti, whose walls can still be seen from inside the *Roma Restaurant* close to the corner of the plaza and Calle Plateros. The plaza's exposed northeastern edge is dominated by the squat **Cathedral**, while the smaller **Iglesia de la Compañía de Jesus**, with its impressive pair of belfries, sits at the southeastern end. To the north of the cathedral is the relatively new **Balcon de Cusco**, a small square with a panoramic walkway leading off it.

The cathedral

The **Cathedral** (Mon–Sat 10am–noon & 2–5pm, Sun 2–5pm; entry by Cusco Tourist Ticket, see p.112) sits solidly on the foundations of the Inca Viracocha's palace, its massive lines looking fortress-like in comparison with the delicate form of the nearby La Compañía. Construction began in 1560, with the cathedral being built in the shape of a Latin cross and its three-aisled nave supported by just fourteen massive pillars. There are two entrances, one via the main central cathedral doors; the other, more usual, way is through the **Triunfo Chapel**, the first Spanish church to be built in Cusco. Check out its finely carved granite altar and huge canvas depicting the terrible 1650 earthquake, before moving into the main cathedral to see an intricately carved Plateresque pulpit and beautiful, cedar-wood seats, as well as a Neoclassical high altar made entirely of finely beaten embossed silver and some of the finest paintings of the Cusqueña school. In the **Sacristy**, on the right of the nave, there's a painting of the crucifixion attributed to Van Dyck. Ten smaller chapels surround the nave, including the **Chapel of the Immaculate Conception**, and the **Chapel of El Señor de los Temblores** (The Lord of Earthquakes), the latter housing a twenty-six-kilo crucifix made of solid gold and encrusted with precious stones. To the left of the cathedral is the adjoining **Iglesia di Jesus Maria**, built in the early eighteenth century.

The cathedral's appeal lies as much in its mingling of history and legend, as in any tangible sights. Local myth claims that an Indian chief is imprisoned in the right-hand tower, awaiting the day when he can restore the glory of the Inca Empire. Here too hangs the huge, miraculous gold-and-bronze bell of Maria Angola, named after a freed African slave girl and reputed to be one of the largest church bells in the world. And on the massive main doors of the cathedral, native craftsmen have left their own pagan adornment – a puma's head.

The Museo Inka

North of the cathedral, slightly uphill beside the Balcon de Cusco, you'll find one of the city's most beautiful colonial mansions, **El Palacio del Almirante** (The Admiral's Palace). Commanding superb views down onto the Plaza de Armas, this palace now houses the **Museo Inka** (Mon–Sat 8am–5pm; $1.7). Again constructed on Inca foundations – this time the Waypar stronghold, where the Spanish were besieged by Manco's forces in 1536 – it is noteworthy for its simple but well-executed Plateresque facade, surmounted by two imposing Spanish coats-of-arms. The museum itself has been recently renovated and is one of the best places in Cusco to see exhibits of mummies, trepanned skulls, Inca textiles and a range of Inca wooden *quero* vases. There are also displays of ceramics, early metalwork in silver and a few gold figurines, but it's the layout and presentation that make this one of the best places to gain a quick understanding of the development of civilization in the Andes, from the pre-ceramic period through to the Inca Imperial.

The Iglesia de La Compañía de Jesus

Looking downhill from the centre of the plaza, the **Iglesia de la Compañía de Jesus** dominates the skyline. First built in the late 1570s, it was resurrected over fifteen years after the earthquake of 1650, in a Latin cross shape, over the foundations of Amara Cancha – originally Huayna Capac's Palace of the Serpents. Cool and dark, with a grand gold-leaf altarpiece, high vaulting and numerous paintings of the Cusqueña school, its transept ends in a stylish Baroque cupola. The guilded altarpieces are made of fine cedar wood and the church contains interesting oil paintings of the Peruvian Princess Isabel Ñusta. Its most impressive features are the two majestic towers of the main facade, a superb example of Spanish colonial Baroque design which has often been described in more glowing terms than the cathedral itself. On the right-hand side of the church, the **Lourdes Chapel**, restored in 1894, is used mostly as an exhibition centre for local crafts.

The Natural History Museum

Alongside La Compañía, an early Jesuit university building houses the **Natural History Museum** (Mon–Fri 9am–noon & 3–6pm; $0.3). The entrance is off an inner courtyard, up a small flight of stairs to the left. The exhibits cover Peru's coast, the Andes and the Amazon jungle with a particularly good selection of stuffed mammals, reptiles and birds. For a small tip, the doorman outside the university building sometimes allows visitors up the stairs to the top of the cupola to admire the view across the plaza.

South to Koricancha

Leading away from the Plaza de Armas, Callejón Loreto separates La Compañía Church from the tall, stone walls of the ancient Acclahuasi, or **Temple of the Sun Virgins**, where the Sun Virgins used to make *chicha* beer for the Lord Inca. Today the Acclahuasi building is occupied by the **Convent of Santa Catalina**, built in 1610, with its small but grand side entrance half a short block down Calle Arequipa; just under thirty sisters still live and worship here. Inside the convent is the **Museo de Arte y Monasterio de Santa Catalina** (Mon–Thurs & Sat 9am–5.30pm, Fri 9am–3pm; entry by Cusco Tourist Ticket, see p.112), with a splendid collection of paintings from the Cusqueña school, as well as an impressive Renaissance altarpiece and several gigantic seventeenth-century tapestries depicting the union of Indian and Spanish cultures. The theme of inter-racial mixing runs throughout much of the museum's fascinating artwork and is particularly evident in the Cusqueña paintings. This artistic movement from the seventeenth and eighteenth centuries, working mainly in oils and blending indigenous and Spanish iconography, was largely created by **Diego Quispe Tito**, an artist of mixed blood whose influential work can be seen on the first floor of the museum – his paintings and idolic images were vital tools of communication used by priests in their attempts to convert the indigenous population of the Andes to Catholicism. A common feature running through much of the Cusqueña art here is the downward-looking, blood-covered disproportionate head, body and limbs of the seventeenth-century depictions of Christ, which represent the suffering of the Andean Indians and originate from early colonial days when Indians were not permitted to look Spaniards in the eyes.

A highlight of the museum, on the first floor at the top of the stairs, is a large fold-up box containing miniature three-dimensional religious and mythological images depicting everything from the Garden of Eden and the flight to Egypt to an image of God with a red flowing cape and dark beard, a white dove and angels playing drums, Andean flutes and pianos. The museum also displays some of the original furniture and objects used by the nuns in previous centuries, and still used by them today when the museum is closed.

On the corner of Maruri and Q'aphchik'ijllu, on the way from Santa Catalina towards Koricancha, there's the **Museo y Sala Cultural** (Mon–Fri 9am–1pm & 4–6pm; free) at the Banco Wiese, where displays include historical documents and archeological and architectural features; exhibitions vary throughout the year. But the focus is often on the restoration work of the Banco Wiese's own premises, an attractive mansion that was once part of the Tupac Inca Yupanqui's Pucamarca palace, which covered the area bounded by Santa Catalina Ancha, San Agustin, Maruri and Santa Catalina Angosta. The bank's section was just the bottom left corner of this much larger building, which over the years became divided between various important Cusco families such as the Astetes. The violent earthquake in the 1950s caused much destruction here, though the walls, built over 600 years earier, stood up to the test.

Koricancha

The supreme example of Inca stonework underlying colonial buildings is just a short walk from the Plaza de Armas, through the Inca walls of Calle Loreto then along the busy Pampa del Castillo. It can't be missed, as the Convento de Santo Domingo rises imposingly but rudely from the impressive walls of **Korincacha** complex (Mon–Sat 8am–5.30pm; $1), which the conquistadores laid low to make way for their uninspiring Baroque seventeenth-century church – a poor contrast to the Inca masonry evident in the foundations and chambers of the Sun Temple. The tightly interlocking blocks of polished andesite abut the street as straight and as firmly rooted as ever, but before the conquistadores set their gold-hungry eyes on it, the temple must have been even more breathtaking, consisting of four small sanctuaries and a larger temple set around the existing courtyard, which was encircled by a cornice of gold (Koricancha means "golden enclosure"). Some of the inner walls, too, were hung with beaten sheets of gold, and in a large, slightly trapezoidal niche on the inside of the curved section of the retaining wall, close to the chamber identified as the Temple of the Sun, there stood a huge, gold disc in the shape of the sun, **Punchau**, which was worshipped by the Incas. Punchau had two companions in the temple: a golden image of **Viracocha**, on the right; and another, representing **Illapa**, god of thunder, to the left. Below the temple, towards the tail of Cusco's puma, was an artifical garden in which everything was made of gold or silver and encrusted with precious jewels, from llamas and shepherds to the tiniest details of clumps of earth and weeds, including snails and butterflies. Not surprisingly, none of this survived the arrival of the Spanish.

Koricancha's position in the Cusco Valley was carefully planned. Dozens of *ceques* (power lines, in many ways similar to ley lines, though in Cusco they appear to have been related to imperial genealogy) radiate from the temple towards more than 350 sacred *huacas*, special stones, springs, tombs and ancient quarries. In addition, every summer solstice, the sun's rays shine directly into a niche – the **tabernacle** – in which only the Inca was permitted to sit. Still prominent today, it must have been incredible when the sun reflected off the plates of beaten gold, studded with emeralds and turquoise. Mummies of dead Inca rulers were seated in niches at eye level along the walls of the actual temple, the principal idols from every conquered province were held "hostage" here, and every emperor married his wives in the temple before taking up the throne. The niches no longer exist, though there are some in the walls of the nearby Temple of the Moon, where mummies of the emperor's concubines were kept in a foetal position (some two hundred Mamaconas, or Sun Virgins, were part of the divine household, their sole purpose to serve Inti).

The **Chapel of Santo Domingo** (Mon–Fri, 9.30–11.30am and 3–5pm) is accessed via the Complex reception desk, or by walking past the Temple of the Moon and the Catholic Sacristy to a tiny section of the inner edge of the vast curved wall which, from the outside, seems to support the Chapel. Indeed, as most guides will tell visitors, major earthquakes have severely damaged the Spanish colonial religious construction, but the dark Inca stone wall never budges. Trapped between the Inca retaining wall and the western end of the Chapel, it is hard not to feel a sense of loss over the destruction of the Sun Temple itself, though as slight compensation, however, you can see the large niche which once held Punchau, the golden sun disc. Returning from here via the Sacristy, it is possible to see the Catholic priest's vestments, some boasting gold thread and jewels.

To reach the **Koricancha Site Museum** (daily 9.30am–6pm; entry by Cusco Tourist Ticket, see p.112), or Museo Arqueologico de Qorikancha, it's a three-minute walk downhill from the Complex reception to the underground museum entrance on block 3 of Avenida Sol. There are only three small rooms here, but each contains a number of interesting pieces. The first houses a mummy, some bi-chrome ceramics of the Killki era (around 800 AD), which reflect the art of the pre-Inca Wari culture. There

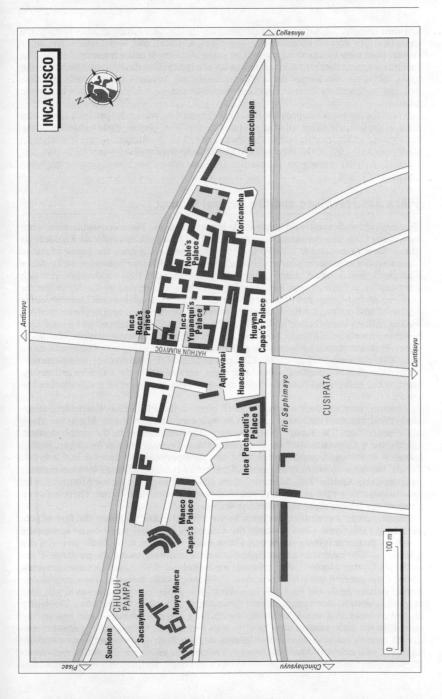

INCA CUSCO

are also some small sacred idols of precious metals plus Chancay and Tiahuanacu ceramics. The second chamber displays Naza, Chancay and Inca textiles, the latter woven from pure vicuna wool, as well as some stone tools and a trepanned skull. The last room is most notable for its presentation of a typical Quechua Indian offering to the gods, including coca leaves, corn, a llama foetus, salt, tobacco, beads, shells and alcohol; also in this room there are further weavings and some historical black and white photos.

From the museum it is possible to access the **garden**, where the pre-Inca spring and bath is particularly beautiful and pertains to the Wari period, clear evidence of the importance of Koricancha before the Incas arrived on the Andean scene. It is thought that, prior to the Incas, the Wari culture had already dedicated the site with its own Sun Temple, possibly known as Inticancha (*Inti* meaning "Sun" and *Cancha* meaning "enclosure").

Plaza San Francisco and the Central Market

Ten minutes' walk southwest along Calle Mantas from the Plaza de Armas, then a left turn along Calle San Bernardo, brings you to the **Iglesia y Convento de La Merced** (Mon–Sat 8.30am–noon & 2.30–5pm; $0.5), sitting peacefully amid the bustle of one of Cusco's more interesting quarters. Founded in 1536 by Brother Sebastian de Trujillo y Castañeda, it was rebuilt some twenty five years after the 1650 earthquake in a rich combination of Baroque and Renaissance styles by such artisans as the native master builders Alonso Casay and Francisco Monya. The façade is exceptional and the roof is endowed with an unusual Baroque spire, while inside there's a beautiful star-studded ceiling, a finely carved chair and a huge silver cross, which is adored and kissed by a shuffling crowd. Its highlight, however, is a breathtaking 1720s monstrance standing a metre high and crafted by Spanish jeweller Juan de Olmos, using over 600 pearls, more than 1500 diamonds and upwards of 22kg of solid gold. The monastery also possesses a fine collection of Cusqueña school paintings, particularly in the cloisters and vestry, but it is the exceptional beauty of the white-stone cloister here that really catches the eye.

Continue another block south and you'll come to the **Plaza San Francisco**, freqeuntly filled with food stalls that couldn't be squeezed into the Central Market or along Calle Santa Clara. The square's southwestern side is dominated by the simply decorated **Museo y Convento de San Francisco** (Mon–Fri 9am–noon & 3–5.30pm; $0.30), founded in 1645 and completed in 1652 and incorporating two facades and a tower. Inside, two large cloisters boast some of the better colonial paintings by local masters such as Diego Quispe Tito, Marcos Zapata, and Juan Espinosa de los Monteros, who was responsible for the massive oil canvas measuring some 12m by 9m. There's also an unusual candelabra made out of human bones.

Passing under a crumbling archway to the left of the church, follow the flow of people along Calle Santa Clara towards the Central Market and you'll come across the small but beautiful **Iglesia de Santa Clara** (daily 6am–6pm; free). Built around a single nave in 1558 by *mestizo* and indigenous master craftsmen under the guidance of the architect Brother Manuel Pablo, it boasts a gold-laminated altar, small mirrors covering most of the interior, and a few canvases. The outside walls, however, show more interesting details: finely cut Inca blocks support the upper, cruder stonework, and four andesite columns, much cracked over the centuries, complete the doorway. The belfry is so time-worn that weeds and wildflowers have taken permanent root. Just up the street, in the busy market area next to San Pedro train station, stands another sixteenth-century colonial church, the **Iglesia de San Pedro**, whose steps are normally crowded with colourful Quechua market traders. The interior is decorated with paintings, sculptures, goldleaf and some wooden carvings, and the elaborate pulpit was carved by Juan Tomás Tuyro Túpac, who was also responsible for the construction of this church. Relatively austere, with only a single nave, its main claim to fame is that somewhere among the stones of its twin towers are ancient blocks dragged here from the small Inca fort of Picchu.

In the area around the **Central Market** (daily 8am–5pm), street stalls sell excellent-value alpaca goods, while the shops around the indoor market building sell antique textiles. At its top end, the Central Market itself is full of stalls selling colourful Andean foods, with a few interesting herb stalls, and magic kiosks displaying everything from lucky charms to jungle medicines. At the bottom end are fruit and vegetable stalls plus some of the best and cheapest street meals in Peru.

Around Plaza Regocijo

The **Plaza Regocijo**, today a pleasant garden square sheltering a statue of Bolognesi, was originally the Inca *cusipata*, an area cleared for dancing and festivities beside the Inca's ancient central plaza. Only a block southwest of the Plaza de Armas, Regocijo is dominated on its northwestern side by an attractively arched municipal building housing the Contemporary Art Museum, with a traditional Inca rainbow flag flying from its roof. Opposite this is the *Hotel Cusco*, formerly the grand, state-run *Hotel de Turistas*, while on the southwest corner of the plaza lies an impressive mansion where more Inca stones mingle with colonial construction, home to the Museo Histórico Regional y Casa Garcilaso. Leading off from the top of Regocijo, **Calle Santa Teresa** is home to the House of the Pumas and leads to the Iglesia di Santa Teresa.

Museo Histórico Regional y Casa Garcilaso

Formerly the home of Garcilaso de la Vega, a prolific half-Inca (his mother may have been an Inca princess), half-Spanish poet and author, the mansion now known as the **Museo Histórico Regional y Casa Garcilaso** (Mon–Sat 8am–5.30pm; entry by Cusco Tourist Ticket, see p.112) is home to significant regional archaeological finds and much of Cusco's historic art. Fascinating **pre-Inca** ceramics from all over Peru are displayed, plus a Nazca mummy in a foetal position and with typically long (1.5m) hair, embalming herbs and unctures, black ceramics with incised designs from the early Cusco culture (1000–200 BC), and a number of **Inca** artefacts such as bolas, maces, architects' plumb-lines and square water-dishes for finding horizontal levels on buildings. Gold bracelets discovered in 1995 at Machu Picchu by Elva Torres Pino, some gold and silver llamas found in 1996 in the Plaza de Armas when reconstructing the central fountain, and some golden pumas and figurines from Sacsayhuaman provide new evidence of Inca offerings at these special sites. From the **colonial** era there are some weavings, wooden *quero* drinking vessels and dancing masks.

THE RISE OF THE CUSQUEÑA SCHOOL OF ART

Cusqueña art was limited to the Cusco region in the sixteenth century, but during the seventeenth century it spread to Titicaca and Bolivi, and much of its technique was developed and elaborated. By the eighteenth century the style had disseminated as far afield as Quito in Ecuador, Santiago in Chile, and even into Argentina, making it a truly South American form and one of the most distinctive indigenous to the Americas. The most famous Cusqueña artists were **Bernardo Bitti** (sixteenth century), **Diego Quispe Tito Inca** (seventeenth century) who was influenced by the Spanish Flamenco school, and **Mauricio Garcia** (eighteenth century) who helped to move the form into a fuller *mestizo* synthesis, mixing Spanish and Indian artistic forms. Many of the eighteenth- and nineteenth-century Cusqueña-*mestizo* works display bold composition and use of colour.

The main exhibition rooms upstairs house mainly period furniture and a multitude of paintings from the **Cusqueña school**, which cross the range from the rather dull (religious adorations) to the more spectacular (like the famous eighteenth-century *Jacob's Ladder*). As you progress through the works you'll notice the rapid intrusion of cannons, gunpowder and violence throughout the 1700s.

The Contemporary Art Museum

The **Contemporary Art Museum** (Mon–Sat 9am–5pm; free) is a welcome and relatively new feature in Cusco, for, as its name suggests, this is an outlet for the work of mainly local artists (of which there are quite a few and whose standard is generally high). **Sala 1** shows images of Cusco, mainly Inca dancers and abstract features, plus some scultpure. **Sala 2** is dedicated to contemporary art and leads off into a large courtyard with a typically attractive colonial fountain; here you'll find glass cases with dolls in traditional costumes, some regional variations of dance masks (from Paucartambo dance groups, for example) and models of buildings in different Cusco styles. The upstairs **Sala 3** houses more images of Cusco, both ancient and modern.

Calle Santa Teresa

On **Calle Santa Teresa** you'll find the **House of the Pumas** (no. 385), though this isn't as grand as it sounds and is now a small café: the six pumas above its entrance were carved into Inca blocks during the Spanish rebuilding of Cusco. Turn right at the end of this street and you pass the **Iglesia de Santa Teresa** (daily 6am–6pm; free), an attractive but neglected church with stone walls, the upper half of which have paintings featuring St Teresa. Inside, the small brick ceiling is finely domed and there's a gold-leaf altar inset with paintings. Next door, along from the church, there's a small **chapel** with intricately painted walls (featuring yet more of St Teresa), usually beautifully candle-lit.

Around Plaza Nazarenas and San Blas

Calle Cordoba del Tucman runs northeast from Plaza de Armas along the northern edge of the cathedral, past the Museo Inka (see p.116) and up to the small, quiet **Plaza Nazarenas**. At the top of this square, the unmistakable **Casa Cabrera** (Mon–Fri 8am–5.30pm, Sat 10am–noon & 3–5pm; free) has a fine open courtyard and some exhibition rooms displaying interesting nineteenth- and twentieth-century and indigenous photography, usually presenting many exhibits by renowned photographer, the late Martin Chambi, plus unusual period artefacts. Once part of Cancha Inka, a busy Inca urban centre prior to the Spanish Conquest, it was occupied by Jeronimo Luis de Cabrera, mayor of Cusco, in the seventeenth century and has been owned by the Banco Continental since 1981.

On the northeastern side of Plaza Nazarenas, the ancient, subtly ornate **Chapel of San Antonio Abad** was originally connected to a religious school before becoming part of the university in the seventeenth century. It's not open to the public, but you can usually look around the courtyard of the **Nazarenas Convent**, virtually next door and home to the plush *Hotel Monasterio* (see p.114); ask permission at the reception desk. Nuns lived here until the 1950 earthquake damaged the building so badly that they had to leave; the central courtyard has since been sensitively rebuilt and has an attractive garden where pricey but good meals and drinks are served. Beside the convent, the rather smelly but quaint Inca passage of Siete Culebras (Seven Snakes) leads onto Choquechaca; just up here on the left, at block 3 of Choquechaca, the **Museo de Arte de Niños "Irq'i Yachay"**, Ladrillos 491 (Wed–Sun 11am–5pm; free), shows paintings by children of the region, including by those from remote villages who are taught by a mobile school.

SAN BLAS

Originally known as T'oqokachi ("salty hole"), the **San Blas** *barrio* was one of twelve administrative sectors in Inca Cusco. After the Conquest it became a colonial parish of some importance and the residence for many defeated Inca leaders. It rapidly grew into one of the more attractive districts in the city, reflecting strong *mestizo* and colonial influences in its architecture and high-quality *artesania* – even today it's known as the *barrio de los artesanos* (artesans' quarter). Hit hard by the 1950 earthquake, it has been substantially restored, and in 1993 was given a major face-lift that returned it to its former glory, and at its centre lies the **San Blas Plazoleta**, on the southeast side of the chapel of San Blas, with 49 gargoyles set on a fountain that's laid out in the form of a *chakana*, or Inca cross, with four corners and a hole at its centre.

San Blas

From Choquechaca, turn left into Cuesta de San Blas and after a short but relatively steep walk past one and a half blocks you'll come to the tiny **Chapel of San Blas** (Mon–Wed, Fri & Sat 10–11am & 2–5.30pm; entry by Cusco Tourist Ticket, see p.112). The highlight here is an incredibly intricate pulpit, carved from a block of cedar wood in a complicated Churrigueresque style; its detail includes a cherub, a sun-disc, faces and bunches of grapes, all believed to have been carved by native craftsman Tomas Tuyro Tupa in the seventeenth century. Outside, along Calle Plazoleta (also called Suytuccato), there are a few art workshops and galleries, the most notable of which is Galeria Olave, at no. 651. The **Museo de Ceramica**, Carmen Alto 133, is worth checking out for its pottery, while on the plazoleta is the quaint **Museo Taller Hilario Mendivil**, containing a number of Cusqueña paintings, some interesting murals and religious icons.

Hathun Rumiyoq and the Museo de Arte Religioso del Arzobispado

Backtracking down the Cuesta de San Blas and continuing over the intersection with Choquechaca, head straight on until you come to the narrow alley of **Hathun Rumiyoq**, the most famous Inca passageway of all. Within its impressive walls lies the celebrated Inca **stone**, perhaps best known through its representation on bottles of Cuzqueña beer. The twelve-cornered block fits perfectly into the lower wall of the Inca Roca's old imperial palace, but you may have to look carefully to find it as it's often hidden behind Quechua women selling crafts.

At the end of Hathun Rumiyoq, and just one block from the Plaza de Armas, along Calle Triunfo, you'll find the broad doors of the **Museo de Arte Religioso del Arzobispado** (Mon–Sat 8–11.30am & 3–5.30pm; entry by Cusco Tourist Ticket, see p.112), housed in a superb Arabesque-style mansion built on the impressive foundations of Hathun Rumiyoq palace. Once home to Brother Vicente de Valarde and the Marquises of Rocafuert, then becoming the archbishop's residence, the museum now contains a valuable collection of paintings, mostly of the Cuzqueña school. There are beautiful mosaics in some of the period rooms, and other significant features include the elaborate gateway, the fine balcony and the gold-leaf craftsmanship on the chapel's altar.

Inca sites near Cusco

The megalithic fortress of **Sacsayhuaman**, which looks down from high above the city onto the red-tiled roofs of Cusco, is the closest and most impressive of several historic sites scattered around the Cusco hills, but there are four other major Inca sites. Not much more than a stone's throw beyond Sacsayhuaman lies the great *huaca* of **Qenko**

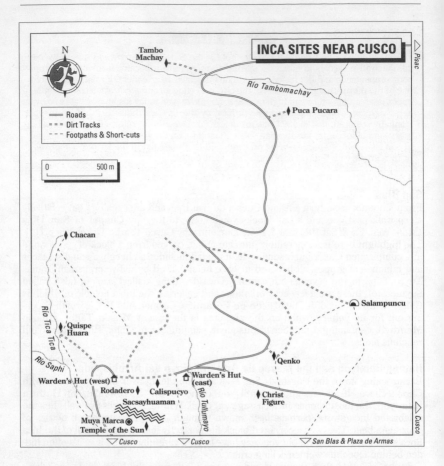

and the less-visited **Salumpuncu**, thought by some to be a moon temple. A few kilometres further on, at what almost certainly formed the outer limits of the Inca's home estate, you come to the small fortified hunting lodge of **Puca Pucara** and the nearby stunning imperial baths of **Tambo Machay**.

All these sites are all an energetic day's **walk** from Cusco, but you'll probably want to devote a whole day to Sacsayhuaman and leave the other sights until you're more adjusted to the rarefied air. If you'd rather start from the top and work your way downhill, it's possible to take a one of the regular **buses** to Pisac and Urubamba, run by Empressa Caminos del Inca (from Calle Huascar 128) and Empressa Urubamba (from Inti Cahuarina 305, 200m from Koricancha, just off Tullumayo). Ask to be dropped off at the highest of the sites, Tambo Machay, from where it's an easy two-hour walk back into the centre of Cusco, or at Qenko, which is closer to Sacsayhuaman and the city. Alternatively, you can take a **horseback tour** incorporating most of these sites, though you will have to get to Sacsayhuaman or Qenko first (a $1–$2 taxi ride from the centre of Cusco).

Sacsayhuaman

Although it looks relatively close to central Cusco, it's quite a steep forty-minute two-kilometre climb up to the ruins of Sacsayhuaman from the Plaza de Armas. The simplest route is up Calle Suecia, then first right (up a few steps) and along the narrow cobbled street of Huaynapata until it meets the even narrower lane of Pumacurco going steeply up (left) to a small café-bar with a balcony commanding superb views over the city; here the lane meets the road coming up from Calle Saphi, via the **Iglesia de San Cristobal**, a fine adobe church next to the even more impressive ruined walls of Kolkampata, the palace of the expansionist emperor Manco Capac, a good diversion to take on your way back down. It's only another ten minutes from the café, following the signposted steps all the way up to the ruins. By now you're beyond the built-up sectors and walking in countryside, and there's a well-worn path and crude stairway that takes you right up to the heart of the fortress.

SACSAYHUAMAN (daily 7am–5.30pm; entry by Cusco Tourist Ticket, see p.112) forms the head of Cusco's ethereal puma, whose fierce-looking teeth point away from the city. The name Sacsayhuaman is of disputed origin, though it may mean "city of stone". Protected by such a steep approach from the town, it only needed defensive walls on one side, and three massive, parallel walls zigzag together for some 600m, bounding what was originally a "spiritual distillation" of the ancient city below, with many sectors named after areas of imperial Cusco. Little of the inner structures remains, yet these enormous ramparts stand 20m high, quite unperturbed by past battles, earthquakes and the passage of time. The strength of the mortarless stonework – one block weighs more than 300 tonnes – is matched by the brilliance of its design: the zigzags, casting shadows in the afternoon sun, not only look like jagged cat's teeth, but also expose the flanks of any attackers trying to clamber up. Recently, however, many sacred and ritual objects excavated here have caused archeologists to consider Sacsayhuaman as more of a ceremonial centre than a fortress, with the zigzag form of these outer walls symbolizing the important deity of lightning.

It was the Emperor Pachacuti who began work on Sacsayhuaman in the 1440s, although it took nearly a century of creative work to finish it. The chronicler Cieza de León, writing in the 1550s, estimated that some twenty thousand men had been involved in its construction: four thousand cutting blocks from quarries; six thousand dragging them on rollers to the site; and another ten thousand working on finishing and fitting them into position. According to legend, some three thousand lives were lost while dragging one huge stone. Various types of rock were used, including massive diorite blocks from nearby for the outer walls, Yucay limestone from more than 15km away for the foundations, and dark andesite, some of it from over 35km away, for the inner buildings and towers. With only natural fibre ropes, stone hammers and bronze chisels, it must have been an enormous task. First, boulders were split by boring holes with stone or cane rods and wet sand; next, wooden wedges were inserted into these holes and saturated to crack the rocks into more manageable sizes; finally the blocks were shifted into place with levers.

Originally, the inner "fort" was covered in buildings, a maze of tiny streets dominated by three major towers. **Muyu Marca**, whose foundations can still be clearly seen, was round, over 30m tall and with three concentric circles of wall, the outer one roughly 24m in diameter. An imperial residence, it apparently had lavish inner chambers and a constant supply of fresh water carried up through subterranean channels. The other two towers – **Salla Marca** and **Paunca Marca** – had rectangular bases about 20m long and were essentially warriors' barracks, and all three were painted in vivid colours, had thatched roofs, and were interconnected by underground passages: in its entirety, the inner fortress could have housed as many as ten thousand people under siege. At the rear of this sector, looking directly down into Cusco and the valley, was a **Temple of the Sun**, reckoned by some to be *the* most important Inca shrine and the most sacred sector of Sacsayhuaman.

In front of the main defensive walls, a flat expanse of grassy ground – the esplanade – divides the fortress from a large outcrop of volcanic diorite. Intricately carved in places, and scarred with deep glacial striations, this rock, called the **Rodadero** ("sliding place"), was the site of an Inca throne. Originally there was a stone parapet surrounding this important *huaca*, and it's thought that the emperor would have sat here to oversee cere-monial gatherings at *fiesta* times, when there would be processions, wrestling matches and running competitions. On the far side of this huge outcrop are larger recreational sliding areas, smoothed by the many centuries of Inca and now tourist's backsides. From here you can see another large circular space called Qocha Chincanas, possibly an Inca graveyard, and on its far side the sacred spring of **Calispucyo**, where ceremonies to ini-tiate boys into manhood were held. Excavations here have uncovered crystals and shells (the latter all the way from Ecuador), a sign usually associated with water veneration.

After the fateful battle of 1536 when the Spanish wiped out the Incas, the conquista-dores wasted little time in dismantling most of the inner structures of the fortress, using the stones to build Spanish Cusco. During the battle, Juan Pizarro, Francisco's younger brother, was killed as he charged the main gate in a surprise assault, and a leading Inca nobleman, armed with a Spanish sword and shield, caused havoc by repulsing every enemy who tried to scale Muyu Marca, the last tower left in Inca hands. Having sworn to fight to the death, he leapt from the top when defeat seemed inevitable, rather than accept humiliation and dishonour. After the battle the esplanade was covered in native corpses, food for vultures and inspiration for the Cusco Coat of Arms which, since 1540, has been bordered by eight condors "in memory of the fact that when the castle was taken these birds descended to eat the natives who had died in it". Today the most dramatic event to take place at Sacsayhuaman is the colourful – if overly commercial – **Inti Raymi festival** in June (see p.107). However, throughout the year, you may stumble across various **sun ceremonies** being performed by mys-tics from the region.

Qenko

An easy twenty-minute walk from Sacsayhuaman, the large limestone outcrop of **QENKO** (daily 7am–5.30pm; entry by Cusco Tourist Ticket, see p.112) was another important Inca *huaca*. Head towards the Cusco–Pisac road along a track from the war-den's hut on the northeastern edge of Sacsayhuaman, and Qenko is just over the other side of the main road; the route is straightforward but poorly signposted.

This great stone, carved with a complex pattern of steps, seats, geometric reliefs and puma designs, illustrates the critical role of the Rock Cult in the realm of Inca cosmo-logical beliefs, and the surrounding foothills are dotted with carved rocks and elaborate stone terraces). The name of the temple derives from the Quechua word *quenqo* mean-ing "labyrinth" or "zigzag" and refers to the patterns laboriously carved into the upper, western edge of the stone. At an annual festival priests would pour *chicha* or sacrificial llama blood into a bowl at the serpent-like top of the main zigzag channel; if it flowed out through the left hand bifurcation, this was a bad omen for the fertility of the year to come. If, on the other hand, it continued the full length of the zigzag and poured onto the rocks below, this was a good omen. Worship in pre-Columbian Peru, from the Chavin era at least (1000 BC), was greatly concerned with the reverence of large (and sometimes small) rocky outcrops.

The rock may be associated with solstice and equinox ceremonies, fertility rites and even marriage rituals (there's a twin seat close to the top of Qenko which looks very much like a lover's kissing bench). Right on top of the rock is a carving with two prominent round nodules carved onto a plinth. These appear to be mini versions of *intihuatanas* ("hitching posts" of the sun), found at many Inca sacred sites – local guides claim that on the summer solstice, at around 8am, the nodules' shadow looks like a puma's face and a condor with wings outstretched at the same time. Along with the serpent-like divinatory channels, this would complete the three main layers of the Inca cosmos: sky (condor), earth (puma) and the underworld (snake). Beneath the rock are several **tunnels and caves**, replete with impressive carved niches and steps and which may have been places for spiritual contemplation and communication with the forces of life and earth. It's been suggested that some of the niches may have been where the mummies of lesser nobles were kept.

At the top end of the *huaca*, behind the channelled section, the Incas constructed an impressive, if relatively small, semicircular **amphitheatre** with nineteen vaulted niches (probably seats for priests or nobles) facing in towards the impressive limestone. At the heart of the amphitheatre rises a natural standing stone, which looks like a frog (representative of the life-giving and cleansing power of rain) from some angles and like a puma from others, both creatures of great importance to pre-Conquest Peru.

Salapunco

A twenty minute stroll uphill and through the trees above Qenko, to the right of the small hill, along the path (keeping the houses to your right), then emerging onto the fields and turning right, leads to **SALAPUNCO**. Yet another sacred *huaca*, though off the beaten track and also known as the Temple of the Moon and locally called Laqo, this large rock outcrop contains a number of small caves where the rock has been painstakingly carved. There's worn relief work with puma and snake motifs on the external rock faces, while in the caves there are altar-like platforms and niches that were probably for holding mummies. The largest of the caves was probably used for full-moon ceremonies (and sometimes is now), when an eerie silver light filters into the usually dark interior. It's possible to walk down from here to Plaza de Armas via interconnecting trails that go initially through some new *barrios* above the main Cusco–Pisac road, then down to San Blas.

Chacan and Quispe Huara

An important but little-visited Inca site, **CHACAN** lies about 5km from Sacsayhuaman on the opposite side of the fortress from Qenko and the road to Tambo Machay. It can be safely reached in the dry season (May–Sept), though not easily, by following the rather indistinct footpaths directly north from the Rodadero at Sacsayhuaman. When you hit the gully coming from the west, follow this up to the site; if you've been walking for ninety minutes or more and haven't found it, the chances are you've already passed it. Chacan itself was a revered spring, and you can see a fair amount of terracing, some carved rocks and a few buildings in the immediate vicinity; like Tambo Machay, it demonstrates the importance of water as an ever changing, life-giving force in Inca religion. A pleasant but more difficult walk leads down the Tica Tica stream (keep to the right-hand side of the stream and stay well above it), until you come to **Quispe Huara** ("crystal loincloth"), where a two- to three-metre-high pyramid shape has been cut into the rock. Close by are some Inca stone walls, probably once part of a ritual bathing location.

At Quispe Huara, cross to the left-hand bank of the stream to follow a path all the way back into Cusco, passing through a stony gorge and some pleasant eucalyptus and bearing left where the Tica Tica stream meets the Río Saphi. However, rains and earthquakes continuously destroy and change the path, which at times follows the upper irrigation channel; be careful on some of the more precipitous corners, always follow the easiest route and keep as high above the river as possible. The last section of the walk is the easiest, with some more Inca terraces at **Moyu Orqo**, open meadows (good for picnicking) and a few rustic dwellings. Ninety minutes or so from Chacan, you'll come to the bottom of the Saphi gully and see the *consejo*'s garbage-truck yard, on the other side of the river. Another ten minutes and you're on Calle Saphi, leading up to Plaza de Armas. It's possible to do the route in reverse, but it is quite an arduous climb from the top end of Calle Saphi.

Puca Pucara

Although a relatively small ruin, **PUCA PUCARA** (daily 7am–5.30pm; entry by Cusco Tourist Ticket, see p.112), meaning "Red Fort", is around 11km from the city, impressively situated overlooking the Cusco valley and right beside the main Cusco–Pisac road. Between one and two hour's cross-country walk, uphill from Sacsayhuaman and Qenko (longer if you keep to the sinuous main road), this area is dotted with cut rocks. The zone was well populated in Inca days, and many of these may have been worked to obtain stones for building.

Although in many ways reminiscent of a small European castle, Puca Pucara is more likely to have been a hunting lodge, or out of town lodgings (a *tambo*, as the Incas would have called this) for the emperor than simply a defensive position. Thought to have been built by the Emperor Pachacutec, it commands views towards glaciers to the south of the Cusco valley. Although easily defended on three sides it could have contained only a relatively small garrison and may have been a guard post between Cusco and the Sacred Valley, which lies to the northeast; it may also have had a sacred function, as it has excellent views towards the Apu of Ausungate – a good example of how the Incas tended to combine comfort and recreation for the elite with social control and military defence. Its semicircle of protective wall is topped by a commanding esplanade, while on the lower levels there are a number of stone-walled chambers; you can still make out the ducts that distributed fresh water from a nearby spring.

Tambo Machay

TAMBO MACHAY (daily 7am–5.30pm; entry by Cusco Tourist Ticket, see p.112), less than fifteen minutes' walk away along a signposted track that leads off the main road just beyond Puca Pucara, is one of the more impressive Inca baths. Situated at a spring near the Inca's hunting lodge, its main construction lies in a sheltered gully where some superb Inca masonry again emphasizes the Inca fascination with, and adoration of, water.

The ruins basically consist of three tiered platforms. The top one holds four trapezoidal niches that were probably used as seats; on the next level, underground water emerges directly from a hole at the base of the stonework, and from here cascades down to the bottom platform, creating a cold shower just about high enough for an Inca to stand under. On this platform the spring water splits into two channels, both pouring the last metre down to ground level. Clearly a site for ritual bathing, the quality of the stonework suggests that its use was restricted to the higher nobility, who perhaps used the baths only on ceremonial occasions.

About 1km further up the gully, you'll come to a small **grotto** where there's a pool large enough for bathing, even in the dry season. Whilst it shows no sign of Inca stonework, the hills on either side of the stream are dotted with stone terraces and caves, one or two of which still have remnants of walls at their entrance. In Inca, *machay* means "cave", suggesting that these were an important local feature, perhaps as sources of water for Tambo Machay and Puca Pucara. Follow the gully up beyond the grotto for another twenty to thirty minutes, past the point where Puca Pucara can be seen poking its head over the horizon, and you come to the boggy source of the present stream. From here there's a pleasant walk back to the road and Puca Pucara.

Eating and drinking

Generally speaking, **eating out** in Cusco is an enjoyable and important part of the city's nightlife, but the food itself is not quite as interesting or as varied as on the coast or in Lima, though there are one or two exceptions. The city prides itself on its traditional foods, and while you'll find it easier to get pizza than roast guinea pig, the more central **cafés and restaurants** accommodate most tastes, serving anything from a toasted cheese sandwich to authentic Andean or *criolla* dishes (a Peruvian form of Creole). The most popular area for restaurants and bars is around the **Plaza de Armas** and along *calles* **Plateros** and **Procuradores**, home to several decent, cheap cafés and a few decent restaurants. The trendy San Blas *barrio* has two excellent restaraunts – *Pacha Papa* and *Greens* – offering something different to the more conventional cuisine found in most places, and there are several vegetarian joints in town. If you're **self-catering**, the Central Market by San Pedro train station sells a wonderful variety of colourful produce including all the usual meats, tropical and imported fruits, local vegetables, Andean cheeses and other basics. The market also has a wide range of daytime hot-food stalls where you can get **takeaway** food (if you have a container to put it in) or eat on the spot.

Cafés and snack bars

Bagdad Café, Portal de Carnes 216, Plaza de Armas. Next to and above *La Yunta*, a popular location not least because it has tables on a colonial balcony overlooking the plaza. Serves good pizzas, breakfasts, sandwiches, some pasta dishes and cool drinks.

Café Allyu, Portal de Carnes 208, Plaza de Armas. Serves one of the best breakfasts in Peru, including fruit, yoghurt and toasted sandwiches, though it's not cheap. Centrally located with downstairs views across the plaza, it's Cusco's most traditional meeting place and the service is fast.

Ethnic Café Bar, Calle Tecsacocha 458. A newish, very trendy place, this smart café serves drinks, cocktails, *piqueos* and delicious cakes. A good meeting place.

Le Paris Snack Bar, Calle Medio 103, corner of Calle Medio and Plaza de Armas. A small, no-frills café with good, fast service with a smile, fairly inexpensive breakfasts and decent enough ice creams.

La Tertulia Café Cultural, Calle Procuradores 50. An interesting travellers' hangout in Cusco's heartland passage, it has a good book exchange, great snacks, some board games and sometimes plays music or presents theatre.

Trotamundos, Portal de Comercio 177, Plaza de Armas. An Internet café that's better known for serving good food and drinks. The Internet section is partitioned off from the café, which has views over the plaza, a good noticeboard, a stove-fire and games.

Varayoc, Calle Espaderos 142. A welcoming *café literario* with a strong Andean intellectual atmosphere. It's okay for snacks, and has a magazine rack and several tables where students, tourists and locals mingle, generally sipping hot chocolate, *pisco* or *mate de coca* (coca-leaf tea – highly recommended for altitude sickness).

La Yunta, Portal de Carnes 214, Plaza de Armas. A groovy eating house right on the plaza, specializing in pizza but also offering large, good-value salads, soups, omelettes, fish, french fries and excellent juices and jugs of *limonada*. Perfect for lunch or supper and a popular meeting place for adventure tour guides in the early evening.

Restaurants

Cusco **restaurants** range from the cheap and cheerful to top quality. Many serve international cuisine but the *quintas*, basic local eating houses, serve mostly traditional **Peruvian food**, full of spice and character in a typical Cusco ambience, though *Pacha Pacha* offers a more refined approach. Generally speaking, trout is plentiful, reasonably priced and usually excellent and roast guinea pig (*cuy*) can usually be ordered, but **pizza** seems to lead in the popularity stakes. This isn't a region particularly noted for its **beef**, but there are a few places serving steaks, and **British** and **oriental** cooking can be found, the latter in some fairly average *chifas*, and one very good **curry** house – *El Grano*. Unless otherwise stated, most restaurants open daily at around 11am and serve until 10.30pm–midnight.

Budget

Cafetería Huaylliy, Plateros 363. Uninspiring décor but some of the best-value breakfasts in Cusco, plus pizzas, *chifa* meals and cakes.

Kaleydaskop Vegetarian Café, Portal de Panes 167 and Triunfo 393 (☎221187). Good vegetarian meals and snacks, with esoteric books on sale, mainly promoting the mystic side of Cusco. The Triunfo branch is the nicer of the two.

Mia Pizza, Procuradores 379, is one of the better places for pizzas and other Italian dishes in this busy alley.

Restaurant Govinda, Calle Espaderos 128. The original vegetarian eating house in Cusco, serving simple healthy food, brilliant fruit-and-yoghurt breakfasts and good-value set lunches. If you get the chance, eat upstairs where there's more atmosphere and more room. Daily 8.30am–7pm

Restaurant Kusikuy, Calle Plateros 354. Increasingly popular with travellers and adventure tour guides, it serves a good set menu at a reasonable price.

Restaurant Mamala, Choquechaca 509 (☎246090). Exceptionally good and very cheap set lunches in a nice ambience, conveniently located between San Blas and the Plaza de Armas.

Restaurant Vegetariano "La Waki de Cristal", Choquechaka 132. A small place with good, wholesome vegetarian snacks and set meals, plus a friendly atmosphere with rainbows and crystals over the doorway.

Restaurant Victor Victoria, corner of Tigre and Teqsecocha. A basic eating house with good, inexpensive set menus, very popular with budget travellers at both lunch and supper. Daily 8am–8pm.

Moderate

Gran Chifa Kam Lung/El Dragon San, Portal Belen 215. A small Chinese restaurant overlooking the Plaza de Armas with good food and service; try the delicious *Kamlu Wantan*, crispy meatballs in a tamarind sauce.

El Grano, Santa Catalina 398 (☎228032). A friendly place serving delicious Asian lunches and suppers, including superb curries, in a pleasant, civilized ambience. They have particularly good deals on set lunch menus (for example, soup and main course for $2).

Pacha Papa, Plaza San Blas 120 (☎233190). A great, inexpensive restaurant set around an attractive courtyard, serving a range of hard-to-find Andean dishes, from a *Gulash de Alpaca* to the highly nutritious *Sopa de Quinoa*. Reservations recommended.

Pucara Restaurant, Calle Plateros 309 (☎222027). A pleasant restaurant, popular with tourists, offering inexpensive set menus, fine salads and well prepared Peruvian cuisine. There's occasional music in the evenings.

Roma Restaurant, Portal de Panes 105 (☎245041). On a busy corner of Plaza de Armas, with Inca stones from the Inca Pachacuti's palace lining the walls. With folklore shows at weekends and evenings, it's worth the extra few soles.

Rosie O'Grady's, Santa Catalina 360 (☎247935). A swish Irish pub and restaurant, serving good beer and even better full meals. The beef steak is among the best in Peru but it has a much wider range, including burgers and snacks.

The Quinta Eulalia, Calle Choquechaca 384 (☎241380). One of the very best and most traditional local eating houses, in a backstreet a few blocks above the Plaza de Armas. Plays fine *criolla* music and is good for *cuy chactado*, (guinea pig fried with potatoes, *tamales* and *rocoto*).

The Quinta Zarate, Totorapaqcha 763 (☎245114). Excellent traditional food and atmosphere, close to the San Blas plazoleta, though it's difficult to find without a taxi.

Expensive

La Estancia Imperial, second floor, Portal de Panes 177 (☎224621). Situated on the Plaza de Armas and specializing in pizzas and chickens, it's worth trying if you can get a table with a view.

Greens, Tandapata 700 (☎651323). British-run restaurant with a very good reputation for Sunday roasts among other excellent dishes, and a very pleasant environment. Reservations are advised.

El Meson de Espaderos, second floor, Calle Espaderos 105 (☎235307). Overlooking the Plaza de Armas and specializing in steaks, grills and *cuy* (traditionally cooked guinea pig).

Pizzeria and Restaurant Machu Picchu, Portal de Escribanos 169, Plaza Regocijo. Upmarket but moderately priced, serving decent pizzas and excellent trout.

Restaurant El Truco, Plaza Regocijo 261 (☎232441). Delicious but expensive traditional Cusco food in one of the city's flashiest restaurants, with fine beef and fish dishes. Music and Andean folk dancing is usually performed during the evenings.

Restaurant Paititi, Portal Carrizos 270, Plaza de Armas (☎252686). Serving both national and international cuisine, this restaurant is open from breakfast and often has folklore shows in the afternoons and evenings.

La Trattoria Adriano, Calle Mantas 105, corner of Avenida Sol (☎233965). Excellent for pasta and wine.

Nightlife and entertainment

Apart from Lima, no Peruvian town has as varied a **nightlife** as Cusco. The corner of Plaza de Armas, where Calle Plateros begins, is a hive of activity until the early hours, even during the week. Most nightspots in the city are simply **bars** with a dance floor and sometimes a stage, but their styles vary enormously, from Andean folk joints with panpipe music through to reggae or jazz joints, and more conventional **clubs**. Most places are within staggering distance of each other, and sampling them is an important part of any stay in Cusco. Many open around 9pm and keep going until 2 or 3am, so it shouldn't be too difficult to manage.

During any of the major **fiestas** (see p.107) you will encounter colourfuly costumed dance groups in the streets, but there few other opportunities to see **folk dancing** beyond the occasional show at a few of the large hotels and more expensive restaurants. Only two groups offer regular performances: Dance Performances, at the Centro Qosqo de Arte Nativo, Avenida Sol 612 (☎227901; 6–10pm); and **Dance Workshops**, at Taller de Danza, Calle Loreto 208 (information from the wooden kiosk at the bottom end of the craft market hidden away at the same location), covering a wide range of Andean and Coastal Peruvian dance steps including Marinera, Tondero, Afro, Cumbia and Huaylas). They're both good and both charge around $5; tickets can be bought on the door or in advance from the venues or from sellers in and around the Plaza de Armas.

Pubs and bars

The Corner Pub, Procuradores 320. Just off the Plaza de Armas, this is very popular with young locals at weekends and plays loud music until late. Can be a bit rough.

The Cross Keys Pub, first floor, Portal Confituras 233. One of the hubs of Cusco's nightlife, this classic drinking dive has the feel of a London pub, with good music, soccer scarves adorning the walls and pool tables. Food is available and there are often English-language newspapers and magazines.

Norton Rats Tavern, second floor, Calle Loreto 115. Just off the Plaza de Armas, with great views over the square, by Iglesia La Compañia. Best known as a drinking establishment it plays rock, blues, jazz and Latin music and has a dartboard. There's also a café serving grills.

Paddy Flaherty's Irish Pub, Calle Triunfo 124 (☎246903). Looking much like a British pub, though its wood-panelled wallls are spattered with Irish artefacts. The atmosphere is pleasant and gets particularly lively at weekends, when they often have live Irish music. Serves Guinness.

Los Perros, Teqsecocha 436. Billing itself as "the original couch bar", *Los Perros* is a trendy hangout where travellers snack, drink and play board games or read from the wide-ranging library and magazines (books can be part-exchanged – give two, take one). There's often jazz music at weekends.

Rosie O'Grady's, Santa Catalina 360 (☎247935). A spacious, tasteful Irish Pub with a range of beers, Guinness included. There's great live music on Thursdays and Fridays, plus a popular Friday evening "boat race" drinking competition.

Clubs and dance bars

KamiKase Bar, Portal Cabildo 274, Plaza Regocijo. One of Cusco's best established nightspots, with modern Andean rock-art decor and basic furnishings. Drinks are quite cheap, though when it hosts live music (most weekends), there's usually a small entrance fee, but it's worthwhile if you're into rock and Andean folk. Happy hour 8.30–9.30pm; live music usually starts around 10pm.

Kerara Discotek, Espaderos 135. A small dance bar with an occasional small entrance fee. The music's pretty good and ranges from rock, Latin and disco to trance, but it can't quite match the atmosphere of most other clubs. Daily 9pm–3am.

Keros Bar-Disco, Procuradores 50. A small club blasting mainly Latino sounds out across the Plaza de Armas every weekend. Its redeeming features are an energetic dance floor, its central position and that it's usually free. Happy Hour 7–10pm. Daily 9.30pm–2am.

Mama Africa, Espaderos 135. A good dance bar with a small entrance fee, popular with an under-thirties crowd of locals and gringos. Drinks are a bit pricey, but they also do food. The music, including reggae, is pretty loud. Daily 9pm–2am, plus it often shows a video at 4.30pm.

El Muki Disco, Santa Catalina Angosta 114 (☎227797). Near the Plaza de Armas, *El Muki* has been pumping out pop every night for over twenty years. With its atmospheric catacomb-like dance floors, it's a traditional, safe space for late-night bopping, charging $2 entrance.

OZ, Santa Catalina Ancha 377. Just over the road from *Rosie O'Grady's* pub, this club has lavish interior décor but somehow lacks the local atmosphere of many other nightspots.

Ukuku's Pub, Calle Plateros 316, down the alley and upstairs. A highly popular venue with one of the best atmospheres in Cusco, thronging with energetic revellers most nights by around 11pm, when the live music gets going. There's a small dance floor and a long bar, with music ranging from live Andean folk with panpipes, drums and *charangos* (small Andean stringed instruments) to taped rock. There's often an entrance charge – usually less than $1.50 – and happy hour lasts from 8pm to 9.35pm and thirty seconds. Daily 7.30pm–2am, plus large-screen movies most afternoons.

UP TOWN, Suecia 302. Easy to spot at weekends thanks to the crowds outside, this is easily the best vibe in Cusco clubland, where local youth meets eurobeat and both keep going virtually all night. Some nights with a strong Latino emphasis. There's a good bar and drinks are inexpensive. Happy Hour 9–10pm & 11–11.30pm

Xcess, Portal de Carnes 298 (☎240901). One of Cusco's most popular dance bars with great décor and lighting, playing a wide range of music, from Latin pop to reggae. Free drinks 10–11.30pm with the pass handed out on the street outside.

Shopping

The main concentration of touristy *artesania* and jewellery **shops** is in the streets around the Plaza de Armas and up Triunfo, though Calle San Agustin (first right off Triunfo as you head towards San Blas), has slightly cheaper but decent shops with leather and alpaca work. It's worth heading off the beaten track to find outlets hidden in the backstreets, and even in the smarter shops, it's quite acceptable to bargain a little. In the markets and at street stalls you can often get up to twenty percent off.

Cusco **opening hours** are generally Monday to Saturday 10am to 6pm, though some of the central gift stores open on Sundays and don't close until well into the evening. If you're worried about being robbed while making a substantial purchase, it's fine to ask the shopkeeper to bring the goods to your hotel so that the transaction can take place in relative safety. However, robberies of this sort are much rarer now than they were during the early 1990s.

Camera equipment

Agfa Foto, Heladeros 172. A small range of films.

Foto Nishiyama, Mantas 109 and Triunfo 346. Both branches stock a wide range of Kodak films as well as other brands and offer good-quality film developing and processing, plus some camera equipment.

Kodak Express, Avenida Sol 180. Sells and develops film.

Camping equipment

Rental or purchase of **camping equipment** is easy in Cusco, but if renting you may be asked to leave your passport as a deposit on more expensive items; always get a proper receipt. For basics such as such as pots, pans, plates and so on, try the stalls in Monjaspata, les than half a block from bottom end of San Pedro market, while others such as buckets, bowls and sheets are sold in various shops along Calle Concebidayoq, close to the San Pedro market area.

Alpaca del Inka, Portal de Confiturias/Comercio 181. Stoves, flashlights, gas and so on.

Expediciones Vilca, see p.137.

Gregory's Tours, Portal Comercio 177. Tents, sleeping bags, bed mats, stoves and gas to rent.

Inkas Trek, Calle Medio 114. All the gear you'll need, and all available to rent.

Killak Sur, Calle Medio 120. A good choice of equipment, plus they change dollars.

Soqllaq'asa Camping Service, Plateros 359 (☎252560). A decent selection of camping equipment, some for rental.

Crafts, artesania and jewellery

Crafts and **artesania** are Cusco's stock in trade, with the best alpaca clothing outside Lima. It's an ideal place to pick up woollen sweaters, ponchos, jackets, weavings or antique cloths, while inexpensive and traditional musical instruments like panpipes, and colourful bags and leather crafts are also common. The unnamed artesans' market in the road running parallel with Santa Clara in the San Pedro district is particularly good value, especially if you bargain. There's also a more central and safer *artesania* market on the right-hand side going up block 1 of Plateros from the Plaza de Armas, and higher up in Calle Saphi there's an *artesania* market area more or less opposite the *Hostal Familiar*. San Blas is home to a number of **jewellers**, art and antique shops, while Hathun Rumiyoq has a few *artesania* shops at its bottom end.

Alpaca 3, Ruinas 472. Good alpaca fabrics, yarns, sweaters and scarves.

Alpaca Golden, Portal de Panes 151, Plaza de Armas. Alpaca sweaters and a range of other well-made items.

Andean Music Museum, Hathun Rumiyoq 487. An interesting range of traditional instruments – *charangos, quenas*, panpipes and drums – plus sheet music and a good selection on books; they also have traditional music workshops on Fridays at around 7pm.

Arte Inkari, Choquechaka 138. A good range of traditional Andean costumes, hats and weavings from the Cusco area, plus some antiques.

Feria Artesanal El Inka, corner of San Andraes and Quera 218. A small but bursting *artesania* market within a stone's throw of Avenida Sol and only a few blocks from the main plaza. Good bargains available, particularly for textiles and ponchos.

Joyeria Oropesa, Portal de Carrizos, corner of Calle Loreto. Jewellery for the seriously wealthy, specializing in silverwork.

Galeria Olave, Calle Plazoleta 651. A superb craft workshop which produces replica religious art and traditional Cusco cabinets and furniture.

La Mamita, Portal de Carnes 244. This excellent shop is an outlet for the Cusco region's more progressive and stylish *artisania*, such as the ceramics of Pablo Seminario (see p.144), basketry, batiks, jewellery and cottonwear.

Manos Magicos, San Blas Plazoleta. Traditional pre-Conquest silver-working techniques combined with local and imported gem stones, inspired by dreamworld imager. Pricey but of phenomenal quality.

Pedazo Arte, Plateros 334b. Stockist of new handicrafts all handmade and of good quality.

Taller de Instrumentos, Hathun Rumiyoq 451 (head through the back to the second patio). Rustic workshop (no entry charge) producing *charangos, quenas* and panpipes, often to professional standards.

Tienda Museo, Calle Plateros 334 and Santa Clara 501. Alpaca and sheep's wool textiles. Their mantas, ponchos and other items are of excellent quality.

Food

Central Market, San Pedro. The best place for generally excellent and very cheap food, provided you feel comfortable with a street-stall standard of hygiene.

El Chinito Grande, Matara 271, a large Chinese-run supermarket with good prices and stocks.

El Croissant, Plaza San Francisco 134. Good French baking.

The Delicatessen, Calle Medio 110. Just off the Plaza de Armas, with a great range of cheeses, wines and dried fruits.

Gato's Market, Santa Catalina Angosta, corner of Plaza de Armas and close to the Cathedral. A good range of typical foods.

Granja Heidi, in the lobby of the *Hostal Colonial*, Matará 288. Delicious organic bioyoghurt and muesli.

El Pepito's, Plaza San Francisco 158. Sweets and chocolates.

Supermercado el Chinito, Avenida Sol 210. General groceries.

The Supermarket, Calle Plateros 346. Small and packed to the gills with food for trekking expeditions – cheese, biscuits, tins of tuna, nuts, chocolate, raisins and dried bananas.

Tierra Atlas, Plaza Nazarenas 211. Natural food products grown at the *Hacienda Yaravilca* (see p.143), in the Urubamba Valley, as part of an effort to cultivate crops and foodstuffs that have disappeared from Peruvian kitchens over the centuries. There are interesting displays on their work.

Newspapers, books, music and videos

New World News, an excellent weekly **English-language newspaper** costing under $1, is available from bookstores and street sellers around Cusco. If you've finished with any books and want to try something new, **book exchange** is available at a number of places, including the *La Tertulia Café Cultural* (see p.129), the South American Explorers Club (see p.136) and *Los Perros* (see p.132).

Agfa Foto, Heladeros 172. A few videos and cassettes amongst the camera films.

Libraria Los Andes, Portal Comercio 125, Plaza de Armas. A good bookshop on Plaza de Armas, with a fair selection of English- and Spanish-language books on Peru and the Cusco region.

El Mini Shop, Portal Confituria 217, Plaza de Armas. Friendly, central and well stocked with interesting guides and history books about Cusco, the Incas and Peru, including ones in English. It also sells educational videos and the cheapest postcards in town.

Music Centre, Avenida Sol 230. The best range of Andean and Peruvian cassettes and CDs in Cusco.

Listings

Airlines Aero Condor, Avendia Sol 789a (☎225000, 252774 or 624005, fax 223393); Aero Continente, Portal de Carnes 245, Plaza de Armas (☎235666, 243031 or 263978, fax 235660, *www.aerocontinente.com.pe*); Helicusco, Calle Triunfo 379 (☎243635, fax 227283, *dfhi@amauta.rcp.net.pe*, *www.rcp.net.pe/HELICUSCO*); Imperial Air, corner of Garcilaso and Plaza San Francisco (☎238000, fax 238877); Lloyd Aereo Boliviano, Avenida Pardo 675b (☎229220); Lan Peru (and Lan Chile), Avenida Sol 620 (☎255552 or 255553), and at the airport (☎255550); TANS, Avenida Sol 565 (☎246513 or 282817). Departure tax is $10 for international departures, $4 for domestic flights.

American Express Lima Tours, Avenida Machu Picchu D-6, Urbina. Manuel Prado (☎228431 or 235241).

Banks and exchange Banco de la Nacion, corner of Avenida Sol and Almagro; Banco de Creditio, Avenida Sol 189; Banco Continental, Avenida Sol 366, change cash and most traveller's cheques; Banco del Sur, Avenida Sol 457, has an external 24hr ATM accepting Visa and Mastercard; Banco Wiese, Jirón Maruri 315–341. There's Mastercard machine outside the *El Dorado Inn*. For faster service and better rates than banks, try Cambio Cusco, Portal Comercio 177, Oficina B (☎238861; daily 9am–10pm) one of the better and more central money changing offices; Casa de Cambio, Oficina 1, Avenida Sol 345, is also good. Lastly, street *cambistas* can be found on blocks 2 and 3 of Avenida Sol, around the main banks.

Bus companies Inter-regional and international buses depart from Terminal Terrestre, except for those run by Cruz del Sur, who leave from Avenida Pachacutec. There is an embarkation tax of $0.3, which you pay before alighting. Recommended operators include: CIVA for Puno and Arequipa; El Chasqui (☎252994) for Arequipa, Tacna and Lima; Cruz del Sur (☎221909 or 233383) for Arequipa and Desaguadero; Expresso Wari (☎261703) for Lima via Abancay and Nazca; Libertad (☎247174) for Juliaca, Puno and Copacabana/La Paz; Ormeño (☎233469) for Espinar, Tintaya, Arequipa, Lima, Copacabana and La Paz; Power (☎246515) for Juliaca and Puno; San Jeronimo (☎261142) for Andahuaylas and Ayacucho; Tours Wari (☎229717) for Puno, Abancay, Nazca and Lima; Trans International Litoral for La Paz; Trans Turismo Colca, for Sicuani and Arequipa; Transportes Pardo for Arequipa and Lima; Tranzela (☎238223) for Puno, Copacabana and La Paz; Turismo Abancay for Abancay; Turismo Ampay (☎227541) for Abancay and Quillabamba; and Urkupiña (☎229962) for Juliaca and Puno.

Cinemas Amauta, Avenida de la Cultura 764 (☎226431); Garcilaso, Union 117 (☎232461); Ollanta, Meloc 417 (☎224052); and Vicoria, Huayruropata 931 (☎233271).

Consulates Bolivia, Avenida Pardo, Pasaje Espinar (☎231412); UK, Avenida Pardo 895 (☎239974); for the USA contact the Instituto de Cultura Peruana Norte Americana, Avenida Tullumayo 125 (☎224112, 222183 or 233541).

Courier services DIIL, Avenida Sol 393 (☎244167).

Cultural centre The Alliance Française, Avenida de la Cultura 804 (☎223755), runs a full programme of events including music, films, exhibitions, theatre and music; phone for details.

Customs office Calle Teatro 344 (☎228181).

Dentists Dr Virginia Valcarcel Velarde, upstairs at Portal de Panes 123, Plaza de Armas (☎231558); and Dr Pintur, Centro Comercial Santa Cecilia, by the Sandy Color Fotografia, Avenida Sol (☎233721 or 651211).

Diners Club Avenida Sol 615 (☎234051 & 236890).

Doctors Dr Oscar Tejada (☎233836, 24hr) is a member of International Assistance for Medical Assistance to Travellers; Dr Dante Valdivia (☎231390, 620588 or 252166), speaks English and German; and Dr Maria Helena (☎650122 or 227385) will visit.

Hospitals and clinics Hospital Regional, Avenida de la Cultura (☎231131); Clinica Pardo, Avenida de la Cultura 710 (☎240387 or 620126), which runs a 24hr service, with some English spoken; Hospital Antonio Lorena, Plaza de Belen (☎226511); and Clinica Laboratorio Louis Pasteur, Tullumayo 768 (☎234727), which has a gynaecologist. For 24hr emergency treatment, try Tourist Medical Assistance, or TMA (☎621838), or Medic Fast (☎688154, 252854 or 273155).

Internet facilities Red Cientifica Peruana INTERNET PERU, upstairs at Portal Comercio 141 (☎229481 or 680354, *rumichip@antara.rcp.net.pe*) has Internet access, Internet phone calls and video conferencing, and they offer a monthly membership (about $10) that gives cheaper rates; Kafe Internet, Plateros 361 (*kfe@latinmail.com*); Internet Station Speed X, Tecsecocha 400, is central, cheap and has a rapid connection; Telser, Calle Medio 125, also has a good link. Expect to pay around $1 an hour for logging on at all places.

Language schools AMAUTA, La Tertulia, second floor, Calle Procuradores 50 (☎ & fax 241422, *amauta@mail.cosapidata.com.pe, www.telser.com.pe/amauta*), offer intensive 8hr Spanish courses. Staff also speak English, French, German and offer combined accommodation and language courses at the *Casa de Campo* (see p.114).

Laundry Ña P'asña, Saphi 578a. Fairly cheap and efficient, with self-service also available; T'Aqsana Wasi, Santa Catalina Ancha 345; and Laundry, Tecsacocha 428.

Post office The main office, at Avenida Sol 800 (☎225232), operates a quick and reliable poste restante system. Mon–Sat 7.30am–8pm, Sun 7.45am–2.30pm.

South American Explorers' Club Avenida Sol 930 (☎223102). Good information sheets, trip reports and files on virtually everything about Cusco and Peru, including transport, trekking, hotels, Internet cafés and tour companies. The excellent clubhouse has a luggage deposit, noticeboard, library and book exchange. Mon–Fri 9.30am–5pm.

Telephones Telefonica del Peru, Avenida del Sol 382; and Telser, Calle Medio 117 (☎242222).

Tourist Police Portal de Belen 115, Plaza de Armas (☎221961 or 223626).

Tourist Protection Service Servicio de Protecion al Turista, Portal de Carrizos 250, Plaza de Armas (Mon–Fri 8am–8pm; ☎ & fax 252974).

Train tickets The Huanchaq station ticket office (Mon–Fri 7am–noon & 2–5pm, Sat 7am–noon, Sun 8–10am; ☎221931 or 221992 for information) sells Puno and Arequipa tickets. For Machu Picchu it's possible to buy tickets from the Peru Rail office in the yard at Huanchaq station (8am–6pm) or from San Pedro station (5–7am & 3–4pm; ☎238722 for reservations and sales).

Vaccinations Cusco Regional Hospital offers free yellow fever inoculations on Sat from 11am to 1pm.

Visas Migraciones, Avenida Sol, 620 (☎222741). Mon–Fri 9am–5pm.

Western Union Santa Catalina Ancha 311 (☎233727); and at Calle Medio 117 (☎242222).

Tours in and around Cusco

Tours in and around Cusco range from a half-day city tour to an expedition by light aircraft or a full-on adventure down to the Amazon. **Prices** range from $20 to over $100 a day, and service and facilities vary considerably, so check exactly what's provided, whether insurance is included and whether the guide speaks English. The main agents are strung along three sides of the Plaza de Armas, along Portal de Panes, Portal de Confiturias and Portal Comercio, up Procuradores and along the *calles* Plateros and Saphi and, although prices vary, many are selling places on the same tours and treks, so always hunt around. Avoid the **tour touts** at the airport or in the plaza at Cusco, and check out the operators in advance at the South American Explorers' Club (see above) if you're able to (members also receive a discount with some outfits). There are also a few Lima-based operators in and around Cusco, and they are listed opposite.

Standard tours around the city, Sacred Valley and to Machu Picchu range from a basic bus service with fixed stops and little in the way of a guide, to a luxury packages including guide, food and hotel transfers. The three- to six-day Inca Trail is the most popular of the **mountain treks**, with thousands of people hiking it every year; many agencies offer trips with guides, equipment and fixed itineraries, but others will just rent you a tent and sleeping bag. Other popular hikes are around the snow-capped mountains of Salcantay (6264m) to the north and Ausungate (6372m) to the south, a more remote trek which needs at least a week plus guides and mules. Less adventurous **walks** or **horse rides** are possible to Qenko, Tambo Machay, Puca Pucara and Chacan, in the hills above Cusco and in the nearby Sacred Valley. You can also rent out **mountain bikes** for trips to the Sacred Valley and around, and some outfits arrange guided tours (or contact Renny Gamarra Loaiza, a good biking guide; ☎231300). Many **jungle trip** operators are based in Cusco, and those that also cover the immediate Cusco area are listed below as well as in Chapter Six (see p.377–380 and p.386–387), where their jungle-specific trips are detailed.

Cusco is also a great **whitewater rafting** centre, with easy access to classes two to five around Ollantaytambo on the Río Urubamba and classes one to three between Huambutio and Pisac, on the Río Vilcanota. From Calca to Urubamba the river runs classes two to three, but this rises to five in the rainy season. Calca to Pisac (Huaran) and Ollantaytambo to Chilca are among the most popular routes, while the most dangerous are further afield on the Río Apurimac. The easiest stretch is from Echarate to San Baray, which passes by Quillabamba. Remember that most travel insurances exclude this kind of adventure activity and always ensure that you are fully equipped with a safety kayak, helmets, and lifejackets.

Cusco tour operators

Apumayo, Calle Garcilaso 265, Oficina 3, Cusco (☎246018, *apumayo@mail.cosapidata.com.pe*). Expert operators offering trekking in the Sacred Valley region, mountain biking around Cusco and the Sacred Valley, historic and archeological tours, tours for disabled people (with wheelchair support for visiting major sites), horse-riding, and rafting on the ríos Urubamba and Apurimac. They can customize their trips to suit your agenda, though note that they usually only work with pre-booked groups.

Chaparral Ranch, Urbino Balconcillo Altok-10 (☎241474; 6–9am & 7–10pm for reservations). Very reasonably priced specialists in horse-riding tours to Qenko, Salampunco, Puca Pucara and Tambo Machay.

Eco Tourism Ch'aska, Calle Garcilaso 265, Cusco (☎240424, *chaskaet@telser.com.pe*). Environmentally and socially aware trail-blazing tours in the Cordillera Urubamba, with an emphasis on archaeology and local culture.

Ecomontana, Calle Garcilaso 265, Oficina 3, Cusco. A professional company with good guides and thirty different mountain bike tours.

Eric Adventures, Plateros 324, Cusco (☎232244, fax 239772, *ericadv@cosapidata.com.pe, www. cuscoonline.com/ericadv*). A good selection of tours, from the Inca Trail to trekking, and with a good reputation for rafting.

Expediciones Vilca, Amargura 101 (☎ & fax 251872, *manuvilca@protelsa.com.pe*), and Plateros 363 (☎244751). A well established trekking company with a variety of treks but they specialize in expeditions to Manu (see p.386). They can rent you any camping gear you need.

Explorandes, Avenida Garcilazo 316-A, Wanchaq (☎238380, fax 233784, *postmast@explorandes. com.pe*); or San Fernando 320, Miraflores, Lima (☎01/445-0532 or 445-8683, fax 445-4686). A long-established company with a range of tours and treks, including the Inca Trail, Cordillera Vilcanota (looping around the peaks of Ausungate and Colquecruz). For their jungle rafting expeditions, see p.379.

Inca Explorers, Calle Suecia 339, Cusco (☎239669, fax 243736, *inqusa@qenco.rcp.net.pe*). A mid range trekking agency with a good reputation for the Inca trail. They have fixed departures on Monday, Tuesday and Thursday and offer a discount to South American Explorers' Club Members.

INSTINCT, Calle Procuradores 50, Cusco (☎238366, *instinct@protelsa.com.pe, www.rcp.net. pe/instinct*). A well-organized company offering rugged river-rafting, willing to tackle some difficult grades.

Kantu, Portal Carrizos 258, Plaza de Armas, Cusco (☎243673). Good for budget rafting, and prices include include food and somewhere to sleep overnight (usually a tent).

Loreto Tours, Calle Medio, Cusco. Particularly recommended for their one-day rafting outings.

Machu Picchu Tours, Portal Comercio 121, Cusco (☎221208, fax 223695). Reliable agent offering decent enough tours of Cusco city sites, as well as the usual Sacred Valley, Machu Picchu and Inca Trail trips.

MANU Aventuras Ecologicas, Portal Carnes 236, Cusco (☎ & fax 233498 or 225562). Jungle specialists (see p.386) but also offering mountain biking and whitewater rafting in the Sacred Valley and personal healing trips involving shamanism.

Manu Expeditions, Avenida Pardo 895, Cusco (☎226671, fax 236706, *Adventure@ ManuExpeditions.com*, *www.ManuExpeditions.com*). Although specialists in trips to Manu (see p.366), they organize other adventure tours, including to Espirito Pampa, the Inca site of Choquequirau through the Vilcabamba mountains, to Machu Picchu from Ollantaytambo via Anacachcocha and the Huyaanay peaks, and more traditional treks like the Inca Trail.

MANU Nature Tours, Avenida Sol 582, Cusco (☎224384, fax 234793, *postmaster@mnt.com.pe*). Good, nature-based adventure travel in the jungle (see p.387), plus longer tours, mountain biking, birdwatching and rafting.

MAYUC, Portal Confiturias 211, Cusco (☎ & fax 232666, *chando@mayuc.com*, *www.mayuc.com*). Highly reliable outfit with the experience to organize any tour or trek of your choice, from an extended Inca Trail to visiting the Tambopata-Candamo area and whitewater rafting.

Peru Expeditions, Avenida Arequipa 5241–504, Miraflores. Lima (☎01/447-2057, fax 445-9683, *peruexpe@amauta.rcp.net.pe*, *www.peru-expeditions.com*). Professional, helpful company specializing in environmentally sound adventure travel in the Cusco region, their leaders are experts in all kinds of adventure activities.

Peruvian Andean Treks, Avenida Pardo 705, Cusco (☎225701, fax 238911, *postmaster@patcusco. com.pe*). Expensive but top-quality options for the Inca Trail, plus treks in Cusco and the Peruvian Andes. Worth contacting in advance for their brochure.

Qosqo Mistic, Calle Procuradores 48, Cusco (☎ & fax 227455). Mystical tours based on the region's archeology, with the focus on Inca beliefs and Andean rituals, usually taking in major sites around town, the Sacred Valley and Machu Picchu.

United Mice, Calle Plateros 351, Cusco (☎ & fax 221139). The top specialists in guided tours of the Inca Trail and reasonably priced, with good guides, many speak of whom speak English. Food is of a high standard and their camping equipment is fine. If anything, their popularity is a drawback, since groups are largish in high season.

Viajes Horizonte, Calle San Jaun de Dios 283, Cusco (☎ & fax 222894). Well-established company offering reasonably priced city tours, airport connections, Machu Picchu visits and trips to the main jungle lodges around Puerto Maldonado. Good English and Italian spoken.

THE SACRED VALLEY AND MACHU PICCHU

The **Sacred Valley**, known as Vilcamayo to the Incas, traces its winding, astonishingly beautiful course to the northwest of Cusco. As a river valley it starts much further upstream to the south and also flows on right down into the jungle to merge with the

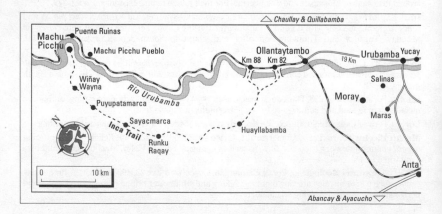

other major headwaters of the Amazon, but the section known as the Sacred Valley lies just between Pisac and Ollantaytambo. Standing guard over the two extremes of the Sacred Valley road, the ancient **Inca citadels** of Pisac and Ollantaytambo hang high above the stunning Río Vilcanota-Urubamba and are among the most evocative ruins in Peru.

Pisac itself is a small, pretty town with a Spanish gridded street plan just 30km from Cusco, close to the end of the Río Vilcanota's wild run from Urcos. It's easily visited in a morning, maybe checking out the market before taking a colectivo on to Ollantaytambo by lunchtime. Further downstream are the ancient villages of **Calca**, **Yucay** and **Urubamba**, the last of which has the most facilities for visitors plus a developing reputation as a spiritual and meditative centre, yet it retains its traditional Andean charm and has a bustling market and one or two good eating houses. At the far end of the Sacred Valley, the magnificent ancient town of **Ollantaytambo** is overwhelmed by the great temple-fortress clinging to the sheer cliffs beside it. It's a very pleasant place to spend some time, perhaps taking a tent and trekking off up one of the Urubamba's minor tributaries, or joining up with the Inca Trail for Machu Picchu.

Beyond Ollantaytambo the route becomes too tortuous for any road to follow, the valley closes in around the rail tracks, the Río Urubamba begins to race and twist below **Machu Picchu** itself, the most famous ruin in South America and a place that – no matter how jaded you are or how commercial it seems – is never a disappointment. If you're tempted to explore further afield, the bus journey to Chaullay is exciting, from where you can set out for the remote ruins of Vilcabamba – Vitcos and Espíritu Pampa – the legendary refuge of the last rebel Incas, set in superb hiking country. The main road itself however, continues to descend towards the jungle, following the presently defunct railway line to the tropical town of Quillabamba, springboard to the Amazon rainforest.

Getting to the Sacred Valley and Machu Picchu

The classic way to arrive at Machu Picchu is to do the three- to five-day **hike** along the stirring Inca Trail, which you can do independently or take one of the guided treks offered by the many operators in Cusco (see p.137). By road, you can follow the Sacred Valley only as far as Ollantaytambo, from where it cuts across the hills to Chaullay, just beyond Machu Picchu. A regular and cheap **minibus** service to Ollantaytambo picks up from the corner of Avenida Collasuyo and Calle Ejercito, a short walk down Recoleta from the heart of Cusco; there are plenty of pick-up points in Pisac, Calca and Urubamba.

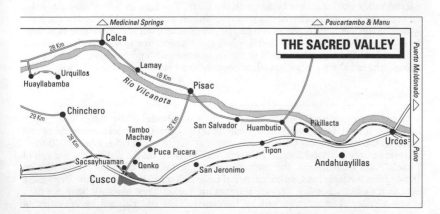

Of the **bus** companies, the best are Empresa Urubamba, departing from Inti Cahuarina 305, 200m from Koricancha just off Tullumayo, and going to Pisac and Urubamba every twenty minutes from dawn till dusk ($2); and Empresa Caminos del Inca, whose depot is at Avenida Huascar 128. **Taxis** to Pisac cost more – about $10 one way. Once you're in the Sacred Valley, hail one of the many cheap buses or colectivos that travel constantly up and down the main road. From Ollantaytambo, afternoon buses to Cusco ($2) leave regularly from the small yard just outside the railway station, often coinciding with the train timetable. In the mornings they mostly depart from Ollantaytambo's main plaza.

The **train** trip from Cusco is almost as spectacular as walking the Inca Trail, but buy your tickets well in advance (see Listings, p.136) as carriages are often fully booked in high season. There are four classes. Economico ($19 return), generally departing from San Pedro station, offers the lowest levels of service and is aimed at locals. Coche Inca ($85 return) and Autowagon ($55 return) offer better comfort than the Backpacker's Express ($30 return), which also stops at the Inca Trail starting point. These three tourist services depart from Huanchaq station at around 6am Monday to Saturday, from where it's just over ninety minutes to Ollantaytambo, then another ninety on to Maccu Pichu. In high season there may be another service laid on at 9am, leaving initially by bus from Huanchaq to Ollantaytambo and switching to the train there. An alternative (and just as dramatic) means of transport is to fly in **by helicopter**; Helicusco, Calle Triunfo 379 (☎243635, fax 227283, *dfhi@amauta.rcp.net.pe, www.rcp.net.pe/HELI-CUSCO*), offer the 25-minute flight there for $85 ($150 return). Fears have been voiced about detrimental effects large helicopters might have on both the stone fabric of the ancient site and its reputed mystical energies. However, they never venture nearer than a couple of kilometres from the most important Inca ruins.

Pisac

A vital Inca road once snaked its way up the canyon that enters the Sacred Valley at **PISAC**, and the ruined **citadel** which sits at the entrance to the gorge controlled a route connecting the Inca empire with Paucartambo, on the borders of the eastern jungle. Nowadays, less than an hour by bus from Cusco, the village is best known for its good Tuesday, Thursday and Sunday morning **market**, held on the town's main square, the Plaza Constitución, where you can buy hand-painted ceramic beads and pick up the occasional bargain. Even when the market's not on, there are still a number of excellent *artesania* shops, particularly along Calle Bolognesi, which connects the Sacred Valley road and river bridge with the plaza. The **Iglesia San Pedro Apostlo**, on the plaza, is an unusually narrow concrete church, rather overshadowed by the lovely nearby trees and the bustle of commerce going on in front of it. The main local **fiesta** – Virgen del Carmen (July 16–18) – is a good alternative to the simultaneous but more remote Paucartambo festival of the same name, with processions, music, dance groups, the usual fire-cracking celebrations, and food stalls around the plaza.

The citadel

It takes a good ninety minutes to climb directly to the **citadel** (daily 7am–5.30pm; entry by Cusco Tourist Ticket, see p.112), heading up through the agricultural terraces still in use at the back of Plaza Constitución. Alternatively, you can catch a bus ($0.2) from the end of Calle Mariscal Castilla (the road that leads off on the right at the top end of Pisac's Plaza Constitución, the market square), or take a taxi, colectivo or pick-up ($3–5) from the main road, on the corner of Calle Bolognesi and close to the Urubamba bridge; it's usually possible to share the cost on market days, when it's busy. Set high above a valley floor patchworked by patterned fields and rimmed by centuries of

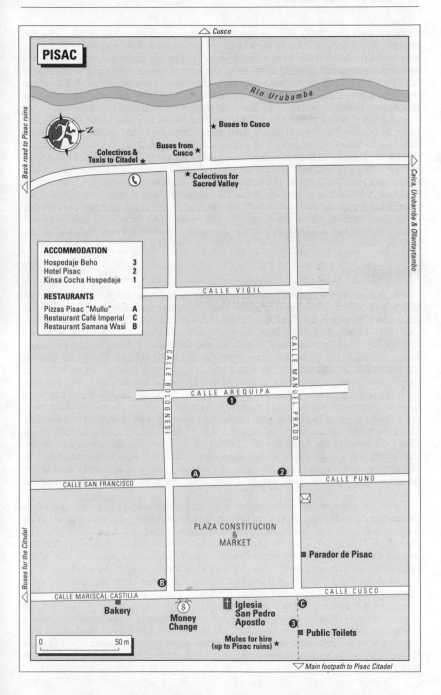

PISAC

△ *Cusco*

Río Urubamba

Back road to Pisac ruins

N

★ Buses to Cusco

Colectivos &
Taxis to Citadel ★

Buses from ★
Cusco

☎

★ Colectivos for
Sacred Valley

▷ Calca, Urubamba & Ollantaytambo

ACCOMMODATION

Hospedaje Beho   3
Hotel Pisac   2
Kinsa Cocha Hospedaje   1

RESTAURANTS

Pizzas Pisac "Mullu"   A
Restaurant Café Imperial   C
Restaurant Samana Wasi   B

CALLE VIGIL

CALLE BOLOGNESI

CALLE MANUEL PRADO

CALLE AREQUIPA

❶

Ⓐ   ❷

CALLE SAN FRANCISCO   CALLE PUNO

✉

Buses for the Citadel

PLAZA CONSTITUCION
&
MARKET

■ Parador de Pisac

Ⓑ

CALLE MARISCAL CASTILLA   CALLE CUSCO

Bakery   ($)   ✝ Iglesia   Ⓒ
                Money   San Pedro
                Change   Apostlo   ❸
                                             ■ Public Toilets
0   50 m   Mules for hire ★
                           (up to Pisac ruins)

▽ Main footpath to Pisac Citadel

terracing amid giant landslides, the stonework and panoramas at the citadel are magnificent. Water ducts and steps have been cut out of solid rock, and the citadel must have had channelled water from a much wider area of this upper mountain to irrigate so extensive a spread of agricultural land. On a large natural balcony, a semicircle of buildings is gracefully positioned under row upon row of fine stone terraces thought to represent a partridge's wing (*pisac* meaning "partridge"). The stonework of these huts is obviously post-Inca, but some of the walls contain striking trapezoidal niches.

In the upper sector of the ruins, the main **Temple of the Sun** is the equal of anything at Machu Picchu and more than repays the exertions of the steep climb. Reached by many of the dozens of paths that criss-cross their way up through the citadel, it's poised in a flattish saddle on a great spur protruding north-south into the Sacred Valley and was built around an outcrop of volcanic rock, its peak carved into a "hitching post" for the sun. The "hitching post" alone is intriguing: the angles of its base suggest that it may have been used for keeping track of important stars, or for calculating the changing seasons with the accuracy so critical to the smooth running of the Inca Empire. Above the temple lie still more ruins, largely unexcavated, and among the higher crevices and rocky overhangs several ancient burial sites are hidden.

Practicalities

The only time when accommodation may be hard to find is in September, when the village fills up with pilgrims heading to the nearby sanctuary of Huanca. The most luxurious **place to stay** is the *Hotel Royal Inca* (☎203064, fax 203067; ⑦), which has a pool and all mod cons, though it's 2km out of the village on the long road that winds up towards the ruins. In Pisac itself there's a good selection of places to stay and some pleasant restaurants. By far the most agreeable is the *Hotel Pisac*, Plaza Constitución 333 (☎203058; ③), with lavishly decorated bedrooms (with or without private bath) and there's also a rock-heated sauna, plus good breakfasts and lunches, including vegetarian food (available to non-residents). They also rent out mountain bikes and can book tours to nearby ruins and change money. Just off the plaza, the *Hospedaje Beho* (☎ & fax 203001; ②) has a large patio with rooms set around it, with or without private bath, plus a few more upstairs, and occasional hot water. Close to the plaza, the friendly *Kinsa Cocha Hospedaje*, Calle Areqiuipa 307 (☎203101; ①) offers simple rooms; run by the Familia Chalco who also have a shop (and sign for the hospedaje). Alternatively, you can usually **rent rooms** at low prices from villagers (ask for details at the *Restaurant Samana Wasi*; see below), or **camp** almost anywhere provided you ask permission first.

There are a few decent **restaurants** in Pisac, but it's hard to better the excellent *Restaurant Samana Wasi*, on the corner of Plaza Constitución 509, with a pleasant little courtyard out the back and very tasty trout, salad and fried potatoes. The *Restaurant Café Imperial,* on the opposite side of the plaza, serves reasonable lunches of local dishes for around $5, while *Pizzas Pisac "Mullu"* on the opposite side of the plaza to the church is a groovy little place offering meals, snacks and drinks. There's a good **shop**, Doña Clorinda, at Bolognesi 592, on the corner of the plaza, selling great cakes and another selling groceries and films next to *Restaurant Samana Wasi*, on the plaza, and a traditional **bakery** with an adobe oven just around the corner in Calle Mariscal Castilla. **Money change** can be had for dollars cash in the jewellers shop on the corner of the plaza close to Samana Wasi, and there's a SERPOST **post office** selling postcards and *artesania*, on the corner of the plaza where Intihuatana meets Calle Comercio. One of the best shops for buying locally crafted beads and *artesania* is at Bolognesi 569.

From Pisac to Urubamba

The first significant village between Pisca and Urubamba is **Lamay**, which has some medicinal springs just 3km away. High above this village, on the other side of the Río Vilcanota and just out of sight, are the fine Inca terraces of Huchiq'osqo. A little further down the road you come to the larger village of **CALCA**, with the popular thermal baths of Machacanca within ninety minutes' walk of the modern settlement, signposted from the town and to which combi colectivos ($0.3; a 15min trip) run quite frequently, particularly on Sunday. Situated under the hanging glaciers of Mount Sahuasiray, this place was favoured by the Incas for the fertility of its soil, and you can still see plenty of maize cultivation. Moving down the valley from here the climate improves and you see pears, peaches and cherries growing in abundance, and in July and August, vast piles of maize sit beside the road waiting to be used as cattle feed.

Crossing the river to Huallabamba, a few kilometres back upstream from Calca the farming initiative, Tierra Atlas, offers comfortable **accommodation** at the splendid, peaceful *Posada Hacienda Yaravilca* (⑦) They're contactable in Cusco at Plazoleta La Nazarenas 211 (☎ & fax 232829, *pmpfink@mail.cosapidata.com.pe*), or in Lima at Los Pinos 584, San Isidro, (☎ & fax 01/440-5476, *tasca@amauta.rcp.net.pe*). The hacienda is experimenting with re-establishing once-important Peruvian foods that have fallen into obscurity, such as the Aguaymanto, a delicious small, yellow fruit also known as the Cape Gooseberry You can try these at the Tierra Atlas shop in Cusco (see p.134) or at the hacienda. There's a lake within hiking distance, high up in the mountains above **Huallabamaba**.

YUCAY, the next major settlement before you get to Urubamba, had its moment in Peruvian history when, under the Incas, Huayna Capac, father of Huascar and Atahualpa, had his palace here, and you can observe the ruined but finely dressed stone walls of another Inca palace, probably the country home of Sayri Tupac though also associated with an Inca princess. Following the stream up behind the village takes you to the village and nevada of San Juan. There are a couple of good **hostals** in Yucay; the *Hostal Y'llary*, Plaza Manco II 107 (☎226607; ③) is comfortable and excellent value with private bathrooms, a lovely garden and large rooms in an attractive old building. More interesting still, the *Posada del Inca*, Plaza Manco II (☎201107, fax 201345, *posada_yucay@el-olivar.com.p*e; ⑤), is based in a beautifully converted eighteenth-century monastery that houses a small museum (open to non-residents) of fine precious metal objects and ceramics. The nearby *Posada del Libertador* (☎201115, fax 201116; ⑥) is another fine colonial mansion noted for accommodating Simon Bolivar when he was in the region with leaders of Peru's pariot army for the public declaration and royal oath of independence sworn in Cusco in 1825; they can help arrange local balloon flights. The *Casa Luna* **restaurant**, Plaza Manco II 107, right next to the Posada, offers great pizzas, sandwiches and drinks in a pleasant environment with Internet and fax services, bike rental, 4x4 tours and also house and bungalow accommodation (③).

Urubamba and around

URUBAMBA, about 80km from Cusco via Pisac or around 60km via Chinchero, is only a short way down the main road from Yucay's Plaza Manco II, and here the Río Vilcanota becomes the Río Urubamba (though many people still refer to this stretch as the Vilcanota). Although it has little in the way of obvious historic interest, the town is well endowed with tourist facilities and is situated in the shadow of the beautiful Chicon and Pumahuanca glaciers.

The attractive Plaza de Armas is laid back and attractive, with palm trees and a couple of pines sourounded by interesting topiary. At the heart of the plaza is a small fountain topped by a maize corn, but it is dominated by the red sandstone **Iglesia San Pedro** with its stacked columns below two small belfries; the cool interior has a vast three-tier gold-leaf altar piece, and at midday, light streams through the glass-topped cupola. At weekends there's a large **market** on Jirón Palacio, which serves the local villages; and at the large **ceramic workshops** set around a lovely garden at Avenida Berriozabal 111, new and ancient techniques are used to produce colourful, Amerindian inspired pots, household items and artistic pieces that you can buy from the shop on site.

Because of its good facilities and position, Urubamba makes an ideal base from which to explore the mountains and lower hills around the Sacred Valley, which are filled with sites. The eastern side of the valley is formed by the Cordillera Urubamba, a range of snowcapped peaks dominated by the summits of Chicon and Veronica. Many of the ravines can be hiked, and on the trek up from the town you'll have stupendous views of Chicon. **Moray**, a stunning Inca site, part agricultural centre part ceremonial, lies about 6km north of Maras village on the Chinchero side of the river, within a two- to three-hour walk from Urubamba. The ruins, are deep, bowl-like depressions in the earth, the largest comprising seven concentric circular stone terraces, facing inward and diminishing in radius like a multilayered roulette wheel.

Also within walking distance, the salt pans of **Salinas**, still in use after more than four hundred years, are situated only a short distance from the village of Tarabamba, 6km along the road from Urubamba to Ollantaytambo. Cross the river by the footbridge in the village, turn right, then after a little over 100m walking downstream along the riverbank, turn left past the cemetery and up the canyon along the salty creek. After this you cross the stream and follow the path cut into the cliffside to reach the salt pans, which are soon visible but still a considerable uphill hike away. The trail offers spectacular views of the valley and mountains. The Inca salt-gathering terraces are set gracefully against an imposing mountain backdrop.

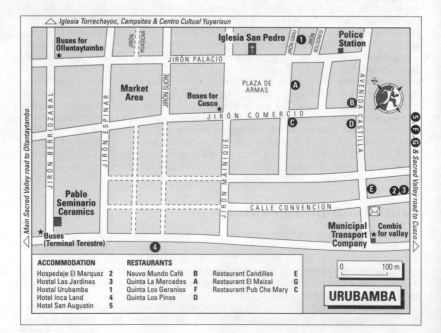

ACCOMMODATION
Hospedaje El Marquez	2
Hostal Las Jardines	3
Hostal Urubamba	1
Hotel Inca Land	4
Hotel San Augustin	5

RESTAURANTS
Neuvo Mundo Café	B
Quinta La Mercedes	A
Quinta Los Geranios	F
Quinta Los Pinos	D
Restaurant Candilles	E
Restaurant El Maizal	G
Restaurant Pub Che Mary	C

URUBAMBA

Practicalities

Regular **buses** connect Urubamba with Cusco, Pisac, Calca and Ollantaytambo. Buses for Cusco and Chinchero leave every thirty minutes from Terminal Terrestre, on the main road more or less opposite the *Hotel Inca Land*. Frequent minibuses to Ollantaytambo can also be caught from the corner of Avenida Castilla and the main Pisca to Ollantay road. The journey takes about twenty minutes. The *Neuvo Mundo Café* (see below) has some local **tourist information**.

The two most upmarket **accommodation** options in town are *Hotel San Augustin,* Km 69, Panamerican Highway (☎201025; ⑦), twenty minutes' walk down the main road towards Cusco, just beyond the bridge over the Río Urubamba, which boasts a small pool and a popular restaurant (delicious buffet lunches served Tues, Thurs & Sun); and the *Hotel INCALAND*, on Avenida Ferrocarril (☎201126 or 201127, fax 201071, *vsagrado@correo.dnet.com.pe, www.enperu.com/incaland/main.htm*; ⑦), a large Best Western hotel and conference centre with a pool and tennis courts, which has plans to develop as a major spa centre and to install three small museums of archeology, Quechua *fiestas* and biodiversity in the region. Cheaper is the basic but friendly *Hostal Urubamba*, Jirón Bolognesi 665 (no phone; ①), behind the police station, one and a half blocks from the Plaza de Armas. The *Hospedaje El Marquez*, Convencion 429 (☎201304; ①) is a clean, family-run hostal, but at no. 459 the *Hostal Las Jardines* (no tel; ②) has better rooms based around a lovely garden. Accommodation and camping are offered by the strongly alternative *Centro Cultural Yuyarisun*, Apartado Postal 345, Correo Central Peru (☎683438; ①), or contactable in Cusco at Hatluun Rumiyoq 487. In a beautiful rural spot about 2km from Urubamba on the Pumahuanca road, by the Q'erokancha canal, they have comfortable rooms, a large garden, and a wooden guesthouse (accessed by ladder) built atop of a vast boulder; the cooking is vegetarian and they sell various homemade and homeopathic items. **Camping** is also available at *Camping Los Cedros* ($3 per tent) and *Los Girasoles* ($2.50 per person), which also has private bungalows (③) and shower facilites. Both sites are on the Pumahuanca road, a few blocks beyond Iglesia Torrechayoc, and are signposted just as the road leaves the built up area of Urubamba.

There is a surprising range of good **places to eat** in and around Urubamba. Try the *Restaurant Pub Che Mary* on Plaza de Armas at the corner of Jirón Comercia and Jirón Grau, a meeting place for travellers, serving juices, drinks and food such as trout and *ceviche*. Nearby, also on the plaza, is the *Quinta La Mercedes*, Comercio 445, which has cheap, set-lunch menus. In line with the alternative feel of Urubamba, there's also *Neuvo Mundo Café*, corner of Avenida Mariscal Castilla and Jirón Comercio, four blocks up from the Texaco petrol station, which serves wholesome vegetarian breakfasts, lunches and dinners on their patio, plus they operate a book exchange and stock trekking food. The *Restaurant Candilles*, Avenida Castilla 207, serves good, reasonably priced chicken, while the *Quinta Los Pinos,* Avenida Castilla 812, specializes in excellent local dishes, served in a pleasant small courtyard. Even better (though pricier) local food can be had by a ten-minute walk along the main Sacred Valley road towards Cusco, on Avenida Conchatupa at the *Restaurant El Maizal* (daily noon–6pm), and the *Quinta Los Geranios* (daily noon–7pm). Both are are pleasant, but *Los Geranios* the better of the two, serving excellent dishes such as *rocoto relleno, chupe de quinoa* and *asado a la olla* in a splendid but usually busy garden environment.

Ollantaytambo and around

On the approach to **OLLANTAYTAMBO** from Urubamba, the river runs smoothly between a series of fine Inca terraces that gradually diminish in size as the slopes get steeper and more rocky. Just before the town, the rail tracks reappear and the road climbs a small hill into the ancient plaza. Built as an Inca administrative centre rather than a town, it's hard not to be impressived by the foundations that abound in the backstreets radiating up from the plaza, especially in Calle Medio. Laid out in the form of a maize corn cob – and one of the few surviving examples of an Inca grid system – the plan can be seen from vantage points high above it, especially from the hill opposite the fortress. An incredibly fertile sector of the Urubamba valley, at 2800m above sea-level and with temperatures of 11–23°C, with good alluvial soils and water resources, it was also the gateway to the Antisuyo (the Amazon corner of the Inca Empire) and a centre for tribute gathering from the surrounding valleys. Beyond Ollantaytambo, the Sacred Valley becomes a subtropical, raging river course, surrounded by towering mountains and dominated by the snowcapped peak of Salcantay.

A very traditional little place, it's worth stopping over for a few days and is particularly colourful during its **fiestas** (the Festival of the Cross, Corpus Christi and Ollantaytambo Raymi fiesta – generally on the Sunday after Cusco's Inti Raymi), or at Christmas, when locals wear flowers and decorative grasses in their hats. On the Fiesta de Reyes, around January 6, there's a solemn procession around town of the three *Niños Reyes* (Child Kings), one of which is brought down from the sacred site of Marcaquocha, about 10km away in the Patacancha valley, the day before. Many local women still wear traditional clothing and it's common to see them in the main plaza with their intricately woven manta shawls, black and red skirts with colourful zig-zag patterns, and inverted red and black hats.

Some history

The valley here was occupied by a number of pre-Inca cultures, notably the Chanapata (800–300 BC), the Qotacalla (500–900 AD) and the Killke (900–1420 AD), after which the Incas dominated only until the 1530s, when the Spanish arrived. Legend has it that **Ollantay** was a rebel Inca general who took arms against Pachacutec over the affections of the Lord Inca's daughter, the Nusta Cusi Collyu, but what is definite is that a fourteen-kilometre canal was built to bring water here from the Laguna de Yanacocha, and it still feeds the town today. It was probably Pachacutec's private estate of the Inca who, in line with his expansionist policies, incorporated the fortress and lookout points. The later Inca Huayna Capac is thought to have been responsible for the trapezoidal Plaza Maynyaraqui and the largely unfinished but impressive and megalithic temples.

As strategic protection for the entrance to the lower Urubamba Valley and an alternative gateway into the Amazon via the Pantiacalla pass, this was the only Inca stronghold to have resisted persistent Spanish attacks. After the unsuccessful siege of Cusco in 1536–37, the rebel Inca **Manco** and his die-hard force withdrew here, with Hernando Pizarro, some seventy horsemen, thirty foot-soldiers and a large contingent of native forces in hot pursuit. But as they approached, they found that not only had the Incas diverted the Río Patacancha to make the valley below the fortress impassable, but that they had also joined forces with neighbouring jungle tribes to form an army so great in numbers that they supposedly overflowed the valley sides. After several desperate attempts to storm the stronghold, Pizarro and his men slunk away uncharacteristically, under cover of darkness, leaving much of their equipment behind. However, more Spanish arrived, and in 1537 Manco retreated further down the valley to Vitcos and Vilcabamba. In 1540, Ollantaytambo was entrusted to Hernán Pizarro, brother of the conquistadore leader. Since the Agrarian reform of 1968, Ollantaytambo has been divided into five rural communities, each with an elected president and a committee of *reidores* who represent peasant interests within local government.

The Town

The main focuses of activity in town are the main **plaza**, the heart of civic life and the scene of traditional folk dancing during festive occasions, the Inca fortress and the train station. The useful **Ollantaytambo Heritage Trail** helps you find the most of the important sites with a series of blue plaques around town. Close to the central plaza there's the recently refurbished **CATCCO Museum** (Tues–Sun 10am–1pm & 2–4pm; $1.75), a small but very interesting museum containing interpretative exhibits in Spanish and English about local history, culture, archeology and natural history. It also has a ceramic workshop and you can buy some good pottery here.

Downhill from the plaza, just across the Río Patacancha, is the old Inca **Plaza Mañya Raquy**, dominated by the fortress. There are a few *artesanía* shops and stalls in here, plus the town's attractive church, the Templo Santiago Apóstal, built in 1620 with its almost Incaic stone belfry containing two great bells supported on an ancient timber. The church's front entrance is surrounded by simple yet attractive and stylized *mestizo* floral relief painted in red and cream. Climbing up through the **fortress** (daily 7am–5.30pm; $4.5, or by Cusco Tourist Ticket, see p.112), the solid stone terraces, jammed against the natural contours of the cliff, remain frighteningly impressive. Above them, huge red granite blocks mark the unfinished sun temple near the top, where, according to legend, the

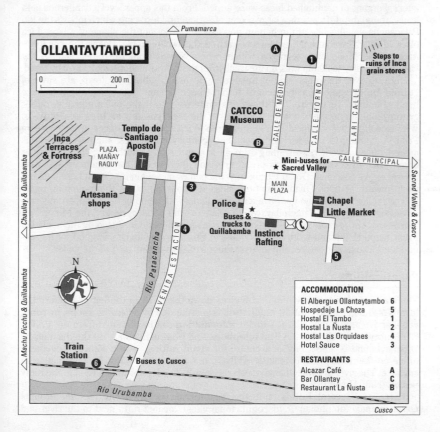

OLLANTAYTAMBO

0   200 m

△ Pumamarca

Steps to ruins of Inca grain stores

CALLE DE MEDIO

CALLE HORNO

LARI CALLE

CATCCO Museum

Templo de Santiago Apostol

Inca Terraces & Fortress

PLAZA MAÑAY RAQUY

Mini-buses for ★ Sacred Valley

CALLE PRINCIPAL

▷ Sacred Valley & Cusco

Artesania shops

Police

MAIN PLAZA

Chapel

Little Market

Buses & trucks to Quillabamba

Instinct Rafting

◁ Chaullay & Quillabamba

Río Patacancha

AVENIDA ESTACION

N

◁ Machu Picchu & Quillabamba

Train Station

★ Buses to Cusco

Río Urubamba

Cusco ▽

ACCOMMODATION

El Albergue Ollantaytambo	6
Hospedaje La Choza	5
Hostal El Tambo	1
Hostal La Ñusta	2
Hostal Las Orquidaes	4
Hotel Sauce	3

RESTAURANTS

Alcazar Café	A
Bar Ollantay	C
Restaurant La Ñusta	B

TREKKING AROUND OLLANTAYTAMBO

Ollantaytambo is an excellent spot to begin **trekking** into the hills. One possibility is to head along the road to Km 82 of the Panamerican Highway, where there's a bridge over the Río Urubamba that's becoming an increasingly popular starting point for the **Inca Trail**. Alternatively, travelling up the Río Patacancha you find the little-visited Inca ruins of **Pumamarca**, on the left of the river where the Río Yuramayu merges with it under the shadows of the Nevada Helancoma. From here the main track carries along the right bank of the Río Patacancha through various small peasant hamlets – Pullata, Colqueracay, Maracocha and Huilloc – before crossing the pass, with the Nevada Colque Cruz on the right-hand side. It then follows the ríos Huacahuasi and Tropoche down to the valley and community of Lares, just before which are some Inca baths. Beyond the village are several more ruins en route to Ampares, from where you can either walk back to Urubamba, go by road back to Cusco, or head down towards Quillabamba. It's at least a two-day walk one way, and you'll need camping equipment and food as there are no facilites at all on the route. Contact the South American Explorer's Club in Cusco for recent trip reports and good maps to use. It's also possible to do it on horseback, or you can organize a guided trek with an agency in Cusco (see p.137).

internal organs of mummified Incas were buried. From this upper level a dangerous path leads around the cliff towards a large sector of agricultural terracing which follows the Río Patacancha uphill, while at the bottom you can still make out the shape of a large Inca plaza, through which stone aqueducts carried the water supply. Below the ruins are Andenes de Mollequasa **terraces** which, when viewed from the other side of the Urubamba valley (a 20min walk up the track from the railway station), look like a pyramid.

High up over the other side of the Río Patacancha, behind the town, are rows of **ruined buildings** originally thought to have been prisons but now thought to have been granaries. To the front of these, it's quite easy to make out a gigantic, rather grumpy-looking profile of a face carved out of the rock, possibly an **Inca sculpture** of Wirraccochan, the mythical messenger from Wiraccocha, the major creator god of Peru. According to sixteeth- and seventeeth-century chronicles, such an image was indeed once carved, representing him as a man of great authority; this particular image's frown certainly implies prescence, and this part of the mountain was also known as Wiraccochan Orcco ("peak of Wiracocha's messenger"). From here, looking back toward the main Ollantaytambo fortess, it's possible to see the mountain, rocks and terracing forming the image of a mother llama with a young llama, apparently representing the myth of Catachillay, which relates to the water cycle and the Milky Way. *The Sacred Valley of the Incas – Myths and Symbols*, published in Cusco by the Sociedad Pacaritanpu Hatha and written by a couple of Cusco archeologists, is good for its useful identification and interesting interpretations of sites in this part of the valley.

Practicalities

The **train station** is a few hundred metres down the track to the left just before the town's traditional little church, which itself is surrounded by *artesania* shops; by **road**, you'll arrive at the main plaza. **Tourist information** can be obtained from the CATCCO Museum, or call ☎204024 The **telephone** and **post offices** are on the main plaza. Ollantaytambo is something of a centre for **river rafting**, with a Rafting Adventure office on the main plaza; contact INSTINCT in Cusco (see p.137), for information in advance. The river around Ollantaytambo is class 2–3 in dry season and 3–4 in the rainy period (Nov–March).

There are several **hotels**, but the best option is the attractive *El Albergue Ollantaytambo* (no phone; ③, discounts to families), located right next to the river and the train station at the bottom end of town (the entrance is on the station platform); write to Casilla 784, Cusco (☎204014, fax 204025) in advance during high season. Its spacious rooms are stylishly rustic, plus there's a sauna, and they serve tasty breakfasts. For full meals (available to non-guests) you need to book in advance. Further up the track from the station towards the town, the *Hostal Las Orquidaes* (☎204032; ③) offers rooms set around a courtyard. The hospitable and good-value *Hostal La Ñusta*, on Carretera Ocobamba (☎204035, 204077; ②), has simple rooms, a comedor, and a patio offering excellent views across to the mountains and the Wiraccochan face. The owner also rents out horses at $10 a day (Pumamarca is reachable in about 2hr). Nearby is the modern and rather plush *Hotel Sauce*, Ventideiro 248 (☎204044, fax 204048, *hostalsauce@tsi.com.pe*; ⑦), which has elegant rooms with fine views. Southeast of the main plaza, the *Hospedaje La Choza*, in Zona Pilquahuasi (no phone; ③) is based in a modern building and is fairly basic, charmless and a little chaotic. The basic, family-run *Hostal El Tambo* (no phone; ②), on Calle Horno, just off the main plaza behind some classical Inca stone walls, is the cheapest accommodation in town.

For a decent **meal**, it's hard to beat *El Albergue* (see above), though there are a couple of good-value cafés in the main plaza, notably the *Bar Ollantay*, often serving superb *quinoa* soup as part of its set-lunch menus. Also on the plaza, the *Café Restaurant Fortaleza* (☎204047) serves good pancakes and inexpensive pizzas and the *Restaurant La Ñusta* (☎204035, 204077) is a very friendly café/shop serving excellent breakfast, snacks and soups made from fresh vegetables (unusual for this region) and runs the hostal of the same name. The *Alcazar Café*, on Calle Medio (☎204034), just a couple of short blocks off the plaza, serves full meals and snacks but doesn't stay open very late. If you want to try the local *chicha* maize beer, pop into any of the private houses displaying a red plastic bag on a pole outside the door – the beer is cheap and the hosts usually very friendly and great fun.

The Inca Trail

The world-famous **Inca Trail** is set in the Sanctuario Historico de Machu Picchu, an area of 32,592 hectares set apart by the Peruvian State for the protection of its flora, fauna and natural beauty. Although just one of a multitude of paths across remote areas of the Andes, what makes it so popular is the fabulous treasure of **Machu Picchu** at the end. It's important to choose your **season** for hiking the Inca Trail. Local tradition states that the perfect time is around the full moon, though May is the best month, with clear views, fine weather and verdant surroundings. Between June and September it's usually a pretty cosmopolitan stretch of mountainside, with travellers from all over the globe converging on Machu Picchu the hard way, but from mid-June to early August it's overly busy (and the campsites are noisy), especially on the last stretch. From October until April, in the rainy season, it's far less crowded but also, naturally, very wet.

As far as **preparations** go, the most important thing is to acclimatize, preferably allowing at least three days in Cusco if you've flown straight from sea level. An **organized hike** with a tour operator (see p.137–138) is much the easiest option, with porters, guidance and specialized knowledge provided. Basic equipment, like tents, sleeping bags and backpacks can be rented in Cusco (see p.133), where you should also pick up a good map. Take at least four days' food (and something to boil water or cook on) as well as iodine or some water sterilizer. Expect to pay $50–$100 for a standard three or four day trek, though competition between the agencies has seen the price drop below $45, but this reduction manifests itself in a lower level of service and, not least, the wages of the porters.

If you decide to do it alone, you will need a map and you should be aware that within the Sanctuario Historico de Machu Picchu, which incorporates the entire trail, you must only camp at a designated site. So many people walk this route every year that toilets have now been built, and hikers are strongly urged to take all their rubbish away with them – there's no room left for burying any more tin cans. It is still possible to hire **pack horses** ($5–10); if they're available you'll spot them by the ticket office (or ask in Huayllabamba) close to the start of the trail to help carry your rucsacks and equipment up to the first pass, but beyond this pack animals are not allowed. **Porters** charge $7–10 a day and can be arranged through trekking agencies in Cusco (see p.137) or in the plaza at Ollantaytambo, distinguished by their colourful dress. If you can only spare three days for the walk, you'll be pushing it the whole way – it *can* be done but it's gruelling. It's far more pleasant to spend five or six days, taking in everything as you go along. Those trekkers who aim to do it in two and a half days should at least give themselves a head start by catching the afternoon train and heading up the Cusichaca Valley as far as possible the evening before.

Setting off

There are two **trailheads** for the Inca Trail. If you're on an organized tour you'll probably approach the trail by road via Ollantaytambo and a dirt track from here to **Chilca** this route adds a few hours to the trail. Minibuses from Ollantaytambo to Chilca cost $1. The **rail trailhead** is at Km 88 along the tracks from Cusco, at a barely noticeable stop announced by the train guard. Have your gear ready to throw off the steps, since the train pulls up only for a few brief seconds and you'll have to fight your way past sacks of grain, flapping chickens, men in ponchos, and women in voluminous skirts.

From the station, a footbridge ($17, including Machu Picchu) crosses the Río Urubamba. Once over the bridge the main path leads to the left, through a small eucalyptus wood, then around the base of the Inca ruins of Llactapata before crossing and then following the Río Cusichaca upstream along its left bank. It's a good two hours' steep climb to **Huayllabamba**, the only inhabited village on the route and the best place to hire horses or mules for the most difficult climb on the whole trail, the nearby **Dead Woman's Pass**. This section of the valley is rich in Inca terracing, from which rises an occasional ancient stone building. To reach Huayllabamba you have to cross a well-marked bridge onto the right bank of the Cusichaca. Many groups spend their first night at Hauyllabamba **campsite**.

The first and second passes

The next five hours or so to the Abra de Huarmihuañusca, **the first pass** (4200m) and the highest point on the trail, is the hardest part of the walk – leave this (or some of it) for the second day, especially if you're feeling the effects of the altitude. There are three possible places to camp between Huayllabmaba and Huarmihuanusca. The first and most popular, known as **Three White Stones**, is at the point where the trail crosses the Río Huayruro, just half a kilometre above its confluence with the Llullucha stream. The next camp, just below the **Pampa Llullucha**, has toilets and space for several tents. Another twenty minutes further up, there's plenty more camping space on the *pampa* within sight of the pass – a good spot for seeing rabbit-like *viscachas* playing among the rocks.

The views from the pass itself are stupendous, but if you're tempted to hang around savouring them, it's a good idea to sit well out of the wind (many a trekker has caught a chill here). From here the trail drops steeply down, sticking to the left of the stream

---

THE CAMINO SAGRADO DE LOS INCAS

The **Camino Sagrado de los Incas**, a truncated Inca Trail, starts at KM104 of the Panamerican Highway, 8km from Maccu Picchu. The footbridge here ($17, including Maccu Pichu) leads to steep climb (3–4hr), past Chachabamba to reach Wiñay Wayna (see p.152), where you join the reminder of the Inca Trail.

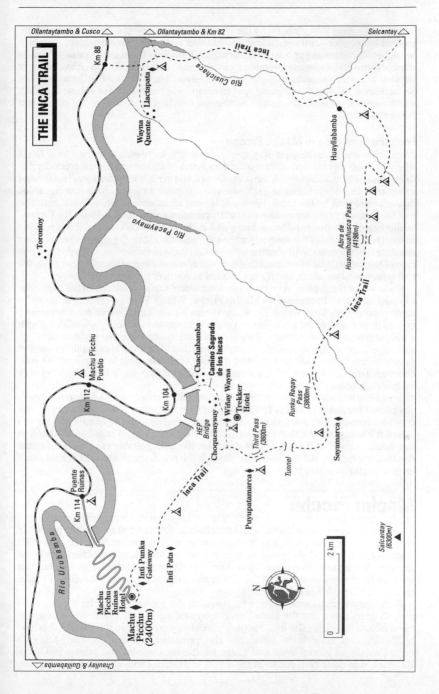

into the Pacamayo Valley where, by the river, there's an attractive spot to **camp**, where you can see playful – and vegetarian – **spectacled bears** if you're very lucky, or take a break before continuing up a winding, tiring track towards the **second pass** – Abra de Runkuracay – just above the interesting circular ruins of the same name. About an hour beyond the second pass, a flight of stone steps leads up to the Inca ruins of **Sayacmarca**. This is an impressive spot to **camp**, near the remains of a stone aqueduct which supplied water to the ancient settlement (the best spots are by the stream just below the ruins).

From the third pass to Machu Picchu

From Sayacmarca, make your way gently down into increasingly dense cloud forest where delicate orchids and other exotic flora begin to appear among the trees. By the **third pass** (which, compared to the previous two, has very little incline) you're following a fine, smoothly worn flagstone path where at one point an astonishing tunnel, carved through solid rock by the Incas, takes you beyond an otherwise impossible climb. The trail winds down to the impressive ruin of **Puyupatamarca** – "Town Above the Clouds" – where there are five small stone baths and in the wet season constant fresh running water. There are places to **camp** actually on the pass (ie above the ruins), commanding stunning views across the Urubamba valley and, in the other direction, towards the snow-caps of Salcantay (Wild Mountain): this is probably one of the most magical camps on the trail (given good weather), and it's not unusual to see deer feeding here.

It's a two- or three-hour, very rough descent along a non-Inca track to the next ruin, a citadel almost as impressive as Machu Picchu, **Wiñay Wayna** – "Forever Young" – another place with fresh water. These days there's an official *Trekker Hotel* here ($8 a bed; $3 floor space; $1 for a hot shower) and restaurant too – nothing splendid, but with a welcome supply of cool drinks. This is usually the spot for the last night of camping, and, especially in high season, the crowds mean that it's a good idea to pitch your tent soon after lunch, but don't be surprised if someone pitches their tent right across your doorway. To reach Machu Picchu for sunrise the next day you'll have to get up very early with flashlight to avoid the rush.

A well-marked track from here takes a right fork for about two more hours through sumptuous vegetated slopes to **Intipunku**, for your first sight of Machu Picchu – a stupendous moment, however exhausted you might be. Aim to get to Machu Picchu well before 9.30am, when the first train hordes from Cusco arrive, if possible making it to the "hitching post" of the sun before dawn, for the unforgettable experience of a sunrise that will quickly put the long hike through the pre-dawn gloom well behind you – bring a torch if you plan to try it.

Machu Picchu

The most dramatic and enchanting of Inca citadels, constructed from white granite in an extravagantly terraced saddle between two prominent peaks, **MACHU PICCHU** (daily 6.30am–5pm; $10) is one of the greatest of all tourist attractions in South America, set against a vast, scenic backdrop of dark-green forested mountains that spike up from the deep valleys of the Urubamba and its tributaries. The distant glacial summits are dwarfed only by the huge sky.

With many legends and theories surrounding the position of Machu Picchu, most archeologists agree that the sacred geography and astronomy of the site were auspicious factors in helping the Inca Pachacuti decide where to build this citadel. It is likely, though, that agricultural influences also prevailed and that the site secured a decent supply of sacred coca and maize for the Inca nobles and priests in Cusco. However, it is quite possible to enjoy a visit to Machu Picchu without knowing too much about the history or archeology of the site or the specifics of each feature; for many it is enough just to absorb the atmosphere. Virtual travellers should check out *www.machupichu.com*

Some history

For years the site of Machu Picchu lay forgotten, except by local Indians and settlers, until it was rediscovered by the North American explorer **Hiram Bingham**, who, on July 24, 1911, accompanied by a local settler who knew of some ruins, came upon a previously unheard of Inca citadel. Bingham's theory was that Machu Picchu was the lost city of Vilcabamba, the site of the Incas' last refuge from the Spanish conquistadores. Not until another American expedition surveyed the ruins around Machu Picchu in the 1940s did serious doubts begin to arise over this assignation, and more recently the site of the Inca's final stronghold has been shown to be Espiritu Pampa in the Amazon jungle (see p.159).

Meanwhile, Machu Picchu began to be reconsidered as the best preserved of a series of agricultural centres which served Cusco in its prime. The city was conceived and built in the mid-fifteenth century by Emperor Pachacuti, the first to expand the empire beyond the Sacred Valley towards the forested gold-lands. With crop fertility, mountains and nature so sacred to the Incas, an agricultural centre as important as Machu Picchu would easily have merited the site's fine stonework and temple precincts.

Arrival and accommodation

If you arrive **by train**, you'll get off at **Machu Picchu Pueblo station**, at the nearest town to the ruins, a place that used to be known (and to many still is) as Aguas Calientes. This settlement has developed tremendously over the last decade or so. From here, you can catch one of the **buses** to the ruins (6.30–11.30am; $9 return), which return between 12.30pm and 5.30pm; services are more frequent at train arrival times. Tickets are stamped with the date, so you have to return the same day. It's possible to walk from Machu Picchu Pueblo to the ruins, but it'll take between one and a half and three hours depending on how fit you are and whether you take the very steep direct path or follow the paved road. **Helicopters** use the small helipad on the opposite side of Machu Picchu Pueblo from the ruins, from where it's a short walk to catch a bus up to the site.

A **cable car** planned to carry visitors straight to the ruins from Pueblo Machu Picchu has cause dconsiderable debate, not least because engineers will blast away a section of the Incas' sacred mountain of Putukusi to site a supporting tower, and while the views from the cable car will no doubt be spectacular, the increased volume in visitors may well prove damaging to the site.

The local *consejo*-run **campsite** ($2, collected every morning), is just over the Río Urubamba on the railway side of the bridge, where the buses start their climb up to the ruins of Machu Picchu. The *Machu Picchu Ruinas* hotel, (☎241777, fax 237111; ⑦) located right at the entrance to the ruins, is something of a concrete block, but it's comfortable and has a restaurant, and staying here allows you to explore the site early in the morning or in the evenings when most others have left. Most people, however, stay, at Machu Picchu Pueblo (see p.156).

Next to the entrance to the ruins there's a **left-luggage office** (no backpacks or camping equipment are allowed inside), toilets, a shop and the **ticket office** (daily 6am–5.30pm; $10 or $5 at night), where you can also hire a guide ($3.5 per person, for a minimum of 6) and buy a **map**.

The ruins

Though it would take a lot to detract from the incredible beauty and unsurpassed location of Machu Picchu, they are zealously supervised, with the site guards frequently

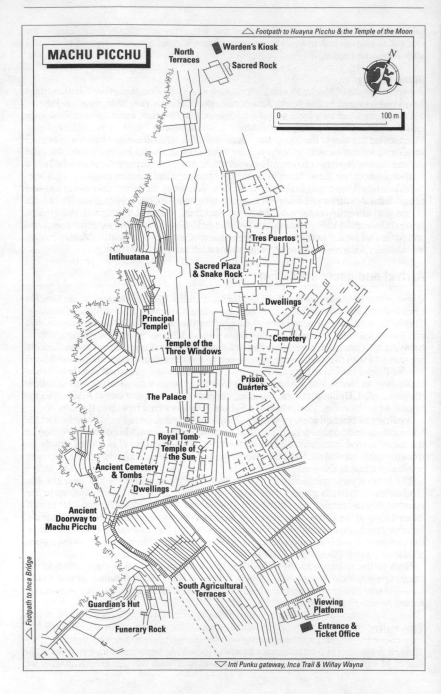

blowing whistles at visitors deviating from one of the main pathways. The best way to enjoy the ruins is to hire a guide, or buy the map and stick to its routes.

Though more than 1000m lower than Cusco, Machu Picchu seems much higher, constructed on dizzying slopes overlooking a U-curve in the Río Urubamba. More than a hundred flights of steep stone steps interconnect its palaces, temples, storehouses and terraces, and the outstanding views command not only the valley below in both directions but also extend to the snowy peaks around Salcantay. Wherever you stand in the ruins, spectacular terraces can be seen slicing across ridiculously steep cliffs, transforming mountain into suspended garden.

Entering the main ruins, you cross over a dry moat. The first site of major interest is the **Temple of the Sun** also known as the *Torreon*, a wonderful, semicircular walled, tower-like temple displaying some of Machu Picchu's finest stonework, carved steps and smoothly joined stone blocks fitted neatly into the existing relief of a natural boulder. The boulder served as some kind of altar and also marks the entrance to a small cave. A window off this temple looks out towards both the June solstice sunrise and the constellation of the Plciades which rises from here over the nearby peak of Huayna Picchu. The Pleiades are still a very important astronomical Andean symbol relating to crop fertility: locals use the constellation as a kind of annual signpost in the agricultural calendar giving information about when to plant crops and when the rains will come. Below the Temple of the Sun is a cave known as the **Royal Tomb**, despite the fact that no graves or human remains have ever been found there. In fact, it probably represented access to the spiritual heart of the mountains, like the cave at the Temple of the Moon (see overleaf).

Retracing your steps 20m or so and following a flight of stone stairs directly uphill, then left along the track towards Intipunku (see p.152), brings you to a path on the right, which climbs up to the thatched **guardian's hut**. This hut is associated with a modestly carved rock known as the **funerary rock** and a nearby graveyard where Hiram Bingham found evidence of many burials, some of which were obviously royal.

Back down in the centre of the site, the next major Inca construction after the Temple of the Sun is the **Three-Windowed Temple**; part of the complex based around the **Sacred Plaza**, and arguably the most enthralling sector of the ruins. Dominating the southeastern edge of the plaza, the attractive Three-Windowed Temple has unusually large windows looking east towards the mountains beyond the Urubamba river valley. From here it's a short stroll to the **Principal Temple**, so-called because of the fine stonework of its three high main walls, the most easterly of which looks onto the Sacred Plaza. Unusually, the main opening of this temple faces south, and white sand, often thought to represent the ocean, has been found on the temple floor, suggesting that it may have been allied symbolically to the Río Urubamba, water and the sea.

A minute or so uphill from here and you come upon one of the jewels of the site, the **Intihuatana**, also known as the "hitching post of the sun". This fascinating carved rock is similar to those created by the Incas in all their important ritual centres, but is one of the very few not to have been discovered and destroyed by the conquistadores. This unique and very beautiful survivor, set in a tower-like position, overlooks the Sacred Plaza, the Río Urubamba and the sacred peak of Huayna Picchu. Intihuatana's base is said to have been carved in the shape of a map of the Inca empire, though few archeologists agree with this. Its main purpose was as an astro-agricultural clock for viewing the complex interrelationships between the movements of the stars and constellations. It is also thought by some to be a symbolic representation of the spirit of the mountain on which Machu Picchu was built – by all accounts a very powerful spot both in terms of sacred geography and its astrological function. Built on a rise above the Sacred Plaza and linked to it by an elaborately carved stone stairway, the Intihuatana appears to be aligned with four important mountains. The snowcapped mountain range of La Veronica lies directly to the east, with the sun rising behind its main summit during the equinoxes; directly south, though not actually visible from here, sits the father of all mountains in this part of Peru, Salcantay, only a few days' walk away; to the west, the sun sets behind the important peak of Pumasillo during the December solstice; while due north stands the majestic peak of Huayna Picchu.

Following the steps down from the Intihuatana and passing through the Sacred Plaza towards the northern terraces, brings you in a few minutes to the **Sacred Rock**, below the access point to Huayna Picchu. A great lozenge of granite sticking out of the earth like a sculptured wall, little is known for sure about the Sacred Rock, but its outline is strikingly similar to the Inca's sacred mountain of Putukusi, which towers to the east.

The prominent peak of **Huayna Picchu** juts out over the Urubamba Valley at the northern end of the Machu Picchu site, and is easily scaled by anyone reasonably energetic. The record for this vigorous and rewarding climb is 22 minutes, but most people take about an hour. Access to this sacred mountain (daily 7am–1pm; last exit by 3pm) is generally controlled by a guardian from his kiosk just behind the Sacred Rock. From the summit, there's an awe-inspiring panorama, and it's a great place from which to get an overview of the ruins suspended between the mountains among stupendous forested Andean scenery.

About two-thirds of the way back down, another little track leads to the right and down to the stunning **Temple of the Moon**, hidden in a grotto hanging magically above the Río Urubamba, some 400m beneath the pinnacle of Huayna Picchu. Not many visitors make it this far and it's probably wise to have a guide (and if you've already walked up Hauyna Picchu, you might want to save this for another day because it's another 45min each way at least). The guardian by the Sacred Rock will often take people for a small fee (around $1 per person, provided there are 2 or more) – but if you do get there, you'll be rewarded by some of the best stonework in the entire site, which suggests that this temple was very important. Its name comes from the fact that it is often lit up by the moonlight, but some archeologists believe the temple is most likely to be dedicated to the spirit of the mountain. The main sector of the temple is in the mouth of a natural cave, where there are five niches set into an elaborate white granite stone wall. There's usually evidence – small piles of maize, coca leaves and tobacco – that people are still making offerings at these niches. In the centre of the cave there's a rock carved like a throne, beside which are five cut steps leading into the darker recesses, where you can see more carved rocks and stone walls. Immediately to the front of the cave is a small plaza with another cut stone throne and an altar. Outside, steps either side of the massive boulder lead above the cave, from where you can see a broad, stone-walled room running along one side of the cave-boulder. There are more buildings and beautiful little stone built sanctuaries just down a flight of steps from this part of the complex.

If you don't have the time or energy to climb Huayna Picchu or visit then Temple of the Moon, simply head back to the guardian's hut on the other side of the site and take the path below it, which climbs gently for twenty minutes or so, up to **Intipunko**, the main entrance to Machu Picchu from the Inca Trail. This offers an incredible view over the entire site with the unmistakable shape of Huayna Picchu in the background.

Machu Picchu Pueblo (Aguas Calientes)

Many people who want to spend more than just a day at Machu Picchu base themselves at the settlement of **MACHU PICCHU PUEBLO** (previously known as Aguas Calientes), which is connected to the ruins by bus and has good accommodation, restaurants and shops. Its warm, humid climate and surrounding landscape of towering mountains covered in cloud forest make it a welcome change to Cusco, but the main attraction (apart from Machu Picchu) is the natural **thermal bath** (daily 6am–9pm; $2), which is particularly welcome after a few days on the Inca Trail or a hot afternoon up at Machu Picchu; right at the end of the main drag of Pachacutec, around 750m uphill from the small plaza, are several communal baths of varying temperatures. There is also a recently restored **trail** (90min each way) up the sacred mountain of Putukusi, starting just outside of the *pueblo*, one a couple of hundred yards on the left if you follow the railway track towards the ruins. The walk offers stupendous views of the town and across to Machu Picchu, but watch out for the small poisonous snakes reported to live on this mountain.

Accommodation

Although there are several **places to stay**, there can be a lot of competition for lodgings in high season (June–Sept), with large groups of travellers turning up and taking over entire hotels. By arriving on an early train you'll have some choice, but for the better places try and book at least a week or two in advance, if not months. Right beside the platform on the river side of the train, the *Hostal Machu Picchu*, Avenida Imperio de los Incas 127 (☎211034, fax 231288; ⑤), is reasonable value, set around a small patio; bathrooms are shared. Almost next door and with the same owner, the more upmarket *Hostal Inca*, Avenida Imperio de los Incas 135 (☎211034, fax 231288; ⑦), is clean, smart and offers private bathrooms, a few with views over the Río Urubamba. Less salubrious, the *Hostal Los Caminantes*, Avenida Imperio de los Incas 138 (☎211007; ②–③), an older building over on the other side of the tracks, has hot water and rooms with or without bath, but is basic. *Gringo Bill's*, Colla Raymi 104 (☎211046, *gringobill@yahoo.com*; ③), also known as the *Hostal Q'oni Unu*, is the best mid-range choice, offering ample hot water, a relaxed environment, breakfasts and evening grills, a book exchange and interesting decoration in the rooms. The *Hostal la Cabaña*, Pachacutec M20-Lot 3 (☎ & fax 211048; ④, includes breakfast) is a friendly pad with comfy, stylish rooms with fresh flowers, open lounge areas, safe and comfortable with a laundry and library (one of the owners is also a local guide). *El Indio Feliz*, Lloque Yupanqui Lote 4m-12 (☎211090; ⑥) is a new and very comfortable place, attached to the excellent restaurant of the same name; rooms have TV and Internet access. The *Machu Picchu Inn*, Avenida Pachacutec 109 (☎211056, fax 211011; ⑧) is plush but plain, though it has a nice geranium garden, pool room, and fine restaurant. The most luxurious choice, on the left just beyond the edge of town as you walk up the rail track towards Cusco, is the *Machu Picchu Hotel*, Km 110, Panamerican Highway (☎220803, *reservas@inkaterra.com.pe*, *www.inkaterra.com.pe*; ⑧), which has its own swimming pool and gardens, and while the rooms are superb, camping is allowed too ($10 per tent).

Camping is also possible at a safe and secure site with evening campfires, just fifteen minutes' walk from Machu Picchu Pueblo at *Campamento Intiwasi* ($3.50 per tent); contact Rikuni Tours, Imperio de los Incas 123 (☎ & fax 211036, *rikuni@ mixmail.com* or *cabi@mixmail.com*). The other camping option is the *consejo*-run site (see p.153).

Eating and drinking

As well as the **foodstalls** specializing in excellent herb teas and fruit juices, which can be found near the little market by the police station, just over the tracks, there are plenty of fully fledged **restaurants** in Aguas Calientes. *Restaurant Aiko*, Imperio de los Incas 153, is one of the closest restaurants to the Machu Picchu end of the tracks in the *pueblo*; it has good service and dishes out reasonably priced meals including trout, soups, pastas and frequently delicious falafels. *Pizzaria Su Chosa*, on Avenida Imperial de los Incas, serves very good pizzas; though a little pricey, it has a pleasant rustic patio upstairs under a tin roof, overlooking the railway tracks and old station. *Donofrio's* ice-cream shop, Pachacutec 120, does reasonable lunch menus. *El Indio Feliz*, Lloque

Yupanqui Lote 4m-12 (☎211090), however, serves exceptional three- or four-course meals of French and local cuisines at remarkably inexpensive prices. Try to reserve a table as far in advance as possible. *Restaurant El Manu*, on Pachacutec has a nice open dining area (sometimes doubling up as a dance space) and specializes in trout and pizzas and gets lively at night. *Trattoria Totos House*, on Avenida Imperio de los Incas, is a vast restaurant with some tables out front by the railway tracks; the food's expensive but quite good. For something a little livelier, *Chez Maggy's*, Pachacutec 156, serves large meals, good-value pizzas, and plays rock music. *Wasicha Pub*, Calle Lloque Yupanqui, Lote 2, M-12 (☎211157) is the loudest, hottest nightspot, with a vibrant dance floor and a good bar. There's a spacious restaurant attached too.

Listings

Exchange Available in the pool room and café next to *Hostal Los Caminantes*.

Internet services Café Internet, corner of Avenida Imperios de los Incas next to the old railway station (☎211077, *rikuni@chaski.unsaac.edu.p*). Decent service plus cakes, snacks and drinks. 6.30am–10pm.

Police, Avenida Imperio de los Incas, next to the small market just down from the old railway station (☎211178).

Post office On the corner of Avenida Imperio de los Incas with Manco Capac.

Telephones Centro Telefonico, Avenida Imperio de los Incas 132 (☎211091, fax 211174). The post office (see above) also has a public phone.

Tour operators Rikuni Tours, Imperio de los Incas 123 (☎ & fax 211036, *rikuni@mixmail.com* or *cabi@mixmail.com*) offer a wide range of local outings, including Machu Picchu by night, the Temple of the Moon, Chaskapata ruins, Wiñay Wayna, and Chacabamba ruins.

Beyond Machu Picchu: into the jungle

The area along the Río Urubamba from Machu Picchu onwards is a quiet, yet relatively accessible, corner of the Peruvian wilderness; as you descend, the vegetation along the valley turns gradually into jungle, thickening and getting greener by the kilometer and the air gets steadily warmer and more humid. It is relatively easy to visit the hilltop ruins of the palace at **Vitcos**, a site of Inca blood sacrifices, and possible, though an expedition of six days or more, to explore the more remote ruins at **Espiritu Pampa**, now thought to be the site of the legendary lost city of Vilcabamba. The easiest way to see the ruins is on a guided tour with one of the adventure tour companies listed on p.137–138. If you'd rather travel independently, at least book a local guide with one of the companies in Cusco before setting off, who can also sell you a good map.

Pukyura

If you want to visit the ruins at Vitcos or Espiritu Pampa independently, it's best to go via the villages of **PUKYURA** and **Huancacalle**, in the Vilcabamba river valley. They are reached in six hours by truck from Chaullay on the Cusco–Quillabamba road. The village has a long history of guerrilla fighting and a tradition of wilful anti-authoritarian independence. Chosen by Manco Inca as the base for his rebel state in the sixteenth century, this area was also the political base for land reformer and Trotskyist revolutionary Hugo Blanco in the early 1960s. **Camping** at Pukyura is possible and you can usually arrange independently for an *arriero* (muleteer) here to take you over the two- or three-day trail to Espiritu Pampa. Narcisco Huaman is recommended ($10 per day, including 2 horses), contactable through Genaro, the Instituto Nacional de Cultura representative in Huancacalle. The hour-long walk uphill to Vitcos from Pukyura is easy to do independently, however. If you're seriously interested in exploring this region, you should also check on the prevailing situation with the Instituto Nacional de Cultura before attempting what is a very ambitious journey.

Vitcos and Espiritu Pampa

In 1911, after discovering Machu Picchu, Hiram Bingham set out down the Urubamba Valley to Chaullay, then up the Vilcabamba valley to the village of Pukyura, where he expected to find more Inca ruins. What he found – **VITCOS** (known locally as Rosapata) – was a relatively small but clearly palatial ruin, based around a trapezoidal plaza spread across a flat-topped spur. Down below the ruins, Bingham was shown a spring flowing from beneath a vast, white granite boulder intricately carved in typical Inca style and surrounded by the remains of an impressive Inca temple. This fifteen-metre-long and eight-metre-high, sacred, white rock – called Chuquipalta by the Incas – was a great oracle where blood sacrifices and other "pagan" rituals took place. According to the chronicles, these rituals had so infuriated two Spanish priests who witnessed them, that they exorcized the rock and set its temple sanctuary on fire.

Within two weeks Bingham had followed a path from Pukyura into the jungle as far as the Condevidayoc plantation, where he found some more "undiscovered" ruins at **ESPIRITU PAMPA** – Plain of the Spirits. After briefly exploring some of the outer ruins at Espiritu Pampa, Bingham decided they must have been built by Manco Inca's followers and deduced that they were post-Conquest Inca constructions since many of the roofs were Spanish tiled. Believing that he had already discovered the lost city of Vilcabamba in Machu Picchu, Bingham paid little attention to the discoveries. Consequently, and in view of its being accessible only by mule, Espiritu Pampa remained covered in thick jungle vegetation until 1964, when serious exploration was undertaken by US archeological explorer Gene Savoy. He found a massive ruined complex with over sixty main buildings and some three hundred houses, along with temples, plazas, wells and a main street. Clearly this was the largest Inca refuge in the Vilcabamba area, and Savoy rapidly became convinced of its identity as the true site of the last Inca stronghold. More conclusive evidence has since been provided by the English geographer and historian John Hemming who, using the chronicles as evidence, was able to match descriptions of Vilcabamba, its climate and altitude, precisely with those of Espiritu Pampa.

THE CUSCO REGION

Cusco is easily the most exciting region in Peru, but all too many visitors overlook the area's lesser-known attractions. Many people choose to spend at least three days in the immediate vicinity of the city, and nearly everyone visits Machu Picchu and the other sites in the Sacred Valley, taking at least another two or three days, but there's a huge number of villages and sites left to stimulate the energetic traveller with more than a week to spend. The Instiuto Nacional de Cultura, for example has identified no fewer than 36,000 known archeological sites in this region. **Chinchero**, an old colonial settlement resting on Inca foundations and boasting a spectacular market, is only forty minutes' drive northwest of the city of Cusco and overlooks the Sacred Valley. To the northeast, towards the jungle, the festive colonial village of **Paucartambo** nestles among breathtakingly high Andean panoramas close to **Tres Cruces**, a remote mountain spot where locals and globetrotters alike go to experience a uniquely spectacular sun rising from the depths of lowland Amazonia. To the south are the superb **ruins** of Tipón, Pikillacta, Raqchi and Rumicolca, the rustic and legendary village of **Urcos**, as well as superb trekking country around the sacred **Nevado Ausungate** (6384m) glaciers between the small settlement of **Ocongate** and the larger town of **Sicuani**. And even if you aren't planning to spend time around Lake Titicaca, the rail journey south to Puno, which starts off through here, is one of the most soul-stirring train rides imaginable, though the track is a little bumpy these days compared to the faster and smoother new road. One last trip, the highland route between Cusco and Lima, passes through Abancay, Andahualays and **Ayacucho**, the latter a beautiful and highly traditional city famous for its churches and *artesania*.

Chinchero

CHINCHERO ("Village of the Rainbow") lies 3762m above sea level, 28km northwest from Cusco and off the main road, overlooking the Sacred Valley, with the Vilcabamba range and the snowcapped peak of Salcantay dominating the horizon to the west. The bus ride here takes you up to the Pampa de Anta, which used to be a huge lake but is now relatively dry pasture, surrounded by snowcapped *nevadas*. The town itself is a small, rustic place, where the local women, who crowd the main plaza during the market, still wear traditional dress. Largely built of stone and abobe, the town blends perfectly with the magnificent display of Inca architecture, ruins and megalithic carved rocks, relics of Inca veneration of nature deities. The best time to visit is on September 8 for the lively traditional **fiesta**. Failing that, the market, smaller but less touristy than Pisac's, has good local craftwork.

The **market** (Sun morning) is in the lower part of town, reached along Calle Manco II. Uphill from here, along the cobbled steps and streets, you'll find a vast **plaza**, which may have been the original Inca market place. It's bounded on one side by a superb wall somewhat reminiscent of Sacsayhuaman's ramparts, though not as massive – it too was constructed on three levels, and some ten classical Inca trapezoidal niches can be seen along its surface. On the western perimeter of the plaza, the raised Inca stonework is dominated by a carved **stone throne**, near which are puma and monkey formations. The plaza is also home to a superb, colonial adobe **church** (daily 7am–5.30pm; entry by Cusco Tourist Ticket, available here or in Cusco – see p.112). Dating from the early seventeenth century, it was built on top of an Inca temple or palace, perhaps belonging to the Inca emperor Tupac Yupanqui, who particularly favoured Chinchero as an out-of-town resort – most of the area's aqueducts and terraces, many of which are still in use today, were built at his command. The church itself boasts decaying frescoes, murals and paintings, many pertaining to the Cusqeña school and celebrated local artist Mateo Cuihuanito. The most interesting depict the late eighteenth-century forces led by local chief Pumacahua against the rebel Tupac Amaru II.

For a quick delve into nearby Inca remains, follow the terraces to the west of the plaza's throne, then drop down a flight of steps towards the stream. You'll soon come across more carved rocky outcrops. and a vast, elaborately worked boulder; to the west a small stone staircase follows the stream down to the base of the rock, where there are two large, square niches cut deep into the boulder, possibly sites for mummies or ceremonial offerings.

Buses ($0.8; a 40min journey) leave Cusco from the compound in Tullumayo, a small road behind Koricancha. There are just two **places to stay** in town, of which the *Hotel Los Incas* (②) is the best value, with a pleasant, rustic restaurant. It's also possible to **camp** below the terraces in the open fields beyond the village, but, as always, ask someone local for permission or advice on this. There are several **restaurants**, all cheap and cheerful, though Camucha, Avenida Mateo Pumacahua 168, at the junction of Calle Manco Capac II and the main road to Cusco, has a good set lunch.

Northeast of Cusco

The two major places to visit northeast of Cusco are **Paucartambo**, 112km from Cusco, and **Tres Cruces**, 50km beyond Puacartambo. The road between the two follows the **Kosnipata Valley**, whose name means "Valley of Smoke", then continues through cloudy tropical mountain scenery to the mission of Shintuya on the edge of the Manu National Park (covered in Chapter Six, p.381–387). Legend has it that the Kosnipata enchants anyone who drinks from its waters at Paucartambo, drawing them to return again and again.

Paucartambo

Eternally spring-like because of its proximity to tropical forest, guarding a major entrance to the jungle zone of Manu, **PAUCARTAMBO** ("The Village of the Flowers") is a pretty village some 110km from Cusco. A slave-driven silver-mining colony in the seventeeth and eighteeth centuries, it's at its best in the dry season between May and September, particularly in mid-July when the annual **Fiesta de la Virgen de Carmen** takes place; visitors arrive in their thousands and the village is transformed from a peaceful habitation into a huge mass of frenzied, costumed dancers.

The beautiful main **plaza**, with its white buildings and traditional blue balconies, has concrete monuments depicting the characters that perform at the *fiesta* – demon-masked dancers, malaria victims, lawyers, tourists and just about anything that grabs the imagination of the local communities. Also on the plaza is the rather splendid, austere **church**, restored in 1998 and full of large Cusqueña school paintings. More importantly, it's also the residence of the sacred image of the Virgen del Carmen,

---

THE FIESTA DE LA VIRGEN DE CARMEN

Paucartambo spends the first six months of every year gearing up for the **Fiesta de la Virgen de Carmen**. It's an essentially female festival: tradition has it that a wealthy young woman, who had been on her way to Paucartambo to trade a silver dish, found a beautiful (if torsoless) head that spoke to her once she'd placed it on the dish, Arriving in the town, people gathered around her and witnessed rays of light shining from it, and henceforth it was honoured with prayer, incense and a wooden body for it to sit on.

The energetic, hypnotic **festival** lasts three or four days (usually July 16–19, but check with the tourist office in Cusco – see p.111), and the town is transformed into a throng of locals in distinctive traditional costumes, dancers and musicians, and market stalls and a small fair spring up near the church. Groups of intricately costumed and masked dancers and musicians process through the streets, the best known of whom are the black-masked Capaq Negro, recalling the African slaves who worked the silver mines. Also memorable are those in grotesque blue-eyed masks and outlandish costumes acting out a parody of the white man's powers – malaria, a post-Conquest problem, tends to be a central theme – in which an old man suffers terrible agonies until a Western medic appears on the scene, with the inevitable hypodermic in his hand. If he manages to save the old man (a rare occurrence) it's usually due to a dramatic muddling of prescriptions by his dancing assistants – and thus does Andean fate triumph over science. On Saturday afternoon there's a procession of the Virgen del Carmen, with a brass band playing mournful melodies as petols and emotion are showered on the icon – an aspect of Pachamama as much as Christianity. The whole event culminates on Sunday afternoon with the dances of the Guerreros (warriors) where good triumphs over evil for another year.

unusual in its Indian (rather than European) appearance: when the Pope visited Peru in the mid-1980s, it was loaded onto a truck and driven to within 30kms of Cusco, then processed on foot to the city centre so that the Pope could bless the image. Even if you don't make it here for the festival, you can still see the ruined *chullpa* burial towers at Machu Cruz, an hour's walk from Paucartambo; ask in the village for directions.

Transportes Gallinos de las Rocas **buses** (☎277255) to Paucartambo leave daily from Avenida Manco Capac 105 at around 10am, plus at 3pm on Tuesdays and Thursdays and at 5am on Sundays ($2; a 4–5hr journey). **Trucks**, which leave from the end of Avenida Garcislaso, beyond the Ormeño office, are slightly cheaper but slower and far less comfortable. Buses generally stop off at the market place, from where you cross the stone bridge into the main part of town up to the plaza, where, during festival times only, there's a **tourist information** office. Whenever you go, it's best to take a tent, because **accommodation** is difficult to find: the only options are the *Albergue Municipal* (no phone; ②) and, by the lower bridge, the *Hotel Quinta Rosa Marina* (no phone; ②), both central and very basic. When the festival is on, they're fully booked, but many of the town people open their houses and it's possible to rent floor space sometimes.

Tres Cruces

The natural special effects during **sunrise** at **TRES CRUCES** are in their own way as magnificent a spectacle as the Fiesta de la Virgen de Carmen. At 3739m above sea level, on the last mountain ridge before the eastern edge of the Amazon forest, the view (at night an enormous star-studded jewel, by day a twisting jungle river system or, when cloudy, an ecosystem of its own) is a marvel at any time. Yet when the sun rises it's spectacular, particularly in June around the southern hemisphere's winter solstice: multi-coloured, with multiple suns, an incredible light show that lasts for hours. **Transport** to Tres Cruces can be a problem, except during the *fiesta*; however, on Monday, Wednesday and Friday, Transportes Gallinos de las Rocas buses (see above) to Paucartambo continue on to Salvacion; beyond Paucartambo, you can disembark at the Tres Cruces turn-off ($2.5; about 8hr from Cusco), but be prepared to walk the remaining 14km into Tres Cruces itself, though you may get a lift with a passing vehicle (especially early in the day from late June to mid-July). Cusco tour operators (see p.137) can organize a trip, or check the noticeboards in the main cafés and backpacker joints in Cusco for people trying to gather together groups to share the cost of a colectivo and driver for the two- to three-day trip – $30–50 a day, plus food and drink for the driver – or even post a notice yourself. The only **accommodation** in Tres Cruces is an empty house that's used as a visitors' shelter, so take a warm sleeping bag, a tent and enough food.

South from Cusco

The first 150km of the road (and rail) south from Cusco towards Lake Titicaca passes through the beautiful valleys of Huatanay and Vilcanota, whence the legendary founders of the Inca Empire are said to have emerged. A region outstanding for its natural beauty and rich in magnificent archeological sites, it's easily accessible from Cusco and offers endless possibilities for exploration or random wandering. The whole area is ideal for **camping** and **trekking**, and in any case, only **Urcos** and **Sicuani** are large enough to provide reasonable accommodation.

South by train and bus

Trains depart from Huanchaq station in Cusco; buy tickets at least one day before travelling and further in advance during high season. As the trains are slow, it makes more sense to take one of the frequent **buses** or **minibuses**; Sol Andino and Oriental run daily services (from 4 or 5am until early afternoon) from Avenida de la Cultura 1624 as far as Urcos and Sicuani, passing all the sites covered below except La Raya. Other buses for Sicuani and Urcos leave from depots in block 19 of Diagonal Angamos, level with blocks 14 and 15 of Avenida de la Cultura.

Heading south from Cusco by road, after about 5km you pass through the little *pueblo* of **San Sebastián**. Originally a small, separate village, it's now become a suburb of the city. Nevertheless, it has a tidy little church, ornamented with Baroque stonework and apparently built on the site of a chapel erected by the Pizarros in memory of their victory over Almagro.

The next place of any interest is picturesque **Oropesa**, traditionally a town of bakers, whose adobe church, boasting a uniquely attractive three-tiered belfry with cacti growing out of it, is notable for its intricately carved pulpit and the beautiful interior murals which correspond to the early Cuzqueña school between 1580 and 1630. However, the town's main attraction is the ruined Inca citadel of **Tipón**, a five- or six-kilometre walk uphill.

The Tipón temples and aqueducts

Both in setting and architectural design, **Tipón ruins** (daily 7am–5.30pm; entry by Cusco Tourist Ticket, see p.112) is one of the most impressive Inca sites. Rarely visited, and with a guard who seems to be permanently on holiday, it's essentially open all the time and free. From Oropesa, the simplest way to reach the ruins is by backtracking down the main Cusco road some 2km to a signposted track. Follow this up through a small village, once based around the now crumbling and deserted hacienda Quispicanchi, and continue along the gully straight ahead. Once on the path above the village, it's about an hour's climb to the first ruins.

Well hidden in a natural shelf high above the Huatanay valley, the **lower sector** of the ruins is a stunning sight: a series of neat agricultural terraces, watered by stone-lined channels, all astonishingly preserved and many still in use. Imposing order on nature's "chaos", the superb stone terracing seems as much a symbol of the Incas' domination over a subservient labour pool as it does an attempt to increase crop yield. At the back of the lower ruins water flows from a stone-faced "mouth" around a spring – probably an aqueduct subterraneously diverted from above. The entire complex is designed around this spring, reached by a path from the last terrace. Another sector of the ruins contains a **reservoir** and **temple block** centred around a large exploded volcanic rock – presumably some kind of *huaca*. Although the stonework in the temple seems cruder than that of the agricultural terracing, its location is amazing. By contrast the construction of the reservoir is very fine, as it was originally built to hold nine hundred cubic metres of water which gradually dispersed along stone channels to the Inca "farm" directly below.

Coming off the back of the reservoir, a large tapering stone aqueduct crosses a small gully before continuing uphill, about thirty minutes' walk, to a vast zone of **unexcavated terraces** and dwellings. Beyond these, over the lip of the hill, you come to another level of the upper valley literally covered in Inca terracing, dwellings and large stone storehouses. Equivalent in size to the lower ruins, these are still used by locals who've built their own houses among the ruins. So impressive is the terracing at Tipón that some archeologists believe it was an Inca experimental agricultural centre, much like Moray (see p.144), as well as a citadel.

With no village or habitation in sight, and fresh running water, it's a breathtaking place to **camp**. There's a splendid stroll back down to the main road taking a path through the locals' huts in the upper sector over to the other side of the stream, and following it down the hillside opposite Tipón. This route offers an excellent perspective on the ruins, as well as vistas towards Cusco in the north and over the Huatanay/Vilcanota valleys to the south.

Pikillacta and Rumicolca

About 7km south of Oropesa, the neighbouring pre-Inca ruins of Pikillacta and Rumicolca can be seen alongside the road. After passing the Paucartambo turn-off, near the ruins of an ancient storehouse and the small red-roofed *pueblo* of Huacarpay, the road climbs to a ledge overlooking a wide alluvial plain and Lucre Lake (now a weekend resort for Cusco's workers). At this point the road traces the margin of a stone wall defending the pre-Inca settlement of Pikillacta.

Spread over an area of at least fifty hectares, **Pikillacta** (daily 7am–5.30pm; entry by Cusco Tourist Ticket, see p.112), "The Place of the Flea", was built by the Huari culture around 800 AD, before the rise of the Incas. Its unique, geometrically designed terraces surround a group of bulky two-storey constructions: apparently these were entered by ladders reaching up to doorways set well off the ground in the first storey – very unusual in ancient Peru. Many of the walls are built of small cut stones joined with mud mortar, and among the most interesting finds here were several round turquoise statuettes. These days the city is in ruins but it seems evident still that much of the site was taken up by barrack-like quarters. When the Incas arrived they modified the site to suit their own purpose, possibly even building the aqueduct that once connected Pikillacta with the ruined gateway of Rumicolca, which straddles a narrow pass by the road, just fifteen minutes' walk further south.

This massive defensive passage, **Rumicolca** (open all day; free), was also initially constructed by the Huari people and served as a southern entrance and frontier of their empire. Later it became an Inca checkpoint, regulating the flow of people and goods into the Cusco Valley: no one was permitted to enter or leave Cusco via Rumicolca between sunset and sunrise. The Incas improved on the rather crude Huari stonework of the original gateway, using regular blocks of polished andesite from a local quarry. The gateway still stands, rearing up to twelve solid metres above the ground, and is one of the most impressive of all Inca constructions.

Andahuaylillas and Huaro

About halfway between Rumicolca and Urcos, the insignificant villages of Andahuaylillas and Huaro hide deceptively interesting colonial churches. In the tranquil and well-preserved village of **Andahuaylillas**, the adobe-towered church sits raised above an attractive plaza, fronted by colonial houses, just ten minutes' walk from the roadside restaurant where buses and minibuses drop off and pick up passengers. Built in the early seventeenth century on the site of an Inca temple, the church has an exterior balconany from which the priests would preach. It has only one nave but is a magnificent example of provincial colonial art. Huge Cusqueño canvases decorate the upper walls, while below are some unusual murals, slightly faded over the centuries: the ceiling, painted with Spanish flower designs, contrasts strikingly with a great Baroque altar and an organ alive with cherubs and angels.

To the south, the road leaves the Río Huatanay and enters the Vilcanota Valley. **Huaro**, crouched at the foot of a steep bend in the road 3km from Andahuaylillas, has a much smaller **church** whose interior is completely covered with colourful murals of religious iconography, angels and saints; the massive gold-leaf altarpiece dominates the entire place as you enter. Out in the fields beyond the village, climbing towards Urcos, you can see boulders which have been gathered together in mounds, to clear the ground for the simple ox-pulled ploughs which are still used here.

Urcos

Climbing over the hill from Huaro, the road descends to cruise past **Lake Urcos** before reaching the town which shares its name. According to legend, the Inca Huascar threw his heavy gold chain into these waters after learning that strange bearded aliens – Pizarro and his crew – had arrived in Peru. Between lake and town, a simple chapel now stands poised at the top of a small hillock: if you find it open, go inside to see several excellent Cusqueño paintings.

The town of **URCOS** rests on the valley floor surrounded by weirdly sculpted hills and is centred around the Plaza de Armas, where a number of huge old trees give shade to Indians selling bread, soup, oranges and vegetables. On one side of the plaza, which is particularly busy during the town's excellent, traditional **Sunday market**, there's a large, crumbling old church; on the other, low adobe buildings.

Practicalities

You can usually find a **room** around the Plaza de Armas. Try *Hostal Luvic*, Belaunde 196 (no phone; ①), just to the right of the church; *Alojamiento Municipal*, Jirón Vallejo 137 (no phone; ①), next to the telephones; the *Alojamiento El Amigo*, half a block up from the left of the church (no phone; ①); or an unnamed place, Calle Arica 316 (no phone; ①), on the street coming from Cusco. All are very basic, crumbling old buildings with communal bathrooms.

There are a couple of reasonable **restaurants** on the Plaza de Armas, notably *El Cisne Azul* and the *Comedor Municipal*, both serving the Andean speciality, *quinoa* soup, made of a highly nutritious grain grown at high altitudes and reputed to be good for skin problems. Although Urcos is not really a tourist town, the occasional traveller is made welcome; in the backstreets you can stop off at one of the *tiendas* (advertised by a pole with a blob of red plastic on the end) for a glass of *chicha* beer and some friendly conversation. Note that **electricity** only lasts until midnight, so take some candles or a torch if you plan to be out late. You can get a truck from Urcos all the way to **Puerto Maldonado** in the jungle, which takes anything from three days to two weeks depending on how much it rains (at its worst between December and March).

VIRACOCHA'S HUACA

One of the unusually shaped hills surrounding Urcos is named after the creator-god **Viracocha**, as he is said to have stood on its summit and ordered beings to emerge from the hill, thus creating the town's first inhabitants. In tribute, an ornate *huaca,* with a gold bench, was constructed to house a statue to the god, and it was here that the eighth Inca emperor received a divinatory vision in which Viracocha appeared to him to announce that "great good fortune awaited him and his descendants". In this way he obtained his imperial name, Viracocha Inca, and supposedly the first inspiration to plan permanent expansion into non-Inca territory, though it was his son, Pachacuti, who carried the empire to its greatest heights

The Temple of Raqchi and Sicuani

Between Urcos and Sicuani the road passes **San Pedro de Cacha**, the nearest village (4km) to the imposing ruins of the **Temple of Raqchi** (daily 9am–5.30pm; $1.75). The temple was evidently built to appease the god Viracocha after he had caused the nearby volcano of Quimsa Chata to spew out fiery boulders in a rage of anger, and even now massive volcanic boulders and ancient lava flows scar the landscape in constant reminder. With its adobe walls still standing over 12m high on top of polished stone foundations, and the site scattered with numerous other buildings and plazas, such as barracks, cylindrical warehouses, a palace, baths and aqueducts, Raqchi was clearly an important religious centre. Today the only ritual left is the annual **Raqchi Festival** (usually June 16–22), a dramatic, untouristy *fiesta* comprising three to four days of folkloric music and dance – bands and dance groups congregate here from as far away as Bolivia to compete on the central stage. The performances are well stage-managed but the site, in a boggy field, can be mahem, with hundreds of food stalls, a funfair, Quechua women selling *chicha* maize beer and their drunken customers staggering through the tightly knit crowds.

SICUANI, about 20km from Raqchi, is capital of the province of Canchis and is quite a thriving agricultural and market town, not entirely typical of the settlements in the Vilcanota Valley. Its busy **Sunday market** is renowned for cheap and excellent woollen artefacts, which you may also be offered on the train if you pass through between Puno and Cusco. Although not a particularly exciting place in itself – with too many tin roofs and an austere atmosphere – the people are friendly and it makes an excellent base for trekking into snowcapped mountain terrain, being close to the vast Nevada Vilcanota mountain range which separates the Titicaca Basin from the Cusco Valley. **Camping** is the best way to see this part of Peru, but if you haven't got a tent there are several **hotels** in town, including the reasonably comfortable *Hostal Tairo*, Calle Mejia 120 (☎351297; ②), and the more basic *Hostal Manzanal*, Avenida 28 de Julio 416 (①). The train journey south continues towards Puno and Lake Titicaca (see pp.160, 163 & 237), with the Vilcanota valley beginning to close in around the line as the tracks climb **La Raya Pass** (4300m), before dropping down into the desolate *pampa* that covers much of inland southern Peru.

From Cusco to Lima: Abancay and Ayacucho

It takes thirty six hours at least to travel **from Cusco to Lima** via Abancay, Andahauylas and Ayacucho then down to the Pisco valley on the coast, which is just a few hours from Lima. A more direct route, though only knocking off around four hours, goes to Abancay then crosses the Andes to join the coast at Nazca (5–6hr from Lima). If you do go on to Ayacucho, it's about another eight to nine hours to Lima.

Whichever route you choose, you'll pass through the village of **Carahuasi**. Within its district are a couple of things to see: by the community of Concacha and some 3500m above sea level, is the archeological complex of Sahuite, comprising three massive, beautifully worked granite boulders, the best of which graphically depict an Inca village (though they have been partially defaced in recent years); while at Conoc there are hot medicinal springs.

About 50km on from Carahuasi is **ABANCAY**, sitting 2378m up in the Andean *departmento* of Apurimac. It's a large market centre in a beautiful area, but with little tourist infrastructure and the best places being hard to reach and little known, it has little to offer the traveller apart from a roof for the night and transport out by truck or bus. For **accommodation**, the most comfortable place is the *Hotel de Turistas*, Avenida Diaz Barcenas 500 (☎ & fax 321017; ④). For money **exchange**, the Banco de Credito is at Libertad 218 and the Banco de la Nacion at Lima 816. Within the locality, overlooking the Apurimac canyon, are the superb Inca ruins of **Choquequirau**, currently accessible only with a planned expedition through one of the Cusco tour operators (see p.137), but with the potential to become a major attraction. From Abancay you can take the (relatively) direct road to Lima, which goes via the coast and the Nazca valley (allow two to three days in the wet season), or you can carry on to **ANDAHUAYLAS**, another potential stopping off point. Again, there's little to see or do in the town, though it is set against the backdrop of a splendid Andean valley. The **airport** here has flights to Arequipa, Cusco and Lima (Aero Continente are at Avenida Peru 137; ☎751515), plus there are **buses** to lima and Cusco (several daily). Of the **hotels**, *El Encanto de Oro Hotel*, Pedro Casafranca 424 (☎ & fax 723066; ③) is pleasant enough; at the budget end of things, the *Hotel Los Libertadores Wari*, Juan Ramos 425 (☎721434; ①) is fairly basic, though the *Hotel Residencial San Juan*, Juan Ramos 126 (☎721119; ②) is slightly better. As for **banks**, the Banco de Credito can be found at Juan Antonio Trelles 255, and the Banco de la Nacion at Ramon Castilla 545.

Ayacucho

Roughly halfway between Cusco and Lima, the city of **AYACUCHO** ("Purple Soul", from its Quechua origins) sits around 2800m high in the Andes in one of the most archeologically important valleys in Peru, with evidence from nearby caves at Pikimachay suggesting that the region has been occupied for over twenty thousand years. Ayacucho was the initial centre of the Huari culture which emerged in the region around 700 AD, spreading its powerful and evocative religious symbolism throughout most of Peru over the next three or four hundred years. The city later became a major Inca administrative centre. The original Spanish site for the city at Huamanguilla was abandoned in favour of the present location and, known then as the city of San Juan de la Frontera, Ayacucho was officially founded in 1540. The bloody **Battle of Ayacucho**, which took place near here on the Pampa de Quinoa in 1824, finally released Peru from the shackles of Spain; indeed Ayacucho was the last part of Peru to be liberated from the colonial power. The armies met early in December, when Viceroy José de la Serna attacked Sucre's Republican force in three columns. The pro-Spanish soldiers, were, however, unable to hold off the Republican forces, who captured the viceroy with relative ease.

Ayacucho is renowned for having over thirty fine **churches**, the exquisite crafts skills of its people and its boisterous **fiestas**. It is also the only city in Peru whose plaza is surrounded on all four sides by stone arches, each facing towards the central monument to Mariscal Antonio José. Its **climate**, despite the altitude, is pleasant all year round – dry and temperate with blue skies nearly every day – and temperatures average 16°C. The surrounding hills are covered with cacti, brooms and agave plants, adding a distinctive atmosphere to the city. Despite the political problems of the last few years (see box on p.169), most people on the streets of Ayacucho, although quiet and reserved, are helpful, friendly and kind. You'll find few people speak any English; Quechua is the city's first language, though most of the town's inhabitants can also speak some Spanish.

Arrival, information and tours

Most visitors arrive in Ayacucho from Lima or Cusco, either on the thirty-minute **flight**, which lands at the airport 4km from town – a taxi into town costs $2–3, buses cost $0.30 and leave from just outside the terminal – or overland by **bus**. Only Aero Continente is presently flying in to Ayacucho but the several bus companies mostly have their depots along Jirón 3 Mascaras or Avenida Mariscal Caceres, both within a few blocks of the Plaza de Armas (see Listings, p.171 for details). **Tourist information** is available from municipalidad building on the Plaza Mayor or at Jirón Asamblea 481 (Mon–Sat

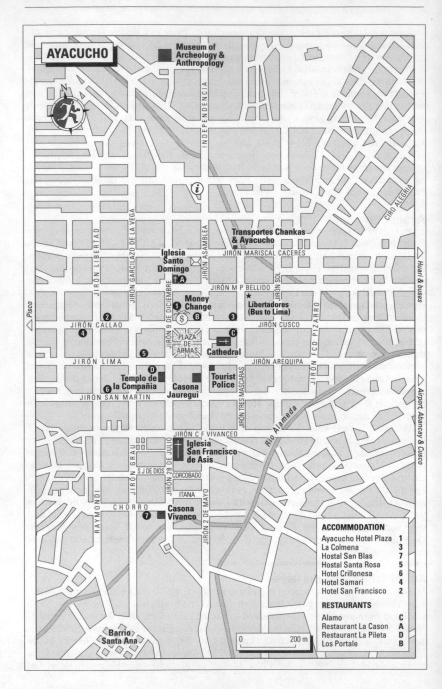

AYACUCHO

N

Museum of
Archeology &
Anthropology

INDEPENDENCIA

CIRO ALEGRIA

Huari & buses

i

JIRÓN LIBERTAD

JIRÓN GARCILAZO DE LA VEGA

JIRÓN ASAMBLEA

Transportes Chankas
& Ayacucho

JIRÓN MARISCAL CACERES

Pisco

Iglesia
Santo
Domingo

A

JIRÓN 9 DE DICIEMBRE

JIRÓN M P BELLIDO

JIRÓN LOS

Money
Change

1

B

3

Libertadores
(Bus to Lima)

JIRÓN CALLAO

2

4

S

PLAZA
DE
ARMAS

5

C

Cathedral

JIRÓN CUSCO

JIRÓN FCO PIZARRO

JIRÓN LIMA

JIRÓN AREQUIPA

Templo de
la Compañia

D

Tourist
Police

6

Casona
Jauregui

JIRÓN SAN MARTIN

JIRÓN TRES MASCARAS

Airport, Abancay & Cusco

JIRÓN GRAU

JIRÓN C F VIVANCEO

Río Alameda

Iglesia
San Francisco
de Asis

JIRÓN 28 DE JULIO

S J DE DIOS

CORCOBADO

ITANA

RAYMONDI

CHORRO

7

Casona
Vivanco

JIRÓN 2 DE MAYO

Barrio
Santa Ana

0   200 m

ACCOMMODATION

Ayacucho Hotel Plaza	1
La Colmena	3
Hostal San Blas	7
Hostal Santa Rosa	5
Hotel Crillonesa	6
Hotel Samari	4
Hotel San Francisco	2

RESTAURANTS

Alamo	C
Restaurant La Cason	A
Restaurant La Pileta	D
Los Portale	B

9am–6pm; ☎064/912548), which has helpful staff, who can arrange trips in the area. One of the easiest ways to visit the sites around Ayacucho is to take a **guided tour**, and all the companies below offer half-day tours to Pikimachay for around $15 and half-day tours to Huari for a similar price. Full-day trips to Huari and Quinua will set you back around $25. Companies to try in Ayacucho include: Ayacucho Tours, San Martin 406; Quinua Tours, Jirón Asamblea 195 (☎064/912191); Urpillay Tours, Jirón Asamblea 145; and Wari Tours, Portal Independencia 91.

Accommodation

Ayacucho Hotel Plaza, Jirón 9 de Diciembre 102 (☎064/912202, fax 912314). Easily the most luxurious hotel in town, with a reasonable restaurant, though service can be slow. Centrally located on the Plaza de Armas. ⑦.

La Colmena, Jirón Cusco 140 (☎064/912146). Clean and good value with the added luxury of a beautiful courtyard full of flowers. ②.

Hostal San Blas, Jirón Chorro 167 (☎064/910552). Good value with friendly service, reasonably comfortable rooms, private bathrooms and a good hot water system. ②.

Hostal Santa Rosa, Jirón Lima 166 (☎064/912083, fax 912083). Only half a block from the Plaza de Armas, with a decent restaurant and with good service. ④.

Hotel Crillonesa, Calle Zazareo (☎064/812350). Hostal with great views of the city and valley from its rooftop terrace, close to Santa Clara Monastery. There's hot water and a laundry service, and rooms are clean and very good value. ①.

Hotel San Francisco, Jirón Callao 290 (☎064/912959). High standards and good value, with a nice café on the roof overlooking town. Rooms have TV and shower. Breakfast included. ③.

Hotel Samari, Jirón Callao 329 (☎064/912442). A fine,welcoming place to relax for a few days, just two blocks east of the Plaza de Armas. ②.

The Town

Ayacucho is an attractive colonial city, with splendid churches and mansions packed together in dense blocks around the central Plaza de Armas (also known as the Plaza

---

THE POLITICAL SITUATION IN AYACUCHO

A radical university town with a long tradition, Ayacucho is known around the world for the outbreaks of **violence** between terrorists and the Peruvian armed forces during the 1980s. Most non-militaristic people in the region remember this era as one where they were trapped between two evils. A large proportion of villagers from remote settlements in the region were forced to leave the area, often moving to the shanty towns around Lima. The exact figure isn't known but something like ten thousand people disappeared (presumed dead) in this region over a twelve-year period. Entire villages were massacred and hundreds of young students evidently liquidated while the army, the media and the Sendero Luminoso argued over who is responsible.

Since the mid-1990s, travellers have returned in force to Ayacucho and many of the refugees who fled their homes in the surrounding area have also returned and begun rebuilding their communities. After more than ten years of terror the city and region regained their previous stability and are now again safe for tourists, which it actively welcomes, both Peruvians and foreigners. There is, though, still an undercurrent of violence that is not apparent when you first visit the town, as it will take a long time for the scars to heal. Sendero Luminoso, however, are no longer very active in the region. You shouldn't have any problems in the area, provided you stick to a few basic ground rules: always stop at any army checkpoints; treat armed soldiers with respect and never try to photograph them. For further details of the Sendero Luminoso and the history and politics of the area, see Contexts (pp.430–433).

If you can be in Ayacucho for **Semana Santa**, the Holy Week beginning the Friday before Easter, you'll see fabulous processions and pageants every day and nightly, candlelit processions centred on the cathedral. But beware of the beautiful procession of the **Virgen Dolores** (Our Lady of Sorrows), which takes place the Friday before Palm Sunday: pebbles are fired at the crowd (particularly at children and foreigners) by expert slingers so that onlookers take on the pain of La Madre de Dios, and so reduce Her suffering. According to Betsy Wagenhauser, of the South American Explorers' Club in Lima, who experienced this procession in March 1988 – "it hurts". Around May 23, there is the elaborate religious procession of the **Fiesta de Las Cruces**, when festivities often involve the local speciality "scissors" folkdance performed by two men, each wielding a rather dangerous pair of cutlasses.

Mayor). The **Templo de San Cristóbal**, dates from the sixteenth century and was the first church built in Ayacucho, but the **Cathedral** (Mon–Sat 11am–3pm; free), just off the Plaza de Armas, is of more interest. Built between 1612 and 1671 by Bishop Don Cristobal de Castilla y Zamora, it has a fine, three-aisled nave culminating in a stunning Baroque wooden and gold-leaf altarpiece. The **Iglesia de Santo Domingo**, block 2 of Jirón 9 de Diciembre, was another early church, founded in 1548, and possesses one of the most beautiful exteriors in the city. In block 1 of 28 de Julio is the **Jesuit Templo de la Compañia**, built in 1605 and renowned for its distinctive Churrigueresque styled main altar. The **Casona Jauregui**, on block 2 of Jirón 2 de Mayo (Mon–Fri 8.30am–4pm; free), is a lovely seventeenth-century mansion built by Don Cayetano Ruiz de Ochon; it has a superb patio and balcony with two lions and a shield displaying a two-headed eagle. Further out, the **Museum of Archeology and Anthropology**, Avenida Independencia (Mon–Sat 9am–noon & 2–6pm, ☎064/912056; $0.5), is full of local finds dating from several millennia ago, plus exhibits from the Chavin, Huarpa, Nazca and Inca eras. The **Museo Pinacoteca de San Francisco de Asis**, in block 3 of 28 de Julio, is known for its library of unique historical works, and there are a couple of **art galleries** in town: the Casona Vivanco, Jirón 28 de Julio 518 (Mon–Sat 10am–1pm & 3–6pm; $0.50), with a particularly good collection of colonial art, and the Popular Art Gallery, Jirón Asamblea 138 (Mon–Sat 9am–6.30pm; free), specializing in regional art.

Arts and crafts in Ayacucho

Many visitors come for the thriving **craft industry** in Ayacucho. The city is a good place to come for woven rugs and *retablos*, finely worked little wooden boxes containing intricate three-dimensional religious scenes made mainly from papier-mâché. Among the best shops for a wide variety of arts and crafts are Artesanias Helme, Portal Unión 49, and Pokra, Jirón 2 de Mayo 128.

If you've got the time to spare, however, it's more interesting and less expensive to visit some of the actual craft workshops and buy from the artisans themselves. Most of the workshops are found in the *barrio* of **Santa Ana**, just uphill from the Plaza de Armas, with some of the best quality *retablos* made by the Jimenez family. Their most simple work is not all that expensive, but if you want to buy one of their more complicated modern pieces illustrating the military/terrorist situation it could cost as much as $300, and take up to three months to complete. For rugs, check out Edwin Sulca – probably the most famous weaver here – who lives opposite the church on the Plaza Santa Ana. His work sells from around $100 (almost double this in Lima's shops), and many of his designs graphically depict the horrors of the recent political situation around Ayacucho. Gerado Fernandez Palomino, another excellent weaver, lives at Jirón Paris 600, also in Santa Ana.

Alabaster stone carvings – known in Peru as **Huamanga stone carvings** – are another speciality of Ayacucho (Huamanga being the old name for the city). Senor Pizarro, Jirón San Cristoval 215, has a reputation as one of the best carvers in town, and the craft co-op Ahuaccllacta, Huanca Solar 130, is also worth checking out. The tourist office can also make a few recommendations.

Restaurants and nightlife

Food and **nightlife** are both surprisingly good in Ayacucho, which has a distinctive cuisine. Try *Puca Picante*, made from pork and potatoes seasoned with yellow chilli peppers and ground toasted peanuts, or the local *chorizo*, which is prepared with ground pork soaked with yellow chilli and vinegar then fried in butter and served with diced fried potatoes. The basic **restaurant** *Los Portales* on the Plaza de Armas is OK, but better is *Alamo*, Jirón Cusco 215, where you can savour the local dishes. *Restaurant La Pileta*, Jirón Lima 166, is excellent for evening meals, while the good-value *Restaurant Tradicional*, San Martin 406, offers a wide range of Peruvian and international dishes in a sophisticated atmosphere, and *Restaurant La Casona*, Jirón Bellido, like *Alamo*, serves excellent Andean *criolle* dishes. The *Restaurant Typic,* Jirón Londres 196, and the *Turistico*, Jirón 9 de Diciembre 396, are both recommended for set-lunch menus at reasonable prices.

If you're after **live music** in the evenings, check out one of Ayacucho's excellent *peñas*. *Arco Blanco*: Jirón Asamblea 280 plays Andean folk music most Friday and Saturday nights from 9pm to midnight, while *Machi*, on Jirón Grau, specializes in *criolla* and *huayno*. *Los Balcones*, block 1 of Jirón Asamblea, plays rock and salsa music and *Los Portales*, Portal Union 33, plays mainly disco music at weekends. *La Casona*, Jirón Bellido 463, is a stylish place combining good food with a pleasant atmosphere and live music. The hippest places these days are *Calle 8*, on Avenida Mariscal Caceres, and *Amor Serrano*, on Garcilaso de la Vega.

Listings

Airline Aero Continente, Jirón 9 de Diciembre (☎064/912816).

Banks and exchange Traveller's cheques can be changed at the Banco de Credito, on the Plaza Mayor (Mon–Fri 9.15am–6pm) or sometimes in the larger hotels. Black market *cambistas* gather on Jirón 9 de Diciembre, near the corner of the Plaza Mayor, giving good rates but will only accept dollars cash.

Bus companies The best company is Cruz del Sur, 9 de Diciembre, for Lima; next up is Ormeño, Jirón Libertad 257 (☎064/812495), also for Lima. Others include: Empresa Libertadores, Jirón 3 Mascaras 496, for Lima, Abancay and Cusco; Empresa Molina, Jirón 3 Mascaras 551, for Huancayo; Transmar, Avenida Mariscal Caceres 896, for Lima, Abancay and Cusco and Transportes Chankas, 3 blocks north of the Plaza Mayor on Jirón Mariscal Caceres, for Andahuaylas.

Post office Asamblea 293 (Mon–Fri 8am–6pm), 2 blocks from the plaza.

Telephone office Jirón Asamblea 293. Daily 8am–10pm.

Tourist Police Corner of 2 de Mayo with Jirón Lima, right on the plaza and close to the cathedral.

TOURS AROUND AYACUCHO

One of the easiest ways to visit the sites around Ayacucho is to take a **guided tour,** and the tourist information office in Ayacucho can arrange trips in the area. Alternatively, all the following companies offer half-day tours to Pikimachay for around $15 and half-day tours to Huari for a similar price. Full-day trips to Huari and Quinua will set you back around $25. Companies to try in Ayacucho include: Ayacucho Tours, San Martin 406; Quinua Tours, Jirón Asamblea 195 (☎064/912191); Urpillay Tours, Jirón Asamblea 145; and Wari Tours, Portal Independencia 91.

Around Ayacucho

Around Ayacucho there are a few interesting places that it's possible to visit, but check with the tourist office beforehand. The political situation is always changing and certain villages are more sensitive than others. The cave of **Pikimachay**, 24km west of Ayacucho, on the road to Huanta, where archeologists have found human (dated to 15000 BC) and gigantic animal remains, is best visited on a guided tour with one of the tour companies listed on p.171. This is also true of the ancient city of **Huari**, sometimes written "Wari", about 20km north of Ayacucho on the road to Huancayo. Covering an area of some 2,000 hectares, historians claim that this site used to house some fifty thousand people just over a thousand years ago. You can still make out the ancient streets, plazas, some reservoirs, canals and large structures. The small site museum displays skulls and stone weapons found here in the 1960s.

About 37km northeast of Ayacucho, the charming and sleepy village of **Quinua** is just a short bus ride away through acres of *tuna cacti*, which is abundantly farmed here for both its delicious fruit (prickly pear) and the red dye (cochineal) extracted from the *cochamilla* – larvae that thrive at the base of the cactus leaves. On the site of the historic nineteenth-century **Battle of Ayacucho**, marked by an obelisk, the village's most characteristic feature is the small, highly ornate ceramic models of churches placed on many of the roofs. There are still some artisans working in the settlement: at San Pedro Ceramics (at the foot of the hill leading to the obelisk) it's often possible to look round the workshops, or try Mamerto Sanchez's workshop on Jirón Sucre. About 120km away, some four hours by road, you can also find **Vilcasayhuaman**, a pre-Conquest construction with a Temple of the Sun, Temple of the Moon and a ceremonial pyramid. Another 25km on from Vilcasayhuaman, at a site called **Intihuatana**, there's another archaeological complex, with a palace, artificial lake and a stone bath that has one big rock with seventeen corners.

travel details

Buses

Cusco to: Abancay (2 daily; 10hr); Arequipa (3 daily; 9hr); Ausungatea (1 daily). Ayacucho (1 daily; 18hr); Buenas Aires, Argentina (3–4 weekly; 3 days); Juliaca (3 daily; 7hr); La Paz (5 weekly; 20hr); Lima via Nasca (1 daily; 30–50hr), via Pisco and Ayacucho (2 weekly; 36–60hr); Puno (1 daily; 8hr); Santiago, Chile (2 weekly; 2 days 6 hr).

Trucks

Cusco to: Atalaya (2 weekly; 20hr); Puerto Maldonado (1 daily; 2–3 days in dry season, up to 7 days in wet season); Atalaya/Shintuya (3–4 weekly; 8–10hr).

Trains

Cusco to: Arequipa (June–Sept daily, Oct–May 4 weekly; 22hr); Juliaca/Puno (June–Sept daily, Oct–May 4 weekly; 10–11hr); Machu Picchu (4 daily; 3hr).

Flights

Cusco to: Arequipa (2 daily; 90min); Ayacucho (2 weekly; 30min); Juliaca (2 daily; 50min); La Paz (2 weekly; 90min); Lima (4 daily; 1hr); Puerto Maldonado (2 daily; 40min).

CHAPTER THREE

THE SOUTH

T he south has been populated as long as anywhere in Peru – for at least nine thousand years in some places – but until this century no one guessed the existence of this arid region's unique cultures, whose enigmatic remains, particularly along the coast, show signs of a sophisticated civilization. With the discovery and subsequent study, beginning in 1901, of ancient sites throughout the coastal zone, it now seems clear that this was home to at least three major cultures: the **Paracas** (500 BC–400 AD), the influential **Nazca** (500–800 AD) and finally, contemporaneous with the Chimu of northern Peru and the Cuismancu around Lima, the **Ica Culture**, or **Chincha Empire**, overrun by and absorbed into Pachacutec's mushrooming Inca Empire around the beginning of the fifteenth century.

The three main towns along the coast, **Pisco**, **Ica** and **Nazca**, all preserve important and intriguing sites from the three cultures. **The Nazca Lines**, a perplexing network of perfectly straight lines and giant figures etched over almost five hundred square kilometres of bleak *pampa*, are just one of southern Peru's many enduring and mysterious archeological features. And for those interested in wildlife, Pisco and Nazca offer three of the most outstanding reserves in the country – the **Ballestas Islands** and **Paracas National Reserve** (outside Pisco), and the rare *vicuña* reserve of **Pampa Galeras** (in the Andes above Nazca).

Arequipa, second city of Peru and a day's journey from Lima, sits in a dramatic setting, poised at the edge of the Andes against an extraordinary backdrop of volcanic peaks. The major centre of the south, Arequipa is an enjoyable place to take it easy for a while, distinguished by its architecture (including the magnificent **Santa Catalina Monastery**) and for several spectacular, if tough-going, excursions into the surrounding countryside where you can explore the **Colca Canyon**, one of the deepest in the world, and watch condors glide gracefully against the backdrop of ancient Inca mountain terraces. Nearby lies the equally stupendous **Cotahuasi Canyon**. The Arequipa region is also the last place to merit a stop before continuing on south to the Chilean border.

Heading inland, you'll probably want to spend time in the **Lake Titicaca** area, getting to know its main town and port – **Puno**, a high, quite austere city with a cold climate and incredibly rarefied air. Alternatively you might fancy a break on one of the huge lake's islands where life has changed little in the last five hundred years. The Titicaca region is renowned for its folk dances and Andean music and, along with Puno, makes an interesting place to break your journey from Arequipa to Cusco or into Bolivia.

ACCOMMODATION PRICE CODES

Unless otherwise indicated, **accommodation** in this book is coded according to the categories below, based on the price of a double room in high season.

① under $5	③ $10–20	⑤ $30–40	⑦ $50–70
② $5–10	④ $20–30	⑥ $40–50	⑨ over $70

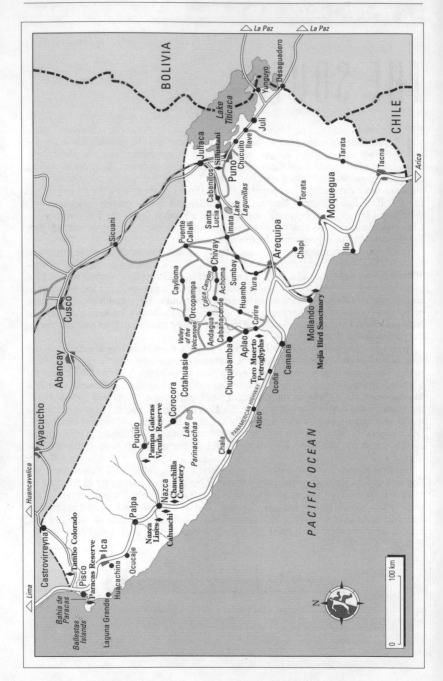

THE COAST

The coastal area between Lima and Arequipa contains enough ancient ruins and unusual landscapes – including some of the best assortments of wildlife in South America – to tempt almost any traveller off the Panamerican Highway, the two-lane road that runs the entire length of Peru. Around **Pisco**, 200km south of Lima, the unspoiled coastline is superb for bird-watching, while the desert plains around **Nazca** are indelibly marked by gigantic, geometric animal and alien-looking figures scratched into the brown earth over a thousand years ago. And, off the beaten track, in the cooler hills above the desert coastal strip you can search out herds of the soft-woolled *vicuña* or see pink flamingos in their natural Andean habitat at the stunning **Lake Parincochas**.

Transport is not usually a problem in this area, with local buses connecting all the towns with each other and with Lima and express buses ploughing along the coastal road between Lima and Arequipa day and night. All the major towns have a decent range of accommodation and restaurants, and wild **camping** is possible in many places, though only Nazca and around Arequipa have formal campsites.

Pisco and around

Less than three hours by bus from Lima, **PISCO** is an obvious and rewarding stop en route south to Nazca and Arequipa. Although of little interest in itself, it makes a pleasant base – and provides access to the **Paracas National Reserve**, the wildlife of the **Ballestas Islands**, and the well-preserved Inca coastal outpost of **Tambo Colorado**. Just off the Panamerican Highway, it is also a crossroads for going up into the Andes: you can take roads from here to Huancavelica and Huancayo, as well as to Ayacucho and Cusco.

Arrival and getting around

If you come into Pisco from Lima, Nazca, Arequipa, Ica, Santiago in Chile or Buenos Aires on one of the frequent **buses** run by Ormeño, you'll arrive at San Francisco 259 (☎034/532764), one block east of the Plaza de Armas. Comité colectivos #3 or #4 from Lima arrive near the Plaza de Armas, while the Peru Bus terminal for Lima and Ica services is at Avenida Ernesto Diez Canseco 41, and if you arrive from Ica by Servitur colectivos, you'll come in at Calle Callao 191. Coming from Huancavelica or Ayacucho on an Oropesa bus, you'll arrive on Calle Commercio.

Getting around Pisco is easy – it's small enough to **walk** around the main places of interest, and a **taxi** anywhere in the central area should cost less than $1. If you're heading for the **Paracas National Reserve** or the **Ballestas Islands**, the cheapest way is to catch a bus from Pisco market, on the corner of *calles* Beatita de Humay and Fermin Tanguis. Most of the buses from here only go as far as the waterfront at **San Andres**, but there are usually at least two buses an hour on to the Playa El Chaco wharf in El Balneario, where you can get a boat to the Ballestas Islands. If you only want to go as far as the San Andres waterfront, you can also take a bus from Calle Pedemonte, two blocks from Plaza de Armas. Most travellers, however, tend to use one of the tour companies (see p.178) in town to get the most out of their time in and around Pisco.

Accommodation

Hostal Callao, Jirón Callao 163 (☎034/532991). One of the cheapest hostals in the town centre, very rudimentary, but some rooms have private bath. ②.

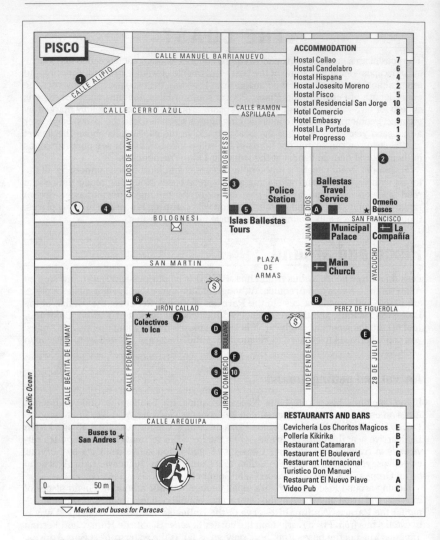

PISCO

CALLE MANUEL BARRIANUEVO

CALLE ALIPIO

CALLE CERRO AZUL

CALLE RAMON
ASPILLAGA

CALLE DOS DE MAYO

JIRÓN PROGRESSO

BOLOGNESI

SAN MARTIN

SAN JUAN DE DIOS

ACCOMMODATION

Hostal Callao	7
Hostal Candelabro	6
Hostal Hispana	4
Hostal Josesito Moreno	2
Hostal Pisco	5
Hostal Residencial San Jorge	10
Hotel Comercio	8
Hotel Embassy	9
Hostal La Portada	1
Hotel Progresso	3

Police Station

Ballestas Travel Service

Ormeño Buses

Islas Ballestas Tours

Municipal Palace

La Compañía

Main Church

PLAZA DE ARMAS

SAN FRANCISCO

AYACUCHO

JIRÓN CALLAO

PEREZ DE FIGUEROLA

Colectivos to Ica

BOULEVARD

JIRÓN COMERCIO

CALLE PEDEMONTE

INDEPENDENCIA

28 DE JULIO

Pacific Ocean

CALLE BEATITA DE HUMAY

CALLE AREQUIPA

Buses to San Andres

N

0   50 m

RESTAURANTS AND BARS

Cevichería Los Choritos Magicos	E
Pollería Kikirika	B
Restaurant Catamaran	F
Restaurant El Boulevard	G
Restaurant Internacional	D
Turistico Don Manuel	
Restaurant El Nuevo Piave	A
Video Pub	C

▽ *Market and buses for Paracas*

Hostal Candelabro, Jirón Callao 190–198 (☎034/532620). Quite luxurious, with excellent service; all rooms boast a minibar, TV and bath. ④.

Hostal Hispana, Avenida Bolognesi 236 (☎034/536363). One of the best choices in Pisco, with excellent information on the region. The place is fresh and well decorated with private bath and constant hot water. ②.

Hostal Josesito Moreno, Ayacucho 250 (☎034/532326). The only thing to recommend this rather noisy *hostal* is its location opposite the Ormeño bus station; only use as a last resort, if everywhere else is full. ③.

Hostal Pisco, San Francisco 115 (☎034/532018). A friendly *hostal* with its own restaurant, in a pleasant position on Plaza de Armas, but quite basic for the price; rooms are with or without private bath. ②–③.

Hostal La Portada, Alipio Ponce 250 (☎034/532098). Located a few blocks from the plaza this is quite good value with pleasant rooms with private bath, hot water and TV. ③

Hostal Residencial San Jorge, Jirón Comercio 187 (☎034/534200). A modern good-value hotel, several blocks north of the town centre. ④.

Hotel Comercio, Jirón Comercio, El Bulevar 168 (☎034/532392). Airy and pleasant; some rooms have hot water. ②.

Hotel Embassy, Jirón Comercio 180 (☎034/532809). Reasonable value but a little run down, with private bathrooms and a rooftop breakfast bar. ③.

Hotel Progresso, Jirón Progresso 254 (☎034/532303). A stylish, old-fashioned building. Quite clean and with lots of rooms, but few have windows or bath and the staff are not particularly helpful. ③.

Out of town

Hostería Paracas, Avenida Los Libertadores, El Balneario. A cheaper alternative to the *Hotel Paracas*, in a good position close to the entrance to Paracas Reserve. ⑤.

Hotel Paracas, Avenida 173, Ribera del Mar (☎034/227022, fax 227023, *hparacas@correo. dinet.com.pe, www.hotelparacas.com*). A luxurious place with pool, excellent bar and restaurant (open to non residents) right on the ocean and the edge of Paracas Reserve, close to Playa El Chaco wharf. Very popular as a weekend retreat for wealthy Limeños and worth the money. Quite good for surfing. ⑥.

The Town

Perhaps because of its ease of access, the Spanish considered making **Pisco** their coastal capital before eventually deciding on Lima. Today the town's old port has been superseded by the smelly fish-meal factories along the bay towards Paracas, and even more so by modern Puerto San Martin north of the Paracas Reserve. There's a small **maritime museum** and **dolphin viewing tower** one block from the pier.

Pisco's focus of activity is the **Plaza de Armas** and adjoining **Jirón Comercio**; every evening the plaza is crowded with people walking and talking, buying *tejas* (small sweets made from pecan nuts) from street sellers, or chatting in one of several laid-back cafés and bars around the square. Clustered about the plaza, with its statue of liberator San Martín poised in the shade of ancient ficus trees, are a few fine colonial showpieces, including the mansion where San Martín stayed on his arrival in Peru; half a block west of the plaza, it's now the **Club Social de Pisco**, but it's still possible to wander in and look around. Another impressive building, inaugurated in 1932 and unusual in its Moorish style, is the **Municipal Palace** (or Consejo Provincial), just to the left if you're facing the church on the Plaza de Armas. One block further away from the plaza down Calle San Francisco, the heavy Baroque **Iglesia de la Compañía**, begun in 1689, boasts a superb carved pulpit and gold-leaf altarpiece.

Restaurants and nightlife

You don't have to look far for good food in Pisco, with most **restaurants** specializing in a wide range of locally caught fish and seafood. **Nightlife** is restricted to the lively *Los Balcones* bar, or the jazzy *Video Pub* dance-spot above *Restaurant Ballestas,* both overlooking the Plaza de Armas.

Cevichería Los Choritos Magicos, 28 de Julio 116. Hidden in a backstreet not far from the Plaza de Armas, its name translates as "the magic mussels" and it's very popular with locals for reasonably priced seafood.

La Estrada, San Francisco 247. A pleasant, small coffee shop next to the Ballestas Travel Service office.

Pollería Kikirika, San Juan de Dios 100. Serves fantastic-value set-lunches in a friendly atmosphere.

Restaurant El Boulevard, on the corner of Calle Arequipa and Jirón Comercio. Serves an interesting selection of juices and seafood.

Restaurant Catamaran, Jirón Comercio. Less than half a block from Plaza de Armas, this is the best place in town for pizzas.

Restaurant Internacional Turistico Don Manuel, Jirón Comercio 187. Just off the Plaza de Armas, serving typical local food and good fish dishes and specializing in fish and shrimps. Good but relatively expensive. Open from 6am for breakfasts.

Restaurant El Nuevo Piave, San Francisco 201. This restaurant, on the corner of Plaza de Armas and popular with travellers and locals alike, serves reasonably priced good, fresh seafood, beer by the jug and has a massive TV screen that's on almost permanently.

Listings

Banks and exchange Banco de Credito, Perez Figuerola 162, and Interbanc, Plaza de Armas, are the only places in town where you can change traveller's cheques. Most hotels and the tour companies will change dollars cash, but the best rates are from the *cambistas* on the corner of the pedestrian boulevard between Comercio and Progresso and Plaza de Armas.

Bus companies Empressa Willy Lily, Calle Callao 172; Ormeño, on the corner of Ayacucho and San Francisco; Oropesa, Calle Commercio; Servitur Colectivos, Calle Callao 191.

Hospital Calle San Juan de Dios 350.

Police Plaza de Armas, Calle San Francisco (☎034/532165).

Post office Calle Bolognesi 173. Mon–Sat 8am–6pm.

Telephone office Calle Bolognesi 298. Daily 7am–11pm.

Tour operators Reservas Tours Pisco, Calle San Francisco 247 (☎034/535472, or 532513), operates excursions to the Islas Ballestas; Ballestas Travel Service, San Franscisco 249 (☎034/533095) has good guides and offers a reliable service, running morning speedboat trips to the Ballestas Islands most days and afternoon tours from town or Playa El Chaco Wharf to Paracas; and Islas Ballestas Tours, San Francisco 109 (☎034/533806), who run similar tours at similar prices, with the Paracas Reserve. These last two companies can also organize tours to Tambo Colorado and offer a discount for ten or more people. The *Hotel Paracas* also offers slightly cheaper tours to the Islas Ballestas.

San Andres, El Balneario and the Ballestas Islands

One of the best trips out from Pisco takes in San Andres, El Balneario and the stunning Ballestas Islands. Local tour operators (see Listings, above), run combined bus and boat tours leaving Pisco early in the morning and returning towards midday. Tickets are best bought the day before and cost $8–10: you'll be picked up around 7am, from the plaza in front of the *Hotel Pisco*, your hotel or the tour company office.

The tour buses – and local buses which leave from Pisco market – run south along the shore past the old port of **San Andres**, where you can watch the fishermen bringing in their catch. The tour buses usually stop here on the way back, so that you can buy fresh *ceviche* or turtle steaks, despite a national ban on eating turtles due to the threat of extinction. Known as the meat with seven flavours because some parts of the creature taste of fish, others of chicken, others of beef, and so on, turtle is still a favourite local food and warm turtle blood is occasionally drunk here, reputedly as a cure for bronchial problems. The plankton in the sea here frequently attracts whales and in 1988 a new, small species – the *Mesoplodon Peruvianus*, which can be up to 4m long – was discovered after being caught accidentally in fishermen's nets.

At the far end of San Andres the road passes the big Pisco Air Force Base before reaching **EL BALNEARIO**, a resort for wealthy Limeños, whose large bungalows line the beach. If you want to stay out here, you can **camp** on the sand, though the Paracas Reserve (see opposite) is a much nicer place to pitch a tent; there are also a couple of hotels here (see Pisco accommodation, p.177). However, most travellers just pass

Cathedral and Plaza Mayor, Lima

Graffiti at Yucay, Urubamba Valley

Machu Picchu, Cusco

Warrior figure at Cerro Sechin   Inti Raymi sun festival, Cusco

Houses decorated with traditional tin crosses, Titicaca region

Llama herding at Sacsayhuaman, Cusco

Chancay funerary ceramic,
Museo Antropología del Peru, Lima

Drying fish on the Uros Floating Islands, Lake Titicaca

Roasted *cuy* (guinea pig)

Cusco, Cathedral rooftop, Plaza de Armas

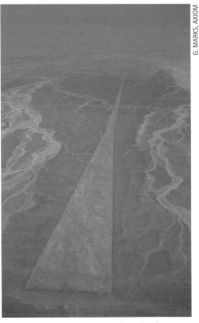
A Nazca Line, Pampa de San José

Plundered grave site, Chauchilla

through using El Balneario as a jumping-off point to visit the Ballestas Islands. Tour buses will drop you here at **Playa El Chaco Wharf**, surrounded by pelicans, where you board speedboats, and zip across the sea, circling one or two of the islands and passing close to the famous Paracas Trident – a huge cactus-shaped figure drawn in the sandstone cliffs (see overleaf).

Often called the Guano Islands, because every inch is covered in bird droppings, a nineteeth-century export, the rocks of the **Ballestas Islands**, which lie off the coast due west from Pisco, seem to be alive and moving with a mass of flapping, noisy pelicans, penguins, terns, boobies and Guanay cormorants. The waters around them are equally full of life, sometimes almost black with the shiny dark bodies of sea lions and the occasional killer whale. The female sea lions have one baby each every year and live in harems of up to fifteen or more per adult male. The largest adult male, with the biggest harem, is known to the locals as Mike Tyson.

Paracas National Reserve

A beautiful peninsula of even greater wildlife interest than the Ballestas Islands, the **Paracas National Reserve**, a few kilometres south of El Balneario, was established in 1975. Its bleak 335,000 hectares of *pampa* are frequently lashed by strong winds and sandstorms (*paracas* means "raining sand" in Quechua). Home to some of the world's richest seas, an abundance of marine plankton give nourishment to a vast array of fish and marine species, who in turn have their attendant predators. It's also a staging point for a host of migratory birds and acts as a sanctuary for many endangered species. Schools of dolphins play in the waves offshore, condors scour the peninsula for food, small desert foxes come down to the beaches looking for birds and dead sealions, and lizards scrabble across the hot sands. Humankind has also been active here – predecessors of the pre-Inca **Paracas** culture arrived here some 9000 years ago, reaching their peak between 2000 and 500 BC.

Plan to stay for a few days, and take food, water and a sun hat – facilities are almost non-existent. It's a twenty-one-kilometre bus journey from Pisco (local buses leave Pisco market every 20min; $0.8 each way), or take an organized tour from one of the operators listed opposite). The reserve's natural attractions include plenty of superb, deserted beaches where you can **camp** for days without seeing anything except the lizards and bird-life, and maybe a couple of fishing boats. **Cycling** is permitted and encouraged in the reserve, though there are no rental facilities and, if you do enter on a bike, keep on the main tracks because the tyre marks will damage the surface of the desert.

On the way to the reserve, the road passes some unpleasant-smelling fish-processing factories, which are causing environmental concern due to spillages of fish-oil that pollute the bay, endangering bird and sea-mammal life. Just before the entrance to the reserve, you'll pass a bleak but unmistakable concrete obelisk in the vague shape of a nineteenth-century sailing boat, built in 1970 to commemorate the landing of San Martín here on September 8, 1820, on his mission to liberate Peru from the Spanish stranglehold.

The **entrance** to the reserve is marked by a barrier-gate and guard post (24hr), just off the Panamerican Highway, where you pay the $1 entrance fee, which permits you to stay in the park for up to a week. From here most of the roads are sand tracks, though one surfaced *carretera* continues along the shore line towards the new port and connects with the park office, museum and track for Lagunillas and the beaches beyond. Not far from the barrier is a **park office**, where maps are sometimes available, and the **Museo de Sitio Julio Tello** (Tues–Sun 9am–5pm; $1), which contains interpretative exhibits relating to the National Park and a wide range of Paracas artefacts – mummies, ceramics, funerary cloths and a reconstructed dwelling.

Right next to the museum is the oldest discovered site in the region, the **Necropolis of Cabeza Largas**, dating from over five thousand years ago and once containing up to

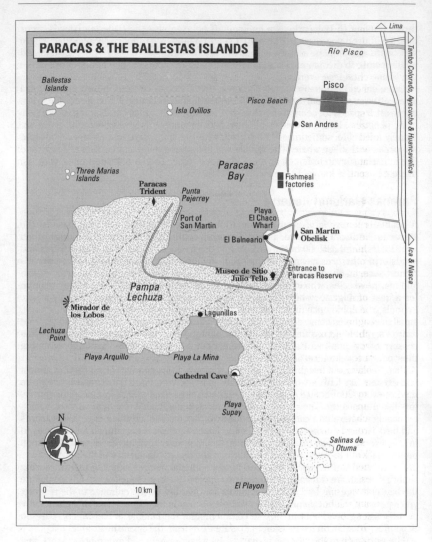

PARACAS & THE BALLESTAS ISLANDS

sixty mummies in one grave. Most were wrapped in *vicuña* skins or rush matting, and buried along with personal objects like shell beads, bone necklaces, lances, net bags and cactus-spine needles. A little further on, near the beach where dozens of pink flamingos hang out between July and November (they return to the high Andean lakes for breeding from December to May), are the remains of a Chavin-related settlement, known as **Disco Verde**, though all there is left to see now are a few adobe walls.

The Paracas Trident (El Candelabro)
Another 2km past the museum you come to a fork in the main road: the paved part continues straight on, parallel to the shore, ending after 20km at **Punta Pejerrey**, which

holds the modern port of San Martin, full of fish canneries. There's nothing of interest here, but just before the port a sandy side road leads away from the sea and around the hills on the outer edge of the peninsula.

This trail, which is poorly signposted and barely passable by car, takes you 13km across the hot desert to **the Trident**, a massive 128-metre-high by 74-metre-wide candelabra carved into the hillside. No one knows its function or its creator, though Eric Von Daniken, author of *Chariots of the Gods*, speculated that it was a sign for extraterrestrial space-craft, pointing the way (inaccurately as it happens) towards the mysterious Nazca Lines that are inland to the southeast (see p.189); others suggest it was constructed as a navigational aid for eighteenth-century pirates. However, it seems more likely that it was a kind of pre-Inca ritual object, representing a cactus or tree of life and that high priests during the Paracas or Nazca eras worshipped the setting sun from this spot.

Lagunillas and around

Unless you want to see the Trident figure, instead of heading on toward Punta Pejerrey, it's a better idea to take the dusty sand track which cuts off to the left of the main road, towards the tiny and likeable port of **Lagunillas**, some 6km from the entrance to the park. A fishing hamlet with no accommodation but a few huts serving *conchitas* (scallops) and other seafood, Lagunillas is really the point on Paracas to make for – a strange, very beautiful part of the peninsula, so flat that if the sea rose just another metre the whole place would be submerged. Pelicans and sea lions hang around the bobbing boats waiting for a fisherman to drop a fish, and little trucks regularly arrive to carry the catch back into Pisco.

From Lagunillas the rest of the Paracas Reserve is at your feet. Nearby are the glorious **beaches** of **La Mina** and **Yimaque**, where you can **camp** for days often without seeing anyone, and a track goes off 5km north to a longer sandy beach, **Arquillo**; on the cliffs a few hundred meters beyond there's a **viewing platform** (Mirador de los Lobos) looking out over a large colony of sea lions (though they were depleted in number by the 1998 El Niño). Another path leads north from here, straight across the peninsula to the Trident and on to Punta Pejerrey. There have been reports of stingrays on some of the beaches, so take care, particularly if you're without transport or company; check first with the fishermen at Lagunillas which beaches are the safest.

South around the bay from Lagunillas, drive or walk along the track turning right across the sandy hills and heading away from the museum, and it's about 4km (a good hour's walk) to the spectacular **cathedral cave** (La Catedral), whose high vaulted ceilings are lined by bats. A family of sea otters (known in Peru as Gatos Marinos, or "Sea Cats") lives under the cave's floor of sea-worn boulders and huge waves pound the rocky inner walls. The cave lies at the end of a vast, curved gravelly beach whose waves are so strong that local fishermen call it **Playa Supay** (or "Devil's Beach"), so don't be tempted to swim – it's far too dangerous. This track continues to the fishing village of **Laguna Grande**, from where it's possible to track back inland to Ocucaje on the Panamerican Highway between Ica and Nazca.

Tambo Colorado

Some 48km northeast of Pisco, the ruins at **TAMBO COLORADO** were originally a fortified administrative centre, probably built by the Chincha before being adapted and used as an Inca coastal outpost. Its position at the base of steep foothills in the Pisco river valley was perfect for controlling the flow of people and produce along the ancient road down from the Andes. You can still see dwellings, offices, storehouses and row upon row of barracks and outer walls, some of them even retaining traces of coloured paints. The rains have taken their toll, but even so this is considered one of the best-preserved adobe ruins in Peru – roofless, but otherwise virtually intact. Though in an odd way reminiscent of a fort from some low-budget Western, it is nonetheless a classic example of a pre-planned adobe complex, everything in its place and nothing out of order – autocratic by intention, oppressive in function, and rather stiff in style.

The easiest way to get to Tambo Colorado is on a **guided tour** from Pisco (see Listings, p.178, for details), which costs less than $15 per person, provided there are at least ten people. You can also travel there independently: take the Ormeño **bus** from Jirón San Francisco or the Oropesa bus from Calle Comercio (both leave most mornings, but check first with the bus company as departure times and frequencies vary from day to day). The bus takes the surfaced Ayacucho road, which runs straight through the site, and the ruins are around twenty minutes beyond the village of Humay.

South from Pisco

South from Pisco, the Panamerican Highway sweeps some 70km inland to reach the fertile wine-producing Ica Valley, a virtual oasis in this stretch of bleak desert. **Pozo Santo**, the only real landmark en route, is distinguished by a small towered and white-washed chapel, built on the site of an underground well. Legend has it that when Padre Guatemala, the friar Ramon Rojas, died on this spot, water miraculously began to flow from the sands. Now there's a restaurant here where colectivo drivers sometimes stop for a snack, but little else.

Beyond Pozo Santo, the Panamerican Highway crosses the Pampa de Villacuri. At the Km 280 marker, there's a track leading north; after about an hour's hike, you'll reach the ruins of an adobe **fortress** complex, where you can see dwellings, a plaza, a forty-metre-long outer wall, and ancient man-made wells, which are still used by local peasants to irrigate their cornfields. Seashells and brightly coloured plumes from the tropical forest found in the graves here suggest that there was an important trade link between the inhabitants of the southern coast and the tribes from the eastern jungles on the other side of the formidable Andean mountain range.

Farther down the Panamerican Highway, the pretty roadside village of **Guadalupe** (at Km 293) signals the beginning of the Ica oasis. To the right there's a large, dark, conical hill, Cerro Prieto, behind which, in amongst the shifting sand dunes, there are even more **ruins**, dating from 500 BC. Just a few kilometres on, beyond a string of wine *bodegas* and shanty-town suburbs, you reach Ica itself.

Ica and around

An attractive old but busy city with around 170,000 inhabitants, **ICA** is famous through-out Peru for its wine and *pisco* production. Its very foundation (in 1563) went hand in hand with the introduction of grapevines to South America, and for most Peruvian visitors it is the *bodegas* or **wineries** that are the town's biggest draw. A further attraction is the **Museo Regional**, whose superb collections of pre-Colombian ceramics and Paracas, Ica and Nazca culture artefacts would alone make the city worth an excursion. Ica's streets and plazas are crowded with hundreds of little *tico* taxis, all beeping their horns to catch potential passengers' attention and making crossing the streets a dangerous affair. Aside from the traffic and the occasional pickpocket – particularly round the market area – Ica is a pleasant but busy place with plenty to do, though after a day or two most visitors are ready to head for the relaxing desert oasis resort of **Huacachina**, a few kilometres to the southwest. On the edge of town is the rather ramshackle suburb of **Cachiche**, known throughout Peru as a traditional sanctuary for white witches.

THE WITCHES OF CACHICHE

In the down-at-heel suburb of Cachiche, history and mythology have merged into the legend of the **witches** of Cachiche. The story appears to date back to the seventeenth century, when, hounded for their pagan beliefs by the Inquisition, Spanish witches apparently emigrated to Peru. However, the persecution in Lima equalled that in their homeland, and they fled to the countryside and, in particular, the Ica Valley, though even then they were forced into outlying villages; the white witches, apparently moved to Cachiche, the black ones to Huamangia, the east of the city. Cachiche resurfaced in the Peruvian consciousness in the 1980s, when a powerful congressman was dramatically cured on TV of a terminal illness by one of the last Cachiche witches.

Arrival, information and city transport

If you arrive in Ica by **colectivo** or Ormeño, Jirón Lambayeque 180 (☎034/215600) or Cruz del Sur **buses**, you'll come in along Prolongación Lambayeque, a few blocks west of Plaza de Armas. Peru Bus fast services from Lima arrive close by on Avenida Matías Manzanilla 130, Expresso Sudamericano arrive at Avenida Municipalidad 336, and Flores come in at Salaverry 396, on the corner with Lambayeque.

To get around the town itself, most people take **taxis**, mostly small, flimsy and dangerous *tico* cars (try to use one of the rarer larger but more solid vehicles), with journeys within town rarely costing more than $2–3. Cheaper still – around $1 for anywhere in town and under $5 to Huacachina – are the **bicycle rickshaw taxis** which can be hailed anywhere in town. For longer journeys to the outlying parts of town, you can take one of the **microbuses**, which leave from Jirón Lima or Prolongación Lambeyeque and have their destinations chalked up on their windscreens. **Tourist information** is available from the official office of Direcíon Subregional de Industria y Turismo, Avenida Grau 150 (☎034/233416). It's also worth trying Pelican Travel Services, Calle Independencia 156 (☎034/225211, 211702 or 235444, fax 225211), and the Automóvil Club at Manzanilla 523.

Accommodation

Hostal Aries, Calle Independencia 181 (☎034/235367). The best of Ica's budget hostals, with clean rooms, though bathrooms are communal; there's a pleasant patio and service is very good. ②.

Hostal Bella Sand, Avenida Casuarines B-1, Residencia La Anostura (☎034/256039, fax 256814). Not central, but reasonable value with a pool, colour TVs and private bathrooms. ④.

Hostal Callao, Jirón Callao 128 (☎034/235976). Very central – just a few metres from the Plaza de Armas – basic, clean and quite friendly. Some rooms have private shower. ②.

Hostal Colibri, Avenida Grau 387 (☎034/231764). A popular little hostal, backpacker-friendly, it has kitchen and laundry facilities, a tourist agency and is very central. ②.

Hostal Diaz, Calle Independencia 165 (☎034/234597) Surprisingly good value, set in a stylish old building, with reasonable service but very basic rooms. ①.

Hostal Europa, Calle Independencia 258 (☎034/232111). Would be good value if it weren't so noisy. Located very close to the market area, it's friendly and clean, with sinks in some rooms but communal toilets. ②.

Hostal Palace, Jirón Tacna 185 (☎034/222882). Modern building with its own café next door; private bathrooms but no single rooms. ③.

Hostal San Isidro, Los Jasminez 127, San Isidro (☎034/235474). Although not particularly central, this pleasant hostal offers economy and comfort in large rooms. Affiliated to Hostelling International. ②.

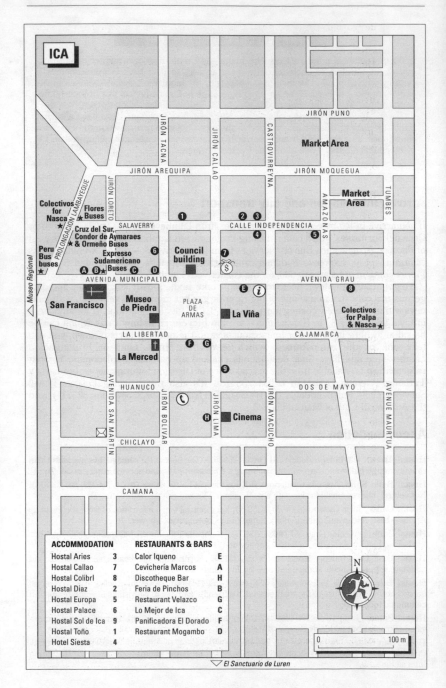

ICA

JIRÓN PUNO

JIRÓN TACNA

JIRÓN CALLAO

CASTROVIRREYNA

Market Area

JIRÓN AREQUIPA

JIRÓN MOQUEGUA

JIRÓN LORETO

PROLONGACION LAMBAYEQUE

Colectivos for Nasca ★

Flores Buses ★

Cruz del Sur, Condor de Aymaraes & Ormeño Buses ★

Peru Bus buses ★

Expresso Sudamericano Buses

A ★ B ★ C D

SALAVERRY

CALLE INDEPENDENCIA

Market Area

AMAZONAS

TUMBES

❶

❷ ❸

❹

❺

❻

Council building

❼ ⓢ

AVENIDA MUNICIPALIDAD

AVENIDA GRAU

San Francisco

Museo de Piedra

PLAZA DE ARMAS

Ⓔ ⓘ

La Viña

❽

Colectivos for Palpa & Nasca ★

△ Museo Regional

AVENIDA SAN MARTIN

LA LIBERTAD

Ⓕ Ⓖ

CAJAMARCA

La Merced †

❾

HUANUCO

JIRÓN BOLIVAR

JIRÓN LIMA

JIRÓN AYACUCHO

DOS DE MAYO

AVENUE MAURTUA

✆

Ⓗ Cinema

CHICLAYO

CAMANA

ACCOMMODATION		RESTAURANTS & BARS	
Hostal Aries	3	Calor Iqueno	E
Hostal Callao	7	Cevichería Marcos	A
Hostal Colibrl	8	Discotheque Bar	H
Hostal Diaz	2	Feria de Pinchos	B
Hostal Europa	5	Restaurant Velazco	G
Hostal Palace	6	Lo Mejor de Ica	C
Hostal Sol de Ica	9	Panificadora El Dorado	F
Hostal Toño	1	Restaurant Mogambo	D
Hotel Siesta	4		

N

0   100 m

▽ El Sanctuario de Luren

Hostal Sol de Ica, Jirón Lima 265, (☎034/236168). Very central, quite modern and clean, with a nice swimming pool, though the building has suffered some earthquake damage. ⑤.

Hostal Toño, Salaverry 146. Clean but noisy and basic, with communal bathrooms. ②.

Hotel Las Dunas, Avenida la Angostura 400, Km 300, Panamerican Highway (☎034/231031, *invertur@invertur.com.pe, www.invertur.com*). Very swish, out-of-town luxury hotel with a pool and plenty of amenities. ⑦.

Hotel Real de Ica, Avenida Los Maestros (☎034/233330 or 233320). Located on the outskirts of town near the hospital and en route to Huacachina. one of a luxury chain of ex-government run *turistas* hotels, with a nice pool open to non-residents for a fee of around $2. Fantastic buffet lunches are served during the main *fiesta* periods. Taxi drivers may still know it as *El Hotel de Turistas*.⑦.

Hotel Siesta, Calle Independencia 196 (☎034/234663). A modernized, very clean, simple hotel used mostly by business types. Service and facilities are superior to others of a similar price in the same road. ④.

The Town

Founded in 1563, and originally called Villa de Valverde de Ica, after only five years the settlement was moved due to earthquake activity in the region and renamed San Jerónimo de Ica. It was moved several times again until finding itself in its present position. It's quite a sprawl these days, and although prone to earthquakes, the flooding caused by El Niño in 1998 resulted in the most recent damage, when the Plaza de Armas and most of the main streets were submerged under more than a meter of water.

Ica's colonial heart – the inevitable **Plaza de Armas**, site of an early declaration of independence from Spain – remains its modern centre, with the inclusion of an obelisk and fountains. Within a few blocks are most of the important **churches**, rarely of great architectural merit but considerably revered within the region. The church of **La Merced**, southwest of the plaza, contains Padre Guatemala's tomb – said to give immense good fortune if touched on New Year's Day. On the main street around the corner, Avenida Municipalidad, is the grander **San Francisco** church, whose stained-glass windows dazzle against the strong Ican sunlight; to the south of the plaza, down Jirón Lima, then left along Prolongación Ayabaca, is a third major church, **El Sanctuario de Luren**. On the site of a hermitage founded in 1556, the present construction, Neoclassical in style and with three brick-built *portales*, houses the Imagen del Señor de Lurin, patron saint of the town, something of a national shrine and centre for pilgrimage on the third Sundays of October and March.

There are a few **mansions** of note in Ica, including the Casona del Marqués de Torre Hermosa, in Calle Libertad and near the plaza, Now belonging to the Banco Continental, it has an interesting doorway and is one of the few examples of colonial

---

FIESTAS IN ICA

There are several important **fiestas** in Ica throughout the year. The most enjoyable time to be in town is in **March** after the grape harvest has been brought in, when there are open-air concerts, fairs, handicraft markets, cockfighting and *caballo de paso* (horse dressage) meetings. Over the **Semana de Ica** (June 12–19) based around the colonial founding of Ica there are more festivities, including religious processions and fireworks, and again in the last week of September for the **Semana Turistica**. On the July 25, there's the nationwide **Dia Nacional de Pisco**, essentially a big celebration for the national brandy (rather than the town of the same name), mostly celebrated in the *bodegas* south of Lima, particularly around Ica. As in Lima, **October** is the main month for religious celebrations, with the focus being the ceremony and procession at the church of El Sanctuario de Luren (main processions on the third Sunday and following Monday of October).

architecture to survive in the earthquake-stricken city. In the first block of Calle 2 de Mayo, you can find the Casona de José de la Torre Ugarte, once home to Iceño, composer of the Peruvian National Anthem. The Casona Alvorado, now belonging to the Banco Latino, at Cajamarca 178, is the region's only example of an architectural copy of the *greco-romana* style, the Casona Colonial El Porton, Calle Loreto 233 conserves some fine colonial architecture and houses a restaurant-*peña* – *Almuerzos Criollos* – (see Bars and Nightlife, p.188).

The Museo Regional

The **Museo Regional Maria Reiche de Ica**, block 8 of Avenida Ayabaca (Mon–Sat 9am–6pm, Sun & *fiestas* 9am–1pm; $1.50, $2 extra if you want to take photos), is one of the best archeological museums in Peru. It's a little way out from the centre on the Prolongación Ayabaca; to get there, take bus #17 from the Plaza de Armas, or walk six blocks down Avenida San Martin from the San Francisco church, then another six blocks right along Ayabaca; either way you can't miss the concrete museum building stuck out on its own in the middle of barren desert parkland. Behind the Museo there's an excellent large-scale model of the Nazca lines.

The most striking and possibly most important of the museum's collections is its display of **Paracas textiles**, the majority of them discovered at Cerro Colorado in the Paracas Peninsula by Julio Tello in 1927. Enigmatic in their apparent coding of colours and patterns, these funeral cloths consist of blank rectangles alternating with elaborately woven ones – repetitious and identical except in their multidirectional shifts of colour and position.

The first room to the right off the main foyer contains a fairly gruesome display of **mummies, trepanned skulls, grave artefacts** and **trophy heads**. It seems very likely that the taking of trophy heads in this region was related to specific religious beliefs – as it was until quite recently among the head-hunting Jivaro of the Amazon Basin. The earliest of these skulls, presumably hunted and collected by the victor in battle, come from the Asia Valley (north of Ica) and date from around 2000 BC.

The museum's main room is almost entirely devoted to pre-Columbian **ceramics and textiles**, possibly the finest collection outside Lima. On the left as you enter are spectacular Paracas urns; one is particularly outstanding, with an owl and serpent design painted on one side, a human face with arms, legs and a navel on the other. There is some exquisite Nazca pottery, too, undoubtedly the most colourful and abstractly imaginative designs found on any ancient Peruvian ceramics. The last wall is devoted mainly to artefacts from the Ica-Chincha culture, which seems to have been specifically marked by a decline in importance of the feline god and a move towards urbanization. A highlight is the beautiful **feather cape**, with multicoloured plumes in almost perfect condition.

Displayed also in the main room are several **quipus**, ancient calculators using bundles of knotted strings as mnemonic devices. According to the historian Alden Mason, these numerical records followed a decimal system very much like our own – a simple knot representing "one", digits from two to nine denoted by longer knots in which the cord was wound or looped a given number of times before it was pulled tight. The concept of zero was shown by the absence of any knot in the expected position, while place value is indicated by any particular knot's distance from the main cord. *Quipu*s were also mnemonic aids for the recitation of ancient legends, genealogies and ballads. They have survived better here on the coast than in the mountains and the Ica collection is one of the best in the country. On the second floor are various (though not signposted) Colonial and Republican exhibits.

Museo de Piedra

Back on the Plaza de Armas, the **Museo de Piedra**, Bolivar 170 (daily 9am–1pm & 4.30–8pm; $5, includes a guided tour), contains a rather bizarre and controversial collection of engraved stones, assembled by Dr Javier Cabrera, a well-respected member of the community. Dr Cabrera claims that the stones are several thousand years old but few people believe this – some of the stones depict patently modern surgical techniques and, perhaps more critically, you can watch artisans turning out remarkably similar designs over on the *pampa* at Nazca. Nevertheless, the stones are remarkable pieces of art and one enthusiastic local guidebook claims that "dinosaur hunts are portrayed, suggesting that Ica may have supported the first culture on earth". The museum doors are often closed, so knock loudly.

Bodegas

The best way to escape Ica's hot desert afternoons is to wander around the cool chambers and vaults and sample the wines at one of the town's **bodegas** or wineries. One of the best is **Vista Allegre** (daily 9am–5pm), easily reached by walking down Avenida Grau from the main plaza, crossing over the Río Ica bridge, then turning left. Follow this road for about twenty minutes until you come to a huge yellow colonial gateway on your right (or take the orange microbus #8 from Avenida Grau or the market); the arch leads via an avenue of tall eucalyptus trees to the *bodega* itself, an old hacienda still chugging happily along in a forgotten world of its own. There's usually a guide who'll show you around free of charge, then arrange for a wine and *pisco* tasting session at the shop. You don't have to buy anything, but you're expected to tip.

If you follow the road beyond Vista Allegre for another 6km you'll come to **Bodega Tacama** (daily 9am–6pm), a larger and slightly more important wine producer about 3km from the centre of Ica, which also offers guided tours and wine and *pisco* tasting. The vineyards here are still irrigated by the Achirana canal, which was built by the Inca Pachacutec (or his brother Capac Yupanqui) as a gift to Princess Tate, daughter of a local chieftain. According to legend, it took forty thousand men just ten days to complete this astonishing canal, which brings cold, pure water down 4000m from the Andes to transform what was once an arid desert into a startlingly fertile oasis. Clearly a romantic at heart, Pachacutec named it Achirana – "that which flows cleanly toward that which is beautiful". About 35km further south, the tourist oasis of **Bodega Ocucaje** is another of Peru's finest vineyards. You can stay here at the *Hotel Ocucaje* (③) and explore the surrounding desert, particularly the Cerro Blanco site where whalebone remains have been found.

Restaurants

Calor Iqueno, Avenida Grau 103. Small and fairly quiet, this snack-bar/coffee shop has great hot drinks, yoghurts and local *empañadas* (pasties filled with meat, onions and olives).

Cevichería La Candella, block 4 of Jirón Lima. Decent food and affordable prices, plus a lively atmosphere and a bar that's open evenings.

Cevichería Marcos, Avenida Municipalidad 350. Good seafood lunches at very reasonable prices.

Chifa Fu Sheng, Jirón Lima 243. Very affordable Chinese restaurant, popular with locals in the evenings.

El Eden, Calle Andaguayllas 204. A popular vegetarian restaurant making good use of local ingredients.

Gran Pollería las Nieves, Calle Piura 400, Plaza Bolognesi. Serves good chicken and chips and is very popular.

Jackeline Cevichería, Calle Tacna 193. Fine traditional cuisine, including lots of fresh seafood. Has an inexpensive set-lunch menu.

Panificadora El Dorado, La Libertad 103. The town's best option for lunch, a bakery-café on the corner of the Plaza de Armas serving cold drinks and savoury and sweet snacks. Pay at the cash till before ordering.

Restaurant Mogambo, Jirón Tacna 137, just off the Plaza de Armas. A popular locals' dive serving big portions of exquisite *aji de gallina* (chicken in chilli sauce) and sometimes the Ica speciality *carapulchra* (pork, chicken and potato casserole). A lively atmosphere, a loud TV and frequent salsa music.

Restaurant Velazco, La Libertad 137, facing the Plaza de Armas. Modern and clean, with a sophisticated atmosphere and food ranging from roast dinners to tasty cakes.

Bars and nightlife

Not surprisingly, Ica wines are very much a part of the town's life and locals pop into a **bodega** for a quick glass of *pisco* at just about any time of the day; most open 9am–9pm. The best places to do likewise are *La Vina*, Jirón Lima 139, on the Plaza de Armas, or the cheaper unnamed shop on the left, half a block further down Jirón Lima. The *Feria de Pinchos* at Avenida Municipalidad 344 serves drinks and sells *artesania*, while *Lo Mejor de Ica*, Avenida Municipalidad 286, is renowned for its wines, *piscos* and local sweets. The only **club** in town is the *Discotheque Bar*, at Jirón Lima 351, opposite the cinema, while the *Almuerzos Criollos* restaurant-*peña* in the Casona Colonial El Porton, Calle Loreto 233, often has shows at weekends.

Listings

Banks and exchange Traveller's cheques and cash can be changed at Banco de Credito, Avenida Grau 109 (Mon–Fri 8am–5pm); Caja Municipa, Avenida Municipalidad 148 (Mon–Fri 8.30am–6pm); ans Banco de La Nacion, Avenida Matias Manzanilla (Mon–Fri 9am–6pm). For dollars cash try any of the *cambistas* on the corners of the Plaza de Armas.

Bus companies Peru Bus, Avenida Matías Manzanilla 150 (☎034/224138), have the fastest and most frequent connections for Pisco and Ica; Condor de Aymaraes, Prolongación Lambayeque 152a; Cruz del Sur, Prolongación Lambayeque 148 (☎034/233333); Expresso Sudamericano, Municipalidad 336; Flores, Salaverry 396; Ormeño, Prolongación Lambayeque 180 (☎034/23262).

Police The Tourist Police are on block 1 of Prolongación Lambayeque (☎034/233632).

Post office San Martin 398, 3 blocks south of Plaza de Armas. Mon–Sat 8am–6.30pm.

Tour operators Pelican Travel Services, Calle Independencia 156 (☎034/225211, 211702 or 235444, fax 225211), employ an excellent and experienced guide to the region.

Huacachina

According to myth, the lagoon at **HUACACHINA**, about 5km southwest of Ica, was created when a princess stripped off to bathe, but, on looking into a mirror, saw that a male hunter was watching her; startled, she dropped the mirror, which turned into the lagoon. The princess eventually became a siren who still comes out at night under the full moon to sing her ancient sacred songs. More prosaically, during the late 1940s, it became one of Peru's most elegant and exclusive resorts, surrounded by palm trees, sand dunes and waters famed for their curative powers, and a delightfully old-world atmosphere. Since then the lagoon's subterranean source has grown erratic and it is supplemented by water pumped up from artesian wells, making it less of a thick, viscous syrup. However, it is still red in colour (and apparently radioactive) and retains considerable mystique, making it a quiet, secluded spot to relax. The **curative powers** of the lagoon attract people from all over: mud from the lake is reputed to cure arthritis and rheumatism if you plaster yourself all over with it; and the sand around the lagoon is also supposed to benefit people with chest problems such as asthma or bronchitis, so it's not uncommon to see locals buried up to the neck in the dunes. **Sand dune surfing** on the higher slopes is all the rage and you can rent wooden boards or foot-skis for around $2 an hour from the cafés along the shoreline.

Practicalities

To get to Huacachina from Ica, take one of the orange **buses** from outside the Sanctuario de Luren, or from Jirón Lima; buses leave at least once every fifteen minutes and the journey takes fifteen to twenty minutes.

The most stylish **accommodation** in Huacachina is the luxurious and exceptionally elegant *Hotel Mossone* (☎034/231651; fax 236137; ⑦), once the haunt of politicians and diplomats, who listened to concerts while sitting on the colonial-style veranda over-looking the lagoon. If your budget won't stretch to this, the *Hotel Salvatierra*, Malecon de Huacachina (☎034/232352; ③), alongside, is excellent value, and has an enormous amount of character; its splendid dining room holds a number of important murals by the Ica artist Servulo Gutierrez (1914–61). Most rooms have private facilities, and the owner will take you to and from Ica in his minibus. It's also possible to **camp** in the sand dunes around the lagoon – rarely is it cold enough to need more than a blanket. The best **restaurant** is *Curasi*, next to the *Hotel Mossone*, with a wide range of reasonably priced Peruvian dishes on offer. The *Mossone* has a wonderful restaurant too, but it's very pricey. There are also three or four other options, mostly temporary shacks serving snacks, cold food and beer, along the eastern margin of the lagoon.

The Nazca Lines

One of the great mysteries of South America, the **Nazca Lines** are a series of animal figures and geometric shapes, none of them repeated and some up to 200m in length, drawn across some five hundred square kilometres of the bleak, stony Pampa de San José. Each one, even such sophisticated motifs as a spider monkey or a hummingbird, is executed in a single continuous line, most created by clearing away the brush and

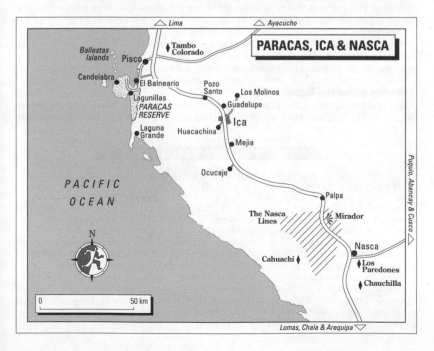

hard stones of the plain to reveal the fine dust beneath. They were probably a kind of agricultural calendar to help regulate the planting and harvesting of crops, while perhaps at the same time some of the straight lines served as ancient sacred paths connecting *huacas*, or power spots. One theory proposes that the Lines were used as running tracks in some sort of sporting competition; whichever theory you favour, they are among the strangest and most unforgettable sights in the country.

Getting to the Lines

The road to Nazca from Ica crosses a large strip of desert named the **Pampa de Gamonal** after the unfortunate man who, as the local story goes, found a vast amount of treasure here, buried it, and then promptly developed amnesia as to its whereabouts. Winds here frequently achieve speeds of up to 45km per hour, bringing sandstorms in their wake. The Lines begin on the tableland above the village of **PALPA** about 70km south of Ica on the Panamerican Highway, where amid orange groves, cherry plantations and date farms are a couple of small **hostals**, the basic *Hostal Palpa* (①) and the simple but clean *Hostal San Francisco* (②) and the **restaurant** *Monterrey*, Avenida Grau 118 (☎034/404062). The annual Fiesta de la Narancja (Orange Festival) on August 15 sees a few days of processions, dancing, singing and drinking.

It's still another 20km until you can actually see the Lines, at Km 420 of the Panamerican Highway, where a tall metal **viewing tower** (or *mirador*, $0.3) has been built above the plain. Unless you've got the time to climb up onto one of the hills behind, or take a **flight** over the Lines (see box), this is the best view you'll get; the **Casa Museo Maria Reiche** (Mon–Sat 9am–5pm; $1), about 1km beyond the *mirador*, contains displays of Maria Reiche's personal possessions and artefacts relating to the Nazca Lines (for more on Maria Reiche, see p.190–191). The vast majority of people base themselves in Nazca and take a **guided tour** (see p.197) or a flight from there. However, you can visit independently; either catch a **local bus** from Nazca ($0.7); a **taxi** from Nazca, which will wait and bring you back again for around $10; or one of the **intercity buses** for Ica and Lima, which leave every couple of hours from the corner of the Panamerican Highway and Jirón Lima on the outskirts of Nazca and will let you off at the *mirador*. The return bus to Nazca passes Km 420 of the Panamerican Highway every couple of hours and can be waved down.

Theories about the Nazca Lines

The greatest expert on the Lines was undoubtedly **Maria Reiche**, who worked at Nazca almost continuously from 1946 until her death in 1998, and who believed that

---

FLYING OVER THE NAZCA LINES

A pricey but spectacular way of seeing the Lines is to **fly** over them. Flights leave from Nazca airstrip, about 3km south of Nazca, and cost $25–70 a person depending on the season, the size of the group, and how long you want to spend buzzing around – they can last from ten minutes to a couple of hours. Bear in mind that the planes are small and bounce around in the changeable air currents, which can cause airsickness, and that you'll get a better view on an early morning trip, since the air gets hazier as the sun rises higher. Some companies flying over the Lines have offices in Nazca, others also have offices in Lima (see p.84), while some are best located at the Nazca airstrip itself. **Flight operators** include Aero Ica, contactable through the *Hotel la Maison Suisse* (see p.194) in Nazca, or see Ica Listings, p.188; Aero Nazca, Calle Lima 165, Nazca (☎ & fax 034/522297, *aeroNazca@Latinmail.com*); Aero Paracas, Jirón Lima 185, Nazca (☎034/521027, fax 522688), or at Nazca airport ☎034/522699, *aeroparacas@wayna.rcp. com.pe*); Alas Peruanas, Jirón Lima 168 (☎ & fax 034/522444, *alasperuanas@nazcaperu. com*). Both Aero Montecarlo and Aero Palpa have offices at the airstrip.

the lines were an astronomical calendar linked to the rising and setting points of celestial bodies on the east and west horizons. She considered the lines and cleared areas to be the most important features, followed by the animals and lastly the spirals. The whole complex, according to her theories, was designed to help organize planting and harvesting around seasonal changes rather than the fickle shifts of weather. In most developed Central and South American cultures there was a strong emphasis on knowledge of the heavens, and in a desert area like Nazca, where the coastal fog never reaches up to obscure the night sky over the *pampa*, this must have been highly advanced.

In the late 1960s an American, **Gerald Hawkins**, computed that two mounds on the *pampa* were aligned with the Pleiades constellation in the era between 600 and 700 AD – during the Nazca period. The Incas revered the Pleiades, calling them Quolqua ("granary") because they believed them to watch over and protect the seeds during germination. This kind of information, if it wasn't already common knowledge in ancient Peru, might have been adopted by the Incas from the Nazca region when it was drawn into their empire in the fifteenth century. Hawkin's computers also suggested, however, that the occasional alignments of the Lines with the sun, moon and stars are barely frequent enough to rise above the level of chance.

In many cases the Lines connect with low hills on the plain or the foothills of the Andes along its edge. Fragments of Nazca pottery found around these hills suggest that they may have been sacred sites, perhaps as important in terms of ritual as the celestial movements. Recent theories regarding the Lines take this as evidence that at least some of them were *ceques*, or sacred pathways, between *huacas*. In Inca Cusco, *ceques* radiated from the Sun Temple, Koricancha, to surrounding *huacas*, many of these being hills on the distant horizon. Each of the *ceques* was under the protection of a particular *allyu* or kinship group. This theory is all the more feasible since, if the Lines were purely for astronomical observations, they wouldn't need to be so long.

Tony Morrisson, one of the proponents of this idea, discovered many similar *ceques* in the mountains between Cusco and La Paz. They were related to *huacas* and still "owned" by specific local kinship groups. Morrisson concludes that the various stone piles often found at the end of lines at Nazca were ancient *huacas*, and the lines were paths between these sacred places. They were in a straight line, he says, simply because this is the shortest distance between any two *huacas*. It follows that the cleared areas were ceremonial sites for larger *allyu* gatherings. The animal figures might be explained by them pre-dating the straight lines; this would fit into the early and late pottery phases (the former being most closely associated with animalistic motifs).

Maria Reiche's theory isn't necessarily contradictory. Many other alignments were confirmed by Hawkins's computer (particularly those for the solar solstices) and even if the Lines and animal designs were made at different times, there's still a connection: designs like the spider and the monkey might be representations of the constellations of Orion and Ursa Major. It's difficult for a Western mind to visualize the constellations except through the stereotyped images we've grown accustomed to. The Nazca people, on the other hand, were free to impose their own ideas and there are remarkable similarities between the motifs they drew on the *pampa* and some of the major constellations.

On a slightly less esoteric level it's interesting to note how many of the extended lines are uncannily straight. One theory is that they were made using three cane poles and a rope, in much the same manner as a surveyor uses ranging sticks and a theodolite; when the late Maria Reiche first came to Nazca some of the locals could indeed remember wooden poles at the end of certain lines – perhaps sighting posts for the stars. How long it took to construct them is a last, inevitable question – and since none of them can be properly seen from the ground it is tempting to believe they must have been the skilled product of numerous generations. In strictly physical terms this isn't necessarily so – a local school once tried building its own line and from its efforts calculated that a thousand patient and inspired workers could have made them all in less than a month.

Nazca and around

Some 20km south of the viewing tower, the colonial town of **NAZCA** spreads along the margin of a small coastal valley. Although the river is invariably dry, Nazca's valley remains green and fertile through the continued application of an Incaic subterranean aqueduct. It's a small town – slightly at odds with its appearance on maps – but an interesting and enjoyable place to stay. Indeed, these days it has become a major attraction, boasting, in addition to the Lines, the excellent **Museo Antoni/Centro Italiano Archaeologico**, adobe Inca ruins of **Paredones** only a couple of kilometres to the south, the **Casa Museo Maria Reiche** (see p.190), with access to several of the Nazca desert's animal figures, and two or three important **archeological sites** within an easy day's range.

Severely damaged by the earthquake of 1996, the face of Nazca has changed recently with the rebuilding of about half the town. The earthquake registered 6.4 on the Richter scale, lasting one minute and fifty two seconds – it only killed ten people in town, but a further three hundred died in nearby mines. Beyond the airport there's ample evidence of the town's rapid development in the form of new squatter settlements parcelled off into 200-square metre plots. After about 6 months the squatters receive their legal right to the land, and water and electricity usually follow a few years later.

September is one of the **best times to visit** Nazca if you want to participate in one of it's *fiestas*, when they venerate the Virgen de Guadalupe (Sept 8) with great enthusiasm. In May, the religious and secular festivities of the Fiesta de las Cruces, too go on for days.

Arrival, information and getting around

Roughly halfway between Lima and Arequipa, Nazca is easily reached by frequent bus, colectivo, or even by small **plane** from Lima with Aero Condor (see p.84 for details); colectivos link the airstrip with *jiróns* Bolognesi and Grau in town. If you're coming in by a **bus** that is going on to Arequipa, Cruz del Sur buses drop off outside the Alegria Tours office Lima–Arequipa service, but it's possible to miss the stop, so ask the driver to tell you when to get off. Ormeño buses arrive at Avenida de Los Incas 112 from Lima and Arequipa several times a day, several times weekly from Cusco; most other buses also stop around the start of Jirón Lima, on Avenida Los Incas. **Colectivos** to and from Ica arrive at and leave close to the presently closed *Hotel Montecarlo*, Jirón Callao 123, on the corner of Avenida Los Incas and Micaelo Bastidas; those from Vista Alegre leave from the corner of Bolognesi and Grau. Wherever you arrive, you'll be besieged by tour touts, who should be ignored (or told firmly that you've already booked a hotel and tour). Most people use the noisy, beeping little *tico* **taxis** or **motorcycle-rickshaws**, which can be hailed anywhere and compete to take you in or around town cheaply – you shouldn't pay more than $2 for any destination in town. Buses leave every hour for the Nazca airstrip, from the corner of Grau with Jirón Bolognesi, and are normally marked *B-Vista Allegre*.

Accommodation

Finding a **hotel** in Nazca is simple enough, with an enormous choice for such a small town; most places are along Jirón Lima or within a few blocks of the Plaza de Armas. There is no official campsite in or around Nazca, but **camping** is sometimes permitted

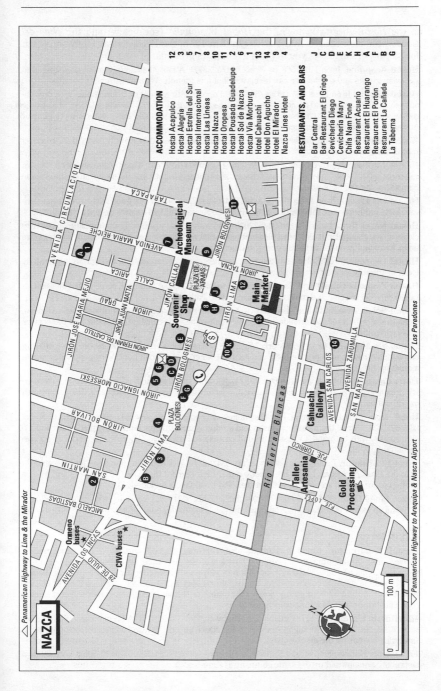

NAZCA

ACCOMMODATION

Hostal Acapulco	12
Hostal Alegría	3
Hostal Estrella del Sur	5
Hostal Internacional	7
Hostal Las Líneas	8
Hostal Nazca	10
Hostal Oropesa	11
Hostal Pousada Guadelupe	2
Hostal Sol de Nazca	6
Hostal Vía Morburg	1
Hotel Cahuachi	13
Hotel Don Agucho	14
Hotel El Mirador	9
Nazca Lines Hotel	4

RESTAURANTS, AND BARS

Bar Central	J
Bar-Restaurant El Griego	C
Cevichería Diego	D
Cevichería Mary	E
Chifa Nam Fone	K
Restaurant Acuario	H
Restaurant El Huarango	A
Restaurant El Portón	F
Restaurant La Cañada	B
La Taberna	G

Archeological Museum

Souvenir Shop

PLAZA DE ARMAS

Main Market

Cahuachi Gallery

Taller Artesanía

Gold Processing

Río Tierras Blancas

Ormeño buses

CIVA buses

▷ Panamerican Highway to Lima & the Mirador

▷ Panamerican Highway to Arequipa & Nasca Airport

▷ Los Paredones

N

0   100 m

at the *Hostal Alegria* in town, the *Hostal Wasipunko* (see below) and the *Nido del Condor*, the closest hotel to the airstrip at Km 447 of the Panamerican Highway, which for $2 per person allows you to pitch a tent in its grounds.

Hostal Acapulco, Jirón Lima 668 (☎ & fax 034/522277). A fairly basic place more accustomed to Peruvian guests and the service can be erratic, but it is friendly. With or without private bath. ②.

Hostal Alegria, Jirón Lima 166 (☎034/522702). Popular with travellers, it has rooms with or without private bath set around an attractive garden, as well as a number of newer, plusher chalet-style rooms with fans and bath. It also has a café, and can arrange tours and bus connections to Lima or Arequipa. Camping is sometimes allowed. ②–③

Hostal Estrella del Sur, Callao 568 (☎034/522764). Good value, though only some of the compact rooms have windows. ②.

Hostal Internacional, Avenida Maria Reiche 112 (☎034/522744). Good value and with its own cafetería; most rooms have private bathrooms, some have TVs; it's got hot water all day and some bungalows out the back. ②.

Hostal Las Lineas, Jirón Arica 299 (☎ & fax 034/522488). Modern and good value, rooms have private bath and hot water, this overlooks the Plaza de Armas and has its own decent restaurant. ④.

Hostal Nazca, Jirón Lima 438 (☎034/522085). Friendly, basic place with shared bathrooms, very clean, airy and popular. It also has a pleasant restaurant and they can exchange dollars and organize taxis, tours and good-value flights over the Lines. ②.

Hostal Oropesa, Jirón Bolognesi 728. Nazca's cheapest accommodation, though not particularly clean or friendly. ②.

Hostal Pousada Guadelupe, San Martin 225 (☎034/522249). A laid-back place with a pleasant little garden. Good value and most rooms have private bath. ②.

Hostal Sol de Nazca, Calle Callao 586 (☎ & fax 034/522730, *dsalasm@Latinmail.com*). Modern, clean hostal with a rooftop breakfast café. Excellent value with constant hot water and the service is very friendly. ③.

Hostal Via Morburg, Jirón Jose Maria Mejia 108 (☎034/522566). A modern, secure place offering comfortable rooms with private bath, constant hot water, and a small pool. Very good value and in a quiet part of town. ③.

Hotel Cahuachi, Jirón Arica 115a (☎034/523786). This spotless, modern hotel overlooks the market area near the river bridge and has a rooftop patio with views to the mountains. Rooms are with or without bath. ③.

Hotel Don Agucho, Avenida Los Paredones, at corner with Avenida San Carlos (☎ & fax 034/522048). One of the nicest options in and around Nazca, this hacienda-style place has comfortable rooms, with bath and TV, based around cactus-filled passages. There's also a pool and a bar-restaurant. ③–④.

Hotel El Mirador, Jirón Tacna 436 (☎ & fax 034/523741). A pleasant new hotel looking straight onto the Plaza de Armas; rooms are mostly rather dark (except those on the top floor) and it has a rooftop patio. Rooms are with or without bath and breakfast is included. ④.

Nazca Lines Hotel, Jirón Bolognesi (☎034/522293, fax 522112). Luxurious, with its own well-kept pool and an excellent restaurant. Non-residents can also use the pool for approximately $5 a day. ⑦.

Out of town

Hostal Wasipunko, Km 457, Panamerican Highway, Pajonal (☎034/522330, *wasipunko@ hotmail.com*). A delightful, rustic country hostal, with its own small ecological and archeological museum. It has no mains electricity, but it's very clean and some rooms have private bath. Rooms are set around a lovely courtyard and the restaurant specializes in tasty pre-Inca food. It is signposted on the right of the highway, some 15km south of Nazca; a taxi from Nazca will cost around $5, or take one of the Marcona colectivos. ③–④.

Hotel de la Borda, Km 447, Panamerican Highway, (☎034/522576). A luxury hacienda hotel set in an oasis just 2km off the highway close to the Nazca airstrip. It also runs tours, including close to wildlife havens on the nearby coast. ⑥.

La Maison Suisse, Km 447, Panamerican Highway, (☎034/221562). A plush joint, with its own swimming pool, owned by the same company as Aero Ica. ⑦.

The Town

As you come into town, Jirón **Bolognesi**, the main street, leads straight into the **Plaza de Armas**. The Municipalidad, once the most impressive building on the plaza, with its steps beautifully tiled with Nazca-style ceramic bird designs, was destroyed by the 1996 earthquake, along with its excellent Archeological Museum. Among the losses were the magnificent bulb-shaped ceramic pot, almost half a metre tall, depicting two stylized monkeys, each one attached to the other by a fish-bone or serpent motif which ended, for one of them, in a condor and vampire bat design. The museum is being rebuilt. A new place, the **Museo Antoni/Centro Italiano Archaeologico**, Avenida de la Cultura 600, was opened in 1999, six long blocks from the Plaza de Armas along Bolognesi and more or less in front of the fire station. It's a fascinating museum, with excellent interpretative exhibits covering the evolution of Nazca culture and a good audio-visual presentation

The **main market** for the town, with the usual food, electronic goods and plastic products, is based in a ramshackle collection of huts and stalls, mostly under cover, on the left just before the river bridge on Calle Arica. The **Taller Artesania**, Pasaje Torrico 240, in Barrio San Carlos, a short walk south of the plaza over the bridge, is worth a visit for its wonderful ceramics; if a few people turn up, they'll demonstrate the process of ceramic-making from moulding to polishing. The San Carlos suburb boasts a couple of other attractions worth seeing: the **Arte Total Cahuachi Gallery**, Avenida San Carlos 241 (daily 9.30am–1pm & 3.30–8pm), a small exhibition and shop displaying local arts and crafts, and about 250m beyond the gallery, a **gold processing** operation. Don't be put off by the fact that it's in someone's back garden – it's fascinating to watch them grind rocks into powder and then extract gold dust from it.

Los Paredones, the graveyard and the Inca canal

The most impressive archeological sites around Nazca are some distance out (see p.197), but if you have an afternoon to spare, there are a few interesting spots you could walk to. The route covered below will take a leisurely three to four hours on foot – if you don't end up staying at the Cantay Cooperative's swimming pool halfway along.

To walk to **Los Paredones**, an Inca trade centre where wool from the mountains was exchanged for cotton grown along the coast, follow Calle Arica from the Plaza de Armas, cross the bridge, and keep going straight (off the main road which curves to the right). The modern road follows the same route as the ancient one from Nazca to Cusco, and passes just below the ruins about 1km ahead, at the foot of the sandy valley mouth, underneath a political slogan – APRA – etched into the hillside.

The buildings, made from adobe with stone foundations, are in a bad state of repair and the site is dotted with *huaquero*'s pits, but if you follow the path to the prominent central sector you can get a good idea of what the town must have been like. Overlooking the valley and roads, it's in a commanding position – a fact recognized and taken advantage of by local cultures long before the Incas arrived. At the foot of the ruins, you can usually look round a collection of funereal pieces collected and displayed by the Pomez family in their adobe home adjacent to the site.

Another 2km up the Puquio road from Los Paredones there's a **Nazca graveyard**, its pits open and burial remains spread around. Though much less extensive than the cemetery at Chauchilla (see p.197), it is still of interest – with subterranean galleries to explore, though they're rather hard to find. A half-hour walk up the valley from the graveyard through the cotton fields and along a track will bring you to the former hacienda of **Cantay**, now a model agricultural co-operative; its central plaza houses a **swimming pool** ($0.5) and a small cafetería. Just a little further above the co-operative settlement, you can make out a series of inverted conical dips, like swallow-holes in the fields. These are the air vents for a vast underground canal system that siphons desperately needed water from the Bisambra reservoir; designed and constructed by the Incas, it is even more essential today. You can get right down into the openings and poke your head or feet into the canals – they usually give off a pleasant warm breeze and you can see small fish swimming in the flowing water. The canals are built out of cut stones, usually about 90cm by 60cm, and run underground in a gentle zigzag fashion.

Eating and drinking

What little nightlife there is in Nazca is mainly based around **restaurants** and **bars**, particularly on Jirón Lima, Plaza de Armas and Jirón Bolognesi. The *Bar Central*, Jirón Bolognesi 500 (Mon–Sat 10am–midnight), is a rough drinking house on the corner of the Plaza de Armas. Another local dive, the *Pub*, Arica 417, is a rather non-descript bar with flashing lights and disco music, but it is popular at weekends.

Bar-Restaurant El Griego, Bolognesi 287. A good local eating house with some decent drinks too, very friendly and reasonably priced. Quite fun in the evening.

Cevichería Diego, Jirón Castillo 375. A nice seafood restaurant, with reasonable prices.

Cevichería Mary, Bolognesi 395. Small and quite basic eating house serving up very cheap and tasty seafood lunches.

Chifa Nam Fone, on the corner of Lima with Grau. The best option in town for a spicy Chinese meal.

Restaurant Acuario, Arica 211. Very good value, particularly the set-menu lunches.

Restaurant Los Angeles, Calle Bolognesi 493 (☎034/522294). A reasonably nice restaurant and soda fountain, close to the centre of Nazca.

Restaurant La Cañada, Jirón Lima 160. Good music, Internet connections and a very pleasant atmosphere, usually full of gringos eating their great seafood.

Restaurant La Encantada, Jirón Callao 592. Excellent *criolla* food in a nice atmosphere, though pricey.

Restaurant El Huarango, Calle Arica 602 (☎034/521287). The finest restaurant in Nazca, with a solid reputation among the locals, it has a rooftop patio and a great ambience. The delicious food is very well priced.

Restaurant Pizzeria-Heladeria Jambouy II, Calle Bolognesi 226. Small and inexpensive, with decent food.

Restaurant El Portón, Calle Ignacio Moresky 120 (☎034/523490). A lively restaurant at night, especially at weekends. Pastas, meat and seafood dishes in a good atmosphere, plus there's a dance floor and a bar. Frequently presents folk music.

Restaurant Turistico Las Lineas, Calle Arica 299. Central place with an unassuming choice of breakfasts and juices.

La Taberna, Jirón Lima 321. Serves a good selection of local and international dishes, plus a variety of drinks; its walls are covered with graffiti scrawled over the years by passing groups of travellers. Lively most evenings until midnight.

Listings

Banks and exchange Banco de Credito, Jirón Lima 495; Interbanc, Calle Arica 363; and Banco de La Nacion, Jirón Lima 463. The best rates for dollars cash are with the *cambistas* in the small park outside the Hotel Nazca, where Jirón Bolognesi and Jirón Lima merge, or outside the Banco de Credito.

Buses companies Cruz del Sur, no office (☎034/522495); Civa, block 1 of Avenida Guardia Civil (☎034/523019), though note that there's a restaurant out front; Cueva, Avenida Los Incas 106 (☎034/523061); Ormeño, Avenida Los Incas (☎034/522058);

Internet facilities Available at *Restaurant La Cañada* (see Eating and drinking, above).

Pharmacy Botica Alejandra, Arica 407.

Police Block 5, Jirón Lima (☎034/522442).

Post office Lima 816. Mon–Sat 7.45am–8pm.

Shopping For food and drink, try the small market, on Jirón Lima, the Panificadora La Esperanza bakery at Jirón Bolognesi 389, and the Licoria liquor store at Arica 401. Camera films can be bought at Comercial Charito, Arica 296, and the unnamed shop at Jirón Bolognesi 600, which also develops. Oscar, Jirón Bolognesi 465, sells local *artesania*

Telephones, Jirón Lima 359. Daily 7am–11pm.

Archeological sites around Nazca

Chauchilla and **Cahuachi**, after the Lines the most important sites associated with the Nazca culture, are both difficult to reach by public transport, and unless your energy and interest are pretty unlimited you'll want to take an organized tour or at least a local guide-cum-taxi driver (see box).

Chauchilla cemetery

Roughly 30km south of Nazca along the Panamerican Highway, then out along a dirt road beside the Poroma riverbed, **Chauchilla Cemetery** certainly rewards the effort it takes to visit. Once you reach the atmospheric site you realise how considerable a civilization the riverbanks must have maintained in the time of the Nazca culture. Scattered about the dusty ground are literally thousands of graves, most of which have been opened by grave robbers, leaving the skulls and skeletons exposed to the sun, along with broken pieces of pottery, bits of shroud fabric and lengths of braided hair, as yet unbleached by the desert sun. Further up the track, near Trancas, there's a small ceremonial **temple** – Huaca del Loro – and beyond this at Los Incas you can find Quemazon **petroglyphs**. These last two are not usually included in the standard tour, but if you hire your own guide, you can negotiate with him to take you there – expect to pay $5 extra.

Cahuachi

The ancient centre of Nazca culture, **Cahuachi** lies to the west of the Nazca Lines, about 30km from Nazca and some 20km from the Pacific. The site consists of a

---

TOURS AROUND NAZCA

Some well-established companies arrange **tours** to the major sites around Nazca, all offering similar trips to Los Paredones, Cantalloc, Cahuachi, Chauchilla and the Lines. Tours out to Chauchilla Cemetery last two and a half hours for about $10 a person; a trip to the viewing tower and the Casa Museo Maria Reiche also takes two and a half hours and costs around $10. Tours out to the ruined temple complex in the desert at Cahuachi (see above) last four hours and cost in the region of $50 for a party of four or five; these need to be arranged in advance. The best **tour operators** are Nazca Trails, Bolognesi 550, Plaza de Armas (☎ & fax 034/522858, *Nazca@correo.dnet.com.pe*)Alegria Tours, Calle Lima 168 (☎034/522444, *info@nazcaperu.com, www.nazcaperu.com*). Otherwise try Tour Peru, Calle Arica 285 (☎034/522481); NaNazca Tours and Souvenirs, Calle Lima 160 (☎ & fax 034/522917, *naNazcatours@yahoo.com*); Huarango Travel Agency, Calle Lima 165 (☎034/522297); and Viajes Nazca, Jirón Lima 185 (☎034/521027). Alternatively you might want to organize a trip with a guide-cum-driver for your own group; **recommended guides** include Orlando Etchebarne, contactable through Nazca Trails; Alex Frank Severino (contact through the *Hotel Sol de Nazca*); Miguel Angel Llaja Chavez, block 3 of Avenida Circunvalacion (☎034/522097); and Jose Bologner, contactable through Oscar's Shop, Jirón Bologner, 465. For **flights** over the Nazca Lines, see the box on p.190.

religious citadel split in half by the river with its main temple (one of a set of 6) constructed around a small natural hillock. Adobe platforms step the sides of this twenty-metre mound and although they're badly weathered today, you can still make out the general form. Separate courtyards attached to each of the six pyramids can be distinguished, but their exact use is unknown.

Quite close to the main complex is a construction known as **El Estaqueria**, The Place of the Stakes, retaining a dozen rows of *huarango* log pillars. *Huarango* trees (known in the north of Peru as *algarrobo*) are the most common form of desert vegetation. Their wood, baked by the sun, is very hard, though numbers are much reduced nowadays by locals who use them for fuel. The Estaqueria is estimated to be 2000 years old, but its original function is unclear, though other such constructions are usually found above tombs. The bodies here were buried with ceramics, food, textiles, jewellery and chaquira beads. Italian archeologist Guiseppe Orefici has worked on Cahuachi for nearly twenty years and has uncovered over 300 graves, one of which contained a tattooed and dreadlocked warrior. Also around 2000 years old, he's a mere whipper snapper compared to other evidence Orefici has unearthed relating to 4000-year-old pre-ceramic cultures.

Cahuachi is typical of a Nazca ceremonial centre in its use of natural features to form an integral part of the structure. The places the Nazcans lived their everyday lives in showed no such architectural aspirations – indeed there are no major towns associated with the Nazcans, who tended to live in small clusters of adobe huts, villages at best. One of the largest of these, the walled village of **Tambo de Perro**, can be found in Acari, the next dry valley. Stretching for over a mile, and situated next to an extensive Nazca graveyard, it was apparently one of the Nazcans' most important dwelling sites.

Until 1901, when Max Uhle "discovered" the Nazca culture, a group of beautiful **ceramics** in Peru's museums had remained unidentified and unclassifiable. With Uhle's work all that changed rapidly (though not quickly enough to prevent most of the sites being ransacked by grave robbers before proper excavations could be undertaken – a problem that continues today) and the importance of Nazca pottery came to be understood. Many of the best pieces were found here in Cahuachi.

Unlike contemporaneous Mochica ware, Nazca ceramics rarely attempt any realistic reproduction of images. The majority – painted in three or four earthy colours and given a resinous surface glaze – are relatively stylized or even completely abstract. Nevertheless, two main categories of subject matter recur: naturalistic designs of bird, animal and plant life, and motifs of mythological monsters and bizarre deities. In later works it became common to mould effigies onto the pots, and in Nazca's declining phases, under Huari-Tiahuanaco cultural influence, workmanship and design became less inspired.

The style and content of the early pottery, however, show remarkable similarities to the symbols depicted in the Nazca Lines, and although not enough is known about this culture to be certain, it seems reasonable to assume that the early Nazca people were also responsible for those drawings on the Pampa de San José. With most of the evidence coming from their graveyards, though, and that so dependent upon conjecture, there is little to characterize the Nazca and little known of them beyond the fact that they collected heads as trophies, that they built a ceremonial complex here in the desert at Cahuachi, and that they scraped a living from the Nazca, Ica and Pisco valleys from around 200 to 600 AD.

The only section of Cahuachi to have been properly excavated so far is the **Templo Escalonado**, a multilevel temple on which you can see wide adobe walls and, on the temple site, some round, sunken chambers. A hundred metres away, from the top of what is known as the main pyramid structure, you can look down over what was once the main ceremonial plaza, though it's difficult to make out these days because of the sands.

East of Nazca

Some 90km inland from Nazca, the Pampa Galeras is one of the best places in Peru to see the *vicuña*, a llama-like animal with very fine wool. The *vicuña* have lived for centuries in the **Pampa Galeras Vicuña Reserve**, which is now maintained as their natural habitat and contains more than five thousand of the creatures. Well signposted at Km 89 of the Nazca to Cusco road, the reserve is easily reached by hopping off one of the many daily Nazca to Cusco buses (Tour Huari run to Puquio at around 4pm; ask the driver to tell you where to get off). The reserve has some shelter in the reserve at the **Park Camp**, but it's a very basic concrete shack with no beds, and you need written permission from the Ministry of Agriculture and Fauna in Lima; it's best to take an organized tour with one of the Nazca companies (see p.197). However, you can **camp** here without a permit.

The *vicuña* themselves are not easy to spot. When you do notice a herd, you'll see it move as if it were a single organism. They flock together and move swiftly in a tight wave, bounding gracefully across the hills. The males are strictly territorial, protecting their patches of scrubby grass by day, then returning to the rockier heights as darkness falls.

Puquio, Coracora, Chumpi and Lago Parinacochas

Head east of the Pampa Galeras Vicuña Reserve along the Cusco road and you reach **PUQUIO**. As soon as you cross over the metal bridge at the entrance to the town, you'll sense that it's very different from the hot desert town of Nazca. In fact, Puquio was an isolated community until 1926, when the townspeople built their own road link between the coast and the *sierra*. If you have to break your journey here, you have a choice of three hostals, though none of them are particularly enticing. The road divides here with the main route continuing over the Andes to Cusco via Abancay.

A side road goes south along the mountains for about 140km to Lago Parinacochas (see below); although frequently destroyed by mudslides in the rainy season, the road always seems full of passing trucks which will usually take passengers for a small price. After about 100km, the road passes the small provincial capital, **Coracora**, a remote town with only one hotel. Around the main plaza there are some reasonable restaurants but there's little here to interest most travellers. Far better to continue the 16km to **Chumpi**, an ideal place to camp amid stunning *sierra* scenery. Within a few hours' walk is the amazingly beautiful lake, **Lago Parinacochas**, named after the many flamingos that live there and probably one of the best unofficial nature reserves in Peru. If you're not up to the walk, you could take a day-trip from Nazca for about $40; try Alegria Tours (see p.197 for details). From Chumpi you can either backtrack to Puquio, or continue down the road past the lake, before curving another 130km back down to the coast at Chala.

South to Arequipa – the Panamerican Highway

There's relatively little of great interest in the 170km of desert between Nazca and Chala. **Sacaco**, a fossil site with a small museum, can be reached on by Cueva bus to Las Lomas – ask the driver where to disembark – after which it's a thirty-minute walk. **LAS LOMAS** itself is an attractive fishing village with a **beach** that's especially good for spotting pelicans, about 90km to the south and off the Panamerican Highway. If you're based in Nazca you can take a tour here (see p.197), often taking in Sacaco, or catch the Cueva bus here (a 1hr journey). The **hotel** *Capricho de Verano* (contact through the *Hotel Don Agucho*, see p.194; ④) has a lovely location looking right down onto the beach, and you can also **camp** in the area.

Avoid **Puerto San Juan**, the one place of any real size on this stretch of coast, but actually just a modern industrial port for local iron-ore and copper mines. Continue on until you find the first break in the area's starkness as you approach Chala, at the olive groves in the Yauca Valley. Just beyond this, at Km 595 of the Panamerican Highway, is a strange uplifted zone, a natural oasis with its own microclimate stretching for about 20km. It's an unusual but interesting enough place to spend some time **camping** and exploring; there are Inca and pre-Inca ruins hidden in the *lomas*, but today the area is virtually uninhabited.

Just 10km before Chala stand the ruins of **PUERTO INCA**, the Incas' main port for Cusco, where there's an excellent **beach** and fine diving and fishing to be had. There's a small **hotel** on the beach, the *Coste Hotel*, Km 603, Panamerican Highway South (☎034/210224; ④). To get to the ruins, take a taxi from Chala (about $10), or catch an Arequipa-bound bus along the Panamerican Highway and ask to be dropped off at Km 603. You can walk the 3–4km from here – a rustic but passable road follows a narrow gully to the coast.

CHALA itself, the main port for Cusco until the construction of the Cusco-Arequipa rail line, is now an agreeable little fishing town, where you can overindulge in fresh seafood. If you want **to stay** in Chala, try the *Hotel de Turistas* (☎014/501110; ④) for a little comfort, or the much more basic *Hotel Grau* (②), close to the pleasant, sandy beach.

Camana

About 200km from Chala, **CAMANA** is a popular Arequipeñan beach resort from December to March, when the weather is hot, dry and relatively windless, but outside this period it has little to offer. The most popular **beach** here is at **La Punta**, around 5km along the Arequipa road. If you do end up here, there are a few decent **places to stay**. The *Hostal Montecarlo*, Avenida Lima 514 (☎054/571101; ③), opposite the hospital, is modern and has reasonable rooms with or without private bath, while the *Gran Hostal Premier*, Garci Carabajal 117 (③) is also fine, if not such good value. The *Hotel de Turistas*, Avenida Lima 138 (☎054/571113 or 571608; ③), is slightly neglected but retains a certain charm. The *Hostal Senor Hans*, on the beach at La Punta (☎054/572288; ③), has great views. For **eating**, the best seafood joints are *Cevichería Los Faroles*, Sebastian Barrianca 254a, hard to beat for its set lunches; *Cevichería Rosa Nautica*, right on the seafront at La Punta, which catches its own fish; and *Restaurant Lider*, Avenida Grau 266. Otherwise, the *Restaurant Turistico Senor Hans*, KM 827, at El Puente, is good for lunch. The *La Noche Disco*, Mariscal Castilla 668, and the nearby *La Miel* are the only worthy **clubs**.

The **Banco de La Nacion** is at Avenida Mariscal Castilla 102, and there's a **telephone** office at Avenida Lima 149 and another at Avenida Lima 300. **Buses** stop right in the centre of town, around the Grifo El Niño petrol station. **Colectivos** for La Punta ($0.3; a 15min journey) are on block 1 of Prolongacion Quilca, not far from the *Hotel de Turistas*.

Continuing toward Arequipa, the road keeps close to the coast wherever possible, passing through a few small fishing villages and over monotonous arid plains before eventually turning inland for the final uphill stretch into the land of volcanos and Peru's second largest city. At Km 916 of the Panamerican Highway, a road leads off into the Maches canyon towards the Toro Muerto petroglyphs, the Valley of the Volcanos and the increasingly popular destination of the great **Canyon de Cotahuasi** (see p.224).

AREQUIPA AND AROUND

It seems probable that the name **Arequipa** is derived from the Quechua phrase "*ari quepay*", meaning "OK, let's stop here", which, according to local legend, is exactly what the fourth Inca Emperor, Mayta Capac, said to his generals when they pestered him to settle here on the way back from one of his conqest trips from Cusco. Situated well above the coastal fog bank, at the foot of an ice-capped volcano – **El Misti** – and close to four other prominent volcanos (Chachani, Ampato, Corpuna and Pichupichu) the place has long been renowned for having one of the most pleasant settings and climates of all Peru's cities. The Ampato volcano is presently active, with wisps of smoke appearing on the horizon.

The Incas were not alone in finding Arequipa to their liking. When Pizarro officially "founded" the city in 1540 he was moved enough to call it Villa Hermosa, or Beautiful Town, and Miguel de Cervantes, author of *Don Quixote*, extolled the city's virtues, saying that it enjoyed an eternal springtime. Today, despite a disastrous earthquake in 1687 it's still endowed with some of the country's finest colonial **churches** and **mansions**, many of which are constructed from white volcanic *sillar*, cut from the surrounding mountains and often flecked with black ash. These buildings – particularly the **Monastery of Santa Catalina**, a complex enclosing a complete world within its thick walls – constitute the city's main appeal to travellers, but the startlingly varied countryside around Arequipa, from the gorges of both the Colca Canyon and the more distant **Cotahuasi Canyon**, to the unsettling isolation of the **Valley of the Volcanos**, is also worth exploring.

Arequipa

An active city, some 2400m above sea level, and with a relatively wealthy population of over three-quarters of a million, **AREQUIPA** maintains a rather aloof attitude toward the rest of Peru. Most Arequipans feel themselves distinct, if not culturally superior, and resent the idea of the nation revolving around Lima, and with **El Misti**, the 5821-metre dormant volcano poised above, the place does have a rather legendary sort of appearance. But besides its widespread image as the country's second biggest and arguably, after Cusco, most attractive city, Arequipa has some very specific historical connotations for Peruvians. Developing late as a provincial capital, and until 1870 connected only by mule track with the rest of Peru, it has acquired a reputation as *the* centre of **right-wing political power**: while populist movements have tended to emerge around Trujillo in the north, Arequipa has traditionally represented the solid interests of the oligarchy. Sanchez Cerro and Odria both began their coups here, in 1930 and 1948 respectively, and Belaunde, one of the most important presidents in pre- and post-military coup years, sprung into politics from one of the wealthy Arequipa families. In recent years, despite the tastefully ostentatious architecture and generally well-heeled appearance of most townsfolk, there has been a huge increase in the number of street beggars and Arequipa typifies the social extremes of Peru more than any other of its major cities.

On of the best times to visit is around August 15, when there's a **festival** celebrating the city's foundation with processions, music and poetry. There's also a folklore festival in the first week of July.

Arrival, information and city transport

Arequipa is the hub of most journeys in the southern half of Peru. As Peru's second city, it has reasonably good road connections and one of the few railway lines, so it's an

CRIME IN AREQUIPA

The worst reports from Arequipa in recent years have concerned a spate of "strangle-muggings" wherein tourists are jumped and strangled to the point of fainting before being robbed. Although rare, it's best to avoid walking along empty streets late at night, especially if alone. Much more common is **pickpocketing**, which is most likely in the Central Market area and on Jerusalen or San Juan de Dios. If you have anything stolen, report it to the **Tourist Police** (see below). If you have problems getting them to believe you, call the **Tourist Protection Service** (☎054/212054), or contact your consulate.

almost unavoidable stopping-off point between Lima and both the Titicaca and Cusco regions. From Arequipa you can continue to either Titicaca or Cusco by bus, train or plane, and over the border to Chile by international bus.

Flights land at Arequipa airport, 7km northwest of the town. A red shuttle bus meets most planes and will take you to any hotel in the town centre for $1; alternatively, a taxi will cost $3–4. **Trains** from Puno or Cusco arrive at the station on Avenida Tacna y Arica 201, seven blocks south of the Plaza de Armas; a taxi from here to the plaza costs around $2. Most long-distance **buses** arrive at the modern, concrete Terminal Terreste bus station or at the newer Terrapuerto, next door, around 4km from the centre of town; a taxi to the Plaza de Armas should cost $2 to $3. For full details of operators, contact details and where they connect to, see Listings, p.214.

Information

Tourist information is available from the official office at Portal de La Municipalidad 112, Plaza de Armas (Mon–Fri 8am–4pm; ☎054/211021, extension 3) where they have maps of the city, information on sights and cultural events and can recommend guides, tour companies and hotels. The **Tourist Police**, Jerusalen 315 (☎054/239888 or 251270), are also particularly helpful with maps and information, plus they have a small exhibition of photos and postcards of major local attractions. The **Terminal Terrestre** also has a kiosk with details of hotels and tour companies, and sometimes maps. For information on **guided tours** of the city and the surounding area, see the box on p.215.

City transport

It's easy enough to **walk** around the city centre, but we've given relevant **bus** services where you might want to avoid a longish walk. If you want a **taxi** it's easy to hail one anywhere in the city; rides within the centre cost about $0.8. For a highly recommended service call Taxi Seguro, Pasaje 7 de Junio 200, Mariano Melgar (☎054/450250) or, second best, Taxi Sur (☎054/465656); an alternative is the *taxista* Abel Cuba, who can usually be found outside the *Casa de mi Abuela hostal* (see p.204), who has reasonable fares for trips to the immediate countryside. **Car hire** is available from AKAL, Avenida Ejercito 311, Oficina 301 (☎054/272663); ALKILA/Localiza, Avenida Villa Hermosa 803, Cerro Colorado (☎054/252499); or AVIS, Palacio Viejo 214 (☎054/282519, fax 212123), and at the airport (☎054/443576).

Accommodation

Arequipa has a good selection of **accommodation** in all price ranges, with most of the better options around the Plaza de Armas or along San Juan de Dios and Jerusalen.

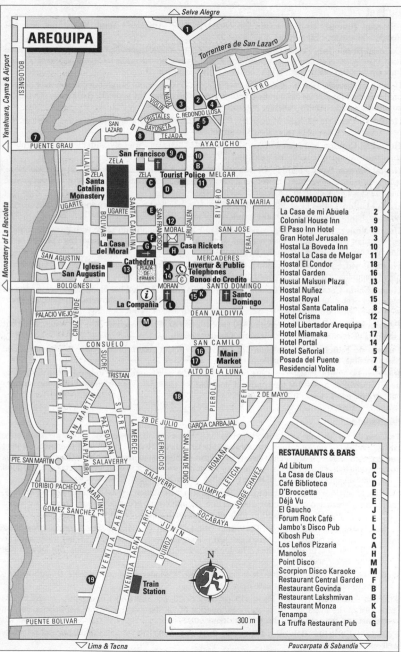

△ *Selva Alegre*

AREQUIPA

Torrentera de San Lázaro

San Francisco

Tourist Police

Santa Catalina Monastery

La Casa del Moral

Iglesia San Agustín

Casa Rickets

Cathedral

Invertur & Public Telephones

Bonco do Credito

Santo Domingo

La Compañia

Main Market

Train Station

ACCOMMODATION

La Casa de mi Abuela	2
Colonial House Inn	9
El Paso Inn Hotel	19
Gran Hotel Jerusalen	3
Hostal La Boveda Inn	10
Hostal La Casa de Melgar	11
Hostal El Condor	18
Hostal Garden	16
Hostal Maison Plaza	13
Hostal Nuñez	6
Hostal Royal	15
Hostal Santa Catalina	8
Hotel Crisma	12
Hotel Libertador Arequipa	1
Hotel Miamaka	17
Hotel Portal	14
Hotel Señorial	5
Posada del Puente	7
Residencial Yolita	4

RESTAURANTS & BARS

Ad Libitum	D
La Casa de Claus	C
Café Biblioteca	D
D'Broccetta	E
Déjà Vu	E
El Gaucho	J
Forum Rock Café	E
Jambo's Disco Pub	L
Kibosh Pub	C
Los Leños Pizzaria	A
Manolos	H
Point Disco	M
Scorpion Disco Karaoke	M
Restaurant Central Garden	F
Restaurant Govinda	B
Restaurant Lakshmivan	B
Restaurant Monza	K
Tenampa	G
La Truffa Restaurant Pub	G

△ *Lima & Tacna*

Paucarpata & Sabandía ▽

Budget

Albergue Juvenil, Ronda Recoleta 104 (☎054/257085). Arequipa's Youth Hostal, out near the Recoleta Manastery. Simple, but it suffices. ②.

Colonial House Inn, Puente Grau 114 (☎054/223533, *colonialhouse@LaRed.net.pe*). Pleasant place with a pretty covered courtyard, electric heated showers, private bathrooms and access to TV and Internet facilities. Well worth it but could do with a paint job. ②.

Hostal La Boveda Inn, Jerusalen 402 (☎054/202562). Cheap and rough but conveniently located on the second floor of an old building, with a vegetarian restaurant beneath. Bathrooms are mostly communal and have fairly constant hot water. ②.

Hostal La Casa de Melgar, Melgar 108-B (☎054/222459). A nice light place, old and stylish; the best rooms are those with views over the street. ③.

Hostal El Condor, San Juan de Dios 525 (☎054/213323). Very friendly, with clean, simple rooms that come with private bath, hot water and TV. ②.

Hostal Garden, San Camilo 116, (☎ & fax 054/237440). A misleading name but still excellent value, with solar-heated communal showers and lovely old-fashioned, clean rooms with or without private bath. Located very close to the central market. ②–③.

Hostal Latino, Carlos Llosa 135 (☎054/244770). Has excellent hot showers and a very trustworthy luggage deposit if you want to make a trek out of town. ②.

Hostal Nuñez, Jerusalen 528, (☎054/218648). A friendly, family-run place with attractive patios, constant hot water, a laundry service and secure luggage deposit; a few rooms have private facilities. You can have breakfast on the terrace. ②–③

Hostal Royal, San Juan de Dios 300-A (☎054/212071). Central, but it's seen better days. Only a couple of rooms have their own private bath. ②.

Hostal Santa Catalina, Santa Catalina 600 (☎054/243705). Pleasant but elementary, set around an old rather drab courtyard; only a few rooms have their own toilets and showers, but there are great views to El Misti from the roof terrace, where you can also dry your clothing. ③.

Posada La Fiorentina, Puente Grau 110 (☎054/242668). This place has 24hr hot water, small but comfortable rooms and a nice courtyard. Good value. ②.

Posada de Sancho, Santa Catalina 213 (☎054/287797). A secure hostal, close to Monasterio de Santa Satalina, and with reasonable rates. ③.

Residencial Yolita, Pasaje Velez 204 (☎054/226505). A new comfortable lodging, close to *La Casa de mi Abuela*, so a possible alternative if you find *La Casa* full. Very friendly, and some upstairs rooms have good views. ②.

Moderate

La Casa de mi Abuela, Jerusalen 606 (☎054/241206, fax 242761, *lperezwi@ucsm.edu.pe*). Innovative family-run hostal, whose name translates as "My Grandma's House", combining elegance, comfort and great value. Rooms are set in a variety of environments around lovely gardens; there are spacious colonial quarters, chalets, family apartments and a fine swimming pool. It's very secure, has a good library and an excellent cafetería. Reserve well in advance during high season. ④–⑤.

Hostal Terrapuerto, in the centre of Terrapuerto bus station (☎054/422277, extension 232). Surprisingly clean and bearable for a bus station, though rooms are windowless. There's hot water, while rooms have TV and are with or without private bath. Has a casino next door. ③–④.

Hotel Miamaka, San Juan de Dios 402 (☎054/288558 or 241496, fax 227906, *miamaka@mil.interplace.com.pe*). Newish, smart and ultra-clean and secure hotel with TV, hot water and carpets in all their decent-sized rooms. The lounge area's nice too. Very good value, but located just outside the better areas. ④.

Hotel Señorial, Carlos Llosa 106 (☎ & fax 054/288061). Modern and comfortable, though with little character. All rooms have private bath. ④.

El Paso Inn Hotel, Avenida Parra 119 (☎054/229523, fax 243649). A new hotel, several blocks southwest of the Plaza de Armas on a continuation of La Merced; has private bathrooms, its own restaurant and the occasional disco at weekends. ③.

Posada del Puente, Bolognesi 101 (☎054/253132, fax 253576). Very comfortable and relatively well situated. ⑤.

Expensive

Gran Hotel Jerusalen, Jerusalen 601 (☎054/244441 or 244481, *jerusalen@mail.interplace.com.pe*). Fairly luxurious and reasonably good value, with TVs and minibars in the carpeted rooms, all of which have private bath. ⑨.

Hostal Maison Plaza, Portal San Augustin 143 (☎054/218929, fax 218931). Pretty plush, and well located on the Plaza de Armas; unusually for Peru the price includes a decent breakfast. ⑦.

Hotel Crisma, Moral 107 (☎054/215290). A relatively smart place with a laundry service, restaurant, and TV in all rooms. Price includes American breakfasts. ⑨.

Hotel Libertador Arequipa, Plaza Bolivar, Selva Alegre (☎054/215110, fax 241933, *www. libertador.com.pe*). Formerly the state-run *Hotel de Turistas*, this luxurious, spacious hotel has a pool and sports facilities and serves excellent breakfasts (not included). In a beautiful setting on the spur above the Barrio San Lazaro, surrounded by the eucalyptus trees of Selva Alegre park, it's quite a few blocks from downtown. ⑥.

Portal Hotel, Portal de Flores 116 (☎054/215530, fax 234374, *reserva@portalhotel.com.pe*). Very smart and central, with a top-class restaurant, views over the plaza, conference rooms and, more importantly, a rooftop pool. All rooms have cable TV, a minibar and an Internet connection. ⑨.

The City

Arequipa's deeply ingrained architectural beauty comes mainly from the colonial period, characterized here by white *sillar* stone and arched interior ceilings. In general, the style is stark and almost clinical, except where Baroque and *mestizo* influences combine, as seen on many of the fine sixteenth- to eighteenth-century facades. Of the huge number of religious buildings spread about the old colonial centre, the **Monastery of Santa Catalina** is the most outstanding and beautiful. However, within a few blocks of the colonial **Plaza de Armas** are half a dozen churches well deserving of a brief visit, and a couple of superb old mansions. Further out, but still within walking distance, you can visit the attractive suburbs of **San Lazaro**, **Cayma** and **Yanahuara**, which is renowned for its dramatic views of the valley with the volcanos, notably El Misti, patiently watching the city from high above.

The Plaza de Armas and around

The **Plaza de Armas**, one of South America's grandest and the focus of social activity in the early evenings, comprises a particularly striking array of colonial architecture, dotted with palms, flowers and gardens. At its heart sits a bronze fountain, topped by an angel fondly known as *turututu* because of the trumpet it carries, but it's the arcades and elegant white façade of the seventeenth-century **Cathedral** (daily 6–11am & 5–7pm; free) that grabs your attention, even drawing your sight away from El Misti towering behind. There are two bronze medallions in the façade symbolizing the Peruvian-Bolivian confederation, and the whole thing looks particularly beautiful when lit up in the evenings. However, apart from the massive Belgian-built organ, said to be one of the largest in South America, and a marble altar created by Felippo Moratillo, the interior is rather disappointing, despite containing over seventy stone columns. Gutted by fire in 1844 and restored in 1868 by Lucas Poblete, it displays some French influence in its neo-renaissance style.

Also on the plaza is the **Casona Flores del Campo**, Portal de Flores 136 (daily 10am–5pm, $0.5), older than most houses in Arequipa, dating back to the sixteenth century (it was apparently once used by Fernando Pizarro), but not completed until 1779 by one Coronel Manuel Flores del Campo. It's quite easy to distinguish different stages in the construction of this *casona*, most notably the double arch and balcony from the late eighteenth century.

On the opposite side of the plaza from the cathedral, and rather more exciting architecturally, is the elaborate **La Compañía** (Mon–Fri 9–11.30am & 3–5.30pm; $0.3), with its extraordinary zigzagging *sillar* stone doorway. Built over the last decades of the seventeenth century, the magnificently sculpted doorway, with a locally inspired *mestizo*-Baroque relief, is curiously two-dimensional, using shadow only to outline the figures of the frieze. Inside, by the main altar hangs a *Virgin and Child* by Bernardo Bitto, which arrived from Italy in 1575. In what used to be the sacristy (now the Chapel of San Ignacio), the polychrome cupola depicts jungle imagery alongside warriors, angels and the Evangelists. Next door to the church are the fine **Jesuit Cloisters** (Mon–Sat 8am–10pm & Sun noon–8pm), superbly carved back in the early eighteenth century. In the first cloister the fine squared pillars support white stone arches and are covered with intricate reliefs showing more angels, local fruits and vegetables, seashells and stylized puma heads. The second cloister is, in contrast, rather austere.

Santo Domingo (daily 7–11am and 3–6pm; free), two blocks east of La Compañía, was built in the seventeenth century but was badly damaged by earthquakes in 1958 and 1960. It was originally built in 1553 and by Gaspar Vaez, the first master architect to arrive in Arequipa, though most of what you see today started in 1650 and was finished in 1698, while the towers were constructed after the 1960 quake. It has been well restored, however, and on the main door you can make out an interesting example of Arequipa's *mestizo* craftsmanship – an Indian face amid a bunch of grapes, fine leaves and even cacti.

Opposite the northeast corner of the cathedral, at Calle San Francisco 108, stands a particularly impressive colonial mansion, **La Casa de Tristan del Pozo**, also known as La Casa Rickets (Mon–Sat 9am–12.30pm & 5–8pm; free). Built in 1737 as a *seminario*, it later became the splendid residence of the Rickets family, who made their fortune from the wool trade in the late nineteenth century, and boasts an extremely fine facade: it's highly intricate and well harmonized, thoughout its design. The stone work above the main door depicts Christ's geneaology with highly stylized plants supporting five discs, or Jesuit medallions, with JHS (the abbreviation for Jesus) at the centre, Maria and Jose to the side of this, and Joaquin and Ana on the extremes. It's also notable for its upper cornice which has zoomorphic gargoyles. Now owned and lavishly restored by the Banco Continental, the mansion houses a small museum and art gallery.

North of the plaza, at Santa Catalina 101, the **Casa Arróspide** (also known as the Casa Iriberry) is home to the Complejo Cultural Chavez de la Rosa (Mon–Sat 10am–6pm; free). This attractive colonial house, built in 1743, belongs to the Law Faculty of the University of San Augustin and hosts changing selections of modern works by mostly Peruvian artists. Around the corner is the eighteenth-century **La Casa del Moral**, Calle Moral 318 (Mon–Sat 9am–5pm & Sun 9am–1pm; $1.8), restored and refurbished with period pieces. Its most engaging feature is a superb stone gateway, carved with motifs that are similar to those on Nazca ceramics – puma heads with snakes growing from their mouths, surrounding a Spanish coat-of-arms. The mansion's name – nothing to do with ethics – comes from an old *mora* tree, still thriving in the central patio. One block down Calle Sucre from the Casa del Moral, the elegant **Iglesia San Agustín**, on the corner with Calle San Agustin (daily 4–9pm; free), boasts one of the city's finest Baroque facades; its old convent cloisters are now attached to the university, while inside only the unique octagonal sacristy survived the 1868 earthquake.

Two blocks down from the Plaza de Armas, on the corner of La Merced with Consuelo, is the **Casa Arango**, owned by the Standard Chartered company. Built in the late seventeenth century in what was then the city's most important street, it brings together a number of architectural styles, including both *mestizo*-Baroque and nineteenth century Neoclassical.

Santa Catalina Monastery

Just two blocks north of the Plaza de Armas, the vast protective walls of **Santa Catalina Monastery** (daily 9am–4pm, last entrance at 4pm; $4.50) housed almost two hundred secluded nuns and three hundred servants until it opened to the public in 1970. The

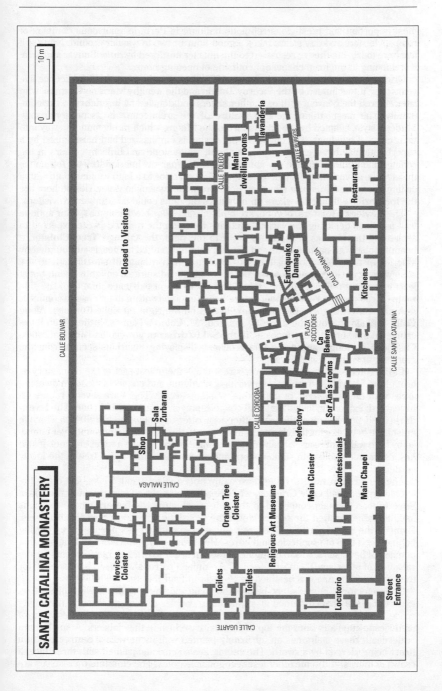

SANTA CATALINA MONASTERY

CALLE BOLIVAR

Closed to Visitors

CALLE TOLEDO

Main dwelling rooms

lavanderia

CALLE BURGOS

Restaurant

Earthquake Damage

CALLE GRANADA

Kitchens

PLAZA SOCODOBE

Ca Bañera

Sor Ana's rooms

CALLE CORDOBA

CALLE SANTA CATALINA

Sala Zurbaran

Shop

CALLE MALAGA

Refectory

Orange Tree Cloister

Main Cloister

Religious Art Museums

Confessionals

Main Chapel

Novices Cloister

Toilets

Toilets

Locutorio

Street Entrance

CALLE UGARTE

0   10 m

most important and prestigious religious building in Peru, its enormous complex of rooms, cloisters and tiny plazas takes a good hour or two to wander around. Nuns still live here today, but they're restricted to the quarter bordered by *calles* Bolivar and Zela, worshipping in the main chapel only outside of opening hours.

Originally the concept of Gaspar Vae in 1570, though only granted official licence five years later, it was funded by the Viceroy Toledo and the wealthy Maria de Guzmán, who later entered the convent with one of her sisters and donated all her riches to the community. The most striking general feature of the architecture is its predominantly Mudéjar style, adapted by the Spanish from the Moors, which rarely found its way into their colonial buildings. The quality of the design is emphasized and harmonized by a superb interplay between the strong sunlight, white stone and brilliant colours in the ceilings and in the deep blue sky above the maze of narrow interior streets. You notice this at once as you enter, filing left along the first corridor to a high vaulted room with a ceiling of opaque *huamanga* stone imported from the Ayacucho valley. Beside here are the **locutorios** – little cells where on holy days the nuns could talk, unseen, to visitors.

The **Novices Cloisters**, beyond, are built in solid *sillar*-block columns, their antique wall paintings depicting the various qualities to which the devotees were expected to aspire and the Litanies of the Rosary. Off to the right, the **Orange Tree Cloister**, a beautiful blue with painted birds and flowers over the vaulted arches, is surrounded by a series of paintings showing the soul evolving from a state of sin through to the achievement of God's grace – perhaps not certain to aid spiritual enlightenment, but at least a constant reminder of the Holy Spirit's permanent existence. In one of the side rooms, dead nuns were mourned, before being interred within the monastic confines.

A new convent, where the nuns now live, is on the right off Calle Cordoba. Along **Calle Malaga** (beyond the doorway marked "M. Colores Llamosa") there's an interesting old mud-brick oven; opposite, in the **Sala Zurbaran** you can find original robes, Cusqueña paintings, and some fine crockery displaying luxurious scenes from the grandeur of early colonial days.

Calle Toledo, a long, very narrow street that's the oldest part of the monastery, is brought to life with permanently flowering geraniums, and connects the main dwelling areas with the *lavandería*, or communal washing sector. There are several rooms off here worth exploring, including small chapels, prayer rooms and a kitchen. The **lavandería** itself, perhaps more than any other area, offers a captivating insight into what life must have been like for the closeted nuns; open to the skies and city sounds yet bounded by high walls, there are 20 halved earthenware jars alongside a water channel. It also has a swimming pool with sunken steps and an Arequipeñan Papaya tree in the lovely garden.

There's a **restaurant**, serving reasonably priced snacks and drinks, just off to the left along the broad Calle Granada, while heading straight on brings you to the **Plaza Socodobe**, a fountain courtyard to the side of which is the **bañera** where the nuns used to bathe. Around the corner, down the next little street, are **Sor Ana's rooms**. Dying at the age of ninety, in 1686, Sor Ana was something of a phenomenon, leaving behind her a trail of prophecies and cures. Her own destiny in Santa Catalina, like that of many of her sisters, was to castigate herself in order to offer up her torments for the salvation of other souls – mostly wealthy Arequipan patrons who paid handsomely for the privilege. Sor Ana was beatified by Pope John Paul II in the 1990s.

The **refectory**, immediately before the main cloisters, is deceptively plain – its exceptional star-shaped stained glass shedding dapples of sunlight through the empty space. Nearby, confessional windows look into the **main chapel**, but the best view of its majestic cupola is from the top of the staircase beside the cloisters. A small room underneath these stairs has an intricately painted wall niche with a centrepiece of a heart being pierced by a sword. The ceiling is also curious, painted with three dice, a crown of thorns, and some other less recognizable items. The **cloisters** themselves are covered with murals following the life of Jesus and the Virgin Mary; though they were originally a communal dormitory, their suberb acoustics make them popular venues for classical concerts and weddings.

Leaving this area and entering the **lower choir room** you can see the **tomb of Sor Ana** and the full interior of the grand, lavishly decorated chapel. Beyond the last sector of the monastery is a rather dark museum full of obscure seventeenth-, eighteenth- and nineteenth-century paintings. The best of these are in the final outer chamber, lined mainly with works from the Cusqueña school. One eye-catching canvas, the first on the left as you enter this room, is of Mary Magdalen. Painted by a nineteenth-century Arequipan, it's remarkably modern in its treatment of the flesh of Mary and the near cubism of its rocky background.

Around Santa Catalina

The **Museo Santivarios Andinos** (Mon–Sat 9am–5.45pm; $1.8), located at Santa Catalina 210 around a pleasant colonial courtyard, has displays of Inca mummies and a range of archeological remains; guides are available if required. Just above Santa Catalina, on the Plazuela de San Francisco, Arequipa's city museum, the **Museo de La Ciudad** (Mon–Fri 8.30am–1pm & 4–6.30pm; $1), devotes itself principally to local heroes – army chiefs, revolutionary leaders, presidents and poets (including the renowned Mariano Melgar). It's rather a dull collection of memorabilia, though some rooms have interesting photographs of the city. Most people find the university museums, located on the outskirts of the city, of much greater interest (see overleaf).

Also on the Plazuela de San Francisco, off Calle Melgar, just one block east of Santa Catalina, you can find a striking Franciscan complex – dominated by the church of **San Francisco** (daily 6–11am & 3.30–7pm; $1.50). Yet another of Gaspar Vaez's projects, this one dating back to 1569, it shows an interesting mix of brick and *sillar* work both inside and on the façade. The central nave was originally covered with paintings by Baltazar de Prado, but these were destroyed by the earthquake of 1604, but it retains its most impressive feature – a pure-silver **altar**. Adjoining the church are rather austere cloisters and the very simple **Chapel of the Third Order** (daily 8–11am & 3–5pm; free), its entrance decorated with modest *mestizo* carvings of Saint Francis and Saint Clare, founders of the first and second orders. The San Francisco Complex also houses a small **Regional History Museum**, containing artefacts from the colonial period and the war with Chile.

Monastery of La Recoleta

Over the Río Chili is the large Franciscan **Monastery of La Recoleta** (Mon–Sat 9am–12am & 3–5pm; $1.8), standing conspicuously on its own on Callejon de la Recoleta, Ronda Recoleta 117. Founded in 1648 by the venerable Father Pedro de Mendoza and designed by Father Pedro de Peñaloza, in 1651 the major and minor cloisters were built, then in 1869 it was converted to an Apostolic Mission school administered by the Barefoot Franciscans. A public museum since 1978, not one of the original buildings is left, but it houses a renowned historic **library** with some 25,000 sixteenth- and seventeenth-century volumes.

Near the Mission Cloisters there's the fascinating **Museo Amazonico**, dedicated to the Franciscans' long-running missionary activity in the Peruvian tropical forest regions and displaying artefacts collected over the years from jungle Indian tribes, and examples of forest wildlife. Based in two main rooms, there's also a collection of fauna and a religious-art museum, with a picture from the Van Dyke school representing the descent of Christ from the cross. The Picture Gallery is home to the most precious paintings owned by the convent, which also has a showcase of pre-Colombian exhibits located in foront of the wake's chapel.

The university museums

San Agustin (Mon–Sat 8.30am–12.30pm & 3–5pm, call first for an appointment on ☎054/29719; $1.50) is the largest of Arequipa's museums, with good collections of everything from mummies and replicas of Chavin artwork to colonial paintings and furniture. Stuck out in the university campus along Avenida Independencia (by the corner with Victor Morales), it's not very far from the road to Paucarpata and the exit route across the mountains to Puno and Cusco. The **Museo Archaeologico de la Universidad de Santa Maria** (Mon–Fri 8am–noon; $1.75, includes a video and a guided tour) belongs to the Catholic University and concentrates on items from pre-Conquest cultures such as the Huari, Tiahuanuco, Chancay and Inca. By far the most interesting exhibit is the 1995 find of Juanita, a superbly preserved Inca maiden who had been offered to a mountain god (*apu*).

The suburbs: San Lazaro, Yanahuara and Cayma

The oldest quarter of Arequipa – the first place the Spaniards settled in this valley – is the *barrio* **San Lazaro**, an uncharacteristic zone of tiny, curving streets stretching around the hillside at the top end of Calle Jerusalen, all an easy stroll from the plaza. If you feel like a walk, and some good views of El Misti, you can follow the stream bed from here to Puente Grau – a superb vantage point. From here, a longer stroll takes you across to the west bank of the Chili, along Avenida Ejercito and out to suburbs of Yanahuara (1–2km) and Cayma (3–4km), quite distinct villages until the railway boom of the late nineteenth century, which brought peasant-migrants to Arequipa from as far away as Cusco. Both are built up now, though they still command stunning views across the valley, above all from their **churches**. Buses and colectivos to these areas leave from *avenidas* Ayacucha and Puente Gran.

The municipal plaza at **Yanahuara** possesses a **viewing point** (*mirador*), whose view of the city, with Misti framed behind by the *mirador's* white stone arches has been made famous by postcards. Buses and colectivos to Yanahuara's *mirador* can be caught from the corner of Grau with Santa Catalina (near the *Hostal Santa Catalina*), or it's a fifteen-minute walk from Puente Grau, between blocks 2 and 3 of Avenida Ejercito. The small **Iglesia Yanahuara** on the tranquil main plaza dates to the middle of the eighteenth century, and its Baroque façade, with a stone relief of the tree of life incorporating angels, flowers, saints, lions and hidden Indian faces, is particularly fine. Next to the church and *mirador* there's the Complejo Parroquial de Yanahuara, which sometimes holds cultural and music events. Exploring the little streets around Yanahuara you'll find several good restaurants and some of the city's more upmarket residences.

Another kilometre or so further out, **Cayma** is a small suburb with some views over the city and, in particular, the Chachani volcano. The **Iglesia de San Miguel**, built in the early eighteenth century, houses the image of the Virgen de la Candelaria, donated to the city by King Carlos V. It's possible to climb up to the roof of the church (daily 9am–4pm).

Eating and drinking

Arequipa boasts all sorts of **restaurants** dotted about the town serving a wide variety of foods, but is particularly famous for a dish called *ocopa*, a cold appetizer made with potatoes, eggs, olives and a fairly spicy yellow chilli sauce. Other delicacies include *rocoto relleno* (a spicy meat-stuffed Andean pepper), *chupe de camarones* (river shrimp casserole) and *adobo* (pork soaked and cooked in vinegar with maize-beer sediment, onions and chillis). As it's not too far from the Pacific, the town's better restaurants are also renowned for their excellent fresh seafood. Unless otherwise indicated, all the places below open daily from 11am to 11pm. **Picanterias** – traditional Peruvian eating houses serving spicy seafood – are particularly well established here.

Cafés and bars

Ad Libitum, San Francisco 300. The café-bar is at the back of the patio: it's quite small but has an interesting modern art display on the walls and occasionally plays funky musics.

Le Bistro, Santa Catalina 208. Claims to have the best coffee in town, and it is pretty good, as are its snacks and cocktails. Has a fun atmosphere with backgammon, chess and domino games.

Burger Express, Portal San Agustin 123. A nice balcony upstairs with tables overlooking the Plaza de Armas, as well as a more ordinary café set-up at street level.

Café Biblioteca, San Francisco. On the left inside the patio, serving drinks and stocking a wide range of books in Spanish and English. Daytime only.

Helados Artika, General Moral 110. Within a block of the Plaza de Armas, this is probably the best ice cream parlour in Arequipa, though it's not cheap.

Los Leños Pizzaria, Jerusalen 407. Just below the corner of Jerusalen with Puente Grau, they have a large range of tasty pizzas and some meat dushes, all of which offer very good value. The walls are covered with graffiti from travellers from every continent.

Manolos, Mercaderes 107. One of Arequipa's longest-established snack bars, offering good service and a tasty range of cakes and sweets.

Restaurant El Café, San Francisco 125. Breakfasts, good juices and fine snacks, but a little on the expensive side. Daily 7am–1am.

Restaurant Lakshmivan, Jerusalen 402. A very popular lunchtime vegetarian cafetería at the back of a small patio, which also sells a range of healthfood products, yoghurts and wholemeal bread; it plays classical music and has a pleasant ambience.

Tenampa, Pasaje Catedral 108. A small vegetarian snack bar in the lane behind the cathedral; has good set menus, great yoghurt and tasty Mexican *tacos*.

Restaurants

Ary Quepay, Jerusalen 502. Traditional local food as well as international dishes and fine *pisco sours*; frequently busy at night, service is good and there's sometimes live folk music.

La Cantarilla, Calle Tahuaycani. A notable modern rather than traditional *picantería*, best at lunchtime.

Chifa Portal, Portal de Flores. The best Chinese restaurant around; quite expensive but very central, just by the Plaza de Armas.

El Gaucho, Portal de Flores 112. On the plaza but below ground level, this is one of the best meat restaurants in town at quite reasonable prices; try the grills or the *lomo gaucho*.

La Palomina, Calle Misti, Yanahuara. One of Arequipa's best and most traditional *picantería* restaurants.

Restaurant Central Garden, San Francisco 127. Specializes in seafood, particularly *camarones*. Open until midnight.

Restaurant El Cerrojo, 111-A, Portal San Augustin. Serves good food on an attractive patio overlooking the Plaza de Armas; excellent value and at its best in the evenings.

Restaurant Cevichería Calamarcitos, San Francisco 129. An inexpensive seafood place. Open until 4.30pm.

Restaurant Govinda, Jerusalen 400b. Excellent breakfasts, natural yoghurt, juices and mueslis plus very good and inexpensive vegetarian set meals. A highly recommended veggie restaurant with a distinctive atmosphere.

Restaurant Monza, Santa Domingo 104. Moderately priced restaurant serving good traditional Arequipan dishes in a distinctly European atmosphere; a favourite with local business people by day and young families in the evenings.

Restaurant Sol de Mayo, Jerusalen 207. Tables set around attractive gardens, live music and superbly prepared traditional Peruvian dishes in a good atmosphere. It's quite expensive but worth it, including the $2 taxi ride out to Yanahuara; alternatively it's a 15-minute walk over Puente Grau, then 5–6 blocks up Avenida Ejercito. Open 10am–7pm.

La Truffa Restaurant Pub, Pasaje Catedral 111. Quality Italian food at rather expensive prices.

Nightlife and entertainment

It's often hard to distinguish between **bars**, restaurants and **nightclubs** (or **discos**, as most are referred to), as many restaurants have a bar and live music while many bars and clubs also serve food. The welcoming **peña** restaurants, for example, concentrated along Santa Catalina, often have better, more traditional music than either the bars or clubs. These reflect Arequipa's very strong tradition of folk singing and poetry and folk musicians will wander from *peña* to *peña*; the most authentic music of the region is *Yaraví* singing, usually lamenting vocalists accompanied by a guitar. Most *peñas* open Thursday to Saturday from 8.30pm to midnight, while discos and nightclubs, many just a couple of blocks from the Plaza de Armas on Palacio Viejo, open nightly until the early hours and usually charge a small entrance fee (around $2.50).

Arequipa's **cinema** scene is based around the Cine Portal, Portal de Fores 112 and the Cine Fenix, General Moran 104. Otherwise the **cultural institutes** put on occasional programmes, especially the Instituto Cultural Peruano-Aleman, San Juan de Dios 202, which shows good films in Spanish and German and sometimes has children's theatre. Also worth a try are the Alianza Francesa, opposite Santa Catalina Monastery, and the Instituto Cultural Peruano Norte Americano, Melgar 109.

Bars

Blue's Bar, San Francisco 319-A. Serves food and drink, accompanied most nights by a variety of music, ranging from classical to rock.

D'Broccetta Pub-Pizzaria, San Francisco 317. A trendy and popular bar that also happens to serve pretty good pizzas and *broccettas*; live music at weekends and a big video screen the rest of the time.

La Casa de Claus, Zela 207. A German drinking house, very popular in the evenings, quite stylish with good music and German food.

Déja Vu, San Francisco 319. Small, trendy and popular, this place serves seafood, spaghetti and meat dishes, plus, of course drinks. Has a big video screen and a nice rooftop patio.

Don Diego's Video Pub, Moral 305-A. Drinks, seafood and other dishes to a backdrop of pop and salsa videos.

Forum Rock Café, San Francisco 317. The liveliest and funkiest scene in the city, with live music on Friday and Saturday. Also has a café, a decent bar and serves snacks.

Kibosh Pub, Zela 205. Good and for beer and pizzas, this busy place is a little exclusive and plays nice Latin music.

El Rome, opposite the Plazuela de San Francisco. Starts its evening entertainment around 8pm and warms up a few hours later with good food and music; at its liveliest at weekends.

Clubs

Cuba Libre, San Francisco 319. A good bar and disco playing mainly Latin music; crowded on Saturday nights.

Delirium Disco, Santa Catalina 406. Almost at Puente Grau this is a small, basic and loud disco, but the drinks are cheap.

Discotek Dady'o, Portal de Flores 112. Right on the Plaza de Armas, this is a bit run down but is still popular with the younger local set. Mainly plays Latin music.

Jambos Disco Pub, Palacio Viejo 125. Rather dark, with a huge video screen and a sunken central dance floor; usually plays pop.

Karaoke Disco Zoom, Santa Catlina 111b. Has two big rooms, a bar and a lounge, a loud sound system and a reasonably large dance floor; slightly seedy, but it plays decent Latin pop and rap.

Papis Bar and AQ Pub, Santa Catalina 200. A large, funky space that occasionally has live music, it's got imaginative cavernous décor, plays Latin music and occasional jazz, and is extremely popular with a young crowd.

Papus Disco Pub, Palacio Viejo 111. Located up an alley, this has the usual video screen but is divided into four different ambiences in balcony, bar, dance and lounge areas. Music is mostly Latino and it gets hectic at weekends.

POINT Disco, Palacio Viejo 204. A disco pub with lots of tables, a video screen and a smallish dance floor.

Scorpion Disco Karaoke, Palacio Viejo 204b. Another fairly ordinary disco, though quite plush, with loud music, a semi-circular dance floor and attendant disco lights. Busy at weekends.

Turbo's Discotheque, block 3 of San Francisco. Popular with young locals and often booked for private parties.

Peñas

Ebano, Zela 202. Small and with an extremely cultured but energetic atmosphere, offering lots of live music, both staged and impromtu.

Marengo Pizzeria, Santa Catalina 221. Good Andean folk music most Saturday evenings.

Restaurant Peña Las Quenas, Santa Catalina 302. One of the better venues in town for authentic Andean music, food and good *pisco sours*; music most weekends and also during the week from June to Sept.

Restaurant El Sillar, Santa Catalina 215. Small, but generally offers live folk music at weekends.

Restaurant La Taberna, Puente Bolognesi 110. Calls itself a piano bar but it's livelier than that suggests, offering good Peruvian *criolla* music most weekends.

Roomies, Plazuela San Francisco. Has good folk and *criolla* music.

Sonccollakta Peña, Santa Catalina 312. A large venue with good folk music at weekends.

Tarasca Café, Santa Catalina 312. A small, fun place which has live folklore music at weekends.

El Tuturutu, Portal San Agustin 105. Right on the Plaza de Armas and overlooking the angel fountain of the same name, this restaurant and *peña* has a great atmosphere when busy at weekends.

La Troica, Jerusalen 522a. A popular folklore venue with music almost every night in high season; good atmosphere, even if well frequented by tour groups.

Shopping

Arequipa's **central market** is one of the biggest and liveliest in Peru, though it's also a prime spot for pickpockets. A couple of blocks down from Santa Domingo, it sells all sorts of food, leather work, musical instruments and even llama and alpaca meat, as well as offering an excellent range of hats, herbs and cheap shoe repairs. You can also get a selection of fruit juices, including some combining with eggs and dark, sweet stout beer. Other places for top-quality **artesania** and **alpaca** goods are El Zanguan, Santa Catalina 105; the stalls and shops around the courtyard at Centro Artesanal Fundo El Fierro, on the second block of Grau; and in the Pasaje Catedral behind the cathedral. For a good selection of colonial and older **antiques**, the Antiques and Art shops at Puente Grau 314b and Santa Catalina 204 are excellent. The tastiest local **sweets** can be bought from Iberica, Jerusalen 136. For picnic food, there's a good **supermarket** at Portal Municipalidad 130, on the Plaza de Armas. The best **bookshop** is the ABC Bookstore, Santa Catalina 217.

Camera film and development is available centrally from Fotos J. Cano, San Juan de Dios 103; Casa Glave, Portal de la Municiplaidad 122, Plaza de Armas; Foto Jerusalen, Jerusalen 503; and Foto Alvis, Portal de Flores 140, Plaza de Armas. For reliable **camera repairs**, go to Fernando Delange, 303 Zela, near the north side of Santa Catalina. **Camping equipment** is best from Campamento Base, Jerusalen 401b, where they stock a good range of tents, sleeping bags and all other essentials, plus maps. They're also a good contact for expert guides. Turandes, Calle Mercaderes 130, rents out equipment and sells maps. Regional maps are also sold at the Instituto de Cultura (see p.212).

Listings

Airlines Aero Continente, Portal San Augustin 113 (☎054/204020 or 203294, fax 219788). Agents for other airlines are mostly on the Plaza de Armas and include: Intertur, Portal San Agustin 125-135 (☎054/212292 or 245923, fax 243404); Morey Representaciones, Portal San Agustin 151 (☎054/216392 or 215056); and Servicio Aereos, San Francisco 106-A (☎054/242030, fax 246580). There's a $5 departure tax on all flights except those to Colca Canyon.

Banks and exchange Banco de Credito, San Juan de Dios 125 (accepts VISA and has an ATM); Banco Continental, block 1 of San Francisco; Banco Latino, San Juan de Dios 112 (Mastercard and American Express); Banco Wiese, Avenida Mercaderes 410; Interbanc, Mercaders 217; or Banco de la Nación, Mercaderes 127. *Cambistas* congregate outside the major banks within a block of the Plaza de Armas, or try American Money, Jerusalen 126, or the camera film shop Fotos J. Cano (see Shopping, previous page).

Bus operators America, Terrapuerto; Angelitos Negros, San Juan de Dios 510 (☎054/213094), for Chapi, Moquegua, Ilo and Tacna; Carhuamayo, Terrestre (☎054/426835), for Cusco and Lima; CIVA, Terrestre or Avenida Salaverry (☎054/426563), for Cusco, Puno & Tacna; Cristo Rey, San Juan de Dios 510 (☎054/213094 or 259848) for Chivay and Cabanaconde; Cromotex, Terrestre (☎054/421555), for Chucquibamba, Cotahuasi, Tomepamap and Alca; Cruz del Sur, Terrestre (☎054/232014), though all departures are from Terrapuerto); Cruz Hermanos, Terrapuerto, for Cusco, Juliaca and Puno; Del Carpio Hermanos, Terrapuerto; Del Carpio, Terrapuerto (☎054/427049 or 430941), for the Majes Valley, Aplao and Pampacolca; El Chasqui, Terrestre (☎054/218142), for Cusco; Empresa Aragon, Terrestre (☎054/693040), for Mollendo, Mejia and La Punta; Enlacesm, Terrapuerto (☎054/430333), for Lima; Flores Hermanos, Terrestre (☎054/244988), for Lima and Tacna; Imaculada Concepion, Avenida Olimpia 109 (☎054/670071), for Julicaca, Puno, Chuquibamba and Salamanca; Ispacas, Avenida Olpimpica 100b (☎054/284936), for Chuquibamba, Andaray, Yanaquilca; Jacanbus, Terrestre, for Lima, Puno and Tacna; Oltursur, Avenida Salaverry 123 (☎054/235110), for the coast to Lima and Trujillo; Ormeño, Terrestre (☎054/218885 or 424187), for the north coast, Lima, Mollendo, Huaraz and Tacna (departures from Terrapuerto and Terrestre); San Cristoval, Terrestre, for Cusco, Puno and Juliaca; San Roman, Terrestre (☎054/425919), for Puno and Juliaca Santa Ursula, Terrestre (☎054/285378), for Mollendo; Santillar, Terrapuerto; Señor de Los Milagros, Avenida Olimpica 109a, for Chuquibamba and Salamanca; Sur Express, San Juan de Dios 537 (☎054/213335) for Chapi, Chivay and Cabanaconde; Tepsa, Terrestre (☎054/212451), for Lima, Mollendo, Tacna, Santaigo, Buenos Aires, Rio de Janiero, Quito and Bogota; Transportes Romaliza, Terrapuerto, for Lima and Cusco; Tranzela, Terrapuerto, for Juliaca, Puno, Cusco and Lima; Tulsa Angeles Tours,Terrestre (☎054/430843), for Puno; Turismo Alex, Avenida Olimpico 203 (☎054/202863) for Andaray, Chuquibamba, Cotahuasi (all departing from Terminal Terrestre); Turismo Expreso Pluma, Terrapuerto, for Lima; TZ Turismo, Terrestre (☎054/421949), for Corire and Aplao; Ultra Tours, San Juan de Dios 510, for Chapi; Valdivia, Avenida Olimpica (☎054/224801), for Juliaca, Puno, Chuquibamba and Salamanca; Zeballos, Avenida Salaverry 107 (☎054/201013) for Lima, Coirire, Aplao and Ilo.

Consulates Bolivia, Piérola 209, Oficina 311 (☎054/213391); United Kingdom, Arica 145 (☎054/241340); Chile, Mercaderes 212, Oficina 401 (☎054/233556).

Courier services DHL, La Merced 106 (☎054/220045 or 234288); and J.L. Bustamante y Rivero, Urbino Monterey A-17 (☎054/422896).

Dentist Dr Morales, Santa Catalina 115; or Clinica dental de Sur, Oficina 1, Avenida Ejercito 803 (☎054/271371).

Doctor Dr Jaraffe (☎054/215115; Mon–Fri 3–7pm).

Hospitals Clinica Arequipa, Avenida Bolognesi (☎054/253416); and the General Hospital, on the corner of Peral and Dom Bosco (☎054/231818).

Internet facilities Netm@nia, Santa Catalina 113a, are the best in town; or try Cabins, San Francisco 202a.

Language courses Centro de Idiomas Europeos, Jasé Santos Chocano 249, Umacollo, in front of the Parque Labertad de Expresion (☎054/252619). Courses in Spanish and Portuguese.

Laundry Lavanderia Rapida, Jerusalen 404b.

Pharmacies Botica Popular, Mercaderes 128; and Farmacia Sudamerica, San Francisco 131.

Police The Tourist Police are at Jerusalen 315 (☎054/251270, 239888 or 254000)

Post office Calle Moral 118 (Mon–Sat 8am–7pm).

Telephone office Telefónica Peru, Portal San Agustin 133.

Tourist Protection Service Calle Mora 315, Cercado (☎054/212054, *tour@indecopigob.pe*).

Visas Migraciones, Urbino Quinta Tristán, Bustamante y Rivero (☎054/421759).

TOURS OF AREQUIPA AND AROUND

Taking a guided tour is the easiest way to get around this otherwise quite difficult region. All operators tend to offer similar packages. **City tours** last around three hours, cost $10–20 and usually include the Santa Catalina Monastery, La Compañia, the Cathedral, San Augustin and the Yanahuara *mirador*. **Countryside tours** (*tur de campiña*) usually consist of a three-hour trip or so to the rural churches of Cayma and Sachaca, the old mill at Sabandia, Tingo lagoon and local *miradors* for $10–30. Most companies offer one- to three-day trips out to the **Colca Canyon** for $20–80 (sometimes with *very* early morning starts) or to the petroglyphs at **Toro Muerto** for $20–40. Trips to the **Valley of the Volcanos** and the **Cotahuasi Canyon** are only offered by a few companies. Specialist adventure activities, eg rafting in the Colca Canyon, can cost up to $120 for a three-day outing.

Competition between companies is high, so check out all the options and determine exactly what you're getting – from the quality of your guide to the standard of transport and accommodation to the quality of equipment used for adventure activities, and whether there may be any supplemental charges (for entry to musuems and so on). Because of the dangers of mountain sickness, also check whether oxygen is provided – even a bus trip to Chivay can bring on *soroche* if you've only recently arrived from sea level.

Campamento Base, Jerusalen 401b (☎054/424223 or 202768). A good camping shop who also have excellent guides for the Colca Canyon and more adventurous treks, including Cananaconde, Tapay and Cotahuasi areas.

EcoAventur, Santa Catalina 114 (☎ & fax 054/231648, *ecoadventure@latinmail.com.pe*). Good guides (English spoken) and excellent treks and canoeing trips to the Colca Canyon, the Río Chili, as well as to the Toro Muerto petroglyphs and the Laguna Salinas area. Will take oxygen on treks if requested to.

Giardino Agencia de Viajes, Jerusalen 606a (☎054/221345, fax 242761, *giardinotours@ chasqui.LaRed.net.pe* or *lperezwi@ucsm.edu.pe*). A well-organized outfit with excellent two-day travels to Colca, including an overnight stay in a hotel in Chivay, trekking and climbing trips, plus the usual city and countryside trips.

Gold Tours, Jerusalen 206-B (☎054/238270). City and countryside tours and one-day trips to Colca, some with English-speaking guides.

Hilton Travel Tour, Santa Catalina 102 (☎054/227297, fax 427787, *hiltontravel@ wayna.rcp.net.pe*). Treks to Colca, plus a 24-hour trip up El Misti and frequent rides to Toro Muerto. Also offer a five-day adventure tour to Cotahuasi Canyon.

Illary Tour, Santa Catalina 205 (☎054/220844). A friendly and professional outfit with English-speaking guides who take enjoyable trips of 2 days and more in the Colca Canyon. They take oxygen, first-aid kits and provide accommodation, folk music and transport.

Invertur, San Juan de Dios 113 (☎054/213585, fax 219526). City and countryside tours, but its speciality is an all-inclusive two-day trip to Colca. Good English-speaking guides are available.

Peru Expeditions, Avenida Arequipa 5241-504, Miraflores, Lima (☎01/447-2057, *peruexpe@amauta.rcp.net.pe, www.peru-expeditions.com*). Highly professional and helpful Lima based company, offering environmentally sound adventure travel in the Arequipa region, including the Colca Canyon and Majes Valley.

Santa Catalina Tours, Santa Catlina 223 (☎ & fax 054/216994, *santacatalina@ rh.com.pe*). City tours, local and Colca Canyon trips, plus ascents up El Misti and occasional rafting on the Río Chili, all at reasonable prices. Good, reliable guides.

Around Arequipa

The spectacular countryside around Arequipa rewards a few days' exploration, with some exciting and adventurous possibilities for trips. Climbing **El Misti** is a demanding but rewarding trek, while the Inca ruins of **Paucarpata** at the foot of the volcano offer excellent scenery, great views and a fine place for a picnic. The attractive village of **Chapi** makes a good day-trip, and just a few hours' drive away from Arequipa, the **Sumbay caves**, on the road towards Caylloma via the austere but stunning Lake Salinas, are hard to reach independently but contain hundreds of unique pre-historic cave paintings.

Further out, 150km to the north, is the **Colca Canyon** one of Peru's major attractions, second only to Machu Picchu and developing fast as trekking and canoeing destination (best in the dry season, May–Sept). Called the "Valley of Marvels" by the Peruvian novelist Mario Vargas Llosa, it is nearly twice the size of Arizona's Grand Canyon and one of the country's most extraordinary natural sights. Around 120km west of Arequipa, you can see the amazing petroglyphs of **Toro Muerto**, perhaps continuing on to hike amid the craters and cones of the **Valley of the Volcanos**. A little further north, and only just opening up to the tourist trail, the **Cotahuasi Canyon** is attempting to usurp Colca's claim to being the deepest canyon in the world.

Getting there

Most people visit these sights on an **organized trip** with one of the tour companies in Arequipa (see box on previous page), which focus on the most interesting sites. If you are prepared to put up with the extra hassle, you can visit many of the sites by much cheaper **public transport**. El Cristo Rey run buses from block 5 of San Juan de Dios in Arequipa daily at 3am and 2pm via Chivay ($2.50, a 3–4hr trip) through the Colca Canyon to Cabanaconde ($3.50, a 6hr trip); these return from Cabanaconde generally around 9am the morning and again at 9pm, but it's always best to check the times on or before arrival. Transportes Colca and Sur Express run twice daily to Chivay (4am from their San Juan de Dios office, 1pm from the Terminal Terreste) and Cabanaconde through the Colca Canyon, returning from Cabanaconde at 4.30pm to arrive in Arequipa around 11pm. Expresso Condor runs a similar service two or three times daily from block 5 of Pizarro. Angelitos Negros buses leave from San Juan de Dios for Chapi at 6am and 7am (3hr; $3). Transportes Mendoza runs two or three buses a week to Toro Muerto, Valley of the Volcanos and the Cotahuasi Canyon from La Merced 301.

Paucarpata and around

For an afternoon's escape into the countryside, **Paucarpata** is a good target. About 7km out of central Arequipa (a good 2hr walk or a quick ride on a local bus, leaving every 30min from the corner of Salverry and San Juan de Dios), it's a large village surrounded by farmland based on perfectly regular pre-Inca terraces, or *paucarpata* – the Quechua word from which it takes its name. Set against the backdrop of El Misti, this is a fine place to while away an afternoon with some wine and a picnic. There's a small colonial church here that contains a few Cusqueña school paintings. Colectivos travel to Paucarpata from the market area or San Juan de Dios in Arequipa for around $0.5.

Another 2–3km beyond Paucarpata is **Sabandia**, where there's a reconstructed colonial **mill** (daily 9am–5pm; $1) with attractive lawns and few alpacas and llamas hanging around. The nearby riverbank is another ideal place for a picnic (no food allowed in the mill itself). Built in 1661 to supply the city, along with three others in the region, it operated continuously for some three hundred years and was capable of milling eight hundred kilos of grain in one eight-hour shift with a single operator. It was only abandoned

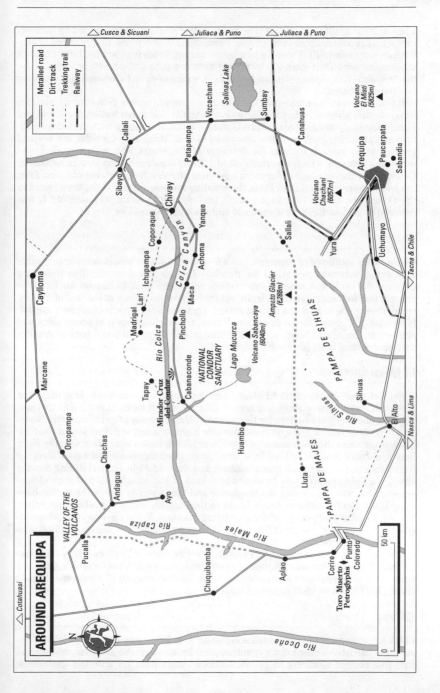

AROUND AREQUIPA

Cusco & Sicuani

Juliaca & Puno

Juliaca & Puno

Salinas Lake

Volcano El Misti (5825m)

Vizcachani

Sumbay

Canahuas

Arequipa

Paucarpata

Sabandia

Callali

Patapampa

Sibayo

Chivay

Volcano Chachani (6057m)

Coporaque

Yanque

Sallali

Uchumayo

Ichupampa

Achoma

Yura

Lari

Maca

Tacna & Chile

Madrigal

Pinchollo

Ampato Glacier (£298m)

Caylloma

Colca Canyon

PAMPA DE SIHUAS

Marcane

Rio Colca

Lago Mucurca

Volcano Sabancaya (6040m)

Tapay

Cabanaconde

Mirador Cruz del Condor

NATIONAL CONDOR SANCTUARY

Sihuas

Rio Sihuas

Orcopampa

El Alto

Huambo

Nasca & Lima

Chachas

Andagua

Luta

Ayo

PAMPA DE MAJES

VALLEY OF THE VOLCANOS

Rio Capiza

Pucalla

Rio Majes

Chuquibamba

Aplao

Corire

Punto Colorado

Toro Muerto Petroglyphs

Rio Ocoña

Cotahuasi

N

Metalled road
Dirt track
Trekking trail
Railway

50 km

0

when industrial milling took root. The surrounding scenery, characterized by Inca terracing and broad vistas of surrounding mountains, is also home to a restored seventeeth-century **windmill**. There's a nearby restaurant, which is expensive but which has a swimming pool. The return-trip by by **taxi** from Arequipa is about $10, or you can take the Arequipa–Paucarpata colectivo (see p.216), which goes on to Sabandia for the same fare from Arequipa.

If you have your own transport, or take a taxi from Arequipa ($15 return), you can travel the ten kilometres beyond here, in the fertile **Socabaya Valley**, the **Casa del Fundador** (daily 10am–5pm), which houses a colonial museum with period furnishings and attractive gardens. Once owned by Garcia Manuel de Carbajal, the original founder of Arequipa, it became the property of the Jesuits, who built a small chapel within the mansion, which was restored in 1821 by the Archbishop Jose Sebastian de Goyeneche y Barreda, one of Arequipa's greatest nineteenth-century benefactors. After the Jesuits were expelled from Peru, the building was bought at auction, then resold to the Goyeneche family, who kept it until 1947 when the estate was sold off; it was restored in the late 1980s by some local architectural enthusiasts.

Chapi

Chapi, 45km southeast of Arequipa, just a few hours away by bus, is easily manageable as a day's excursion (see p.215 for details). Though less dramatic than the Colca Canyon, the landscape here is still magnificent. Chapi itself is famous for its white church, the **Sanctuary of the Virgin**, set high above the village at the foot of a valley which itself is the source of a natural spring. Thousands of pilgrims come here annually on May 1 to revere the image of the Virgin, a marvellous burst of processions and *fiesta* fever. There's no hotel, so if you intend to stay overnight you'll need a tent, but there are several basic places to eat.

El Misti

If you feel compelled to climb **El Misti**, 20km northeast of Arequipa, bear in mind that it's considerably further away and higher (5821m) than it looks. It is a perfectly feasible hike, allowing just two days for the ascent with another day to get back down. Buses (marked "Chiguata"; a 1hr trip) leave Avenida Sepulveda and will drop you at the trailhead, from where there's a seven- to eight-hour hike to **base camp**. To spend the night here you'll need at the very least food, drink, warm clothing, boots and a good sleeping bag. Your main enemies will be the altitude and the cold night air, and during the day strong sunlight requires you to wear some kind of hat, sunglasses and a good sunscreen; note that the climate is changeable and that water is scarce. From the base camp it's another breathless seven hours to the summit, with its excellent panoramic views across the whole range of accompanying volcanos. Any of the tour companies listed on p.215 can drop walkers off at a higher starting point than Chiguata, cutting off a few hours of the first day.

The largest protected area in this region, covering some 300,000 hectares of plateau behind El Misti is **Aguada Blanca**, 4000m above sea level. A cold and dry *puna*, it's home to *vicuña*, *guanacos* and *vizcachas*, while its reservoirs of El Farile and Aguada Blanca are known for their excellent trout fishing.

Chivay

CHIVAY, 150km north of Arequipa and just three to four hours by bus from there, lies amongst fantastic hiking country, surrounded by some of the most impressive and intensive ancient terracing in South America. Apart from its inherent quaintness,

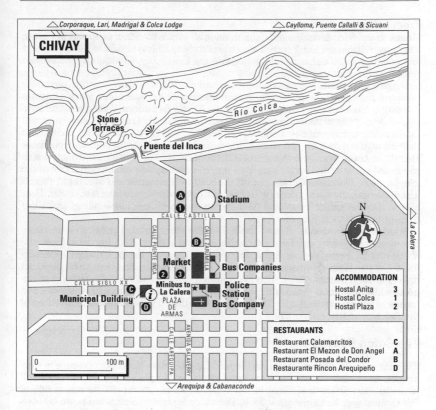

Chivay is just one of fourteen sixteeth-century settlements founded by the Spanish colonial Viceroy Toldeo in an effort to group together the scattered poulation of the Collaguas tribe, who traditionally live in this region. Of all these *reducciones*, **Yanque**, on the road to the Cruz del Condor *mirador* (see overleaf), preserves the best Inca ruins and the original settlement structure of long, straight and narrow streets imposed on the local population by the would-be social architect Toledo. The town's church is an open-plan chapel, designed to allow its parishioners to see the images of the saints and the local idol, the Virgen de la Candelaria, during Mass. The chapel's baptistry contains some seventeeth- and eighteenth-century murals representing Christ's Baptism.

Today, Chivay is notable as a market town that dominates the head of the Colca Canyon. It's not the best place to see the canyon from, but with a growing range of accommodation, restaurants and good bus services, it makes a reasonable place to stay while you acclimatize to the high altitude, before exploring the region by bus or on foot. Some 5km east of town, slightly further up the Colca Valley, the road passes mainly through cultivated fields until it reaches the tiny settlement of **La Calera**, which boasts one of Chivay's main attractions – a wonderful series of hot spring-water **pools and chambers** ($1.2), fed by the bubbling, boiling brooks which emerge from the mountain sides all around. You can walk there from Chivay in an hour or take one of the colectivos that leave approximately every twenty minutes from the church-side corner of Plaza de Armas in Chivay ($0.25). Chivay also makes a good base if you want to go whitewater rafting on the Río Colca.

Practicalities

Buses to and from Arequipa and Cabanaconde all stop at the Plaza de Armas in Chivay. The most reliable are Sur Express who travel daily to Chivay ($3.50, a 3–4hr journey) and continue on to Cabanaconde; otherwise try Cristo Rey, Chasqui or Transportes Andalucia (see Listings, p.214).

Despite its periodic problems with water and electricity, Chivay boasts a surprising choice of reasonably comfortable **accommodation**. The *Hostal Plaza*, Plaza de Armas 705 (①), is basic but clean and set round a small courtyard adorned with beautiful flowers, while the *Hostal Anita*, Plaza de Armas 607 (☎054/521114; ②), is also basic, but modernizing fast. *Hostal Colca*, Salaverry 307 (☎054/521111 or 255055; ③), is clean and modern with private bath, hot water and a decent restaurant, or there's the dependable *Hostal Los Leños*, Francisco Bolognesi 906 (☎054/521028 or 286828; ②), which is simple, excellent value and very clean. Well into the countryside on the north side of the canyon, some 8km from Chivay just off the road to Ichupampa and Madrugal, there's a new *albergue*, the *Colca Lodge* (☎054/212813, *colcalodge@grupoinca.com.pe*; ④). They offer a thermal spring swimming pool and mountain biking, horse-riding, and short treks or tours to local sites of interest.

Tourist information is often available from the Municipalidad building on the plaza. For **money** in Chivay, the Banco de la Nacion is at Cabildo 311. For local **food**, the *Restaurant El Mezon de Don Angel,* Salaverry 321, serves the best dishes, especially trout. On the Plaza de Armas, *Restaurante Rincon Arequipeño* offers tasty, basic set menus at rock bottom prices. The *Restaurant Calamarcitos*, on Calle Siglo, is pretty good, while *Restaurant Posada del Condor*, Avenida Salaverry, is popular with locals and travellers alike for its well-priced dishes. For **nightlife**, try the rock and latino vibes of the *Pub Wititer Bar*, Galvez 210.

The Colca Canyon

Claiming to be the deepest canyon in the world at more than 1km from cliff-edge to river bottom, the **Colca Canyon** is a vast and incomparable place, its sharp terraces still home to more-or-less traditional Indian villages, despite its rapidly becoming one of Peru's most popular tourist attractions. The valley is highly scenic with its pre-Inca terracing, huge herds of llamas, massive mountains and traditionally dressed Andean peasants. Many of its small villages have unusually grand and Baroque-fronted churches, underlining the importance of this region's silver mines during the seventeenth and eighteenth centuries. In the mountains to the southwest, dominated by the glaciers of Ampato and Hualca, the volcano Sabancaya can often be seen smoking away in the distance. The **Mirador Cruz del Condor** ($2), 200km and five hours from Arequipa between Pinchillo and Cabanaconde, is the most popular viewing point for looking into the depths of the canyon – it's around 1200m deep at this point – and where you can almost guarantee seeing a condor or two circling against breathtaking scenery (best spotted 8–9am). For safety's sake, however, stand well back from the edge.

You'll need a couple of days to begin exploring the area and three or four to do it any justice, but in the dry season (May–Sept) several tour companies offer one-day tours as well as extended trips with overnight stops in either Chivay or a *posada* on the road to Cabanaconde (see p.215 for details). Although you can travel along the northern edge of the Colca Canyon by local transport from Chivay, most people take one of the Arequipa buses passing through Chivay around 7 or 8am and follow the southern rim of the valley via the small hamlets of Yanque (with its early eighteenth-century chapel), Achoma, Maca and Pinchillo to Cabanaconde.

The nearest **accommodation** and **restaurant** to the *mirador* is in the village of **MACA**, about 15km back towards Chivay, at *El Albergue* (④) and, at Cabanaconde, a new hostal, the *Valle del Fuego – Rancho del Sol* (②), based in converted cattle sheds

---

TREKKING IN AND AROUND THE COLCA CANYON

There are dozens of **treks** in the Colca Canyon, but if you're planning on descending to the **canyon floor**, even if just for the day, it's best to be fit and prepared for the altitude – it's tough going and becomes quite dangerous in sections. Because of this and the myriad trails, guides are recommended; several tour operators offer this service (see p.215), for which you'll pay $35–70 a day per person. For decent **maps**, contact the South American Explorers' Club in Cusco.

Alternative routes include a popular seven-hour hike from Cabanaconde to **Lake Mucara**, where the beautiful Ampato volcano is reflected in its crystalline waters. From here you can walk on along a trail to Ampato. A quieter, seven-hour route goes from Huambo down to the hacienda at **Canco**, where the Río Huambo meets the Río Colca. It's another day's hike up to **Ayo**, a wine-making settlement, from where the road and buses go to Andagua. There's also a well-used trekking route connecting Cabanaconde with the small settlement of **Tapay**, a four-day hike through fine scenery and the tiny villages of Cosnihua and Malata as well as various Inca and pre-Inca ruins. There are no facilities at all in the area.

---

around a central courtyard with very basic rooms, though the toilets and showers are surprisingly good; simple meals are available. For something slightly out of the ordinary, you can stay with local families ($4 a day for full board) in the villages of Coporaque, Ichupampa and Madigal, a good way to sample local life; you can get information on this from the Municipalidad building in Chivay, on the plaza.

The local bus continues for twenty minutes (a 3hr walk) beyond the *mirador* to the tiny village of **CABANACONDE** (2hr from Chivay), at an altitude of around 3200m; the village boasts a general store and the large but relatively plain church of San Pedro de Alcántera, and some quite basic accommodation. The bus terminates here, and the road becomes a little-used dirt track continuing down the valley via Huambo and Sihuas to the coastal Panamerican Highway where you can catch buses back to Arequipa to complete the circuit. Few trucks use this route and it's only recommended in the dry season (June–Sept) for those well prepared with food and camping equipment. The owner of the rustic *Hostal del Fuego* (☎054/280376; ②) is a good local **guide**.

Toro Muerto and the Valley of the Volcanos

It's difficult not to be overwhelmed by the sheer size and isolation of **Toro Muerto** and the **Valley of the Volcanos**. These two locations, though over 100km apart, are linked by the fact that the rocks on which the Toro Muerto petroglyphs are carved were spewed out by volcanos, possibly from as far away as Coropuna or Chachani during the Tertiary period, about fifty million years ago. Both Toro Muerto and the valley can be visited on guided tours from Arequipa (see p.215 for details of tour companies), but many people choose to do one of the most exciting – albeit long and exhausting – trips in southern Peru independently. To combine these two sites by public transport you'll need at least four or five days. Wandering around the petroglyphs takes a day or maybe two; catching the next bus on to the valley will give you another couple of days' camping and hiking; before returning to Arequipa by the same route, or by continuing up the valley and circling back via Caylloma and Chivay, or meeting up with the Arequipa–Cusco/Puno roads high up on the Altiplano.

Getting to Toro Muerto

Leaving Arequipa the bus follows the Lima road to **Sihuas**, a small oasis town where you can see drainage channels cut into the hillside waiting for water to irrigate the desert *pampa* north of the town. At present, the fertile strip of Sihuas is very narrow –

little more than 200m in width in 1983 – but recently sprinklers have begun to water the sandy plain above and small patches of alfalfa have been planted. This is the first stage of the vast $650 million **Majes Project**, which plans to irrigate 150,000 acres of the dry *pampa*, build two hydroelectric power plants, and develop a number of new towns to house some two hundred thousand people. With costs escalating to more than $10,000 an acre, many people consider the project a complete waste of time and money, despite the fact that the plans are very similar in theory to successful Inca irrigation projects, like the Achirana aqueduct, which still maintains the Ica oasis after five hundred years.

Just beyond the sprinklers, a few kilometres north of Sihuas, the bus turns off the Panamerican Highway, at a junction marked by an archway over the road and a few restaurants, to head east across stony desert. After around 20km you find yourself driving along the top of a cliff, a sheer drop of almost 1000m separating the road from the Majes Valley below. This striking contortion was created by a fault line running down the earthquake belt which stretches all the way from Ayacucho. Descending along winding asphalt, you can soon see right across the well-irrigated valley floor, the cultivated fields creating a green patchwork against the stark, dusty yellow moonscape. At the bottom, a steel-webbed bridge takes the road across the river to the small village of **Punto Colorado**, dwarfed below a towering and colourful cliff – an ancient river bluff. At the *Condesuyos* **restaurant** here, on the left just after the bridge, they serve fresh river crayfish caught locally. It's just 3km from here to the turn-off to the Petroglyphs, which is marked by a large sign on the left – "Petroglifos de Torro Muerto", close to the chapel and before the petrol station. From here a track runs almost another 2km to a T-junction by some sandy cliffs; turn right here and continue to the hamlet, keeping left at the electricity pylon. The **entrance to Toro Muerto** is slightly uphill, on the left, where there's a gate-barrier and ticket hut ($1). The petroglyphs are still a stiff kilometre or so, uphill along a dersert track from here – ask for directions at the entrance.

The best **place to stay** locally is **CORIRE**, about 2km further down the main road from the signposted turn-off to Torro Muerto to Corire – just keep going past past the petrol station. There are a few good **hostals** at Corire and one or two restaurants. The *Hostal El Molino*, Progreso 121 (☎054/472056 or 472002, or in Arequipa ☎054/449298; ②) is very pleasant and is a good contact for canoeing or 4x4 tours in the valley, or less adventurous visits to the local *pisco*-producing hacienda. The *Hostal Solar*, on the corner of the plaza (②), is good value with solar-heated hot water and rooms with bath and TV; and *Hostal Willy*, on Avenida Progreso (☎054/472180, or in Arequipa ☎054/251711, fax 257157; ②) is a very reasonable hostal, most rooms having private bath and a few with TV. There's a *chifa* **restaurant** under *Hostal Willy* and the *Snack-Bar Pollería El Molino* is great, with fresh chicken and chips on Sundays. This small town is well endowed with a **Banco de Credito**, block 1 of 28 de Julio and a **casa de cambio,** Don Rufo, nearby. There are public **telephones** at Avenida Progreso 121.

There are fairly regular daily **buses** to Corire from Arequipa. Operating from early morning to early evening, the most regular are with Transportes Zeballos, with others run by TZ Turismo and Del Carpio (see Listings, p.214). Returning buses depart from the Plaza de Armas in Corire and, unless full, can be flagged down on the main road at the Torro Muerto turn-off.

The Toro Muerto petroglyphs

The **Toro Muerto petroglyphs** consists of carved boulders strewn over a kilometre or two of hot desert. More than a thousand rocks of all sizes and shapes have been crudely, yet strikingly, engraved with a wide variety of distinct representations. No archeological remains have been directly associated with these pictures but it is thought that they date from between 1000 and 1500 years ago, largely attributed to the Wari culture, though with probable additions during subsequent Chuquibamba and Inca periods of domination in the region. The engravings include images of humans, snakes, llamas, deer, parrots, sun discs and simple geometric motifs. Some of the figures appear to be dancing, others look like spacemen with large round helmets – obvious potential for the author Eric Von Daniken's extraterrestrial musings, particularly in view of the high incidence of UFO sightings in this region.

Curiously, and perhaps the main clue to their origin, there are no symbols or pictures relating to coastal life. One possibility is that they were a kind of communal drawing session during a tribe's long migration from the mountains towards the coast. Some of the more abstract geometric designs are very similar to those of the Huari culture, who may well have sent an expeditionary force in this direction, across the Andes from their home in the Ayacucho basin, around 800 AD. To be certain, however, archeological traces would have to be found along the route, and no such work has been undertaken as yet.

There's no very clear route to the **petroglyphs**, which are a good hour's walk from the road, and at least 500m above it. What you're looking for is a vast row of **white rocks**, which were thought to have been scattered across the sandy desert slopes by a prehistoric volcanic eruption. After crossing through corn, bean and alfalfa fields on the valley floor, you'll see a sandy track running parallel to the road along the foot of the hills. Follow this to the right until you find another track heading up into a large gully towards the mountains. After about 1km – always bearing right on the numerous crisscrossing paths and trying to follow the most well-worn route – you should be able to see the line of white boulders: over three thousand of them in all. The natural setting is almost as magnificent as the petroglyphs themselves, and even if you were to camp here for a couple of weeks it would be difficult to examine every engraved boulder. Unfortunately many have been smashed to make portable souvenirs for the tourist market, and this highly illegal, "entrepreneurial" behaviour continues to destroy the boulders.

Getting to the Valley of the Volcanos

Going on to the **Valley of the Volcanos**, the bus winds uphill for at least another ten hours. After tracing around Mount Coropuna, the second highest Peruvian peak at 6450m, the little town of **Andagua**, at a mere 3450m, appears at the foot of the valley. Buses continue to Orcopampa, from where you can walk the whole 60km or so down the valley, if you have the energy; however, most passengers get off and base themselves at Andagua. The mayor of Andagua offers a roof and meals to travellers when he's in town, but there are no hotels or restaurants as such. However, the local people are generally very hospitable, often inviting strangers they find camping in the fields to sleep in their houses. Because this is a rarely visited region, where most of the locals are pretty well self-sufficient, there are only the most basic of shops – usually set up in people's houses.

From Andagua, you can get a bus two or three times a week for the six-hour journey to Cotahausi, or, from Orcopampa, there are infrequent buses and occasional slow trucks that climb up the rough track to **Caylloma**, from where there's a bus service to Chivay and Arequipa; however, it is actually quicker to backtrack to Arequipa via Toro Muerto, on the bus, due to the appalling state of the roads and transport connections. Returning via Caylloma and Chivay, however, rewards with exceptional scenery and an opportunity to see the colonial churches of Caylloma. A small town now, it was important during the colonial period because of its mines, the wealth behind which generated these notable constructions and the fine religious art contained within them.

The Valley of the Volcanos

At first sight just a pleasant Andean valley, the **Valley of the Volcanos** (Valle de Los Volcanos) is in fact one of the strangest geological formations you're ever likely to see, its surface scored with extinct craters varying in size and height from 200 to 300m, yet perfectly merged with the environment. The main section of the valley is about 65km long; to explore it in any detail you'll need to get **maps** (two adjacent ones are required) from the South American Explorers' Club or the Instituto Geográfico in Lima (see p.21 and 00), or from the Instituto de Cultura in Arequipa (see Entertainment, p.212). You won't need a tent to **camp** here – a sheet of plastic and a good sleeping bag will do – but you will need good supplies and a sun hat; the sun beating down on the black ash can get unbelievably hot at midday.

The best overall view of the valley can be had from Anaro Mountain (4800m), looking southeast towards the Chipchane and Puca Maura cones. The highest of the volcanos, known as Los Gemelos (The Twins) are about 10km from Andagua. To the south, the Andomarca volcano has a pre-Inca ruined settlement around its base.

Cotahuasi Canyon

First navigated by a Polish expedition in 1981 and declared a Zona de Reserva Turística Nacional in 1988, the magnificent **COTAHUASI CANYON** (Cañon de Cotahuasi), 378km from Arequipa, has since opened up to visits that don't necessarily involve major rafting trips. However, getting to this wild and remote place is more adventurous and less frequently attempted than the trip to the Valley of the Volcanos. Another claimant to the title of world's deepest canyon, along with nearby Colca and the Grand Canyon in the USA, it runs more or less parallel to the Cordillera de Chila, and is in possession of some pretty impressive staistics: around 3400m deep and over 100km long, it effectively divides the earth's crust between the towering volcanos of Coropuna (6425m) and Ampato (6325m). In 1982, the mountain from where the Río Cotahuasi gushes forth, at over 4000m above sea level, was recognized by the National Geographic Society as the source of the Amazon. **Cotahuasi pueblo** has a variable climate but isn't particularly cold and is rapidly developing a name as an adventure travel destination. About 40km from Cotahuasi, the Wari ruins of **Marpa** can be seen straddling both sides of the river, but another hour away is the larger and better preserved Wari city of **Maucallacta**.

Cotahuasi Canyon practicalites

The remote and attractive *pueblo* of **Cotahuasi** (2684m above sea level), with its quaint narrow streets and a small seventeenth-century church, makes a good base for exploring the canyon. Some 375km north of Arequipa along a rough road, the easiest way to get here is to take a **guided tour** from Arequipa (see p.215); the tour specialist for Cothuasi is Canyon Tours, San Pedro 139, Arequipa (☎054/288081), or for an independent guide, try Marcio Ruiz Sánchez (☎054/581050). Cromotex and Turismo Alex **buses** run the twelve-hour route from Arequipa (see Listings, p.214 for details); Cromotex also have an office and alighting point at Calle Arequipa 100, by the plaza in Cotahuasi. The main plaza has a few places to stay, most of which also provide **information** about visiting the canyon. The **Banco de la Nacion** is at Plaza de Armas 104.

South from Arequipa:
Tacna and the Chilean frontier

The one place worth stopping at south of Arequipa – and this only really during the summer months (Dec–April) – is **Mollendo**, a coastal resort for Arequipa and home of the **Mejia bird sanctuary**. Most travellers, however, tend to go straight past on the bus, through the old colonial town of **Moquegua** and on to sprawling **Tacna**, whose only attraction is that it's the jumping-off point for crossing the border into Chile.

Mollendo and the Mejia bird sanctuary

A little more than an hour and a half away from Arequipa, **MOLLENDO** is a pleasant old port with a decent beach and a laid-back atmosphere. It's a relaxed spot to spend a couple of days chilling out on the beach and makes a good base from which to visit the nearby nature reserve lagoons at Mejia, also known as the **Mejia Bird Sanctuary**. These can be easily reached, only 4kms south of Mejia, by colectivos from the top end of Calle Castilla (every 10min).

Several **buses** daily arrive from Arequipa, Moquegua and Tacna, including Empresa Aragon, Calle Comercio, four blocks north of Plaza de Armas; Tepsa, Alfonso Ugarte 320 (☎054/532872); and Cruz del Sur, on Alfonso Ugarte. Mollendo has a reasonable choice of **accommodation**: the *Hostal Brisas del Mar*, Tupac Amaru (☎054/533544; ④), is a popular place close to the beach, while *Hostal El Muelle*, Arica 144 (☎054/533680; ③), is clean, friendly and good value. *Hostal Paraiso*, Arequipa 209 (☎054/533245; ③), fills up very quickly in January but has nice rooms and a pleasant outlook, while *Hostal Cabaña*, Comercio 240 (☎054/533833; ③), with private bathrooms and good hot water, is the best value in town. *El Hostalito*, Mayor Blondell 169 (☎054/533674; ③), is a pleasant little place, but rather out of the way.

As befits a coastal holiday town, Mollendo has a good selection of **restaurants**. First choice is the superb seafood restaurant *Cevichería Alejo*, Panamerican Highway South, Miramar – it's a little out of town, but worth the twenty-minute walk for excellent, reasonably priced seafood. At the lower end of the budget, there's a decent pizzeria on the Plaza de Armas, or try the excellent *Chifa Restaurant*, Comercio 412, serving tasty Chinese meals for under $3.

If you need to change **money**, you'll get the best rates for dollars cash from the *cambistas* on Plaza Bolognesi; for traveller's cheques, try the Banco de La Nacion, Areqipa 243; the Banco de Credito, Comercio 323; or the Banco del Sur, Plaza Bolognesi 131.

The National Sanctuary and Lakes of Mejia

The **National Sanctuary and Lakes of Mejia**, 7km south of Mollendo, is an unusual ecological niche consisting of almost 700 hectares of lakes separated from the Pacific Ocean by just a sand bar, and providing an important habitat for many thousands of migratory birds. Of the 157 species sighted at Mejia, around 72 are permanent residents; the best time for sightings is early in the morning. To get there, take an Empresa Aragon **bus** from Arequipa (see above); you'll see the lagoons just before you get to Tambo Valley.

Moquegua

An exceptionally dry and dusty colonial town, **MOQUEGUA** is characterized by winding streets, an attractive plaza and a lot of adobe houses roofed in thatch and clay. On the northern edge of the Atacama desert, the vast majority of which lies over the border in Chile, this area is traditionally and culturally linked to the Andean region around Lake Titicaca, and many ethnic Colla and Lupaca from the mountains live here. The local economy is based on copper mining, fruit plantations and wine, this last product being frequently exported south to Chile.

There's little in town, save the **Iglesia de Santo Domingo,** which has a large single nave, two finely worked *retablos*, and a handful of museums. The **Museo Contisuyo**, Calle Tacna 294 (Tues 8am–noon & 4.30–6pm, Wed–Sun 8am–1pm & 2.30–5pm; free) is a new archeological museum in the town centre, exhibiting relics from the region; the **Museo Regional de Tacna**, Apurimac 202 (Mon–Fri 8am–3.30pm; $0.5) houses a few more such items and some colonial exhibits; while the **Museo de Alto de la Alianza**

(Mon–Sun 9am–5pm), close to the entrance to the city, houses some war exhibits but little else. About 24km away, **Torata** is a picturesque district with country homes demonstrating traditional *mojinete* roofs. There's also an imposing church and old stone mill, both from the colonial period. You can get there by bus from the Carretera Binacional ($1, a 30min journey), and there are a few decent restaurants.

Practicalities

For **buses** serving Arequipa, Mollendo and Tacna, Empresa Aragon have offices on Calle Balta, four blocks southwest of the Plaza de Armas; Cruz del Sur can be found at Avenida La Paz 296 (☎054/762005); Tepsa, at Avenida del Ejercito 18 (☎054/761171); and San Martin at Grau 301 (☎054/762122). Altiplano, Avenida Ejercito 444 (☎054/726672) runs direct services to Puno (9hr). **Tourist information** is available from the Dirección de Industria y Turismo, Jirón Callao 435 (☎ & fax 054/762236).

If you need to stay here, you have the choice of a few reasonable **hotels**: *Hostal Adrianella*, Miguel Grau 239 (☎054/763469; ③), with private baths, colour TVs and good hot water; the more basic *Hostal Paraiso*, Moquegua 151 (☎054/762659; ②); the excellent-value *Hostal Comercio* (②) on Calle Moquegua, half a block east of Plaza de Armas; and *Hostal Limoñeros*, Jirón Lima (③), one and a half blocks northwest of the plaza which has attractive gardens and a swimming pool of sorts. The best **food** in town is served at the *Chifa*, Lima 965, an inexpensive Chinese restaurant. **Money** can be changed at the Banco de La Nacion, Jirón Lima 616, the Banco de Credito on the corner of Tarapaca with Moquegua, or with the *cambistas* outside Plaza Bolivar.

Tacna

Over three hours south of Moquegua and five times larger, **TACNA,** at 552m above sea level, has a nice climate but more importantly is the last stop in Peru. Cave paintings at nearby Toquepala, a small mining settlement, confirm that the area has been occupied for at least 9000 years. More recently, the people of Tacna suffered Chilean occupation from May 1880 until the Treaty of Ancón was signed in August 1929, after a local referendum. Tacna, in fact, has long been noted for its loyalty to Peru and was also highly active in Peruvian emancipation from Spain, though nowadays it's more notorious as an expensive city that's renowned for both its contraband and pickpockets. The only real reason to stop is if you're coming from or going over the border into Chile (see box opposite)

The main focus of activity in this sprawling city is around the **Plaza de Armas** and along the tree-lined Avenida Bolognesi. At the centre of the plaza, the ornamental *pileta*, designed by D'Len Hard, has a Neoclassical base depicting the four seasons while on top of the main fountain are four children holding hands. The nearby Arco Parabólico was erected in honour of the Peruvian dead from the War of the Pacific. Fronting the plaza is the **Cathedral**, designed by Eiffel in 1870 (though not completed until 1955) and built from *cantera* stones quarried from the hills of Intiorko and Arunta. Around the corner there's the **Museo Histórico** (Mon–Sat 9am–6pm; free) where, if you have an hour to spare, you can browse around the pre-Conquest artefacts and exhibitions related to the nineteenth-century wars with Chile. The **Casa de Zela**, Calle Zela 542, houses a small archeological museum exhibiting ceramics largely discovered in the region.

For rail enthusiasts there's the **Museo Ferroviario** (Mon–Fri 9am–5.30pm, Sat 9am–1pm; $0.3), on the corner of Calle Albarracíon and Avenida Dos de Mayo, just five minutes' walk from the plaza, containing locomotives, machinery and documents mainly relating to the Tacna-Arica line, but also a philatelic collection of train-related stamps from around the world. There's also a **Parque de la Locomotora**, based on Avenida Grau, dedicated exclusively to housing the antique Locomotive No. 3, which carried troops to the historic battle of Morro de Arica.

Practicalities

Buses leave three times a week from outside the train station, or from the bus terminal on Hipolito Unanue, for Lake Titicaca along the back road via Tarata which emerges
300km east at the small settlement of **Llave**, but this route is often impassable between
January and March. From Llave several buses and colectivos a day head north for the
one-hour journey **to Puno**, or south **to La Paz**: for this latter option, you'll need to visit
the Bolivian consulate (on the corner of San Martin, and Libertad) before leaving
Tacna. Alternatively, Altiplano buses run three times a week from Avenida
Circunvalacion 1013 (☎054/726672) to Puno (12hr) via Moquegua. For **Lima** (18hr)
and **Cusco** (18hr), daily Cruz del Sur buses leave from Avenida Manuel Odría, bays 16
and 17 (☎054/724341); CIVA, for Arequipa, Puno, Cusco, and the coast, also depart
from Manuel A. Odría, bays 8 and 9 (☎054/741543); while Tepsa run from the Terminal
Terrestra (☎054/711333) to all coastal destinations. The best **taxi** service is offered by
Radiotaxi, Gral. Valera 397 (☎054/726532).

If you do need a **place to stay**, the cheap and reasonable *Hotel San Diego,* Ayacucho
86a (③), is good value. Alternatively, the *Hotel Las Lido,* Calle San Martin 876 (②), is
comfortable and centrally located just off the Plaza de Arma; the *Hospedaje Lima*,
Avenida San Martin 442 (☎054/711912; ④), is also by the Plaza de Armas, and has private baths, hot water, TVs, a cafetería and its own small disco. The *Hostal Hogar*, 28 de
Julio 146 (☎054/711352, fax 726811; ④) is good value, secure and has nice rooms with
private baths and TV. The best place for a cheap **meal** is the *Comedor* in the market, but
the more upmarket *Al Carbon*, Avenida Bolognesi 260, serves good grills and salads.
The *Cevichería a Todo Vapor*, Alfonso Ugarte 419 has fine seafood, and the popular
Restaurant El Pacífico, Olga Groomau 739, also serves good seafood and a range of
other Peruvian dishes. **Tourist information** is sometimes available from offices at
Avenida Bolognesi 2088 (Mon–Sat 8am–3pm; ☎054/713501 or 713778), slightly out of
the town centre, and at San Martin 405 (Mon–Fri 9am–6pm & Sat 9am–1pm;
☎054/715352), on the Plaza de Armas. Failing that, try the Dirección Regional de
Industria y Turismo, Jirón Blondell 506. For **money** matters, cash and traveller's

CROSSING THE CHILEAN BORDER

The **border with Chile** (daily 9am–10pm) is about 40km south of Tacna. Regular buses
and colectivos to Arica (25km beyond the border) leave from the modern bus terminal,
on Hipolito Unanue in Tacna, and three trains a day depart from the station, on Calle
Coronel Albarracin (at 7am, 8.30am and 3pm). At around $3.50, the **train** is the cheapest
option, but it's slow and you have to visit the Passport and Immigration Police, on Plaza
de Armas, and the Chilean Consulate, Presbitero Andia, just off Coronel Albarracin,
beforehand. You will already have cleared Peruvian customs control on your way into
Tacna, along the Panamerican Highway. Tepsa (Leguis 981) and Ormeño (Araguex 698)
buses leave the bus terminal every couple of hours or so for the one-to two-hour journey to Arica ($4). **Colectivos** (normally $6) are quicker and slightly more expensive
than the bus, but well worth it given the hassle saved, since they'll wait at the border controls while you get your Peruvian exit stamp and Chilean tourist card.

Arica, the first town in Chile, is a fun town and a good place to get acquainted with the
excellent Chilean wines. Bus and air services from here to the rest of Chile are excellent.
The *Hotel Casa Blanca*, General Lagos 557, is cheap and very pleasant, and the moderately priced *Hostal Muñoz*, Calle Lynch 565, is excellent value. Good restaurants abound.

Coming back into Peru from Arica is as simple as getting there. Colectivos run
throughout the day and the train leaves at the same times as the one from Tacna. Night-
travellers, however, might be required to have a *salvoconducto militar* (safe-conduct
card), particularly in times of tension between the two countries. If you intend to travel
at night, check first with the tourist office in Arica, Calle Prat 305, on the second floor.

cheques can be changed at the Banco de la Nacion, San Martin 320, on the Plaza de Armas; Banco del Sur, Apurimac 245; Banco Continental, San Martin 665; Banco de Wiese, at Avenida San Martin 476; Banco de Credito, San Martin 574; and the Banco Latino, San Martin 507. *Cambistas* hang around in *avenidas* Bolognesi and Mendoza. It's a good idea to get rid of your extra nuevo soles before going into Chile (exchange them for US dollars or, if not, Chilean *pesos*), and the *cambistas* in Tacna usually offer better rates than those in Santiago or Arica anyway.

East from Arequipa to Puno

Heading **east from Arequipa**, you cross the 4500-metre-high Meseta del Collao through some of the most stunning yet bleak Andean scenery in southern Peru. It's a long and not particularly comfortable journey, however, either by train or by bus, travelling at very high altitudes for many long and weary hours. When running by day, the **train** is the better option, allowing you to stop off at the hot springs near **Yura** or to have a look at the rock paintings in the mountains around **Sumbay**. The **bus** is slightly faster (10hr to Puno), more comfortable and takes a largely dirt road that runs to the south of the rail line – crossing the *pampa* at Toroya (4693m) and passing the spectacular **Lake Salinas**, in the shadow of Peru's most active volcano, Ubinas. This icy-blue lake is frequently adorned with thousands of flamingos and the surrounding landscape is dotted with herds of llamas, alpacas and the occasional flock of fleet-footed *vicuñas*. Salinas is particularly worth visiting in June, when hundreds of pink Andean flamingos wade along its shores; you could do both the reserve and the lake in a day from Arequipa on an organized trip (see p.215) or hire a car or colectivo, but it'll take around six hours.

Arequipa to Puno and Cusco by train

Much of the account below describes the train journey by day, and although the train currently only travels at night, there is every likelihood that day journeys will be resumed once the privatization of the Peruvian rail system is completed. The night train has a bad reputation for thieves so always strap your luggage to the racks, hide your valuables around your body and be particularly careful at stops. It's also a good idea to carry a flashlight. The altitude can make you feel sick or bring on a thumping headache as the train reaches the highest point; if this happens, ask the waitress or guard for oxygen (*oxigeno*).

It's a ten- or eleven-hour trip from **Arequipa to Puno**, but the schedules are in a state of flux, so always check with the station first. The **train station** can be easily found on Avenida Tacna y Arica 201, seven blocks south of the Plaza de Armas; a taxi from the plaza costs around $2. Buy your **tickets** at least one day in advance from the office at the station (Mon–Fri 7am–noon & 2–5pm, Sat 7am–noon, Sun 8–10am) and cost up to $40 to go all the way to Cusco in Turismo class. Services depart Wednesdays and Sundays at 9pm, arriving the next day in Juliaca at 6am, in Puno at 7am, and ending up in Cusco at 6pm.

Yura, 30km up the tracks, is perched right on the side of Mount Chachani, and although marred by a modern cement works, the views from here are stupendous. There are well-maintained **thermal baths** here, as well as a *Hotel de Turistas* and a more basic hostal, but it's not a very inviting place to stay. Beyond Yura, you ascend almost continually for the next five hours, a strange process that never really gives you the feeling of entering the mountains. Instead you edge slowly through a series of deceptively small-looking hills and across apparently flat *pampa*. The tufted grass looks like electrified sea urchins, with powerful sprays extended towards the sun, and you can get occasional glimpses of *vicuña* herds, darting away en masse when they spot the train's approach. There are llamas, too, along with alpacas, sheep and cows, tended by the occasional herder, sitting here on top of the world.

After about three hours you reach **SUMBAY**, basic and little visited with few facilities. To stay here you'll have to **camp**, which is really the best way to visit the place – waking up to the morning sun on this high *pampa* is always exhilarating. Approximately 6km from Sumbay are a series of eight-thousand-year-old rock paintings, mostly found in small **caves**, representing people, pumas and *vicuñas*. The surrounding countryside is amazing in itself: herds of alpacas roam gracefully around the plain looking for *itchu* grass to munch, and vast sculpted rock strata of varying colours mix smoothly together with crudely hewn gullies.

In another couple of hours the train stops briefly at **Crucero Alto**, the highest point on the track at 4476m. At this altitude many people feel pretty terrible, and the only thing for it is a cup of *maté de coca*, served on the train, and a packet of glucose tablets.

After crossing an even sparser stretch of *pampa*, covered in vast volcanic boulders, the train stops at **Imata** – a largish settlement dependent upon the rail line, and surviving on sheep and alpaca wool spinning. From here on it's all downhill into the lakeland region of the Titicaca Basin: another shift of scene to a landscape which, apart from the flamingos, is reminiscent of the Scottish Highlands.

Santa Lucia (7hr 30min from Arequipa) is a lively, tin-roofed town with a small hotel, closely followed by the old colonial buildings of **Cabanillos**, where – at 3885m – the air is still quite thin. It's another hour to Juliaca, the junction for Cusco, where there's often a long wait as scores of Indian women pile onto the train to peddle their ponchos, scarves, sweaters and socks. Initial prices are reasonable, but they get even better as the train begins to pull out for the last 45 minutes of the journey to Puno.

Juliaca

Unless you're making an early morning connection, there's no particular reason to stop in **JULIACA**, in many ways an uninspiring and very flat settlement. It certainly isn't an inviting town, looking like a large but down-at-heel and desert-bound work camp. However, there are some good **artesania stalls** and shops on the Plaza Bolognesi, and abundant and excellent woollen goods can be purchased extremely cheaply, especially at the **Monday market**. The daily market around the station is worth a browse and sells just about everything – from stuffed iguanas to second-hand bikes.

If you get stranded here and need to sample one of Juliaca's several bland **hotels**, first choice is the comfortable and safe *Hostal Peru*, San Ramon 409 (②) on the rail plaza. Alternatively, try the immaculate *Hostal Royal,* San Roman 158 (③), or the more upmarket *Hotel Santa Maria*, one block from the plaza along Avenida Noriega (③). Frequent **colectivos** to Puno (45min; $2) and Lake Titicaca leave from Plaza Bolognesi and from the service station Grifo Los Tres Marias, off Avenida Noriega, two blocks from the plaza. Cruz del Sur **buses** leave from Huancane 443 (☎054/322011) twice a day for Arequipa and Lima; Empresa San Martin operate from Jirón Tumbes 920 to Puno and Moquegua; San Ramon, for Arequipa, are next door at no. 918 (☎054/324583). Local buses and colectivos to Puno leave every thirty minutes ($1.50, a 1hr trip) from Plaza Bolognesi, outside the station, and from the airport, or you can take a taxi for around $10 or a colectivo for $2. **Flights** leave daily from the Aeropuerto Manco Capac, 2km north of Juliaca, for Cusco, Arequipa and Lima: Aero Peru, S. Roman 160 (☎054/322490); Americana, Jirón Noriega 325 (☎054/321844) and at the airport (☎054/325005); and Faucett, Loretto 113–140 (☎054/321966) all have reliable and regular flights (departure tax is $9). You can **change money** with the street dealers on Plaza Bolognesi, with the *casa de cambio* J.J. Peru, on Mariano Nuñz or with the money changing shops on block 1 of San Martin; alternatively, banks include the Banco de La Nacion, Lima 147; Banco Continental, San Roman 441; Banco del Sur, San Roman

301, at the corner of San Roman with San Martin; the Banco Wiese, Jirón San Martin 510; the Banco de Credito, Mariano Nunez Butron 136; and the Banco Latino, Avenida Mariano Nuñez 570. However, if you can wait, you'll get a much better rate in Puno.

PUNO AND LAKE TITICACA

An immense region both in terms of its history and the breadth of its magical landscape, the **Titicaca Basin** makes most people feel like they are on top of the world. The skies are vast and the horizons appear to bend away below you. The high altitude ensures that recent arrivals from the coast take it easy for a day or two, though those coming from Cusco will already have acclimatized. The scattered population of the region are descended from two very ancient Andean ethnic groups or tribes – the Aymara and the Quechua. The Aymara's Tiahuanaco culture predates the Quechua's Inca civilization by over three hundred years.

The first Spanish settlement at **Puno** sprang up around a silver mine discovered by the infamous Salcedo brothers in 1657, a camp that forged such a wild and violent reputation that the Lima viceroy moved in with soldiers to crush and finally execute the Salcedos before things got too out of hand. At the same time – in 1668 – he created Puno as the capital of the region and from then on it developed as the main port of Lake Titicaca and an important town on the silver trail from Potosi. The arrival of the railway, late in the nineteenth century, brought another boost, but today it's a relatively poor, rather grubby sort of town, even by Peruvian standards, and a place that has suffered badly from recent drought and an inability to manage its water resources.

On the edge of the town spreads the vast **Lake Titicaca** – enclosed by white peaks and dotted with unusual **floating islands**, basically huge rafts built out of reeds and home to a dwindling and much-abused Indian population. More spectacular by far are two of the populated fixed islands, **Amantani and Taquile**, whose ongoing traditional life gives visitors a genuine taste of pre-Conquest Andean Peru. Densely populated since well before the arrival of the Incas, the lakeside Titicaca region is also home to the curious and ancient tower tombs known locally as **chullpas**, which are rings of tall, cylindrical stone burial chambers, often standing in battlement-like formations.

Puno

With a dry, cold climate – frequently falling below freezing in the winter nights of July and August – **PUNO** is just a crossroads to most travellers, en route between Cusco and Bolivia or Arequipa and maybe Chile. In some ways this is fair, for it's a breathless place (at 12,700ft above sea level), with a burning daytime sun in stark contrast to the icy evenings, and a poor reputation for pickpockets, particularly at the bus and train terminals. Yet the town is immensely rich in traditions and has a fascinating ancient history with several stone *chullpas* nearby. Puno's port is a vital staging point for exploring the northern end of Lake Titicaca, with its floating islands and beautiful island communities of Amantani and Taquile just a few hours by boat. Perhaps more importantly, though, Puno is famed as the folklore capital of Peru, particularly relevant if you can visit in the first two weeks of February for the **Fiesta de la Candelaria**, an great folklore dance spectacle, boasting incredible dancers wearing devil-masks; the festival climaxes on the second Sunday of February. If you're in Puno at this time, it's a good idea to reserve hotels in advance (though hotel prices can double). The **Tinajani Festival of Dance**, based around June 27, is set in the bleak Altiplano against the backdrop of a huge wind-eroded rock in the Canyon of Tinajani. Off the beaten trail but, it's well worth checking out for its raw Andean music and dance, plus its large sound systems;

ask in the tourist offices in Puno or Cusco for details. Just as spectacular is the **Semana Jubilar** (Jubilee Festival) in the first week of November, which takes place partly on the Ilsa Esteves and celebrates the Spanish founding of the city and the Inca's origins, which legend says are from Lake Titicaca itself. Even if you miss the festivals, you can find a group of musicians playing brilliant and highly evocative music somewhere in the labyrinthine town centre on most nights of the year.

Arrival and information

However you arrive in Puno, you'll be immediately affected by the altitude and should take it easy for at least the first day, preferably for the first two, although if you arrive from Cusco or Bolivia, the chances are you will already be accustomed to the altitude. Arriving **by bus** you are most likely to end up somewhere central on Jirón Tacna or a few blocks east towards the lake, along Avenida Titicaca or Jirón Melgar; see Listings (p.235) for details of the different companies and their terminals. Colectivos to and from Juliaca and **Juliaca Airport** (Aeropuerto Manco Capac) also use Jirón Tacna. If you're coming in from Arequipa or Cusco by train, you'll arrive at the **train station** (information on ☎054/351041) on Avenida la Torre. Taxis and motorcycle rickshaws leave from immediately outside the station and will cost less than $2 to anywhere in the centre of town. The main **port**, used by boats from Bolivia (contact Capital del Puerto, Avenida El Sol 725, for information), as well as the Uros Islands, Taquile and Amantani, is a fifteen to twenty minute walk from the plaza de Armas down, straight up Avenida El Puerto, crossing over Jirón Tacna, then up Jirón Puno.

The helpful and friendly **tourist information office** is at Jirón Lima 585 (Mon–Fri 7.30am–7pm & Sat 8am–1pm) and can provide photocopied town plans, leaflets and other information. The **tourist police**, Jirón Deusta 538, are very helpful and also give out free maps.

Accommodation

There is no shortage of **accommodation** in Puno to suit all budgets, but the town's busy and narrow streets make places hard to locate, so you may want to make use of a taxi or motorcycle rickshaw.

Budget

Hostal Europa, Jirón Alfonso Vgarte 112 (☎054/353023). Good rates, friendly and popular with travellers, with 24hr hot water but few private bathrooms. ②.

Hostal Monterrey, Lima 447 (☎054/351691). Quiet, central and pretty basic but nevertheless pleasant; has rooms with or without bath. ②.

Hostal Nesther, Deustrua 268 (☎054/363308). All rooms have private bath and hot water, but it hasn't got much style and has seen better days. Nevertheless it's a reasonably priced and central option. ②.

Hostal Presidente, Tacna 248 (☎054/351421). Excellent value with a lot of character; hot water most evenings, all rooms with private baths. Has a nice, small café on the first floor for breakfast. ②.

Hostal Q'oña Wasi, Avenida la Torre 119 (☎054/353912). An inexpensive hostal close to the station, with or without private bath in the rooms, with its own breakfast room. Friendly but a bit run down and dingy. ②.

Hotel Extra, Moquegua 124 (no tel). An old building set around a small colonial courtyard, but very run down and with basic facilities. ②.

Hotel Torina, Libertad 126 (☎054/351061). Very basic, but incredibly cheap. ①.

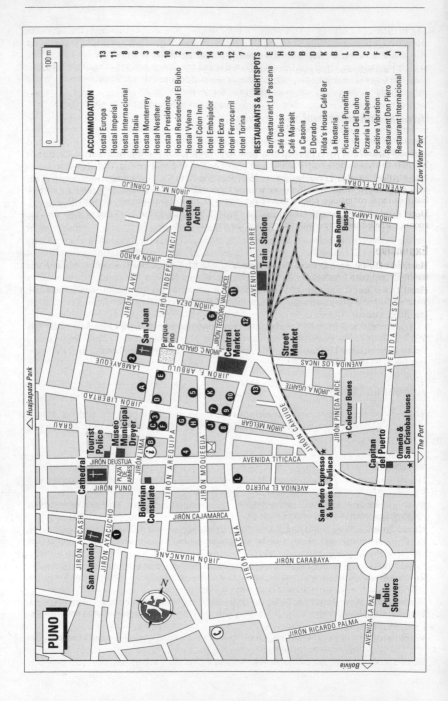

PUNO

ACCOMMODATION

Hostal Europa	13
Hostal Imperial	11
Hostal Internacional	8
Hostal Italia	6
Hostal Monterrey	3
Hostal Nesther	4
Hostal Presidente	10
Hostal Residencial El Buho	2
Hostal Vylena	9
Hotel Colon Inn	14
Hotel Embajador	5
Hotel Extra	12
Hotel Ferrocarril	7
Hotel Torina	

RESTAURANTS & NIGHTSPOTS

Bar/Restaurant La Pascana	E
Café Delisse	H
Café Marselt	G
La Casona	B
El Dorado	D
Hilda's House Café Bar	K
La Hosteria	B
Picantería Puneñita	L
Pizzeria Del Buho	D
Pizzeria La Taberna	C
Positive Vibration	F
Restaurant Don Piero	A
Restaurant Internacional	J

San Antonio

Cathedral

Tourist Police

Museo Municipal Dreyer

Bolivian Consulate

San Juan

Parque Pino

Deustua Arch

Central Market

Train Station

Street Market

San Roman Buses

San Pedro Expresso & buses to Juliaca

Capitan del Puerto

Ormeño & San Cristobal buses

Colectur Buses

Public Showers

Huajsapata Park

Low Water Port

The Port

Bolivia

JIRÓN ANCASH
JIRÓN AYACUCHO
JIRÓN HUANCANE
JIRÓN TACNA
JIRÓN DEUSTUA
JIRÓN PUNO
JIRÓN CAJAMARCA
JIRÓN CARABAYA
JIRÓN RICARDO PALMA
AVENIDA LA PAZ
AVENIDA EL PUERTO
AVENIDA TITICACA
JIRÓN LIMA
JIRÓN AREQUIPA
JIRÓN MOQUEGUA
JIRÓN LIBERTAD
GRAU
LAMBAYEQUE
JIRÓN LLAVE
JIRÓN INDEPENDENCIA
JIRÓN M. H. CORNEJO
JIRÓN PARDO
JIRÓN DEZA
JIRÓN C. GRADO
JIRÓN TEODORO VALCARCEL
JIRÓN F. ARBULU
AVENIDA LA TORRE
JIRÓN A. UGARTE
JIRÓN PINEDA ARCE
JIRÓN MELGAR
JIRÓN CANUDE
AVENIDA LOS INCAS
AVENIDA EL SOL
AVENIDA FLORAL
JIRÓN LAMPA

0   100 m

Moderate

Hostal Imperial, Jirón Teodoro Valcarcel 145 (☎054/352386). Has private baths and hot water from 6 to 10am and 6 to 10pm; modernish and quite comfortable but relatively pricey. ③.

Hostal Internacional, Libertad 161 (☎054/352109). A modern building, with clean and well-kept rooms; cheaper accommodation available without private baths. ③.

Hostal Italia, Teodoro Valcarcel 122 (☎054/352521, fax 352131). A tastefully furnished, warm and comfortable haven; highly recommended. All rooms have private baths and hot water 24hr a day. ③–④.

Hostal Residencial El Buho, Lambayeque 142 (☎ & fax 054/366122, *zuluqv@mix.mail.com*). A pleasant and comfortable place with private baths in all rooms and hot water much of the time; also has its own tour company. ③–④.

Hostal Vylena, Jirón Ayacucho 505 (☎ & fax 054/351292). Very clean and quite smart, this friendly family run hotel offers excellent value; has its own small restaurant and lounge areas. ③–④.

Hotel Allyu, Avenida Laykakota 299 (☎054/351555, fax 354372, *h-allyu@post.cosapidata.com.pe*, *www.unap.edu.pe/allyu*). A well-run, smart new hotel with friendly service, frequented by several European tour companies. Many rooms have superb views; friendly and good service. ④.

Hotel Embajador, Avenida Los Incas 289 (☎054/352072, fax 352562). Plenty of nice modern rooms, carpeted and warm, with hot water in the mornings. ④.

Expensive

Hacienda Hostal, Jirón Deustua 297 (☎ & fax 054/356109). Very comfortable and stylish, with hot water, TV and private bath in the rooms, and luggage storage facilities. ⑤.

Hotel Colon Inn, Tacna 290 (☎054/351432). Newly converted and very plush, with carpets and heating, excellent value; private baths and constant hot water. ⑤.

Hotel Ferrocarril, Avenida la Torre 185 (☎ & fax 054/351752 or 352011). Very close to the station and reasonably priced with good, old-fashioned service and an excellent restaurant. Rooms have private bath but can get cold at night. ⑥.

Hotel Libertador, Isla Esteves (☎054/353870, *www.libertador.com.pe*). Flashy former *Hotel de Turistas* on an island out to the north of town, with an excellent restaurant and far from the fray of Puno's daily life. ⑦.

Hotel Qelqatani, Jirón Tarapaca 355 (☎054/366172, fax 351053, *www.punonet.com/qelqatani*). Modern and very smart, the rooms in this attractive new hotel have TV and private baths, and there's a bar and restaurant. Security is excellent, plus there are fax and Interenet facilities. ⑦.

Hotel Sillustani, Lambayeque 195 (☎054/351881 or 352641, *htl-sill@unap.edu.pe*). A bright, airy place that's excellent value, with private bath, TV, fridge-bar and telephone in all rooms. There's also a pleasant dining room. ⑦.

Hotel Taypikala, Chucuito (☎054/356042, fax 355887). A new, rather fanstastic and stylish New Age hotel, built next to the Templo de la Fertilidad. Superb rooms, pool and meditation suites. ⑥.

The Town

Puno is one of the few Peruvian towns where the motorized traffic seems to respect pedestrians. Busy as it is, there is less of a sense of manic rush here than in most coastal or mountain cities, perhaps because of the altitude. It lacks the colonial style of Cusco or the bright glamour of Arequipa's *sillar* stone architecture, but it's a friendly town, whose sloping corrugated iron roofs reflect the heavy rains that fall between November and February.

There are three main points of reference in Puno: the spacious **Plaza de Armas**, the **train station** several blocks north, and the vast strung-out area of old, semi-abandoned docks at the ever-shifting **Titicaca lakeside port**. It all looks impressive from a distance, but, in fact, the real town-based attractions are few and quickly visited.

The seventeenth-century **Cathedral** on the Plaza de Armas (daily 7.30am–6pm; free), is surprisingly large with an exquisite Baroque facade, and, unusually for Peru, very simple and humble inside, in line with the local Aymara Indians' austere attitude to religion. Opposite its north face, the **Museo Municipal Dreyer**, Conde de Lemos 289 (Mon–Sat 8am–2pm; $1), contains an interesting collection of archeological pieces, including ceramics, textiles and stone sculptures, mainly removed from some of the region's *chullpas*. The nearby **Church of San Antonio**, on Jirón Ayacucho, one block to the south, is smaller and much simpler externally, though, inside, it is colourfully lit by ten stained-glass circular windows. The church's complex iconography, set into six wooden wall niches, is highly evocative of the Catholic and Indian mix.

High up, overlooking the town and Plaza de Armas, the **Huajsapata Park** sits on a prominent hill, a short but steep climb up Jirón Deustua, right into Jirón Llave, left up Jirón Bolognesei, then left again up the Pasaje Contique steps. Often crowded with young children playing on the natural rock-slides and cuddling couples, Huajsapata offers stupendous views across the bustle of Puno to the serene blue of Titicaca and its unique skyline, while the pointing finger on the large white statue of Manco Capac reaches out towards the lake from here.

In the northern section of town, at the end of the pedestrianized Jirón Lima, you'll find an attractive busy little plaza called **Parque Pino**, dominated in equal parts by the startlingly blue **Church of San Juan** and the scruffy, insistent shoe-shine boys. Two blocks east from here, towards the lake, you find the **old central market**, which is small and very dirty with rats and dogs competing for scraps, and beaming Indian women selling an incredible variety of fruits and vegetables. Head from here down Avenida los Incas, initially between the old railtracks, and you'll find a much more substantial **street market**, whose liveliest day is Saturday.

Moored down in the port, the nineteenth-century British-built steamship, the **Yarari** (Wed–Sun 8am–5pm; free; for guided tours call ☎054/622215), provides a fascinating insight into maritime life on Lake Titicaca over a hundred years ago and the military and entrepreneurial mindset of Peru in those days. Delivered by mule from the coast of Peru in over 1300 different pieces, it started life as a Peruvian navy gunship complete with bullet-proof windows, but ended up delivering the mail around Lake Titicaca.

Eating, drinking and nightlife

Puno's **restaurant** and **nightlife** scene is fairly busy and revolves mainly around Jirón Lima, but bear in mind that places shut relatively early – not much happens after 11pm on a weekday. The city's strong tradition as one of the major Andean folklore centres in South America means that you're almost certain to be exposed to at least one live band an evening. Musicians tend to visit the main restaurants in town most evenings from around 9pm, playing a few folk numbers in each, usually featuring music from the *altiplano* – drums, panpipes, flutes and occasional dancers. The food in Puno is nothing to write home about, but the local delicacies of trout and kingfish (*pejerey*) are worth trying and are available in most restaurants.

Restaurants and cafés

Bar Delta Café, Jirón Lima 284. Excellent for snacks and early morning breakfasts; located on the Parque Pino.

Bar/Restaurant La Pascana, Jirón Lima 339–341. Particularly good for evening meals, with a fine selection for vegetarians and interesting murals on the walls.

Café Delisse, Moquegua 200. A small, pleasant vegetarian restaurant that serves great healthy breakfasts.

Café Marselt, Libertad 215. Small and a bit dingy, but serves very good breakfasts.

La Casona, Jirón Lima 517. The best restaurant in town, particularly for evening meals, serving excellent *criolla* dishes in an attractive traditional environment. It is also something of a museum, with antique exhibits everywhere, and is very popular with locals.

El Dorado, Jirón Lima 371. Very friendly place with good service serving tasty International and Chinese food, including trout.

Hilda's House Café Bar, Moquegua 189. Open for breakfast; serves good pancakes and fish, and has taped music in the evenings.

Picanteria Puneñita, Tacna 429. Serves very cheap lunchtime set menus and good-value breakfasts.

Pizzerria La Taberna, Jirón Lima 453. A lively evening spot serving warming alcoholic drinks and scrumptious pizzas; the garlic bread baked in a real-fire oven is particularly good.

Quinta Bolivar, Avenida Simon Bolivar 405, Barrio Bellavista. Quite far from the centre, but worth the trip for its wide range of quality local foods in a traditional setting.

Restaurant Don Piero, Jirón Lima 364. A favourite with travellers, it's relatively inexpensive, has good breakfasts, a fine selection of cakes and a magazine rack for customer use.

Restaurant Internacional, corner of Libertad and Moquegua. Popular with locals for lunch and supper, who come for its good range of reasonably priced meals; upstairs has the best atmosphere.

Restaurante La Pyramide, Jirón Theodoro Valcarcel 158. A simple and very small vegetarian restaurant that isn't always open but when it is, usually for lunches, the food is pretty good, including their natural yoghurts.

Bars and nightlife

Nightlife centres around Jirón Lima, a pedestrian precinct where the locals, young and old alike, hang out, parading up and down past the hawkers selling woollen sweaters and craft goods or cigarettes and sweets. Most **bars** are open Monday to Friday 8 to 11pm or midnight, but keep going until 2am at the weekends.

Apu Salcantay, Jirón Lima 425. Good drinks and food at this bar, and the disco is accompanied by the latest Latin and European pop videos.

Casa del Abuelo, on the corner of Tarapaca and Libertad. A folklore *peña* at its most lively on Sat nights.

Discoteca Monaco, Jirón Monaco 108. A popular, modern, dance music dive, packed with young locals at the weekend.

La Hosteria, Jirón Lima 501. A smart pizzeria and bar, busy in the evenings and a good meeting place.

Pizzeria Del Buho, Libertad 386 and Jirón Lima 347. Probably the best pizzas in Puno and a warm pleasant environment to boot; a crowded and popular spot with travellers on Puno's cold dark evenings; serves delicious mulled wines and often has good music.

Positive Vibration, Jirón Grau 148. A decent bar or pub environment, trendy and polular with young locals and travellers alike; also serves decent breakfasts and plays hot rock and reggae music.

Listings

Airline Faucett, Libertad 265 (☎054/355860 or 351301).

Banks and exchange Banco Continental, Lima 400; Banco de La Nacion, on the corner of Grau and Ayacucho 269; Banco de Credito, on the corner of Lima with Grau; and Banco del Sur, Arequipa 459. *Cambistas* hang out at the corner of Jirón Tacna near the central market. There are *casas de cambios* at Tacna 232, Lima 440, and at Vilca Marilin, Tacna 255.

Bus companies Jirón Tacna, Jirón Melgar and Avenida Titicaca are the main areas for buses, but always check who is leaving for where and when. Companies and their terminals include: Altiplano, Avenida Titicaca 270 (☎054/369592), for Moquegua and Ilo; Cruz del Sur, Avenida Sol 668 (☎054/352451) for Cusco, Arequipa, the coast, Desaguaderos and La Paz; Dur Oriente, Avenida Titicaca 254 (☎054/368133), for Moquegua and Tacna; Expreso San Ramon, Jirón Lampa 301 (☎054/352121), for Arequipa; Huanca, Melgar 250 (☎054/364335), for Cusco and Arequipa; Latino Tours, Avenida Titicaca 238 (☎054/364260), for Deasaguaderos, Moquegua, Tacna and Ilo; Ormeñol, Melgar 338 (☎054/352321) for Lima and Arequipa; Porvenir, Avenida Titicaca 258 (☎054/363627), for Moquegua and Tacna; Rodriguez, Melgar 328 (☎054/363741) for Lima and

Arequipa; San Cristoval, Melgar 338 (☎054/352321) for Lima and Arequipa; San Martin, Avenida Titicaca 210 (☎054/363326), for Juliaca, Moquegua and Puno; Señor de Los Milagros, Melgar 308 (☎054/351481), for Lima; and Tranzela, Melgar 300 (☎054/364192), for Cusco and Arequipa.

Cinemas Ciné Puno, Arequipa 135; and Cine Teatro Municipal, Arequipa 101.

Consulate Bolivia, Jirón Arequipa 120 (☎054/351251).

Couriers DHL services are available from Tur Puno, Lambayeque 175.

Dentist Dental Valencia, Jirón. Tarapaca 179 (☎054/363379).

Hospital For emergencies call ☎054/352931. Otherwise, try Clinica los Pinos (☎054/351071) or the Hospital Regional, Avenida El Sol (☎054/351020).

Internet facilities *The Café Internet*, Jirón Lima 425 (☎054/363955), is the best for speed and prices; also try TM at corner of Jirón Puno with Jirón Arequipa (☎054/352900); or J. M. Data, Pasaje Grau 140 (☎054/356437).

Migraciones Libertad 403 ☎054/357103 or 352801.

Police The Tourist Police are at Jirón Deusta 538 (☎054/357100).

TOURS AROUND PUNO

The streets of Puno are full of touts selling guided tours and trips, but don't be swayed, always go to a respected, established **tour company**, such as one of those listed below. There are four main local tours on offer in Puno, all of which will reward you with abundant bird and animal life, immense landscapes and genuine living traditions. The trip to **Sillustani** normally involves a three- or four-hour tour by minibus and costs $5–8 depending on whether or not entrance and guide costs are included. Most other tours involve a combination of visits to the nearby **Uros Floating Islands** (half-day tour; $5–10), **Taquile and the Uros Islands** (full day from $7, or from $12 overnight), and **Amantani** (2–5 days from $7 a day, including transport and food). Of the independent tour **guides** operating in Puno, Andres Puelino Arucutipa Inta (☎054/353847 or 689775) is reliable and knowledgeable about the sites around Puno and Titicaca, while Andres Lopez is good and can be contacted through any of the town's hotels.

All Ways Travel, Jirón Tacna 234 (☎ & fax 054/355552, *awtperu@mail.cosapidata. com.pe*). The most progressive of the tour companies in Puno and the Titicaca region, running most of the usual tours but also offering trips to the wildlife and haven of Anapia, close to the Bolivian border, where they work with locals on a sustainable tourism project.

Cusi Travel, Theodoro Valcarcel 103 (☎054/369072). Better than you'd think at first glance, this reliable company offers all the usual tours at reasonable prices.

Edgar Adventures, Jirón Lima 328 (☎054/353444, fax 354811, *edgaradventures@ viaexpresa.com.pe*). Islands tours at average prices, but more interestingly they also go to Chucuito and the Templo de Fertilidad for about $10 a person, as long as there are four or more in the group.

Feiser, Jirón Teodoro Valcarcel 153 (☎054/353112 or 355933, *feiser@puno.perured.net*). Offers the standard tours at pretty reasonable prices; can also arrange short trips onto the lake in faster boats, or pleasure rides on reed boats from Isla Esteves.

Kontiki Tours, Jirón Melgar 188 (☎054/355887, fax 353473). A bit out of the ordinary, this company offers mystic tours focussing on the ancient power centres of the region. They are reliable, very professional and work in other regions too, such as Cusco and Nazca.

Lake Country Treks, Lima 458 (☎054/355785 or 352259). Standard tours plus a range of more outward-bound options and alternative trips to Taquile or even to *chullpas* at Cutimbo and the Templo de Falos near Chucuito.

Tur Puno, Lambayeque 175 (☎054/352001, *turpuno@via_expresa.com*). The normal tours and, for groups, with very good deals on the one-day Taquile trip. Also free transport to Jualica if you buy your air travel with them.

Transturin, Libertad 176 (☎054/352771). Travel agent offering catamaran trips to Bolivia.

BY TRAIN TO AREQUIPA AND CUSCO

Trains from **Puno to Arequipa** depart Monday and Friday at 7.45pm, arriving at 6am ($19 Pullman, $10 Economico); **Puno to Cusco** trains leave Monday, Wednesday, Thursday and Saturday at 8am and pull in at 6pm ($23 Turismo Inka, $19 Pullman, $7 Economico) However, the railway has recently been privatized, so always check with the ticket office at the station (Mon & Wed 6.30–10.30am & 4–8pm, Tues 6.30–10.30am & 2–6pm, Thurs 7am–3pm, Sat 6.30–8.30am & 6–8pm, Sun 4–6pm). It's best to buy your seats a day in advance and as with all train journeys in Peru, keep your valuables well hidden and a good eye on your gear as you board the carriage and find your seat.

It's worth noting, however obvious, that if you book train (or for that matter, bus) tickets through an agent you will inevitably pay more for them than if you buy them directly yourself.

The first town out of Puno towards Cusco is **Juliaca** (see p.229), an hour away across a grassy *pampa*, where it's easy to imagine a straggling column of Spanish cavalry and footmen followed by a thousand Inca warriors – Almagro's fated expedition to Chile in the 1530s. Today, much as it always was, the plain is scattered with tiny isolated communities, many of them with conical kilns, self-sufficient even down to kitchenware.

Passing beyond here through a magnificent glacial landscape, the train pulls up outside **Ayavari** station (3903m). Once a great Inca centre with a palace, sun temple and well-stocked storehouses, it's now a market town, notable for the women's weird and wonderful hats. You can see an interesting old church from the train – low but with two stone towers and a cupola – and it's a perfect place for trekking if the urge grabs you.

Next stop is **La Raya**, a scenic pass between the Vilcanota Valley in the Amazon watershed and the Titicaca Basin which flows down into the Pacific. Enclosed by towering mountains, some of them snowcapped, it's the sort of spot that makes you feel like leaving the train and heading for the horizon. See Chapter Two for accounts of the villages north of La Raya pass.

Post office Moquegua 269.

Shopping The unnamed shop at Jirón Arbulu 231 sells most traditional Andean musical instruments; instruments can be bought extremely cheaply in the street market, on Avenida los Incas. Laboratorio Fotografico, Jirón Lima 120, Foto Prisma, Lima 389, and Full Color Lima 525, sell camera film and develop film.

Taxis ☎054/351616 or 332020.

Telephones and faxes Telefonica del Peru, corner of Federico More and Moquegua (daily 7am–11pm); and Mabel Telecommunications, Jirón Lima 224 (Mon–Fri 7am–noon & 2–7pm).

Theatre The Teatro Municipal, block 1 of Arequipa, has folklore music, dance and other cultural events displays; for details of what's on, check at the box office.

Lake Titicaca

Lake Titicaca is an undeniably impressive sight. A National Reserve since 1978, it has over sixty varieties of birds, fourteen species of native fish and eighteen types of amphibians. It's also the world's largest high-altitude body of water, at 284m deep and more than 8500 square kilometres in area, fifteen times the size of Lake Geneva in Switzerland and higher and slightly bigger than Lake Tahoe in the US. It's often seen as three separate regions: Lago Mayor, the main, deep part of the lake; Wiñaymarka, the area incorportaing various archipelagos that relate to both Peruvian and Bolivian Titicaca; and the Golfi de Puno, essentially the bay encompassed by the peninsulas of Capachica and Chucuito. The villages that line its shores depend mainly on grazing, since the altitude limits the growth potential of most crops. Titicaca is where the

Quechua Indian language and people merge with the more southerly Aymaras. Curious Inca-built **Chullpa burial tombs** circle the lake and its man-made **Uros Floating Islands**. These islands have been inhabited for centuries since their construction by retreating Uros Indians. Today, they are a major tourist attraction – floating platform islands, weird to walk over and even stranger to live on. More powerful and self-determined are the communities who live on the fixed islands of **Taquile** and **Amantani**, often described as the closest one can get to heaven by the few travellers who make it out this far into the lake. There are, in fact, more than seventy islands in the lake, the largest and most sacred being the **Island of the Sun**, an ancient Inca temple site on the Bolivian side of the border which divides the southern section of the lake. Titicaca is an Aymara word meaning "Puma's Rock", which refers to an unusual boulder on the Island of the Sun. The island is best visited from Copacabana in Bolivia, or trips can be arranged through some of the tour companies in Puno (see p.236).

Not surprisingly, fish is an important part of the diet of the Titicaca inhabitants, both the islanders and the ibis and flamingos which can be seen along the pre-Inca terraced shorelines. The most common fish is a small piranha-like specimen called *carachi*. Trout arrived in the lake, after swimming up the rivers, during the first or second decade of the twentieth century. *Pejerey* (Kingfish) established themselves only thirty years ago but have been so successful that there are relatively few trout left.

The Uros Floating Islands

Although there are more than forty islands, most guided tours limit themselves to the largest island, **Huacavacani**, where several Indian families live alongside a floating Seventh Day Adventist missionary school. The islands are made from layer upon layer

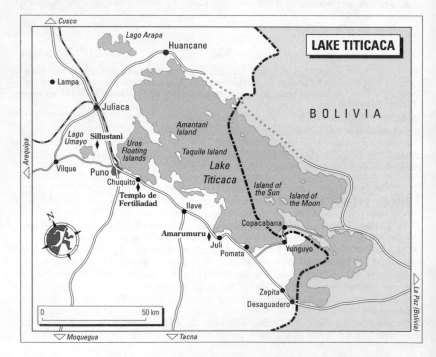

of **tortora reeds**, the dominant plant in the shallows of Titicaca and a source of food as well as the basic material for roofing, walling and fishing rafts. During the rainy season months of November to February it's not unusual for some of the islands to move about the surface of the lake.

The easiest way to get to the islands is on a short three- to four-hour trip with one of the tour agencies in Puno (see p.236). Alternatively, you can go independently with the skipper of one of the many launches that leave from the port in Puno about every thirty minutes, or take the daily public transport boat leaving at 9am, usually getting back for 12–1pm (always check with the captain for the time they plan to depart the islands).

There are only a few hundred **Uros Indians** living on the islands these days, and many of those you might meet actually live on the mainland, only travelling out to sell their wares to the tourists; most are a mixture of the original Uros and the larger Aymara tribe. When the Incas controlled the region, they considered the Uros so poor – almost subhuman – that the only tribute required of them was a section of hollow cane filled with lice.

Life on the islands has certainly never been easy: the inhabitants have to go some distance to find fresh water, and the bottoms of the reed islands rot so rapidly, that fresh matting has to be constantly added above. More than half the islanders have converted to Catholicism, and the largest community is very much dominated by its evangelical school. Thirty years ago the Uros were a proud fishing tribe, in many ways guardians of Titicaca, but the 1980s, particularly, saw a rapid devastation of their traditional values. Many foreign visitors are put off by what they experience on landing at the island – a veritable mobbing by young children speaking a few words of English ("sweets", "money", "what's your name?" and "give it to me") and fighting each other for your gifts. However, you do get a glimpse of a very unusual way of life and the opportunity to ride on a *tortora* reed raft.

Taquile and Amantani

Two genuine – non-floating – islands in Titicaca can also be visited. **Taquile** and **Amantani**, peaceful places that see fewer tourists, are both around 25–30km across the water from Puno, just beyond the outer edge of the Gulf of Chucuito. Amantani is the least visited of the two and, consequently, has fewer facilities and costs slightly more to reach by boat.

Daily **boats** for Taquile leave at 8am, returning by around 5.30 or 6pm, while for Amantani they usually leaving at 9am, returning at 4–4.30pm; as usual, check with the captain for the time they plan to depart the islands. You can go on an organized trip with one of the tour companies listed on p.236, but the agencies use the same boats and charge at least twice the going rate. The sun's rays reflected off the lake can burn even well-tanned skins so it's a good idea to protect your head and shoulders during this voyage. The launches tend to be ageing wooden boats with engines from old North American cars, like the 1962 Dodge which belongs to one of the island captains. Most boats return after lunch the same day, but since this doesn't give you enough time to look around, many visitors prefer to stay a night or two in bed and breakfast **accommodation** (from around $3). The only way to guarantee a place to stay is to book in advance through one of Puno's tour agencies (see p.236); if you arrive on spec, you could ask the relevant island authorities or talk to the boat's capitain and you may be lucky, but don't bank on it. Sleeping bags and toilet paper are recommended, and fresh fruit and vegetables are appreciated by the host-islanders.

Taquile

The island of **Taquile** has been inhabited for over ten thousand years, with agriculture being introduced about 4000 BC. It was dominated by the Aymara-speaking

Tiahuanuco culture until the thirteenth century, when the Incas conquered it and introduced the Quechua language. In 1580, the island was "bought" by Pedro Gonzalez de Taquile and so came under Spanish influence. During the 1930s it was used as a safe exile/prison for troublesome characters like former president Sanchez Cerro, and it wasn't until 1937 that the residents – the local descendants of the original Indians – regained legal ownership by buying it back.

Approaching Taquile, the most attractive of the islands and some 1km-by-7km, it looks like a huge ribbed whale, large and bulbous to the east, tapering to its western tailend. The horizontal striations of the island are produced by significant amounts of ancient terracing along Taquile's steep-sided shores. Such terraces are of an even greater premium here in the middle of the lake where soil erosion would otherwise slowly kill the island's largely self-sufficient agricultural economy, where potatoes, corn, broad beans and the hardy *quinoa* are the main crops. Without good soil Taquile could become like the main floating islands, depending almost exclusively on tourism for its income.

The main heart of the island is reached by some 525 gruelling steps up a steep hill from the small stone harbour. The view from the top is spectacular – looking towards the southeast of the island you can see the hilltop ruins of Uray K'ari, built of stone in the Tiahuanuco era around 800 AD; looking to the west you may glimpse the larger, slightly higher ruins of Hanan K'ari. On arrival you'll be met by a committee of locals who delegate various native families to look after particular travellers – be aware that your family may live in basic conditions and speak no Spanish, let alone English (Quechua being the first language). There is no electricity on the island, apart from a solar-powered community loudspeaker and one or two individual houses with solar lighting, so take a torch and candles. There are no medical facilities or hotels either, though there is a small store and a few **places to eat** around the small plaza, where fish and chips and honey pancakes are the specialities.

Most of Taquile's population of 1200 people are weavers and knitters of fine alpaca wool – renowned for their excellent cloth and unusual designs and among the most skilled weavers in the Andes. You can still watch the locals drop-spin, a common form of hand-spinning that produces incredibly fine thread for their special cloth. The men sport black woollen trousers fastened with elaborate waistbands woven in pinks, reds and greens, while the women wear beautiful black headscarves, dark shawls and skirts trimmed usually with shocking pink or bright-red tassles, sweaters or fringes.

Amantani

Like nearby Taquile, **AMANTANI**, a basket-weavers' island and the largest on the lake, has managed to retain some degree of cultural isolation and autonomous control over the tourist trade. The ancient agricultural terraces are maintained in excellent condition and traditional crafts of stone masonry are still practised, as are the old Inca systems of agriculture, labour and ritual trade. The islanders eat mainly vegetables, with meat and fruit being rare commodities, and the women dress in colourful clothes, very distinctly woven. The island is dominated by two small hills: one is the **Temple of Pachamama** (Mother Earth) and the other the **Temple of Pachatata** (Father Earth). Around February 20, the islanders celebrate their main festival with half the five thousand-strong population going to one hill, the other half gathering at the other. Following ancient ceremonies, the two halves gather together to celebrate their origins with traditional and colourful music and dance.

Currently the only available **accommodation** is staying in an islander's house (see above) though there are plans to build a hostal. There are no restaurants, but you can buy basic supplies at the *artesania* trading post in the heart of the island. If you're lucky, the mayor of Amantani may be available to act as a guide for a few dollars a day; unsurprisingly, he is very knowledgable about the island and its history.

The Chullpa Tombs of Sillustani

Scattered all around Lake Titicaca you'll find *chullpas*, gargantuan white stone towers up to 10m in height in which the Colla tribe, who dominated the region before the Incas, buried their dead. Some of the most spectacular are at **SILLUSTANI**, set on a little peninsula in Lake Umayo overlooking Titicaca, 30km northwest of Puno. This ancient temple-cum-cemetery consists of a ring of stones more than five hundred years old – some of which have been tumbled by earthquakes or, more recently, by tomb-robbers intent on stealing the rich goods (ceramics, jewellery and a few weapons) buried with important mummies. Two styles predominate at this site: the honeycomb *chullpas* and those whose superb stonework was influenced by the advance of the Inca Empire. The former are set aside from the rest and characterized by large stone slabs around a central core; some of them are carved, but most are simply plastered with white mud and small stones. The Inca-type stonework is more complicated and in some cases you can see the elaborate corner jointing more typical of Cusco masonry.

The easist way to get here is on a **guided tour** from Puno (see p.236); alternatively, you can take a **colectivo** from Avenida Tacna most afternoons at around 2–2.30pm, for under $5. If you want to **camp** overnight at Sillustani (remembering how cold it can be), the site guard will show you where to pitch your tent. It's a magnificent place to wake up, with the morning sun rising over the snowcapped Cordillera Real on the Bolivian side of Titicaca.

South to Bolivia

The most popular routes to Bolivia involve overland road travel, crossing the frontier either at **Yunguyo** or at the river border of **Desaguaderos** (this latter route is little frequented these days due to the poor condition of the road). En route to either you'll pass by some of Titicaca's more interesting colonial settlements, each with its own individual styles of architecture. Several **bus companies** run services from Puno over these routes: Empresa Los Angeles has twice weekly buses to Desaguaderos ($1.50, a 3hr trip); Tour Peru runs daily to Copacabana ($1.50, also 3hr) and La Paz ($6, a 7hr trip); Altiplano Buses go most days to La Paz ($6); Colectur runs to Copacabana and La Paz daily for around $5; and San Pedro Express runs daily to Yunguyo, Desaguaderos and Copacabana ($8). From Yunguyo some buses connect with a minibus service to Copacabana, then a Bolivian bus on to La Paz, though many buses go through to Copacabana and some on to La Paz itself, especially between June and August; see Puno Listings, p.235, for addresses and phone numbers of bus companies.

Chucuito to Juli

CHUCUITO, 20km south of Puno, is dwarfed by its intensive hillside terracing and by huge igneous boulders poised behind the brick and adobe houses. Chucuito was once

---

BY FERRY INTO BOLIVIA

Until recently, the best way into Bolivia was undoubtedly on the **steam ship** across Lake Titicaca from Puno to Guaqui; tickets were available from the jetty in Puno's main port and cost $10–$25. The steamer is currently not running, but it's worth checking with the tourist office or at the jetty for up-to-date information. Expensive, irregular **hydrofoils** from Puno to La Paz are run by Crillon Tours in the US (1450 South Bayshore Drive, Suite 85, Miami, FL 33131; ☎305/358-5353), also bookable through the tourist office or tour operators in Puno, but you need to book well in advance in all cases. A similarly upmarket **catamaran** service runs on demand; contact Transturin (see p.236) for details.

a colonial town and its main plaza retains the **pillory** (*picota*) where the severed heads of executed criminals were displayed. Close to this there's a **sundial**, erected in 1831 to help the local Aymara people regulate their working day according to European hours. The base is made from stones taken from the Inca **Templo de Fertilidad**, itself located behind the *Hotel Taypikala*, which remains Chucuito's greatest treasure. Inside the main stone walls are around a hundred phalluses. Also on the plaza is the **Iglesia Santo Domingo**, constructed in 1780 and displaying a very poor image of a puma. For **accommodation**, try the *Hotel Las Cabañas*, Jirón Bolognesi 334 (☎054/351276), affiliated to Hostelling International and where you stay in small huts with constant hot water and a fire for the cool nights.

CROSSING THE BOLIVIAN BORDER

Yunguyo–Copacabana

The **Yunguyo–Copacabana** crossing is by far the most enjoyable route into Bolivia, though unless you intend staying overnight in Copacabana (or taking the 3hr Puno–Copacabana minibus) you'll need to set out quite early from Puno; the actual **border** (8am–6pm) is a two-kilometre walk from Yunguyo. The Bolivian passport control, where there's usually a bus for the 10km or so to Copacabana, is a few hundred metres on. The best **hotel** in Yunguyo is the *Hostal Residencial Isabel* San Francisco 110 (☎054/856084; ②), which has hot water but only communal bathrooms. You can change money at the Banco de La Nacion at Triunfo 219 and 28 de Julio, but there are several *casas de cambio* and street *cambistas* nearby, usually offering better rates and dealing in a greater variety of currencies, though even then only change enough to get you to La Paz, as the rate is poor. The cheap afternoon bus service from Copacabana takes you through some of the most exciting scenery of the basin. At Tiquina you leave the bus briefly to take a passenger ferry across the narrowest point of the lake, the bus rejoining you on the other side from its own individual ferry. Officially all travellers have to report to the Bolivian Naval Office – this is one of the few landlocked countries in the world which has a navy – beside the passenger ferry terminal before crossing the lake; but in practice there are often too many people and there's a very real danger of missing the bus (and your luggage) on the other side by hanging around in a hopeless queue; once across the lake it's a four- to five-hour haul on to La Paz.

The Desaguaderos Crossing

Very little traffic now uses the **Desaguaderos Crossing** over the Peru–Bolivia border; it's less interesting than going via Yunguyo, but has the advantage of passing the Bolivian ruined temple complex of Tiahuanuco. If you do want to travel this route, take one of the early morning colectivos (6–9am) from Jirón Tacna in Puno to **Desaguaderos** ($2, a 3–4hr trip); you'll need to get a stamp in your passport from the Peruvian control by the market and the Bolivian one just across the bridge. If you arrive here by bus, it's a short walk across the border and you can pick up an Ingravi bus on to La Paz more or less hourly (4–5hr), which goes via Tiahuanuco. Money can be changed on the bridge approach but the rates are poor, so buy only as much as you'll need to get you to La Paz.

From Bolivia to Peru

For anyone **coming into Peru from Bolivia** by either route, the procedure is just as straightforward. One difference worth noting is that when leaving Copacabana, a customs and passport check takes place in two little huts on the left just before the exit barrier. Now and again Bolivian customs officials take a heavy line and thoroughly search all items of luggage. In some cases bribery has to be resorted to, simply to avoid undue hassle or delay. If you get stranded crossing the border and need a basic **hostal**, try the *Hotel Amazonas,* on the main plaza in Yunguyo (②); the only option in Desaguaderos is the rather sordid *Alojamiento Internacional* on the central plaza (①).

Some eight kilometres beyond Chucuito you pass through the **Aymara** settlement of Plateria, once famous and so named for the coins manufactured here in colonial days, but there's little to stop here for. Similarly, the next village, **Acora**, has a busy Sunday market and is renowned for its fish, but little else. Off the main road, however, some 6km south-east of Acora there are vestiges of the Tiahuanuco culture and the Chullpas of Molloq'o.

About halfway between Puno and Juli you pass through the village of **ILAVE**, where a major side road heads off directly down to the coast for Tacna (320km) and Moquegua via Trata (231km). As an an arterial road intersection, Ilave is quite an important market town and has a large Sunday **market** selling colourful clothing and coca-leaves, plus a few shamanic fortune-tellers. It also has a surprisingly large and modern Terminal Terrestre, where all the **buses** from Puno stop and from where it's possible to catch services to Tacna and Moquegua on the coast. The town has a large Plaza de Armas, where there's a statue to Coronel Francisco Bolognesi, hero of the Arica battles between Peru and Chile. Half a block to the south, the ancient and crumbling **Iglesia de San Miguel** has an impressive cupola and belfry. If you want a **place to stay**, the very basic *Hostal Grau*, on the plaza at Jirón Dos de Mayo 337 (①) is just about bearable. For **food**, try the *Polleria Ricos Pollo*, Jirón Andino 307, towards the market from the plaza.

After crossing the bridge over the Río Ilave, the road cuts 60km across the plain towards Juli, passing by some unusual rock formations sacttered across the *altiplano* of the Titicaca basin, many of which have ritual significance to the local Aymara population. The most significant of these is the rock that's been worked to represent the face of **Amarumuru**, said by indigenous mystics to have been transformed by a race of giants and to act as a doorway into another dimension

A few kilometres on from Amarumuru, the relatively large town of **JULI**, now bypassed by the new road, but nestling attractively between gigantic round-topped and terraced hills is known locally as Pequeña Roma (Little Rome) because of the seven prominent mountains immediately surrounding it, each one of them of spiritual significance to the indigenous inhabitants in terms of earth-magic, healing and fertility. Perhaps because of this, the Jesuits chose Juli, at 3800m above sea level, as the site for a major mission training centre, which prepared missionaries for trips to the remoter regions of Bolivia and Paraguay. The concept they developed, a form of community evangelization, was at least partly inspired by the Inca organizational system and was extremely influential throughout the seventeenth and eighteenth centuries. Their political and religious power was and still is reflected in the almost surreally extravagant church architecture.

Fronting the large open plaza is the stone-built parish church of **San Pedro**, known for its intricately carved plateresque side altars. Constructed in 1560, it has an impressive cupola, and the cool, serene interior, awash with gold leaf, is home to many superb examples of the Cusqueña school. Behind the altar there's a wealth of silver and gold, the woodwork dripping with seashells, fruits and angels. In front of this church you'll often see local shamanic fortune tellers. Across the plaza from here is the amazing-looking **Casa Zavala** (House of the Inquisition), with thatched roof and fantastically carved double doors, opposite the church and known as *el carcel* ("the prison"). Juli's numerous other churches display superb examples of the Indian influence, particularly the huge brick and adobe **Iglesia San Juan** (Mon–Sat 9am–5pm; $1.20), with its *mestizo* stonework on some of the doors and windows. Cold and musty but with a rather surreal interior, due in part to the play of light through its few high windows, this *iglesia* was founded in 1775 but is now dedicated to being an excellent museum of religious art and architecture, which handsomely rewards the inquisitive visitor. Of the few **hostals** here, try the basic *Hostal Treboles* (②) on the main plaza, or the *Hostal Municipal* (②) on the left as you enter the town from Puno road.

Twenty kilometres on lies the historic town of **POMATA**, with its pink granite church of **Santaigo Aposto**, built in 1763. Outside the church, in a prominent location overlooking the lake, is a circular stone construction known as the **glorieta**; crumbling today, it's still the site where local authorities meet for ceremonial purposes. Pomata's name is derived from the Aymaru for "puma", and you'll see the puma symbol all over the fountain in the Plaza de Armas and outside the church. If you happen to be around the area in October, try to get to Pomata for the **Fiesta de la Virgen de Rosaria** on the first Sunday of the month, a splendid celebration with processions, music and folk dancing, as well the usual drinking and feasting.

travel details

Buses and colectivos

Arequipa to: Chivay (6 daily; 3–4hr); Colca (3 daily; 5–6hr); Cusco (several daily; 10–12hr); Lima (8–10 daily; 14–18hr); Moquegua (4 daily; 3–4hr); Paucarpata (every 30min; 15min); Puno (daily; 12hr); Tacna (2–3 daily; 5hr).

Ica to: Arequipa (6 daily; 14hr); Lima (12 daily; 4hr); Nazca (6 daily; 2hr).

Nazca to: Arequipa (1 nightly, several daily; 12hr); Cusco, via Arequipa (daily; 35hr); Lima (2–3 daily; 5hr).

Pisco to: Ayacucho (3 weekly; 14hr); Lima (3 daily; 3hr); Ica (10 daily; 1hr); Nazca (2 daily; 3hr).

Puno to: Cusco (8 daily; 12–14hr); Juliaca (3–4 hourly; 30–40min); La Paz via Desaguaderos (2 daily; 7–9hr), via Yunguyo (6–8 daily; 7–8hr); Moquegua (daily; 10–12hr); Tacna (3 weekly; 17hr).

Tacna to: Arequipa (5 daily; 6–7hr); Arica (10 daily; 1–2 hr); Lima (4 daily; 22hr); Puno (3 weekly; 17hr).

Trains

Arequipa to: Cusco (2 weekly; 20–22hr); Puno (2 weekly; 11hr).

Puno to: Arequipa (4 weekly; 11hr); Cusco (4 weekly; 10hr), via Juliaca (1hr 30min) and Sicuani (6hr 30min).

Flights

Arequipa to: Cusco (2 daily; 1hr); Juliaca, for Puno (4 weekly; 40min); Lima (3 daily; 1hr).

Juliaca (Puno) to: Arequipa (daily; 40min); Cusco (daily; 40min); Lima (daily; 2hr).

CHAPTER FOUR

ANCASH AND HUÁNUCO

Sliced north to south by parallel ranges of high Andean peaks, the **Ancash and Huánuco** areas of central Peru offer more in terms of trekking and climbing, beautiful snowcapped scenery, flora and fauna, glaciated valleys, history and traditional cultures than anywhere else in the country. The *departmento* of **Ancash** unfurls along an immense desert coastline, where pyramids and ancient fortresses are scattered within easy reach of several small resorts linked by vast, empty Pacific beaches. Behind, range the barren heights of the Cordillera Negra, and beyond that the spectacular backdrop of the snowcapped Cordillera Blanca; between the two the **Callejón de Huaylas**, a 200-kilometre-long valley some 3000m above sea level, offers some of the best hiking and mountaineering in South America. Nestling in the valley, the *departmento's* capital, **Huaraz** – seven hours or so by car from Lima – makes an ideal base for exploring some of the best mountain scenery in the Andes. Over the last twenty years or so, this region has become a major focus for mountaineers, and Huaraz, the vital centre of this inland region, is the place to stock up, hire guides and mules, and relax after a breathtaking expedition. The city is close to scores of exhilarating mountain trails, as well as the ancient Andean treasure, **Chavín de Huantar**, an impressive stone temple complex which was the heart of a puma-worshipping religious movement 2500 years ago.

Separated from the coast by the western Andes, and with a distinct cultural tradition, the *departmento* of **Huánuco** is less visited than Ancash but still offers some spectacular, if remote, destinations en route to the central jungle, as well as a range of fascinating nearer sites. From the eponymous regional capital – the thriving market city of **Huánuco** – it's possible to visit a series of unique archeological ruins, above all the huge and puzzling complex at **Tantamayo**, and the deserted expanse of **Huánuco Viejo**, a remarkably well-preserved Inca city. It's just a short trip from Huánuco to **Tingo Maria** and the luxuriant rainforest regions, where the eastern slopes of the Andes merge into the jungle of the Amazon Basin.

The connecting road between Huánuco and Huaraz via **La Unión** is little more than a barely passable track, a delicate thread connecting two large but separate economic and political regions. Some terrorist activity has been reported in this remote mountain area, though the route is currently being travelled safely by more intrepid visitors; always check the situation before setting off with the South American Explorers' Club (see p.21), a reliable tour company in Huaraz or Caraz or the tourist offices in Huaraz or Huánuco.

ACCOMMODATION PRICE CODES

Unless otherwise indicated, **accommodation** in this book is coded according to the categories below, based on the price of a double room in high season.

① under $5	③ $10–20	⑤ $30–40	⑦ $50–70
② $5–10	④ $20–30	⑥ $40–50	⑧ over $70

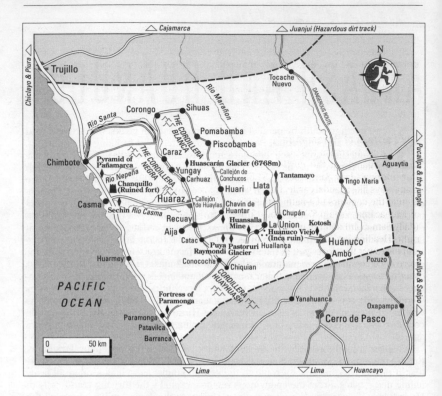

THE ANCASH COAST

Most people travelling along the **Ancash coast** between Lima and Trujillo do the whole trip in a single eight-hour bus ride along the Panamerican Highway. If you're short of time you'll probably want to do the same, but it's worth at least considering a stop at the small beach resort of **Barranca** or the farming and fishing villages of **Casma** or **Chimbote** – all three of which have some intriguing archeological sites nearby, as well as offering alternative routes up into the **Callejón de Huaylas**. Facilities for tourists are hardly overwhelming, and the towns themselves have developed as road- and seaside urban sprawls, but the zone is relatively well serviced.

Barranca, Patavilca and the Fortress of Paramonga

North of Lima, the **Fortress of Paramonga** is the first site of real interest, the best preserved of all Peru's coastal outposts, built originally to guard the southern limit of the powerful Chimu empire. To explore the ruins, it's best to base yourself at **BARRANCA**, 7km before the fortress, where there are a few simple **hotels** and two or three places to eat. The *Hotel Jefferson*, at Jirón Lima 946 (②), is cheap and quite comfortable, or there's the basic *Hostal Colón*, Jirón Galvez 407 (①). The best place to eat is at the excellent Chinese **restaurant** on the main street. Nearly all buses and colectivos on their way between Lima and Trujillo or Huaraz stop at Barranca.

Five kilometres north of Barranca is the smaller town of **PATAVILCA**, where Bolivar planned his campaign to liberate Peru. The main Tarmacked road to Huaraz and the Cordillera Blanca leaves the Panamerican Highway here and heads up into the Andes, but the only facilities in the village are a basic café, the *Restaurant Conejo*, and a small **museum** (Mon–Sat 9am–5pm; $0.5), containing local archeological finds, including ceramics.

The Fortress of Paramonga

To get from Barranca to Paramonga, take the efficient local bus service, which leaves from the garage at the northern end of town, every hour or so. The **Fortress of Paramonga** (daily 8am–5.30pm; $1.5) sits less than 1km from the ocean and looks in many ways like a feudal castle. Constructed entirely from adobe, its walls within walls run around the contours of a natural hillock similar in style and situation to the Sun Temple of Pachacamac (see p.87). As you climb up from the road, by the small site **museum** (daily 8am–5pm) and the ticket office, you'll see the main entrance to the fortress on the right. Heading into the maze-like **ruins**, you'll find the rooms and sections get smaller and narrower the closer you get to the top – the original palace-temple. From here there were once commanding views across the desert coast in either direction; today, looking south, you see vast sugar-cane fields, now farmed by a co-operative, but formerly belonging to the US-owned Grace Corporation, once owners of nearly a third of Peru's sugar production. In contrast to the verdant green of these fields, irrigated by the Río Fortaleza, the fortress stands out in the landscape like a huge, dusty yellow pyramid.

There are differences of opinion as to whether the fort had a military function or was purely a ritual centre, but as most pre-Conquest cultures built their places of worship around the natural personality of the landscape (rocks, water, geomorphic features and so on), it seems likely that the Chimu built it on an older *huaca*, both as a fortified ritual shrine and to mark the southern boundary of their empire. It was conquered by the Incas in the late fifteenth century, who built a road down from the Callejón de Huaylas and another that ran along the sands below the fortress. Hernando Pizarro was the first Spaniard to see Paramonga, arriving in 1533 en route from Cajamarca to Pachacamac. He described it as "a strong fort with seven encircling walls painted with many forms both inside and outside, with portals well built like those of Spain and two tigers painted at the principal doorways". There are still red- and yellow-based geometric murals visible on some of the walls in the upper sector, as well as some chess-board patterns.

Huarmey and around

North of Paramonga, sand dunes encroach on the main coastal road as it continues the 75km to **HUARMEY**, where you'll find the exhilarating and usually deserted beaches of La Honda, El Balncario and Tuquillo. If you want **accommodation**, there's the basic *Hotel Venus* (②), plus there's a 24-hour **restaurant**, *El Piloto*, geared towards truckdrivers. Leaving Huarmey, the road closely follows the shoreline, passing the magnificent **Playa Grande**, a seemingly endless beach with powerful rolling surf – often a luminous green at night due to phosphorescent plankton being tossed around in the white water crests – and a perfect spot for **camping**. Some of the desert you pass through has no plant life at all, beyond the burned-out tumbleweed that grows around the humps and undulations fringed with curvy lines of rock strata – intrusions of volcanic power from the ancestral age. In places, huge hills crouch like sand-covered jellyfish squatting on some vast beach.

Casma and around

The town of **CASMA**, 70km north of Huarmey, marks the mouth of the well-irrigated Sechin river valley. Surrounded by corn and cotton fields, this small settlement is peculiar in that most of its buildings are just one storey high and all of them are modern. Formerly the port for the Callejón de Huaylas, the town was razed by the 1970 earthquake, whose epicentre was just offshore. There's not a lot of interest here and little reason to break your journey, other than to explore the nearby ruins, such as the temple complex of **Sechin**, the ancient fort of **Chanquillo**, or the **Pañamarca Pyramid**, 20km north.

The town boasts several roadside cafés and a small selection of **hotels**: the *Hotel El Farol*, Tupac Amaru 350 (☎044/711064; ③), two blocks from the Plaza de Armas, is clean, friendly and comfortable with a decent restaurant; the *Hostal Gregori*, Calle Ormeño 579 (☎044/711073; ③), is also very clean and almost as comfortable; or try the basic *Hotel Indoamerica*, Huaraz 132 (☎044/711395; ②), close to the Plaza de Armas. En route to the Sechin ruins there's the well-run *Hospedaje Las Dunas* (no tel; ②), which also has a good **restaurant** and is only ten minutes from town by motorcar. Turismo Chimbote **buses** run at least three times a day to Lima (5hr) and Chimbote (40min); Huandoy, Avenida Luis Ormeño 158 (☎044/712336), connect with Huaraz and Caraz; while Empresa Moreno buses take the scenic but dusty track three times a week, over the Cordillera Negra via the Callan Pass to Huaraz (5hr).

The Sechin Ruins

Just over an hour's walk from Casma – head south along the Panamerican Highway for 3km then up the signposted side road to Huaraz for about the same distance – lies the ruined temple complex of **SECHIN** (daily 9am–6pm; $2). The main section of the site, unusually stuck at the bottom of a hill, consists of an outer wall clad with around ninety monolithic slabs engraved with sometimes monstrous representations of bellicose warriors and mutilated sacrificial victims or prisoners of war. Some of these stones, dating from about 750 BC, stand 4m high. Hidden behind the standing stones is an interesting looking inner sanctuary – a rectangular building consisting of a series of superimposed platforms with a central stairway on either side – but it is currently closed to the public. The site also has a small museum, the **Museo Max Uhle**, which displays photographs of the complex plus some of the artefacts uncovered here.

It is rare for granite stone to be used so extensively in coastal construction, which generally favoured adobe. Some of the original temple constructions have been found to predate the Chavín de Huantar complex (see p.275) and have consequently put into doubt some basic assumptions about the evolution of religious and ceremonial construction in ancient Peru. Some of the ceremonial centres at Sechin were built before 1400 BC, including the massive U-shaped **Sechin Alto** complex, at the time the largest construction in the entire Americas. Around 300m long by 250m wide, the massive stone-faced platform predates the similar ceremonial centre at Chavín de Huantar possibly by as much as four hundred years. This means that Chavín could not have been the original source of temple architectural style, and that much of the iconography and legends associated with what has until recently been called the Chavín cultural phase of Peruvian prehistory, actually began 3500 years ago down here on the desert coast.

If you're not up to the walk here, your best option is to take a **motorcycle taxi** from Casma, for $1–2. There are no buses, but some local **colectivos** come here in the mornings from the market area of Casma; alternatively, there are **taxis** from the Plaza de Armas, for around $10 including an hour's wait.

Chanquillo and Mojeque

Several other lesser-known sites dot the **Sechin Valley**, whose maze of ancient sandy roadways constituted an important pre-Inca junction. The remains of a huge complex of dwellings can be found on the **Pampa de Llamas**, though all you will see nowadays are the walls of adobe huts, deserted more than a thousand years ago. At **Mojeque**, you can see a terraced pyramid with stone stairs and feline and snake designs. Both these sites are best visited from Casma by taxi; expect to pay around $5–10.

Some 12km southeast of Casma lies the ruined, possibly pre-Mochica fort of **Chanquillo**, which you can wander around freely. Trucks leave for here every morning at around 9am from the *Petro Peru* filling station in Casma – ask the driver to drop you off at "El Castillo", from where it's a thirty-minute walk uphill to the fort. It's an amazing ruin set in a commanding position on a barren hill, with four walls in concentric rings and watchtowers in the middle, keeping an eye over the desert below.

The Pyramid of Pañamarca

Heading north from Casma, the first major landmark is the Nepeña river valley. At Km 395 of the Panamerican Highway there is a turn-off on the right that leads 11km to the ruined adobe pyramid of **Pañamarca**. Three large painted panels can be seen here, and on a nearby wall a long procession of warriors has been painted – but both have been badly damaged by rain. Although an impressive monument to the Mochica culture, dating from around 500 AD, it's not an easy site to visit; the best way is to get a **taxi** from the Plaza de Armas in Casma for around $5.

Chimbote

Until the early part of this century, **CHIMBOTE** – another 25km beyond the turn-off to Pañamarca – was a quiet fishing port and popular honeymoon spot. Now, it's a busy, modern city, rather ugly and characterized by the stench of fish, and with little of interest for tourists. Its sprawling development, which constitutes the country's most spectacular urban growth outside Lima, was stimulated by the Chimbote–Huallanca rail line (built in 1922), a nearby hydroelectric plant, and by government planning for an anticipated boom in the anchovy and tuna fishing industry. The population grew rapidly from 5000 in 1940 to 60,000 in 1961 (swollen by squatter settlers from the mountains), nearly tripling in the next decade to an incredible 159,000 – making it Peru's fifth-largest city, despite the destruction of nearly every building during the 1970 earthquake.

Chimbote has more than thirty fish-packing factories, boasting some of the world's most modern canning equipment. Unfortunately the fishing industry has been undergoing a crisis since the early 1970s – overfishing and El Niño have led to bans and strict catch limits for the fishermen. However, more than 75 percent of Peru's fishing-related activity continues to take place here.

Practicalities

Although not as bad as it used to be, it still often smells too awful to **stay** very long in Chimbote (although the locals say you get used to it after a while) and most travellers remain overnight at most. The *Hotel Venus*, on Avenida Prado (☎044/321339; ③), is bearable and not too expensive. The *Hostal El Ruedo*, Lote 15, Urbino Los Pinos (☎044/335560; ②), is fine and relatively free of the smell, a little way from the noisy town centre. The *Gran Hotel Chimú*, Jirón José Galvez 109, on the Plaza 28 de Julio (☎044/321741; ⑤), is reasonably priced offering comfortable rooms and mod cons, and its restaurant, though not cheap, serves some of the best food found along this coast.

Almost all the coastal **buses** travelling north to Trujillo and south to Lima along the Panamerican Highway stop along Bolognesi, just off the Plaza 28 de Julio; Movil Tours, Turismo Chimbote, Expresso Huandoy and Trans Moreno all run daily buses to Huaraz via Pativilca and Casma and mostly nightly services to Caraz via Huallanca (Cañon del Pato) from Jirón Pardo, between Jirón José Galvez and Manual Ruiz.

Turismo Huaraz run the only Chimbote–Huaraz day bus (8.3km), from Avenida Galvez 1178. **Colectivos** to Trujillo (2–3hr away) leave regularly from opposite the *Hostal Los Angeles*, while colectivos to Lima hang around on Manual Ruiz, one block towards the sea off Avenida Prado. The **tourist office**, Bolognesi 421 (Mon–Sat 9am–5pm), can advise on transport to sites nearby and sometimes stocks town and regional maps. The **post office** (Mon–Sat 8am–6pm) is on Avenida Prado, between Tumbes and Jirón José Galvez and the **Telefónica Peru** (daily 7am–11pm) is at Tumbes 356.

The Great Wall of Peru

The desert area around Chimbote, though rarely visited, is littered with archeological remains, including an enormous defensive wall known as the **Great Wall of Peru**, thought to be over a thousand years old. Twenty kilometres north of Chimbote, the Panamerican Highway crosses a rocky outcrop into the Santa Valley, where the wall – a stone and adobe structure more than 50km long – rises from the sands of the desert. The enormous structure was first noticed in 1931 by the Shippee-Johnson Aerial Photographic Expedition, and there are many theories about its construction and purpose. Archeologist Julio Tello thought it was pre-Chimu, since it seems unlikely that the Chimu would have built such a lengthy defensive wall so far inside the limits of their empire. It may, however, have been constructed prior to a second phase of military expansion or, as the historian Garcilaso de la Vega believed, the Spaniards might have built it here as a defence against the threat of Inca invasion from the coast or from the Callejón de Huaylas.

In its entirety, the wall stretches from Tambo Real near the Santa estuary in the west up to Chuqucara in the east, where there are scattered remains of pyramids, fortresses, temples and stone houses. To see the wall, take any Trujillo bus north from Chimbote (see previous page) along the Panamerican Highway, and get off when you see a bridge over the Río Santa. From here, simply head upstream for three to four hours and you'll arrive at the best surviving section of the wall, just to the west of the Hacienda Tanguche, where the piled stone is cemented with mud to more than 4m high in places.

Further up the valley lies a double-walled construction with outer turrets, discovered by Gene Savoy's aerial expedition in the late 1950s. Savoy reported 42 stone-built **strongholds** in the higher Santa Valley in only two days' flying, evidence that supports historians' claims that this was the most populated valley on the coast prior to the Spanish Conquest. Hard to believe today, it seems more probable if you bear in mind that this desert region, still alive with wildlife such as desert foxes and condors, is fed by the largest and most reliable of the coastal rivers. In 1962 Savoy led an expedition into the area on foot, finding that most of the parapeted defensive structures he had seen from the air were well hidden from the valley floor. Once you climb up to them, however, you can see (on a clear day) the towering peaks of the Cordillera Blanca to the east and the Pacific Ocean in the west. The climate here is hot but ideal for **camping**, and the only things you'll need to carry are a sunhat, sunblock, enough food, ample drinking water and a sleeping roll (blanket and mat); detailed **maps** of the region are available from the Instituto Geográfico Militar in Lima (see p.21). Remember though that this is off the beaten track and there is no tourism infrastructure whatsoever, so make sure someone knows where you're going and your expected return date.

The Viru Valley

Continuing north towards Trujillo, the Panamerican Highway cuts up the usually dry river-bed of Chau, a straggling, scrubby green trail through the absolutely barren desert of the **Viru Valley**. In the Gallinazo period, around 300 AD, the Viru Valley saw great changes: simple dwelling sites became fully fledged villages consisting of large groups of adjacent rooms and stone pyramids; improved irrigation produced a great population increase; and a society with complex labour patterns and distribution systems began to develop. The Gallinazo started to build defensive walls, just prior to being invaded by the Mochicas (around 500 AD) on their military conquests south as far as the Santa and Nepeña valleys. Later on, during the Chimu era, the population was dramatically reduced again, perhaps through migration north to Chan Chan, capital of this highly centralized pre-Inca state.

Viru and around

The main town in the valley is **Viru**, a small place at Km 515 of the Panamerican Highway, with a bridge over the river bed that, in the dry season, looks as though it has never seen rain. An impressive cultural centre around 300 AD, when it was occupied by the Gallinazo or Viru people, the town today offers very little to the tourist. The only reason to consider staying here is to visit the abundant **archeological remains** in the vicinity, though you're probably better off taking a guided tour from Trujillo with one of the companies listed on p.296.

The closest of the sites to town is **Cerro Prieto**, near the fishing village of Guanape – a three-kilometre walk from the northern side of the bridge in Viru towards the mouth of the Río Viru. There's little to see other than several dusty mounds, but this ancient rubbish dump was the site of an agricultural settlement in around 1200 BC, and some of the earliest ceramics on the coast were found here.

A far more interesting ruin, however, is the **Grupo Gallinazo** near Tomabal, 24km east of Viru up a side road just north of the same bridge. Here in the valley you can see the dwellings, murals and pyramids of a significant religious and administrative centre, its internal layout derived from kinship networks. The site covers an area of four square kilometres and archeologists estimate that it held over thirty thousand rooms. All the buildings at the site are built entirely of adobe, with separate cultivation plots irrigated by an intricate canal system. You can also make out the adobe walls and ceremonial platform of a Gallinazo temple, on top of one of the hilltops at Tomabal.

From Viru, the Panamerican Highway cuts north across a desert plain, close to the sea. Before reaching Trujillo, the road runs down into the expansive plains of the Moche Valley, with its great Mochica temples of the Sun and Moon (see p.304).

HUARAZ AND THE CORDILLERA BLANCA

Situated in the steeply walled valley of the **Callejón de Huaylas**, **Huaraz** is the focal point of inland Ancash. Although not one of Peru's most interesting towns, Huaraz has a lively atmosphere and makes an ideal springboard for exploring the surrounding mountains. It is dominated by the **Cordillera Blanca**, the highest tropical mountain range in the world, and **Huascarán**, Peru's highest peak. Only a day's bus ride from Lima or Trujillo, it's one of the best places to base yourself if you have any interest in hiking. The best weather in the region comes between May and September when the skies are nearly always blue and it rains very little. Between October and April, however, the skies are often cloudy and most afternoons you can expect some pretty heavy rains.

Besides the mountain scenery, the region boasts spectacular ruins such as **Chavín de Huantar**, at the bottom end of the parallel valley the **Callejón de Conchucos**, the natural thermal baths at **Monterrey** and **Chancos**, and immense glacial lakes, like **Lago Parón**, the largest and surrounded by some snowcapped peaks, and the beautiful **Llanganuco**. Throughout the whole area, too, you come upon unusual and exotic flora like the enormous, tropical *Puya Raymondi* plants, and traditional mountain villages where unwritten legends are encapsulated only in ancient carved stones and the memories of the local peasant population.

Huaraz

Less than a century ago, **HUARAZ** – some 400km from Lima – was still a fairly isolated community, barricaded to the east by the dazzling snowcapped peaks of the Cordillera Blanca and separated from the coast by the dry, dark Cordillera Negra. Between these two mountain chains the powerful Río Santa has formed a valley, the **Callejón de Huaylas**, a region with strong traditions of local independence. In 1885 the people of the Callejón waged a guerrilla war against the Lima authorities, which led to the whole valley being in rebel hands for several months. The revolt was sparked off by a native leader, the charismatic Pedro Pablo Atusparia, and thirteen other village mayors protesting over excessive taxation and labour abuses. They were sent straight to prison and humiliated by having their braided hair (a traditional sign of status) cut off, so the local peasants reacted by overrunning Huaraz, freeing their chieftains, and expelling all officials before looting the mansions of wealthy landlords and merchants (many of them expatriate Englishmen who had been here since the Wars of Independence). The rebellion was eventually quashed by an army battalion from the coast, which recaptured Huaraz while the Indians were celebrating their annual *fiesta*. But even today, Atusparia's memory survives close to local hearts, and inhabitants of the areas' remote villages remain unimpressed by the claims of central government.

Arrival and information

Most people arrive in Huaraz by **bus** from Lima, which takes eight or nine hours; the road is pretty good and so are the buses. You can expect to pay $8–12 for the journey, depending on the level of comfort; Cruz del Sur and Movil Tours both offer day and night buses and a range of services from standard to deluxe, which includes a packed lunch and video. Some cheaper bus companies, as well as Colectivos Comité 14, also run daily services here from Jirón Leticia, in Lima Centro. Companies coming from and going to Trujillo (8–10hr; around $8) include Cruz del Sur, Turismo Chimbote and Colectivos Comité 14. Coming from or going to Chimbote (5–7hr; $7) or Caraz (6–8hr; $7), you'll probably travel with Turismo Chimbote, Rodriguez or Empressa Huandoy; arriving direct from Casma (4–5hr; $6) you'll almost certainly travel on Empresa Moreno. All the above buses come in at and leave from or close to their companies' offices (see p.261 for details).

Few people arrive in the Callejón de Huaylas **by air** since there is no regular service, though Aero Condor fly from Lima around once a week between June and August. If you do arrive by air, you're dropped off at a small airstrip close to the village of Anta, some 23km north of Huaraz; from here it's thirty minutes into the city by colectivo or bus, both of which leave from the main road outside the airstrip.

Tourist information is available from the Oficina de Promocion Turistica, Pasaje Alfonso Martel Oficina 1, just off Avenida Luzuriaga by the Plaza de Armas (Mon–Fri 9am–1pm & 5–8pm, Sat 9am–1pm). Staff are very helpful and offer free photocopies of trekking maps but do not often have any city maps; these, though, can usually be obtained from good hotels or tour companies.

City transport

The **Avenida Luzuriaga is** the north–south axis of the town centre, where most of the restaurants, nightlife and tour agencies are based. The **Parque Ginebra**, set just behind Luzuriaga and the Plaza de Armas, is a pleasant little plaza but something of an afterthought in terms of city planning and not yet fully integrated into the network of roads. A city centre **taxi** ride costs less than $1, while motorbike rental can be arranged through the *Restaurant Monte Rosa* (see p.260) any afternoon or evening.

Colectivos and **local buses** connect Huaraz with all the main towns and villages north – Anta, Marcara, Carhuaz, Yungay and Caraz – at very reasonable rates ($0.5–2 for up to 2hr); these can be caught from just over the river bridge from the town centre, on either side of the main road, beside the Río Quillcay. Just before the bridge in Huaraz colectivos heading south to Catac ($0.8) and Olleros ($1) can be caught daily every thirty-minutes from the end of Jirón Caceres, just below the market area. Buses to Chiquian are run by Chiquian Tours from block 1 of Calle Huascarán, near the market, and leave every hour or so. For short journeys **within the city**, the best option is one of the regular colectivos, which run on fixed routes along *avenidas* Luzuriaga and Centenario ($0.4–0.6).

Accommodation

Even in the high season, around August, it's rarely difficult to find **accommodation** at a reasonable price. Within the centre of town, from the Plaza de Armas along Avenida Luzuriaga, there are countless **hostals** and many smaller places renting out rooms; outside of high season it is definitely worth bargaining.

Budget

Casa Alojamiento La Cabaña, Jirón José de Sucre 1224 (☎044/723428). A popular and really friendly *pension* with safe, comfortable accommodation, a dining room and hot water all day. Rooms have private bath and TV, while guests also have access to kitchen and laundry facilities, plus a dining room. ②.

Edward's Inn, Avenida Bolognesi 121 (☎ & fax 044/722692, *edwars@pol.com.pe*, *www/edwards@pol.com.pe*). One of the most popular trekkers' *hostals*, located just below the market area (at the end of Jirón Caceres) and offering an excellent range of services in a very pleasant atmosphere. Rooms come with or without private bath, and hot water is almost always available. The owner, who speaks English, is a highly experienced trekker, climber and mountain rescuer. ②–③.

Hostal Churup, Jirón Pedro Campos 735, La Soledad (044/722584). Just 5 minutes' walk from Plaza de Armas and with a garden, this great-value establishment has a family atmosphere and offers laundry, kitchen and left-luggage facilities. They also have lots of info about trekking. ②–③.

Hostal Galaxia, Jirón Juan de La Cruz Romero 638 (☎044/722230, fax 726535). Quite central and amicable staff, with hot water and private bathrooms. ③.

Hostal Gyula, Parque Ginebra 632 (☎044/721567, *hotelperu@infoweb.com.pe*). Located above an Internet office, this is relatively plain but excellent value and is bright and cheerful with great views, private bathrooms and access to kitchen facilities. ②.

Hostal Huaraz, Avenida Luzuriaga 529 (☎044/721982). Centrally located, simple and basic, this place has little character but is cheap even for rooms with private bath. ②.

Hostal Landauro, Jirón José de Sucre 109 (☎044/721212). One of the cheapest places in town, right on the Plaza de Armas, with pleasant but small rooms (with or without bath) set along narrow balconies boasting views over the town towards the Cordillera Blanca. ②.

Hostal Los Andes, Tarapaca 316 (☎044/721346). A pleasant enough family run hostal, in a slightly noisy street, it has a useful noticeboard and some information on trekking; rooms are with or without private bath. ②.

Hostal Rinconcito, Avenida Firtzcarrald 236 (☎044/727591). A bit near the bus terminals, but very good value for a slightly better than basic pad. Reasonably clean and with private baths. ②.

Hostal Wilkahuain, Avenida Centenario 1167 (☎044/727331 or 722211). Situated on the northern edge of town opposite the *Gran Hotel Huascarán*, this offers excellent value and is pretty friendly if a bit rough; the rooms are basic and the bathrooms shared. ②.

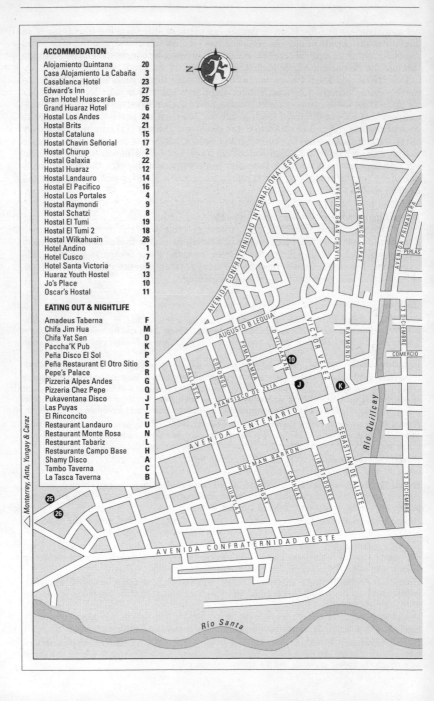

ACCOMMODATION

Alojamiento Quintana	20
Casa Alojamiento La Cabaña	3
Casablanca Hotel	23
Edward's Inn	27
Gran Hotel Huascarán	25
Grand Huaraz Hotel	6
Hostal Los Andes	24
Hostal Brits	21
Hostal Cataluna	15
Hostal Chavin Señorial	17
Hostal Churup	2
Hostal Galaxia	22
Hostal Huaraz	12
Hostal Landauro	14
Hostal El Pacifico	16
Hostal Los Portales	4
Hostal Raymondi	9
Hostal Schatzi	8
Hostal El Tumi	19
Hostal El Tumi 2	18
Hostal Wilkahuain	26
Hotel Andino	1
Hotel Cusco	7
Hotel Santa Victoria	5
Huaraz Youth Hostel	13
Jo's Place	10
Oscar's Hostal	11

EATING OUT & NIGHTLIFE

Amadeus Taberna	F
Chifa Jim Hua	M
Chifa Yat Sen	D
Paccha'K Pub	K
Peña Disco El Sol	P
Peña Restaurant El Otro Sitio	S
Pepe's Palace	R
Pizzeria Alpes Andes	G
Pizzeria Chez Pepe	Q
Pukaventana Disco	J
Las Puyas	T
El Rinconcito	E
Restaurant Landauro	U
Restaurant Monte Rosa	N
Restaurant Tabariz	L
Restaurante Campo Base	H
Shamy Disco	A
Tambo Taverna	C
La Tasca Taverna	B

△ Monterrey, Anta, Yungay & Caraz

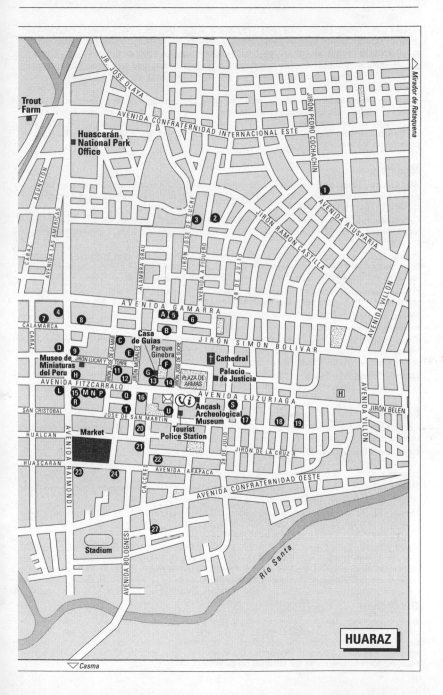

HUARAZ

Hotel Cusco, Jirón Cajamarca 204 (☎044/722561). A modernized place that's friendly, clean and fairly central, though hidden away up a side street off Avenida Raimondi; communal bathrooms only. ②.

Huaraz Youth Hostel, Parque Ginebra 28-G (☎044/721811, fax 722306). Located on a quaint little plaza in the streets behind Avenida Luzuriaga, this place is modern and very clean, with communal rooms and showers at reasonable rates. You can safely leave baggage here while out of town on trekking expeditions. ②.

Jo's Place, Jirón Daniel Villarzan 276 (☎044/725505). Located north of the main street in Huaraz, some 10 minutes' walk from the town centre, over the river bridge then fourth street on the right. Its relaxed, secure atmosphere, comfortable rooms and great value make it popular with backpackers. It also has a large garden and terrace and views across to the Cordillera Blanca. English newspapers are available. ②.

Moderate

Alojamiento Quintana, Juan de la Crus Romero 411 (☎044/726060). An increasingly popular backpacker joint, less than 3 blocks from the Plaza de Armas. Clean, comfortable and well managed, and most rooms have private bath. ③.

Grand Huaraz Hotel, Jirón Larrea y Loredo 721 (☎044/722227, fax 726536). This new and comfortable hotel offers the usual mod cons – TV, private bath – plus, unusually, it includes breakfast in the price. ⑤.

Hostal Los Portales, Avenida Raimondi 903 (☎044/728184). A spacious but strangely soulless hotel, well situated for most bus terminals and with a large safe luggage store for trekkers. Rooms are clean and comfortable with private baths, and there's a restaurant. ⑤.

Hostal Raymondi, Avenida Raimondi 820 (☎044/721082). Large, clean with a spacious, old-fashioned lobby. Full of character, it has plenty of rooms with private bath. ④.

Hostal Schatzi, Jirón Simón Bolivar 419 (☎044/723074, *schatzihs@yahoo.com*). A lovely little place set around a lush garden patio; very friendly. ③.

Hotel Santa Victoria, Avenida Gamarra 690 (☎044/722422, fax 724870). Pretty good value, offering fairly modern rooms with TV and private shower (which usually have hot water); ask for a room with a view towards the Cordillera Blanca. ⑤.

Oscar's Hostal, Jirón José de la Mar 624 (☎ & fax 044/722720, *marciocoronel@hotmail.com*). Pretty central but a bit dark and uninspiring, though the rooms are very clean and many have private bath. ③.

Expensive

Casablanca Hotel, Avenida Tarapaca 138 (☎044/722602, fax 724801). Quite a comfortable and upmarket hotel in a surprisingly downmarket street; used by a lot of tour groups. ⑥.

Gran Hotel Huascarán, block 10 of Avenida Centenario (☎ & fax 044/721640, 722821 or 721709, *jezquerra@infotex.com.pe*). The biggest hotel in Huaraz with cabins and suites. It's quite plush, with carpeting, good service a games room and pleasant bedrooms. ⑦.

Hostal Brits, Jirón Mariscal Caceres 399 (☎ & fax 044/722771). A smart new place, rooms have private bath and colour TV. Other comforts include a restaurant and bar. ⑥.

Hostal El Tumi, Jirón José de San Martin 1121 (☎044/721784 or 721913, *hottumi@net. cosapidata.com.pe*). Reasonable value with clean, comfortable rooms with private bath and TV. There's also a large restaurant and a travel agent. ⑥.

Hotel Andino, Jirón Pedro Cochachín 357 (☎044/721662, fax 722830, *andino@mail.cosapidata. com.pe*). An uphill hike away from the centre of town, with beautiful views over the Cordillera Blanca and plush rooms in the best hotel in town. A variety of rooms to choose from, with or without terraces and fireplaces. The food is also excellent. ⑦–⑧.

Out of town

Centro Turistico Las Cordilleras, Yungar (☎044/614530, fax 721111, *cordilleras@rocketmail. com*). Excellent value in a beautiful setting, most rooms are cabins with fine views, or you can camp here ($2 per person). Horse-riding is offered around the Cordillera Negra, but even if you don't intend to stay here, it's worth visiting for the views from its restaurant *El Herraje*, which serves excellent local cuisine under the shade of avocado trees. ④.

Hotel Eccame, Km 18 from Huaraz towards Carhuaz (☎044/721933). A full-on Peruvian holiday resort offering stylish accommodation, a restaurant, sports facilities and horse-riding. ⑤.

Hostal Nogal, Jirón Los Libertadors 106, Monterrey (☎044/725929). Just a couple of hundred yards from the thermal baths at Monterrey, this offers very good value with hot water; rooms or slightly more expensive suites (these with TV) are available. ④–⑤.

Hostal El Patio, Avenida Monterrey, Monterrey (☎044/724965; reservations ☎01/449-6295, fax 448-0254). Located in the village of Monterrey and just a couple of hundred yards from the thermal baths. A luxurious complex of rooms and more expensive bungalows based around an attractive patio and lovely gardens. ⑥–⑧.

Hostal Las Retamas, Cascapampa 250 (☎044/721722, fax 722191). Located just before the turn-off to Wilkawain, over the bridge beyond the *Gran Hotel Huascarán*, this is a pleasant place with rooms and bungalows based around a grassy garden. It also has a games room, a nice lounge and a cafetería. Discounts for mountaineers. ⑤.

Hostal Sterling, Tarica (☎044/790299). A kilometre or so beyond Paltay, just off the road to Carhuaz, this is a rather quaint, friendly place with a rustic restaurant attached. The village of Tarica itself doesn't have much to offer, but it does have the usual views and is a quiet spot not too far out of Huaraz. ③.

Hotel Monterrey, Avenida Monterrey, Monterrey (☎044/721717). An old hotel full of character and style and attached to thermal baths to which residents have free access. The fine rooms have hot showers, and there's a splendid restaurant overlooking the heated pool. They also have bungalows, which cost a bit more. ④–⑥.

The City

Some 3060m above sea level, the **city of Huaraz** has become almost cosmopolitan, having developed rapidly in terms of tourism and commerce since the completion of the highway through the river basin from Paramonga, though there's a distinct lack of cultural emphasis within the tourist trade here. Virtually the entire city was levelled by the 1970 earthquake, and the old houses have been replaced with single-storey modern structures topped with gleaming tin roofs. Surrounded by eucalyptus groves and fields, it must have been really beautiful once, but it's a decent enough place in which to recuperate from the rigours of hard travel. There are many easy walks just outside of town, and if you fancy an afternoon's stroll you can simply go out to the eastern edge and follow one of the paths or streams uphill.

With glaciated peaks and significant trekking country close to the city, Huaraz is dominated by the prospect of mountaineering, and the city's only real tourist attraction is the **Ancash Archeological Museum**, on Avenida Luzuriaga 762, facing the modern Plaza de Armas (Mon–Sat 8.30am–6.30pm & Sun 9am–noon; $1.50). Fronting attractive, landscaped gardens, this small but interesting place contains a superb collection of Chavín, Chimu, Wari, Moche and Recauy ceramics, as well as some expertly trepanned skulls. It also displays an abundance of the finely chiselled stone monoliths typical of this mountain region, most of them products of the Recuay and Chavín cultures. One of its most curious exhibits is a *goniometro*, an early version of the surveyor's theodolite, probably over a thousand years old and used for finding alignments and exact ninety-degree angles in building construction. On the other side of the Plaza de Armas from the museum is the **Cathedral** (daily 7am–7pm; free). Completely rebuilt after being destroyed in the 1970 earthquake, it has nothing special to see inside, but its vast blue-tiled roof makes a good landmark and, if you look closely, appears to mirror one of the glaciated mountain peaks, the Nevado Huanstán (6395m), behind. Also close to the Plaza de Armas, the Banco Wiese has a **Sala Cultural** where they rotate exhibitions of photos or artwork, mainly relevant to the city or region (Mon–Fri 9am–1pm & 4.30–6.30pm; free). The only other museum to merit a brief visit is the **Museo de Miniaturas del Peru** (Mon–Fri 9am–5.30pm; $0.85), in the gardens of the *Gran Hotel Huascarán*, which contains an interesting collection of pre-Hispanic art from the Huaraz region and a range of local folk art and crafts, including the fine red Callejón de Huaylas ceramics. It also displays a small model of Yungay (see p.268) prior to the entire town being buried under a mudslide caused by the 1970 earthquake.

A fifteen-minute walk up Avenida Raimondi from the centre of Huaraz, then left over the Río Quillcay bridge a little way down the Avenida Confraternidad Internacional Oeste brings you to the regional **Trout Farm** (daily 7am–6pm; $0.20, includes guided tour), or *Estacion Pesqueria*, run by the Ministero de Pesqueria. It breeds thousands of rainbow trout every year and you can observe the process from beginning to end (more interesting than you might think) and much of the excellent trout available in the restaurants of Huaraz comes from here.

There are one or two vantage points on the hills around the city of Huaraz, but the best and most accessible is probably the **Mirador de Rataquenua**, about a two-hour walk, each way, above the town to the southeast – follow Avenida Villón out beyond the cemetery and up through the woods to the cross. This is very popular with visitors since you get splendid views across the town, over the Callejón de Huaylas – one of the most beautiful valleys in the Andes – and towards Peru's highest and most breathtaking snowcapped peak, Huascarán. Most taxi drivers will take you there and back for less than $8.

Hiking in the Huaraz region

In 1932 a German expedition became the first succesful venture to scale Huascarán and the concept of *Andinismo* – Andean mountaineering – was born. However, you don't have to be a mountaineer to enjoy the high Andes of Ancash, and there is plenty of scope for trekking as well in the two major mountain chains accessible from Huaraz. The closest is the **Cordillera Blanca**, detailed on p.270. The **Cordillerra Huayhuash**, about 50km south of the Cordilerra Blanca is still relatively off the beaten tourist trail. About 31km long it is dominated by the Yerupajá glacier, and *Andinistas* claim it to be one of the most spectacular trekking routes in the world. Wherever you end up, be sure to pay heed to the rules of **responsible trekking**: carry away your waste, particularly above the snow line, where even organic waste does not decompose (if you can pack it in the first place, you can pack it back up). Note too that you should always use a camping stove – campfires are strictly prohibited in Huascarán National Park, and wood is scarce anyway.

If you intend to hike at all, it's essential to spend at least a couple of days **acclimatizing** to the altitude beforehand. Although Huaraz itself is 3060m above sea level, most of the Cordilleras' more impressive peaks are over 6000m. If you're going to trek in Huascarán National Park, register beforehand with the **Park Office**, at the top end of Avenida Raymondi (☎044/722086), and at the **Casa de Guias**, Parque Ginebra 28-G (Mon–Fri 9am–1pm & 4–8pm, Sat 9am–1pm; ☎044/721811, fax 722306, *agmp@ net.telematic.com.pe*, *clientes.telematic.com.pe/agmp*), where there's also a good contact noticeboard, worth checking to see if there are any groups about to leave on treks that you might want to join. Ideally you should have detailed maps and one or other of the excellent **guidebooks**, *Backpacking and Trekking in Peru and Bolivia*, *Trails of the Cordillera Blanca and Huayhuash*, or *The High Andes: a guide for climbers* (all detailed on p.475). These aren't always available in Huaraz, though you should be able to get them at the South American Explorers' Club in Lima (see p.21). **Maps**, too, are available there, or from the Casa de Guias, where there's also a list of official local mountain guides, as well as lots of local expertise and the Andean Mountain Rescue Corp on hand. Both the Casa de Guias and the park office can give you up-to-the-minute advice on the best and safest areas for trekking, since this region is not without its political danger zones. For additional information on trekking in the region, try the tourist information office (see p.252), one of the tour and travel companies listed on p.262, or the guides listed opposite. Peruvian **mountaineering associations** are all based in Lima, including the Club de Montañismo Américo Tordoya, which is based in Lima at Tarapacá 384 (☎01/460-6101 or 431-1305); the Club de Andinismo de la Univeridad de Lima, Avenidajavier Prado Este, Lima 33 (☎01/437-6767, extension 30775); and the Club Andino Peruano, Avenida Dos de Mayo 1545, Oficina 216, Lima 27.

There are three levels of **guides** available: certified mountain guides, who cost from $60 a day; mountain guides undergoing the one year trial period after training, from $40 a day; and trekking guides, who cost from $30 a day. Note that these costs don't include transport or accommodation. Recommended guides include Alberto Cafferata, a trekking guide contactable through Pony Expeditions (see p.262); David Gonzales Castromonte, Pasaje Coral Vega 354, Huarupampa, Huaraz (☎044/722213); Oscar Ciccomi who is based in Lima and is contactable through Viajes Vivencial, Los Cerezos 480, Chaclacayo, Lima (☎ & fax 01/497-2394); or Eduardo Figueroa, at *Edward's Inn* (see p.253). All speak English and Spanish. For local **tour operators** offering guided treks, see the box on p.262).

Porters cost between $15 and $20 a day, depending on whether they are leaders or assistants, and are not supposed to climb over 6000m, while **mule drivers** (*arrieros*) charge from $5 to $8 a day, plus around $4 a day per animal. Expedition **cooks** usually charge the same as *arrieros*. **Llama-packing**, whereby llamas carry the baggage, is a new initiative designed to promote eco-tourism in the region; contact Jorge Martel Alva, calle Agustin Loli 43, Plazuela de la Soledad, Huaraz (☎ & fax 044/721266) or ask for details in the Casa de Guías, Parque Ginebra, Huaraz (☎044/721811).

Eating, drinking and entertainment

There's no shortage of **restaurants** in Huaraz, though they do vary considerably in value and quality. There's also a lively nightlife scene, with several **peñas** hosting traditional Andean music, as well as a few **clubs** where locals and tourists can relax, keep warm and unwind during the evenings or at weekends. Nightlife joints start to open from 7pm and can go on til 3am. There's a **cinema** next to Banco de Wiese, on Jirón José de Sucre.

Restaurants

Café de Paris, Jirón San Martin 687. Open 24hr for breakfast, snacks, kebabs and French pastries.

Chifa Jim Hua, Avenida Luzuriaga 643. A good-value, small restaurant offering a broad selection of Chinese and Peruvian meals in a friendly environment.

FIESTAS IN HUARAZ

Throughout the year various **fiestas** take place in the city and its surrounding villages and hamlets. They are always bright, energetic occasions, with *chicha* (beer) and *aguardiente* flowing freely, as well as roast pigs, bullfights, and vigorous communal dancing with the town folk dressed in outrageous masks and costumes. The main festival in Huaraz city is usually in the first week of **February** and celebrates Carnival. In **June** (check with the tourist office for exact dates each year), Huaraz hosts the Semana del Andinismo, the Andean Mountaineering and Skiing Week, which includes trekking, climbing and national and international ski competitions, on the Pastoruri Glacier. However, unless this is precisely your cup of tea, the city is probably best avoided during this period, since prices of hotels and restaurants increase considerably. Other festivals include the folklore celebrations in the first week of **August** for Coyllur-Huaraz, plus the Virgin de la Asunción, in Huata and Chancas during mid-August. Late **September** sees the festival of the Virgen de Las Mercedes, celebrated in Carhuaz, and other rural get-togethers that you'll often come across en route to sites and ruins in the Callejón de Huaylas.

Chifa Yat Sen, on the corner of Avenida Raimondi and Comercio. A pleasant little Chinese restaurant, offering amazing value ($1.50) 3-course set lunches with a Peruvian twist; it also has a range of standard Chinese dishes available most evenings from around 6pm.

Crêperie Patrick, Avenida Luzuriaga 422. Centrally located close to the corner with Avenida Raimondi, serving excellent crêpes at bearable prices.

La Estacion, Avenida Luzuriaga 1045 (☎044/723190). A grill restaurant with a video-bar that's fun at weekends.

Monttrek Pizza-pub, Luzuriaga 646. A very popular place with trekkers and a great meeting place with a good notice board for contacting like-minded backpackers.

Pepe's Palace, Avenida Raimondi 622. Dishes up decent international food, including pizzas, and is a good place to meet fellow trekkers, though it's only open June–Sept.

Pizza BB, José de La Mar 674. Cheap take-away or stand-up pizzas at this hole in the wall.

Pizzeria Alpes Andes, Parque Ginebra 28-G. A pleasant, modern restaurant in the same building as *Huaraz Youth Hostel*. It serves excellent pizzas, spaghetti and vegetarian dishes at reasonable prices, and is a good place to meet trekkers and mountaineers.

Pizzeria Chez Pepe, Avenida Luzuriaga 570. Run by the same Pepe of *Pepe's Palace*; again, the food is good, but more importantly this is the place to make contact with other trekkers and local trek leaders. Pepe will also change dollars cash.

Pizzeria Monteros, Jirón Jose de La Mar 661. An upmarket pizzeria with good beer and excellent meat dishes.

Las Puyas, Jirón Morales 535. An old-fashioned restaurant popular with visitors and locals, serving cheap breakfasts, snacks and lunches of all kinds.

Restaurant Alpes Andes, Parque Ginebra 28 (☎044/721811). Commonly thought of as the Casa de Guias restaurant because of its location in the same building, this dishes up superb pizzas and pastas for very good prices, and great mulled wine.

Restaurant Bistro de Los Andes, Jirón Julián de Morales 823 (☎044/726249). A great place for breakfast or lunch with seats outside, and popular during the evening. It also has a book exchange.

Restaurante Campo Base, Avenida Luzuriaga 407. A relatively expensive restaurant that aims at the trekking and climbing crowd. Excellent food and a good range of drinks, often hosting live folk music at weekends. It's the best place in the city for *cuy à la Huaracina* (guinea pig, Huaraz style).

Restaurant Landauro, Jirón José de Sucre 109. Well worth visiting for its cheap pizzas, though gets very busy on weekend evenings.

Restaurant Monte Rosa, Avenida Luzuriaga 496. Excellent pizzas and one or two other Italian dishes, plus a wide range of snacks and cold drinks; popular with travellers but not that cheap.

Restaurant Tabariz, corner of *avenidas* Raimondi and Fitzcarral. A solidly local eating house, it has a wide range of snacks, soups and meals at reasonable prices in a hectic environment, with old-fashioned décor. Good set menus.

Restaurant Vegeteriano Nuevo Horizonte, Jirón Sucre 476. An inexpensive café that serves mainly but not exclusively vegetarian meals and snacks. Specialities include muesli and yoghurt breakfasts, pizzas and vitamin-enhanced specials.

Tequila, Mz. Unica Lote 28, Parque Ginebra. A funky eating and drinking spot, right next to the Casa de Guias; serves excellent Mexican food and margaritas.

Vegetarian Café, Avenida Luzuriaga 502. A small place serving good simple vegetarian fare and selling a range of vitamins, wholefoods and health products.

Pubs, music bars and clubs

Amadeus Taberna, Parque Ginebra. Situated at the back of the Interbanc, in an alley between the Plaza de Armasand Parque Ginebra, this is Huaraz's most established nightclub. It serves meals and plays popular dance music, as well as hosting Andean folk groups. Entry $1.

Paccha'K Pub, Centenario 290. A good trekkers' joint with a noticeboard for messages that hosts lively Andean folk music shows most weekends.

Peña Disco El Sol, Avenida Luzuriaga. The liveliest disco in the city, particularly during October and November, when high school kids visit the region en masse. Entry $1.

Peña Restaurant El Otro Sitio, 28 de Julio 570. More of a restaurant than a nightclub, though there's good live folk and *criolla* music at weekends.

Peña Tio Tiburcio, 28 de Julio 560. Just one block up from the Plaza de Armas, this popular spot with locals and travellers hosts Andean folk and pop most weekends.

El Refugio, Jirón Teofilo Castillo 556. A video-pub with a pretty good range of Latin and European sounds and a three-hour happy "hour".

El Rinconcito, Julian de Morales 757. A video-pub with quite a few movies, good food and snacks.

Shamy Disco, Avenida Gamara 678. A popular disco and video bar, playing mostly international and Latin pop. Entry $1.

Tambo Taverna, Jirón José de la Mar 776. A restaurant-cum-*peña* serving good drinks, with occasional live music after 10pm – one of Huaraz's best nightspots.

La Tasca Taberna, Simon Bolivar 653. A small, friendly video bar with some decent Latin music and international pop and rock.

Shopping

Huaraz is a noted **crafts** centre, producing, in particular, very reasonably priced handmade leather goods (custom made if you've got a few days to wait around). Other bargains include woollen hats, scarves and jumpers, embroidered blankets, and interesting replicas of the Chavín stone carvings. Most of these items can be bought from the stalls in the small **artesania market** in covered walkways set back off Avenida Luzuriaga (daily 2pm–dusk), or, for more choice, in the Mercado Model. For individual shops, try Tierras Andinas, Parque Ginebra, which has some fine handicrafts and local artwork, or the Centro Artesanal, next to the Post Office on the plaza, which sells textiles, ceramics, jewellery, stone and leather work.

Huaraz is also renowned for its **food**, in particular its excellent local cheese, honey and *manjar blanco* (a traditional sweet made out of condensed milk). These can all be bought in the **food market**, in the backstreets around Avenida José de San Martin (daily 6am–6pm). Market Ortiz, Avenida Luzuriaga 401, is one of the best **supermarkets** in town, while Centro Naturista, Fitzcarrald 356, is good for natural medicines, yoghurt, herbs and cosmetics.

Photographic equipment can be bought from Shala, Firzcarrald 369; Photo Blas, Avenida Luzuriaga 547; Video River, Avenida Luzuriaga 641; Kodak Shop, Avenida Luzuriaga 625; and Foto Shop, Avenida Luzuriaga 419, which also does one-hour developing. **Camping equipment** is available to rent from most of the adventure-tour companies (see overleaf) plus Mount Climb, Jirón Mariscal Caceres 421, which also sells trekking foods, has a contact noticeboard and stocks a range of tents, boots, sleeping bags, crampons, ice axes and other essentials for rent. Galaxia Expeditions, Leonisa y Lescanao 603, also has mountaineering equipment for sale and rental. Other places to try include Pizzeria Monteros, Jirón Jose de La Mar 661; Lobo Adventure, Avenida Luzuriaga 557; Andean Sports Tours, Avenida Luzuriaga 571; and Edward's Inn, Avenida Bolognesi 121.

Listings

Banks and exchange All banks open Mon–Fri 9am–6pm. Try Banco Wiese, Jirón José de Sucre 766; Interbanc, on Plaza de Armas; Banco de Credito, Avenida Luzuriaga 691; and Banco de la Nacion, Avenida Luzuriaga. *Cambistas* gather where Morales and Luzuriaga meet, or try the *casa de cambio* at Luzuriaga 614, and Oh Na Nay, on the Plaza de Armas, for good rates on dollars.

Buses For local colectivos and buses to Anta, Marcara, Carhuaz, Yungay and Caraz, see "City transport", p.252. Other companies include: Chavín Express, Jirón Mariscal Caceres 338 (☎044/724652), for Sihuas, Chavín, Huari and other destinations; Colectivos Comité 14, Avenida Fitzcarral 216

TOURS AND ACTIVITIES IN AND AROUND HUARAZ

Most of the tour agencies in Huaraz are located along Avenida Luzuriaga and offer guided **city tours**, including stopping at all the major panoramic viewpoints (4hr, $8). For the surrounding area the most popular outings are to the **Llanganuco Lakes** (8hr, $10–15 per person), **Chavín de Huantar** (9–11hr, $10–15 per person), including lunch in Chavín before exploring ruins, and to the edge of the **Pastoruri Glacier** at 5240m (8hr, $10 per person), where you can walk on the ice and explore naturally formed ice caverns beneath the glacier's surface. This last tour, which usually includes a visit to see the *Puya Raymondi* plants (see p.266), is rather commercialized and there is often a lot of rubbish lying around the most commonly visited parts of the glacier; it's also worth remembering that Pastoruri is very high and can be bitterly cold, so make sure you're well acclimatized to the altitude, and take warm clothing with you. Most agents also can arrange trips to the thermal baths at **Chancos** (4hr, $8) and **Caraz** (6hr, $10), and some offer **adventure activities** in the area. Always check if the guide leading your tour speaks English.

Baloo Tours, Avenida Julian de Morales 605, Huaraz (☎044/727830, fax 725994, *nilocamp@hotmail.com*). Expeditions throughout the Cordillera Blanca and Huayhuash, with mountaineering equipment for rent, including tents.

Chavín Tours, Avenida Luzuriaga 502, Huaraz (☎044/721578, fax 724801, *Chavín@telematic.edu.pe*). Runs most of the standard tours, including around the city, Wilcahuain and Monterrey, plus day-trips to Llanganuco, Pastorurri/Puya Raimondi, and to Chavín de Huantar. Can also organize canoeing and rafting on the Río Santa.

J.M. Expeditions, Avenida Luzuriaga 465, Oficina 4, Huaraz (☎ & fax 044/728017, *mmazuelos@hotmail.com*); main shopfront and store in the Centro Comercial, Manzana Unica, Lote 35, between the Casa de Guias and Luzuriaga. Lot's of mountaineering equipment to rent and some professional high mountain guides on call.

Monttrek, Avenida Luzuriaga 646, Huaraz (☎044/721124). Climbing, guides, treks, horse-riding, river rafting and snow-boarding in the region, and stocks new and used camping and climbing equipment. The office is a great place to meet other trekkers.

Mountain Bike Adventures, Castilla Postal 111, Jiron Lucre y Torre 530, Huaraz (☎044/724259, *julio.olaza@terra.com.pe*). Customizable guided bike tours with mountain bikes to rent. They also have English speaking guides and offer a book exchange in their office. For cyclists with particular interests they offer a variety of alternative routes.

Pablo Tours, Avenida Luzuriaga 501, Huaraz (☎ & fax 044/721145, *pablot@net. telematic.com.pe*). One of the best agencies for standard tours and good for organized treks, though they get booked up very quickly.

Peru Trek Expeditions, Avenida Luzuriaga 502, Huaraz (☎044/721578 or 722602). Adventure trips, such as rafting on the Río Santa, as well as reasonably priced tours to Llanganuco, Pastoruri, Chavín and around the city.

Pony Expeditions, Sucre 1266, Caraz (☎ fax 044/791642, *ponyexp@terra.com.pe*). A very professional organization that outfits and guides expeditions in the area. They also run treks in other regions, such as the Cordillera Huayhuash, the Inca Trail and Ausungate.

Wilcahuain Tours, Avenida Luzuriaga 534, Oficina 202, Huaraz (☎044/723186). Offers most of the standard tours, plus one that finishes with a visit to the Fountain of Youth thermal baths and natural cave saunas at Chancos.

(☎044/721202 or 721739), for Lima and Trujillo; Cruz del Sur, Jirón Lucar y Torré 585 (☎044/722491), for Lima and Trujillo; El Aguila, Raymondi 901 (☎044/726666) for Trujillo and Lima; Empresa Sandoval, Tarapaca 582 (☎044/726930), for Catac, Chavín, Pomacha, Huari; Empresa Condor de Chavín, Jirón Tarapaca 312 (☎044/722039), for Chavín and Lima; Empresa Huandoy, Avenida Fitzcarral 261 (☎044/722502); Empresa Huascaran, Jirón Tarapaca 133 (☎044/722208), for Chavín; Empresa Rapido, Jirón Huascaran 117 for Chiquián; Empresa Rosario, Jirón Caraz 605, for Pomabamba, La Union and

Huánuco; Expresso Ancash/Ormeño, Avenida Raimondi 527 (☎044/721102, 724915), for Lima and Caraz; Movil Tours, Avenida Raimondi 730 (☎044/722555), for Lima, Chimbote and Trujillo; Rodriguez Tarapaca 629 (☎044/722631 or 721353), for Lima; Turismo Atusparia, Tarapaca 574 (☎044/726745), for Lima; Turismo Chimbote, Avenida Raimondi 815 (☎044/721984), for Chimbote and Lima; Turismo Huaraz, Jirón Caraz 605, for Caraz, Piscobamba, Pomabamba and Chimbote; and Yungay Express, Avenida Fitzcarrald 261 (☎044/727507), for Cimbote and Pativilca.

Doctors and dentists Dr Simon Komori, Jirón 28 de Julio 602 (☎044/613100; 24hr); or try the surgery at Avenida Luzuriaga 618 (Mon–Fri 9am–5pm).

Hospital Avenida Luzuriaga (☎044/721861).

Internet facilities Cabinas Publicas Internet, Parque Ginebr; Andes on Line, Jirón Morales 759, upstairs; and the basic public cabins at Avenida Centenario 577.

Laundry Lavanderia BB, Jiron la Mar 674, is the best; otherwise, try Lavandería Huaraz, on Avenida Fitzcarral, close to the bridge; and Lavandería El Amigo, on the corner of Jirón Bolivar and Jirón José de Sucre.

Police The Tourist Police are at Jirón Larrea y Loredo 716 (☎044/721341, extension 315).

Post office Plaza de Armas, on the corner of Jirón José de Sucre and Avenida Luzuriaga. Mon–Sat 8am–8pm & Sun 9am–1pm.

Telephones Cabinas de Teléfono, Jirón José de Sucre 409. Daily 6am–11pm.

Tourist Protection Service ☎044/613542.

Western Union Avenida Luzuriaga 556 (☎044/726410).

Around Huaraz

There are a number of sites within easy reach of Huaraz. Only 7km north are the natural thermal baths of **Monterrey**; a similar distance, but higher into the hills, is the dramatic **Wilkawain temple**, its inner labyrinths open for exploration. On the other side of the valley, just half an hour by bus, **Punta Callan** is an ideal spot for magnificent views over the Cordillera Blanca, while to the south of the city you can see the intriguing cactus-like *Puya Raymondi* in the **Huascarán National Park**.

Monterrey

Just fifteen minutes by colectivo from the centre of Huaraz (every 10min or so from the corner of avenidas Fitzcarral and Raimondi; 40c), the vast **thermal baths of Monterrey** (daily 7am–6pm; $1) include two natural hot spring swimming pools and a number of individual and family bathing rooms. Luxuriating in these slightly sulphurous hot springs can be the ideal way to recover from an arduous mountain trekking expedition, but make sure you are fully acclimatized, otherwise the effect on your blood pressure can worsen any altitude sickness. The complex attracts locals as well as visitors to the area, and if you're staying at the wonderful old *Hotel Monterrey* (p.257) the baths are free. There's also an impressive **waterfall** just ten minutes' walk behind the hotel and baths. As far as eating goes, the best **restaurant** is *El Monte Rey*, opposite Artesania Johao, the ceramic workshop on the main access lane to the baths, which serves great local food at excellent prices. A close second is the *Hotel Monterrey* itself, which serves very reasonable dishes in some style in their elegant, old-fashioned restaurant.

The Temple at Wilkawain

Wilkawain, 8km from Huaraz, can be reached from the centre of the city by following Avenida Centenario downhill from Avenida Fitzcarral, then turning right up a track (just about suitable for cars) a few hundred metres beyond the *Gran Hotel Huascarán*. From here, it's about an hour's stroll, winding slowly up past several small hamlets, to

the signposted ruins. If there are four or five of you, a taxi there and back shouldn't come to more than about $3 each.

The **temple** is an unusual two-storey construction, with a few small houses around it, set against the edge of a great bluff. With a torch you can check out some of its inner chambers, where you'll see ramps, ventilation shafts, and the stone nails that hold it all together. Most of the rooms, however, are still inaccessible, filled with the rubble and debris of at least a thousand years. The temple base is only about 11m by 16m, sloping up to large slanted roof slabs, long since covered with earth and rocks to form an irregular domed top. The construction is a small replica of the Castillo at Chavín de Huantar (see p.275), with four superimposed platforms and stairways, and a projecting course of stones near the apex, with a recessed one below it. There was once a row of cats' heads beneath this, which is a typical design of the Huari-Tiahuanucu culture that spread up here from the coast some time between 600 and 1000 AD.

Punta Callan

Some 24kms kilometres west of Huaraz, **Punta Callan** is reached in about two hours on the Casma bus from Avenida Raymondi 336. Ask the driver to drop you off at Callan,

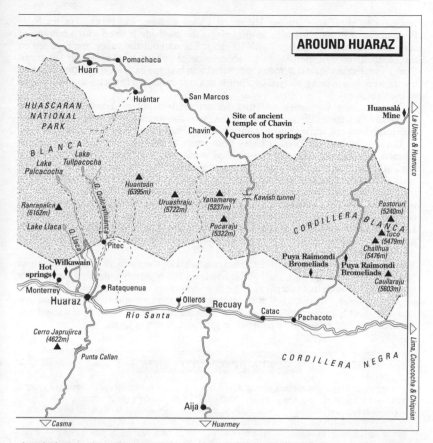

shortly before the village of Pira along the road to Casma; from here it's a twenty-minute walk up the path to the promontory. No other spot can quite match the scintillating views of the Cordillera Blanca, so save it for a really clear afternoon when you can see Huascarán's towering ice-cap at its best. Callan and Pira are surrounded by grazing land as pleasant as you could find for a picnic, and it's a relatively easy walk of a few hours back down the road to Huaraz. Passing trucks or buses will usually pick up anyone who waves them down en route. Go early in the day, to make sure you can get a bus on or back.

North to Caraz and the Cordillera Blanca

No one should come to the **Callejón de Huaylas** without visiting the northern valley towns, and many travellers will want to use them as bases from which to explore one or more of the ten snow-free passes in the Cordillera Blanca. Simply combining any two of these passes makes for a superb week's trekking. Travelling north along the valley from Huaraz you'll immediately notice the huge number of **avocado** trees, particularly when they are in fruit during the rainy season (Nov–Feb). One of the first villages you pass through after leaving Huaraz is called **Paltay**, which, unsurprisingly, is Peruvian for avocado. Just outside the village, the roadside is lined with a number of ceramics workshops, which sell good pottery. Throughout the valley, you'll notice on the pantiled roofs of the houses an abundance of ornate crosses, which represent Christ's protection against demons, witchcraft and bad spirits, a local tradition that also involves the house being blessed by a priest at a communal party during the final stages of construction.

Further along the valley are the distinct settlements of **Yungay** and **Caraz**. Physically they have little in common – Yungay is the tragic site of several catastrophic natural disasters, while Caraz has survived the centuries as one of Peru's prettiest little towns – but both are popular bases from which to begin treks into the **Cordillera Blanca**. The highest range in the tropical world, the Cordillera Blanca consists of around 35 peaks poking their snowy heads over the six-thousand-metre mark, and until early this century, when the glaciers began to recede, this white crest could be seen from the Pacific. Of the many mountain lakes in the range, **Lake Parón**, above Caraz, is renowned as the most beautiful. Above Yungay, and against the sensational backdrop of Peru's highest peak, **Huascarán** (6768m), are the equally magnificent **Llanganuco Lakes**, whose waters change colour according to the time of year and the sun's daily movements, and are among the most accessible of the Cordillera Blanca's three hundred or so glacial lakes.

Fortunately, most of the Cordillera Blanca falls under the auspices of the **Huascarán National Park**, and as such the habitat has been left relatively unspoiled. Among the more exotic **wildlife** that hikers can hope to come across are the *viscacha* (Andean rabbit-like creatures), *vicuña*, grey deer, pumas, foxes, the rare spectacled bear, and several species of hummingbirds. All of these animals are shy, so you'll need a good pair of binoculars and a fountain of patience to get close to any of them.

THE PUYA RAYMONDI

The gigantic **Puya Raymondi** plants, up to 12m high and with a lifespan of around forty years, are found in the **Huascarán National Park**. Most people assume the *Puya Raymondi* is a type of cactus, but it is, in fact, the world's largest bromeliad, or member of the pineapple family. Known as *cuncush* or *cunco* to locals (and *Pourretia gigantea* to botanists), it only grows between altitudes of 3700m and 4200m, and is unique to this region; May is the best month to see them, when they are in full bloom and average eight thousand flowers and six million seeds per plant. Dotted about the Quebrada Pachacoto slopes like candles on an altar, the plants look rather like upside-down trees, with the bushy part as a base and a phallic flowering stem pointing to the sky. Outside of late April, May, and early June, the plants can prove disappointing, often becoming burned-out stumps after dropping their flowers and seeds, but the surrounding scenery remains sensational, boasting grasses, rocks, lakes, llamas and the odd hummingbird.

By far the easiest way to see the *Puya Raymondi* is on an **organized tour** with one of the companies listed on p.262; most of the Pastoruri Glacier tours include a stop here. Alternatively, you could take a **combi colectivo** to Catac, leaving daily every thirty minutes from the end of Jirón Caceres in Huaraz ($0.8). From Catac, 45km south of Huaraz, there are a few buses and trucks each day down the La Unión road, which passes right by the plants. Alternatively, get off the combi colectivo 5km beyond Catac at Pachacoto (where there are a couple of cafés often used as pit-stops by truck drivers) and hitch from here along the dirt track which leads off the main road across barren grasslands. This track is well travelled by trucks on their way to the mining settlement of Huansala, and after about 15–20km – roughly an hour's drive – into this isolated region, you'll be surrounded by the giant bromeliads. From here, you can either continue on to La Unión (see p.279), via the Pastoruri Glacier, or return to Huaraz by hitching back to the main road.

The number of possible **hikes** into the Cordillera depends more than anything on your own initiative and resourcefulness. **Maps** of the area, published by the Instituto Geográfico Militar, are good enough to allow you to plot your own routes, or you can follow one of the standard paths outlined in books such as *Backpacking and Trekking in Peru and Bolivia* by Hilary Bradt or *Trails of the Cordillera Blanca and Huayhuash of Peru* by Jim Bartle (see p.475 for details). The most popular hike is the **Llanganuco to Santa Cruz Loop** (outlined on p.270), which begins at Yungay and ends at Caraz.

Chancos

Known traditionally as the Fountain of Youth, the **thermal baths of Chancos**, 30km north of Huaraz, consist of a series of natural saunas inside caves, with great pools gushing hot water in a beautiful stream, and the Nevado Copa glacier looming 3000m above (daily 8am–6pm; $0.5–1 depending on treatment). It is claimed that the thermal waters are excellent for respiratory problems, but you don't have to be ill to enjoy them, and they make an ideal end to a day's strenuous trekking.

To get there take any of the frequent **buses** or **colectivos** along the valley towards Yungay or Caraz, from the first block of Avenida Fitzcarral or the market area in Huaraz. Get off at **Marcara** (an attractive little village whose name, aptly, means maizecorn village) and follow the rough road uphill for about 4km, passing several small peasant settlements en route, until you reach the baths. There's no accommodation in Chancos, but the valley bus service is good enough to get you back to Huaraz within an hour or so, or you could **camp**. There are a couple of basic **restaurants** on hand which are famous for their strong *chicha*, and are particularly popular with locals on Sunday afternooons.

From Chancos a small track leads off to the hamlet of **Ullmey**, following the contours of the Legiamayo stream to the upper limit of cultivation and beyond into the barren zone directly below the glaciers. Keeping about 500m to the right of the stream, it takes ninety minutes to two hours to reach **Laguna Legia Cocha**, at 4706m above sea level. Hung between two vast glaciers and fed by their icy melted water, the lake is an exhilarating spot, with the added bonus of amazing views across the Santa Valley – to Carhuaz in the north, Huaraz in the south, and Chancos directly below. If you leave Huaraz early in the morning, you can do a fine day-trip, stopping here for lunch, then heading down to Chancos for a stimulating bath before catching the bus back into town from Marcara.

Carhuaz and Mancos

One of the major towns along the valley, **CARHUAZ**, some 30km from both Huaraz and Yungay, has an attractive central Plaza de Armas, adorned with palm trees, roses and labyrinths of low cut hedges and dominated by the solid concrete **Church of San Pedro** on its south side. On Sundays the streets to the north and west of the plaza are home to a thriving traditional **market**, where Andean and tropical foodstuffs, herbs and crafts, in particular gourd bowls, can be bought very cheaply. The colourfully dressed women here often sell live guinea pigs from small nets at their feet, and wear a variety of wide-brimmed hats – ones with blue bands indicate that they are married, ones with red bands show that they are single. Many also wear glass beads, on their hats or around their necks, as a sign of wealth.

Combi **colectivos** to Huaraz ($0.5), Chancos ($0.3) and Caraz ($0.4) leave from one block beyond the market side of the plaza, while the **buses** to Lima, Huaraz and Caraz leave from a terminal on block 2 of Avenida La Merced, which is a continuation of the road from the market side of the plaza to the main highway. In the unlikely event that you'll need them, **the local police** can be called at ☎044/794197.

There are a few basic **hostals** in Carhuaz: the *Hostal La Merced*, Jirón Ucayali 600 (☎044/794241; ③) has comfortable rooms with or without private bath; the *Hostal Residencial Huaraz*, Avenida Progreso 586 (☎044/794139; ②) is relatively comfortable and attractive, with hot water and clothes washing facilities at good value, and the *Hostal Las Delicias*, Avenida progreso 117 (☎044/794132; ②), closer to the main road towards Caraz and a couple of blocks from the Plaza de Armas, is slightly cheaper but not as nice. On the east side of the plaza, *Restaurant Heladería Huascarán*, Avenida Progresso 757, has good local **food**, including trout and ice cream; and the *Café Heladería El Abuelo* also serves ice creams, snacks and meals (ask for the local delicacy of beanshoots); the *Restaurant y Peña La Punta Olimpica*, Avenida La Merced 500 specializes in fish dishes and *comida criolla*, is good and cheap with music at weekends.

In the 1980s a **cave** was discovered a few kilometres north of Carhuaz, on the other side of the Río Santa in the Cordillera Negra. It can be accessed in just over an hour's walk, beyond the sports stadium and up the stream past the unusual church, which sits beside the road from Carhauz to Yungay. The cave contained bones of mastodons and llamas and suggested human occupation dating from as far back as 12000 BC. Situated close to a natural rock formation which looks vaguely like a guitar, the site is now known as the cave of Hombre Guitarrera (Guitar Man).

A little further on from Carhuaz, a small river bridge brings the road to the village of **MANCOS,** where there's an unusually attractive plaza, with palm trees and a quaint but modern church with twin belfreys sitting under the glistening glacier of Huascaran. On the square there's **accommodation** at the *Casa Alojamiento* (②), which offers clean, comfortable rooms and shared bathrooms, and there are several restaurants around and about. The village's main **fiesta**, August 12–16, is in honour of its patron, San Royal de Mancos., and the plaza becomes the focus of highly colourful religious processions and dancing and, later, bull-fighting.

Yungay

YUNGAY, a mere 58km along the valley from Huaraz, was an attractive, traditional small town until it was obliterated in seconds at 3.23pm on May 31, 1970, during the major **earthquake**, which registered 7.7 on the Richter Scale. Long before its final destruction the "Pearl of the Huaylas Corridor" had shown itself to be unwisely situated: in 1872 it was almost completely wiped out by an avalanche, and on a *fiesta* day in 1962 another avalanche buried some five thousand people in the neighbouring village of Ranrahirca. The 1970 quake also arrived in the midst of a festival, and although casualties proved impossible to calculate with any real accuracy, it's thought that over seventy thousand people died. Almost the entire population of Yungay, around 26,000, disappeared virtually instantaneously, though a few of the town's children survived because they were at a circus located just above the town, which fortuitously escaped the landslide. Almost eighty percent of the buildings in neighbouring Huaraz and much of Carhuaz were also razed to the ground by the earthquake.

The **new town** has none of the beauty of the original, an uninviting conglomeration of modern buildings – including some ninety prefabricated cabins sent as relief aid from the former Soviet Union – has been built around a concrete Plaza de Armas. It still cowers beneath the peak of Huascarán, but hopefully is more sheltered than its predecessor from further dangers. On the way into town from Carhuaz, a car park and memorial monument mark the entrance to the site of the buried **old town** of Yungay (daily 8am–6pm; $0.50), which has developed into one of the region's major tourist attractions. The site, entered through a large, blue concrete archway, is covered with a grey flow of mud and moraine, now dry and solid, with a few stunted palm trees to mark where the old Plaza de Armas once stood. Thousands of rose bushes have been planted over the site – a gift from the Japanese government. Local guidebooks show before and after photos of the scene, but it doesn't take a lot of imagination to reconstruct the horror. You can still see a few things like an upside-down, partially destroyed school bus, stuck in the mud. The **graveyard** above the site, which predates the 1970 quake, is known as Campo Santo and gives the best vantage point over the devastation. A tall statue of Christ holds out its arms from here towards the deadly peak of Huascarán itself, as if pleading for no further horrors.

The best reason for staying here is to make the trip up to the Llanganuco Lakes and Huascarán (trucks leave most mornings from the Plaza de Armas) or simply as a base for exploring from the heart of the Callejon de Huaylas. Despite its looks, modern Yungay is a reasonable place to stay, and there are a number of acceptable **hostals**: The best value and thus the most popular is the *Hostal Gledel* on Avenida Aries Graziani (☎044/793048; ②), at the northern end of town; it has small rooms and shared toilet facilities but it is spotlessly clean and is a very pleasant environment, with a dining room where excellent food is served. Nearby there's the *Alojamiento La Suiza Peruana*, Avenida Aries Graziani, Lote 7 (☎044/793003; ②) which has shared bathrooms and a bar with games set around a patio. For those on a tight budget, try the very basic *Hostal Sol de Oro* (①), or you can **camp** in a eucalyptus wood at *Hostal Blanco*, next to the hospital, which also has doubles (③). The *Hostal Yungay*, on the Plaza de Armas (②), gives out free **maps** and information on the area. Also on the plaza is a reasonable **café**, the *Comedor Yungay*, which offers good, cheap set-lunch menus; and the Banco de La Nacion (Mon–Fri 8.30am–1.30pm & 2.15–4pm) for **money change**.

Llanganuco Lakes

The **Llanganuco Lakes**, at 3850m above sea level, are only 26km from Yungay (83km from Huaraz), but take a good ninety minutes to reach by bus or truck, on a road that crawls up beside a canyon that is the result of thousands of years of Huascarán's meltwater. On the way you get a dramatic view across the valley and can clearly make out the path of the 1970 devastation. The last part of the drive – starkly beautiful but no fun for vertigo sufferers – slices through rocky crevices, and snakes around breathtaking precipices surrounded by small, windbent *quenual* trees and orchid bromeliads known locally as *weclla*. Well before reaching the lakes you pass through the entrance to the **Huascarán National Park** (daily 6am–6pm; $2 or $20 for hikers and mountaineers), located over 600m below the level of the lake; from here it's another 30 minutes or so by bus or truck to the lakes.

The first lake you come to after the park entrance, is **Chinan Cocha**, named after a legendary princess. You can rent rowing boats here to venture onto the blue waters ($0.8 for 15min), and buy a picnic from the foodstalls, at the end of the lake. The road continues around Chinan Cocha's left bank and for a couple of kilometres on to the

---

THE LEGEND OF ICHIC OLLCO

According to local legend, a goblin called **Ichic Ollco** once lived around the Llanganuco Lakes, a little man with pointed ears, a grotesque face, small legs, massive arms and a penchant for stealing small children and pretty young women. One day, a child went up on a mountain near Llanganuco and met Ichic Ollco, who played with him, but when the child wanted to go home the goblin persuaded him to stay another hour – then another, and then another. After several hours, Ichic Ollco gave the child permission to go home on the condition that he returned again one day. When the child arrived home, a stranger answered the door and told him that his parents had died many years before. In tears, the young boy started back up the mountain; as he went up he got older and older with every step, eventually turning into a pile of dust as he reached the Llanganuco Lakes.

second lake, **Orcon Cocha**, named after a prince who fell in love with Chinan. The road ends here and a **loop trail** begins (see below). A third, much smaller, lake was created between the two big ones, as a result of an avalanche caused by the 1970 earthquake, which also killed a group of hikers who were camped between the two lakes.

Immediately to the south of the lakes is the unmistakable sight of the massive **Huascarán ice cap**, whose imposing peak tempts many people to make the difficult three-thousand-metre climb to the top. Surrounding Huascarán are scores of lesser glaciated mountains stretching for almost 200km and dividing the Amazon Basin from the Pacific watershed.

Hiking in the Cordillera Blanca

There are a multitude of excellent hikes in the Cordillera Blanca, almost all of which require acclimatization to the rarified mountain air, a certain degree of fitness, good camping equipment, all your food and good maps. Hiking in this region is a serious affair and you will need to be properly prepared. Bear in mind that for some of the hikes you may need guides and mules to help carry the equipment at this altitude. One of the most popular routes, the **Llanganuco to Santa Cruz Loop** (see below), is a well-trodden trail offering spectacular scenery, some fine places to camp and a relatively easy walk that can be done in under a week even by inexperienced hikers. There are shorter walks, such as the trails around the **Pitec Quebrada**, within easy striking distance of Huaraz, and a number of other loops like the **Llanganuco to Chancos** trek. Experienced hikers could also tackle the circular **Cordillera Huayhuash** route. Detailed information on all these walks is available from the South American Explorers' Club in Lima (see p.21), the Casa de Guias (see p.258), the tourist office (see p.252), or tour companies in Huaraz (see p.262).

The Llanganuco to Santa Cruz Loop

The **Llanganuco to Santa Cruz Loop** starts at the clearly marked track leading off from the end of the road along the left bank of Orcon Cocha. The entire trek shouldn't take more than about five days for a healthy (and acclimatized) backpacker, but it's a perfect hike to take at your own pace. It is, however, essential to carry all your food, camping equipment and, ideally, a medical kit and emergency survival bag. Along the route there are hundreds of potential **camp sites**. The best time to attempt this trek is in the dry season, between April and October, unless you enjoy getting stuck in mud and being soaked to the skin.

From Orcon Cocha the main path climbs the **Portachuelo de Llanganuco pass** (4767m), before dropping to the enchanting beauty of the **Quebrada Morococha**, through the tiny settlement of **Vaqueria**. From here you can go on to Colcabamba and Pomabamba, in the Callejón de Conchucos (though not in the rainy season, when you may well find yourself stranded), or continue back to the Callejón de Huaylas via Santa Cruz. The Loop Trail heads north from Vaqueria up the **Quebrada Huaripampa** and around the ice cap of **Chacraraju** (6000m) – a stupendous rocky canyon with a marshy bottom, snowy mountain peaks to the west, and Cerro Mellairca to the east. Following the stream uphill, with the lakes of Morococha and Huiscash on your left, you pass down (via Punta Union, 4750m) into the Pacific watershed along the **Quebrada Santa Cruz**. Emerging eventually beside the calm waters of **Lake Grande**, you go around the left bank and continue down this perfect glacial valley for about another eight hours to the village of **SANTA CRUZ**, which has very basic accommodation. From here it's just a short step (about 2km) to the inviting thermal baths of **Shangol** (daily 8am–5pm; $0.75), and there's a road or a more direct three-hour path across the low hills south to Caraz.

Caraz and around

The attractive town of **CARAZ**, known for its honey and milk products, is little less than 20km down the Santa Valley from Yungay and sits quietly at an altitude of 2285m well below the enormous Huandoy Glacier. Palm trees and flowers adorn a classic colonial **Plaza de Armas**, while the small daily **market**, three blocks north of the plaza, is normally vibrant with activity, good for fresh food, colourful basketry, traditional gourd bowls, religious candles and hats. Nearby there are the interesting archeological ruins of **Tunshucayco**, a couple of kilometres northeast of town along 28 de Julio, close to the Lago Parón turn off; probably the largest ruins in the Callejon de Hualyas they apparently date back to pre-Chavín era, later influenced by the Huaylas culture and perhaps, after that, the Wari. A possible ceremonial centre, it may well also have had a defensive function given its dominating position overlooking the valley.

The best place to **stay** is the brand new *Hostal Perla de Los Andes,* Plaza de Armas (☎044/792007; ③) – spic, span and thus completely out of character with the rest of Caraz – offering comfortable rooms with hot water, private bath and TV; it also has a very nice restaurant. Across the plaza, the attractive old *Hotel la Suiza Peruana*, at Jirón San Martin 1133, close to the Plaza de Armas (☎044/722166; ②), is cheap and basic but is in an interesting old building with a small but verdant patio; it also has a restaurant. Also near the plaza, the better organized and cleaner *Hostal Chavín*, Jirón San Martin 1135 (☎044/791171; ②), is good value and some rooms have private bath, while the cheapest place in town is the *Alojamiento Ramirez*, Daniel Villar 407 (no tel; ①). One other rather unusual hostal is the *Hostal Chamanna*, a little out of town down 28 de Julio, at Avenida Nueva Victoria 185 (☎044/682802, fax 791642, *chamanna@usa.net*, *www.welcome.to/chamanna*; ④). Set in a lovely labyrinth of gardens, streams and patios, not all rooms have private bath but they are very stylish and have distinctive ethnic murals.

For **places to eat**, try the *Café de Rat*, just down from the Plaza de Armas, which serves pasta and pizzas, pancakes and vegetarian food, as well as having darts, maps, guide books, music and Internet access. Also on the plaza, the *Polleria El Mirador* does reasonably priced lunches and evening meals of Peruvian and international food. Just up above the plaza, on block 10 of Jirón San Martin, the restaurant *La Boca del Lobo* serves good local food in a vibrant atmosphere, often accompanied by loud music. The helpful **tourist information** office (Mon–Sat 7.45am–1pm & 2.30–5.30pm), with maps and brochures covering the attractions in the immediate area, is on the Plaza de Armas, while the **telephone office** is at Raimondi 410. For **money** exchange there's a Banco de Credito at Jirón Daniel Villa 217 or there's the Banco de la Nación on Jirón Raimondi, half a block from the Plaza de Armas. For trekking **guides**, local information or help organizing or fitting out an expedition, the excellent Pony Expeditions (see p.262) can't be beaten.

Most of the **bus** offices are along *calles* Daniel Villar and Cordova, within a block or two of the Plaza de Armas: Chinachasuyo serve Trujillo; Empresa Turismo go to Lima and Chimbote; Ancash to Lima; Movil Tours to Huraz and Lima; Region Norte runs buses to Yungay, Huaraz and Recauy; and Transporte Moreno to Chimbote. **Colectivos** for Huaraz leave from just behind the market more or less every thirty minutes.

Huata

Nine kilometres across the Río Santa from Caraz, set on the lower slopes of the Cordillera Negra, is the small settlement of **HUATA**, a typical rural village with regular truck connections from the market area in Caraz. The village is a good starting point for a number of easy **walks**, such as the eight-kilometre stroll up to the unassuming lakes of **Yanacocha** and **Huaytacocha** or, perhaps more interesting, north about 5km along a path up Cerro Muchanacoc to the small Inca **ruins of Cantu**.

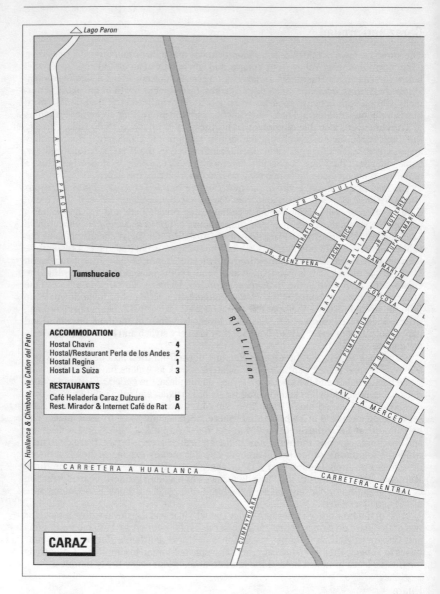

ACCOMMODATION

Hostal Chavin	4
Hostal/Restaurant Perla de los Andes	2
Hostal Regina	1
Hostal La Suiza	3

RESTAURANTS

Café Heladería Caraz Dulzura	B
Rest. Mirador & Internet Café de Rat	A

Lake Parón

The deep-blue **Lake Parón** (4185m), some 3km long and 700m wide, is sunk resplendently into a gigantic glacial cirque, hemmed in on three sides by some of the Cordillera Blanca's highest ice caps. There's a mountain **refuge** at the lake, run by the private company which operates the electricity plant at Huallanca; but there are only basic facilities available (toilet and hot water). It's always open for access, however,

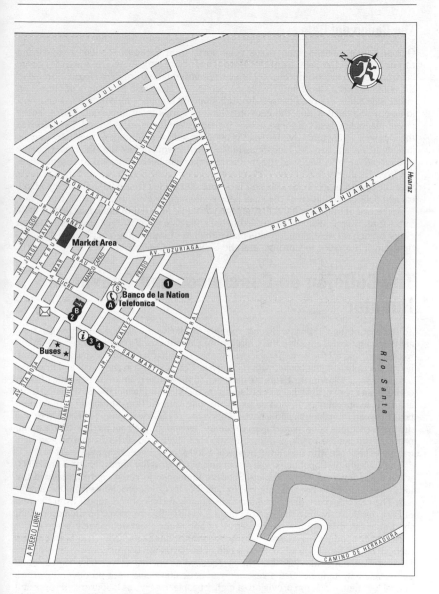

since two guards (one a radio operator) live there. **Camping** is possible at the refuge or on the east side of the lake, to which there's a clear path on the north bank. **Buses** and **colectivo**s (4.50am & 1pm; $1) from Caraz market travel up to Pueblo Parón, from where it's a 9km (3hr) hike up a further 900m in altitude to the lake. The last transport back from Pueblo Parón to Caraz is usally at 2.30pm. **Taxis** to the lake (about $10 per person) leave most days from the Plaza de Armas in Caraz.

The Cañon del Pato

One of Peru's most exciting roads runs north from Caraz to Huallanca, squeezing through the spectacular **Cañon del Pato** (Duck's Canyon). An enormous rocky gorge cut from solid rock, its impressive path curves around the Cordillera Negra for most of the 50km between Caraz and Huallanca. Sheer cliff faces rise thousands of metres on either side while the road passes through some 39 tunnels – an average of one every kilometre. Situated within the canyon is one of Peru's most important hydroelectric power plants; the heart of these works, invisible from the road, is buried 600m deep in the cliff wall. Unfortunately, the road is often closed for a number of reasons – causes include terrorists, bandits, landslides in the rainy season, or just the sheer poor quality of the road surface. Much of the the first section has been improved in recent years, but from Huallanca to Chimbote it's more like a dry river bed than a dirt track. Check with the tourist office in Huaraz and local bus companies (see p.261) about the physical and political condition of the road before attempting this journey.

At the end of the canyon the first village you come to is **Huallanca**, reached by daily buses from Huaraz (9am–6.30pm). From here, it's 8km on to Yuramarca where you can either branch off west along an alternative road to Chimbote (another 140km), or continue along the valley to Corongo and the Callejón de Conchucos.

The Callejón de Conchucos and Chavín de Huantar

To the east of the Cordillera Blanca, roughly parallel to the Callejón de Huaylas, runs another long natural corridor, the **Callejón de Conchucos**. Virtually inaccessible in the wet season, and off the beaten track even for the most hardened of backpackers, the valley makes a challenging target, with the town of **Pomabamba** in the north and the spectacular ruins at **Chavín de Huantar** just beyond its southern limit. There's little of interest between the two; the villages of **Piscobamba** (Valley or Plain of the Birds) and **Huari** are likely to appeal only as food stops on the long haul (141km) through barren mountains between Pomabamba and Chavín. This is one of the few regions of Peru where bus drivers sometimes allow passengers to lounge around on the roof as they career along precipitous mountain roads, plummeting into each steep drop of the dusty road – an electrifying experience with the added bonus of a 360-degree, ever-changing view.

The Callejón de Conchucos was out of bounds to travellers between 1988 and 1993, when it was under almost complete Sendero Luminoso terrorist control; many of the locals were forced to flee the valley after actual or threatened violence from the terrorists. The region's more distant history was equally turbulent and cut-off from the rest of Peru, particularly from the seat of colonial and Republican power on the coast. Until the Conquest, this region was the centre of one of the most notoriously fierce of the ancient tribes – the Conchucos – who surged down the Santa Valley and besieged the Spanish city of Trujillo in 1536. By the end of the sixteenth century, however, even the fearless Conchuco warriors had been reduced to virtual slavery by the colonial *encomendero* system: besides a vast array of agricultural and craft produce, the area's annual levy demanded the provision of eighty people to serve as labourers, herders and servants in the distant town of Huánuco.

Pomabamba

The small town of **POMABAMBA**, 3000m up in dauntingly hilly countryside, is surrounded by little-known archeological remains which show common roots with

Chavín de Huantar (see below). Originally named Puma Bamba, the Valley or Plain of the Pumas, this may reveal direct links with the ancient Chavín cult of the feline deity. Today the town makes an excellent trekking base; from here you can connect with the **Llanganuco to Santa Cruz Loop** (see p.270) by following tracks southwest to either Colcabamba or Punta Union. Or, a hard day's hike above Pomabamba, you can walk up to the stone remains of **Yaino**, an immense fortress of megalithic rock. On a clear day you can just about make out this site from the Plaza de Armas in Pomabamba; it appears as a tiny rocky outcrop high on the distant horizon. The climb takes longer than you might imagine, but locals will point out shortcuts along the way. The area also abounds in little explored **ruins**; try Pony Expeditions in Caraz (see p.262) for further information on these as well as maps, equipment and advice on trekking in this region.

Practicalities

Direct Empresa Los Andes **buses** leaves from the Plaza de Armas in Yungay at 8.30–9am, while Turismo Huaraz in Huaraz (see Listings, p.261) go to Piscobamba and Pomabamba. Alternatively there are sometimes buses from the Plaza de Armas in Caraz at around 5.30am for Corongo via the Cañon del Pato (see p.274). From Corongo, there are usually two trucks daily (at least between April and Oct) on to Pomabamba. Alternatively, you can get here from Huaraz via Chavín, on a bus from Lima which comes north up the Callejón de Conchucos more or less every other day. Pomabamba has a few small **places to stay**, the best being the Hotel Estrada (②) one block from the plaza on Calle Lima; the others are more basic, simple and slightly cheaper: the *Hostal Pomabamba* (no tel; ①) is just off the Plaza de Armas, and the *Hotel San Martin* (no tel; ②) is on the edge of town, though you'll undoubtedly be better off taking a tent and asking the locals for good **camping** spots.

Chavín de Huantar

Only 30km southeast of Huari or a five-hour journey from Huaraz, the magnificent temple complex of **CHAVÍN DE HUANTAR** is the most important site associated with the Chavín cult (see box on p.277), and although partially destroyed by earthquakes, floods and erosion from the Río Mosna, enough of the ruins survive to make them a fascinating sight for anyone even vaguely interested in Peruvian archeology. The religious cult that inspired Chavín's construction also influenced subsequent cultural development throughout Peru, right up until the Spanish Conquest some 2500 years later, and the temple complex of Chavín de Huantar is equal in importance, if not grandeur, to most of the sites around Cusco.

Getting there

The vast majority of people approach the temple complex from Huaraz. Empresa Condor de Chavín, Empresa Huascarán and Chavín Express and Empresa Sandoval **buses** leave Huaraz daily around 10am ($4, a 3–4hr trip) for Chavín (see p.261 for bus company details), while all the tour companies in Huaraz (see p.262) offer a slightly faster though more expensive service ($10–15, a 3hr trip). The buses turn off the main Huaraz to Lima road at the town of **Catac**, and take a poor quality road which crosses over the small Río Yana Yacu (Black Water River). It then starts climbing to the beautiful **Lake of Querococha** (*quero* is Quechua for "teeth", and relates to the teeth-like rock formation visible nearby), which looks towards two prominent mountain peaks — **Yanamarey** and **Pucaraju** ("Red Glacier" in Quechua). From here the road, little more than a track now, climbs further before passing through the **Tunel de Cahuish**, which cuts through the solid rock of a mountain to emerge in the **Callejón de**

Conchucos, to some spectacular but quite terrifying views. A couple of the more dangerous and precipitous curves in the road are known as the **Curva del Diablo** and **Salvate Si Puedes** ("Save Yourself If You Can"), from which you can deduce that this journey isn't for the squeamish or for vertigo sufferers.

A more adventurous way to reach Chavín is by following the two- to four-day **trail** over the hills from **Olleros**. Colectivos leave daily every thirty minutes from the end of Jirón Caceres, for Olleros ($1), from where the hike is fairly simple and clearly marked all the way. It follows the Río Negro up to Punta Yanashallash (4700m), cuts down into the Marañón watershed along the Quebrada Shongopampa, and where this meets the Jato stream coming from north, the route follows the combined waters (from here known as the Río Huachesecsa straight down, southwest to the Chavín ruins another 1500m below. It's quite a hike, so take maps and ideally a guide and pack-llamas (see p.259). A good account of this walk is given in Hilary Bradt's *Backpacking and Trekking in Peru and Bolivia* (see Contexts, p.475), and the South American Explorers' Club in Lima (see p.21) can give advice and information about it.

The temple complex

North of Lima, the magnificent temple complex of **Chavín de Huantar** daily 8am–5pm; $1) evolved and elaborated its own brand of religious cultism during the first millennium BC. The original temple was built here by at least 800 BC, though it was not until around 400 BC that the complex was substantially enlarged and its cultural style fixed. Some archeologists claim that the specific layout of the temple, a U-shaped ceremonial courtyard facing east and based around a raised stone platform, was directly influenced by what was, in 1200 BC, the largest architectural monument in the New World, at Sechin Alto (see p.248). By 300 BC, Sechin Alto had been abandoned and Chavín was at the height of its power and one of the world's largest religious centres, with about three thousand resident priests and temple attendants. Most archeologists agree that the U-shaped temples were dedicated to powerful mountain spirits or deities, who controlled meteorological phenomena, in particular rainfall which was vital to the survival and wealth of the people. These climactic concerns became increasingly important as the ancient Peruvians became increasingly dependent on agriculture rather than hunting.

The complex's main building consists of a central rectangular block with two wings projecting out to the east. The large, southern wing, known as the **Castillo**, is the most conspicuous feature of the site: enlarged three times it now stands some 10m high. Massive, almost pyramid shaped, the platform is built of dressed stone with gargoyles attached, though few remain now.

Some way in front of the Castillo, down three main flights of steps, is the **Plaza Hundida**, or sunken plaza, covering about 250 square metres with a rectangular, stepped platform to either side. Here, the thousands of pilgrims thought to have worshipped at Chavín would gather during the appropriate *fiestas*. And it was here that the famous Tello Obelisk (now in the Archeological and Anthropological Museum in Lima; see p.71) was found, next to an altar in the shape of a jaguar and bedecked with seven cavities forming a pattern similar to that of the Orion constellation.

Standing in the Plaza Hundida, facing towards the Castillo, you'll see on your right the **original temple**, now just a palatial ruin dwarfed by the neighbouring Castillo. It shows several stages of construction, although it has always maintained its roughly east–west orientation. It was first examined by Julio Tello in 1919 when it was still buried under cultivated fields; during 1945 a vast flood reburied most of it and the place was damaged again by the 1970 earthquake and the rains of 1983. Evolving between 850 and 200 BC, it began with a small temple area separated from a village dwelling complex. Over the centuries the village was abandoned in favour of sites focusing around the temple itself. Among the fascinating recent finds from the area are bone

THE CHAVÍN CULT

The **Chavín cult** had a strong impact on the Paracas culture, and later on the Nasca and Mochica civilizations. Theories as to the origin of its religious inspiration range from extraterrestrial intervention to the more likely infiltration of ideas and individuals or entire tribes from Central America. There is an affinity between the ceramics found at Chavín and those of a similar date from Tlatilco in Mexico, yet there are no comparable Mexican stone constructions as ancient as these Peruvian wonders. More probable, and the theory expounded by Julio Tello, is that the cult initially came up into the Andes (then down to the coast) from the Amazon Basin via the Marañón Valley. The inspiration for the beliefs themselves may well have come from visionary experiences sparked by the ingestion of **hallucinogens**: one of the stone reliefs at Chavín portrays a feline deity or fanged warrior holding a section of the psychotropic mescalin cactus – San Pedro – still used by *curanderos* today for the invocation of the spirit world, thus providing an Amazonian link.

Chavín itself may not have been the centre of the movement, but it was obviously an outstanding ceremonial focus: the name of Chavín comes from the Quechua *chaupin*, meaning navel or focal point. As such, it might have been a sacred shrine where natives flocked in pilgrimage during festivals, much as they do today, visiting important *huacas* in the *sierra* at specific times in the annual agricultural cycle. The appearance of the Orion constellation on Chavín carvings fits with this since it appears on the skyline just prior to the traditional harvest period in the Peruvian mountains. This may have been the moment, too, for marriage rituals and even intergroup truces.

snuff tubes, beads, pendants, needles, ceremonial shells (imported from Ecuador) and some quartz crystals associated with ritual sites. One quartz crystal covered in red pigment was found in a grave, placed after death in the mouth of the deceased.

Behind the original temple, there are two entrances leading to underground passages. The one on the right leads down to an underground chamber, containing the awe-inspiring **Lanzon**, a prism-shaped block of carved white granite that tapers nearly 4m down from a broad feline head to a point stuck in the ground. The entrance on the left takes you into the labyrinthine inner chambers, which run underneath the Castillo on various levels and are connected by ramps and steps. In the seven major subterranean rooms you'll need a torch to get a decent look at the carvings and the granite sculptures (even when the electric lighting is switched on), while all around you can hear the sound of water dripping.

Another large stone slab discovered at Chavín in 1873 – the Estela Raymondi, also now in the Archeological and Anthropological Museum – was the first of all the impressive carved stones to be found. This, too, seems to represent a monstrous feline deity, the same one that frequently recurs both in human form with snake appendages and as a bird figure, sometimes both at the same time. The most vivid of the carvings remaining at the site are the gargoyles (known as Cabeza Clavos), guardians of the temple that again display feline and birdlike characteristics.

Most theories about the **iconography** of these stone slabs, all of which are very intricate, distinctive in style and highly abstract, agree that the Chavín people worshipped three major gods: the Moon (represented by a fish), the Sun (depicted as an eagle or a hawk), and an overlord, or creator divinity, normally shown as a fanged cat, possibly a jaguar. It seems very likely that each god was linked with a distinct level of the Chavín cosmos: the fish with the underworld, the eagle with the celestial forces, and the feline with earthly power. This is only a calculated guess, and ethnographic evidence from the Amazon Basin suggests that each of these main gods may have also been associated with a different subgroup within the Chavín tribe or priesthood as a whole.

Practicalities

The pretty village of **Chavín de Huantar**, with its whitewashed walls and traditional tiled roofs, is just a couple of hundred metres from the ruins and has a reasonable supply of basic amenities. The best **accommodation** is at the relatively new and very good-value *Hotel La Casona de JB*, Wiracocha 130 (☎044/754020; ③), just next door to the town hall on the plaza, with hot showers. There's also a friendly family lodging at the *Casa del Senor Chapaco* (②), while *Hotel Inca* (②), at Wiracocha 160, has hot water most evenings but shared bathrooms, or try the basic but clean *Hotel Monte Carlo*, at Calle 17 de Enero 1015 (②), on the plaza. Alternatively, you can **camp** by the Baños Quercos thermal springs (daily 7am–6pm; $0.5) some twenty minutes' stroll from the village, 2km up the valley. For **places to eat** the best bets are the *Restaurant Chavín Turistico*, 17 de Enero Sur 439, or the *Restaurant La Ramada*, a few doors further up the same road at 17 de Enero 577. Getting back to Huaraz or Catac, there are buses daily from Chavín, more or less on the hour from 3 to 6pm. There's a **post and telephone office** at Calle 17 de Enero 365 (6.30am–10pm), plus a small **tourist information** office on the corner of the Plaza de Armas, next to the market, though it doesn't have regular hours.

North from Chavín

Some 8km north of Chavín is the lovely village of **SAN MARCOS**, a good base for mountain hiking. There are **buses** every hour from Chavín, or you can walk there in well under two hours. **Accommodation** is available at the *Casa del Senor Luis Alfaro* (②), though it's a good idea to take a tent just in case his rooms are full. From San Marcos you can climb up another 300m in altitude to the smaller community of **Carhuayoc**, a hundred-year-old village whose population specialize in the production of fine textiles, mainly blankets and rugs (its a 9hr round trip). About 35km from San Marcos, the town of **Huari** is a good base for a short trek to the scenic Lago Purhuay; it's only 8km from the town and a climb of some 400m, but it usually takes between five and six hours to get there and back. To continue on to Pomabamba from here, there are **buses** every other day, usually leaving Huari at 9pm ($5, a 7hr journey).

HUÁNUCO

On the main road from Lima to the central jungle region of Pucallpa and the vast Río Ucayali, the *departmento* of **Huánuco** offers the possibility of several fascinating excursions – the four-thousand-year-old **Temple of Kotosh** and the impressive ruins at **Tantamayo**, to name but two – as well as the option of penetrating the wilder parts of the Amazon Basin. Its capital, also called **Huánuco**, is a well-serviced market town and an ideal stopping point on the way to the jungle town of **Tingo Maria** and the coca-growing slopes at the upper end of the Río Huallaga. The region is usually reached via the Central Highway and La Oroya, then north through Cerro de Pasco. However, for anyone already in and around Huaraz, or those willing to risk possible hardship and delays in return for magnificent scenery, there is a direct route over the Cordillera Blanca which takes you to **La Unión** and the preserved Inca ruins of **Huánuco Viejo**, before continuing to the modern city.

Overland from Huaraz to La Unión and Huánuco

A dusty minor road to **La Unión** turns off the main Huaraz to Lima road 7km beyond Catac, cutting through the Huascarán National Park past the Puya Raymondi and Pastoruri Glacier. From **Catac**, it's possible to hitch a ride in a truck to the rather cold, bleak and miserable mining settlement of **Huansala** (an hour or two up the road), but try not to get stuck here overnight, as there are no facilities for travellers. From Huansala, you can either get one of the daily buses, or walk the 10km to Huallanca, where there are frequent trucks all the way to La Unión; with luck you can do the whole trip in a day. However, most people will take the much easier route via Conococha and Chiquian (9hr). Empresa Rapido run buses from Huaraz daily ($3, a 4–5hr journey), from where they continue directly to La Unión. If snow makes the pass difficult, the bus arrives at 8–10pm, making a stopover in La Unión pretty inevitable.

La Unión

LA UNIÓN, a small market town high up on a cold and bleak *pampa*, is a base for visiting the Inca ruins of Huánuco Viejo, a two- or three-hour hike away. If you do need a **place to stay**, there's the very basic, dirty *Hostal Dos de Mayo* (no tel; ①), or *Hostal Turista* (no tel; ②), which is slightly more salubrious but still has shared bathrooms. There are one or two **restaurants** around the market area, including the *Restaurant El Danubo*, for simple meals such as rice, chicken and stews.

There are usually two or three **buses** a day to Huánuco from the market area in La Unión, with the last one leaving around 11pm for the nine-hour ($5) journey. Alternatively, you can ride on top of one of the **trucks** which leave La Unión market for Huánuco most mornings. There are no buses or public transport to Huánuco Viejo and the only way to get there is to walk, or take a **taxi** from the Plaza de Armas ($4–5).

Huánuco Viejo

From La Unión a dusty track continues along precipitous and winding mountain roads that are frequently washed away in places during the rainy season. The journey can be done in half a day but it often takes a few hours longer to reach the superb Inca stonework of **HUÁNUCO VIEJO** (daily 8am–6pm; free), virtually untouched by the Spanish conquistadores and with no later occupation, lying on the edge of a desolate *pampa*. Although abandoned by the Spanish shortly after their arrival in 1539, the city became a centre of native dissent – Illa Tupac, a relative of the rebel Inca Manco and one of the unsung heroes of the Indian resistance, maintained clandestine Inca rule around Huánuco Viejo until at least 1545. As late as 1777 the royal officials were thrown out of the area in a major – albeit shortlived – insurrection.

One of the most complete existing examples of an Inca provincial capital and administrative centre, Huánuco Viejo gives a powerful impression of a once-thriving city – you can almost sense the activity even though it's been a ghost town for four hundred years. The grey stone houses and **platform temples** are set out in a roughly circular pattern radiating from a gigantic *unsu* (Inca throne) in the middle of a plaza. To the north are the **military barracks** and beyond that the remains of suburban dwellings. Directly east of the plaza is the palace and temple known as Incahuasi, and next to this the Acllahuasi, a separate enclosure devoted to the Chosen Women, or Virgins of the Sun. Behind this, and running straight through the Incahuasi, is a man-made water channel diverted from the small Río Huachac. On the opposite side of the plaza you can make out the extensive administrative quarters.

Poised on the southern hillside above the main complex are over five hundred **storehouses** where all sorts of produce and treasure were kept as tribute for the emperor and sacrifices to the sun. Well away from the damp of the valley floor, and separated from each other by a few metres to minimize the risk of fire, they also command impressive views across the plain.

Arriving here in 1539, the Spanish very soon abandoned the site of Huánuco Viejo to build their own colonial administrative centre at a much lower altitude, more suitable for their unacclimatized lungs and with slightly easier access to Cusco and Lima. The modern city, built along the standard city plans specified by royal decree, grew thoroughly rich, but was still regarded by the colonists as one of those remote outposts (like Chile) where criminals, or anyone unpopular with officialdom, would be sent into lengthy exile.

Huánuco and around

The charming modern city of **HUÁNUCO**, more than 100km east of the deserted Inca town, and around 412km from Lima, sits nestled in a beautiful Andean valley some 1900m above sea level. The relatively peaceful city, located on the left bank of the sparkling Río Huallaga, depends for its livelihood on forestry, tea and coca, along with a little low-key tourism. Its old, narrow streets ramble across a handful of small plazas, making a pleasant environment to spend a day or two preparing for a trip down into the jungle beyond Tingo Maria or exploring some of the nearby archeological sites, such as the **Temple of Kotosh** and the ruins at **Tantamayo**.

The City

The city itself boasts no real sights, save a handful of fine old churches and a small natural history museum. The sixteenth-century church, **San Francisco** (daily 6am–9pm; free), houses the tomb of the town's original founder and shows a strong indigenous influence, its altars richly carved with native fruits – avocados, papayas and pomegranates. It also boasts a small collection of sixteenth-century paintings. The church of **La Merced** (daily 6am–9pm; free) is worth a brief look around for its spectacular gold-leaf altarpiece. The **San Cristobal** church (daily 7am–9pm; free) also has some fine gold-leaf altarpieces, and is said to be built on the site where the chief of the Chupacos tribe once lived and where Portuguese priest Pablo Coimbra celebrated the first Mass in the region. The natural history museum, **Museo de Ciencias**, Jirón General Prado 495 (Mon–Fri 9am–6pm, Sat 9am–1pm; $0.75), houses archeological finds, mainly pottery, from the region and a small display of Andean flora and fauna.

Practicalities

The best of the budget **accommodation** options is the downmarket *Hotel Astoria*, Jirón General Prado 988 (☎064/512310; ②), a couple of blocks from the Plaza de Armas, with shared bathrooms, or the clean but basic *Hostal Residencial Huánuco*, Calle Huánuco (☎064/512050; ③), an attractive colonial building that's also close to the plaza. Pricier options include the *Hotel Cusco*, on Calle Huánuco 616 (☎064/512244; ④), just one and a half blocks from the plaza, which has private bathrooms, while the much more upmarket and very comfortable *Gran Hotel Huánuco* (☎064/512410; ⑤), sits right on the Plaza de Armas in the shade of some beautiful old trees. Alternatively, you can **camp** down by the Río Huallaga near the stadium, but watch out for the active insect life.

FIESTAS IN HUÁNUCO

If you can, you should aim to be in Huánuco around August 15, when **carnival week** begins and the city's normal tranquillity explodes into a wild *fiesta* binge. **Peruvian Independence Day** (July 28) is also a good time to be here, when traditional dances like the *Chunco* take place throughout the streets; at Christmas time, children put on their own dance performances. On January 1, 6 and 18, you can witness the **Dance of the Blacks** (El Baile de los Negritos) when various local dance groups, dressed in colourful costumes with black masks, run and dance throughout the main streets of the city; food-stalls stay open and drinking continues all day and most of the night.

El Café, on the Plaza de Armas, is the best **restaurant** for international cuisine, as well as a variety of Peruvian *criolla* dishes, though the *Restaurant Vegetariano,* Dos de Mayo 751, three blocks from the plaza, has nicer food. For a better atmosphere in the evenings and the local speciality, *picante de queso* – a spicy sauce made from yellow chillis and onions, poured over cold cheese and potatoes – try *La Casona de Gladys* at General Prado 908.

Tourist information is available from ICTA-Huánuco, Jirón General Prado 722, right by the Plaza de Armas (Mon–Fri 9am–1pm & 4–6pm). The **post office** is on the Plaza de Armas (Mon–Sat 8am–7pm), and the **telephone office** is two blocks away along 28 de Julio (daily 8am–9pm). You can change **money** with the *cambistas* on the corner of Dos de Mayo and the Plaza de Armas, or at the Banco de Credito, on Dos de Mayo, less than a block up from the plaza. **Guided tours** to places of interest in the locality, such as Kotosh, are available from Ecotur Tour and Travel Agent, 28 de Julio 1033 (☎064/512410).

Buses to La Unión (8–9hr) leave daily at 8am from the market area, while buses, colectivos and trucks to Tingo Maria (4–5hr) and Pucallpa leave daily from Jirón General Prado, just three blocks east of the Plaza de Armas, over the Río Huallaga bridge. Direct Leon de Huánuco buses to Lima ($12, a 10–12hr trip), via the Central Highway and La Oroya, leave daily from the terminal on Jirón Ayacucho, close to the river. Trucks and buses for Tantamayo ($8, a 14hr trip) leave most days at around 6pm from the market area, close to the corner of Jirón Aguilar with Calle San Martin. There are no direct buses from Huánuco to Junin and Huancayo; the best you can do is try to catch one of the Lima buses that passes through La Oroya, where you should disembark and catch a bus or colectivo to Huancayo area from here.

The Temple of Kotosh

Only 6km from Huánuco along the La Unión road, the fascinating, though poorly maintained, **Temple of Kotosh** lies in ruins on the banks of the Río Tingo. At more than four thousand years old, this site predates the Chavín era by more than a thousand years. Between 1960 and 1962 a team of Japanese archeologists excavated the large mound which had been created by the fallen debris of the original temple: its occupation proved to span six phases, the first town of which falls into the Early Agricultural Period, when ceramic arts were beginning to develop rapidly. Potsherds found here bear clear similarities to works from the lower jungle areas.

The first evidence of massive stone constructions from about 2000 BC suggests that complicated building work began here centuries before anywhere else on the American continent. More or less permanent settlement continued here throughout the Chavín era (though without the monumental masonry and sculpture of that period) and Inca occupation, right up to the Conquest. One unique feature of the Kotosh complex is the **crossed-hands symbol** carved prominently in stone – the gracefully executed insignia of a very early culture about which archeologists know next to nothing.

To get to the site, you can either walk along the La Unión road, or take the La Unión bus (see above) from Huánuco, and ask the driver to drop you off at the path to Kotosh. Alternatively, a **guided tour** from Huánuco will cost around $10 per person (see above), or a **taxi** from the Plaza de Armas will cost around $8.

Tantamayo

About 150km north of Huánuco, poised in the mountainous region above the higher reaches of the Río Marañón, lies the small village of **TANTAMAYO**, with its nearby extensive ruins. In the village you can hire local **guides** (from $5 a day) to take you on the two- to three-hour hike to the scattered site, and excellent **accommodation** is offered at the Swiss-style tourist lodge known as the *Hotel Turistica* (no tel; ④), where English is spoken, and there are a couple of other more basic *hostals.*

The ruins of Tantamayo

The precise age of the remote pre-Columbian **ruins of Tantamayo** is unknown. Its buildings appear to fit into the later TiaHuánuco-Huari phase, which would make them some 1200 years old, but physically they form no part of this widespread cultural movement and the site is considered to have developed separately, probably originating from tribes migrating to the Andes from the jungle and adapting to a new environment over a long period.

At Tantamayo the architectural development of some four centuries can be clearly seen – growing from the simplest of structures to complex edifices. Tall buildings dot the entire area – some clearly **watchtowers** looking over the Marañón, others with less obvious functions, built for religious reasons as temple-palaces, perhaps, or as storehouses and fortresses. One of the major constructions, just across the Tantamayo stream on a hill facing the village, was named Pirira by the Incas who conquered the area in the fifteenth century. At its heart there are concentric circles of carved stone, while the walls and houses around are all grouped in a circular formation – clearly this was once an important centre for religious ritual. The **main building** rises some 10m on three levels, its bluff facade broken only by large window niches, changes in the course of the stone slabs, and by centuries of weathering.

A detailed archeological survey of the ruins may well reveal links with Chavín (see p.277) and Kotosh (see previous page). In the meantime, the thirty separate, massive constructions make an impressive scene, offset by the cloudforest and jungle flourishing along the banks of the Marañón just a little further to the north.

From Huánuco to the jungle

The Amazon is the obvious place to move on to from Huánuco unless you're heading back to Lima and the coast. The spiralling descent north **from Huánuco** is stunning, with views across the jungle, as thrilling as if from a small plane, at their best in the **Pass of Padre Abad** with its glorious waterfalls. By the time the bus reaches **Tingo Maria**, the Huallaga has become a broad tropical river, navigable downstream in shallow canoes or by balsa raft. And the tropical atmosphere, in the shadow of the forested ridges and limestone crags of the **Bella Durmiente** (Sleeping Beauty) mountain, is delightful. From Tingo Maria you can continue the 260km directly northeast through virgin forest to Pucallpa, jumping-off point for expeditions deep into the seemingly limitless wilderness of tropical jungle (see Chapter Six).

Tingo Maria

Once known as the Garden City, the ramshackle settlement of **TINGO MARIA**, 130km north of Huánuco, lies at the foot of the Bella Durmiente mountain, where, according to legend, the lovesick Princess Nunash awaits the waking kiss of Kunyaq, the sorcerer. These days the town welcomes few travellers due to the proliferation of the **cocaine trade** that grew up in the surrounding regions during the 1980s, and the gang and terrorist control of such large-scale illicit operations. Despite its striking setting – 670m above sea level on the forested eastern slopes of the Andes, amid the fecund tropical climate of the *ceja de selva* – Tingo Maria, today, is a tatty, ugly town, on which the ravages of Western civilization have left their mark. Dominated by sawmills and plywood factories financed by multinational corporations, and with a booming trade in stolen goods and cocaine, the town displays all the symbols of relative affluence, but the tin roofs and forest of TV aerials spattered across the township betray the poverty of the majority of its inhabitants. There's little for visitors to see, beyond the rather sorry **zoo and botanical gardens** (Mon–Fri 9am–5pm; free) attached to the university on the edge of town, or – about 14km out of town

– the **Cueva de las Lechuzas** (Owls' Cave), the vast, picturesque and dark home to a flock of rare nocturnal parrots (you'll need a torch). If you're here in the last week of July, you'll coincide with Tingo Maria's major **fiesta** period – a lively and fun time to be be in town, but on no account leave your baggage unattended then.

Practicalities

Accommodation is available at the *Hotel Viena*, Tulumayo 245 (☎064/562194; ②), which is surprisingly comfortable as well as reasonably priced; the simple but excel-lent-value *Hostal La Cabaña* at Avenida Raymondi 342 (☎064/562146; ①), where the rooms are small and all bathrooms shared; and the clean and friendly *Hotel Royal* on Avenida Benavides 206 (☎064/562166; ③). However, the best option is the upmarket *Madera Verde Hotel* (☎064/562047, fax 561608; ⑤–⑥), 2km south of town, with its own pool (open to non-residents for around $1), and clean, comfortable rooms, most with private bath. For **food** it's hard to beat the *Café Rex* at Avenida Raymondi 500, while *La Cabaña* serves up tasty Peruvian evening meals and lunches.

Into the jungle

The **bus** from Tingo Maria to Pucallpa ($9) leaves three times a day from Avenida Raymondi; the journey takes twelve to sixteen hours, depending on whether it's the dry (May–Oct) or rainy (Nov–April) season. Leon de Huánuco travel this road from Lima via Tingo to Pucallpa more or less daily and can be picked up in town, or Transtel Buses leave from Avenida Raymondi. However, you should always book in advance – nearly all the buses arrive full on their way from Lima and Huánuco. Colectivos leave at all times for both Pucallpa and Huánuco from the corner of Callao with Raymondi, about five blocks from the Plaza de Armas. If you do get stuck you can always **fly** to Pucallpa ($40–60), with Aero Condor or Aero Continente, bookable through Tingo Maric Travel, Avenida Raimondi (☎064/562501).

Buses and **trucks** leave from Avenida Raymondi just about every day to **Tarapoto** (24hr), along the road that follows the Huallaga Valley north via Juanjui (18hr), but this route is NOT recommended for travellers in view of the high level of cocaine smug-gling, terrorist activity and army presence in this remote region.

travel details

Buses, Trucks and Colectivos

Barranca to: Casma (6 daily; 2hr); Chimbote (8 daily; 3hr); Huaraz (8–10 daily; 5hr); Lima (8–10 daily; 3hr).

Chimbote to: Caraz (mostly daily; 6–7hr) Huaraz (3–4 daily; 8hr); Lima (8 daily; 6–8hr); Trujillo (8 daily; 3hr).

Huánuco to: La Unión (1 daily; 8hr); Lima (2 daily; 12hr); Pucallpa (4 daily; 19hr); Tantamayo (1 daily; 12–14hr); Tingo Maria (3 daily; 4–5hr).

Huaraz to: Casma (3 daily; 6hr); Chavín (2 daily; 3–4hr); Chimbote (3–4 daily; 7–8hr); La Unión (1 daily; 9–12hr); Lima (5–6 daily; 8hr); Trujillo (2–3 daily; 8–10hr).

La Unión to: Huánuco (1 daily; 7–10hr); Huaraz (1 daily; 9–12hr); Lima, via Chiquián (3–4 weekly; 14hr).

Tingo Maria to: Huánuco (3 daily; 5hr); Lima (3 daily; 16–17hr); Pucallpa (4 daily; 14hr).

Flights

Chimbote to: Lima (1 daily; 1hr); Trujillo (1 daily; 1hr).

Huánuco to: Lima (daily; 1hr); Tarapota (1 daily; 2hr); Tingo Maria (1 daily; 1hr).

Huaraz to: Lima (occasionally in high season; 1hr).

Tingo Maria to: Huánuco (4 weekly; 1hr); Lima (4 weekly; 1hr 30min); Pucallpa (4 weekly; 1hr).

CHAPTER FIVE

TRUJILLO AND THE NORTH

Though less known and less visited than the regions around Cusco, Ancash or Lima, the northern reaches of Peru definitely repay the time spent exploring. It's an immensely varied, often intriguing corner of the country, ranging from a handful of culturally vital cities that stand out as welcoming oases along the desert coast, up to secluded villages in the Andes where you may well be the first foreigner to pass through for years. On top of this, the entire area is brimming with Inca and pre-Inca sites, some of them uncovered in the last decade or two, making it among the most historically and archeologically important parts of Peru.

Trujillo, which rivals Arequipa for the title of Peru's second city, is one of the country's undiscovered jewels, located on the seaward edge of the vast desert plain at the mouth of the Moche Valley. It's an interesting colonial city with all the usual modern amenities and is something of a northern capital, even if few people have heard of it before they arrive. Its attraction lies partly in its nearby ruins, notably **Chan Chan** and the huge sacred pyramids of the **Huaca del Sol** and **Huaca de la Luna**, partly in the city itself, and partly in its excellent beaches. **Huanchaco**, 12km from Trujillo, is a good case in point, essentially a fishing village and a likeable resort within walking distance of sandy beaches and massive ancient ruins.

The so-called "Northern Circuit" is a variety of established touring routes through the Andean region above Trujillo, all of which take the beautifully situated mountain town of **Cajamarca** as their main focus. It was here that Pizarro first encountered and captured the Inca Emperor Atahualpa to begin the Spanish conquest of Peru, and around the modern city are a number of fascinating Inca ruins – many linked with water and ritualized baths. Cajamarca is also one of the springboards for the smaller town of **Chachapoyas** and the ruined city complex of **Kuelap**, arguably the single most overwhelming pre-Columbian site in Peru. Beyond, there are two possible routes down Amazon headwaters to the **jungle** town of Iquitos – both long and arduous, but well worth it if you have the time, enthusiasm and necessary equipment. Alternatively, you could take the well travelled circular route back to the coast via **Jaen** and **Olmos**, or head back to Trujillo via the old colonial outpost of **Huamachuco** and, for the really adventurous, visit the remote ruins of **Gran Pajaten**.

ACCOMMODATION PRICE CODES

Unless otherwise indicated, **accommodation** in this book is coded according to the categories below, based on the price of a double room in high season.

① under $5	③ $10–20	⑤ $30–40	⑦ $50–70
② $5–10	④ $20–30	⑥ $40–50	⑧ over $70

The coastal strip north of Trujillo, up to **Tumbes** by the Ecuadorean border, is for the most part a seemingly endless desert plain, interrupted by many small isolated villages but only two substantial towns, **Chiclayo** and **Piura**. Just outside Chiclayo, however, near the small settlement of **Lambayeque**, archeologists have discovered some of the coast's most important temple ruins whose tombs contain a wealth of precious-metal ceremonial items associated with the Sican culture. You may well decide to pass straight through on the Panamerican Highway, but you'd miss out on some interesting **archeological sites**, such as the ancient **Temple of Sipán**, the adobe pyramids of **Túcume**, and the ceremonial centre and ecological reserve at **Batan Grande**. There are also a couple of adventurous routes into the Andes, and, best of all, a number of beach resorts, such as **Chicama** and **La Pimentel**, along the only stretch of coast in Peru where the sea is ever really warm.

TRUJILLO AND AROUND

Peru's northern capital, **Trujillo** is small enough to get to know in a couple of days, and has the feel of a lively, cosmopolitan regional city. The pleasant coastal **climate** here is warm and dry without the fogs you get around Lima, but not as hot as the deserts further north.

One of the main reasons for coming to Trujillo is to visit the numerous archeological sites dotted around the nearby Moche and Chicama valleys. There are three main zones of interest within easy reach, first and foremost being the massive adobe city of **Chan Chan** on the northern edge of town. To the south, standing alone beneath the Cerro Blanco hill, you can find the largest mud-brick pyramids in the Americas, the **Huaca del Sol** and **Huaca de la Luna**, while further away to the north of Trujillo, in the **Chicama Valley**, the incredible remnants of vast pre-Inca irrigation canals, temples, and early settlement sites stand in stark contrast to the massive green sugar-cane plantations of the haciendas. In many ways these sites are more impressive than the ruins around Cusco – and most are more ancient too; yet apart from Chan Chan they have been underpromoted by the Peruvian tourism authorities.

Trujillo

Pizarro, on his second voyage to Peru in 1528, sailed by the site of ancient Chan Chan, then still a major city and an important regional centre of Inca rule. He returned to establish a Spanish colony in the same valley, naming it **TRUJILLO** in December 1534 after his birthplace in Estremadura, and officially founding it in March 1535. A year later, in 1536, the town was besieged by the Inca Manco's forces during the second rebellion against the conquistadores. Many thousands of Conchuco Indian warriors, allied with the Incas, swarmed down to Trujillo, killing Spaniards and collaborators on the way and offering their victims to Catequil, the tribal deity. Surviving this attack, Trujillo grew to become the main port of call for the Spanish treasure fleets, sailors wining and dining here on their way between Lima and Panama. By the seventeenth century it was a walled city covering three square miles, with 56 blocks that contained some three thousand houses. The only sections of the walls remaining are the Herrera rampart and a small piece of the façade on Avenida España.

Trujillo continued to be a centre of popular rebellion, declaring its independence from Spain in the Plaza de Armas in 1820, long before the Liberators arrived. The enigmatic APRA (American Popular Revolutionary Alliance) leader, Haya de la Torre, was born here in 1895, running for president, after years of struggle, in the elections of 1931. The dictator, Sanchez Cerro, however, counted the votes and declared himself

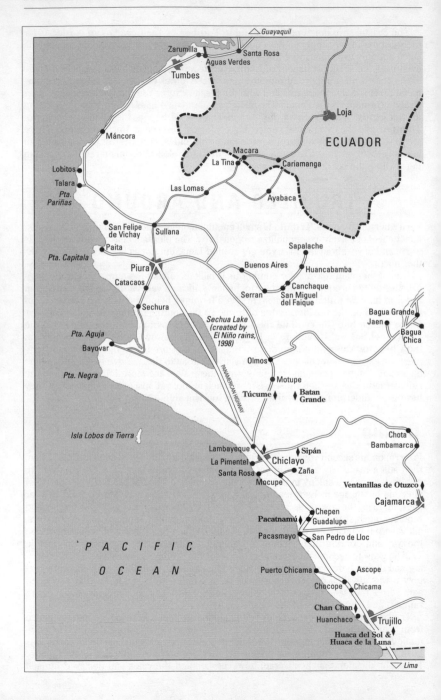

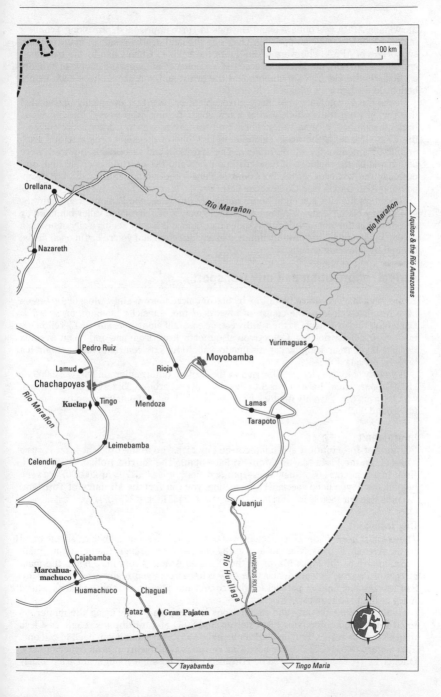

the winner. APRA was outlawed and Haya de la Torre imprisoned, provoking Trujillo's middle classes to stage an uprising. Over one thouand deaths resulted, many of them supporters of APRA, who were taken out to the fields of Chan Chan by the truckload and shot. Even now, the 1932 massacre has a resonance amongst the people of Trujillo, particularly the old APRA members and the army, and you can still see each neighbourhood declaring its allegiance in graffiti.

It was the Revolutionary Military government in 1969 that eventually unshackled this region from the stranglehold of a few sugar barons, who owned the enormous haciendas in the Chicama Valley. Their land was given over to worker cooperatives – the Casa Grande, a showcase example, is now one of the most profitable and well-organized agricultural ventures in Peru. The mid-1980s and early 1990s, however, were dominated by the violence of Sendero Luminoso and the corruption of the first, and probably the last ever, APRA President of Peru – the young, charismatic but disappointing Alan Garcia (see Contexts, p.429).

Nowadays the city, just eight hours north of Lima along the Panamerican Highway, looks every bit the oasis it is, standing in a relatively green, irrigated valley bounded by arid desert at the foot of the brown Andes mountains. It hardly seems a city of nearly a million inhabitants – walk twenty minutes in any direction and you're out in open fields, hedged by flowering shrubs.

Arrival, information and city transport

You're most likely to arrive in the city by bus or colectivo from Lima. Most of the **buses** have terminals close to the centre of town near the Mansiche Stadium, on *avenidas* Daniel Carrion or España to the southwest, or east of it along *avenidas* or Ejercito (see Listings, p.295, for details). **Colectivos** also mostly leave from and end up on Avenida España. If you're arriving by day it's fine to walk to the city centre, though at night it's best to take a taxi ($2–3).

If you **fly** into the city, you'll arrive at the airport (information on ☎044/246000 or 252301), near Huanchaco. Taxis into the city will cost around $5, or you can get a bus, which leaves every twenty minutes from the roundabout just outside the airport gates, for around $0.5.

Information
For **tourist information** and photocopied city maps, go to the office at Jirón Pizarro 412–414, on the Plaza Mayor (Mon–Fri 9am–5pm). The **tourist police**, at POLTUR, Jirón Independencia 630 (daily 9am–1pm & 4–7pm; ☎044/291705 or 200200) are very helpful, too. If you need specialist information, you can visit the **Ministry of Tourism**, Avenida España 1800 (Mon–Fri 9am–5pm; ☎044/245345, fax 245797).

City transport
The colonial heart of the city consists of about fifty relatively small bocks, all encircled by the Avenida España. More or less at the centre of the circle is the ubiquitous main plaza, known as the Plaza Mayor or the Plaza de Armas. From here begin the main streets of Pizarro, Independencia; the only other streets you really need to know are San Martín and Bolivar, parallel to Pizarro and Independencia, and Gamarra, where many of the banks are to be found.

Getting around the city and its environs is cheap and easy, using the numerous **local buses** and **colectivos** (flat rates around $0.7) and **minibuses**. **Taxis** cost less than $3 for ride within Trujillo and can be hailed anywhere, but if you need to call one, Taxi Seguro (☎044/253473) are best. **Car rental** is available from Jirón Ayacucho 414, Oficina 11 (☎ & fax 044/234985). **Hitchhiking** is possible though not particularly

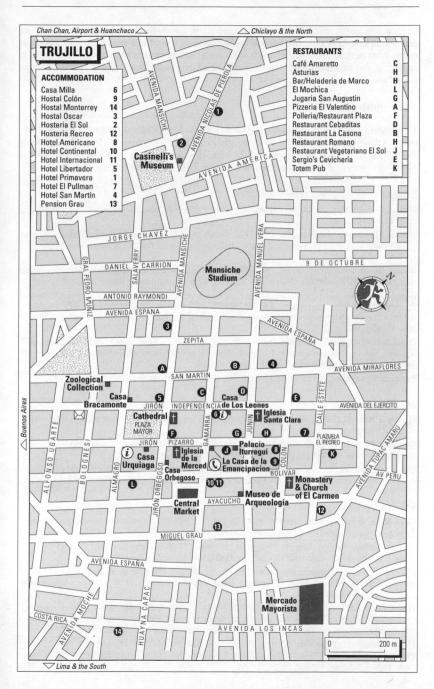

Chan Chan, Airport & Huanchaco △   △ Chiclayo & the North

TRUJILLO

ACCOMMODATION

Casa Milla	6
Hostal Colón	9
Hostal Monterrey	14
Hostal Oscar	3
Hosteria El Sol	2
Hosteria Recreo	12
Hotel Americano	8
Hotel Continental	10
Hotel Internacional	11
Hotel Libertador	5
Hotel Primavera	1
Hotel El Pullman	7
Hotel San Martín	4
Pension Grau	13

RESTAURANTS

Café Amaretto	C
Asturias	H
Bar/Heladeria de Marco	L
El Mochica	G
Jugaria San Augustin	A
Pizzeria El Valentino	F
Polleria/Restaurant Plaza	D
Restaurant Cebaditas	B
Restaurant La Casona	H
Restaurant Romano	J
Restaurant Vegetariano El Sol	E
Sergio's Cevichería	K
Totem Pub	

Casinelli's Museum

Mansiche Stadium

Zoological Collection

Casa Bracamonte

Cathedral
PLAZA MAYOR

Casa de Los Leones

Iglesia Santa Clara

Casa Urquiaga

Iglesia de la Merced

Palacio Iturregui

Casa Orbegoso

La Casa de la Emancipacion

Central Market

Museo de Arqueología

Monastery & Church of El Carmen

Mercado Mayorista

0   200 m

easy; going north towards Huanchaco and Chan Chan, the best places to start from are beside the stalls near the Mansiche Stadium, or from the Petro Peru filling station at the start of the Panamerican Highway. Going south, your best bet is the big service station at the junction where the Panamerican Highway heads towards Moche and Chimbote.

Accommodation

The majority of Trujillo's **hotels** are within a few blocks of the central Plaza Mayor: most of them are to the south, but a number of reasonable ones are to be found along Jirón Pizarro, Independencia and San Martín. However, many people prefer to stay out of the city centre, at the nearby beach resort of Huanchaco (see p.296).

Budget

Hostal Colón, Colón 568 (☎044/234545). A pleasant place with simple rooms, with or without private bath. ②–③.

Hostal Monterrey, Avenida Los Incas 256 (☎044/241673). One of the more basic hostals in Trujillo, with simple small rooms and shared bathrooms, all a bit run-down; nevertheless, the staff are helpful. ②.

Hostal Oscar, Jirón Orbegoso 172 (☎044/257033). Cheap, with small, very simple rooms, though with private bath. Reasonably clean and central but security might be an issue. ②.

Hotel Americano, Jirón Pizarro 765 (☎044/241361). A superb old building with around 120 rooms. Plenty of character but a bit shabby, and the rooms aren't spotless. This is a favourite with travellers, not least because it's friendly and good value, especially if you get one of the rooms with a view over Jirón Pizarro. ②.

Hotel Internacional, Bolivar 646 (☎044/245392). Located in a fairly central and grand old building, with clean if very basic rooms. It's good value but not that comfortable; some rooms have toilets but no showers, while a few have full bathrooms. ②.

Pension Grau. Good central location, basic but clean and with some private bathrooms. ②.

Moderate

Hosteria Recreo, Calle Estete 647 (☎044/246991). A very comfortable hotel with its own restaurant and friendly service. ④.

Hosteria El Sol, Los Brillantes 224 (☎044/231933). Built in the shape of a Bavarian castle, it's slightly out of the way but has good rooms with private bath. ③.

Hotel San Martín, San Martín 743–749 (☎044/235700, fax 252311). Lots of decent rooms in a large, relatively modern though tired-looking building. Good service, and all rooms have private bath. ④.

Expensive

Casa Milla, Jirón Independencia 618 (☎044/291133, fax 292532). An attractive, central place, where they speak some English, plus there's a patio and cafetería. Rooms are fine and have TV. ⑤.

Hostal Portada del Sol, Avenida 28 de Julio 140 (☎044/245346). Some 5 or 6 blocks from the main plaza, it has modern rooms with TVs, private baths, laundry and restaurant. ⑦.

Hotel Continental, Gamarra 663 (☎044/241607, fax 249881). Plain but centrally located and popular with Peruvian business types. Rooms are clean with private bath and TV, and hot water is available. Breakfast is included. ⑤.

Hotel Libertador, Jirón Independencia 485 (☎044/232741, fax 235641, *www.libertador.com.pe*). Formerly the *Hotel de Turistas*, this place is particularly grand, with excellent service and a superb restaurant renowned for its *criolla* dishes. The large, plush rooms have all mod cons. ⑦.

Hotel Primavera, Avenida Nicolas de Pierola 872 (☎044/231915). Located close to the Panamerican Highway, this concrete building lacks style but offers air-conditioned comfort, large clean rooms and good service. ⑤.

Hotel El Pullman, Pizarro 833 (☎ & fax 044/203624, *pullmanhotel@ots.com.pe*). One of the city centre's newest and nicest hotels, it is cool and plush with solar water heating, good restaurant and bar plus all modern conveniences. ⑤.

The City

From the graceful colonial mansions and Baroque churches at its heart, Trujillo's grid system gives way to commercial buildings, light industry and shantytown suburbs, before thinning out into rich sugar-cane fields that stretch far into the neighbouring Chicama Valley. At the city's centre is its dominating force – the university **La Libertad**, founded by Bolivar in 1824, and surrounded by elegant, Spanish-style streets, lined with ancient green ficus trees and overhung by long wooden-railed balconies. **Gamarra** is the main commercial street, dominated by ugly, modern, brick and glass buildings, shops, hotels and restaurants. The other main street, older and more attractive, is **Jirón Pizarro**, where much of the city's nightlife can be experienced and which has been pedestrianized from block 8 to the pleasant **Plazuela El Recreo**. Life for most Trujillanos still revolves around the old town, centred on **Plaza Mayor** and bounded roughly by San Martín, Ayacucho, Almagro and Colón.

In addition to the city's many **churches**, Trujillo is renowned for its **colonial houses**, most of which are in good repair and are still in use today. These should generally be visited in the mornings (Mon–Fri), since many of them have other uses at other times of day; some are commercial banks and some are simply closed in the afternoons.

Around Plaza Mayor

Commissioned and built by Miguel de Estete, Trujillo's **Plaza Mayor** (also known as the Plaza de Armas) is packed with sharp-witted shoe-shine boys around the central statue – the *Heroes of the Wars of Independence*, created by a German sculptor. Although the plaza is sinking noticeably year by year, subsidence doesn't seem to have affected the two colonial mansions that front it, both of which have been tastefully restored. The **Casa Bracamonte**, Jirón Independencia 441, is closed to visitors but has some interesting cast ironwork around its patio windows, while the **Casa Urquiaga** (also known as Casa Calonge), Jirón Pizarro 446 (Mon–Fri 9am–1pm; free), said to be the house where Bolivar stayed when visiting Trujillo, is home to some first-class Rococo-style furniture and a fine collection of ancient ceramics.

Plaza Mayor is also home to the city's **Cathedral** (daily 6–9am & 5–9pm; free), built in the mid-seventeenth century, then rebuilt the following century after earthquake damage. Known locally as the Basilica Menor, it's plain by Peruvian standards but houses some colourful Baroque sculptures and a handful of paintings by the Quiteña school (a style of painting that originated in eighteenth-century Quito). Inside the cathedral, a **museum** (daily 8am–2pm; $2) exhibits a range of mainly eighteenth- and nineteenth-century religious paintings and sculptures.

Just behind the plaza at San Martín 368, is a **zoological collection** (9am–1pm; $0.3), full of dozens of bizarre stuffed animals from the coastal desert and Andean regions.

From Plaza Mayor to the Central Market

Just off the plaza, the **Iglesia de La Merced**, Jirón Pizarro 550 (daily 8am–7pm; free), built in 1636, is worth a look for its unique priceless Rococo organ, plus its attractive gardens. Around the corner from here, between the Plaza de Armas and the Central Market, stands the most impressive of Trujillo's colonial houses – the **Casa Orbegoso**, at Jirón Orbegoso 553 (Mon–Sat 9am–4pm; free). This old mansion was the home of Orbegoso, former president of Peru, and houses displays of period furniture, glass and silverware amid very refined decor. Born into one of the city's wealthiest founding families, Orbegoso fought for independence and became president of the republic in 1833 with the support of the liberal faction. However, he proved to be the most ineffective of all Peruvian leaders, resented for his aristocratic bearing by the *mestiso* generals, and from 1833 to 1839, although still officially president, he lost control of the country – first in civil war, then to the invited Bolivian army, and finally to a combined rebel and Chilean force. Orbegoso's rule marked a low point in his country's history, and he disappeared from the political scene to return here to his mansion in disgrace. Today even his family home has been invaded – although it's still in perfect condition and outstandingly elegant, the main rooms around the courtyard have been converted into offices.

Trujillo's main market, the **Central Market**, is 100m from here, on the corner of Ayacucho and Gamarra. As well as selling most essentials, such as juices, food and clothing, it has an interesting line in herbal stalls and healing or magical items – known locally as the Mercado de los Brujos (the Witches' Market) – not to mention unionized shoe-cleaners. There's a second, much busier market, the Mercado Mayorista, further out, on Avenida Costa Rica in the southeast corner of town.

From the market, head along Ayacucho until you reach the the the corner of Junin, and you'll find University's **Museo de Arqueología y Antropología**, Jirón Junin 602, (Mon 9.30–2pm, Tues–Fri 3–7pm, Sat & Sun 9.30–4pm; $1), which is pretty good, specializing in ceramics, early metallurgy, textiles and featherwork.

East of Plaza Mayor

East of the plaza, on the corner of Jirón Pizarro and Gamarra, stands another of Trujillo's impressive mansions, **La Casa de la Emancipacion**, at Jirón Pizarro 610 (Mon–Sat 10am–8pm; free), known as a republican rather than a colonial house. The building was remodelled in the mid-nineteenth century by the priest Pedro Madalengoitia (which is why it is also sometimes known as the Casa Madalengoitia), and is now head office of the Banco Continental. The main courtyard and entrance demonstrate a symmetrical and austere design, while the wide gallery has some impressive marble flooring. Inside, there are a couple of interesting late eighteenth-century murals depicting peasant life, and paintings or historical photographs are usually exhibited in at least one of its rooms.

Further down the same road, two blocks east of the Plaza Mayor, is the **Palacio Iturregui**, Jirón Pizarro 688 (Mon–Fri 8.30–10.30am; free), a striking mid-nineteenth-century mansion. The highlight of the building is its courtyard in pseudo classical style, with tall columns and an open roof. The courtyard is encircled by superb galleries, and gives a wonderful view of the blue desert sky. Built by the army general Don Juan Manuel de Iturregui y Aguilarte, the house is used today by the city's *Central Club*, who allow visitors to look round some of the interior rooms. The courtyard can be seen at any time of the day, just by popping your head inside.

At the eastern end of Jirón Pizarro, five blocks from the Plaza Mayor, there's a small but attractive square known as the restored **Plazuela El Recreo** where, under the shade of some vast 130-year-old ficus trees, a number of bars and foodstalls present a focus for young couples in the evenings. This little plaza was, and still is, an *estanque de agua* – a water distribution point – built during colonial days, but tapping into more ancient irrigation works.

A couple of minutes' walk south from the Plazuela, on the corner of Colón and Bolivar, stands the most stunning of the city's religious buildings, the **Monastery and Church of El Carmen** (Mon–Sat 9am–1pm; $1). Built in 1759 but damaged by earthquake in the same year, its two brick towers were then reconstructed of bamboo for safety. The church was also built above ground level to save it from El Niño's periodic flooding. Inside you can see the single domed nave, with exquisite altars and a fine gold-leaf pulpit. The processional and recreational cloisters, both boasting fine vaulted arches and painted wooden columns, give access to the **Pinacoteca** (picture gallery), where Flemish works include a *Last Supper* (1625) by Otto van Veen, one of Rubens' teachers. There are also some interesting figures carved from *huamanga* stone and a room showing the process of restoring oil paintings.

Northeast of Plaza Mayor

Jirón Independencia runs northeast from the Plaza Mayor and boasts a couple of minor attractions. Just one block from the plaza, at Independencia 628, stands the **Casa de Los Leones** (Mon–Fri 9am–6pm; free), a colonial mansion that's larger and more labyrinthine than it looks from the outside and which holds exhibitions of photos, art, culture, crafts and wildlife. A few minutes further along Jirón Independencia, on the corner of Junin, you'll find the most architecturally interesting of the city's churches, the **Iglesia Santa Clara** (daily 8am–9pm; free). Make sure you look inside its chapel to see the altar covered with gold-leaf and the pulpit with high relief carvings.

Casinelli's Museum

The most curious museum in Trujillo is set in the middle of the road, just north of the large Mansiche Stadium, in the basement of the Petro Peru filling station at Nicolas de Pierola 601. **Casinelli's Museum**, (Mon–Sat 9.30–1pm & 3.30–6.30pm, Sun 10am–1pm & 4–6pm; $1.50), is stuffed with pottery and artefacts spanning thousands of years, collected from local *huaqueros*. The Salinar, Viru, Mochica, Chimu, Nasca, Huari, Recuay and Inca cultures are all represented, with highlights including **Mochica pots** with graphic images of daily life, people, animals and anthropomorphic deities, and two ceramic men, one with a fine beard, the other, with a moustache, sitting in a lotus position. Señor Casinelli sometimes shows his visitors around personally and will point out his exquisite range of **Chimu silver artefacts**, including a tiny set of panpipes. Also of note are the owl figures, symbols for magic and witchcraft, and the perfectly represented **Salinar houses**, which give you an idea of the ancient culture much more successfully than any site restoration.

Eating and drinking

There's no shortage of **bars** or **restaurants** in Trujillo. Some of the liveliest are along Jirón Independencia, Jirón Pizarro, Bolivar and Ayacucho, to the east of Plaza Mayor. A speciality of the city is good, reasonably priced **seafood**, which is probably best appreciated on the beach at the nearby resorts of Buenos Aires or Huanchaco (see p.296).

Asturias, Jirón Pizarro 739. Tasty fruit juices plus alchoholic drinks, meals and snacks at this busy coffee bar.

Bar/Heladeria de Marco, Jirón Pizarro 725. A flashy, Italian-style ice-cream parlour cum bar. A limited menu is also offered.

Le Boulevard, Pizarro 844. A pleasant lunchtime spot in the pedestrianized section of Pizarro, with a nice little patio and very good, inexpensive, set-lunches.

Café Amaretto, Gamarra 368. Great coffee and good cakes, breakfast and snacks.

Chifa Vegetariano "La Nueva Eden", Pizarro 687. Chinese health-food and vegetarian dishes with yoghurts, *quinoa* with *maca*; it has cheap set lunches.

Govinda, Jirón Estete 361. A solid health-food and vegetarian restaurant, known for its great fruits salads and yogurts.

Jugaria San Augustin, Jirón Pizarro 691 (☎044/259591). An excellent juice bar offering an enormous choice of tropical drinks, beers and sandwich snacks in a plastic but friendly environment that's very popular with Trujillo's youth. Will take phone orders and deliver to your door.

El Mochica, Bolivar 462. A superb, smart restaurant that offers reasonably priced seafood and exquisite *criolla* dishes.

Pizzeria El Valentino, Jirón Orbegoso 224. Opposite the Ciné Primavera, this flashy place serves fast Italian food of all kinds and gets very busy at weekends.

Polleria/Restaurant Plaza, Jirón Pizarro 501. A very popular roast chicken joint on the corner of the Plaza Mayor; the fried potatoes aren't bad either.

Restaurant Cebaditas, Junin 336. A simple little place, excellent for snacks, sandwiches and breakfasts.

Restaurant La Casona, San Martín 677. A modest, quiet restaurant serving local dishes; excellent lunches at fantastically cheap prices.

Restaurant Romano, Jirón Pizarro 747 (☎044/252251). Small, friendly restaurant specializing in good Peruvian and Italian dishes. Good-sized portions, and exceptional value with its *economico familia* or *turistico* set menu, but it gets very busy in the evenings, so reservations are advised.

Restaurant Vegetariano El Sol, Jirón Pizarro 660. Open for lunches and evening meals, *El Sol* serves simple vegetarian fare at reasonable prices, mostly based on rice, alfalfa, soya, maize and fresh vegetables. It's particularly popular with locals at lunchtime.

Sergio's Cevicheria, Independencia 925. A small and surprisingly cheap seafood restaurant that serves very fresh food and is excellent value for lunch.

Totem Pub, Jirón Pizarro 922. A pleasant restaurant-cum-bar on the Plazuela El Recreo, with a romantic atmosphere in the evenings. It serves good drinks and freshly grilled kebabs, accompanied by taped music from the likes of Frank Sinatra.

Nightlife and entertainment

Trujillo boasts a fairly active **nightlife**, a characteristic of this being its **drive-in disco pubs**, mostly associated with motels, and located around the outskirts of the city; try *Pussy Cat*, Avenida Nicolas de Pierola 716, or *La Herradura*, Avenida Teodoro Valcarcel 1268, both in Urbino Primavera. Occasional exhibitions, performances and films are shown at some of the **cultural centres**: the Instituto Nacional de Cultura is at Independencia 572, half a block from the plaza, behind the cathedral; the Instituto Cultural Peruano-Norte-Americano at Avenida Venezuela 125, Urbino El Recreo (☎044/245832); and the Alliance Française at San Martín 862.

Clubs and peñas

Burbujas Night Club, Avenida Tupac Amaru 340, Urbino H. Grande. A classic drinking and dancing club, popular with most age groups.

La Canana, San Martín 791. A highly popular restaurant-*peña* serving excellent meals, a great atmosphere and good danceable shows that generally start after 10pm and carry on into the early hours.

Disco Pub Kuntur Huasi, Pasaje Santa Luisa, Lote 3, Urbino Santa Leonor. On the outskirts of the city, this is one of the best places for international pop, though it occasionally hosts salsa evenings too.

Disco Pub Las Tinajas, corner of Pizarro and Almagro. Very central and lively at weekends. Plays rock and pop.

Peña El Estribo, San Martín 810. A large, lively dance and music venue with great weekend shows of coastal folklore and *musica negra*.

Peña/Restaurant El Maizal, Jirón Pizarro 654. A rustic, lively and informal atmosphere. Great *criolla* food and music, plus Peruvian *musica negra* most Friday and Saturday nights.

Cinema

In the 1950s, the writer George Woodcock noted, after a few nights at local cinemas, that the uninhibited and infectious response of Trujillo's movie-going audiences "made one realize how much the use of sound in films had turned audiences into silent spectators instead of vociferous participants". Trujillo's audiences are still undaunted by the technology of the screen: however boring the film, you always leave with the feeling that you've shared a performance. It may not be as strong now as in the 1950s, with videos and satellite TV having taken their toll, but Trujillo still offers a better range of films than in most Peruvian towns.

The vast majority of cinemas show **original language films**, with Spanish subtitles, so you should be able to watch any mainstream US movie. There are several **cinemas** clustered within a few blocks of the Plaza Mayor, showing anything from old classics to Hollywood's latest. The most popular downtown esablishment is the Ciné Primavera, on Jirón Orbegoso, one and a half blocks northwest of the Plaza Mayor.

Fiestas

Trujillo's main **fiestas** turn the town into even more of a relaxed playground than it is normally, with the **marinera** dance featuring prominently in most celebrations. This regional dance originated in Trujillo and is accompanied by a combination of Andalucian, African and Aboriginal music played on the *cajón* (rhythm box) and guitar. Previously known as the Chilena, it was patriotically renamed such during the 1879 war with Chile to honour the feats of Admiral Grau against the Chilean forces. Energetic and very sexual – traditionally seen as the seduction by a servant man of an elegant, upper-class woman – the *marinera* involves dancers holding handkerchiefs above their heads and skilfully prancing around each other. You'll see it performed in *peñas* all over the country but rarely with the same spirit and conviction as here in Trujillo. The last week in January is the main **Festival de la Marinera**, with a National Marinera Competition taking place during the entire month.

The main **religious fiestas** are in October and December, with October 17 seeing the procession of El Señor de Los Milagros, and the first two weeks of December being devoted to the patron saint of Huanchaco – another good excuse for wild parties in this beach resort. February, as everywhere, is **Carnival** time with even more *marinera* dancing evenings taking place throughout Trujillo.

Listings

Airlines Aero Condor, Bolivar 613 (☎044/256794 or 232865); Aero Continente, Avenida España 307 (☎044/244592); Air Lider (☎044/204470); TANS, Avenida España 106 (☎044/255722); VARIG, Independencia 533 (☎044/254763). All flights out of Trujillo airport are liable to $4 airport tax.

Banks and exchange Banco de Credito, Jirón Gamarra 562; Banco Wiese, Jirón Pizarro 314; Banco Latino, Jirón Gamarra 574; Banco de La Nacion, Jirón Almagro 297. America Tours, Jirón Pizarro 470, Casa de Cambio, Jirón Pizarro 336, or the Casa de Cambios Martelli, Jirón Bolivar 665, give the best rates in town for dollars cash, or try the *cambistas* on the corner of Jirón Pizarro and Gamarra, or on the Plaza Mayor.

Buses Alto Chicama, José Sabogal 305, Urbino Palermo (☎044/203659), for Chicama; Cruz del Sur, Amazonas 437 (☎044/261801), for all coastal destinations, Cajamarca and Huancayo; El Aguilla, Nicaragua 220 (☎044/243211), for Lima, Chimbote and Huaraz; El Dorado, Avenida D. Carrion 1164 (☎044/242880), for Chiclayo, Tumbes and Lima; Leon del Norte, Avenida Manseriche 413 (☎044/260906), for Piura Mercurio, Avenida Mansiche 413 (☎044/250906), for Cajamarca; Movi, Avenida America del Sur 3959 (☎044/286538), for Huaraz and Lima; Ormeño, Avenida Ejercito 233 (☎044/259782), for the coast and international destinations; Palacios, Avenida España 1005 (☎044/233902), for Huamachuco; San Pedro Express, Avenida Manseriche 375, for Chepen; San Pedro Express, Avenida Mansiche 335 (☎044/528039) for the north coast; Trans Negreiros, Zarumilla 199, Prolognacion C. Vallejo (☎044/210725), for Huamachuco; Trans Sanchez Lopez, 1 block from Negreiros, for Huamachuco; Transportes Guadalupe, Avenida Manseriche 331 (☎044/246019), for Tarapoto, Yurimaguas and Juanjui; Turismo Chimbote, Jirón Nicaragua 194–198 (☎044/245546), for Chimbote, Casma, Huaraz and Caraz; Turismo Expreso Chan Chan, Orbegoso 308 (☎044/234111), for Chimbote, Lima and Huaraz; Vulcano, Avenida Daniel Carrion 140 (☎044/235847), for Chiclayo, Cajamarca and Piura;

Consulates UK, Avenida Jirón Nazareth 312 (☎044/235548).

Courier service DHL, Jirón Pizarro 356 (☎044/220916, fax 203689).

Hospital Bolivar 350 (☎044/245281).

Internet facilities A 24hr service is available at Interc@ll, Zepita 728 (☎044/246465); otherwise, there's also El Navigante, San Martín 622 and Web@café, Orbegoso 529.

Laundry The two best places in town are Luxor, Jirón Grau 637, and Lavanderia El Carmen, Pizarro 759.

Post Independencia 286. Mon–Sat 8am–6pm.

Shopping For traditional musical instruments, try the shop at Jirón Pizarro 721; for *artesania* go to Los Tallanes, San Martín 455; for films and photographic equipment, try Foto Para Ti, Jirón Pizarro 645 or Foto Expres Trujillo, Pizarro 582.

Telephones Telefónica del Peru, Bolivar 658 (daily 7am–11pm). There's also a telephone and fax office at Bolivar 611.

Tour operators and guides Most companies offer tours to Chan Chan for $15–20 (including the site museum, Huaca Arco Iris and Huaca Esmeralda), and to *huacas* del Sol and Luna from $8. For Chicama sites, expect to pay $20 plus. Recommended operators include Condor Travel, Jirón Pizarro 576 (☎044/254763); Guia Tours, Independencia 580 (☎044/245170, fax 246353); Trujillo Tours, Diego de Almagro 301 (☎044/233091, fax 257518, *ttours@pol.com.pe*); and America Tours, Jirón Pizarro 470 (☎044/235182 or 247049). Good, English-speaking guides for Trujillo and around include Bravo Díaz Clara (☎044/243347); Takanga López Edith (☎044/222705); Soto Ríos José (☎044/251489); and Fajardo Linares Luis (☎044/248917)

Tourist complaints ☎ & fax 044/204146.

Tourist Police ☎044/200200.

Western Union Pizarro 203 (☎044/257501, fax 243913).

Around Trujillo

The closest of the coastal resorts to Trujillo is the beachfront *barrio* of **Buenos Aires**, a five-kilometre stretch of sand southwest of Trujillo – very popular with locals and constantly pounded by surf. Like other coastal resorts, its seafood restaurants are an attraction, though it doesn't have as much style or life as Huanchaco or Las Delicias.

Two kilometres south of Trujillo, after crossing the Río Moche's estuary, you come to the settlements of **MOCHE** and **Las Delicias**, both within an easy bus ride of the Huaca del Sol and Huaca de la Luna (see p.304). Moche is a small village, slightly inland from the ocean and some 4km south of the city, blessed with several **restaurants** serving freshly prepared seafood, including one of the best in the whole Trujillo region, the *Restaurant Mochica* (try the *shamba*, a substantial soup). Close by, Las Delicias, 5km south of Trujillo, boasts a fine long beach and a handful of restaurants. For **accommodation**, the clean and pleasant *Hostal Janita*, Calle Montero 340 (☎044/485286; ③), in Las Delicias, overlooks the sea and is the only choice at the moment. Las Delicias' main claim to fame is that the *curandero* El Tuno once lived at Lambayeque 18, right on the beach. By arrangement with his family there you can witness the fascinating diagnostic healing sessions that are now practiced by El Tuno's apprentices, often involving rubbing a live guinea pig over the patient's body, then splitting the animal open; its innards are removed for inspection while the heart is still pumping. It might not do much for your appetite, but apparently reveals the patient's problems and he or she is sent away with a mix of healing herbs. To reach Las Delicias from Trujillo, catch the direct **bus** marked "Delicias" from the corner of Avenida Moche and Avenida Los Incas.

Huanchaco

Although no longer exactly a tropical paradise, **HUANCHACO** is still a beautiful and relatively peaceful resort, 12km west, or twenty minutes by bus, from Trujillo. Until the

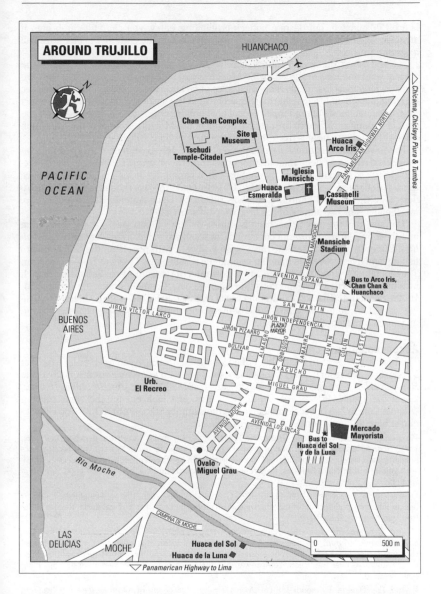

AROUND TRUJILLO

HUANCHACO

Chan Chan Complex
Site Museum
Tschudi Temple-Citadel

PACIFIC OCEAN

BUENOS AIRES

Huaca Arco Iris

Iglesia Mansiche

Huaca Esmeralda

Cassinelli Museum

Mansiche Stadium

Bus to Arco Iris, Chan Chan & Huanchaco

JIRÓN VÍCTOR LARCO

SAN MARTIN

JIRÓN INDEPENDENCIA
PLAZA MAYOR
JIRÓN PIZARRO
BOLIVAR

AVENIDA ESPAÑA

ALMAGRO
ORBEGOSO
GAMARRA
JUNIN
COLON
CALLE ESTETE

Urb. El Recreo

AYACUCHO

MIGUEL GRAU

AVENIDA LOS INCAS

AVENIDA MOCHE

Ovalo Miguel Grau

Río Moche

LAS DELICIAS

MOCHE

CAMPIÑA DE MOCHE

Mercado Mayorista

Bus to Huaca del Sol y de la Luna

Huaca del Sol
Huaca de la Luna

0   500 m

△ *Panamerican Highway to Lima*

△ *Chicama, Chiclayo Piura & Tumbes*

PANAMERICAN HIGHWAY NORTE

AVENIDA MANSICHE

1970s, Huanchaco was a tiny fishing village, quiet and little-known to tourists. Today it is one of the fastest growing settlements in Peru, and is slowly spreading back towards Trujillo as half-finished adobe houses, concrete hotels and streets appear beside the main road. However, it still makes an excellent base for visiting many of the sites around the region, in particular the nearby ruins of Chan Chan, and the development hasn't entirely diminished its intrinsic fishing village appeal. There is a long jetty which is a bit dilapidated, but despite notices prohibiting entry, you can still climb onto it alongside fishermen jostling for the best positions. Just at the entry to the pier is a small *artesania* **market**.

Stacked along the back of the beach, you'll see rows of *caballitos del mar* – the ancient seagoing rafts designed by the Mochicas and still used by locals today. They are constructed out of four cigar-shaped bundles of *tortora* reeds, tied together into an arc tapering at each end. The fishermen kneel or sit at the stern and paddle, using the surf for occasional bursts of motion. The local boat builders here are the last who know the craft of making *caballitos* to the original design of the Mochicas. Some of the fishermen offer 10–15 minute **boat trips** ($1.50) on the back of their *caballitos*.

The town's only historical sight is the old, square **Iglesia Soroco**, perched high on the coastal cliffs – a fifteen-minute walk uphill from the seafront. Claiming to be the second church in Peru to be built by the Spanish, it sprang up in 1540 on top of a pre-Inca temple dedicated to the idol of the Golden Fish; the earthquakes of 1619–1670 destroyed the original church and it was rebuilt by Dean Antonio de Saavedra, who, incidentally was also author of the first World Water Code.

The best time to visit Huanchaco is during its June **fiesta** week, at the end of the month when a large *tortora* raft comes ashore accompanied by a smaller flotilla of *caballitos*. But even out of season the town is always lively, with people on the beach, others fishing, and a few travellers hanging around the restaurants. To get to Huanchaco from Trujillo, take the frequent orange-and-yellow **microbus** from Avenida España, or pick up a bus or colectivo from the Petro Peru garage over Casinelli's museum (see p.293). On the way out to Huanchaco the bus travels the whole length of Calle Estete (returning via Colón); to get back into the city there's normally a line of microbuses picking up passengers from the waterfront.

Accommodation

The town is well served by the kind of accommodation range you'd normally expect at a popular beach resort. Many families also put people up in **private rooms**, such as the *Hospedaje Las Gaviotas*, Los Pinos 535 (☎044/461858; ②) or the *Hospedaje Jimenez*, Colon 378 (☎044/461844; ②). To locate others, just look out for the signs reading "Alquila Cuarto" on houses, particularly in the summer (Dec–Feb). It's also possible to **camp** here, in the grounds of *Hostal Bracamonte*.

Hospedaje Familiar La Casa Suiza, Los Pinos 451 (☎044/461285, *casasuiza.peru@mailcity.com*, *http://come.to/casasuiza.peru*). One of the best and most popular budget places with backpackers in Huanchaco, with a range of different rooms (some with bath) and a lovely rooftop terrace. There are laundry and Internet facilities, they rent out body boards and surfboards, and good English is spoken. ②.

Hostal Ancla, La Rivera 101 (☎044/461030). Overlooking the beach, this well-established lodging has an interesting collection of old photos and memorabilia in its bar and cafetería. Rooms at the front can be noisy, though. ③.

Hostal Bracamonte, Los Olivos 503 (☎044/461162, fax 461266, *hostalbracamonte@yahoo.com*, *http://welcome.to/hostal_bracamonte*). A lovely complex of different-sized chalets with solar-heated showers. It also has a pool, a games room, Internet access, a laundry, a good restaurant, and terraces with views over the ocean. You can camp in the grounds for $3 per person or $12 including tent rental. ④.

Hostal Las Brisas, Raimondi 146 (☎044/461186, fax 244605, *lasbrisas@hotmail.com*). Clean and modern, though somewhat lacking in character. ③.

Hostal Caballitos de Tortora, La Ribera 219 (☎ & fax 044/461004). Right on the seafront, this place offers rooms with ocean views plus cheaper less panoramic options. There's also a small pool, garden, cafetería and sun terraces. ④–⑤.

Hostal Los Esteros, Avenida Larco 618 (☎044/461272). An attractive place with sea views. The tidy rooms all come with private bath and hot water. ③.

Hostal Solange, Los Ficus 484 (no tel). This is a small family run hostal where you can do your own cooking if you wish; just 2 blocks from the beach. ②.

Huanchaco Hostal, Victor Larco 287 (☎044/461272). Good-value, comfortable hostal with pleasant gardens, a cafetería and a small pool. The service is excellent and all rooms have TV and private bath. One of the entrances faces the sea, and the other onto the tiny but attractive Plaza de Armas. ④.

Eating and nightlife

There are seafood **restaurants** all along the front in Huanchaco, one or two of them with verandas extending to the beach. Not surprisingly seafood is the local speciality, including excellent crab, and you can often see women and children up to their waists in the sea collecting shellfish. The fishermen can also be seen returning usually around 3–4pm on their *caballitos*. A kilo of fresh fish can be bought for just $1–2, but the catches these days aren't huge.

Anyone looking for **nightlife** should check out *Sun Kella Bar*, at the southern end of the beach. Alternatively there's the *Sunset Pub*, on la Ribera, just one block from the pier with a balcony overlooking the sea. Both are popular hangouts with young locals and visiting surfers.

Club Colonial, at Grau 272 (☎044/461015). A beautifully restored colonial house with paintings, old photos and fine stained-glass work adorning it. The food is sumptuous, with an extensive menu of traditional dishes, but it's not cheap. The garden is the residence of some penguins and a couple of rare Tumbes crocodiles.

Huanchaco Beach Restaurant, Malecón Larco 602. Very tasty fish dishes, and excellent views across the ocean and up to the cliff-top Iglesia Soroco.

El Pescadito, block 3 of Calle Grau. One of the smaller, less expensive restaurants located in the backstreets of Huanchaco; the views are not so good as those from along the seafront, but the seafood is just as fresh and well prepared.

Restaurant El Caribe, on Atahualpa. Just around the corner from the seafront to the north of the pier, this place has great *ceviche* and is very popular with locals.

Restaurant El Erizo, Avenida La Rivera 269. Virtually on the beach, and within a stone's throw of the pier, *El Erizo* ("the sea urchin"– a local delicacy and reputedly a strong aphrodisiac) serves good seafood dishes, including excellent crab and sea urchin if you're lucky.

Restaurant Estrella Marina, Malecón Larco 594. Very good, fresh *ceviche* served in a seafront restaurant, which often plays loud salsa music and is popular with locals.

Restaurant Miramar, Avenida Victor Larco 525. Just north of the pier, this is another good seafood restaurant with great views of the pier and ocean.

Restaurant Pisagua, on the seafront. Just to the north of the pier, serving excellent *ceviche*.

The Chan Chan complex

The ruined city of **CHAN CHAN** stretches across a large sector of the Moche Valley, beginning almost as soon as you leave Trujillo on the Huanchaco road, and ending just a couple of kilometres from Huanchaco. A huge complex, it needs only a little imagination to raise the weathered mud walls to their original grandeur, and picture the highly civilized, rule-bound society, where slaves carried produce back and forth while artisans and courtiers walked the streets slowly, stopping only to give orders or chat with people of similar status. On certain days there were great processions through the streets, the priests setting the pace, loaded down with gold, silver jewellery, and dressed in brightly coloured feather cloaks as they made their way to one of the principal temples along roads lined by ten-metre-high adobe walls.

Chan Chan was the capital city of the **Chimu Empire**, an urban civilization which appeared on the Peruvian coast around 1100 AD. The Chimu-built cities and towns throughout the region stretch from Tumbes in the north to as far south as Paramonga. Their cities were always extremely elaborate with large, flat-topped buildings for the

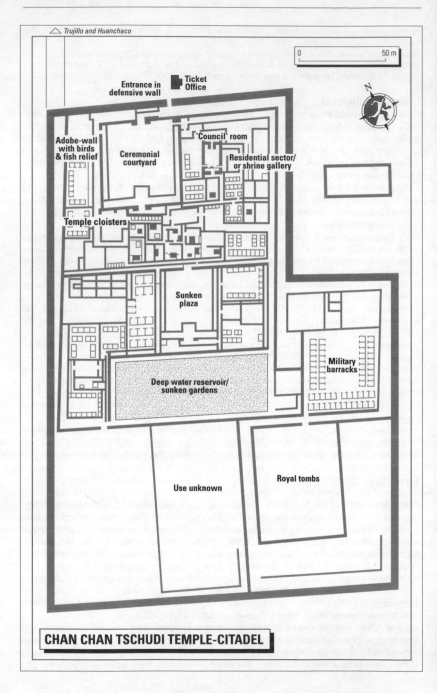

△ Trujillo and Huanchaco

0   50 m

N

Entrance in
defensive wall

Ticket
Office

'Council' room

Adobe-wall
with birds
& fish relief

Ceremonial
courtyard

Residential sector/
or shrine gallery

Temple cloisters

Sunken
plaza

Military
barracks

Deep water reservoir/
sunken gardens

Use unknown

Royal tombs

CHAN CHAN TSCHUDI TEMPLE-CITADEL

nobility and intricately decorated adobe pyramids serving as temples. The Chimu artwork, particularly ceramics, was essentially mass produced, with quantity being much more important than quality. Food was rationally distributed among the population that grew it, while nobles involved themselves in politics, religion and commerce – bringing treasures such as gold, silver, gems, skins and plumes into the heart of the empire.

Recognized as fine goldsmiths by the Incas, the Chimu used to panel their temples with gold and cultivate palace gardens where the plants and animals were made from precious metals. Even the city walls were brightly painted, and the style of architecture and relief decoration is sometimes ascribed to the fact that the Mochica migrated from Central America into this area, bringing with them knowledge and ideas from a more advanced civilization, like the Maya. But although this is possible, it's not really necessary to look beyond Peru for inspiration and ingenuity, as the Chimu inherited ideas and techniques from a host of previous cultures along the coast, and, most importantly, adapted the techniques from many generations of trial and experiment in irrigating the Moche Valley. In the desert, access to a regular water supply was critical in the development of an urban civilization like that of Chan Chan, whose very existence depended on extracting water not only from the Río Moche but also, via a complicated system of canals and aqueducts, from the neighbouring Chicama Valley.

With no written records, the **origins of Chan Chan** are mere conjecture, but there are two local legends. According to one, the city was founded by **Taycanamu**, who arrived by boat with his royal fleet; after establishing an empire, he left his son, Si-Um, in command and then disappeared into the western horizon. The other legend has it that Chan Chan was inspired by an original creator deity of the same name, a dragon who made the sun and the moon and whose earthly manifestation is a rainbow – sign of life and energy, evidence of the serpent's body. Whatever the impulse behind Chan Chan, it remains one of the world's marvels and, in its heyday, was one of the largest pre-Columbian cities in the Americas. By 1450, when the Chimu empire stretched from the Río Zarumilla in the north to the Río Chancay in the south and covered around 40,000 square kilometers, Chan Chan was the centre of a chain of provincial capitals. These were gradually incorporated into the Inca Empire between 1460 and 1480.

The events leading to the city's demise are better documented than those pertaining to its birth: in the 1470s Tupac Yupanqui led the Inca armies down from the mountains in the east and cut off the aqueducts supplying Chan Chan with its vital water supply. After lengthy discussions, the Chimu council managed to persuade its leader against going out to fight the Incas, knowing full well that resistance would be met with brutality, and surrender with peaceful takeover. The Chimu were quickly deprived of their chieftains, many of them taken to Cusco (along with the highly skilled metallurgists) to be indoctrinated into Inca ways. These turbanned aliens from the coast must have been a strange sight there – strutting around Cusco's cold stone streets with huge golden nose ornaments dangling over their chins. Sixty years later when the first Spaniards rode through Chan Chan they found only a ghost town full of dust and legend, as the Incas had left to fight their civil war and the remaining Chimu were too dispirited to organize any significant urban life.

The ruins

Of the three main sectors specifically opened up for exploration, the **Tschudi temple-citadel** is the largest and most frequently visited. Not far from Tschudi, **La Huaca Esmeralda** displays different features, being a ceremonial or ritual pyramid rather than a citadel. The third sector, the **Huaca El Dragon** (or **Arco Iris**), on the other side of this enormous ruined city, was similar in function to Esmeralda but has a unique design which has been restored with relish if not historical perfection. Entrance to all three sectors of the ruins is included on the same **ticket**, which is valid for two days (daily 8.30am–6pm, last entry 4pm, closed Christmas week & May; $3, including the Museo de Sitio). Although you can visit each sector separately, there is only one **ticket office**, at the entrance to the Tschudi temple-citadel, where there's also a small interpretative centre, toilets, cafetería and souvenirs, plus a full-size model of a Chimu warrior in full regalia. **Guided tours** are easily arranged (around $5), and are worthwhile provided the guides can speak English or you can understand Spanish; guides usually hang around at Tschudi, but will take you round the *huacas* too. In addition, there's a **Museo de Sitio** (daily 9am–4pm; $1, or included on the main ticket), a few hundred metres before the entrance to the Tschudi temple-citadel. The museum uses models, ceramics and other archeological finds to reconstruct an image of what life must have been like here almost one thousand years ago in the hot but irrigated desert before Trujillo was built.

THE TSCHUDI TEMPLE-CITADEL

The Tschudi temple-citadel is the best place to get an idea of what Chan Chan must have been like, even though it's now stuck out in the desert among high ruined walls, dusty streets, gateways, decrepit dwellings and open graves. Only a few hundred metres from the ocean at Buenos Aires beach, and bordered by corn fields, this was once the imperial capital and power base from which the Chimu elite ruled their massive domain. To reach Tschudi take the orange-and-yellow Huanchaco-bound **microbus** from Avenida Mansiche in the city, getting off at the concrete Tschudi/Chan Chan signpost about 2km beyond the outer suburbs. From here, just follow the track to the left of the road for ten to fifteen minutes until you see the ticket office (on the left), next to the high defensive walls around the inner temple-citadel.

All the inner courtyards and passages of the **citadel** are laid out according to a well-ordered and preordained plan – and all have been carefully restored and enclosed. Very little is known about the history or even the daily life of those who lived in Tschudi; unfortunately, the Chimu didn't leave such a graphic record as the earlier Mochica culture, whose temples were built on the other side of the Moche Valley. But following the marked route around the citadel through a maze of corridors, chambers, and amazingly large plazas, you will begin to form your own picture of this ancient civilization. In a courtyard just past the entrance gateway, some 24 seats are set into niches at regular intervals along the walls, and you can experience an unusual acoustic effect. This area is now roped off, but by sitting in one niche and whispering to someone in another, this simply designed **council room** amplifies all sounds, and the niches sounding like they're connected by adobe intercoms.

Beyond the citadel extend acres of ruins, untended and, according to the locals, dangerous for foreigners – some certainly have been robbed after wandering off alone. This is frustrating, since Tschudi is thought to have been the central citadel among a group of at least ten complexes, each divided by wide streets and clearly forming separate wards or sacred urban areas. Like Tschudi, each of these distinct sectors was designed along typical Chimu lines – with a rectangular layout and divided by enormous trapezoidal walls. As you walk from the road towards Tschudi, you will pass at least four other citadels, though it's difficult to make them out clearly: **Bandelier** and **Uhle** to the left, **Velarde** and **Laberinto** on the right. Each of these individual complexes was most likely based around a royal clan with its own retinues.

LA HUACA ESMERALDA

One of the most beautiful and possibly the most venerated of Chimu temples, **La Huaca Esmeralda** lies in ruins a couple of kilometres before Tschudi, just off the main Trujillo to Huanchaco road. Unlike Tschudi, the *huaca*, or sacred temple, is on the very edge of town, stuck between the outer suburbs and the first cornfields. To get here, catch the orange-and-yellow Huanchaco-bound **microbus** from Avenida Mansiche and get off at the colonial church of **San Salvador de Mansiche,** then follow the path along the right-hand side of the church for three blocks (through the modern *barrio* Mansiche), until you reach the *huaca.*

La Huaca Esmeralda (Emerald Temple) was built in the twelfth or early thirteenth century – at about the same time as the Tschudi temple-citadel – and is one of the most important of the *huacas* scattered around Trujillo. It was uncovered only in 1923, but its adobe walls and decorations were severely damaged in the freak rains of 1925 and 1983. Today, because of the rains, you can only just make out what must have been an impressive multicoloured **facade.** All the relief work on the adobe walls is original, and, unusually, shows marine-related motifs including friezes of fishing nets containing swimming fishes, waves, a flying pelican, a sea otter and frequent repetitive patterns of geometrical arabesques. The *huaca* has an unusually complex structure, with two main platforms, a number of surrounding walls, and several sloping pathways giving access to each section. From the top platform, which was obviously a place of worship and possibly also the cover to a royal tomb, you can see across the valley to the graveyards of Chan Chan, out to sea, over the cultivated fields around the site, and into the primitive brick factory next door. Only some shells and *chaquiras* (stone and coral necklaces) were found when the *huaca* was officially dug out some years ago, long after centuries of *huaqueros* (treasure hunters) had exhausted its more valuable goods.

You may still be offered strings of *chaquiras* to buy, by the people of **Mansiche,** a small settlement next to the *huaca.* Apparently direct descendants of the Chan Chan people, the Mansiche locals claim that the stone and coral necklaces came from remote graves in the Chan Chan complex, though this is highly unlikely.

LA HUACA ARCO IRIS

La Huaca Arco Iris – the Rainbow Temple – is the most fully restored ruin of the Chan Chan complex. Its site is just to the left of the Panamerican Highway, about 4km north of Trujillo in the middle of the urban district of La Esperanza. To get there, take the regular Comité 19 red-and-blue **microbus** from the centre of Trujillo, or across the road from the Petro Peru filling station. Get off the bus at the blue concrete sign on the side of the main road, and you'll see the *huaca,* surrounded by a tall wall and set back a few hundred metres to the west of the highway.

The *huaca,* which flourished under the Chimu between the twelfth and fourteenth centuries, consists of two tiers. The **first tier** is made up of fourteen rectangular chambers, possibly used for storing corn and precious metals for ritual purposes. A path slopes up to the **second tier,** a flat-topped platform used as a ceremonial area where sacrifices were held and the gods spoke. From here there is a wide view over the valley, towards the ocean, Trujillo, and the city of Chan Chan.

Several interpretations have been made of the **central motif,** which is repeated throughout the *huaca* – some consider it a dragon, some a centipede, and some a rainbow. The dragon and the rainbow need not exclude one another, as both can represent the creator divinity, though local legend has it that the rainbow is the protector of creation and, in particular, fertility and fecundity. The centipede, however, is a fairly widespread motif (notably on the Nasca ceramics), though its original meaning seems to have been lost. Most of the main **temple inner walls** have been restored, and they are covered with the re-created central motif. Originally, the outer walls were decorated in the same way, with identical friezes cut into the adobe, in a design that looks like a multi-legged serpent arching over two lizard-type beings. Each of the serpents' heads, one at either end of the arc, seems to be biting the cap (or tip of the head) off a humanoid figure.

Huaca del Sol and Huaca de la Luna

Five kilometres south of Trujillo beside the Río Moche, in a barren desert landscape, are two temples that really bring ancient Peru to life. The stunning **Huaca del Sol** (Temple of the Sun) is the largest adobe structure in the Americas, and easily the most impressive of the many pyramids on the Peruvian coast. Its twin, **La Huaca de la Luna** (Temple of the Moon), is smaller, but more complex and brilliantly frescoed.

Although very much associated with the Moche culture and nation (100–600AD), there is evidence of earlier occupation at these sites, dating back 2000 years to the Salinar and Gallinazo cultures, indicated by constructions underlying the *huacas*. It continued to be held in high regard after the collapse of the Moche culture, with signs of Wari, Chimu and Inca offerings here demonstrating a continued importance. The latest theory suggests that these *huacas* were mainly ceremonial centres, separated physically by a large graveyard and an associated urban settlement. Finds in this intermediate zone have so far revealed some fine structures, plus pottery workshops and storehouses.

Collectively known as the Huacas del Moche, these sites make a fine day's outing and shouldn't be missed. To get there from Trujillo take one of the golden coloured **colectivos**, which run every thirty minutes from the corner of Suarez with Los Incas, near the market, to the base of Huaca del Sol (\$.3).

Huaca del Sol

The **Huaca del Sol** (9am–4pm; \$1.50) was built by the Mochica around 500 AD, and, although very weathered, its pyramid edges still slope at a sharp 77 degrees to the horizon. Although still massive, what you see today is about thirty percent of the original construction. The largest part of the structure, which you come to first, is made up of a lower-level base platform. On top of this is the demolished stump of a four-sided, stepped pyramid, surmounted about 50m above the desert by a ceremonial platform. From the top of the ceremonial platform you can see clearly how the Río Moche was diverted by

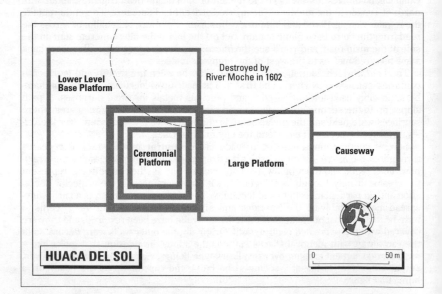

Lower Level Base Platform

Destroyed by River Moche in 1602

Ceremonial Platform

Large Platform

Causeway

HUACA DEL SOL

0   50 m

the Spanish in 1602, in order to erode the *huaca* and find treasure. They were quite successful at washing away a large section but found precious little, except adobe bricks. The first scientific, archeological work here was done by Max Uhle in the early 1900s; he discovered more than 3400 objects and ceramics, most of which were taken to the University of California at Berkeley museum. New excavations may begin here soon.

Estimates of the pyramid's **brickwork** vary, but it is reckoned to contain somewhere between fifty million and 140 million adobe blocks, each of which was marked in any one of a hundred different ways – probably with the maker's distinguishing signs. It must have required a massively well-organized labour supply to put together – Calancha, a Spanish historian, wrote that it was built in three days by two hundred thousand Indians, though three days might actually mean three stages. How the Mochica priests and architects decided on the shape of the *huaca* is unknown, but if you look from the main road at its form against the silhouette of Cerro Blanco, there is a remarkable similarity between the two, and if you look at the *huaca* sideways from the vantage point of the Huaca de la Luna, it has the same general outline as the hills behind.

Huaca de la Luna

Clinging to the bottom of Cerro Blanco, just 500m from the Sun Temple, is another Mochica edifice, the **Huaca de la Luna** (9am–4pm; $1.50), a ritual and ceremonial centre that was constructed and utilized in the same era as the Huaca del Sol. What you see today is only part of an older complex of interior rooms built over six centuries, a maze of interconnected patios, some covered and adorned lavishly with painted friezes. The friezes are still the most striking feature of the site, rhomboid in shape and dominated by an anthropomorphic face surrounded by symbols representing nature spirits, such as the ray fish (symbol of water), pelicans (symbol of air), and serpent (symbol of earth). Twisting, flame-like rays emanating from it and its feline fangs and boggle-eyes are stylizations dating back to the early Chavín cult, and it's similar to the face of the Winged Decapitator, an image associated with Sipán but known to the Moche as **Ai-Apaec**, master of life and death. The god that kept the human world in order, he has been frequently linked with human sacrifice, and in 1995, archeologists found 42 skeletons of sacrificial victims here. Sediment found in their graves indicates that these sacrifices took place during an El Niño weather phenomenon, something that would have threatened the economic and political stability of the nation. Ceramics dug up from the vast graveyard that extends between the two *huacas* and around the base of Cerro Blanco suggest that this might have also been a site for a cult of the dead, while the fact that it is built at the foot of the sacred Cerro Blanco and incorporates some rocky outcrops into one of the patios suggests that this may also have been somewhere honouring *apus*, or mountain spirits.

Behind the *huaca* are some frescoed rooms, discovered by a grave robber in the early 1990s, displaying murals with up to seven colours (mostly reds and blues). The most famous of these paintings has been called *The Rebellion of the Artefacts* because, as is fairly common on Mochica ceramics, all sorts of objects are depicted attacking human beings, getting their revenge, or rebelling. Unfortunately, this is not presently accessible.

The Chicama Valley

Chicama is the next valley north of the Río Moche, 35km from Trujillo and the heart of its fertile plain. In the Mochica and Chimu eras the Río Chicama was connected to the fields of Chan Chan by a vast system of canals and aqueducts over 90km long, and the remains of this irrigation system, fortresses, and other evidence from over six thousand years of residence can still be seen around the valley.

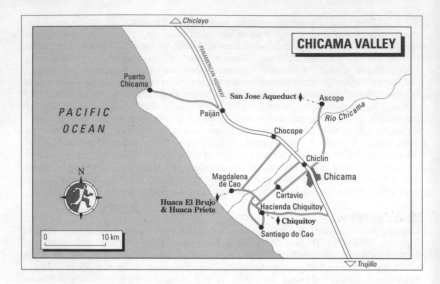

Today, however, the region appears as a single enormous sugar-cane field, although in fact it's divided among a number of large sugar-producing co-operatives, originally family-owned **haciendas** that were redistributed during the military government's agrarian reforms in 1969. The sugar cane was first brought to Peru from India by the Spaniards and quickly took root as the region's main crop. Until early this century, the haciendas were connected with Trujillo by a British-operated rail line, whose lumbering old wagons used to rumble down to Trujillo full of molasses and return loaded with crude oil; they were, incidentally, never washed between loads. Although the region still produces nearly half of Peru's sugar, it has diversified within the last thirty years or so to specialize in wheat, rice and mechanical engineering as well. The haciendas are also renowned for the breeding of **caballos de paso** – horses reared to compete in dressage and trotting contests – a long-established sport that's still popular with Peruvian high society. The isolated seaside village of **Puerto Chicama**, 65km north of Trujillo, offers rather more laid-back opportunities to surf.

Like the Moche, the Chicama Valley is full of **huacas** and ancient sites – **Huaca El Brujo**, **La Huaca Prieta**, **Chiquitoy** and **Ascope** – and the locals have a long tradition as *huaqueros*, or grave robbers. Rumours abound about vile deaths from asphyxiation, a slow process sometimes lasting days, for anyone who ventures into a tomb: "*Le llamó la huaca*", they say – "the *huaca* called him".

Getting there

There are buses and colectivos to the sites in the Chicama Valley, but it is a good day-trip from Trujillo and many people prefer to go on a **guided tour** from there (see p.296), or to hire a **taxi** with driver and guide for the day ($20–30). The whole valley is also well served by local colectivos, and although they have no fixed timetables, it's quite easy to get from one village or site to another. If you want to go by public transport from Trujillo, catch one of the **buses** marked "Puerto Chicama", "Paiján", "Chicama" or "Ascope", which leave every thirty minutes from opposite Casinelli's Museum, or from the Mercado Mayorista (where most of them start). To get to El Brujo or Chiquitoy from Trujillo, take a bus to Chocope from the Chicago bus terminal

Typical beach along the Peruvian Pacific coast

Sealions, Ballestas Islands

Iguana, beside the Río Amazonas

Chan Chan temple city ruins, Trujillo

Plaza de Armas, Arequipa

The Panamerican Highway as it runs through coastal desert

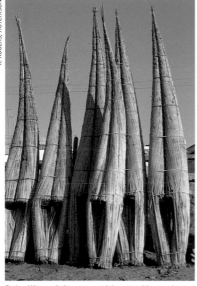

Caballitos del mar reed boats, Huanchaco   Aymara dancers at wedding celebrations

Huandoy glacier, in the Cordillera Blanca

Amarakaeri baby, Peruvian Amazon

Yellow-ridged toucan

Lago Sandoval, in the Amazon

on Avenida America Sur, then pick up a colectivo from Chocope. For Chiquitoy to Cartavio and for El Brujo to Magdalena de Cao, from where it's a 8km walk to the site, colectivos run every 10–15 minutes to Cartavio ($0.5) and every thirty minutes to Magdalena ($0.25) from Chocope. If you can't face the walk, you can usually find taxis in Chicama or Chocope who'll take you to the sites for a few dollars per person.

Huaca El Brujo

Fifty kilometres north of Trujillo, the **Huaca El Brujo** (Mon, Sat & Sun; free), whose name means "Temple or Tomb of the Wizard", is a Mochica-built complex of associated adobe temple ruins incorporating the Huaca Cao Viejo to the south and the Huaca Cortada, slightly to the north. Most of the recent discoveries have been made in Huaca Cao Viejo, and investigations at the site mean that the whole place is closed to the public, although tour operators sometimes secure permission to visit. Otherwise, there's a good exhibition about the site at the Museo de la Nacion in Lima.

Large adobe temple constructions dominate the actual site, some of whose walls are adorned with figures in high relief and painted murals, discovered here as recently as 1990. On the top, third layer of the Huaca Cortado there's a painted character, with startled eyes, a sacrificial knife in one hand and a decapitated head in the other, decapitation apparently being common practice amongst the Mochica. Below this executioner figure, on the second level, there is a long line or chain or figures looking forward, holding hands and wearing headdresses. The Huaca Cao Viejo is a larger pyramid, topped by a ceremonial platform some 30m high, 90m wide and 100m long, and clearly of great significance to the Mochica ceremonial world and religious hierarchy.

To get to the *huaca*, you have to pass through the nearby village of **Magdalena de Cao**, home to an attractive colonial church, and the ideal place to sample *chicha del año*, an extra-strong form of maize beer brewed in the valley.

La Huaca Prieta

Quite literally a heap of rubbish, **La Huaca Prieta** sits right next to the Playa El Brujo at the edge of the ocean, ten minutes' walk west of the Huaca El Brujo. It may be a garbage dump but it is one that has been accumulating rubbish for some 6500 years, and is crowded with evidence and clues about the evolution of culture and human activity on this coast. This small, dark hill is about 12m high and owes its coloration to thousands of years of decomposing organic remains. On the top, there are signs of subterranean dwellings, long since excavated by archeologists Larco Hoyle and Junius Bird.

Chiquitoy

The well-preserved ruins of **Chiquitoy** (daily 8am–6pm) are rarely visited – stuck out as they are on an empty desert plain unconnected by any road. To reach the site from Hacienda Chiquitoy, take the right track which leads off into the desert (ask at the hacienda, if you're not sure about which track); follow this across the flat *pampa* for 5–6km (an hour's walk) and you can't miss the site. Chiquitoy's **ruins** consist of a temple complex with a three-tiered pyramid – very Mayan-like – in front of a walled, rectangular sector. There is evidence of some dwellings and a large courtyard, too, though little is known about its history. Chiquitoy is well worth the walk, if only because of its location and the good condition of the pyramid.

Ascope

Twelve kilometres northeast of Chicama, on a small road off to the right of the Panamerican Highway, the settlement of **ASCOPE** is principally of interest for its great earthen **aqueduct**, just a couple of kilometres away. Standing 15m high and still an impressive site even after 1400 years, it carried water across the mouth of this dry valley up until 1925, when it was damaged by heavy rains. The *San Jose*, as the aqueduct is known, was one of a series of canal bridges traversing ravines along the La Cumbre irrigation system, which joined the Moche and Chicama valleys during the Mochica and Chimu periods.

Puerto Chicama

PUERTO CHICAMA, known also as MALABRIGO, 13km northwest of Paijan, is a small fishing village which used to serve as a port for the sugar haciendas, but is now a **surfers'** centre, with the best surfing waves on Peru's pacific coast. If you want a **place to stay**, try the *Hostal El Hombre*, the traditional surfers' place, or *Hostal Chicama*, both with a nice sea view.

CAJAMARCA AND THE NORTHERN CIRCUIT

Whether or not you are planning to venture to the eastern sites or the rainforest, **Cajamarca** is worth a visit. A *sierra* town, it is second only to Cusco in the grace of its architecture, the drama of its mountain scenery, and, above all, the friendliness of its people. From Trujillo there are two main routes, each exciting and spectacular. The speediest way is to head up the coast via **Pacasmayo**, then turn inland along a relatively new paved road which follows the wide Río Jequetepeque valley, passing small settlements and terraced fields. Regular buses and colectivos from Trujillo do this route, completing the journey in about eight hours. A slower route (2 days at least) is by bus along the old road, currently in a poor state of repair, from Trujillo through **Huamachuco** and **Cajabamba**. Adventurous travellers may choose to make a loop, known as the **Northern Circuit**, going up by one route and returning by the other.

The proud and historic city of Cajamarca remains relatively unaffected by the tourist trade, despite its intrinsic appeal as the place where Pizarro captured and eventually killed the Inca emperor, Atahualpa. It also makes a very dramatic starting point for visiting the ruins of **Chachapoyas** and the jungle regions around **Tarapoto** and **Yurimaguas**, although most people choose the faster and more frequented route from Chiclayo via Olmos and Jaen to access this region.

Cajamarca and around

An attractive city that's almost Mediterranean in appearance, **CAJAMARCA**, at more than 2700m above sea level, squats below high mountains in a neat valley. Despite the altitude, the city's climate is surprisingly pleasant, with daytime temperatures ranging from 6°C to 23°C; the rainy season is between the months of December and March. The city's stone-based architecture reflects the cold nights up here – charming as it all is, with elaborate stone filigree mansions, churches and old Baroque facades, most buildings are actually quite austere in appearance. Cajamarca is never overcrowded with tourists; in fact, it's unusual to see any foreign travellers outside of the main season, June to September. The narrow streets are, however, usually thronging with locals going to and from the market or busy at their daily toil. However, all this may change as a result of the discovery of Peru's largest **gold mine** at nearby Yanacocha, in the hills to the west of the city, and another at Cerro Negro, which are likely to make a significant difference to both the economy and the look and feel of the city over at least the next few years, and problems with associated immigration and river pollution have already begun to manifest themselves.

Some history

The fertile Cajamarca basin was domesticated long before cows arrived to graze its pastures, or fences were erected to parcel up the flat valley floor. As far back as 1000 BC it was occupied by well-organized tribal cultures, the earliest sign of the Chavín culture's influence on the northern mountains. The existing sites, scattered all about this region, are evidence of advanced civilizations capable of producing elaborate stone constructions without hard metal tools, and reveal permanent settlement from the **Chavín** era right through until the arrival of the conquering **Inca** army in the 1460s. Then, and over the next seventy years, Cajamarca developed into an important provincial garrison town, evidently much favoured by Inca emperors as a stopover on their way along the Royal Highway between Cusco and Quito. With its hot springs, it proved a convenient spot for rest and recuperation after the frequent Inca battles with "barbarians" in the eastern forests. The city was endowed with sun temples and sumptuous palaces, and their presence must have been felt even when the supreme Lord was over 1000km away to the south, paying homage to the ancestors in the capital of his empire.

Atahualpa, the last Inca Lord, was in Cajamarca in late 1532, relaxing at the hot springs, when news came of **Pizarro** dragging his 62 horsemen and 106 foot soldiers high up into the mountains. Atahualpa's spies and runners kept him well informed of the Spaniards' movement, and he could quite easily have destroyed the small band of weary aliens in one of the rocky passes to the west of Cajamarca. Instead he waited patiently until Friday, November 15, when a dishevelled group entered the silent streets of the deserted Inca city. For the first time, Pizarro saw Atahualpa's camp, with its sea of cotton tents, and an army of men and long spears. Estimates varied, but there were between thirty thousand and eighty thousand Inca warriors, outnumbering the Spaniards by some two hundred to one.

Pizarro was planning his coup along the same lines that had been so successful for Cortés in Mexico: he would capture Atahualpa and use him to control the realm. The plaza in Cajamarca was perfect for the following day's operation, as it was surrounded by long, low buildings on three sides, so Pizarro stationed his men there. The next morning, nothing happened and Pizarro became anxious. In the afternoon, however, Atahualpa's army began to move in a ceremonial procession, slowly making their way across the plain towards the city of Cajamarca. Tension mounted in the Spanish camp. As the Indians came closer they could be heard singing a graceful lament and their dazzlingly bright clothes could be made out.

Leaving most of his troops outside on the plain, Atahualpa entered with some five thousand men, unarmed except for small battleaxes, slings and pebble pouches. He was being carried by eighty noblemen in an ornate litter – its wooden poles covered in silver, the floor and walls with gold and brilliantly coloured parrot feathers. The emperor himself was poised on a small stool, dressed richly with a crown placed upon his head and a thick string of magnificent emeralds around his aristocratic neck. Understandably bewildered to see no bearded men and not one horse in sight, he shouted – "Where are they?"

A moment later, the Dominican friar, Vicente de Valverde, came out into the plaza; with the minimum of reverence to one he considered a heathen in league with the devil, he invited Atahualpa to dine at Pizarro's table. The Lord Inca declined the offer, saying that he wouldn't move until the Spanish returned all the objects they had already stolen from his people. The friar handed Atahualpa his Bible and began a Christian discourse which no one within earshot could understand. After examining this strange object Atahualpa threw it on the floor, visibly angered. Vicente de Valverde, horrified at such a sacrilege, hurried back to shelter screaming – "Come out! Come out, Christians! Come at these enemy dogs who reject the things of God".

Two cannons signalled the start of what quickly became a massacre. The Spanish horsemen flew at the five thousand Indians, hacking their way through flesh to overturn the litter and capture the emperor. Knocking down a two-metre-thick wall, many of the Inca troops fled onto the surrounding plain with the cavalry at their heels. The foot soldiers set about those left in the square with such speed and ferocity that in a short time most of them were killed. Not one Indian raised a weapon against the Spaniards.

To the Spanish, it was obvious why Atahualpa, an experienced battle leader, had led his men into such a transparent trap. He had underestimated his opponents, their crazy ambitions, and their technological superiority – steel swords, muskets, cannons, and horse power. Perhaps the Inca Lord knew differently, however; perhaps the oracles had warned him that even if he defeated Pizarro others would follow, maybe even more ruthless, and subjugate his people. Whatever the explanation, it must surely be one of the world's most horrific massacres of indigenous people, and it represents a bloody beginning to Cajamarca's colonial history.

Arrival and information

Most people arrive in Cajamarca **by bus**, at one of the main bus company offices on the third block of Avenida Atahualpa (see Listings, p.315, for details), a major arterial route running almost directly east out of the city. If you **fly** into Cajamarca on the daily Aero Continente or Aero Condor flights from Lima ($90, a 2hr trip), or with Aero Condor on one of its daily connections with Trujillo and Chimbote, you'll arrive at the airport, 3km out of town along Avenida Arequipa. Buses leave from just outside the airport every twenty minutes or so for the market area, a couple of blocks below the Plaza de Armas in the city ($0.4). Alternatively, a motorcycle taxi there costs less than $1, or a taxi will be around $1.5–2.

Free maps and **tourist information** are available from the ITINCI office in the Belén Complex, on block 6 of Calle Belen (Mon–Fri 7.30am–1pm & 2.15–7pm; ☎044/822903). Alternatively, any of the tour companies listed on p.296 can give advice and information; Cumbe Mayo Tours and Cajamarca Tours are among the most helpful. Free tourist information is also available from the University office at Batan 289, next door to the museum.

Accommodation

Most of Cajamarca's **accommodation** is in the centre of the city, around the Plaza de Armas, although there are also some interesting options, such as the *Hostal Galvez* with its natural hot spring baths, a few kilometres away at Baños del Inca.

Hostal Los Balcones de La Recoleta, Amalia Puga 1050 (☎ & fax 044/823003, *hscajama@correo.dnet.com.pe*). A beautifully restored late nineteenth-century building with rooms set around a courtyard full of flowers. All rooms have private bath and some have period furniture. ③–④.

Hostal Cajamarca, Jirón Dos de Mayo 311 (☎044/821432). A pleasant colonial building set around an attractive courtyard with an excellent restaurant, *Los Faroles*; comfortable and reasonable value. ⑤.

Hostal Colonial Inn, Los Heroes 350 (☎ & fax 044/825300). Halfway between the town centre and the bus offices, in an old, brightly painted building. Rooms are without or with bath, plus it has a Chinese restaurant. ②–③.

Hostal El Dorado, Urrelo 908 (☎044/826641). Marginally the best of the large relatively modern hostals, but it doesn't have any balconies or terraces. ②.

Hostal Los Jazmines, Amazonas 775 (☎044/821812). A pleasant new hostal in a converted colonial house with a courtyard. Some rooms have private bath. ②.

Hostal La Merced, Chanchamayo 140 (☎044/822171). A small, friendly hostal which offers good value; clean, with private bath and access to laundry facilities. ②.

Hostal Plaza, Amalia Puga 669 (☎044/822058). Situated in a lovely old building on the Plaza de Armas, but a bit run down. It's still good value though, and rooms come with or without private bath. ③.

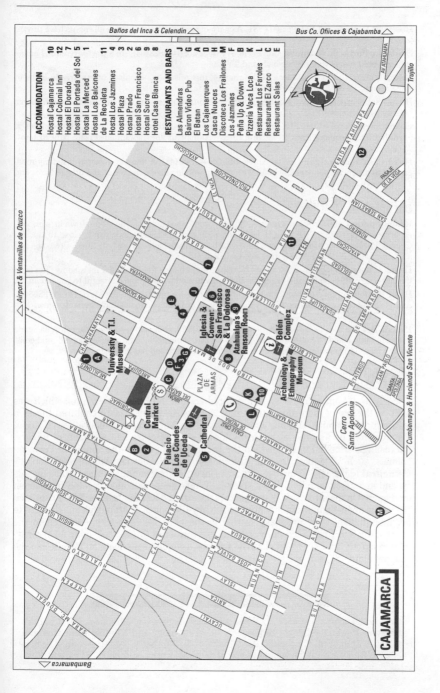

△ Baños del Inca & Celendin

Bus Co. Offices & Cajabamba △

ACCOMMODATION
Hostal Cajamarca	10
Hostal Colonial Inn	12
Hostal El Dorado	7
Hostal El Portada del Sol	5
Hostal La Merced	1
Hostal Los Balcones de La Recoleta	11
Hostal Los Jazmines	4
Hostal Plaza	3
Hostal Prado	2
Hostal San Francisco	6
Hostal Sucre	9
Hotel Casa Blanca	8

RESTAURANTS AND BARS
Las Almendras	J
Bairon Video Pub	G
El Batan	A
Los Cajamarques	D
Casca Nueces	H
Discoteca Los Frailones	M
Los Jazmines	F
Peña Up & Down	B
Pizzeria Vaca Loca	K
Restaurant Los Faroles	L
Restaurant El Zarco	C
Restaurant Salas	E

△ Airport & Ventanillas de Otuzco

△ Bambamarca

Trujillo ▽

Cumbemayo & Hacienda San Vicente ▽

University & T.I. Museum

Central Market

Palacio de Los Condes de Uceda

Cathedral

Iglesia & Convento San Francisco & La Dolorosa

Atahualpa's Ransom Room

Belén Complex

Archeology & Ethnography Museum

Cerro Santa Apolonia

PLAZA DE ARMAS

CAJAMARCA

Hostal El Portada del Sol, Pisagua 731. A charming colonial house, where all rooms have private bath. ④.

Hostal El Portal de Marques, Comercio 644 (☎ & fax 044/828464). An attractive colonial house with carpeted rooms with private bath and TV. ④.

Hostal Prado, La Mar 580. Close to the market, this relatively new place offers private baths in some rooms, TV in all; very good value. ③.

Hostal San Francisco, corner of Belen with Amazonas. Quite similar to the *Sucre*, though rooms have small balconies. ②.

Hostal Sucre, Amalia Puga 815. Just off the Plaza de Armas, this is one of the most basic places in town, but its redeeming features include many rooms with fine views, and private bath in most. ①–②.

Hotel Casa Blanca, Jirón Dos de Mayo 446 (☎044/822141). A fine old mansion tastefully modernized to produce a comfortable hotel with rickety wooden floors, hot water and private baths and TVs in every room. ④.

Out of town

Hostal Fundo Campero San Vicente, 3km towards Baños del Inca, then 2km down its signposted driveway (☎044/821237). An old hacienda with gardens and its own dairy, close to the Río Chonta. There are open fireplaces and all rooms have private bath and are fully fitted. Breakfast and a ride on their *caballos de paso* horses are included. ⑥.

Hostal Galvez, Manco Capac 552 (☎044/820203). Right beside the Baños del Inca, some 6km from the city centre, this comfortable hotel has thermally heated water pumped straight to your room. ⑤.

Hotel Hacienda San Vicente, 2km west of the city centre towards Cumbe Mayo (☎044/822644). A luxuriously renovated hacienda with the full range of facilities. Rooms have been designed with reference to Gaudi. ⑦.

Posada del Puruay, 5km north of the city (☎044/827928, *postmast@p-puruay.com.pe*). A hacienda converted into a luxury hotel-museum. All rooms have colonial furniture as well as full mod cons, but the place is especially notable for its ecological approach and has an organic garden. ⑧.

The City

The city is laid out in a grid system centred around the **Plaza de Armas**, which was built on the site of the original triangular courtyard where Pizarro captured the Inca leader Atahualpa in 1532. Four centuries on, it not surprisingly looks rather different, distinguished by its greenness, lovely low trees, fine grass and a wealth of topiary: interestingly trimmed bushes adorn the square, most cut into the shapes of Peruvian animals, such as llamas. On one side of the plaza is the late seventeenth-century **Cathedral** (daily 7am–7pm; free), its walls incorporating various pieces of Inca masonry, and its interior lifted only by a splendid Churrigueresque altar created by Spanish craftsmen. On the other side of the plaza is the strange-looking **Iglesia San Francisco** (Mon–Fri noon–6pm; free), in whose sanctuary the bones of Atahualpa are thought to lie, though they were originally buried in the church's cemetery. Attached to the church, the **San Francisco convent** houses a **museum** (Mon–Sat 3–6pm; $0.5) devoted to religious art – not as good as the one in Cusco, but still giving an insight into the colonial mind.

CAJAMARCA ENTRANCE TICKETS

One **ticket** allows entrance to three of Cajamarca's main attractions, **Atahualpa's Ransom Room**, the **Iglesia Belén**, and the **Archeology and Ethnography Museum** (all open Mon, Wed, Thurs & Fri 9am–1pm & 3–5.45pm, Sat & Sun 9am–1pm). The ticket costs $1.50, and can be bought at any of the three sites.

One of Cajamarca's unique features was that, until relatively recently, none of the churches had towers, in order to avoid the colonial tax rigidly imposed on "completed" religious buildings. The eighteenth-century chapel of **La Dolorosa** (Mon–Sat 10am–5pm; free), next to San Francisco, followed this pattern; it does, however, display some of Cajamarca's finest examples of stone filigree, both outside and in.

Around the Plaza de Armas

The most famous sight in town, the so-called **Atahualpa's Ransom Room** or El Cuarto del Rescate, at Amalia Puga 722, is the only Inca construction still standing in Cajamarca. Lying just off the Plaza de Armas, over the road from the Iglesia San Francisco, the Ransom Room can, however, be a little disappointing, especially if you've been waiting a long time to see it: it is simply a small rectangular room with Inca stonework in the back yard of a colonial building. It has long been claimed that this is the room which Atahualpa, as Pizarro's prisoner, promised to fill with gold in return for his freedom. It's true that the room fits the dimensions described in detail by the chroniclers, but this is unsurprising considering the symmetry and repetitiveness of Inca design, and historians are still in disagreement about whether this was just Atahualpa's prison cell, rather than the actual Ransom Room which was filled with precious metal. There is, however, a line drawn on the wall at the height it was supposed to be filled to, and you can also see the stone on which Atahualpa is thought to have been executed. The room's bare Inca masonry is notably poorer than that which you find around Cusco, and the trapezoidal doorway is a post-Conquest construction – probably Spanish rather than native. A far better example of colonial stonecraft can be seen at the **Palacio de los Condes de Uceda** (9am–4pm; free), Apurimac 719, one block the other side of the plaza, beyond the cathedral. This splendid colonial mansion has been taken over and conserved by the Banco de Credito, but you are free to wander in and have a look around.

A block north of the Plaza de Armas, in the streets around Apurimac, Amazonas, Arequipa and Leticia, you'll find Cajamarca's **Central Market** (daily 6am–5pm). Because Cajamarca is the regional centre for a vast and important area, its street market is one of the largest and most interesting in Peru – you can find almost anything here from slingshots, herbs and jungle medicines to exotic fruits and vegetables as well as the usual cheap plastic imports. It is generally a busy, friendly place, but beware of pickpockets.

Slightly further north along Arequipa is the **University Museum**, at no. 289 (Mon–Sat 7am–2.45pm; $0.35), chiefly of interest for its collections of ceramics, textiles and other objects spanning some three thousand years of culture in the Cajamarca basin. Look out for the work of Andres Zevallos, whose representations of local people is reminiscent of Ribera and whose landscapes are in the style of Matisse.

The Belén Complex

The **Belén Complex** of buildings, on Calle Belén, houses a variety of institutions, including two hospitals (in the lower part, the Hospital de Hombres has an exceptionally attractive stone-faced patio with fountains), a small medical museum, part of the university administration, the National Institute of Culture, and the **Iglesia Belén**, whose lavish interior boasts a tall cupola replete with oversized angels.

However, the most interesting part of the complex is the **Archeology and Ethnography Museum**. Located in what used to be the Hospital de Mujeres, over the road from the main complex, the museum displays ceramics and weavings from the region, as well as one or two objects that have been brought here from the jungle tribes to the east. Look out for the elaborate stone carvings on the archway at the entrance to the museum, which depict a locally infamous woman with four breasts and symbolize female fertility, and which date from the time when the building was a women's hospital.

Eating and drinking

Las Almendras, Amazonas 801. A small, friendly café that opens early for decent breakfasts.

El Batan, Del Batan 369. Set in a converted colonial building, there's an art gallery on the first floor and other paintings adorn the dining room wall. Good food, including local dishes that don't appear on the tourist menus, plus live music on Fridays and Saturdays.

Los Cajamarques, Amazonas 770. An upmarket restaurant whose walls are decorated with colonial paintings, weapons and other artefacts. The cooking is good, though portions aren't generous.

Casca Nueces, Amalia Puga 554. Very popular with locals for its delicious *humitas* (sweet maize-meal pasties) and large slices of cream cake.

Los Jazmines, Amazonas 775. Located in the hotel of the same name, it serves a good selection of snacks in an attractive courtyard.

Pizzeria Vaca Loca, San Martín 330. If you can stomach the name (Mad Cow), this busy place serves the town's best pizzas.

Restaurant Los Faroles, *Hostal Cajamarca*, Jirón Dos de Mayo 311. One of the best restaurants in town for *criolla* dishes, served in a quiet, plush atmosphere.

Restaurant Salas, Amalia Puga 637 (☎044/922876). A small restaurant with an old-fashioned atmosphere and good service. Similiar to *El Zarco*, but slightly more upmarket and with better food, particularly the breakfasts.

Restaurant El Zarco, Jirón del Batan 170 (☎044/923421). One of the few local cafés to stand out in Cajamarca, *El Zarco* is always heaving with locals. It plays a wide range of mostly Latin music and offers an enormous variety of tasty dishes (excellent trout). By no means upmarket, but its plethora of friendly red-coated waiters gives it a 1920s atmosphere.

Nightlife and entertainment

Nightlife isn't really Cajamarca's strong point, but it does have a few venues playing very vibrant local music, often incorporating violins as well as the more usual Andean instruments and guitars. During *fiesta* times in particular, you should have no trouble finding traditional music and dancing. At weekends, many of the **peñas** host good live music, and the clubbier **video pub** or **disco** scene is at its liveliest.

Discos and peñas

Bairon Video Pub, Amalia Puga 699, on the corner of the Plaza de Armas. Serves a good range of drinks to a background of ultraviolet lighting and a loud video screen blasting out pop and salsa hits. Upstairs is for couples only.

Discoteca Las Frailones, corner of Peru with Cruz de la Piedra, 6 blocks up Santa Apolonia from the plaza. All kinds of music and fantastic views over the city from the dance floor.

Peña Up & Down, Tarapaca 782. Something for everyone, with a *peña*, pub and disco on different floors, but the rooms are small and it can get quite crowded.

Peña Usha Usha, Amalia Puga 320. One of the best venues in town for *criolla* music, particularly at weekends.

Video Club Casablanca, Jirón Dos de Mayo 448, on the Plaza de Armas, above the *Hotel Casa Blanca*. Spacious and upmarket video bar offering karaoke. Gets very lively at weekends.

Fiestas

The best time to visit Cajamarca is during May or June for the **Festival of Corpus Christi**. Until eighty years ago this was the country's premier festival, coinciding with the traditional Inca Sun Festival and led by the elders of the Canachin family who were directly descended from local pre-Inca chieftains. The procession still attracts Indians from all around, but increasing commercialism is eating away at its traditional roots.

Nevertheless it's fun, and visited by relatively few non-Peruvian tourists, with plenty of parties, bullfights, *caballos de paso* meetings, and an interesting trade fair. The city's other main *fiesta* is **Cajamarca Day**, usually around February 11, which is celebrated with music, dancing, processions and fireworks.

Listings

Airlines Aero Continente, 2 de Mayo 574; Aero Condor, Jirón Dos de Mayo 323 (☎044/825674).

Banks and exchange Banco Continental, Jirón Tarapaca 725; Banco de Credito, Calle Comercio 679; Banco de la Nacion, Jirón Tarapaca 647; and Interbanc, Plaza de Armas. *Cambistas* hang out along Jirón del Batan, between *Restaurant El Zarco* and the Plaza de Armas.

Buses Cruz del Sur, Avenida Atahualpa 313; Empresa Arberia, Avenida Atahualpa 315 (☎044/826812); Expreso Cajamarca and Transportes Arberia, Atahualpa 290 (☎044/823337); Palacios, Independencia 350 (☎044/822600); El Cumbe, Independencia 270; Vulkano, Avenida Atahualpa 318 (☎044/821090); Transportes Atahualpa, Atahualpa 330; and Emtrafesa, Atahualpa 316.

Car rental Promotora Turistica, Manco Capac 1098, Baños del Inca (☎044/823149); and Cajamarca Tours, Jirón Dos de Mayo 323 (☎044/822813 or 822532).

Hospital Mario Urteaga 500 (☎044/822156).

Police Plaza Amalia Puga 807 (☎044/822944).

Post office Amazonas 443. Mon–Sat 8am–7pm.

Shopping For leathercraft, ceramics, woollens, jewellery and local hats (*sombreros de paja*) famous throughout Peru for their quality, try the inexpensive *artesania* stalls lining the steps up to the sanctuary on Cerro Santa Apolonia and also in block 7 of Calle Belen; or try Los Cajachitos, 2 de Mayo 379, Artesania, Jirón Dos de Mayo 381, La Tienda Amalia Puga 653, or Artesania Cajamarca at Amalia Puga 689. For photographic equipment, try Video Plaza Filmaciones, Amalia Puga 681, or Foto Andina, Amalia Puga 663.

Taxis Taxi Seguro, Avenida Independencia 373 (☎044/825103) are the best.

Telephone office Telefónica del Peru, on the Plaza de Armas at Calle Comercio. Daily 8am–10pm.

Tour and travel agents Aventura Cajamarca, Jirón Dos de Mayo 444 (☎044/822141); Cajamarca Tours, Jirón Dos de Mayo 323 (☎044/822813 or 825674); Cumbe Mayo Tours, Amalia Puga 635 (☎044/822938); Inca Bath Tours, Amalia Puga 807 (☎044/821828). Most tours cost about $6 for a long half day to local sites or $10–15 for a full day.

Around Cajamarca

Within a short distance of Cajamarca, there are several attractions which can easily be visited on a day-trip from the city. The closest is the **Cerro Santa Apolonia**, with its carved pre-Inca rocks, though these are not nearly as spectacular as the impressive aqueduct at **Cumbe Mayo**, or the ancient temple at **Kuntur Huasi**. However, the most popular trip from Cajamarca is to the steaming-hot thermal baths of **Baños del Inca**, just 5km from the city centre.

Cerro Santa Apolonia

A short stroll southeast from Cajamarca's Plaza de Armas, two blocks along Jirón 2 de Mayo, brings you to a path up the **Cerro Santa Apolonia**, a hill that overlooks the city and offers great views across the valley. At the top of the hill are the sensitively landscaped and terraced gardens known as the **Parque Ecologia** (daily 7am–6pm; $0.5), whose entrance is beside the Iglesia Santisima Virgen de Fatima, a small chapel at the top of the steps as you walk up from town. At the highest point in the park, originally a sacred spot, you'll find what is thought to have been a sacrificial stone dating from around 1000 BC. It is popularly known as the Inca's Throne, and offers a great overview

AROUND CAJAMARCA

of the valley. Just 2km southwest of the hill, along the road to Cumbe Mayo, is a further group of ruins – prominent among them an old pyramid, known to the Spanish as a temple of the sun, but now called by the locals Agua Tapada, "covered water". Quite possibly, there is a subterranean well below the site – they're not uncommon around here and it might initially have been a temple related to some form of water cult.

Baños del Inca and the Ventanillas de Otuzco

Many of the ruins around Cajamarca are related to water, in a way that seems both to honour it in a religious sense and use it in a practical way. A prime example of this is the **Baños del Inca** (daily 5am–8pm; $0.5–$1, depending on the type of bath), just 5km east of the city. It's a fifteen-minute bus ride from block 10 of Amazonas; local buses leave when full, usually every ten minutes or so ($0.25). As you approach you can see the steam rising from a low-lying set of buildings and hot pools. The baths, which date from pre-Inca times, are very popular with locals, though the whole place could do with a bit of a face-lift. Having said that, wallowing in the thermal waters is a glorious way to spend an afternoon. No doubt, it was even more wholesome some 470 years or so ago when Atahualpa camped here at the time of Pizarro's arrival, and it was from here that the Inca army marched to their doom.

An enjoyable two-hour walk from the baths, following the Río Chonta gently uphill to its source, brings you to another important site, the **Ventanillas de Otuzco** ($1). The

Ventanillas (Windows) are a huge pre-Inca necropolis where the dead chieftains of the Cajamarca culture were buried in niches, sometimes metres deep, cut by hand into the volcanic rock. If you don't fancy the walk, you can take one of the **colectivos** direct from Cajamarca to the Ventanillas ($0.25), which leave every twenty minutes or so from Arequipa, just below the Central Market.

Aylambo

A four-kilometre-walk along Avenida R. Castilla to the south of Cajamarca brings you to the small village of **Aylambo**, known for its ceramics workshops. You can buy a wide range of locally made earthenware products or even try your hand at making your own pottery. Special workshops are also laid on for children; ask at one of the tour agents in Cajamarca for details (see p.315). There are plenty of **buses** here from Avenida Independencia in Cajamarca (15min; $0.25), if you want to save your legs for the many trails which wind around the village through attractive forestry land.

Cumbe Mayo

Southwest of Cajamarca stands the ancient aqueduct and canal of **Cumbe Mayo**, stretching for over 1km in an isolated highland dale. Coming from Cajamarca just before you reach Cumbe Mayo, you'll see a odd natural rock formation, the Bosque de Piedras (Forest of Stones), where clumps of eroded limestone taper into thin, figure-like shapes – known locally as *los frailones* (the friars). A little further on, you'll see the well-preserved and skilfully constructed canal, built perhaps 1200 years before the Incas arrived here. The amount of meticulous effort which must have gone into this, cut as it is from solid rock with perfect right angles and precise geometric lines, suggests that it served a more ritual or religious function rather than being simply for irrigation purposes. In some places along the canal there are rocks cut into what look like tables, which were left by the quarrying of stones during the construction of the canal. Cumbe Mayo originally carried water from the Atlantic to the Pacific watershed (from the eastern to the western slopes of the Andes) via a complex system of canals and tunnels, many of which are still visible and in some cases operational. To the right-hand side of the aqueduct (with your back to Cajamarca) there is a large face-like rock on the hillside, with a man-made **cave** cut into it. This contains some three-thousand-year-old petroglyphs etched in typical Chavín style (you'll need a torch to see them) and dominated by the everpresent feline features.

There are no buses from Cajamarca, and only infrequent trucks, but you can **walk** here in two to four hours, starting from the back of the Cerro Santa Apolonia. Most people, though, take a **tour** ($6–8 per person, 9am–2pm) with one of the companies listed on p.315, or, if you really want to do it independently, hire a **taxi** for $5–8. The *Parador Turístico* (no phone; ②) in Cumbe Mayo has pleasant **rooms** and a small cafetería, so you can now stay out here without camping.

Kuntur Huasi

From Cumbe Mayo it's possible to walk the 90km to a second ancient site – **Kuntur Huasi** – in the upper part of the Río Jequetepeque valley, to the east of the Cajamarca Basin. This, however, takes three or four days, so you'll need a tent and food. Hilary and George Bradt's *Backpacking and Trekking in Peru and Bolivia* (see p.475) has a detailed description and sketch map of the route: you'll need this, or at least a survey **map** of the area since the site is not marked. If you can't face the walk, you can get on the Trujillo bus from Avenida Atahualpa in Cajamarca to Chilete, a small mining town about 50km along the paved road to Pacasmayo. Here, you need to change to a local bus (leaving every hour or so) to the village of **San Pablo** (with two small, basic hotels), from where it's just a short downhill walk to the ruins. The journey can take from two to five hours by public transport, so most people choose the easiest option – an **organized tour** from Cajamarca for $15–25 per person (see p.315).

Although Kuntur Huasi has lost what must once have been a magnificent temple, you can still make out a variation on Chavín designs carved onto its four stone monoliths. Apart from Chavín itself, this is the most important site in the northern Andes relating to the feline cult; golden ornaments and turquoise were found in graves here, but so far not enough work has been done to give a precise date to the site. The anthropomorphic carvings indicate differences in time, suggesting Kuntur Huasi was built during the late Chavín era, around 400 BC. Whatever its age, the pyramid is an imposing ruin amid quite exhilarating countryside.

South to Huamachuco and Gran Pajaten

It's a long and quite rough but rewarding journey south from Cajamarca to the small town of **Huamachuco**, jumping-off point for visiting the remote ruins of **Gran Pajaten**. The whole journey from Cajamarca to the ruins takes at least five days, and involves a combination of bus and hiking. To get to Huamachuco, take a Palacios **bus**, which leaves three times a week from Avenida Atahualpa in Cajamarca, for the five-hour ride to Cajabamba, where you need to change to a more local bus for the three-hour journey on to Huamachuco. Virgen del Rosario buses from Atahualpa 315 in Cajamarca offer the fastest direct service to Cajabamba; Transportes Atahualpa are good too, but they're en route from Lima and can sometimes be delayed arriving in Cajamarca. Both leave in the early afternoon, along with Transportes Dias, who also offer an evening service, but if you can do it by day you'll be rewarded by the spectacular views coming down from the green pastures of Cajamarca and across the almost tropical Condebamba valley before ascending to Cajabamba.

In **CAJABAMBA**, a small market town, the best **accommodation** is at the *Hostal Flores*, L. Pradon 137 (☎044/851086; ②), on the plaza, where the simple rooms have private bath and are set around a pleasant courtyard. For **eating**, try the *Restaurant Cajabambino II*, at Grau 1193, next to the market, which serves up tasty plates of local trout and chicken dishes. The *Café Grau*, on Grau, just before the plaza, offers excellent fruit salads and *alfajores*. All the **bus companies** are located within a block of the market; those running between Cajabamba and Huamachuco include Transportes Anita (the fastest) and Transportes Gran Turismo. Both leave at 4am from in front of the market for the three-hour journey along a poor road.

Huamachuco

Infamous in Peru as the site of the Peruvian army's last ditch stand against the Chilean conquerors back in 1879, **HUAMACHUCO**, at 3180m, is a fairly typical Andean market town, surrounded by partly forested hills and a patchwork of fields on steep slopes. The site of the battle is now largely covered by the small airport, while the large Plaza de Armas in the centre of town possesses an interesting colonial archway in one corner, which the Liberator Símon Bolivar once rode through. Now, however, it's flanked by the modern, rather ugly Cathedral.

From the plaza you can take a three-hour walk for about 6km to the dramatic circular pre-Inca fort of **Marca Huamachuco** (daily 6am–6pm; free), the main reason most travellers end up in this neck of the woods. On top of one of several mountains dominating the town, it's hard to get a taxi to take you there, although Alosio Rebaza, at D. Nicolau 100 (☎044/441488) will transport people in his 4x4 vehicle ($10 for up to 4, or $20 if you want him to wait for you). Some 3km long, the **ruins** date back to around 300 BC, when they probably began life as an important ceremonial centre, with additions between 600 and 800 AD. The fort was possibly adopted as an administrative outpost during the Huari-Tiahuanuco era (600–1100 AD), although it evidently maintained its independence from the powerful Chachapoyas nation, who lived in the high forested regions to the north and east of here (see p.320–324). An impressive, commanding and easily defended position, Marca Huamachuco is also protected by a massive eight-metre-high wall surrounding its more vulnerable approaches. The *convento* complex, which consists of five circular buildings of varying sizes towards the northern end of the hill, is a later construction and was possibly home to a pre-Inca elite ruler and his selected concubines; the largest building has been partially reconstructed. A guardian controls entry to the *convento* buildings and should be offered a small tip ($1 per person). An information sheet providing a plan of the site and some brief details is available from the Municipalidad in Huamachuco.

Practicalities

Of the **bus** companies, Gran Turismo pull in at Balta 790; Anita at San Martín 700; Palacios at Castilla 167; Negreiros at Suarez 721 (off Balta); Agreda at block 7 of Balta; and Sanchez Lopez at Balta 1030 (though their booking office is on the plaza. Air Lider, at the airport, offer daily **flights** to Trujillo and Huamachuco ($50 one way) in ten-seater planes.

For **accommodation**, try the *Hostal Huamachuco*, at Castilla 354 (☎044/441393; ②), near the Plaza de Armas, for rooms with or without bath in their old building with a courtyard. There's also the *Noche Buena* (③), on the plaza adjoining the Cathedral, which is modern, clean and has private bath and TV; slightly cheaper but just as good is *Hotel San José* (☎044/441044; ②) on the plaza, while the *Casa de Hospedaje Las Hortencias* (☎044/441049; ②), Castilla 130, has fairly basic rooms with bath in a friendly family house with a nice courtyard where you can lounge around. All get full during festival times when you should try to book in advance.

The best bets for food are the **restaurants** *El Karibe*, on the Plaza de Armas, which serves guinea pig and goat, and the place in *Las Hortencias* hotel, which serves a delicious *caldo de gallina* and a limited choice of other dishes. The *Café Venezia*, at San Martín 780, does great desserts and excellent coffee made from beans fresh from the Marañon valley, while the *Bar Michi Wasi*, at San Ramon 461 on the plaza, is small but trendy, and with a nice atmosphere it's definitely the place to press locals for information about the local attractions. For **nightlife** there's *Cachimil*, Esquinas 5, two blocks from the plaza towards Trujillo, which also does good food and is a *peña* with dancing to traditional as well as Latino music. On the first weekend in August the **Fiesta de Waman Raymi** is held at nearby Wiracochapampa, bringing many people from the town and countryside to the Inti Raymi-style celebrations. Other festivals in the region include the **Fiesta de Huamachuco** (celebrating the founding of the city) on August 13–20, a week of festivities including a superb firework display on August 14 and aggressive male *turcos* dancers during the procession.

Money can be changed at the Caja Municipal or the Caja Rural, both on the plaza, or in several of the shops along the first few blocks of San Martín. The **market** is on block 9 of Balta.

The ruins of Gran Pajaten

Agreda **buses** connect Huamachuco twice weekly (Wed & Sat) with the village of **Chagual** (around 12 very bumpy hours) from where it's possible to hire mules and guides (from $5 a day per mule) for the four- or five-day trek via the settlements of Pataz (20km, a 6hr walk from Chagual) and Los Alisos (another 8km or 3hr walk), the true trailhead for the extremely remote ruins of **Gran Pajaten** – a further three or four days' walk. Occasional mining vehicles also go from Chagual to Pataz. If you're interested in seeing these fantastic ruins of a sacred city, **permission** must first be obtained from the Insituto Nacional de Cultura (see p.44), which is generally only given to those who can demonstrate a serious and specific interest and reason for visiting this special site. The South American Explorers' Club in Lima (see p.21), can also give advice.

From Cajamarca to Chachapoyas

There are two routes up to **Chachapoyas** from the coast, both of them arduous, bumpy and meandering. By far the easiest is the **northern route** from Chiclayo via Olmos, Jaen and Bagua, involving fewer climbs than the Cajamarca route and crossing the Andes by the Porculla Pass, the lowest possible track. Daily buses cover the entire Chiclayo to Chachapoyas route (10–12hr in the dry season; up to 20hr from Nov to March), but seats get booked up days in advance.

The **road from Cajamarca** is certainly more memorable and spectacular, though it is also more dangerous both in terms of the precipitous nature of the roads and the, nowadays very rare, possibility of buses being held up by robbers. The route winds through green mountain scenery, past dairy herds and small houses built in a variety of earthy colours, and crosses into the Marañon Valley beyond Leimabamba, reaching heights of almost 4000m before descending to the town of Chachapoyas. The whole trip takes at least twenty hours, and involves changing buses at **Celendin**. Palacios run daily services along the 112-kilometre route from Cajamarca to Celendin ($5, a 5hr trip), where you can get twice-weekly Transportes Virgen del Carmen and Empresa Jauro buses (Thurs & Sun) from Jirón Caceres 108 (7 blocks from the Plaza de Armas), for the fourteen-hour ($7) journey to Chachapoyas. The seats are often sold out the day before, so buy tickets in advance if possible. If you have to break the journey overnight at Celendin and need **accommodation**, try the *Hotel Loyers* (②), on Jiron Galvez, or *Hotel Amazonas* (③), Jiron 2 de Mayo; alternatively the *Hotel Celendin,* on the Plaza de Armas (③), which has private baths and its own restaurant, or the nearby *Hotel Amazonas,* on Jirón Galvez (②), which is slightly cheaper and more basic, but has a good reputation. If you happen to be here on a Sunday, check out the great **market**, which has particularly good bargains in leather goods.

Chachapoyas

CHACHAPOYAS, the unlikely capital of the *departmento de Amazonas*, is poised on an exposed plateau between two river gorges, at 2234m above sea level. In Aymara, Chachapoyas means "the cloud people", perhaps a description of the fair-skinned tribes who used to dominate this region, living in one of at least seven major cities, each one located high up above the Utcubamba Valley on prominent, dramatic peaks and ridges. Many of the local inhabitants still have light-coloured hair and remarkably pale faces. The town today, although friendly and attractively surrounded by wooded hills, is of no particular interest to the traveller except as a base from which to explore the area's numerous archeological remains – above all the ruins of **Kuelap**. Even at the close of the twentieth century, Chachapoyas remains well off the beaten track, though it has become a firm favourite for those who have made it to this remote and beautiful destination.

A small town by Peruvian standards, Chachapoyas was once a colonial possession rich with gold and silver mines as well as extremely fertile alluvial soil, before falling into decline during the Republican era. Recently, however, with the building of the Cajamarca road and the opening up of air travel, it has developed into a thriving little market town supporting a mostly Indian population of some seven thousand, with a reputation of being among the most friendly and hospitable in Peru. The pleasant **Plaza** de Armas contains a colonial bronze fountain, a monument to Toribio Rodriguez de Mendoza, the Cathedral and the municipal buildings. The town also possesses a couple of churches of some interest, notably the **Iglesia del Señor de Burgos**, known for its attractive colonial imagery, and the **Iglesia de Santa Ana**, the first of its kind built by the Spanish. There is very little tourism infrastructure in Chachapoyas or the surrounding region, but, if you are prepared to camp, you can explore a wealth of interesting sites in little charted territory.

Accommodation

Gran Vilaya Hotel, Jirón Ayacucho (☎074/757208). Comfortable and warm hotel, with its own restaurant; all rooms have private bath and hot water. ⑥.

Hostal Amazonas, Jirón Grau 565 (☎074/757199). A popular budget place on the Plaza de Armas, with an attractive patio. Hot water and rooms with or without bath are available. ②.

Hostal Kuelap, Jirón Amazonas 1057 (☎074/757136). Clean and friendly, but most rooms have shared baths and no hot water. ②.

Hotel El Dorado, Jirón Ayacucho 1062 (☎074/757047). Comfortable, with hot water and some rooms have private bath. ②–③.

Hotel Revash, on the Plaza de Armas. This is comfortable and good value, with private bath and hot water. ②.

Restaurants

Las Chozas de Marlissa, Jirón Ayacucho 1133. A friendly restaurant where typical local food combines tropical dishes with staple mountain meals based on rice and potatoes; at night it is also a good bar.

Cuyería, Pollería y Panadería Virgen Asunta, Jirón Puno 401. *The* place to go for roast guinea pig, though you have to order it a couple of hours in advance.

La Huerta de mi Amada, slightly out of town; ask a motorcycle taxi to take you (under $2). Has lovely gardens with great views and typical, if slightly pricey, local lunches.

La Olla de Barro, Avenida Sarafin Filomeno. A good selection of local dishes at very reasonable prices.

Restaurant Chacha, Jirón Galvez, next to the *Hotel Amazonas*. An excellent restaurant serving well-priced and well-prepared Peruvian fare.

Restaurant Kuelap, Jirón Ayacucho. Serves reasonably priced Peruvian dishes.

Restaurant Las Vegas, Jirón Amazonas 1091. Good for basic hot meals, snacks and drinks.

Arrival, information and getting around

Chachapoyas airport is 4km from the town (taxis cost $4–5), and has flights from Lima ($95–120) and Chiclayo ($75) a couple of times a week, and from Cajamarca ($50) three times a week; all flights should be booked as far in advance as possible. Calibri, on the Plaza de Armas, and Grupo Ocho (☎074/757391) and Transportes Aereas Andahuaylas, both based at the airport, are the main companies serving Chachapoyas. **Transport around town** tends to be by motorcycle rickshaws, which cost a flat rate of $0.3. For general **tourist information** ask at the Dirección Subregional de Industria y Turismo, Calle Chincha Alta 445 (9am–5.30pm Mon–Fri; ☎074/758355), but for advice on local archeological sites, try the **National Institute of Culture**, second block, Avenida Libertad (Mon–Fri 9am–6pm). The Banco de Credito, on the Plaza de Armas, will change dollars cash, traveller's cheques and can sometimes give cash against Visa cards. The **post office** (Mon–Sat 8am–7pm) is at Dos de Mayo 438, though note that it's usually quicker to wait and post your letters from a coastal city. The only official local **guide** is Martín Chumbe, Jirón Piura 909 (☎074/757212), also contactable through the *Gran Vilaya Hotel* (see above), who speaks some English and charges $25–30 a day for tours of sites in the region, including Kuelap.

Kuelap and Gran Vilaya

The main attraction for most travellers in the Chachapoyas region is the unrestored ruin of **Kuelap**, one of the most overwhelming pre-Inca sites in Peru. Just 40km south of Chachapoyas (along the Cajamarca road), the ruins were discovered in 1843, above the tiny village of Tingo in the remote and verdant Utcubamba Valley. In 1993, Tingo was partly destroyed by flash floods, when more than a hundred homes were washed away, but it is still the main point of access for visiting the ruins. Also best reached from Tingo, but far less accessible – a minimum of two days' walk – are the collection of ruins known as **Gran Vilaya**. If you intend to venture beyond Kuelap to Gran Vilaya, you must first obtain **permission** from the National Institute of Culture in Chachapoyas (see previous page).

Getting to the ruins

If you're coming from Cajamarca and Celendin, the bus passes right through Tingo. It's possible to visit the ruins independently by taking a colectivo from the corner of Grau and Salamanca (6am or 7am) **from Chachapoyas to Tingo**. Alternatively, you can go on an organized day tour with a guide (from $20 per person; see p.321), or rent a horse at El Chillo ($5–10 per day), on the road to Tingo.

To get **from Tingo to Kuelap**, it's a hard but hugely rewarding 1500-metre climb (around 4hr up and about 2 back down) from the west bank of the Río Utcubamba. Leave early to avoid the mid-morning sun, and remember to carry all the water you'll need with you. Mules or horses are usually available to hire from the hostal in Tingo ($5–10 per day). Alternatively, colectivos go from Tingo to the Kuelap parking lot (3hr).

Colectivos also go **from Tingo to Choctamal**, and it's then another five hours' or so walk **from Choctamal to Gran Vilaya**'s remote, largely unexplored and hard-to-find sites. The best way to reach them is with a decent guide and some mules – try Oscar Arce at El Chillo (see *Estancia Chillo hostal*, opposite) He can also take you to see the impressive ruins of **Santa Cruz**, **Machu Llaqta** and **Las Pilas**, all relatively easy one-day walks through stunning cloud forest. Note that once you get beyond Choctamal, it's often hard to use money and it can prove handy to have some trade goods with you – pencils, fruit, chocolate, bread, canned fish or biscuits – and, of course, camping gear unless you want to be completely dependent on the local hospitality.

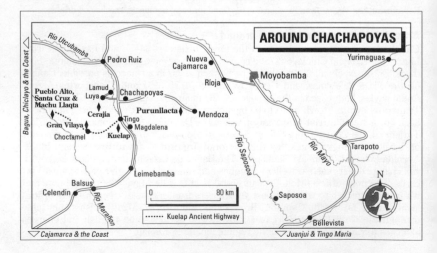

Accommodation

Most people coming to see the ruins **camp** (you'll need a sleeping bag), but there are also a few **hostals** in the area. **Tingo** has the very basic, unamed hostal (no tel; ①), or, if you arrive too late to get into the hostal, you can sometimes shelter in the village police station. Surprisingly, there's a small hostal with dormitory accommodation at the **Kuelap** site itself, the *Albergue de Kuelap* (no tel; ①), run by the site guardian who also sometimes provides food. Another equally basic place, the *Hostal El Bebedero* (①), is situated about ten minutes' walk down the hill from the *Albergue*. A few kilometres beyond Tingo, in a place called **Chillo**, there's an eco-*hostal*, the *Estancia Chillo* (no tel; ③), which has private baths, generates its own electricity, and whose owner is a reliable guide. For those continuing on to Gran Vilaya, there's also a small hostal in **Choctamal** (no tel; ②).

The Kuelap ruins

The ruined citadel of **Kuelap** (daily 8am–2pm; $4) is situated high on a ridge, about 3000m above sea level, commanding terrific views of the surrounding landscape, but it is the structure itself which immediately arrests your attention. Its enormous walls tower up to 20m high, and are constructed from gigantic limestone slabs arranged in geometric patterns, with some sections faced with rectangular granite blocks over forty layers high. Inside the ruins you come across hundreds of round stone houses decorated with a distinctive zigzag pattern (like the local modern ceramics), small carved animal heads, condor designs, and intricate serpent figures. There are also various enclosures and huge crumbling watchtowers partly covered in wild subtropical vegetation, shrubs, and even trees. One of these towers is an inverted, truncated cone containing a large, bottle-shaped cavity, possibly a place of torture, since archeologists have found the remains of wild animals, snakes and pumas with human bones above them, though these could date from after the original inhabitants of Kuelap had abandoned the citadel.

It has been calculated that some forty million cubic feet of building material was used at Kuelap, three times the volume needed to construct the Great Pyramid of Egypt. An estimated three thousand people would have lived here at its height, working mainly as farmers, builders and artisans and living in little round stone houses. It is the strongest, most easily defended of all Peruvian fortress cities and, occupied from about 600 AD by the Chachapoyas tribe, is thought to be the site which the rebel Inca Manco considered using for his last-ditch stand against the conquistadores in the late 1530s. He never made it here, ending up instead in the equally breathtaking Vilcabamba, northeast of Cusco.

The only resident today is the guardian from INC (Instituto Nacional de Cultura), who runs the hostal (see above), and sells soft drinks and sometimes beer near the top of the ruins. He can also give information about the other, smaller ruins in the immediate vicinity such as **Revash**, near the village of Santo Tomas, and can direct you to the village of Choctamal, a five-hour walk.

The Gran Vilaya ruins

The name **Gran Vilaya** refers to a superb complex of almost entirely unexcavated ruins scattered over a wide area. Explorer Gene Savoy claimed to have "discovered" them in 1985, though travellers have been hiking into this area for years and there were several sketch maps of the ruins in existence years before he arrived. Despite Savoy's claim to have found thousands of buildings, a more conservative estimate puts the record at some 150 sites divided into three main political sections. About thirty of these sites are of note, and about fifteen of these are of real archeological importance.

Purunllacta

Among other charted ruins in the Utcubamba Valley are those of the archaic metropolis of **Purunllacta**. This can be reached fairly easily by taking the daily bus from Grau in Chachapoyas to Pipos on the Mendoza road. Get off here and walk to the village of **Cheto**, from where it's a short climb to the ruined city itself. The return trip is possible the same day, though it's more enjoyable to camp at the site.

Purunllacta was one of the seven major cities of the Chachapoyas culture – and probably the capital – before all of them were conquered by the Inca Tupac Yupanqui in the 1470s. The **site** consists of numerous groups of buildings scattered around the hilltops, all interconnected by ancient roads and each one surrounded by elegant agricultural terraces. At the centre of the ruined city you can clearly make out rectangular stone buildings, plazas, stairways and platforms. The most striking are two storeys high, and made of carved limestone blocks. The explorer Gene Savoy estimated that the entire complex covered about 150 square kilometres – and even if the truth amounts to only a third of this calculation, it is an astonishing accomplishment.

Carajía and Pueblo de los Muertos

A characteristic of the Chachapoyas region is its **sarcophagi**, elaborately moulded, earthernware coffins, often stuck inaccessibly into horizontal crevices high up along cliff faces and painted in vivid colours. A fine example – and a rewarding excursion from Chachapoyas – are the sarcophagi at **Carajía**. To get here, catch one of the early morning colectivos or pickups headed for **Luya Vieja** from Grau and Salamanca in Chachapoyas. At Luya Vieja ask for directions to **Shipata**, where the path to the sarcophagi begins. From Shipata, walk down one side of the valley, over a bridge and then up the other side for about five minutes before taking a less clearly marked path to your right. The entire, spectacular walk from Luya Vieja takes about 4 hours.

Another good example of sarcophagi is at the **Pueblo de los Muertos** (City of the Dead), some 30km to the north of Chachapoyas. Up to 2m high and carved with human faces, they stare blankly across the valley from a natural fault in the rock face. Each one has been carefully moulded into an elongated egg-like shape from a mixture of mud and vegetable fibres, then painted purple and white with geometric zigzags and other superimposed designs. Savoy described them aptly as "standing like ten pins in a bowling alley", and most of them are still intact. If you get close, you can see that the casings are hollow, and some contain mummies wrapped in funerary shrouds; others are just filled with sun-bleached bones. Protected as they are from the weather by an overhang, these ancestors of the Chachapoyas race may well be watching over their land for another thousand years to come, though recent reports suggest that they have been looted and partially destroyed.

The Pueblo de los Muertos is easily reached by taking the daily Chiclayo bus from the market in Chachapoyas to Puente Tingobamba, at the settlement of Lamud. The sarcophagi are about three hours' walk from Puente; ask for directions there.

Into the jungle: downriver to Iquitos

A very adventurous **journey by land and river** will take you on from Chachapoyas to the Peruvian jungle capital of Iquitos (see p.398) on the Amazon, not far from the Brazilian border. It's difficult to estimate the duration of this trip – there are always waits for connections and embarkations – but you'd be unlikely to do it in much less than a week's hard travelling, unless you take the easy way out, catching a scheduled internal flight from **Moyobamba** (though the airstrip is actually in nearby Rioja) or

Yurimaguas. However, most travellers opt for the main overland route to Iquitos,
which involves one of Peru's best Amazon river trips – not as long as most, and reasonably straightforward.

Moyobamba

It takes about nine to ten hours in the dry season (and up to 15hr Dec & March) to
reach **MOYOBAMBA**, 160km east of Chachapoyas. Situated just above the Río Mayo
in a hot, humid, tropical forest environment, the town was founded in 1539 by Don
Alonso de Alvarado on one of his earliest explorations into the Amazon jungle.
Although a small town, it is the capital of the large, though sparsely populated *departmento* of San Martín. During the colonial period it was a camp for pioneers, missionaries and explorers, like **Pedro de Urzúa**, who used it as a base in his search for
cinnamon. Having noticed Indians using dry buds that tasted of cinnamon in cooking,
Urzúa kept his men busy looking for the potentially profitable spice. If he had been successful in finding cinnamon plantations in the jungles, where the Indians traded for it,
then the Portuguese monopoly with the Spice Islands could have been challenged,
Columbus's original aspirations fulfilled, and Moyobamba transformed into a rich city.
As you can see today, however, Urzúa failed in his attempt, and Moyabamba is much
the same as any other jungle town – hot, muddy and laid back, with a cathedral and a
few, but not many, decent hotels. The town was shaken up by a fairly heavy earthquake
back in 1991, and signs of this are still visible, with some buildings still in disrepair.

An hour's walk (5km) south of the town are the hot thermal springs of **San Mateo**
(daily 10am–6pm; $0.3); some 6km from town there are also the natural sulphur baths of
Oromina which are renowned for their medicinal properties. While about 15km south of
the town, you can see the spectacular waterfalls, **Cataratas de Gera**. To get to the falls
take a bus from Calle Miguel Grau some 21km to the village of Jepelacio ($1), then walk
the 3km from here. Note that you need to obtain a free permit from Moyobamba's
National Institute of Culture, block 3, Jirón Benavides, before visiting the falls.

Practicalities

To get to Moyobamba from Chachapoyas, take a colectivo along the Mayo Valley to
Pedro Ruiz ($3, a 2hr trip), then take another colectivo to **Rioja** ($10, a 7hr trip),
where you need to change to yet another colectivo to Moyobamba ($1.50, a 1hr trip).
Moyobamba is also served by the **airstrip** at nearby Rioja (see "Travel details" on p.356
for information about flights).

The cheapest **accommodation** in town is the *Quinta El Mayo*, Calle Canga (no tel;
②), closely followed by the *Hostal Albricias* (③), and the slightly more basic *Hostal
Monterrey*, Calle Aguila (☎094/562145; ③). Mid-range options include the clean *Hostal
Inca* (④), the *Hotel Royal* (④), both on Calle Alvarado, and the good-value, comfortable
Puerto Mirador (☎094/562594; ⑤), on Calle Sucre, twenty minutes' walk or a $3 taxi ride
from the town centre, with its own pool. The *Hostal Marcantonio* (☎094/562319; ⑦) is
by far the swishest place; it's very clean with good service and an excellent restaurant.

Tarapoto and around

Though much larger than Moyobamba, **TARAPOTO**, known as the City of Palms, has little to recommend it, except as a reasonable base in which to prepare for a jungle trip, or to do some **whitewater rafting** on the Río Mayo (ask at the tour company on the Plaza de Armas for details). The town, founded on August 20, 1772, lies just 420m above sea level and has an average daily temperature range of between 29 and 37 degrees centigrade. The Río Huallaga flows on from here, via the Amazon, until it finally empties into the Atlantic Ocean many thousands of kilometres away. A strange sort of place, Tarapoto has a large **prison** and a big drug-smuggling problem, with people flying coca paste from here to Colombia, where it is processed into cocaine for the US market.

Practicalities

From the Plaza de Armas in Moyobamba there are several **colectivos** a day to Tarapoto ($6, a 4–5hr journey). Alternatively, you could catch the daily Chiclayo to Tarapoto **bus** ($14, a 20–22hr trip), which also stops at the Plaza de Armas; the Moyabamba to Tarapota leg takes five hours and costs $7. Tarapoto has its own **airport**, too, 5km from the centre of town (see "Travel details" on p.356 for information about flights). The best **accommodation** in Tarapoto is at the comfortable *Hotel Rio Shilcayo*, Pasaje Las Flores 224, Banda de Shilcayo (✆094/522225; ⑤), with its own swimming pool. The *Hotel San Antonio*, less than a block southwest of the Plaza de Armas (③), is better value for money, but only some rooms have private baths. The cheapest options are the basic *Hostal Pasquelandia*, on Pimental (①–②), the *Hostal Melendez*, Calle Ursua (①), and the *Hostal Central*, on Jirón San Martín (✆094/522234; ①).

Eating out is surprisingly good, especially at the *Real*, Jirón Moyabamba 331, which serves superb evening meals including a mix of standard Peruvian dishes augmented with jungle produce such as yucca, plantains or large fish steaks. The *Restaurant El Mesón*, on the Plaza de Armas, offers a good, cheap set-lunch menu, while *El Camarón*, on Jirón San Pablo de la Cruz, is renowned for its delicious Amazon river shrimp. Further afield – 45 minutes by colectivo – the pleasant restaurant *El Mono y El Gato* (meaning "chalk and cheese", because the couple who run it are so different to each other) serves interesting local dishes, and is very close to the *Cataratas de Ahuashiyacu*, a popular local swimming spot.

Lamas

A pleasant day-trip from Tarapoto is to the nearby village of **LAMAS**, folklore capital of the *departmento* of San Martín, about 20km up into the forested hills and sur-

---

SOUTH FROM TARAPOTO

The route **south from Tarapoto** via Juanjui (150km) and Tingo Maria (a further 350km) through wild frontier jungle territory is not currently recommended for travellers. It passes through one of the most dangerous areas in Peru, dominated by the illegal **coca-growing industry**, as is most of the Huallaga Valley. This is inevitably associated with **drug smuggling**, which attracts big money to buy **arms** for terrorist groups, and the army have been present in the region for years. Now and again there are confrontations, Wild West-style shoot-outs involving all the interested parties, and the region remains more or less beyond the control of law and order. The situation suits some locals, and the illegal drug money and machine guns have a large influence on many people's lives, and, all current advice suggests that it's not worth the risk of travelling here at the moment.

rounded by large pineapple plantations. Colectivos to Lamas leave every hour or so from the Plaza de Armas in Tarapoto and take around thirty minutes ($1). The inhabitants of this small, exotic, native settlement, and particularly the quarter known as Barrio Huayco, are reputed to be direct descendants of the Chanca tribe that escaped from the Andes to this region in the fifteenth century, fleeing from the conquering Inca army. The people keep very much to themselves, carrying on a highly distinctive lifestyle which displays an unusual combination of jungle and mountain Indian cultures – the women wear long blue skirts and colourfully embroidered blouses, and the men adorn themselves on ceremonial occasions with strings of brightly plumed, stuffed macaws. Everyone goes barefoot and speaks a curious dialect, a mixture of Quechua and Cahuapana (a forest Indian tongue), and the town is traditionally renowned for its *brujos* (wizards), who use the potent hallucinogen ayahuasca, for their nocturnal divinatory and healing sessions. The best month to visit is August when the village **festival** is in full swing. The days are spent dancing, and drinking, and most of the tribe's weddings occur at this time. There's no hotel here, but villagers may let you camp in their gardens; alternatively, you can easily make it here and back from Tarapoto in a day.

Yurimaguas

From Tarapoto it's another 140km north along pretty but rough jungle tracks to the frontier town of **YURIMAGUAS**. In the dry season you can do this journey by one of the frequent colectivos ($10) in about five or six hours, but from November to March it's more likely to take between eight and ten hours. Try and travel this route by day if possible, because there's less risk of being robbed or encountering trouble on the road. The bustling little market town of Yurimaguas has little to recommend it, other than its **three ports**, giving access to the Río Huallaga. The most important is the downriver port of **La Boca**, where all the larger boats leave from, including those to Iquitos. The port is located some fifteen to twenty minutes' walk from the town centre, or $1 in a motorcycle rickshaw. The second, middle port, known as **Puerto Garcilaso**, is closer to the heart of Yurimaguas and mainly used by farmers bringing their produce into town from the nearby farms in smaller boats. The third, upper port, called **Puerto Malecón Shanuse**, is used primarily by fishermen.

Accommodation options in Yurimaguas include the *Hostal Cesar Gustavo* (②), the most comfortable and friendly of the basic hostals, and the good-value *Hostal La Estrella* (②). Slightly pricier, but better quality and with a good restaurant, is the *Hostal el Naranjo* (☎044/352650; ③), while the *Hostal de Paz* (☎044/352123; ③) is clean and friendly. For food, try the *Restaurant Copacabana*, which serves a range of Peruvian and standard international dishes, or the *Polleria Posada*, for chicken and fries. The *Café La Prosperidad* specializes in delicious fruit juices, and there's an excellent *cevichería, El Dorado,* by the Puerto Malecón Shanuse in Barrio La Loma.

Downriver to Iquitos

From Yurimaguas, you can travel all the way **to Iquitos** by river ($15–20 on deck or $20–30 for cabins, a 3–5 day trip). As soon as you arrive in Yurimaguas, head straight to La Boca port to look for boats, since they get booked up in advance. Boats leave regularly though not at any set times; it's simply a matter of finding a reliable captain (preferably the one with the biggest, newest or fastest-looking boat) and arranging details with him. The price isn't bad and includes food, but you should have your own hammock if you're sleeping on deck, and bring clean bottled water, as well as any extra treats, like canned fish, and a line and hooks (sold in the town's *fereterías*) if you want to try fishing.

The scenery en route is electric: the river gets steadily wider and slower, and the vegetation on the river banks more and more dense. Remember, though, that during the day the sun beats down intensely and a sunhat is essential to avoid **river fever** – cold sweats (and diarrhoea) caused by exposure to the constant strong light reflected off the water. On this journey the boats pass through many interesting settlements, including Santa Cruz and Lagunas, starting point for trips into the huge Pacaya-Samiria National Reserve (see p.407).

THE NORTHERN DESERT

The **Northern Desert** remains one of the least visited areas of Peru, due as much to its distance from Lima and Cusco as its lack of obvious attractions. Despite the fact that it offers a considerable amount in terms of landscape, wildlife and history, with a complex cultural identity that's quite distinct and strongly individualistic, its popular image is of a desolate zone of scattered rural communities – a myth that belies both its past and its present. Today, its main cities of **Chiclayo** and **Piura** are both important and lively commercial centres, serving not only the desert coast but large areas of the Andes as well. Before Pizarro arrived in this region during the sixteenth century to begin the Conquest, the Northern Desert had formed part of both the Inca and Chimu empires and hosted a number of local pre-Columbian cultures, and in recent years the **Lambayeque Valley**, near Chiclayo, has become a focus of interest for archeologists. Various tombs and temples, full of gold, silver and precious stones such as emeralds, have been discovered, providing substantial information about life around here some thousand years ago.

The coastal resorts, such as **La Pimentel**, are among the best reasons for stopping: though small, they usually have at least basic facilities for travellers, and, most importantly, the ocean is warmer here than anywhere else in the country. This region has much historic interest, too, in **Túcume** and **Batan Grande**, two immense pre-Inca ceremonial centres within easy reach of **Chiclayo**. With the Andes rising over 6000m to the east, this northern coastal strip of Peru has always been slightly isolated and access even today is restricted to just a few roads, including the main north–south Panamerican Highway, a new cross-desert road linking Chiclayo and Piura, and two minor routes straggling over the Andes.

If, like a lot of travellers, you decide to bus straight through from Trujillo to the Ecuadorean border town beyond **Tumbes** (or vice versa) in a single journey, you'll be missing out on all of this – and also the region's strong sense of **history**. It was at Tumbes that Pizarro's Andalucian sea pilot, Bartholomew Ruiz, discovered the first evidence of civilization south of the equator – a large balsa sail raft – in 1527. And, five years on, it was off this northern coast that Pizarro and the conquistadores first dropped anchor, before coming ashore to change the course of Peru's history.

The Panamerican Highway from Trujillo to Chiclayo

The **Panamerican Highway**, mainstay of the north's transport system, offers the fastest route north from Trujillo, passing through an impressively stark and barren landscape with few towns of any significance – though the valleys here have yielded notable archeological finds dating from Peru's Early Formative period.

San Pedro de Lloc, the first settlement of any real size, stands out from miles around with its tall, whitewashed buildings and its old town walls that contain the one mansion of note, the Casa de Raymondi (ask in the Biblioteca for the key holder). There are a few reasonable restaurants here, including the *Bar-Recreo Los Espinos*, Jirón 2 de Mayo 720. Some 3km from the town, at Cerro Chilco, it's still possible to visit the ruins of the ancient Indian settlment of Loc. Generally, though, a quiet little village with little to see, San Pedro's only claim to fame is its local culinary delicacy of stuffed lizards.

If these don't appeal, you may prefer to press on 10km north to the growing port and town of **Pacasmayo**. Despite the town's grim initial appearance, the area around the old jetty is not unattractive and posesses some dilapidated colonial mansions, and it's a good spot to get **buses** on to Cajamarca or back down the coast to Trujillo and Lima. Expresso Cajamarca, Roggero, Transportes Atahualpa and Vulkano all stop in the main street of Leoncio Prado; Emtrafesa's depot is at Avenida 28 de Julio 104, just around the corner; while Cruz del Sur are at Jirón Espinar C-7/90. The seafront has one or two good seaside **hotels**, such as the *Hotel Pakatnamu*, Malecon Grau 103 (☎044/522368, fax 521051; ⑤) which has rooms with TV and there's a weeekend disco in the summer. *Hostal Cesar's Palace*, Leoncio Prado 1a (☎044/521945; ③) is also decent enough, with fairly comfortable rooms with TV. The seafront also has a good **restaurant**, *El Encuentro de Ignacio*, or try *Chifa Tip Top*, at Leon Prado C/18, which is cheap and very popular with locals. The **Banco de Credito** is on the small Plaza de Armas, near the seafront.

The one historical site along this stretch of road is a few kilometres beyond Pacasmayo, just before the village of **Guadalupe**, where a track leads off left to the well-preserved ruins of **Pacatnamú** (The City of Sanctuaries), overlooking the mouth of the Río Jecetepeque. Being off the main road and far from any major towns, the ruins of this abandoned city have survived relatively untouched by treasure hunters or curious browsers. The remains were first excavated in 1938 and 1953 by archeologist Ubbelonde-Doering, who found a great complex of pyramids, palaces, storehouses and dwellings. Digging up the forecourts in front of the pyramids and some nearby graves, he discovered that the place was first occupied during the Gallinazo period (around 350 AD), then was subsequently conquered by the Mochica and Chimu cultures. You can get here by colectivo or bus from Pacasmayo, but you'll have to walk the 6km from the main highway to the site. Note that it gets very hot around midday, and there's little shade and no food or drink available at the site, so bring your own.

Chiclayo and around

Some 770km north of Lima, and rapidly becoming one of Peru's larger cities, **Chiclayo** is an active commercial centre thanks more to its strategic position than to any industrial development. Originally it was just a small annexe to the old colonial town of **Lambayeque**, 12km north, but things have swung the other way over this century, and Lambeyeque is now a tiny, almost two-street town, with a great ceramics museum, while all the vibrancy and energy are concentrated in Chiclayo. The city itself has little of architectural or historical interest, but it makes a good base for visiting Lambayeque, and the nearby archeological sites.

Despite being the northern base of several successive ancient cultures, the Chiclayo region's most interesting period was during the first millennium AD in the Lambayeque Valley. First came the Mochica-dominated settlements, which produced such magnificent treasures as were recently encountered at the **Temple of Sipán**. Then followed the Sican culture, which was equally rich in iconographic imagery and fine ritual objects and garments, and was responsible for the enormous desert temple complex of **Batan Grande** and the city of pyramids at **Túcume**, which some archeologists believe to be at least as important as the Chimu settlement of Chan Chan (see p.299), near

Trujillo. More recent and far less inscrutable ruins are to be found in the colonial ghost town of Zaña.

Apart from the historical interest, there are also a few attractive resorts and coastal towns to relax in and catch some sun, such as **La Pimental** and **Santa Rosa**. Most places can be reached independently by taking a **colectivo** from the market area of Chiclayo, but you'll find it much easier to see all the archeological sites if you've got your own transport. You'll probably get the most out of these, however, by going with a knowledgable local guide on an organized tour from Chiclayo.

Chiclayo

Chiclayo is the commercial centre of northern Peru, so it's better famed for its banks than its heritage. Nevertheless it has its attractions, even if most of the city is an urban sprawl modernizing and growing by the month. The heart of **CHICLAYO** is the central plaza, known as the **Parque Principal**, where there's a futuristic foun-

CHICLAYO

ANDRES RASURI

M. PARDO

ANGAMOS

UNIVERSO

M. PARDO

Mercado Modelo

AMAZONAS

ARICA

AVENIDA LUIS GONZALES

ALFONSO UGARTE

R. CIVILES

T. PINGLO

LETICIA

AVENIDA SAENZ PENA

PEDRO RUIZ

8 DE OCTUBRE

SIETE DE ENERO

LEONCIO PRADO

FERRE

LEONCIO PRADO

LORA Y CORDERO

Bus Terminal

SAN MARTIN

VICENTE DE LA VEGA

Central Market

Palacio Municipal

M. CAPAC

$

①

PLAZA ELIAS AGUIRRE

SAN JOSE

Parque Principal

Cathedral

ELIAS AGUIRRE

③ ④

Centro Civico

Hospital Las Mercedes

⑤ MARIA IZAGA

AVENIDA JOSE BALTA SUR

M. CASTILLA

N

TORRES PAZ

FCO. CABRERA

L. APOINI

COLON

AVENEDA JOSE BALTA SUR

TACNA

STA. ISABEL

ACCOMMODATION

Gran Hotel Chiclayo **2**
Hostal Sican **5**
Hotel Costa de Oro **4**
Hotel Europa **3**
Hotel Garza **6**
Hotel Royal **1**

Scale unknown

AVENEDA BOLOGNESI

Lambayeque & Túcume ②

Ferreñafe & Batan Grande ▷

Lima ▽

⑥

tain that's elegantly lit at night. You'll also find the Neoclassical **Cathedral** here, built in 1869 and with its main doorway supported by Doric columns, and the **Palacio Municipal**, a Republican edifice built in 1919. Along Calle San José, you'll find the **Convento Franciscano Santa Maria**, built in the early seventeenth century but destroyed, apart from the second cloister, by El Niño rains in 1961. But the main focus of activity is along **Avenida Jose Balta**, between the plaza and the town's fascinating **Central Market**. Packed daily with food vendors at the centre, and other stalls around the outside, this is one of the best markets in the north – and a revelation if you've just arrived in the country. The market boasts a whole section of live animals, including wild fox cubs, canaries, and even the occasional condor chick, and you can't miss the rayfish known as *la guitarra* hanging up to dry in the sun before being made into a local speciality – *pescado seco*. But the most compelling displays are the herbalists' shops, selling everything from herbs and charms to whale bones and hallucinogenic cacti.

Elsewhere in town there's the small, attractive chapel of **La Véronica** on Calle Torres Paz. Built at the end of the nineteenth century, its most notable feature is the altar piece of silver- and gold-leaf. The **Plazuela Elías Aguirre**, just around the corner from here is a small shady square which has a statue in honour of the *comandante* of this name, who was a local hero serving the Republicans in the Battle of Angamos.

At weekends, Chiclayo families crowd out to the **beaches** of **Santa Rosa** and **La Pimentel** – each well served by buses from the market area. Santa Rosa is the main fishing village on the Chiclayo coast, from where scores of big, colourful boats go out early every morning, along with the occasional *caballito de tortora*, reed canoes that have been used here for almost two thousand years. On Sunday afternoons, *Chiclayanos* congregate for the **horseraces** at the town's Santa Victorial Hipodromo, 2km south of the Plaza de Armas just off the Avenida Roosevelt.

Arrival, information and city transport

The José Abelado Quiñones González **airport** is 2km east of town, and easily reached by taxi for $3–5. **Buses** connecting Chiclayo with Pimental and Lambayeque use the Terminal Terrestre Oeste, on the first block of Angamos, just off block one of San José. Services for all the southern cities – Trujillo, Lima and so on – use the Terminal Terrestre La Victoria on Calle Mochica, where it meets the Panamerica Sur, where there's a waiting area, a left-luggage deposit and a hostal. For **tourist information** go to Sáenz Peña 838 (9am–5.30pm Mon–Fri, 9am–1pm Sat; ☎074/233132, fax 238112), or San José 733 (Mon–Sat 8am–6pm, Sun 8am–noon; ☎074/232231), or the information desk at the *Hotel Garza* (see overleaf). Alternatively, you can contact the tourist police (see "Listings", overleaf).

The centre of town is fine to **walk** around, but if you need a **taxi** try Chiclayo Rent-a-Car, Avenida Grau 520, Santa Victoria (☎074/229390, fax 237512) which also has offices at the *Gran Hotel Chiclayo* (see below) and the airport (☎074/244291).

Accommodation

Finding a place to stay is relatively simple in Chiclayo. Most of the good, reasonably priced **hotels** are around the Plaza de Armas. The *Hotel Royal*, San José 787 (☎074/233431; ②) is the best budget option, offering rooms with or without private bath, or there's the comfortable *Hotel Costa de Oro*, Avenida José Balta 399 (☎074/232869; ④–⑤), which also has rooms with or without bath. The *Hotel Europa* on Elías Aguirre (☎074/237919; ③) is very clean and has excellent service, and the *Hostal Sican*, at Avenida Izaga 356 (☎074/237618; ④) is nicely decorated, central and friendly, but significantly more luxury can be found at the *Gran Hotel Chiclayo*, Avenida Federico Villareal 115 (☎074/234911, fax 223961, *granhotel@lima.business.com.pe*, *www.business.com.pe/granhotel*; ⑦), the best hotel in town and with its own pool, though a little way from the centre. The *Hotel Garza*, Bolognesi 756 (☎074/228172; ⑦) is more central and pretty comfortable, with a pool and sauna, good food and useful tourist information. They also rent out cars and jeeps. If you'd rather stay out at one of the beaches, you can **camp** at both Santa Rosa and La Pimentel, provided you ask local permission first, and there's a cheapish hotel at Santa Rosa.

Restaurants and nightlife

The best of Chiclayo's **restaurants** is the excellent *Las Tinajas*, Elías Aguirre 134, which serves local dishes including a delicious *arroz con pato* (rice with duck) and a *seco de cabrito* (roast goat with spicy gravy sauce). If you can't get in here, try the *Restaurant Mi Tia*, Elías Aguirre 698, for snacks, pasta and goat dishes at very reasonable prices. Specializing in typical Chiclayano cooking, there's the good-value *Restaurant Roma*, Avenida Balta 548, or, right on the Plaza de Armas, the *Restaurant Las Americas*, Elías Aguirre 824, which offers decent international dishes and good, basic *criolla* fare. Slightly more upmarket is *El Huaralino*, La Libertada 155, Urbino Santa Victoria, which does Chiclayano dishes, including *tortilla de raya*. The *Pueblo Viejo*, Izaga 900, is one of the city's best *criolla* restaurants and is excellent value, though it's better still when there's live music on Fridays.

For a little **nightlife**, try the *Centro Turistico El Señorio*, Izaga 654, which has food and live *criolla* music on Friday and Saturday after 10.30pm. For more up-tempo music, try the trendy but friendly *Yomiuri*, Saenz Peña 997 which serves drinks and Japanese food in the evenings but doesn't warm up until quite late. The **disco** *Excess*, on Virgilio D'Allors, is lively, while *La Gaviota*, another disco, at Alfonso Ugarte 401 in Pimentel, can be fun at weekends.

Listings

Airlines Aero Andino, Los Cirpreses 191, Los Parques, Chiclayo (☎074/233161, fax 224351, *aeroandino@llampayec.rcp.net.pe*); Aero Continente, Los Cipreses 191, Urbino Los Parques (☎074/233161); LanPeru, Avenida Saenz Peña 637 (☎074/236475); and Expreso Aereo, 7 de Enero 873 (☎074/241688).

Banks and exchange The main banks are concentrated around the Parque Principal. *Cambistas* can be found on the corners of the Parque Principal, particularly José Balta, or there's the *casa de cambio* Hugo Barandiaran at Avenida Balta 586.

Buses Civa, Bolognesi 757 (☎074/242488), for Chachapoyas and Lima; Cruz del Sur, Bolognesi 751 (☎074/242164) for Lima; Empresa El Cumbe, Quiñones 425 (☎074/231454) for Cajamarca; Oltursur, Avenida Balta 598 (☎074/237789), for Trujillo and Tumbes; Tepsa, Bolognesi 536 (☎074/236981), for Tumbes and Tacna; Transportes Arberia, Bolognesi 536 (☎074/234421), to Cajamarca; and Vulcano, Bolognesi 638 (☎074/233497), for Trujillo and Cajamarca.

Courier sevice DHL Elías Aguirre 576.

Internet Abaco Internet Cabins, Avenida Luis Gonzales 507; and Internet Cabins, San José 104.

Post office Elías Aguirre, 7 blocks west of the plaza (Mon–Sat 8am–7pm).

Telephones Telefónica del Peru, Elías Aguirre 919.

Tour operators Tours around the area include trips to Túcume, Batan Grande and the Museo Brúning, plus occasional shamanic tours, last 4–8hr and cost $15–30. The best are offered by Avanti Travel Service, Izaga 725, Oficina 301 (☎074/241728), and Sipán Tours, 7 de Enero (☎ & fax 074/229053, *Sipántours@kipu.rednorte.com.pe*). Other companies include: Andina Tours, Avenida El Dorado 1875 (☎074/243126); Mochica Tours, Luis Gonzales 946 (☎074/229305); and Tumi Tours, Elías Aguirre 598 (☎074/225371); Sobre Vuelos Turisticos offer flights over the main archeological sites and panoramas with Aero Andino.

Tourist Police ☎074/236700.

Western Union Elías Aguirre 576.

La Pimental, Santa Rosa, Monsefú and Etén

An attractive beach resort with a population of some 23,000 just 14km southwest of Chiclayo, **La Pimentel** offers a decent, safe **beach** for swimming and **surfing** (competitions take place in Dec and Jan). It became a busy port under military rule in the 1970s, exporting agricultural products from the co-operative haciendas, but it's now better known for its small-scale fishing industry, much of it using the traditional *caballitos de tortora*. For a small fee ($0.25) you can access the long pier that divides the seafront *malecon* in two, and you can see the fishermen. There are plenty of seafood **restaurants** at the south end near to where the *caballitos de tortora* are stacked.

More picturesque is the small fishing village of **La Caleta Santa Rosa**, about 5km south of Pimentel. Here the beach is crowded with colourful boats and fishermen mending nets; the best and freshest *ceviche* in the Chiclayo area can be found in the **restaurants** on the seafront here (try the *Restaurant Puerto Magnolia*). The area known as El Faro (the lighthouse), slightly to the south of Santa Rosa, is the best location for **surfing**. Continuing from here along the road inland for about 5km, you come to the small town of **Monsefú**, known as the "city of flowers" because of the local cottage industry that supplies blooms to the area. It's also known for its fine straw hats, straw-rolled cigarettes and the quality of its cotton, all of which you can buy at the daily market. Another 4km south from here you come to the colonial village of **Etén** and its nearby ruined church, the Capilla del Milagro, built after of a vision of the Christ child in 1649. Southwest, towards the sea, lie the wide avenues of **Puerto Etén**, just another 4km away. The town has some well tended plazas, but its most interesting feature is a derelict iron pier built in 1873 to receive and export goods by rail; nearby there are abandoned nineteenth century train carriages.

La Pimentel is easily reached by **bus** every thirty minutes from Vicente Vega 420 in Chiclayo ($0.3). Regular **colectivos** from Avenida Ugarte connect Chiclayo with Pimentel, Santa Rosa and Monsefú and Puerto Etén ($0.3).

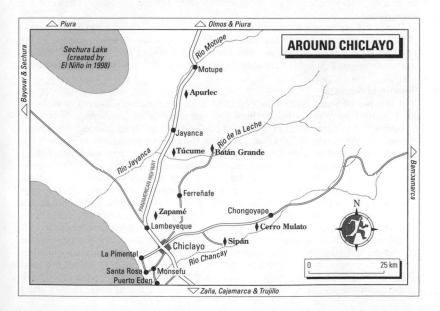

AROUND CHICLAYO

Zaña

The ruined colonial settlement of **Zaña** sits in the desert about 12km away from the modern town of Mocupe, itself 38km south of Chiclayo along the Panamerican Highway. Elaborate arches, columns and sections of old churches, such as the once elegant Convento de San Agustín, stand partly overgrown by shrubs, but it was once an opulent city. Founded in 1553, it became a centre for meting out justice to thieves, witches and errant slaves, but its wealth actually originated from the nearby port of Cherrepe, from where it controlled the passage of vessels along the coast between Lima and Panama. It rapidly grew rich, and its subsequent excesses were soon notorious, attracting the attention of pirates, including a band led led by one Edward Davis, who sacked the place in 1668. The city subsequently lost much of its prestige and most of the important families moved out, the rest following a few years later when news arrived of another English pirate off the Peuvian coast – Francis Drake. The final blow came in 1720, when the waters of the Río Zaña swept through the streets, causing such damage that the settlement was abandoned. **Buses** to Mocupe and Zaña can be caught hourly from 7 de Enero 1349 in Chiclayo ($0.5, a 45–60min trip).

Ferrañape and the Temple of Sipán

Ferrañape, founded in 1550 by Captain Alfonso de Osorio, and, was once known as the "land of two faiths" because of the local tradition of believing first in the power of spirits and second in the Catholic church. Today, it's known mainly for its young women having won the Miss Peru title more than girls from any other town. Whether this has anything to do with the place's proximity to Batan Grande's ancient moon ceremonies is unclear, but one thing that's certain is that you'll only be visiting Ferrañape if you're en route to that same centre of Sican culture. Nevertheless, the town, just 18km northeast of Chiclayo, has some fine old buildings, recently repainted in traditional colonial blue, and the unspectacular late nineteenth-century **Iglesia de Santa Lucía** on the main plaza.

Buses to Ferrañape leave from the centre of Chiclayo every hour and, if you want to stay over, there are several restaurants and two basic **hostals**, including one run by the municipalidad, named, prosaically, the Hotel Municipalidad (③). Leaving Ferrañape from the cemetery end of town, the new road heads for Batan Grande (see opposite).

Temple of Sipán

The **Temple of Sipán** (daily 8am–6pm; $1), 33km southeast of Chiclayo, was discovered in 1987 by Walter Alva, archeologist and director of Lambayeque's Brüning Museum, in the heart of an area farmed by the sugar growing co-operative Agraria Pomalca, in the district of Zaña, just 2km from the present community of Sipán. It has proved to be one of the richest tombs in the entire Americas. Every important individual buried here, mostly Mochica nobles from around 200–600 AD, was interred prostrate with his or her own precious metal grave goods, such as gold and silver goblets, headdresses, breastplates and jewellery including turquoise and lapis lazuli. The most important grave uncovered was that of a noble known today al **El Señor de Sipán**, the Lord of Sipán. He was buried along with a great many fine golden and silver decorative objects adorned with semi-precious stones and shells from the Ecuadorian coast.

There's not a huge amount to see at the site, although there are two large adobe **pyramids**, including the Huaca Rajada, in front of which there was once a royal tomb; but the place certainly gives you a feel for the people who lived here almost two thousand years ago, and it's one of the few sites in Peru whose treasures were not entirely plundered either by the conquistadores or more recent grave robbers. There's also a

THE SICAN CULTURE

Having come to light in the early 1990s, the **Sican culture** is associated with the Naymlap dynasty, based on a wide-reaching political confederacy emanating from the Lambayeque Valley between around 800 and 1100 AD. Legend has it that a leader called **Naymlap** arrived by sea with a fleet of balsa boats, his own royal retinue and a female green stone idol. Having been sent to establish a new civilization, Naymlap set about building temples and palaces near the sea in the Lambayeque Valley. On his death, Naymlap was entombed and his spirit was said to fly away to another dimension. The region was successfully governed by Naymlap's twelve grandsons, until one of them was tempted by a witch to move the green stone idol. Legend has it that this provoked a month of heavy rains and flashfloods, rather like the effects of El Niño today (see p.45), bringing great disease and death in its wake. Indeed, glacial ice cores analyzed in the Andes above here have shown the likelihood of a powerful El Niño current around 1100 AD.

The Sican civilization, like that of Mochica culture in the Moche Valley around Trujillo, depended on a high level of irrigation technology combined with a tight political coherence, not least concerning the difficult issues surrounding rights of access to water supplies in such a vast and dry desert region. The civilization also had its own copper money and sophisticated ceramics, many of which featured an image of the flying **Lord of Sican**. The main thrust of the Lord of Sican designs is a well-dressed man, with small wings, a nose like a bird's beak and, sometimes, talons rather than feet. Quite possibly a representation of Naymlap himself, the Lord of Sican is often seen flying on a double-headed snake, a motif widely used by the Mochica culture. The Sican culture showed a marked change in its burial practices from that of the Mochicas, almost certainly signifying a change in the prevalent beliefs about life after death. Whilst the Mochica were buried in a lying position – like the Mochica warrior in his splendid tomb at Sipán (see opposite) – the new Sican style was to inter its dead in a sitting position.

The Sican monetary system, the flying Lord of Sican image and much of the culture's religious and political infrastructures were all abandoned after the dramatic environmental disasters caused by the 1100 AD El Niño. Batan Grande, the culture's largest and most impressive city, was partly washed away and a new centre, now known as the city of El Purgatorio, was constructed in the Leche Valley. This relatively short-lived culture was taken over by Chimu warriors around 1370 AD, who absorbed the Lambayeque Valley, some of the Piura Valley area and seventy percent of the Peruvian desert coast into their empire.

site museum, displaying photos and illustrations of the excavation work plus replicas of some of the discoveries.

To get here take one of the combi **colectivos** ($0.8, a 40min trip) which leave every morning from Jirón 7 de Enero 1552 in Chiclayo. If you want to stay overnight at the site, there are a couple of **rooms** available at the *Parador Turistica* (②), or you can **camp** ($1) in the grounds.

Batán Grande and Cerro Mulato

The site at **Batán Grande**, 57km southeast of Chiclayo, incorporates over twenty pre-Inca temple pyramids, and over ninety percent of Peru's ancient gold artefacts are estimated to have come from here, where, as you'll notice, there are over 100,000 holes dug over the centuries by treasure hunters. However, the treasures may have been imported here from the Río Marañon region to the east and the Río Chinchipe to the north in Ecuador over 1000 years ago, although the Huaca Corte has been associated with ceramic work over 4000 years old. Batan Grande is also known to have developed its own copper-smelting works, which produced large quantities of flat copper plates between 5 and 10cm long. These artefacts, called *naipes*, are thought by archeologists to have been used and exported to Ecuador as a kind of monetary system.

The centre of Sican culture, Batan Grande was abandoned in the thirteenth century and the Sican moved across the valley to Túcume (see opposite), possibly following devastation by drought or an epidemic. There is some evidence that the pyramids were deliberately burnt, supporting the latter theory, but ceramic evidence also suggests that the move coincided with a shift in emphasis from ceremonial to urban centres.

The main part of the **site** that you visit today was largely built between 750 and 1250 AD, comprising the Huaca del Oro, Huaca Rodillona, Huaca Corte and the Huaca Las Ventanas, where the famous **Tumi de Oro** was uncovered in 1936. The tomb of **El Señor de Sican** (not to be confused with the tomb of El Señor de Sipán), on the north side of the Huaca del Oro, contained a noble with two women and two children and five golden crowns; these finds will be exhibited in an as yet unbuilt museum in Ferrañape. From the top of these pyramids you can just about make out the form of the ancient ceremonial plaza on the ground below.

The **interpretative centre here** has a cafetería, hostal **accommodation** (no tel; ②), a **camping** area, and a small, interesting archeological museum with a scale model of the site. It also frequently offers **horse-riding** access to the main temple complex. To visit the site in just one day, it's best to take a **guided tour** from Chiclayo (see p.332), though you could take public transport: **colectivos** to Batan Grande pueblo (10km beyond the site) leave each morning from block 16 of 7 de Enero in Chiclayo – go as early as possible and ask to be dropped at the interpretative centre ($1.50, a 2hr trip; check with the driver for return journey times). **Buses** for Batan Grande pueblo also pass the interpretative centre, leaving the Terminal Terrestre Norte in Chiclayo from 6.30am daily, with the last one leaving Batan Grande pueblo for Chiclayo at around 4.30pm. To speed things up, it's sometimes possible to hire a taxi in Batan Grande pueblo for half a day ($15–20).

Part of the beauty of this site comes from its siting at the heart of an ancient forest dominated by *algarrobo* trees spreading out over some 13,400 hectares, a veritable oasis in the middle of the desert landscape. Now the **Reserva Natural de Batán Grande,** it's the largest dry forest in western South America. A kilometre or so in from the interpretative centre you'll find the oldest *algarrobo* tree in the forest, the **arbol milenario**; over a 1000 years old, its spreading, gnarled mass is still the site for pagan rituals, judging from the offerings hanging from its twisted boughs, but it's also the focus of Fiesta de Las Cruces on May 3. In the heart of the reserve is a section known as the Bosque de Poma, where over forty species of birds have been identified and most visitors see some iguanas and lizards scuttling into the undergrowth. Rarer, but still hanging around, are wild foxes, deer and anteaters.

Cerro Mulato

Also worth a visit is the site of **Cerro Mulato**, near the hill town of **Chongoyape**, some 80km out of Chiclayo along the attractive Chancay Valley. At Cerro Mulato, you can see some impressive Chavín petroglyphs (engraved stones), and in the surrounding region, a number of Chavín graves dating from well into the fifth century BC. **Buses** to Chongoyape leave every hour or so from Pedro Ruiz in Chiclayo ($1.50, a 2hr trip).

Lambayeque

A short **colectivo** ride of 12km from Chiclayo market, **LAMBAYEQUE** is an old colonial town that must have been a grand place in the seventeenth century but fell into decay in the twentieth. It's now, however, showing signs of recovery, not least because of its important museum and its vibrant Sunday **markets**. Of the town's buildings worth seeing, the early eighteenth-century church of **San Pedro**, parallel to the main square between the two principal streets of 2 de Mayo and 8 de Octubre, is still holding up and is the most impressive edifice in the town, with two attractive front towers and fourteen balconies. But the dusty streets of Lambayeque are better known for their handful of colonial *casonas*, such as **La Casa Cúneo**, 8 de Octubre 328, and a few doors down the **La Casa Descalzi**, which has a fine *algarrobo* doorway in typical Lambayeque Barroque style. The **La Casa de La Logia Masónica** (Masonic Lodge), at the corner of *calles* 2 de Mayo and San Martín, is also worth checking out for its superb balcony, which has just about lasted for 400 years and, at 67m, is thought to be the longest in Peru.

Lambayeque's main draw, however, is the modern **Museo Arqueológico Nacional Brüning** on block 7 of Avenida Huamachuco (Mon–Sun 9am–6pm; $1.5). Named after its founder, an expert in the Mochica language and culture, the museum possesses superb collections of early ceramics and metal work, in particular a large collection of gold, silver and copper objects from the tomb of **El Señor de Sipán** (see p.334). The Lambayeque Valley has long been renowned for turning up pre-Columbian metallurgy – particularly gold pieces from the neighbouring hill graveyard of **Zacamé** – and local treasure hunters have sometimes gone so far as to use bulldozers to dig them out, but it's the addition of the Sipán treasures that's given the biggest boost to Lambayeque's reputation, and the museum is now one of the finest in South America. However, it is also brimming over with artefacts from elsewhere, including golden Tumi back-protectors, one embossed with the image of **Ai-Apaec**, the deity thought to be the lord of life and death and quaintly known as the "winged decapitator". Another depicts a woman copulating over the rising moon (thus combining fertility with creation), roofed over by a series of horned heads.

On a rather more prosaic note, Lambayeque is also known for its sweet pastry cakes – filled with *manjar blanca* and touted under the unlikely name of *King-Kongs*. In any of the town's streets, you'll be bombarded by street vendors pushing out piles of the cake, shouting "King-Kong! King-Kong!". For **accommodation**, the *Hostal Brunning*, Avenida S. Bolivar 578 (☎074/283549; ③) is fine. To exchange **money, the** Banco de Credito is opposite the main market, on Ramon Castillo at the corner with Atahualpa.

Túcume, Túcume Viejo and Apurlec

The site of **Túcume** (daily 8am–6pm; $1, guides from $2), also known as the **Valley of the Pyramids**, contains twenty-six adobe pyramids, many clinging to the naturally protruding relief of the desert landscape around the hill of **El Purgatorio** (197m), also known as Cerro La Raya (after a legendary ray fish that lives within it), some 33km from Chiclayo.

Covering more than 200 hectares, Túcume was occupied initially by the **Sican** culture, who began building here around 1100AD after abandoning Batan Grande. At its peak, in the thirteenth and early fourteenth centuries, it was probably a focus of annual pilgrimage for a large section of the coastal population, whose Sican leaders were high priests with great agro-astological understanding, adept administrators, a warrior elite, and expert artisans. However it wasn't long before things changed, and around 1375 AD the **Chimu** invaded from the south. They added a little to the structures and the area's irrigation complex during their occupation, but within another hundred years the **Incas** had arrived, though they took some twenty years to conquer the Chimu, during which time it appears that Túcume played an important role in the military, magical and diplomatic intrigues. Afterwards, the Incas transported many of Chimu warriors to remote outposts in the Andes, in order to maximize the Incas' political control and minimize the chances of rebellion. By the time the **Spanish** arrived, just over half a century later, Túcume's time had already passed.

Today, it remains an extensive site with the labyrinthine ruins of walls and court-yards still quite visible, if slightly rain-washed by the impact of recent heavy El Niño weather cycles, and you can easily spend two or three hours exploring. There's a **viewing point**, reached by a twisting path which leads up El Purgaotia hill, from where you can get a good view of the whole city. The largest of the pyramids, the **Huaca Larga**, is 700m long by 280m wide and, like the majority of them, stands just over 30m tall. The **Huaca de la Piedra Sagrada** (Temple of the Sacred Stone) was found to contain signs of human and animal sacrifice. Miniature metal and some shell offerings were also found as well as ritually important seeds, textiles and ceramics. Chimu and Inca offerings have also been found here, indicating that these conquering cultures respected this temple's importance.

The excellent and architecturally distinctive **Museo de Siteo**, at the entrance to the site, has exhibits relating to the work of Thor Heyerdahl, who found in Túcume the inspiration for his *Kon Tiki* expedition, as he tried to prove a link between civilizations on either side of the Pacific. The museum also covers the work of Wendell Bennet, the first person to scientifically excavate at the site, a scale model of the Huaca de la Piedra Sagrada, and some excavated objects. More esoterically, Túcume has a local reputation for magical power, and a section of the museum has been devoted to a display of local *curanderismo*, Peru's ancient healing art; *curanderos* still perform rites around the site. There's also an attractive picnic area, and a ceramic workshop where they use 2500-year-old techniques. Beside the museum the local community have kitchens where they prepare and sell traditional regional **food**.

To get to the site from Chiclayo, take a **colectivo** marked "Túcume" ($1.25, a 50min trip), which leaves every thirty minutes or so from block six of Manuel Pardo (they can be picked up as they pass through Lambayeque) or from the corner of Pedro Ruiz and Avenida Ugarte in Chiclayo. Get off at the small fork in the sandy road just a few kilometres beyond the town of **Mochumi** (where there's a well signposted **tourist information** centre on the main road, Avenida Federico Villareal just before turn-off to the plaza, if you want to stop here first) and a kilometre or two before the village of Túcume (look out for the pyramids and the signs to the Museo de Sitio). Follow the dusty track signposted to the right for 50m or so to reach the ticket office.

Túcume Viejo

Less than 2km from the Túcume ruins is the village of **Túcume Viejo**, reached by turning left along the sand track at the fork in the road just before you get to the site museum. Although there are no tourist facilities as such, it makes for an interesting thirty-minute walk, checking out the crumbling colonial adobe walls and a once painted adobe brick gateway as well as the church, all of which have an elegant and rather grandoise feel, suggesting perhaps that the early colonists were trying to compete for attention with the Valley of Pyramids. There's also the **Museo Santos Vera**, a local *curandero*'s museum full of magical paraphernalia, less than a kilometre beyond the entrance to the village.

Apurlec

Apurlec, some 60km north of Chiclayo, is another vast adobe settlement a little further north of Túcume. First occupied in the eighth century BC, it was still flourishing five hundred years later under the great Chimu planners and architects. Scattered over a huge area, the adobe remains of pyramids, forts, palaces, temples, storehouses and long city streets have been eroded over the years by heavy rains but remain quite recognizable. To get here, stay on the Túcume colectivo (see above) for another fifteen minutes or so (ask the driver where to get off), and make sure you bring some drink and a sunhat, as Apurlac has no shade or refreshments.

North to Piura: through the Sechura Desert

Buses and colectivos between Chiclayo and Piura tend to use the Panamerican Highway, cutting across the **Sechura Desert** and bypassing the town of Olmos. To the west of the road, at the close of the twentieth century, you could still see the remains of the lake created by the heavy El Niño weather of 1998. Chiclayo bus companies (see p.332) do the journey in three hours ($3), while plenty of slightly faster colectivos ($6, a 3hr trip) leave daily from Pedro Ruiz and Luis Gonzalez.

A few colectivos take the old **coastal route** to Piura, via the oil refinery of **Bayovar** and the beach resort of **Sechura**, a journey of around six hours. These buses run towards the Bayovar turn-off, then switch up to the coast at a vast obelisk and round-about right in the middle of one of the world's driest deserts. To the south, accessible only on foot or 4x4 vehicles, are the **Sechura hills** – an isolated and unoffical wildlife reserve of wild goats, foxes, and the occasional condor. There is no **water** in the region, and it's a good three-day walk from the road to the beach; maps are available in Lima, however, if you're interested in a serious exploration. The beaches here, on the **Bahia de Nonura**, are really the last of Peru's remaining virgin coastline, and there's more wildlife here, including dolphins, turtles, sea lions, sometimes penguins, and a host of different seabirds – but no people once you're away from the oil refinery. It's also reputed to have Peru's best **surfing**, but note that a special entry permit is required from Petro Peru at their headquarters in Lima (Avenida Paseo de La Republica 3361; ☎01/442-5000 or 442-5033) to get to the best (and the only accessible) sections beyond the refinery. You can only camp here and there are no facilities what-soever.

North of the roundabout there is little more than a handful of hermit goat-herders and two or three scattered groups of roadside restaurants, until just before Sechura, where you'll find a few tiny hamlets – basically clusters of huts on the beach – inhabit-ed by the same fishing families since long before the Conquest. The last of these, **Parachique**, has recently developed into a substantial port with its own fishmeal fac-tory; the others are all very simple, their inhabitants using sailing boats to fish, and often going out to sea for days at a time.

Sechura

The small town of **SECHURA**, 52km south of Piura, has a quaint seventeenth-century **church**, on the main square, whose tall twin towers lend the town an air of civilization. Local legend has it that the church was built over an ancient temple, from where an underground tunnel containing hidden treasure led out to the ocean. To the south of the town – between the sea and road – a long line of white crescent **dunes**, or *lomas*, reaches into the distance. Local people claim that these were used by Incas as land-marks across the desert.

If you want to **stay** overnight here you can **camp** virtually anywhere (including the beach), or stay in a **hostal**, such as the *Hospedaje de Dios* (③). There are several **restaurants**, the best being *Don Gilberto's* on the main plaza. The town's **food market**, just off the main square, takes place on weekdays and is good for picnic supplies.

Piura and around

The city of **Piura** feels very distinct from the rest of the country, cut off to the south by the formidable Sechura Desert, and to the east by the Huancabamba mountains. The people here see themselves primarily as Piurans rather than Peruvians, and the city has a strong oasis atmosphere, entirely dependent on the vagaries of the Río Piura – known colloquially since Pizarro's time as the Río Loco, or Crazy River. In spite of this precarious existence, Piura is the oldest colonial city in Peru. And this century – despite weathering at least two serious droughts and eight major floods (the last in 1998) – it has grown into a *departmento* of well over 1.5 million people, around a quarter of whom actually live in the city. With temperatures of up to 38°C from January to March, the region is known for its particularly wide-brimmed straw sombrero, worn by everyone from the mayor to local goat herders. You'll have plenty of opportunites to see these in **Piura Week**, (first two weeks of Oct), when you'll find the town in high spirits, but beds are a little scarce so it's best to book in advance.

Francisco Pizarro spent ten days in Piura in 1532 en route to his fateful meeting with the Inca overlord, Atahualpa, at Cajamarca. By 1534 the city, then known as San Miguel de Piura, had well over two hundred Spanish inhabitants, including the first Spanish women to arrive in Peru. All were hungry for a slice of the action – and treasure – but although Pizarro kept over 57,000 pesos of his spoils looted from the native inhabitants, he only gave 15,000 to the Piurans, which was the cause of some considerable resentment, and possibly the origin of the town's isolationist attitude. Pizarro did, however, encourage the development here of an urban class, trained for trade rather than war. As early as the 1560s, there was a flourishing trade in the excellent indigenous Tanguis cotton, and Piura today still produces a third of the nation's cotton.

Arrival, city transport and information

El Dorado **buses** from Trujillo and Tumbes, Dorado Express buses from Tumbes, Sullana and Aguas Verdes, buses from Chiclayo, and EPPO buses from Talara and Máncora all arrive around blocks 11 and 12 of Avenida Sanchez Cerro. All other buses arrive at their companies' offices (see "Listings", p.343 for addresses). **Colectivos**, mainly from Tumbes and Talara, also arrive and depart from the middle of the road at block 11 of Avenida Sanchez Cerro, ten minutes' stroll from the centre of town. If you arrive by one of the daily **planes** from Lima, Trujillo, Talara or Tumbes, you'll land at Piura airport (for flight information call ☎074/327733), 2km east of the city; a taxi into the centre costs $2–3. The quickest way of getting around the city is by the ubiquitous **motocycle rickshaw**, which you can hail just about anywhere for $0.50. In-town **taxi** rides are set at $1.

There is no official tourist office in Piura, though **information** and advice can sometimes be obtained from a desk at the airport (daily 9am–6.30pm), or from the Ministry of Tourism, Jirón Lima 775 (Mon–Fri 9am–1pm & 4–6pm; ☎074/327013). Failing these, your best bet is one of the helpful tour companies listed on p.344.

Accommodation

A wide range of **hotels** and **hostals** is spread throughout the town, with most of the cheaper ones on or around Avenida Loreto or within a few blocks of Avenida Grau and the Plaza de Armas.

Budget

Hostal California, Junin 835 (☎074/328789). A family-run establishment, brightly painted and decorated with plastic flowers giving it a somewhat kitsch feel. Good value and popular with backpackers, there are no private baths. ②.

Hostal Capullanca, Junin 925. Clean, friendly and all doubles have private bath, plus there are some cheaper singles. ②.

Hostal Moon and Night, Junin 899 (☎074/336174). Offers more modern comforts, private bath, TV, spacious rooms and is clean. ③.

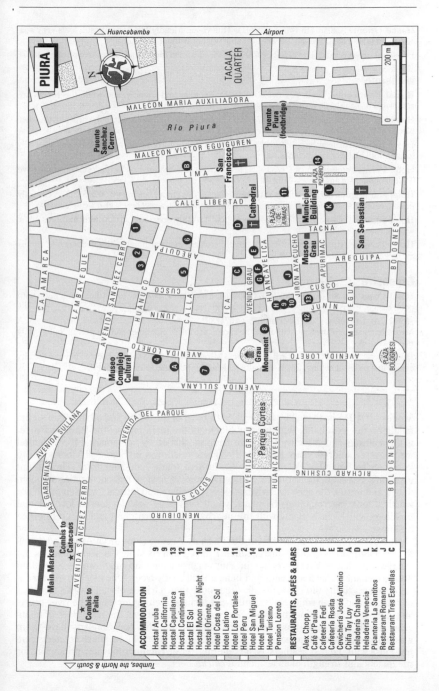

PIURA

△ Huancabamba   △ Airport

TACALA QUARTER

200 m

MALECON MARIA AUXILIADORA

Río Piura

Puente Sanchez Cerro

Puente Piura (footbridge)

MALECON VICTOR EGUIGUREN

LIMA

San Francisco

CALLE LIBERTAD

Cathedral

Municipal Building

San Sebastian

PLAZA PIZARRO

PLAZA DE ARMAS

TACNA

AREQUIPA

Museo Grau

CAJAMARCA

LAMBAYEQUE

AVENIDA SANCHEZ CERRO

HUANUCO

AREQUIPA

CUSCO

CALLAO

ICA

AVENIDA GRAU

HUANCAVELICA

APURIMAC

JIRON AYACUCHO

CUSCO

BOLOGNESI

JUNIN

JUNIN

Museo Complejo Cultural

AVENIDA LORETO

Grau Monument

AVENIDA SULLANA

AVENIDA LORETO

MOQUEGUA

PLAZA BOLOGNESI

AVENIDA SULLANA

DEL PARQUE

AVENIDA DEL PARQUE

Parque Cortes

AVENIDA GRAU

HUANCAVELICA

BOLOGNESI

LAS GARDENIAS

LOS COCOS

RICHARD CUSHING

BOLOGNESI

MENDIBURO

Main Market

★ Combis to Catacaos

AVENIDA SANCHEZ CERRO

★ Combis to Paita

Tumbes, the North & South ▽

ACCOMMODATION	
Hostal Aruba	9
Hostal California	9
Hostal Capullana	13
Hostal Continental	12
Hostal El Sol	1
Hostal Moon and Night	10
Hostal Oriente	6
Hotel Costa del Sol	7
Hotel Latino	8
Hotel Los Portales	11
Hotel Peru	2
Hotel San Miguel	14
Hotel Tambo	5
Hotel Turismo	3
Pension Loreto	4

RESTAURANTS, CAFÉS & BARS	
Alex Chopp	G
Café d'Paula	B
Cafeteria Fedi	F
Cafeteria Rosita	E
Cevicheria José Antonio	H
Chifa Tay Loy	A
Heladeria Chalan	D
Heladeria Venecia	L
Picanteria La Santitos	K
Restaurant Romano	J
Restaurant Tres Estrellas	C

Hostal Oriente, Callao 446 (☎074/328891). This clean, friendly family-run hostal feels very spacious and is well managed. Rooms are available with or without bath. ②.

Pension Loreto, Avenida Loreto 532 (☎074/300607). Clean and friendly, all rooms have private bath. ②.

Moderate

Hostal Continental, Junin 924 (☎074/334531). Spotless and friendly, and while the rooms are somewhat basic they do come with or without bath. ③.

Hostal El Sol, Sanchez Cerro 411 (☎074/324461, fax 326307). Clean and largely carpeted, this cool place has pleasant rooms (the front ones can be noisy) with TV and air conditioning. ④.

Hotel Latino, Huancavelica 720 (☎074/335123). A large, fairly modern establishment, centrally located with all the usual facilities. ④.

Hotel Peru, Arequipa 476 (☎074/333421, fax 331530). Good-value hotel whose smart rooms have TV, telephone, fan and private bath. ④.

Hotel San Miguel, corner of Lima with Apurimac on the Plaza Pizarro (☎074/305122). A decently priced, comfortable hotel with some rooms overlooking the plaza. There's also a cafetería. ④.

Hotel Tambo, Callao 546 (☎074/326440 or 325379). A tidy, spacious hotel, where all rooms come with private bath and a fan. ③.

Hotel Turismo, Huanuco 526 (☎074/325950). A clean, modern hotel, with good service; rooms available with or without baths. ③.

Expensive

Hotel Costa del Sol, loreto 649 (☎074/302864, *tcosol@peru.itete.com.pe*). A luxurious hotel with pool, casino, Internet facilities, car park, restaurant. ⑧.

Hotel Los Portales, Calle Libertad 875 (☎074/321161, fax 325920, *hoteles@peru.itete.com.pe*). A luxury hotel set in a lovely old building; the rooms are full of character and very clean, but slightly overpriced. ⑧.

Hotel Vicus, Avenida Guardia Civil B-3, Urbino Miraflores (☎074/341186). Located beyond the city centre in a pleasant setting, this is a comfortable and quiet hotel with good service. ⑥.

The City

Modern **PIURA** is divided by the river, with most of the action and all the main sights falling on the west bank. Within a few blocks of the main bridge, the **Puente Piura**, is the spacious and attractive **Plaza de Armas**, shaded by tall tamarind trees planted well over a hundred years ago. On the plaza you'll find a "Statue of Liberty", also known as La Pola (The Pole), and the **Cathedral** (daily 7am–7pm: free). Though not especially beautiful, the cathedral boasts impressive bronze nails decorating its main doors, and inside, the spectacularly tasteless, gilt altars and intricate wooden pulpit are worth a look. Surrounding the plaza, you'll see some pastel-coloured low colonial buildings which clash madly with the nearby tall, modern glass and concrete office buildings.

One block towards the river from the Plaza de Armas, along Jirón Ayacucho, you'll find a delightful elongated square, called **Plaza Pizarro**, which is also known as the Plaza de 3 Culturas. Every evening the Piurans promenade up and down here, chatting beside elegant modern fountains and beneath tall shady trees. One block to the east of here, you reach the Río Piura, usually little more than a trickle of water with a few piles of rubbish and some white egrets, gulls and terns searching for food. The river bed is large, however, indicating that when Piura's rare rains arrive, the river rises dramatically; people who build their homes too close to the dry bed regularly have them washed away. The river is spanned by the old bridge, Puente Piura, which connects central Piura with the less aesthetic east-bank quarter of **Tacala**, renowned principally for the quality and strength of its fermented *chicha* beer.

A block south of the Plaza de Armas, along Tacna, you'll find the **Museo Grau** (Mon–Sat 8am–1pm & 4–7pm; free), nineteenth-century home of Admiral Miguel Grau, one of the heroes of the War of the Pacific (1879–80), in which Chile took control of Peru's valuable nitrate fields in the south and cut Bolivia's access to the Pacific. The museum's exhibits include a model of the British-built ship, the *Huascar*, Peru's only successful blockade runner, as well as various military artefacts. A display of the region's archeological treasures, and in particular the ceramics from Cerro Vicus (see p.344), can be found at the **Museo Complejo Cultural** (Mon–Fri 9am–5.30pm, Sat 9am–1pm; $1) on Huanuco, one block west of Avenida Loreto.

The town's daily **market**, in the north of the city, is worth a visit for its well-made straw hats (invaluable in the desert), ceramics made in the village of Simbila, and a variety of leather crafts.

Eating, drinking and nightlife

Most of Piura's **restaurants** and **cafés** are centred around the Plaza de Armas area, with many of the cafés specializing in delicious ice cream. In the evenings, you'll find most Piurans strolling around the main streets, chatting in the plazas, and drinking in the cheap **bars** along the roads around Junin. Piura's speciality is a very sweet toffee-like delicacy, called *natilla*, which can be bought at street stalls around the city. For a spot of late-night **drinking and dancing**, try block 5 of Ayacucho, where you'll find *Bloom Moon*; *Bohemio's* and *Flamingos*; *Alex Chopp* (see below) is also pretty good.

Alex Chopp, Huancavelica 538. A popular nightspot with a friendly atmosphere, serving good beers and fine seafood in the evenings.

Café d'Paula, Lima 541. This is a smart new café serving delicious cakes and good coffee.

Cafetería Fedi, Arequipa 780. A good all round choice, this is a dignified and very pleasant coffee house.

Cafetería Rosita, Avenida Grau 223. Serves delicious sandwiches and green *tamales*, savoury maizemeal cakes typical of the region, as well as great breakfasts.

Cevichería José Antonio, corner of Junin with Huancavelica. Good for seafood dishes and other local specialities.

Chifa Tay Loy, Callao 828. Dishes up the best Chinese meals in town, in a stylish Mandarin environment.

Heladeria Chalan, Plaza de Armas. Excellent service in a bright and busy atmosphere; serves sandwiches, juices, cakes and wonderful ice creams; they also have a smarter, newer place behind the Cathedral.

Heladeria Venecia, Calle Libertad 1007. Choose your ice cream from a wide variety of flavours and enjoy it on the cool and elegant patio.

Picanteria La Santitos, La Libertad 1014. Only open for lunches, it serves a good choice of traditional *criolla* dishes such as *majado de yuca* (mashed *yuca* with pieces of pork) and *seco de chavelo* (mashed plantain with pieces of beef), in a renovated colonial house.

Restaurant Romano, Ayacucho 580. A popular local eating house serving a host of reasonably priced dishes.

Restaurant Tres Estrellas, Arequipa 702. The best restaurant in town for serious *criolla* dishes; try the goat (*cabrito*) with rice and *tamales*.

Listings

Airlines Aero Conintente, Calle Libertad 951 (☎074/325635); and TANS, Libertdad 422.

Buses CIAL, Bolognesi 817 (☎074/304250), for Huaraz, Lima and Tumbes; Cruz del Sur, Libertad 1176 (☎337094), for Lima and the coast; Entrafesa, Los Naranjas 235 (☎074/337093), for Chiclayo, Trujillo and Tumbes; Etrans-Chiclayo, Sanchez Cerro 1121 (☎322251) for Chiclayo; Tepsa, Avenida

Loreto 1195 (☎074/323721), for Trujillo and Tumbes; Trans Piura, Loreto 1253 (☎074/329131), for Tumbes, Chiclayo, Trujillo and Lima; Transa/Vulcano, Sanchez Cerro 1215 (☎074/327821), for Trujillo and Chiclayo; and Trans-EPPO, Sanchez Cerro 1141 (☎074/331160), for Talara and Máncora.

Banks and exchange The Banco Continental is on the Plaza de Armas, at the corner of Ayacucho and Tacna. *Cambistas* are at block 7 of Avenida Arequipa, near the corner of Avenida Grau.

Post office Plaza de Armas, on the corner of Calle Libertad and Ayacucho. Mon–Sat 9am–7pm.

Tour operators Piura Tours, Ayacucho 585 (☎074/328873); and Tallan Tours, Tacna 258n (☎074/334647).

Catacaos

Just 12km south of Piura is the friendly, dusty little town of **CATACAOS**, worth a visit principally for its excellent, vast **market**. Just off the main plaza – which boasts a public TV given to the town by the mayor – the market sells everything from food to crafts, even filigree gold and silverwork, with the hammocks hanging colourfully about the square being a particularly good buy. The town is also renowned for its **picanterías** (spicy food restaurants), which serve all sorts of local delicacies, such as *tamalitos verdes* (little green-corn pancakes), fish-balls, *chifles* (fresh banana or sweet potato chips), goat (*seco de cabrito*) and the local *chicha* beer. One of the better restaurants is *La Chayo*, San Francisco 493, which is friendly and serves huge portions and lets you sample the *chicha* before buying. While you're here you could also try the sweet medicinal drink *algarrobina*, made from the berries of a desert tree, and available from bars and street stalls. The **church** is worth a peep, too, having been recently repainted rather brightly.

From Piura, regular combi **colectivos** for Catacaos leave when full, usually every twenty minutes or so, ($0.25, a 20min trip) from the terminal in block 12 of Sanchez Cerro.

Cerro Vicus

At **Cerro Vicus**, 27km east of Piura on the old route to Chiclayo, you'll find an interesting pre-Inca site, just 500m to the left of the main road. There are no buildings still visible at the site, probably due to the occasional heavy rains which can destroy adobe ruins, but you can see a number of L-shaped tombs, some up to 15m deep. These graves contained ceramics and metal artefacts revealing several styles, early Mochica being the most predominant. The artefacts were superbly modelled in a variety of human, animal and architectural forms, and you can see good examples of them in the Museo Complejo Cultural in Piura (see p.343).

To reach Cerro Vicus, take any of the Olmos **buses** or **colectivos**, which leave every hour or so from Sanchez Cerro in Piura. Ask to be dropped off at Km 449 of the Panamerican Highway, then walk across the sand to the tombs on the hill. Most buses, and some trucks, will stop if you wave them down beside the road for the return trip to Piura.

Paita and Colán

Fifty kilometres northwest of Piura lies its port and closest major settlement, **PAITA**. Set on a small peninsula a little south of the mouth of the Río Chira, it is Peru's fifth largest port, but is best known to many Peruvians as the former home of **Manuela Saenz**, the tragic mistress of Simón Bolivar during the Wars of Liberation. After the 1828 skirmishes with Colombia (of which Bolivar was dictator), Manuela was ostracized by Peruvian society, dying here in poverty in 1856. Her house (it has a plaque on

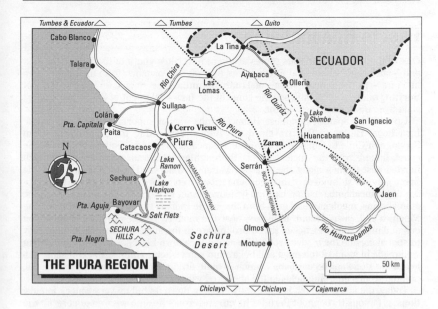

Map: THE PIURA REGION

it) is in the old quarter of town, just up from the petrol station and across from the market, but it is not open to the public. A good **place to stay** is the *Hotel Las Brisas*, Aurora 201, (☎074/611023; ②) on the seafront, while the *Chifa Hong Kong*, Junin 358, is well known amongst locals for its authentic **food**. For a beer with a view, try the *Club de La Libertad*, on the seafront; it's a crumbling old wooden building commanding a fine panorama across the bay and port from its terrace.

To the north of Paita, you'll find the once exclusive bay of **COLÁN**. This is still a good place to swim, though the old seaside residences that used to echo with the chatter of wealthy land-owning families are now pretty much destroyed, many washed away in 1983 by the swollen Río Chira amid the dramatic floods of that rainy season, with others currently looking ready to tumble into the sea. The **church** in Colán (ask for the key holder in the village), however, is a state-protected building and has been recently renovated, due to its claim to be the oldest church in Peru and the first where Mass was said in South America. From the tower there are fine views over the pueblo of San Lucas de Colán, the sandy spit on which the beach settlement sits, and the salt flats between the two, which, incidentally is a great spot for bird-watching and sometimes floods, cutting off the two communities. There are a couple of expensive **lodges** here, the *Sol de Colán* (⑥) and the *Colán Lodge* (⑤), both offering a range of bungalows, pool, cafetería and games rooms. The only other place is the *Hospedaje Frente el Mar* (☎074/615465; ③); it's small and basic, perhaps slightly overpriced, but the sea comes right up to the terrace. There are a few decent small beaches nearby, including **Yacila** and **Cangrejos**.

Buses and **colectivos** to Paita ($0.75, a 1hr trip) and Colán leave from Sanchez Cerro in Piura every hour or so, the latter generally when full. Your best bet is Transportes Dora, Sanchez Cerro 1387, which has a direct service from Piuera to Paita (most of the others stop en route). For Colán from Paita, combi colectivos leave when full (usually every hour), from the top end of the market ($0.50, a 20min journey).

East to Huancabamba

One of the more adventurous routes around Piura takes you into the hills to the east and – after some 215km and fifteen hours by daily bus or truck from the market area in Piura – to the remote village of **Huancabamba**. The road goes via the town of **Serran**, where you can still see the ruins of the Inca settlement of Zaran, just a short walk from the modern settlement.

Up until the Spanish Conquest, Huancabamba was an important crossroads on the Inca Royal Highway. This traversed the Andes, connecting the Inca Empire from Santiago in Chile to Quito in Ecuador. At Huancabamba a side road went down to the coast, linking with the ancient desert thoroughfare at Zaran, while another branch headed east to Jaen along the forested Marañon watershed, a trading link with the fierce jungle headhunters of the Aguaruna tribe. Even before the Incas arrived, the people of Huancabamba had an extremely active trade, ferrying goods such as feathers, animal skins, medicines and gold from the jungle Indians to the coastal cultures of the Mochica and, later, Chimu. In places, near the modern village of Huancabamba, you can still make out stretches of that thoroughfare in the ancient stone slabs, quite easy to spot alongside the modern road. The actual Inca town here has been lost but, being well made of stone, it too must still be around somewhere. *Huancabamba* means "valley of the stone spirit guardians", which is quite fitting, since you can still see the tall, pointed stones guarding fields in the sheltered valley.

Today, the village, which is apparently slipping down its hill on very watery foundations, is famous throughout Peru for its **curanderos** – healing wizards or curers, who use herbal and hallucinogenic remedies in conjunction with ritual bathing in sacred lagoons such as Lake Shimbe, 2000m and seven hours' mule ride above the town. These *curanderos* are still visited by Peruvians from all walks of life. The lake area above the town is unhospitable, with sparse, marshy vegetation. It is usually possible to hire mules and a guide from Huancabamba to take you up to **the lakes** – or even on the five-day trek, following the route of the old Inca Highway, to **Ayabaca** and the nearby Inca fortress of **Ayapate**. These trips, though, are only for the really adventurous, and it's not a good idea to go alone or without a local guide.

HOW PIZARRO FOUND ATAHUALPA

It was at Serran, then a small Inca administrative centre, that **Pizarro** waited in 1532 for the return of a small troop of soldiers that he had sent up the Inca Royal Highway on a discovery mission. It took the soldiers, led by Hernando de Soto, just two days and a night to reach the town of Cajas, now lost in the region around Huancabamba and Lake Shimbe. At Cajas, the Spaniards gained their first insight into the grandeur and power of the Inca Empire, although, under orders from Atahualpa, the two-thousand-warrior garrison had slunk away into the mountains. The Spaniards were not slow to discover the most impressive Inca buildings – a sacred convent of over five hundred virgins who had been chosen at an early age to dedicate their lives to the Inca religion. The soldiers raped at will, provoking the Inca diplomat who was accompanying de Soto to threaten the troop with death for such sacrilege, especially as they were only 300km from Atahualpa's camp at Cajamarca. This information about Atahualpa's whereabouts was exactly what de Soto had been seeking. After a brief visit to the adjacent, even more impressive, Inca town of Huancabamba – where a tollgate collected duties along the Royal Highway – he returned with the Inca diplomat to rejoin Pizarro. Realizing that he had provided the Spanish with vital information, the Inca diplomat agreed to take them to Atahualpa's camp – a disastrous decision resulting in the massacre at Cajamarca (see pp.309–310).

North of Piura: Talara and Cabo Blanco

Leaving Piura, the Panamerican Highway heads directly north, passing through the large town of **SULLANA** after 40km. This major transport junction has little of interest to travellers, except perhaps as a rest before or after taking the inland route to Ecuador. If you do stop, take a quick look at the **Plaza de Armas**, which boasts fine views over the Río Chira, and is the location for the old church of La Santisima Trinidad. There are many **hotels** between Avenida lama and the Plaza: try the *Hostal El Chorre*, Tarapaca 501 (☎074/507006; ③), which is decent value and offers private bathrooms, TVs, laundry and a cafetería; the *Hostal Tarapaca*, Tarapaca 731 (☎074/503786; ②), which also has private baths and is quiet and friendly, though slightly more basic; and the *Hospedaje San Miguel*, Farfan 204 (☎074/502789; ①), the cheapest of the lot, with rooms off a central passageway that share bathrooms, but it's clean. For **eating**, one of the best places is *Bima Chopp*, in the plaza, which has good set menus and is popular with locals; for Chinese food, the best is the *Chifa Kam Loy*, at San Martín 925. Most **bus companies** have their offices on or just off Avenida Lama; EPPO and Emtrafesa, are at the corner of Callao with Pierola, offering regular departures to Talara. EPPO also have buses twice daily to Máncora, while Emtrafesa serves Tumbes and Chiclayo. There are regular **combis** from Avenida Lama to Piura and Paita, each one hour away ($0.75), while the faster **colectivos** cost slightly more. Combis for the inland border crossing with Ecuador at la Tina leave in the morning from Avenida Buenos Aires, close to the main market.

Talaria

TALARA, some 70km further north, would be more attractive if it wasn't for the entrance to the city being strewn with rubbish, a depressing sight of plastic bags impaled on bushes for almost a kilometre. All roads into the town are in a poor state of repair. Until 1940, it was no more than a small fishing hamlet, though its deep-water harbour and tar pits had been used since Pizarro's time for caulking wooden ships – Pizarro had chosen the site for the first Spanish settlement in Peru, but it proved too unhealthy and he was forced to look elsewhere, eventually hitting on Piura. Talara takes its name and function from the country's most important coastal oilfield, and it was the town's oil reserves that were directly responsible for Peru's last military coup in 1968. President Belaunde, then in his first term of office, had given subsoil concessions to the multinational company IPC, declaring that "if this is foreign imperialism what we need is more, not less of it". A curious logic, based on his impressions of superior conditions at the plant, it led to the accusation that he had signed an agreement "unacceptable to true Peruvians". Within two months of the affair, and as a direct consequence, he was deposed and exiled. One of the initial acts of the new revolutionary government was to nationalize IPC and declare the Act of Talara null and void. Today the town is highly industrialized, with several fertilizer plants as well as the oil business, although you can find an unpolluted **beach** at La Pena, 2km away.

If you need to spend the night, there are a few reasonable **hotels** in the commercial centre, such as the *Hotel Gran Pacifico*, on Avenida Aviacion, (☎074/385450; ⑦), which has a fantastic swimming pool, or the more modest *Hostal Talara*, Avenida Ejercito 217 (☎074/382186; ③), where there are rooms with or without bath.

Cabo Blanco

Thirty kilometres or so beyond Talara, there's a turning off the highway to the old fishing mecca of **CABO BLANCO**. It is just off the cape here that the cold Humboldt Current meets the warm equatorial El Niño – a stroke of providence that creates an extraordinary abundance of marine life. Thomas Stokes, a British resident and fanatical fisherman, discovered the spot in 1935, and it was a very popular resort in the post-war years. Hemingway stayed for some months in 1951, while two years later the largest fish ever caught with a rod was landed here – a 710-kilo black marlin. Changes in the offshore currents have brought a decline in recent years, but international fishing competitions still take place and the area is much reputed for swordfish. The fishing club where Hemingway is supposed to have written *The Old Man and the Sea* offers accommodation (⑥), which includes access to a nice pool, an excellent seafood restaurant, and fishing and watersports facilities. It also has one of the few free and official **campsites** in Peru.

From here to Tumbes the Panamerican Highway cuts across a further stretch of desert, for the most part keeping tightly to the Pacific coastline. It's a straight road, except for the occassional detour around bridges destroyed by the 1998 El Niño. but not a dull one, with immense views along the rolling surf and, if you're lucky, the occasional school of dolphins playing close to the shore. To the right of the road looms a long hill, the **Cerros de Amotape**, the largest bump along the entire Peruvian coast that isn't actually a proper Andean foothill. Amotape was a local chief whom Pizarro had killed in 1532 as an example to potential rebels; just to the north of this wooded hill is the ancient Inca Highway, though it can't be seen from this road.

Tumbes and around

About 30km from the Ecuadorean border and 287km north of Piura, **TUMBES** is usually considered a mere pit-stop for overland travellers. However, the city has a significant history and, unlike most border settlements, is a surprisingly warm and friendly place. On top of that, it's close to some of Peru's finest **beaches** and the country's only serious mangrove swamp, **Los Bosques de Manglares**. In the rural areas around the city, nearly half of Peru's tobacco leaf is produced.

Tumbes was the first town to be "conquered" by the Spanish and has maintained its importance ever since – originally as the gateway to the Inca Empire and more recently through its strategic position on the controversial **frontier with Ecuador**. Despite three regional wars – in 1859, 1941–42 and 1997–98 – the exact line of the border remains a source of controversy, although relations at the close of the millenium seemed to be at an all time high, with huge numbers of Peruvians crossing the border to buy cheaper Ecuadorian products. Maps of the frontier vary depending on which country you buy them in, with the two countries claiming a disparity of up to 150km in some places along the border. The traditional enmity between Peru and Ecuador and the continuing dispute over the border, means that Tumbes has a strong Peruvian army presence and a consequent strict ban on photography anywhere near military or frontier installations. Most of the city's hundred thousand population are engaged in either transport or petty trading across the frontier, and are quite cut off from mainstream Peru, being much nearer to Quito than Lima, 1268km to the south.

Some history

Pizarro didn't actually set foot in Tumbes when it was first discovered in 1527. He preferred to cast his eyes along the Inca city's adobe walls, its carefully irrigated fields, and its shining temple, from the comfort and safety of his ship. However, with the help of translators he set about learning as much as he could about Peru and the Incas during this initial contact. An Inca noble visited him aboard ship and even dined at his table. The noble was said to be especially pleased with his first taste of Spanish wine and the present of an iron hatchet.

The Spaniards who did go ashore – a Captain Alonso de Molina and his black servant – made reports of such grandeur that Pizarro at first refused to believe them, sending instead the more reliable Greek cavalier, Pedro de Candia. Molina's descriptions of the temple, lined with gold and silver sheets, were confirmed by Candia. He also gave the people of Tumbes their first taste of European technological might – firing his musket to smash a wooden board to pieces. With Candia's testimony, Pizarro had all the evidence he needed; after sailing another 500km down the coast, as far as the Santa Valley, he returned to Panama and then back to Spain to obtain royal consent and support for his projected conquest.

The Tumbes people hadn't always been controlled by the Incas. The area was originally inhabited by the **Tallanes,** related to coastal tribes from Ecuador who are still known for their unusual lip and nose ornaments. In 1450 they were conquered for the first time – by the **Chimu**. Thirteen years later came the **Incas,** organized by Topac Inca, who bulldozed the locals into religious, economic, and even architectural conformity in order to create their most northerly coastal terminus. A fortress, temple and sun convent were built, and the town was colonized with loyal subjects from other regions – a typical Inca ploy, which they called the *Mitimaes* system. The valley had an efficient irrigation programme, allowing them to grow, among other things, bananas, corn and squash.

It didn't take Pizarro long to add his name to the list of conquerors. But after landing on the coast of Ecuador in 1532, with a royal warrant to conquer and convert the people of Peru to Christianity, his arrival at Tumbes was a strange affair. Despite the previous friendly contact, some of the Spanish were killed by Indians as they tried to beach, and when they reached the city it was completely deserted with many buildings destroyed, and, more painfully for Pizarro, no sign of gold. It seems likely that Tumbes's destruction prior to Pizarro's arrival was the result of intertribal warfare directly related to the **Inca Civil War**. This, a war of succession between Atahualpa and his half-brother, the legitimate heir, Huascar, was to make Pizarro's role as conqueror a great deal easier, and he took the town of Tumbes without a struggle.

Arrival, city transport and information

Most **buses** coming to Tumbes arrive at offices along Avenida Tumbes Norte (also known as Avenida Teniente Vasquez), or along Piura, although a new Terminal Terrestre is planned for the near future. Ormeño and Continental buses from Ecuador stop at Avenida Tumbes Norte. 216. See "Listings", p.352, for full details of bus company offices. Comite **colectivos** also pull in on Tumbes Norte, at no. 308 (☎074/525977) If you're **flying** in from Lima, note that Tumbes airport is often very quiet, particularly at night, when there's no access to food or drink. A taxi into town should cost around $5, about a twenty-minute journey.

Tumbes is quite pleasant and easy to get around **on foot**, or you can hail down one of the many **motorcycle rickshaws**, which will take you anywhere in the city for around $0.50. **Tourist information** is available from the first floor of the Centro Civico, on the Plaza de Armas (8am–1pm & 2–6pm).

Accommodation

Central Tumbes is well endowed with places **to stay**. Some of the better budget options are strung out from the Plaza de Armas along Calle Grau, an attractive old-fashioned hotchpotch of a street, lined with wooden colonial buildings.

Hostal Chicho, Avenida Tumbes Norte 327 (☎074/522282). New and good value; some rooms come with private bath and TV. Ones at the back are quieter. ③.

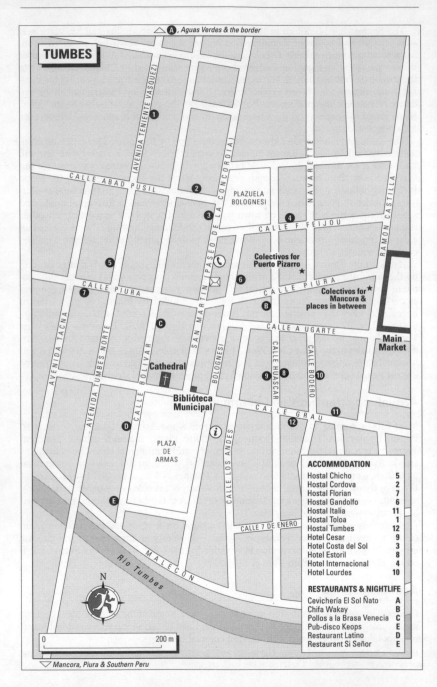

TUMBES

△ **A**, *Aguas Verdes & the border*

AVENIDA TENIENTE VASQUEZ

CALLE ABAD PUSIL

PASEO DE LA CONCORDIA

PLAZUELA BOLOGNESI

NAVARETTE

RAMON CASTILLA

CALLE F FEIJOU

Colectivos for Puerto Pizarro ★

CALLE PIURA

CALLE PIURA

Colectivos for ★
Mancora & places in between

AVENIDA TACNA

SAN MARTIN

BOLOGNESI

CALLE A UGARTE

Main Market

AVENIDA TUMBES NORTE

CALLE BOLIVAR

CALLE HUASCAR

CALLE BODERO

Cathedral

Biblióteca Municipal

CALLE GRAU

CALLE LOS ANDES

i

PLAZA DE ARMAS

CALLE 7 DE ENERO

MALECON

Río Tumbes

N

0   200 m

▽ *Mancora, Piura & Southern Peru*

ACCOMMODATION

Hostal Chicho	5
Hostal Cordova	2
Hostal Florian	7
Hostal Gandolfo	6
Hostal Italia	11
Hostal Toloa	1
Hostal Tumbes	12
Hotel Cesar	9
Hotel Costa del Sol	3
Hotel Estoril	8
Hotel Internacional	4
Hotel Lourdes	10

RESTAURANTS & NIGHTLIFE

Cevichería El Sol Ñato	A
Chifa Wakay	B
Pollos a la Brasa Venecia	C
Pub-disco Keops	D
Restaurant Latino	E
Restaurant Si Señor	E

Hostal Cordova, Jirón Abad Pusil 777 (☎074/523981). Some rooms have private bath, and although comforts are minimal, it's reasonable value. ②.

Hostal Gandolfo, Bolognesi 118 (☎074/522868). Small, budget rooms that are decent for the price. ①.

Hostal Florian, Calle Piura 414 (☎074/522464, fax 524725). A large hotel, slightly down-at-heel, but with comfortable beds at reasonable rates. Most rooms have private bath. ③.

Hostal Italia, Calle Grau 733 (☎074/526164). Slightly run down, but it's a characterful old building. Rooms are with or without bath. ③.

Hostal Toloa, Avenida Tumbes Norte 430 (☎074/523771). A reasonable choice, but the road outside is very noisy and it's opposite a large military establishment. ②.

Hostal Tumbes, Calle Grau 614 (☎074/522203). Very pleasant rooms with showers that are excellent value, although the ones upstairs have better light. ②.

Hotel Cesar, Calle Huascar 333 (☎074/522883). Small, very friendly and good value, with simple rooms. ③.

Hotel Costa del Sol, San Martín 275 (☎074/523991, fax 525862). A smart revamped hotel on the Plazuela Bolognesi; all rooms have TV, minibar, air conditioning and private bath with hot water. ⑤.

Hotel Estoril, Huascar 317 (☎074/524906). Small and plain, but with friendly staff and exceptionally good value. ②.

Hotel Internacional, Calle F. Feijou 185 (☎074/525976). An airy but rather run-down place. All rooms have private bath. ②.

Hotel Lourdes, Bodero 118 (☎074/522126, fax 522758). Located in a quiet side street, it has private bathrooms and is clean, good value and friendly. ③.

The City

Although it has very few real sights, Tumbes is a surprisingly elegant city, at least in the centre where its broad **Plaza de Armas** is bounded by the **Biblióteca Municipal** and the plain **Cathedral**, which dates from 1903, and with an amphitheatre at its southern end. An attractive pedestrian precinct, the **Paseo de la Concordia**, decorated with colourful tiles and several large sculptures and statues, leads off the plaza between the cathedral and the *biblióteca* to the Plazuela Bolognesi. Older and slightly grubby is the long **Malecón** promenade that runs along the high riverbanks of the Río Tumbes, a block beyond the southern end of the Plaza de Armas. At the western end of the Malecón, you can see a massive Modernist **sculpture** *Tumbes Paraiso del Amor y el Eterno Verano* (Tumbes Paradise of Love and Eternal Summer), depicting a pair of lovers kissing.

Restaurants and bars

Tumbes has some excellent **restaurants** and is the best place in Peru to try *conchas negras* – the black clams found only in these coastal waters, where they grow on the roots of mangroves. The *Pub-disco Keops*, Bolivar 121, on the plaza, has a rustic style **bar** at the front with a music scene going on behind it; at weekends they sometimes have live music.

Cevichería El Sol Ñato, Bolivar 608. The best place in town for a wide range of seafood, but only open for lunches; try a *ceviche* with *conchas negras* or a huge steaming dish *of sudado de pescado*.

Chifa Wakay, Calle Huascar 417. Dishes up well priced, tasty Chinese dishes.

Pollos a la Brasa Venecia, Bolivar 237. Does exactly what it says in its name – a great place for chicken.

Restaurant Latino, Calle Bolivar 163. Right on the Plaza de Armas, this old-fashioned place specializes in excellent Continental and American breakfasts.

Restaurant Si Señor, Calle Bolivar 119. Serves mostly beer and seafood, right on the Plaza de Armas.

Listings

Airlines Aero Continente, Tumbes Norte 217 (☎074/522350).

Banks and exchange Banco de Credito, Calle Bolivar 227, and Banco de la Nacion, on the corner of Calle Grau and Calle Bolivar, by the Plaza de Armas. *Cambistas* are at the corner of Bolivar with Piura.

Bus companies CIAL, Avenida Tumbes Norte 586, for Lima; Cruz del Sur, Avenida Tumbes Norte 319 (☎074/522350), for Lima and the coast; El Dorado, Piura 454, for Máncora. Emtrafesa, Avenida Tumbes Norte 581 (☎074/524616), for Chiclayo and Trujillo; Nor Pacifico, Avenida Tumbes Norte, for Piura, Chiclayo and Máncora; Ormeño and Continental, Avenida Tumbes Norte 319, for Trujillo; Santa Rosa, Avenida Tumbes Norte, for Piura, to Piura and Máncora; Tepsa, Tacna 216 (☎074/522428), for Lima; Trans Olano, Avenida Tumbes Norte 324; and Transportes Chiclayo, Avenida Tumbes Norte 466 (☎074/525260), for Chiclayo.

Photographic equipment Foto Estudio Gunes, Bolognesi 127.

Post office San Martín 240. Mon–Sat 7am–7pm.

Telephones The Telefónica del Peru office is on San Martín in the same block as the post office. Ravitel telephone and fax point is at Avenida Tumbes Norte 322.

Tour operators Tumbes Tours, Avenida Tumbes Norte 341 (☎074/522481), runs a number of tours including a 4-day/3-night trip exploring the nearby Puerto Pizarro mangrove swamp and beaches from $20 per person per day, depending on size of group. Manglares Tours, Avenida Tumbes Norte 313 (☎074/522887), can organize local tours with guides, though they specialize in air tickets. Preferencial Tours, Grau 427, are good for tourist information and are very friendly.

Around Tumbes

Along the coast around Tumbes you'll find some of the best **beaches** in the country, with pleasantly warm sea. Among them are Caleta de la Cruz, 23km southwest (45min), reputed to be the bay where Pizarro first landed, **Punta Sal**, 50km southwest (1–2hr), Zorritos, 34km southwest (1hr) and **Máncora**, about 100km to the south (2hr). Buses to all four resorts leave daily from the main market in Tumbes, on Ramon Castillo, but return buses aren't that frequent, so check return times with the driver before you leave Tumbes. Nor Pacifico and Santa Rosa buses (see "Listings", above) also go to Máncora from their offices in Tumbes.

The ruined Inca city of **San Pedro de Las Incas** lies 5km south of the modern town in the village of Corrales and although there's not a lot that you can make out these days it's a pleasant walk, and both the temple and fortress are recognizable. It used to be on the Inca coastal highway to Cajamarca, which was vital in Pizarro's rapid advance towards the Inca Stahuallpa. The ruins are 1km from the modern Panamerican Highway, and cows and goats from the nearby hamlet of San Pedro wander freely among the ancient adobe walls, devastated by centuries of intermittent flooding.

Puerto Pizarro

If you've never seen a mangrove swamp, **PUERTO PIZARRO** is perhaps worth a visit, 13km further on, though it has no specific link with the conquistador and the waterfront today is full of rubbish. This ancient fishing port was a commercial harbour until swamps grew out to sea, making it inaccessible for large boats and permanently disconnecting Tumbes from the Pacific. You can take short **boat trips** ($12 per person) out to the **Isla de Amor**, a bathing beach and some **mangrove creeks** where it's possible to see the *rhizopora* tree's dense root system and wildlife. Overlooking the port, the brightly painted bungalows of the **hotel** *Puerto Pizarro* (③) occupy the only nice bit of waterfront; the hotel has a pool, private bathrooms, palm trees and restaurant-café. **Combis** leave every thirty minutes or so from the corner of Calle Piura with Navarette in Tumbes (50¢, 20mins), or you can take an organized tour from one of companies in "Listings" above.

THE TUMBES PROTECTED AREAS

The Tumbes region is well endowed with natural resources, not least the three major **protected areas** of the Sanctuario Nacional Los Manglares de Tumbes, the Parque Nacional de Cerros de Amotape and the Zona Reservada de Tumes. These, plus the El Angulo Hunting Reserve, encompass many habitats only found in this small corner of the country. If you're short of time it is just about possible to travel between these in just a day, but contact the local conservation organization – Pronaturaleza (☎074/523412) Avenida Tarapaca 4-16, Urbino Fonavi, on the outskirts of Tumbes – beforehand for impartial, expert advice. Permission from **INRENA**, opposite Pronaturaleza's office, is needed to enter all of these areas, though this is a formality for which no fees are payable.

The **Sanctuario Nacional Los Manglares de Tumbes** covers 3000 hectares of of the remaining 4750 **mangrove swamps** left in Peru, which are under serious threat from fishing and farming (shrimp farming in particular), to which an equal amount of land is already dedicated around Tumbes. The best way to visit the sanctuary is via the Pronaturaleza centre near Zarumilla, here called **CECODEM** (Centro de Conservacion para el Desarrollo de los Manglares); combis run from Tumbes market to Zarumilla regularly ($0.5, a 20min trip), from where it's only 7km down a track to CECODEM; a motorcycle taxi will cost $1.50, and you can arrange for the driver to retun to pick you up. If arranged in advance with Pronaturaleza in Tumbes (at least one day before), CECODEM offer a 2–3 hour walking **tour** following a raised walkway through the mangroves and a canoe trip with a guide ($12 for up to 6 people). The centre also presents a lot of interpretative material about the mangroves, of which there are five species here. Red mangrove is the most common and this is where the *conchas negras* thrive, although the 1998 El Niño weather introduced large amounts of fresh water into the shell beds here, causing significant damage. The mangroves also contain over 200 bird species, including eight endemic species, such as the rather splendid mangrove eagle.

The **Zona Reservada de Tumbes**, which extends right up to the Ecuadorian border, covers 75,000 hectares of mainly tropical forest. The best route is inland, due south from Tumbes via Pampas de Hospital and El Caucho to El Narranjo and Figueroa on the border, but transport from Tumbes is only regular as far as Pampas de Hospital, and only occasional further on to El Caucho, which is where the best forest is. Like all tropical forests it has a clear structure, with a canopy and emergent trees. Potential sightings include monkeys, many bird species, small cats and snakes, while the Río Tumbes crocodile is a highly endangered species, found only at two sites along this river. There is some small hope for this unique creature in the form of a local breeding programme, but the whole area is under threat from gold-mining, mainly from across the border in Ecuador at the headwaters of the river. Pollution, too, from Tumbes is generating further disturbance.

The **Parque Nacional Cerros de Amotape** covers over 90,000 hectares which contain seven distinct habitats, including the best-preserved region of dry forest anywhere along the Pacific coast of South America. Access is via Corrales, 5km south of Máncora, or via Chillo, just north of Sullana; you'll need permission from INRENA to visit (see above, or if coming via Chillo you can visit them en route at Encuentro de Los Pilares). Animals that you just might see here include the Black parrot, desert foxes, deer, white-backed squirrels, *tigrillos* (ocelots), puma and white winged turkeys. Remember to take all your drinking and other water needs with you when entering this zone.

Punta Sal

Punta Sal, considered by many to be to be the best beach in Peru, has extensive sands and attractive rocky outcrops, swarming with crabs at low tide. It's a safe place to swim and is a heavenly spot for diving in warm, clear waters. Several **hotels** here were destroyed by the 1998 El Niño, but for now the best place to stay is the friendly *Hotel Caballito del Mar* (☎074/608077; ⑤), overlooking the sea at the southern end of the beach, with its own swimming pool by the beach, a restaurant, sun terraces and comfortable rooms. Less expensive is the *Hostal Hua* (④), towards the midlle of the beach, an older more rustic wooden building, where some rooms have sea views and the service is decent, plus there's a restaurant; **camping** is also permitted. There are no shops in Punta Sal, so you unless you want to be totally dependent on the hotels and restaurants, take some food and drink with you. In the low season you'll probably have a beautiful beach pretty much to yourself; in high season it's a good idea to book your accommodation in advance.

Máncora

Máncora is an enjoyable stopover when travelling along the north coast, well served by public transport and, though spread out along the Panamerican Highway, parallel to a pleasant sandy beach with safe swimming. It's also the north coast's current major **surfing** centre, and you can hire gear from the *Godwanaland* restaurant for around $1.50 each per hour. All the main hotels are located between the bridge at the entrance to town and the plaza towards the north end, though there are several cheaper basic **hostals** strung out along the southern end of the Panamerican Highway: the *Hospedaje Crillon* (☎074/858000; ②) is one block back from it, with small basic rooms and shared bathrooms, but it's clean and friendly; the comfortable *Hostal Sausalito* (☎074/858058; ③) is pretty comfortable and has private bathrooms, with quieter rooms to the back and the price includes breakfast; the *Hostal Sol y Mar* (no tel; ②), popular with the surfing crowd, is right on the beach, has private baths, and boasts its own shop and Internet café; the *Hostal El Mar* (⑤) overlooks the sea, has smart cabin-like rooms, private baths, hammocks and meals are included; and the *Hostal Las Olas* (☎074/858109; ③–④) also overlooks the sea, and is great value with prices including either breakfast or full board. For eating, there's a surplus of **restaurants** in the centre of town, mainly along the Panamerican Highway. One of the best is the *Restaurant Arplan*, opposite this are the *Espada* and the *San Pedro*, all pretty reasonable and offering a range of fish dishes, including surprisingly affordable lobster. The *Restauarnt Stephanies*, overlooking the beach serves *fuentes* dishes sufficient for two or three people; while the *Café Regina's*, in the centre, is good for fruit salads and breakfasts. The *Café La Bajadita* is the place to hang out in the evenings, serving gooey chocolate cake and *majar blanco* pancakes to the rhythms of Bob Marley.

Transportes EPPO run five **buses** between here and Piura ($3, a 3hr journey) from their office just north of the plaza, towards the northern end of Máncora. Other bus companies, including Nor Pacifico, and Santa Rosa stop at the plaza on route between Tumbes and Piura. **Colectivos** depart from near the EPPO office for Los Oreganos ($0.50, a 30min trip), from where there are other **combis** to Talara ($1, a 1hr trip). Colectivos also patrol up and down the Panamerican Highway looking for passengers for Tumbes ($2, A 2hr trip).

Crossing the border at Aguas Verdes

Crossing the border is relatively simple in either direction. Two kilometres before the busy frontier settlement of **Aguas Verdes**, you'll find the **Peruvian immigration office** (daily 9am–noon & 2–5pm) where you get an exit or entry stamp and tourist card for your passport. Once past these buildings, it's a fifteen-minute walk or a short drive to Aguas Verdes. **Combis** for the border leave Tumbes from block 3 of Tumbes Norte, but ensure that it's going all the way to the border; some continue to Zarumilla or Aguas Verdes. A **taxi** from Tumbes costs $4–5. From Aguas Verdes, you just walk over the bridge into the Ecuadorean border town of **Huaquillas**, and the **Ecuadorean immigration office** (daily 8am–1pm & 2–6pm) where you'll get your entry or exit stamps and tourist card. If coming from Ecuador to Peru, Tumbes is the nicer place to stay close to the border; it has a greater choice of hotels and restaurants and it's much easier to make southerly connections from here. If going north, frequent buses depart to all the major destinations in Ecuador from Huayquillas. The best bet is to go on to Cuenca (5hr), an attractive small Ecaudorian city and a major cultural centre.

In both directions the authorities occasionally require that you show an onward ticket out of their respective countries. Unless you intend to recross the border inside a week or two, it's not worth taking out any local currency: changing Peruvian nuevo soles in Ecuador or Ecuadorean sucres in Peru usually involves a substantial loss, and inflation is such that even two weeks can make quite a difference. The area of **no-man's-land** between the two countries' posts is basically a street market where everyone gets hassled to change money – grab a taxi to ease the passage. The best policy is to change as little money as possible (because of the por exchange rates mentioned above) and, if you take a taxi, be firm on the price in advance.

The **Peruvian customs** point, a purpose-built concrete complex in the middle of the desert between the villages of Cancas and Máncora and more than 50km south of the border, was inactive following the 1999 agreements between Ecuador and Peru. When it is operating, however, most buses are pulled over and passengers have to get out and often have to show documents to the customs police while the bus and selected items of luggage are searched for contraband goods. This rarely takes more than twenty minutes, as they are quite efficient.

Crossing the border at La Tina

The alternative frontier crossing between **La Tina** and **Macará** is easiest approached by combi from Sullana, leaving from Avenida Buenos Aires, near the main market, in the mornings ($3, a 3hr trip). Hours for the **Peruvian immigration office** are the same as at Aguas Verdes (daily 9am–noon & 2–5pm), as are those for the **Ecuadorian immigration office** (daily 8am–1pm & 2–6pm).

There's nowhere to stay in La Tina, but a couple of basic **hostals** are to be found in Macará. Buses on for Loja (5hr) depart from Macará and it may be possible to connect on arrival and travel from Sullana to Macará in one day. Macará is 3km from the border, **motocycle taxis** ($0.5, a 10min trip) take people from the border into town. The journey to or from the border and Macará is extremely hot – take or drink plenty of fluids. You can change **money** (dollars, sucres or soles) in Macará, and in La Tina or at the bank (Mon–Fri) on the Ecuadorian side of the international bridge. The main advantage of this route is bascially the scenery en route to Loja.

travel details

Buses and Colectivos

Cajamarca to: Celendin (6 daily; 5hr); Chachapoyas (2 weekly from Celendin; 20hr); Chiclayo (10 daily; 7–9hr); Lima (several daily; 17hr); Cajabamba (6 daily; 5hr).

Chachapoyas to: Cajamarca (2 weekly from Celendin; 20hr); Chiclayo (several daily; 10–12hr); Rioja/Moyabamba (3 daily; 9–12hr).

Chiclayo to: Cajamarca (10 daily; 7–9hr); Chachapoyas (1 daily; 10–12hr); Huancabamba (2 weekly; 15–20hr); Lima (6–8 daily; 14hr); Piura (12 daily; 4hr); Trujillo (12 daily; 3hr); Tumbes (6 daily; 10hr).

Piura to: Chiclayo (12 daily; 4hr); Huancabamba (2–3 daily; 13–18hr); Lima (10 daily; 13–15hr); Tumbes (8 daily; 4–6hr).

Rioja/Moyabamba to: Chachapoyas (3 daily; 9–12hr); Tarapoto (5 daily; 4–5hr).

Trujillo to: Cajamarca (several daily; 8hr); Chiclayo (12 daily; 3hr); Lima (12 daily; 9hr);

Piura, via Chiclayo (8 daily; 7hr); Yurimaguas (2–3 daily; 12–15hr).

Tumbes to Aguas Verde (hourly; 20min); Chiclayo (8 daily; 10hr); Lima (8 daily; 23hr); Puerto Pizarro (hourly; 25min).

Flights

Cajamarca to: Chachapoyas (2 weekly; 1hr); Chimbote (3 weekly; 1hr 30min); Lima (1 daily; 2hr); Trujillo (3 weekly; 1hr).

Chachapoyas to: Cajamarca (2 weekly; 1hr); Chiclayo (2 weekly; 1hr 30min); Lima (3 weekly; 2hr).

Chiclayo to: Cajamarca (1 daily; 40min); Chachapoyas (2 weekly; 1hr 30min); Iquitos (1 daily; 2hr); Lima (2 daily; 2hr); Piura (2 daily; 30min); Talara (1 daily; 1hr); Rioja/Moyabamba (2 weekly; 1hr); Tarapoto (2 weekly; 90min);

Trujillo (1 daily; 45min); Tumbes (1 daily; 75min).

Piura to: Lima, via Chiclayo (2 daily; 2hr); Trujillo (1 daily; 1hr).

Rioja/Moyabamba to: Chiclayo (2 weekly; 1hr); Iquitos (3 weekly; 1hr 30min); Lima (6 weekly; 2hr); Tarapoto (2–4 weekly; 30min); Trujillo (1 weekly; 75min).

Tarapoto to: Iquitos (6 weekly; 1hr 30min); Lima (daily; 1hr 30min); Rioja/Moyabamba (2–4 weekly; 30min); Yurimaguas (1–2 weekly; 25min).

Trujillo to: Chiclayo (1 daily; 45min); Iquitos (4 weekly; 2hr); Lima (2 daily; 2hr 30min); Piura (1 daily; 1hr); Rioja/Moyabamba (1 weekly; 75min).

Tumbes to: Chiclayo (1 daily; 75min); Lima (1 daily; 2hr 30min).

Yurimaguas to: Iquitos (3 weekly; 90min); Lima (1 daily; 2hr 30min); Tarapoto (1–2 weekly; 25min).

CHAPTER SIX

THE JUNGLE

Whether you look at it up close, from the ground or a boat, or fly over it in a plane, the Peruvian **jungle** seems endless. In fact, it is disappearing at an alarming rate. However, while awareness of its importance as a unique eco-system and as a vital component of the global environment (not to mention the wealth of wildlife and sheer beauty of the vegetation) has brought it into the inter-national spotlight, few people think of Peru in terms of jungle. In fact, well over half the country is covered by dense tropical rainforest, with its eastern regions offering unri-valled access to the world's largest and most famous jungle, the **Amazon.**

Of the Amazon's original area, around four million square kilometres (about 80 per-cent) remain intact, fifteen percent of which lie in Peru, where they receive over 2000mm of rainfall a year and experience average temperatures of 25–35°C. Considered as *El Infierno Verde* – "the Green Hell" – by many Peruvians who've never been here, it's the most bio-diverse region on Earth, and much that lies beyond the main waterways remains relatively untouched and often unexplored. Jaguars, anteaters and tapirs roam the forests, huge anaconda snakes live in the swamps, toothy caimans (of the South American *Alligatoridae* family) sunbathe along riverbanks, and trees like the giant Shihuahuaco, strong enough to break an axe head, rise from the forest floor. Furthermore, there are over fifty indigenous tribes scattered throughout the Peruvian section alone, many surviving primarily by hunting, fishing and gathering, as they have done for thousands of years.

At about six times the size of England, or the size of California, it's not surprising that the Peruvian Amazon possesses a variety of ecotypes. Easier to access than many other South American jungle regions, increasing numbers of travellers are choosing to spend time here, and the tangled, sweltering and relatively accessible **Amazon Basin** never fails to capture the imagination of anyone who ventures beneath its dense canopy. In the **lowland areas**, away from the seasonally flooded riverbanks, the landscape is dom-inated by red, well-drained loamy soil, which can reach depths of fifty metres. Reaching upwards from this, the primary forest – mostly comprising a huge array of tropical palms, with scatterings of larger, emergent tree species – regularly achieves evergreen canopy heights of fifty metres. At ground level the vegetation is relatively open (most-ly saplings, herbs and woody shrubs), since the trees tend to branch high up, restrict-ing the amount of light available. At higher altitudes, the large belt of **cloud forest** (**ceja de selva**) that sweeps along the eastern edges of the Andes has been the focus of significant oil-prospecting during the last decade and has revealed some of the world's largest remaining fossil-fuel reserves.

The biggest river in the world, the **Río Amazonas** originally flowed east to west, but when the Andes began to rise along the Pacific edge of the continent around one hun-dred million years ago, the waters became an inland sea. Another forty million years of geological and climatic action later saw this "sea" break through into the Atlantic, which reversed the flow of water and gave birth to the mighty 6500-kilometre river. Starting in Peru as an insignificant trickle on Cerro Huagra, the waters cascade through the *ceja de selva* down some 4450m in just under 1000km, passing through the Toto, Santiago, Apurimac, Ene and Tambo valleys until they reach the Ashaninka trib-al territories in the Gran Pajonal. From here, where the **Río Tambo** meets the **Río**

Urubamba to form the larger **Río Ucayali**, the river is less than 200m above the level of the Atlantic, and from **Atalaya** onwards, the river and its tributaries – still the basis of jungle transport – are characterized by slow, meandering courses broken occasionally by tumultuous rapids (*pongos*). Erosion and deposits continue to shift these courses, and oxbow lakes are constantly appearing and disappearing, adding enormous quantities of time and fuel to any river journey in the lowlands. In fact, as it languidly meanders past **Iquitos**, an isolated, land-locked city, on its way towards Brazil and eventually the Atlantic, it's still at least ten days by boat to the mouth of a river which, at any one moment carries around twenty percent of the world's fresh water.

Some history

Many archeologists think that the initial spark for the evolution of Peru's high cultures came from the jungle. Evidence from **Chavin**, **Chachapoyas** and **Tantamayo** cultures seems to back up such a theory – they certainly had continuous contact with the jungle areas – and the **Incas** were unable to dominate the tribes, their main contact being peaceful trade in treasured items such as plumes, gold, medicinal plants and the sacred coca leaf. At the time of the **Spanish Conquest**, fairly permanent settlements seem to have existed along all the major jungle rivers, the people living in large groups to farm the rich alluvial soils, but the arrival of the Europeans appears to have begun the process of breaking these up into smaller and scattered groups (a process exacerbated by the nineteenth-century rubber boom – see overleaf).

Yet the Peruvian jungle still resisted major colonization. Although **Alonso de Alvarado** had led the first Spanish expedition, cutting a trail through from Chachapoyas to Moyabamba in 1537, most incursions ended in utter disaster, defeated by the ferocity of the tribes, the danger of the rivers, climate, and wild animals – and perhaps by the inherent alienness of the forest. Ultimately, apart from the white man's epidemics (which spread faster than the men themselves), the early conquistadores had relatively little impact on the populations of the Peruvian Amazon. Only **Orellana**,

---

INDIGENOUS JUNGLE TRIBES

Outside the few main towns, there are hardly any sizeable settlements, and the jungle population remains dominated by between 35 and 62 **indigenous tribes** – the exact number depends on how you classify tribal identity – each with its own distinct language, customs and dress. After centuries of external influence (missionaries, gold seekers, rubber barons, soldiers, oil companies, anthropologists, and now tourists), many jungle Indians speak Spanish and live pretty conventional, Westernized lives, preferring jeans, football shirts and cola to their more traditional clothing and manioc beer (the tasty and nutritious *masato*). But while many are being sucked into the money-based labour market, others, increasingly under threat, have been forced to struggle for their cultural identities and territorial rights, or to retreat well beyond the new frontiers of so-called civilization. In 1996 for instance, oil workers encountered some previously uncontacted groups while clearing tracts of forest for seismic testing in the upper Río de Las Piedras area of Madre de Dios, northwest of Puerto Maldonado. In this region it appears that some of the last few uncontacted tribal communities in the Amazon – Yaminahua, Mashco Piro and Amahuaca Indians – are keeping their distance from outside influences (for more on this, see Contexts, p.463–467).

For most of these traditional or semi-traditional tribes, the jungle offers a quasi-nomadic existence, and in terms of material possessions, they have very little. Communities are scattered, with groups of between ten and two hundred people, and their sites shift every few years. For subsistence they depend on small cultivated plots, fish from the rivers, and game from the forest, including wild pigs, deer, monkeys and a great range of edible birds. The main species of edible jungle fish are *sabalo* (a kind of oversized catfish), *carachama* (an armoured walking catfish), the feisty piranha (not really as dangerous as Hollywood makes out), and the giant *zungaro* and *paiche* – the latter, at up to 200kg, being the world's largest freshwater fish. In fact, food is so abundant that jungle dwellers generally spend no more than three to four days a week engaged in subsistence activities.

on his intrepid explorations along the Río Amazonas, managed to glimpse the reality of the rainforest, though even he seemed to misunderstand it when was attacked by a tribe of blond women, one of whom managed to hit him in the eye with a blow-gun dart. These "women" are nowadays considered to be men of the Yagua tribe (from near Iquitos), who wear straw-coloured, grass-like skirts and headdresses.

By the early eighteenth century the **Catholic Church** had made serious but vulnerable inroads into the region. Resistance to this culminated in 1742 with an indigenous uprising in the central forest region led by an enigmatic character from the Andes calling himself Juan Santos Atahualpa. Many missions were burnt, missionaries and colonists killed, and Spanish military expeditions defeated. The result was that the central rainforest remained under the control of the indigenous population for the next 90 years or so; in fact, as recently as 1919 the Ashaninka Indians were blockading rivers and ejecting missionaries and foreigners from their ancestral lands.

As "white-man's" technology advanced, so too did the possibilities of returning to Amazonia. The 1830s saw the beginning of one hundred years of massive and painful exploitation of the forest and its population by **rubber barons**. Many of these wealthy men were European, eager to gain control of the raw material desperately needed following the discovery of the vulcanization process, and during this era the jungle regions of Peru were better connected to Brazil, Bolivia, the Atlantic and ultimately Europe, than they were to Lima or the Pacific coast. The peak of the boom, from the 1880s to just before World War I, had a prolonged effect. Treating the natives as little more than slaves, men like the notorious **Fitzcarrald** made overnight fortunes, and large sections of the forests were explored and subdued. In 1891, for example, the British-owned Peruvian Corporation was granted the 500,000 hectare "Perene Colony" in the central rainforest in payment of debts owed by the Peruvian state. That the land so granted was indigenous territory was ignored – the Ashaninka who lived in the area were considered a captive labour force that was part of the concession. The process only fell into decline when the British explorer Markham took Peruvian rubber plants – via Kew Gardens – to Malaysia, where the plants grew equally well but were far easier to harvest.

Nineteenth-century colonialism also saw the progression of the **extractive frontier** along the navigable rivers, which involved short-term economic exploitation based on the extraction of other natural materials, such as timber and animal skins; coupled to this was the advance of the **agricultural frontier** down from the Andes. Both kinds of expansion assumed that Amazonia was a limitless source of natural reserves and an empty wilderness – misapprehensions that still exist today. The agricultural colonization tended to be by poor, landless peasants from the Andes and was concentrated in the Selva Alta, on the eastern slopes of that range. From the 1950s these *colonos* became a massive threat when, supported by successive government land grants, credit and road building, subsistence farmers and cattle ranchers inflicted large-scale deforestation.

In the 1960s, President Belaunde saw the colonization of Amazonia as central to his political platform, a verdant limitless and "unpopulated" frontier that was ripe for development, offering land to the landless masses. New waves of *colonos* arrived and, once again, indigenous inhabitants were dispossessed and yet more rainforest cleared. Things quietened down between 1968 and 1980, during the Military Regime, but when Belaunde returned to power in 1980, peasant colonization continued, by and large along tenuous penetration roads built by the government, but also with further state sponsorship and funding by international banks. Between 1985 and 1995, new factors began to threaten the cultures and environment of the Peruvian Amazon – the rise of terrorism and the illegal cocaine industry.

The threat to the forest

Over the last few decades, the intrusion of **oil and timber companies** has seen repeated exploitation of the rainforest. Even worse, vast tracts of forest have disappeared as successive waves of *colonos* have cleared trees to grow cash crops (especially coca). Since the late 1980s, conservationists have shown that this large-scale, haphazard **slash-and-burn agriculture** is unsustainable. The rainforest's nutrients are held in the vegetative and animal life-forms that live, die and are consumed and transformed into new life, mainly by fungal and insect species; the soil itself contains less than twenty percent of the nutrients, so jungle quickly turns to desert when its plant life is destroyed. The decline in nutrient yields has been irreversible.

When the Peruvian economy began to suffer in the mid-1980s, foreign credit ended and those with substantial private capital fled, mainly to the US. The government, then led by the young Alan Garcia, was forced to abandon the jungle region, and both its colonist and indigenous inhabitants were left to survive by themselves. This effectively opened the doors for the **coca barons**, who had already established themselves during the 1970s in the Huallaga Valley, and they moved into the gap left by government aid in the other valleys of the *ceja de selva* – notably the Pichis-Palcazu and the Apurimac-Ene. During the next ten years, illicit coca production was responsible for some ten percent of deforestation in the twentieth century; furthermore, trade of this lucrative crop led to significant corruption and, more importantly, supported the rise of **terrorism**. Strategic alliances between coca-growers (the colonists), smugglers (Peruvians and Colombians) and the terrorists (mainly, but not exclusively, Sendero Luminoso) led to a large area of the Peruvian Amazon being utterly lawless. Each party to this alliance gained strength and resources whilst the indigenous peoples of the region suffered, stuck seemingly powerless in the middle.

Over the last ten years the Peruvian authorities have persecuted the *colonos* for the one crop that made them money, and their greatest successes in this area have come largely from the tenacity and lust for cultural and territorial survival among the indigenous groups themselves, like the Ashaninka tribe. Armed by the authorities, they were among the vanguard of resistance to the narco-terrorists, whose movement, once rooted in politics and agriculture, had become blood-thirsty, power-hungry and highly unpopular. In the aftermath of this civil war, which began to fizzle out with the capture of Sendero's leader in 1992, the international financial institutions, whose earlier loans had helped fund the disastrous colonization, started to determine development policy in the Peruvian Amazon at least partly so that those same loans could be repaid, and resources such as fossil-fuels, lumber and land were privatized and sold to the highest bidder.

President Fujimori's neo-liberal agenda led to new investment in this legitimate exploitation, but this was mirrored by a huge increase in **illegal mining** by the informal sector, in many ways beyond the control of the government. Hordes of landless peasants from the Cusco region also flocked into the Madre de Dios to make their fortune from **gold mining**. In itself this was neither illegal nor an environmental threat, but the introduction of front-loader machines and trucks – which supplanted child-labour in the mines in the early 1990s – increased the environmental damage and rate of territorial consumption by this unregulated industry. By 1999, a massive desert had appeared around Huaypetue, previously a small-time mining frontier town, and the neighbouring communities of Amarakeiri Indians (who have been panning for gold in a small-scale, sustainable fashion for some 30 years) are in serious danger of losing their land and natural resources.

As the danger from terrorism faded in the mid-1990s, **oil and gas exploration** by multinational companies began in earnest. Initially the Peruvian government appeared to be bending over backwards to assist them, and the reserves discovered – mainly in the Madre de Dios and the Camisea – were believed to be of world-shattering importance, with only the Amazonian indigenous organizations and environmental conservationists active in opposition. For the moment, the momentum seems to have slowed right down, as the decision to drill in the Río de las Piedras has been reversed and work has stopped in the Camisea. However, at macro-economic and political levels this appears to be due more to an unforeseen extension of Fujimori's policies than genuine concern for environmental protection or the territorial and resource rights of the tribal groups. Ultimately, the Peruvian government was not prepared to offer the multinational oil companies as big a monopoly over the country's power supply industry as they desired.

In the late 1990s, the price of coca continued to drop in Peru as production shifted to Colombia, and many peasants and jungle Indians alike were looking seriously for **alternative cash crops**, such as the traditional chocolate and coffee products or newer options like *uña de gato* (a newly rediscovered medicinal herb) and *barbasco* (a natural pesticide). The way things are going, though, it's hard to see how much longer the indigenous peoples can maintain their culture or their traditional territories. The present forest-dwellers' children will be without a means of earning a living if the forest disappears, but there is still time to save most of it.

Getting into the jungle

Given the breadth and quality of options, it's never easy to decide which bit of the jungle to head for. Your three main criteria will probably be budget, ease of access, plus

JUNGLE HAZARDS

Going even a little off the beaten track in the jungle is real travelling, through an intense mesh of plant, insect and animal life. It's an environment that's not to be taken lightly: apart from the real chance of getting lost (see p.366), the image of poisonous snakes, jaguars and mosquitos is based on fact, though these dangers don't actually come hunting for you. Always consult your doctor on how to prevent diseases before departing for Peru if you are planning to spend *any* time in the rainforest regions.

•**DENGUE FEVER** There is no inoculation against **Dengue fever**, a mosquito-transmitted viral infection that occurs mainly in urban Amazonia, and the best prevention is by avoiding bites (see "Malaria" below, though note that the Dengue mosquito is primarily diurnal). Symptoms include high fevers, headache, severe pains in muscles and joints, vomiting and a red skin rash after the first few days. The illness usually lasts around ten days and can be treated with Paracetamol. If haemorrhaging occurs, see a doctor immediately. Recovery is usually complete within a few weeks.

•**JIGGERS** Small insects that live in cut grass, **jiggers** can also be a very irritating problem; they stick to and bury their heads in your ankles before slowly making their way up your legs to the groin, causing you to itch furiously. You can either pick them out one by one as the natives do, or apply sulphur cream (ask for the best ointment from a *farmacia* in any jungle town).

•**LEISHMANIASIS** Endemic to certain zones, **Leishmaniasis** (known in Peru as *uta*) is transmitted by sandfly bites and is rare for short-term visitors to the jungle. Symptoms start with skin sores that begin to ulcerate, followed by fever and swelling of the spleen. There is no prophylactic and if untreated it can lead to severe degeneration of skin and facial tissue, usually around the upper lip and lower nose areas. There is treatment in the form of heavy metal injections, but many untreated cases among relatively malnourished Peruvian peasants and Indians have resulted in permanent and quite horrific disfigurement.

•**MALARIA** The most significant disease in the Amazon, **malaria** has two common forms in South America; *Plasmodium vivax* and *Plasmodium falciparum*. The latter is the most common, but both are found in the Peruvian Amazon and both are thought to be fast adapting to modern medicines. Of the **prophylactics**, many have side-effects (some psychological, others physiological), so do some independent research as well as consulting your doctor. Mosquitos are mainly, but not exclusively nocturnal, coming out at

the depth and nature of jungle experience you're after. Flying to any of the main jungle towns is surprisingly cheap and can save an arduous few days' journey overland, and once you've arrived a number of **excursions** can be made easily and cheaply, though the best experience comprises a few nights at one of the better **jungle lodges**. For more intimate (but often tougher) contact, it's easy enough to arrange a **camping expedition** and a guide, travelling in canoes or speedboats into the deeper parts of the wilderness. A further, costlier option, mainly restricted to a few operators based in Iquitos, is to take a **river cruise** on a larger boat. This offers two significant advantages: firstly, the boats are comfortable, with good service and food; and secondly, the programmes take you to remote areas in style, and can then pentrate the deeper forest (such as the rarely visited Pacaya Samiria National Reserve) in well-equipped speedboats. Unlike lodge-based operations, both canoe expeditions and cruises aren't fixed to specific locations, so they can customize programmes and routes. Hotels and tours tend to work out cheaper while there is less demand due to the annual cycle of USA and European holiday seasons, though growing trends in **ecological tourism** and, more recently, psychedelic or jungle **mystic experiences**, are bringing groups throughout the year.

dusk and disappearing at sunrise; the best **protection** is to use roll-on DEET (diethyltoluamide) repellents; to wear clothing that's treated with diluted DEET repellant and covers exposed skin; and to sleep under mosquito nets. Note that DEET harms plastics. Even with the best effort possible, you can't be sure of avoiding bites, especially when camping in the rainforest or on night-walks, so always take what your GP prescribes. Malaria starts three or four weeks after contact, usually with a combination of severe nausea, high fevers, delirium and chills; get medical help as soon as possible if you have these symptoms – it's easier to treat in the early stages.

•**PARASITES Parasites** are quite common, so it's best to **boil drinking water** and use sterilizing tablets or crystals. Around human settlements, including the muddier parts of larger towns, you can pick up parasites through the soles of your feet; the best precaution is to wear shoes rather than flip-flops or sandals. Also, get a medical check-up at a centre that specializes in tropical diseases when you return home.

•**RIVER SICKNESS** The most likely hazard you'll encounter is **river sickness**, a general term for the effect of the sun's strong rays reflected off the water. After several hours on the river, particularly at midday and without a hat, you may get the first symptom – the runs – sometimes followed by nausea or shaking fever; in extreme cases these can last for a day or two. Anti-diarrhoea medicine should help (Lomotil, Imodium, or something similar); otherwise drink plenty of fluids and take rehydration salts dissolved in water.

•**SNAKES** It's unlikely that you will encounter any **snakes**. If you do, nearly all of them will disappear as quickly as they can – only the *shushupe* (a bushmaster) is fearless. The Fer-de-lance, or *jergon*, is also quite common; it's smaller and packs less venom than the bushmaster, but can still be deadly. Most bites occur by stepping on a sleeping snake or picking it up with a handful of vegetation; be constantly aware of this possibility. If anyone does get bitten, the first thing to remember is to keep calm – most deaths result from shock, not venom. Try to kill the snake for identification, but, more importantly, apply a temporary tourniquet above the bite and find medical help *immediately*. Some natives have remedies even for a potentially deadly *shushupe* bite.

•**YELLOW FEVER Yellow fever** is simple to prevent by a jab that covers you for ten years. Consult your doctor to find the nearest inoculation centre, and remember to obtain a **certificate of inoculation**, which you are sometimes required to show on entry into many of Peru's jungle regions. If you can't, you run the risk of being subject to on-the-spot inoculation, wherever you may be.

Cusco is the best base for trips into the southern jungle, with road access to the frontier town of **Puerto Maldonado**, itself a good base for budget travellers. The nearby forests of **Madre de Dios** boast the **Tambopata-Candamo Reserved Zone** and the **Bahuaja-Sonene National Park**, an enormous tract of virgin rainforest close to the

JUNGLE ESSENTIALS

All visits
- certificate of inoculation against yellow fever (check with your embassy for prevailing health requirements).
- malaria pills (start course in advance as directed by prescribing doctor).
- roll-on insect repellent containing DEET.
- suitable clothing (wear socks, trousers and long sleeves in the evenings).
- toilet paper.
- waterproof poncho, cagoule or overclothes.

3–5 days at a lodge or basic facility
- anti-diarrhoea medicine (eg Lomotil or Imodium).
- blanket or thick cotton sheet for sleeping.
- mosquito net for sleeping under.
- multipurpose knife (with can and bottle opener).
- plastic bags for packing and lining your bags with (a watertight box is best for camera equipment and other delicate valuables). Note that cardboard boxes dissolve on contact with an Amazon river or rain shower.
- sun hat (especially for river travel).
- torch and spare batteries.
- waterproof matches and a back-up gas lighter.

5 days or more away from facilities
- candles.
- compass and a whistle (in case you get lost).
- cooking pots and stove (or the ability to cook over a fire and a supply of dry wood), plus eating utensils.
- filled water container (allow for a gallon a day).
- first-aid box or medical kit (including tweezers, needles, scissors, plasters, bandages, adhesive tape, sterile dressings, antiseptic cream, antibiotics and painkillers).
- fishing line and hooks (unsalted meat makes good bait).
- food supplies (mainly rice, beans, cans of fish, crackers, noodles and fruit; chocolate is impractical, as it melts).
- gifts for people you might encounter (batteries, knives, fish hooks and line, camera film, and so on).
- a hammock or mat, plus a couple of blankets.
- insect-bite ointment (antihistamines, tiger balm, or *mentol china*; toothpaste as a last resort).
- a good knife and machete.
- quick-dry clothing.
- petrol for boats, useful for bargaining for rides.
- rope.
- running shoes, sandals (ideally plastic or rubber); rubber boots or strong walking boots if you're going hiking.
- water sterilizers (good tablets, crystals or a decent filter).

Bolivian border. Many naturalists argue that this region is the most bio-diverse on Earth, and that it's the best place to head for wildlife. An expedition into the **Manu Reserved Zone** (part of the larger **Manu National Biosphere Reserve**), will also bring you into one of the more exciting wildlife regions in South America, but for a quicker and cheaper taste of the jungle, you can go by bus from Cusco via Ollantaytambo to **Quillabamba**, on the Río Urubamba. Flowing north along the foot of the Andes, through the dangerous and unforgettable whitewater rapids of the **Pongo de Mainique**, the Urubamba merges with the Ucayali to flow past **Pucallpa**, a large (and rapidly growing) industrialized jungle town, best reached by scheduled airflights or the largely paved road from Lima. Nearby is **Lago Yarinacocha**, an attractively developed lake resort that has declined in popularity as a major destination since the mid-1980s, mainly due to a combination of terrorist infiltration, over-industrialization and the improvement of facilities in other competing jungle regions. However, it remains a good introduction to the rainforest and is reached by a relatively easily over-land trip from Lima.

From Pucallpa it's possible, if somewhat uncomfortable, to take a boat upriver to Iquitos, the jungle's only real city, although it's easier to come by speedboat from Brazil or to fly from Lima. It's also accessible from the northern coast via an increasingly popular and adventurous route that takes the Río Huallaga from Yurimaguas, a four- to five-day boat journey that can be broken by a visit to the immense **Pacaya Samiria National Reserve** at the heart of the upper Amazon. Capital of the remote and massive frontier region of Loreto, **Iquitos** is one of Peru's most welcoming cities, despite the presence of oil wells, cocaine traffickers and the US Drug Enforcement Agency. It's also the most organized and established of the Peruvian Amazon's tourist destinations, and has many reputable companies offering a range of jungle visits, from luxury lodges to rugged survival expeditions. From Iquitos you can catch a ferry downstream to the growing town of **Requena**, similar to how Iquitos was around fifty years ago.

Getting around the jungle

The three most common forms of **river transport** are canoes (*canoas*), speedboats (*deslizadoras*), and larger riverboats (*lanchas*). Whichever you choose, it's a good idea to make sure you can get along with the boatman (*piloto*) or captain and that he really does know the rivers. **Canoes** can be anything from a small dugout with a paddle, useful moving along small creeks and rivers, to a large eighteen-metre canoe with panelled sides and a *peque-peque* (on-board engine) or a more powerful outboard motor. **Speedboats** tend to have lightweight metal hulls and are obviously faster and more manoeuvrable, but more expensive. **Riverboats** come in a range of sizes and vary considerably in their river-worthiness, and you should always have a good look at the boat before buying a ticket or embarking on a journey – note that the smaller one- or two-deck riverboats are frequently in worse condition (and noisier) than larger ones. The best are the Iquitos-based tour boats, with cabins for up to thirty passengers, dining rooms, bars, sun-lounges and even Jacuzzis on board. Next best are the larger vessels with up to three decks that can carry two hundred passengers, with hammock spaces and a few cabins (for which you pay two to three times as much); if you're over 1.8m tall, it's best take a hammock in any case as the bunks may be too small. Always try to get a berth as close as possible to the front of the boat, away from the noise of the motor. On the larger riverboats (especially between Pucallpa and Iquitos, or Tabatinga and Iquitos) you can save money on hotels by literally hanging around in your hammock, as most captains allow passengers to sling one up and sleep on board for a few days before departure. Riverboats travelling upstream tend to stay close to the bank, away from the fast central flow, and while this means longer journeys, they're much more visually interesting than travelling up the middle of the river, particularly on the larger ones where it can be hard to make out even huts on the banks.

JUNGLE PERMITS

To enter certain areas, such as the Pacaya Samiria National Reserve, or the Manu and Tambopata-Candamo Reserved Zones, you'll need to obtain permission first. This is often done for you if you're on an organized tour; otherwise, contact the **Instituto Nacional de Recursos Naturales (INRENA)**, Calle Diesisiete 355, Urbino El Palomar, Lima 27 (☎01/224-3298; Mon–Fri 9am–5pm) or Pevas 350–363, Iquitos (☎094/231330, fax 234861, *rnps-zrg@aeci.org.pe*). It's not usually difficult to get a permit unless there's a good reason, such as specially restricted areas (eg in Manu Biosphere Reserve – see p.381) or suspected hostility from indigenous locals (in 1980, for example, a German-led wildlife expedition was attacked by Indians – the first thing they knew about it was a sheet of arrows flying towards their canoe).

Anyone who intends **hitching** along the river system should remember that the further you are away from the town, the harder it is to lay your hands on **fuel** (even if you should come across a multinational company drilling in the middle of the forest). You'll always be expected to contribute financially, but however much you offer, no one will take you upriver if they're short on fuel – and most people are most of the time. Taking your own supply (a 55-gallon container, for example) is a little difficult but isn't a bad idea if you're going somewhere remote. As a last resort it's possible to get hold of a **balsa raft** and paddle (downstream) from village to village, but this has obvious dangers: in addition to rapids, you may well get stuck for the night (or even a week in many areas) in some godforsaken place. It certainly isn't advisable without the help of someone who knows the river extremely well.

A basic rule of thumb is to make sure that reliable guidance is always available, and wherever you venture, try to be with a **local guide**. They don't need to have official status but they should be experienced in the region and willing to help out; natives are often the best guides. There are several ways of enlisting this kind of help: by paying significant sums for a commercially operated jungle tour; by going to the port of a jungle town and searching for someone who will hire out his boat and services as a guide; or by travelling within the boundaries of friendly settlements, hopping along the rivers from one village to the next with someone who is going that way anyway and who will be able to introduce you to the villagers at the next stage. This last and most adventurous option will normally involve long waits in remote settlements, but the jungle is an essentially laid-back place, and if there's one thing certain to get a *selvatico* (jungle dweller) mad, it's a gringo with a loud voice and pushy manner. If you choose to travel this way, remember that you are imposing yourself on the hospitality of the locals and that you are dependent on them: be sensitive to their needs, their privacy and their possessions and take **goods and cash** to offer them in return for any help that might be offered. Fishing hooks, nylon fishing line, tins of fish, trade cloth, clothes, fresh batteries and even shotgun cartridges are usually appreciated.

Getting lost is no fun and can happen very easily. Just by straying a hundred metres from camp, the river, or your guide, you can find yourself completely surrounded by a seemingly impenetrable canopy of plant life. It's almost impossible to walk in a straight line through the undergrowth, and one trail looks very much like the next to the unaccustomed eye. Your best bet, apart from shouting as loud as you can or banging the base of big buttress-root trees as Indians do when they get lost on hunting forages, is to find moving water and follow it downstream to the main river, where someone will eventually find you waiting on the bank. If you get caught out overnight, the two best places to sleep are beside a fire on the river bank, or high up in a tree that isn't crawling with biting ants.

THE SOUTHERN JUNGLE: MADRE DE DIOS

A large forested region, with a manic climate (usually searingly hot and humid, but with sudden cold spells – *friajes* – between June and August, due to icy winds coming down from the Andean glaciers), the **southern jungle** has only been systematically explored since the 1950s and was largely unknown until the twentieth century, when rubber began to leave Peru through Bolivia and Brazil, eastwards along the rivers.

Named after the broad river that flows through the heart of the southern jungle, the still relatively wild *departmento* of **Madre de Dios**, like so many remote areas of Peru, is changing rapidly. One of the last places affected by the rubber boom at the turn of the century, the natives here – many of whom struggle to maintain their traditional ways of life, despite the continuing efforts of *colonos* and some of the less enlightened Christian missionaries – were left pretty much alone until the push for oil in the 1960s and 1970s brought roads and planes, making this now the most accessible part of the Peruvian rainforest. As the oil companies moved out, so prospectors took their place, panning for gold dust along the river banks, while agribusiness moved in to clear mahogany trees or harvest the bountiful Brazil nuts. Today the main problems facing the Indians are loss of territory, the merciless pollution of their rivers, devastating environmental destruction (caused mainly by large scale gold-mining), and new waves of oil exploration by multinationals.

Nearly half of Madre de Dios *departmento*'s 78,000 square kilometres are accounted for by national parks and protected areas such as **Manu Biosphere Reserve** and **Tambopata-Candamo Reserved Zone**, between them encompassing some of the most exciting jungle and richest flora and fauna in the world. The latest, **Bahuaja-Sonone National Park**, created in 1996, is surrounded largely by a massive rainforest area formed by the Tambopata-Candamo Reserved Zone confirming the Peruvian government's support for this region as an ecological treasure. Taken together, these comprise some 1.5 million hectares, almost the size of Manu (15,000 square kilometres), and if you add on the Maididi National Park – just across the border in Bolivia – the protected area in this corner of the Amazon exceeds 50,000 square kilometres.

The **Río Madre de Dios** is fed by two main tributaries, the **Río Manu** and the **Río Alto Madre de Dios**, which roll off the Paucartambo Ridge (just north of Cusco), which divides the tributaries from the **Río Urubamba** watershed and delineates Manu Biosphere Reserve. At Puerto Maldonado, the Madre de Dios meets with the **Río Tambopata** and the **Río de las Piedras**, then flows on to Puerto Heath, a day's boatride away on the Bolivian frontier. From here it continues through the Bolivian forest into Brazil to join the great Río Madeira, which eventually meets the Amazon near Manaus.

Madre de Dios is still very much a frontier zone, centred on the rapidly growing river town of **Puerto Maldonado**, near the Bolivian border, supposedly founded by legendary explorer and rubber baron **Fitzcarrald**. The town extends a tenuous political and economic hold over the vast *departmento*, and has a population of over 25,000, a city centre with one or two traffic policemen, and evening classes where row upon row of young locals train for the future in front of the glare of PC monitors. But while the *departmento*'s scattered towns and villages are interesting for their Wild West energy and spirit, most visitors come for the wildlife, especially in the strictly protected Manu Biosphere Reserve – still essentially an expedition zone – and the cheaper, less well-known Tambopata-Candamo Reserved Zone, chiefly visited by groups stay-

ing at lodges. As in all jungle regions, human activity here is closely linked to the river system, and these two are actually among the most easily reached parts of the Amazon: from Cusco, Manu is either a day's journey by bus then a couple days more by canoe, or a thirty-minute flight in a light aircraft; Tambopata, meanwhile, is a forty-minute scheduled flight (or 3- to 10-day truck journey), plus a few hours in a motorized canoe.

Slightly less accessible, but nevertheless rewarding for many budget travellers staying in Puerto Maldonado, are **Lago Sandoval** and the huge expanse of **Lago Valencia**, both great wildlife locales east along the Río Madre de Dios and close to the Bolivian border. At the least, you're likely to spot a few caimans and the strange hoatzin birds, and if you're lucky, larger mammals such as capybara, tapir, or, less likely, a jaguar – and at Valencia, you can fish for piranha. A little further southeast of here, less than a couple of hours in a decent motorized launch, brings you to **Las Pampas del Heath**, the only tropical grassland within Peru. It now lies within the Bahuaja-Sonene National Park, so special permission is needed from the INRENA office (see p.366) to visit it. The grasslands extend eastward across northern Bolivia to the Pantanal region of Brazil, itself one of the wildlife jems of the Americas.

Madre de Dios indigenous groups

Off the main Madre de Dios waterways, within the system of smaller tributaries and streams, live a variety of different **indigenous groups**. All are depleted in numbers due to contact with this century's Western influences and diseases, but while some have been completely wiped out over the last twenty years, several have maintained their isolation. Many tribes were acculturated as late as the 1950s and 1960s, and occasionally "uncontacted" groups turned up during the 1980s and 1990s. These are, however, usually segments of a larger tribe that split or dispersed with the arrival of the rubber barons, and they are fast being secured in controllable mission villages. Most of the native tribes that remain in, or have returned to, their traditional territories now find themselves forced to take on seasonal work for the *colonos* who have staked claims around the major rivers. In the dry season (May to November), this usually means panning for gold – the region's most lucrative commodity. In the rainy season, Brazil nut (or, rather, Peru nut) collection takes over. The timber industry, too, is well established, and most of the accessible large cedars have already gone.

If you go anywhere in the jungle, especially on an organized tour, you're likely to stop off at a **tribal village** for at least half an hour or so, and the more you know about the people, the more you'll get out of the visit. Downstream from Puerto Maldonado, the most populous indigenous group are the **Ese Eja** tribe (often wrongly, and derogatorily, often called Huarayos by *colonos*). Originally semi-nomadic hunters and gatherers, the Ese Eja were well-known warriors who fought the Incas and, later on, the Spanish expedition of Alvarez Maldonado – eventually establishing fairly friendly and respectful relationships with both. Under Fitzcarrald's reign, they apparently suffered greatly. Today they live in fairly large communities and have more or less abandoned their original bark-cloth robes in favour of shorts and T-shirts.

Upstream from Puerto Maldonado live several native tribes, known collectively (again, wrongly and derogatorily) as the Mashcos but actually comprising at least five separate linguistic groups – the **Huachipaeri**, **Amarakaeri**, **Sapitoyeri**, **Arasayri** and **Toyeri**. All typically use long bows – over 1.5m – and lengthy arrows, and most settlements will also have a shotgun or two these days, since less time can be dedicated to hunting when they are panning for gold or working timber for *colonos*. Traditionally, they wore long bark-cloth robes and had long hair, and the men often stuck eight feathers into the skin around their lips, making them look distinctively fierce and cat-like. Having developed a terrifying hatred of white people during the rubber era, they were eventually conquered and settled by missionaries and the army about forty years ago. Many Huachipaeri and Amarakaeri groups are now gaining an insight into the realities of the outside world, and some of their young men and women have gone through university education and are returning to their villages.

Puerto Maldonado

A remote settlement even for Peru, **PUERTO MALDONADO** is a frontier colonist town with strong links to the Cusco region and a great fervour for bubbly jungle *chicha* music. With an economy based on gold-panning and Brazil-nut gathering from the rivers and forests of Madre de Dios, it has grown enormously over the last twenty years. From a small, laid-back outpost of civilization to a busy market town, it has become the thriving, safe (and fairly expensive) capital of a region that feels very much on the threshold of major upheavals, with a rapidly developing tourist industry.

It was rubber, however, that led to the settlement's establishment at the turn of the century. During the 1920s came the game hunters, who dominated the economy of the region, and after them, mainly in the 1960s, came the exploiters of mahogany and cedar trees – leading to the construction of Boca Manu airstrip, just before the oil companies moved in during the 1970s. Most of the people, riding coolly around on Honda motorbikes, are second-generation *colonos*, but there's a constant stream of new and hopeful arrivals – rich and poor boys from all parts of South America, and even the occasional gang from the US.

The lure, inevitably, is **gold**. Every rainy season the swollen rivers deposit a heavy layer of gold dust along their banks and those who have been quick enough to stake

THE SAGA OF FITZCARRALD

Fitzcarrald (often mistakenly called Fitzcarraldo) is associated with the founding of Puerto Maldonado, but he actually died some twelve years before the event, though his story is relevant to the development of this region. While working rubber on the Río Urubamba, Fitzcarrald evidently caught the gold bug after hearing rumours from local Ashaninka and Machiguenga Indians of an Inca fort protecting vast treasures, possibly around the Río Purus. Setting out along the Mishagua, a tributary of the Río Urubamba, he managed to reach its source, and from there walked over the ridge to a new watershed which he took to be the Purus, though it was in fact the Río Cashpajali, a tributary of the Río Manu. Leaving men to clear a path, he returned to Iquitos, and in 1884 came back to the region on a boat called *La Contamana*. He took the boat apart, and, with the aid of over a thousand Ashaninka and other Indians, carried it across to the "Purus". But, as he cruised down, attacked by tribes at several points, Fitzcarrald slowly began to realize that the river was not the Purus – a fact confirmed when he eventually bumped into a Bolivian rubber collector.

Though he'd ended up on the wrong river, Fitzcarrald had discovered a link connecting the two great Amazonian watersheds. In Europe, the discovery was heralded as a great step forward in the exploration of South America, but for Peru it meant more rubber, a quicker route for its export, and the beginning of the end for Madre de Dios's indigenous tribes. Puerto Maldonado was founded in 1902, and as exploitation of the region's rubber peaked, so too was there an increase in population of workers and merchants, with Madre de Dios ultimately becoming a *departmento* of Peru in 1912. German director Werner Herzog thought this historical episode a fitting subject for celluloid, and in 1982 directed the epic *Fitzcarraldo*.

claims on the best stretches have made substantial fortunes. In such areas there are thousands of unregulated miners, using large front-loader earth-moving machines, destroying a large section of the forest, and doing so very quickly. Gold-lust is not a new phenomenon here – the gold-rich rivers have brought Andean Indians and occasional explorers to the region for centuries. Even the Incas may well have utilized a little of the precious stuff – the Inca emperor Tupac Yupanqui is known to have discovered the Río Madre de Dios, naming it the Amarymayo ("serpent river"). Perhaps, too, it's more than coincidental that one suggested location for the legendary city of **"El Dorado"**, known in southern Peru as **Paititi** and where the Incas hid their most valuable golden objects from the Spanish conquerors, is in the high forests close to the Río Alto Madre de Dios.

In town, the main street, **León de Velarde**, immediately establishes the town's stage-set feel, lined with bars, hardware shops, and a pool-room. At one end is the **Plaza de Armas**, with an attractive if bizarre Chinese pagoda-style clocktower at its centre, and along another side a modern **Municipalidad** – where, not much more than ten years ago, a TV was sometimes set up for the people to watch an all-important event like a soccer game. These days there are satellite TV dishes all over town and the youth of Puerto Maldonado are as familiar with computer software as they are with jungle mythology. The streets, mostly muddy but for a few concreted main drags, show few signs of wealth, despite the gold dust that lures peasants here from the Andes; for these *colonos*, who now and then arrive to sell a few grams to one of the many *compro oro* (gold-buying) offices in town, Puerto Maldonado is their main source of manufactured goods. Occasionally, too, a small group of local Indians visit town to buy or trade for cloth, fish hooks, machetes or consumer goods such as radios and ghetto-blasters. If you're considering a river trip, or just feel like crossing to the other side for a walk, follow Jirón Billingshurst, or take the steep steps down from the Plaza de Armas to the **main port**, situated on the Río Madre de Dios – one of the town's most active corners.

There are two main routes out of Puerto Maldonado: Avenida Fitzcarraldo brings you out at the cattle ranches on the far side of the airstrip; while if you turn off on 28 de Julio, you can take the road as far as you like in the direction of Laberinto, Quincemil and Cusco. A regular bus and colectivo ($5) service now connects Puerto Maldonado with **Laberinto** (leaving from the *Hotel Wilson*, or from the main market on Ernesto Rivero), some ninety minutes away. Formerly a gold-mining frontier settlement, since the early 1990s it has been superseded by the settlement of **Masuko**, deeper into the forest, and is now important mainly for its role as an upriver port for Puerto Maldonado; most boats going upstream start here, though if you're planning to visit Manu Biosphere Reserve, you should set out from Cusco (for more details, see p.383).

Arrival, information and getting around

If you arrive by plane, the blast of hot, humid air you get the moment you step out onto the **airport**'s runway is an instant reminder that this is the Amazon Basin. Aero Continente operate daily jets from Lima via Cusco, while Aero Condor and Aero Santander offer cheaper, daily propeller planes from Cusco. Military Grupo Ocho planes also jet in from Cusco several times weekly, but you need to check their schedule at Cusco airport. There are also two or three flights weekly to other jungle destinations in Madre de Dios, such as Iberia; check with travel agents or the new airline companies on arrival in Peru. Unless you're being picked up as part of an organized tour, **airport transfer** is simplest and coolest by *motokar*, costing around $2.50 for the otherwise very hot eight-kilometre walk.

Most of the **trucks** from Cusco arrive after a tough five-hundred-kilometre journey at Puerto Maldonado main market on Calle Ernesto Rivero, or block 19 of La Union, also by the market. It's a laborious, three- to ten-day journey down from the glacial highlands, depending on how much it's raining; the worst period is generally between December and March. After passing into the *ceja de selva*, the muddy track winds its slippery way through dense tropical vegetation, via the small settlement at Quincemil.

The quickest way of **getting around town** and its immediate environs is to hail a *motokar* ($0.75 in-town flat rate, but check before getting on) or passenger-carrying motorbikes ($0.3, also a flat rate). If you fancy doing a bit of running about on your own, or have a lot of ground to cover in town, moped rental is a useful option; you'll find a reasonable place at Avenida Gonzalez Prada 321, by the *Hotel Wilson* ($1 for 1hr, $10 for 12hr; no deposit, but passports and driving licences required). Make sure there's ample petrol in the tank.

Puerto Maldonado has two main **river ports**, one on the Río Tambopata, at the southern end of León de Velarde, the main street, the other on the Río Madre de Dios, at the northern end of León de Velarde; from the former, there's a very cheap **ferry** service across the river to the newish road to Brazil. From either it's possible to hire a **boatman and canoe** for a river trip; prices usually start at $25 per person for a day journey, for a minimum of two people; this rises to $35 for trips of two to four days. Boats are equipped with a *peque-peque* or small outboard motor, and usually take up to twelve people (see also "Around Puerto Maldonado", pp.375–377). If you're prepared to pay significantly more (from $100 a day per person, again for a minimum of two), you can find boatmen with speedboats and larger outboard motors.

However you get here, you have to go through a yellow fever **vaccination checkpoint** at Puerto Maldonado's small but clean, modern and air-conditioned airport, where there's also a **tourist information** kiosk and *artesania* shops. For entry and exit stamps, the **immigration office** is at 26 de Diciembre 356, one block from the Plaza de Armas.

PUERTO MALDONADO

Rio Madre de Dios

Airport, Laberinto & Cusco

BILLINGHURST

LORETO

National Police &
Immigration Office ❶

Port area
(Madre de Dios)

Viewing Platform ❷
over river

CARRION

Ⓐ

Captain
of the Port

Ⓑ

CUSCO

✆

Municipal
Building

PLAZA
DE
ARMAS

2 DE MAYO

Cinema

Ⓒ ⓢ ⓢ

Cabaña Quinta **3**

Banco
de la Nación

Banco de Credito

PIURA

ERNESTO RIVERO

G PRADA

Explorer's Inn
Offices

AREQUIPA

Ⓓ Ⓔ

Ⓕ

Aero Continente

Ⓖ

La Mascota
(hammock shop)

26 DE DICIEMBRE

N

J TRONCOSO

LEON DE VELARDE

Old
Market **5**

Market

MOQUEGUA

TACNA

Ⓗ

ⓢ

Money
Change

ICA

| 0 | 200 m |

✉

ACCOMMODATION		RESTAURANTS	
Cabaña Quinta	3	Chifa Wa Seng	F
Hotel Wilson	5	Club Witite	A
Moderno	1	La Casa Nostra	G
Reyport	4	La Tiendacita Blanca	H
Wasai	5	Pizzaria Chez Maggy	C
		Pollos a la Brasa La Estrella	D
		Restaurant Califa	B
		Tu Dulce Espera	E

▽ *Hotel de Turistas & Port Area (Río Tambopata)*

Accommodation

Puerto Maldonado has a reasonable range of **hotels**, most of them either on or within a couple of blocks of León de Velarde. All the better hotels offer protection against mosquitos and some sort of air conditioning. Of the more **expensive options**, the best is the *Wasai*, on Billinghurst (☎ & fax 084/571355, *wasai@telematic.edu.pe*; ⑤), which offers fine views over the Río Madre de Dios, and a swimming pool with a waterfall and bar set among trees, overlooking a canoe-builders yard. All rooms are cabin-style with

---

ACCOMMODATION PRICE CODES

Unless otherwise indicated, **accommodation** in this book is coded according to the categories below, based on the price of a double room in high season.

① under $5	③ $10–20	⑤ $30–40	⑦ $50–70
② $5–10	④ $20–30	⑥ $40–50	⑧ over $70

COMPULSORY TOURISM

To ensure that a greater proportion of income generated by tourism stays in town, the local council is threatening to insist all tourists stay at least one night in Puerto Maldonado during their visit to the area. While this may not suit everyone, it is in line with one of the basic tenets of sustainable tourism (to maximize economic incentives to locals for tourism's use of their natural resources). Since most jungle lodge operators are from outside the area, this policy may well be implemented by the year 2001; ask about this before you book a lodge-based tour to this region.

TV and shower, and staff here also staff organize local tours and run the *Wasai Lodge* (see p.380). The *Cabaña Quinta*, Cusco 535 (☎084/571863, fax 571890; ④), is also very comfortable, with rooms surrounded by an attractive garden, plus there's an excellent bar-restaurant. A few blocks south of the town centre, there's the fine *Don Carlos*, Velarde 1271 (☎084/571029, fax 571323; ④), which overlooks the Río Tambopata. Outside the heart of town, the *Libertador*, Libertad 433 (☎084/572661; ③), is a relatively good deal, not least because it has a small pool. Some 6km northwest from the town centre, but only five minutes from the airport, the *Hotel Iñapari* (no tel; ③) is run by a Spanish couple, Isabel and Javier. Accommodation is in bungalows next to the forest, an atmospheric place to start a visit to the jungle (Javier organizes several trips), and the price includes excellent breakfasts and dinners.

The best of the **cheaper options** is the *Royal Inn*, 2 de Mayo 333 (☎084/571048; ②), which is clean, though noisy once the *motokars* get going in the mornings, usually around 5am. The *Reyport*, Velarde 457 (☎084/571177; ②), is also acceptable, but similarly noisy. Among the more basic establishments the *Hotel Wilson*, Avenida Gonzalez Prada 335 (☎084/571086; ①), has private bathrooms but is rather neglected. The older *Moderno*, Billinghurst 357 (☎084/571063; ①), is brightly painted and well kept, with something of a frontier-town character.

Eating, drinking and nightlife

You should have no problem finding a good **restaurant** in Puerto Maldonado. Delicious river fish are always available, even in *ceviche* form, and there's venison or wild pig fresh from the forest (try *estofado de venado*). One of the best (though also priciest) establishments is the one in the *Wasai* (see p.372), where you can enjoy an enormous plate of food while watching life pass by along the river. The restaurant at the *Cabaña Quinta* (see above) is hard to beat for its excellent three-course set lunches, often including fresh river fish and fried manioc, while just around the corner, on Piura, the *Restaurant Califa* serves great lunches and specializes in fish and jungle crops.

The cosy *Pizzaria Chez Maggy*, on the Plaza de Armas, is very popular with travellers and locals alike, and at weekends you may have to wait a while for a table; there are no exotic toppings, but it's hard to imagine how they can produce such good **pizzas** in this jungle environment. If you like grilled **chicken**, you're spoiled for choice; try *Pollos a la Brasa La Estrella*, Velarde 474 for the tastiest. On 2 de Mayo, at no. 253, *Chifa Wa Seng* successfully combines traditional **Chinese** meals with an abundance of jungle foodstuffs. For **vegetarian food** there's *Natur*, at Velarde 928, but their dishes are a little uninspiring.

Along León de Velarde are a number of **cafés and bars**, one or two of which have walls covered in typical *selvatico*-style paintings, developed to represent and romanticize the dreamlike features of the jungle – looming jaguars, brightly plumed macaws talking to each other in the treetops, and deer drinking water from a still lake. Locals are very keen on sweet and savoury **snacks**, and if you fancy trying some yourself pop in to *Tu Dulce Espera*, *La Tiendacita Blanca* or *La Casa Nostra*, all on the fifth block of Velarde. The first sells typical sweets, while the latter two offer traditionally prepared, delicious tropical fruit **juices** (including mango, passionfruit, pineapple and carambola – a local favourite), for less than $0.5 a glass, as well as *tamales, papas rellenas* (stuffed potatoes) and a range of exotic looking cakes. Also on León de Velarde, the old **market** (mornings only) has excellent juices, fresh fruit and vegetables, while the best place for Brazil nuts is the general store at Velarde 570. Delicious (but hard to eat) aguaje palm fruits are sold at several street corners along Velarde.

There's very little **nightlife** in this laid-back town, especially during the week – most people just stroll around, stopping occasionally to sit and chat in the Plaza de Armas or in bars along the main street. At weekends and *fiesta* times, however, it's possible to sample *chicha* music (one of the jungle's greatest delights for many people), *salsa*, which has infiltrated the jungle over the last ten years, and a more recent arrival, the Colombian rhythms of *cumbia* – the latest fads being *technocumbia* and *chichiperalta*. All are loud and easy to move to, and on Friday and Saturday nights, you can usually pinpoint a concert just by following the sound of an electric bass guitar. The best **club** in town is *Witite*, at Velarde 153 (Fri & Sat; $0.5 for men on Sat), which has a surprisingly advanced sound system that plays the whole range of Latino music – though spiders' webs frequently adorn the speakers at this cool spot. Other **music bars** (weekends only) cluster around the plaza.

Listings

Airlines Aero Condor, León de Velarde 545 (no tel); Aero Continente, León de Velarde 506/508 (☎084/572285); Aero Santander, 2 de Mayo 294 (☎084/573120 or 571754); and Grupo Ocho, block 6 of 2 de Mayo (no tel).

Banks and exchange There are two banks on the plaza: Banco Credito, Arequipa 334; and Banco de la Nación, Jirón Daniel Carrion 233 (both Mon–Fri 9am–1pm & 5–7pm). *Cambistas* usually hang out on the corner of Prada and Puno, near the *Hotel Wilson*. Your hotel might also change dollars.

Captain's Office León de Velarde, between Avenida Gonzalez Prada and 2 de Mayo. For permits to travel by river into the jungle. Mon–Sat 8am–6pm.

Post office León de Velarde 675, opposite the corner of Jirón Jaime Troncoso. Mon–Sat 7.45am–8.15pm, Sun 7.45am–3pm.

Shopping Excellent-value hammocks are available from La Mascota, León de Velarde 599, on the corner of Gonzalez Prada.

Telephones The main offices of Telefónica del Peru are on block 7 of Puno (daily 7am–11pm). There are also public phones in most parts of town.

Onward travel: into Brazil

The route into Brazil was first opened for use by trucks in the late 1980s and is still not commonly used by independent travellers. The dirt road was significantly improved in the late 1990s, though it still might take a while for vehicles during the rainy season, particularly the section between Iberia (close to the Brazilian frontier) and Iñapari (see opposite); generally speaking, you should reach **Iñapari** within a day or two. There is almost no forest along the road now, just secondary growth and *chacra* farms and gardens.

There are currently no regular flights to Brazil from Puerto Maldonado, but details about ad-hoc services can be obtained from Oeste Redes Aereo on Prada, opposite the *Hotel Wilson*; prices cost about $40–80. A daily bus to Iberia departs at 8am ($3; a 5–6hr journey) from the quay opposite town over the Río Madre de Dios; several colectivos also make this trip ($7; a 4hr journey). Just outside Iberia is an interesting **Reserve and Information Centre** set up by the local Rubber Tappers Association.

From Iberia, regular, if infrequent, colectivos travel the remaining 70km to the border settlement of **IÑAPARI** ($3, a 90min trip), where there are a couple of basic hostals. Note that **exit stamps** are obtained in Iñapari, rather than Puerto Maldonado. In the dry season it's possible to walk across the Río Acre into **ASSIS**, in Brazil; otherwise you have to take the ferry. The **hostal** (②) here, on the main plaza, is much nicer than those in Iñapari. Regular buses and colectivos travel from Assis to **Brasileia** (by no means to be confused with the capital) where Brazilian **entry stamps** can be obtained, then on to **Xapuri** and **Río Branco** (totalling another day or two at most).

Around Puerto Maldonado

Madre de Dios boasts spectacular virgin lowland rainforest and exceptional wildlife. Brazil-nut tree trails, a range of lodges, some excellent local guides and ecologists, plus indigenous and colonist cultures are all within a few hours of Cusco. Serious jungle trips can be made here with relative ease and without too much expense, and this part of the Amazon offers easy and uniquely rewarding access to rainforest that is much less disturbed than that around Iquitos, or Manaus in the heart of the Brazilian Amazon, for example. There are two main ways to explore: firstly, by arranging your own boat and boatman; and secondly, though considerably more expensive, by taking an excursion up to one of the lodges.

Less than one hour downriver from Puerto Maldonado (90min on the return upriver) is **LAGO SANDOVAL**, a large lake where the Ministry of Agriculture have introduced the large *paiche* fish. At its best on weekday mornings (it gets quite crowded at other times), there are decent opportunities for spotting wildlife, in particular **birds** similar to those at Lago Valencia. You may even spot a **giant otter** (*Pteronura brasilensis*); for more on these endangered creatures, see p.381. It's also possible to walk to the lake (about 1hr), and once here boatmen and canoes can usually be obtained by your guide for a couple of hours, as can food and drink. Incidentally, if you're travelling to the lake by river, most guides show you the ruined hulk of an old boat. If they claim it had anything to do with Fitzcarrald, don't believe them; it may be similar in style to Fitzcarrald's, but in fact it's smaller and is a far more recent arrival – it's a hospital boat that was in use until two or three decades ago.

It takes the best part of a day by canoe with a *peque-peque*, or around two hours in a *lancha* with an outboard, to reach the huge lake of **LAGO VALENCIA** from Puerto Maldonado. On the way you can stop off to watch some gold panners on the Madre de Dios and visit a small settlement of Ese Eja Indians; about thirty minutes beyond, you turn off the main river into a narrow channel that connects with the lake. Easing onto the lake itself, the sounds of the canoe engine are totally silenced by the weight and expanse of water. Towards sunset it's quite common to see caimans basking on the muddy banks, an occasional puma, or the largest rodent in the world, a capybara, scuttling away into the forest. Up in the trees around the channel lie hundreds of hoatzin birds, or *gallos* as they are called locally – large, ungainly creatures with orange-and-brown plumage, long wings and distinctive spiky crests. The strangest feature of the hoatzin are the claws at the end of their wings, which they use these to help them climb up into overhanging branches beside rivers and lakes. They have almost lost the power of flight.

There's a police control post on the right as you come out onto the lake, where you must register passports and show your port **captain's permit** (see p.374). Beyond, reached via a slippery path above a group of dugout canoes, is the lake's one real settlement, a cluster of thatched huts around a slightly larger schoolhouse. Fewer than fifty people live here – a schoolteacher, a lay priest, the shop owner, and a few fishing families. Some tour groups stay in a small **camp** further down, a seasonal nut-

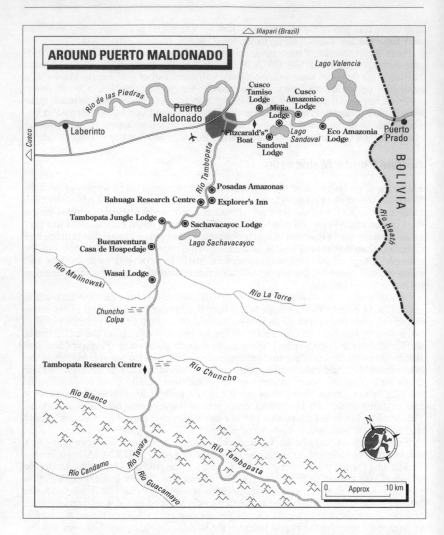

AROUND PUERTO MALDONADO

collectors' *campamento*, comprising just one cooking hut with an adjacent sleeping plat-form. By day most people go for a **walk in the forest** – something that's both safer and more interesting with a guide, though whichever way you do it you'll immediately sense the energy and abundance of life. Quinine trees tower above all the trails, sur-passed only by the Tahuari hardwoods, trees so tall and solid that jungle shamans describe themselves in terms of their power. Around their trunks you'll often see *pega-pega*, a parasitic ivy-like plant that the shamans mix with the hallucinogenic *ayahuasca* into an intense aphrodisiac. Perhaps more useful to know about are the liana vines; one thin species dangling above the paths can be used to take away the pain from a *shushupe* snake-bite. Another, the *maravilla* or *palo de agua*, issues a cool stream of fresh water if you chop a section, about half a metre long, and put it to your lips. You may come upon another vine, too – the sinister *matapalo* (or *renaco*), which sometimes extends over dozens of trees, sucking the sap from up to a square kilometre of jungle. Hideously formed, these are known as a place where demons dwell, zones where native children can mysteriously vanish.

You can also take a **canoe up the lake** for a bit of fishing, passing beaches studded with groups of lazy-looking turtles sunning themselves in line along the top of fallen tree trunks – when they notice the canoe, each one topples off, slowly splashing into the water one after another. It takes a bit more to frighten the **white caimans** away; many can be seen soaking in the sun's strong rays along the margin of the lake. Sometimes over 2m in length, they are a daunting sight, although they won't bite unless you happen to step on one. At night, it's possible to glide along the water, keeping close to the bank looking for the amber glint reflected from a pair of caiman eyes as the beam from your torch catches them. This is how the locals hunt them, fixing the crocs with a beam of light, then moving closer before blasting them with a shotgun; unless you're really hungry (the meat is something of a delicacy), it's best just to look into their gleaming eyes in the pitch darkness. The only sound on the lake will be the grunting of corvina fish vibrating up through the bottom of the canoe.

Both Lago Valencia and Lago Sandoval are superbly endowed with **bird-life**. In addition to the hoatzin there are kingfishers, cormorants, herons, egrets, pink flamingos, skimmers, macaws, toucans, parrots and gavilans. And behind the wall of trees along the banks hide deer, wild pigs and **tapir**. If you're lucky enough to catch a glimpse of a tapir you'll be seeing one of South America's weirdest creatures – almost the size of a cow, with an elongated rubbery nose and spiky mane. In fact, the tapir is known in the jungle as a *sachavaca* ("forest cow" – *sacha* is Quechua for "forest" and *vaca* is Spanish for "cow"). The easiest fish to catch are **piranha** – all you need is some line, a hook, and a chunk of unsalted meat; throw this into the lake and you've got yourself a piranha.

Another good trip, if you've got at least three days to spare (two nights minimum), is up to the **Río Heath**, a national rainforest sanctuary, though while the **Pampas del Heath** are excellent for macaws they don't have the primary forest necessary for a great variety of wildlife. A shorter trip – five hours up and about two hours down – is to **Tres Chimbales**, where there are a few houses belonging to the Infierno community on the Río Tambopata; it's possible to spend two or three days watching for wildlife, walking in the forest and fishing. From here you can visit **Infierno** village itself – spread out along the river, you can see glimpses of thatched and tin-roofed huts.

One other possibility, though something not commonly done by gringos, is to **travel into Bolivia** on one of the cargo boats that leave more or less every week. Before embarking on this, however, you'll have to clear your passport and visa with the Puerto Maldonado police and Migraciones offices (see p.371). Puerto Pardo is the last Peruvian frontier settlement (Bolivian formalities can usually be dealt with at the frontier post of Puerto Heath, from where you continue by river to Riberalta). Be aware that the journey from Puerto Maldonado to Riberalta is rough and usually takes ten to fourteen days; always make sure that the boat is going all the way or you might get stuck at the border, which, by all accounts, is not much fun, and you might have to wait days for another boat. From Riberalta there are land and air connections with the rest of Bolivia, as well as river or road access into Brazil via the Río Madeira or Guajara-Mirim.

Organized tours

Compared to independent travel, an **organized excursion** saves time and adds varying degrees of comfort. It also ensures that you go with someone who knows the area, who probably speaks English, and, if you choose well, can introduce you to the flora, fauna and culture of the area (although a couple of lodges have seen fit to establish "monkey islands", which could be seen as giving in to the desires of tourism rather than educating visitors about underlying issues). It's also worth noting that you are less likely to get ripped off with a registered company with a fixed office and contact details, especially if you should need redress afterwards.

Most people book a trip in Cusco before travelling to Puerto Maldonado, though it is possible to contact most of the operators in Puerto itself, either at the airport or through one of the offices (see below), or through the cafés on León de Velarde. Flying from Cusco is the quickest way to reach Puerto Maldonado, and most Cusco agencies will organize plane tickets ($40–50) for you if you take their tours. The cheapest option is a two-day and one-night tour, but on these you can expect to spend most of your time travelling and sleeping. Frankly, the Amazon deserves a longer visit, and you're only looking at $25–50 more for an extra day.

Of the ever-increasing number of **lodges** and **tour operators** around Puerto Maldonado, mainly on the *ríos* Madre de Dios and Tambopata, all offer a good taste of the jungle, but the quality of the experience varies from area to area and lodge to lodge – all lodges tend to offer full board and include transfers, though always check the level of service and ask to see photos at the lodges' offices in Cusco or Lima. It's also worth checking out what costs will be once you're there; complaints are common about the price of drinks (soft drinks and beer), although given the distance they've travelled, the mark-up is hardly surprising. Remember, too, that even the most luxurious place is far removed from normal conveniences, and conditions tend to be rustic and relatively open to the elements. Varying in capacity (the largest can accommodate up to a hundred, the smaller no more than a dozen or so), most lodges have huts, cabins or bungalows built from wood and palm fronds gathered from the forest. Toilets can be anything from standard WC closets covered in mosquito netting to earth privies, while sleeping arrangements can range from bunk rooms to pretty comfy twin doubles with doors and mosquito-net windows. Food is generally good, though you might want to take supplements or treats. Note that most lodges require guests to get up very early in the morning of the day of departure in order to arrive at Puerto Maldonado airport in good time – generally speaking, the nearer the lodge to the town, the longer you can sleep in.

LODGES AND TOUR OPERATORS

Bahuaja Research Centre ☎ & fax 084/573348. A small lodge aimed at the less wealthy traveller. It's fairly basic – toilets and showers are shared – but has a pleasant setting. Visits go to Tres Chimbadeas and Lago Sachavacayoc lake, with guiding in English and Spanish, plus there are extensive trails in the surrounding forest. The research side of the operation is associated with the UK organization Greenforce. From $165 per person for 4 days and 3 nights.

Buenaventura Casa de Hospedaje, ☎084/572590, *jerko_herrera@exite.com.pe*. Located in the community of Baltimore, 4hr upriver from Puerto Maldonado (6–7hr by *peque-peque*). Adjoining a family home and *chacra* gardens, this is a good but basic place, with shared toilets and showers. The trail system is quite limited, but trips go to the nearby waterfall and Chuncho *colpa* (guides speak Spanish only). $20 per day per person full board, $15 without.

TREES IN TAMBOPATA

In 1999, the Tambopata-Candamo Reserved Zone was subject to a widespread local consultation process to prepare a management plan and decide how best to zone activities in the region to ensure a sustainable future. At that time too, Mobil decided to pull out of this area, and the limits of the Bahuaja Sonene National Park now look likely to expand following the companies release of its exploration concession there. **TReeS** (c/o John Forrest, Tambopata Reserve Society, 64 Belsize Park, London, NW3 4EH, UK), is a UK organization with strong links with the Tambopata area and should be able to offer you detailed and up-to-date information on the situation and the environmental work going on there. They also know many of the lodges well and can advise you about them.

Casa Machiguenga, contactable through Manu Expeditions (see p.386). Owned by the Machiguenga Indian communities of Tayakome and Yombebato, though run by a German NGO as the Machiguenga are still undergoing a capacity-building programme. It's pretty rustic, with accommodation in huts, though with mod cons such as hot water and showers available. $35–45 per night per person.

Cusco Amazonico Lodge, Pasaje J. C. Tello C-13, Urbanización Santa Monica, Cusco (☎084/235314; in Lima ☎01/422-6574, fax 422-6574, *reservas@inkaterra.com.pe*). Set up by a French-Peruvian venture in 1975, comforts here include a cocktail bar and good food (often a buffet). The main excursion is to Lago Sandoval, some twenty minutes upriver, and guides speak several languages. The lodge owns 10,000 hectares of forest surrounding it and has recently established a monkey island. From $160 per person for 3 days and 2 nights ($25 supplement for a single).

Cusco Tambo Lodge, Plateros 351, Cusco (☎084/236159); or at the airport in Puerto Maldonado. A little basic for accommodation (wooden huts with bunks and mosquito nets) and not quite such a beautiful location as the others, this isn't for those seriously interested in wildlife. Although classified as a jungle trip, it's only about 11km from Puerto Maldonado and there's little forest in the area; instead, you get *chacra* fields and gardens. However, it's reliable and inexpensive, you don't have to invest heavily in food or equipment, plus it offers airport transfers. There are jungle walks, visits to Lago Sandoval and a gold-panning beach upstream, plus a viewing tower from which to see the distant forest. $30–35 per person per night.

Eco Amazonia Lodge, Portal de Panes 109, Oficina 6, Cusco (☎084/236159, fax 225068, *ecolodge@chasqui.unsaac.edu.pe*); Avenida Larco 1083, Oficina 408, Miraflores, Lima (☎ & fax 01/242-2708); *www.unsaac.edu.pe/CUSCO/TURISMO/Agencia/EcoAmazonia*. Less than two hours downriver of Puerto Maldonado, this large establishment offers basic bungalows and dormitories. The area abounds in stunning oxbow lakes but can't claim the variety of flora and fauna of the Tambopata-Candamo Reserved Zone, though it is recommended for bird-watching, plus it has swamp forest platforms and is the only lodge in the area with tree-canopy access. Packages usually include visits to Lago Sandoval, about 30min upriver, plus organized visits can be made to the Palma Real community, though this is often anticlimactic and of dubious value to both tribe and tourist. There's also a monkey island. From $30 per person per night according to length of stay.

Explorandes, San Fernando 320, Miraflores, Lima (☎01/445-0532, fax 445-4686, *Postmast@Exploran.com.pe*). A veteran company operating whitewater rafting expeditions, including a 12-day trip starting out from Puno by road, then travelling down through cloud forest, and finally rafting through Class III to V rapids along the Río Tambopata to Puerto Maldonado, where the last night is spent in a lodge. $1495 per person, for a minimum of four people.

Explorer's Inn, Plateros 365, Cusco (☎084/235342); c/o Peruvian Safaris, Avenida Garcilazo de la Vega 1334, Lima 1 (☎01/316330 or 313047, fax 328866). In the Tambopata-Candamo Reserved Zone, 58km (about 3hr) in a motorized *canoa* upriver from Puerto Maldonado, this is a large, well-organized lodge where research has contributed towards building a world-record list of species (580 birds and 1230 butterflies). Spanish- or English-speaking guides are available (boots are provided for jungle walks), and there are excellent displays, mostly in English, about rainforest ecology, plus there are radio links to the outside world. Food is good, and accommodation is generally in twin rooms with private bath, and full board is included. The price includes airport transfers, with expeditions to a nearby macaw salt-lick (*colpa*) – generally requiring one night camping out – plus there's a superb network of well-marked jungle trails. From $180 per person for 3 days and nights; enquire about rates for special-interest visitors (eg ornithologists).

Mejia Lodge ☎084/571428. On the shores of the popular Lago Sandoval, this rustic-style lodge is good for canoe exploration of the lake. It's rarely full, so it's fine to just turn up here by canoe from Puerto Maldonado without prior arrangement (get the boatman to drop you off on the trail). One of two lodges on the lake, this is an expanded family home with ten doubles and basic, shared toilet facilities. $15–$20 per person per day (dependent on season and open to negotiation), including food.

Posadas Amazonas Lodge and Tambopata Research Centre, contact through Rainforest Expeditions, Aramburu 166, 4B, Lima 18 (☎01/421-8347 or 221-4182, fax 421-8183, *postmast@ rainforest.com.pe*,). *Posadas* is probably the region's best lodge for its relationship with locals – it's owned by the Ese Eja community of Infierno (though mainly non-native members work here) – and for its wildlife research. There's great bird diversity in seven distinct, easily accessible habitats, plus good populations of primates and large mammals. Resident researchers act as guides (different languages available), and most packages include a visit to Lago Tres Chimbadas; additional trips to the

Tambopata macaw *colpa* (6–8hr upriver) can be arranged, involving a night at the remote Tambopata Research Center (TRC); a minimum of 6 days is recommended for complete tours. The lodge itself features large, stylish doubles with shared bath, set in three native-style buildings, plus a central dining area-cum-bar and lecture room. From $90 per day per person.

Sachavacayaco Lodge, contact through the *Cabaña Quinta* (see p.373). A small lodge offering a relatively rustic, more intimate and quiet experience than most, 3–4hr upriver from Puerto Maldonado. Visits usually go to Lago Sachavacayoc, with mostly Spanish-speaking guides. From $150 for 3 days and 2 nights per person, minimum of 4 people.

Sandoval Lodge, Inkanatura, Avenida Benadvides 3634, Oficina 301, Lima (✆01/271-8156) or Avenida Sol 821, second floor, Cusco (✆084/226392, *inkanatura@chavin.rcp.net.pe*). On the shores of Lago Sandoval, and usually accessed by canoe, this is the only lodge offering regular trips to this zone. It's medium-sized and features one large communal building as a bar and dining room, plus it boasts electricity and hot water. Most groups spend time on the lake or explore the small, well-trodden surrounding trail system, and there's also a small platform on the Río Heath. Guides speak several languages, including English. From $60 to $80 per person per day, depending on size of group, nature of visit and length of stay.

Tambopata Jungle Lodge, Pardo 705, Cusco (✆084/238911, *postmast@patcusco.com.pe*). Located in the Tambopata-Candamo Reserved Zone, 12km up the Río Tambopata from the *Explorer's Inn*, nearly 4hr from Puerto Maldonado. The lodge has comfortable, individual cabin-style accommodation and offers excellent tours of the forest, mainly in Spanish and English. It's located quite close to a community of *colonos*, some of whom farm while others pan for gold. Trips include a visit to Lago Condenado and sometimes Lago Sandoval, plus the Chuncho *colpa* by arrangement. From $160 per person for 3 days/2 nights.

Wasai Lodge, owned by the *Wasai* hotel in Puerto Maldonado (see p.372). Four hours upriver from Puerto Maldonado is this relatively new and smallish lodge set in the forest, with a pleasant jungle bar and dining area. Spanish and English speaking guides are available, with 15km of trails in the vicinity plus trips to the Chuncho *colpa* on request. $170 per person for 3 days and 2 nights; $250 for 4 days/3 nights, including a visit to Lago Sandoval plus the last night at the *Wasai* (avoiding the early morning start); $500 for 7 days and 6 nights, including a visit to the *colpa*.

Independent travel

Travelling independently can be rewarding, though note that most of the major river trips (including Lago Valencia) require visitors to obtain **permission** from the Captain's Office in Puerto Maldonado (see "Listings" p.374) – though boatman and guides generally do this and organize payment of entry fees for you at the **INRENA office** in Iquitos at Pevas 350–363 (✆084/231330, or 232980, fax 234861, *rnps-zrg@aeci.org.pe*). Even if you do end up doing this yourself it's normally quite straightforward, though it can be a battle to be heard over the *chicha* music on the Captain's radio.

Fortunately, it's still possible to get your own expedition together without spending a fortune. For limited excursions all you need is a boat and boatman, permission from the Captain's Office and basic essentials (see box on p.364). One of the most important aspects of any boat trip is finding the right boatman: three **recommended guides** include Willy Wither, who has lived many years in the area and is pretty reliable and well-organized, going to a wide range of places by canoe and on foot (he usually meets flights at Puerto Maldonado airport and speaks mainly Spanish); Javier Salazar, who owns the *Hotel Iñapari* (see p.373) and often takes groups up the Río de las Piedras and guides in English, Spanish or French; and Romel Nacimiento, a boat-owner and guide who specializes in day trips to Lago Sandoval, and who can usually be found at the Madre de Dios river port (ask around to find out where he is). Alternatively, ask around town or go down to the port to speak to a few of the guys who have canoes and motors. If there are six or more of you, these do-it-yourself trips (*always* go with a guide) can cost under $25 a day per person, all-inclusive; expect to pay between $50 and $120 a day for a reasonable launch (big enough for eight), with a decent outboard motor, a guide-cum-boatman, and fuel. All guides should have a Ministerio de Turismo *carnet* (ID card).

Whichever way you organize it, if you have the opportunity to spend several days exploring the Río Tambopata, try and get up as far as the mouth of the Río Tavara, where the wildlife is still abundant. No *colonos* have ever settled this far upstream and the jungle is wild, though not totally virgin – when Colonel Fawcett came through here, rubber extraction was already going on and a mule track running from Puno down the Tavara valley had been established.

Manu Biosphere Reserve

Encompassing almost two million hectares of virgin cloud and rain forest on the foothills of the eastern Andes, the Manu area was created in 1973 as a National Park, and then elevated to the status of Biosphere Reserve by UNESCO in 1977. In 1987 it became a World Natural Heritage Site. About half the size of Switzerland, the **Manu Biosphere Reserve** covers a total of 1,881,200 hectares of relatively pristine rainforest, from crystalline cloud-forest streams and waterfalls down to slow-moving, chocolate-brown rivers in the dense lowland jungle – a uniquely varied environment. The only permanent residents within this vast area are the teeming forest wildlife, a few virtually uncontacted native groups who have split off from their major tribal units (Yaminahuas, Amahuacas and Matsiguengas), the park guards, and the scientists at a biological research station situated just inside the park on the beautiful Lago Cocha Cashu, where flocks of macaws pass the time cracking open Brazil nuts with their powerful, highly adapted beaks.

For **flora and fauna**, it's pretty much unbeatable in South America, being home to 20,000 vascular plant types (one five-square-kilometre area was found to contain 1147 species of vascular plants, almost as many as the whole of Great Britain), with over 5000 flowering plants, 1200 species of butterfly, 1000 types of bird, 200 kinds of mammal and an unknown quantity of reptiles and insects. Rich in macaw salt-licks, otter lagoons, prowling jaguars, there are also thirteen species of monkey and seven species of macaw in Manu, and it still contains other species in serious danger of extinction, such as the giant otter and the black caiman (*Melanosochus niger*).

The reserve is divided into three zones. **Zone A** is the core zone, the **National Park** (1,532,806 hectares), which is strictly preserved in its natural state. **Zone B** is a Buffer Zone (257,000 hectares), generally known as the **Reserved Zone** and set aside mainly for controlled research and tourism. **Zone C** is the Transitional or **Cultural Zone** (91,394 hectares), an area of human settlement for controlled traditional use. Accessible only by boat, any expedition to Manu is very much in the hands of the gods,

---

THE OTORONGO OTTERS

The **giant otters** of Lago Otorongo are one of the world's most endangered species, and contact with people has to be minimized for their safety and long-term conservation. They are also bio indicators of the environment, since they only live where there is clean, healthy water and a wide choice of fish, so conservation of this rainforest environment is of primary importance. Only the oldest female of the group is mated with, so reproduction is very slow – the "queen" otters only have two or three cubs a year, usually around October, who can be expected to live for around 30 years. The top-ranking male otters are responsible for defending the group and do very little fishing, taking the catch from younger males instead.

Although they appear friendly as they play in their large family groups, they can be very aggressive, able to keep jaguars at bay and kill caimans who approach their lakeside nesting holes, which they mark by mixing male urine with clay at the entrance. This particular family, however, has learnt that the floating platform is not a threat.

thanks to the changeable jungle environment; the region experiences a rainy season from December to March, but is best visited between May and August when it's much drier, although at that time the temperatures often exceed 30°C.

The highlight of most organized visits to Manu is the trail network and lakes of **Cocha Salvador** (the largest of Manu's oxbows, at 3.5km long) and **Cocha Otorongo**, bountiful jungle areas rich in animal, water and bird-life. The latter is best known for the family of **giant otters** who live here; because of this, canoeing is not permitted, but there is a floating platform which can be manoeuvred to observe the otters fishing and playing from a safe distance (though your guide has to book a time for this): 50–30m is good enough to observe and photograph them, though as this is Manu's tourist honey-pot, you're likely to meet other groups and there can be severe competition for access to the platform. Other wildlife to look out for includes the plentiful **caimans**, including the two- to three-metre white alligators and the rarer three- to five-metre black ones, and you can usually see several species of **monkey** (including Dusky Titis, Woolly Monkeys, Red Howlers, Brown Capuchins and the larger Spider Monkeys – known locally as *Maquisapas*). Sometimes big mammals such as **capybara** or **white-lipped peccaries** (called *sajinos* in Peru) also lurk in the undergrowth.

The flora of Manu is as outstanding as its wildlife. Huge **cedar trees** can be seen along the trails, covered in hand-like vines climbing up their vast trunks (most of the cedars were taken out of here between 1930 and 1963, before it became a protected area). The giant **Catahua trees**, many over 150 years old, are traditionally the preferred choice for making dugout canoes – and some are large enough to make three or four – though second choice is the **lagarto tree**.

Just east of Zone B, but often visited in combination with it or with Zone C, is the **Manu Wildlife Centre**, a comfortable lodge some ninety minutes downriver from Boca Manu by motorized dugout. Owned by Manu Expeditions (see p.387) and the non-profit-making Selva Sur Conservation Group, it's located on privately owned rainforest and is built of the same sustainable local materials that the native Machiguenga Indians use – bamboo, wood, and palm-frond roofing – and all rooms are screened with mosquito nets. It operates hides close to a superb salt-lick where small parrots and larger more colourful macaws can be seen. It claims to be strategically located in an area of forest that counts on the highest diversity of micro-habitats in the Manu, and tierra-firme (lowland forest that doesn't get flooded), transitional floodplain, varzea and bamboo forest are all found close by, and an astounding 530 bird species have been recorded in one year alone. The Blanquillo macaw and parrot salt-lick is only thirty minutes away by river, with floating blinds to access the wildlife attracted here. About an hour's walk through the forest there's also a large *colpa* where tapirs and Brocket deer regularly come. The centre also features mobile canopy towers, making it possible to see more birds and even monkeys; access to these is by rope and harness, but there's also a static canopy platform with a spiral stairway.

The only viable way of **visiting Manu** is by joining an organized tour through one of the main Cusco agents, which is safer and generally cheaper than doing it yourself; you share the work and responsibilities, you can look after each other if you get ill or something goes wrong, and there's security in numbers. However, you can travel independently as far as Boca Manu, but unless you've secured a highly elusive special permit (see box opposite), you then have to head away from the reserve on one of the canoes that go most weeks (cargo and river permitting) to Puerto Maldonado. For this you'll need to be well stocked and prepared for a rough voyage of a several days – plus a few more if you have to hitch along the way. The only significant settlement en route is **Boca Colorado** at the confluence of the Río Colorado and Río Madre de Dios, a small gold-miner's service town full of rodent rats and human sharks. Remember, this region is well off the beaten tourist trail and is relatively wild territory, where *colonos*, indigenous Indians, and even smugglers and terrorists hang out.

Into the reserve

Manu Biosphere Reserve is better reached from Cusco than it is from Puerto Maldonado. Flying direct to Boca Manu (see p.386) will dramatically affect the price and the amount of time you get in the reserve (it's only a 30–45min flight but costs $300–400), and twin-engined planes can be chartered from the airport in Cusco. Most people, however, travel there on transport organized by their tour operators; otherwise, **buses** operated by Gallito de las Rocas (Avenida Manco Capac 105, Cusco; ☎084/277255) go to Pilcopata and usually beyond to Salvacíon at about 10am most Mondays and Fridays ($7; a 10–14hr journey depending on road conditions). **Trucks**, generally loaded to the brim with beer, fuel and passengers, leave Cusco from Avenida Huascar, and some from the Coliseo, every Monday, Wednesday, Friday and Sunday for Shintuya ($6; a 20–30hr journey in good conditions). All of the necessary **provisions and equipment** (see box on p.364) should be bought in Cusco, and this is one journey where you'll definitely need as much petrol as you can muster (a 55-gallon drum is probably enough). A sleeping mat is also a good idea even if only to sit on during the long journey to Shintuya; if the truck is carrying fuel, wear old clothes and cover your baggage properly. If you can afford one luxury, make it a sturdy pair of binoculars, preferably brought with you from home.

The first four- to six-hour stage is by road to the attractive town of **Paucartambo** (see p.161), over stupendous narrow roads with fine panoramas of the region's largest glaciated mountain of Ausungate, a major Apu – or god – for the Incas and also the locals today. From Paucartambo onwards, the precipitous and gravelly nature of the road down through the cloud forest to the navigable sections of the Río Alto Madre Dios means that access is supposedly limited to one direction per day, except Sunday, when it's a free for all. You can travel down on Monday, Wednesday and Friday, and back up on Tuesday, Thursday and Saturday.

It's another 30km to the turn-off to **Tres Cruces** (see p.162); from here the road winds down, at times along narrow stretches of quite bad track with drops of well over 300m only a few feet away. Somehow the beauty overrides the scariness for most people, and a surprising amount of wildlife can usually be spotted as the track continues downhill – Andean Guans, Mountain Motmots, Woodcreepers, Oropendulas and the brilliant-red Gallo de las Rocas (the national bird of Peru) can all be seen. Of course, you're more likely to get a glimpse of these if you're travelling with a good guide who has a well-trained eye.

MANU PERMITS

Permits to visit Manu are granted to groups only (mainly to established tour companies operating out of Cusco), and done so according to quotas, in order to limit the number of people in the reserve at any one time and throughout any particular year. It's virtually impossible to get permission by going it alone, and no settlers, hunters or missionaries are allowed in, while tourists are allowed into Zones B and C only as part of organized visits with guides, following the basic rules of non-interference with human, animal or vegetable life; Zone A is restricted to the occasional scientist (usually biologists or anthropologists) and indigenous groups, including the recently contacted Nahua people. Very rarely, however, if you're a naturalist, photographer, or can demonstrate a serious interest, then it is sometimes possible to gain a **special permit** for restricted areas; contact INRENA in Lima (see p.366).

The first settlement you come to in the high jungle is **Chontachaca**, which is Quechua for "Chonta Bridge" (*chonta* being the common hardwood palm whose wood is used throughout the Peruvian Amazon for Indian bows and arrow points). Vehicles rarely stop here, and shortly beyond, you pass through the slightly larger **Patria**, another frontier-type village, where coca is grown in some quantities. Turkeys, pigs and children play beside the road and the town's grassed-over, neglected concrete fountain says a lot about this place, which is more famous for its cock-fighting *fiestas* than anything else. Twenty-metre high electricity posts (made of concrete to stop the termites destroying them) line the settlement. Around here the jungle is being cleared for cash crops and, occasionally during the 1990s, so much vegetation was being burned that planes were occasionally unable to land in Cusco because of the rising smoke.

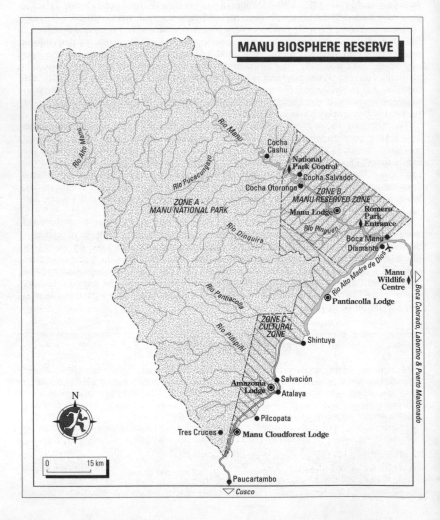

THE DIAMANTE PIRO

The Diamante community of **Piro Indians** were brought to the region from the lower Urubamba river, way beyond the Manu area, by rubber barons over a hundred years ago. Some of the community are said to want to return to the Urubamba, but are scared to travel there overland because of possible retribution by other indigenous groups who live in the reserve and who still, generations later, hold grudges against them for the violence during the rubber era. In 1987, some Piro guides and the Peruvian president Belaunde were attacked by sheets of arrows as they travelled in the then-National Park.

At the next town, **PILCOPATA**, the road crosses a river over a new steel bridge; to the right, a rickety old wooden one is left to decay in memory of a truck that collapsed it and fell into the water in the mid-1990s. Most buses and trucks stop here for the night, and there's a basic **hotel**, a few small shops and a simple market here. The road then skirts the Río Alto Madre de Dios, which eventually merges with the Río Manu to form the great Río Madre de Dios. The forest around here hides some fascinating **petroglyphs**, etched onto boulders by Indians before the Spanish arrived. However, these are along the Río Pishiyura river, hidden in the restricted area of Manu and reported to be protected by a still largely unacculturated group of Mashco-Piro Indians, who shoot arrows at intruders. This is also one of the areas where the legendary Inca city of gold – **El Dorado**, or **Paititi** – is reputed to lie.

The following day takes you on to the small riverside settlement of **ATALAYA** (10–12hr from Cusco), some tours cross the river to spend the night at an old tea hacienda which has been converted into an attractive tourist **lodge** – *Amazonia Lodge* (⑤ half board) 600m above sea level on the edge of the cloud forest. The food here is excellent and it's one of the few Peruvian jungle lodges to have solar-heated showers; the owners can be contacted in Cusco (Ramiro Yabar Calderon, Calle Matara 334, Cusco; ☎084/231370, *amazonia@correo.dnet.com.pe*). They offer full board and excursions in the region and frequently work with Manu Expeditions (see overleaf). There are also few restaurants in town.

Twenty minutes down the road from Atalaya, at the pueblo of **Salvación**, 28km before Shintuya, the Manu National Park has an office and your guide will usually be expected to show his permits. There are also a couple of rough hostals and one or two places to catch some **food** – a bowl of jungle soup or, if you're lucky, river fish with manioc. Trucks, mostly carrying timber, go from here to Cusco every Tuesday, Thursday and Saturday. Two hours beyond Atalaya, at **SHINTUYA**, the road finishes. The **Dominican Mission** here has been in existence for forty years, though recently many of the indigenous members have left after making good money with their chainsaws – some of them now own trucks to facilitate the supply of timber out to Cusco and beyond. There's no hotel, but there's no problem about **camping** if you ask permission – the best spot is beside the small stream that enters the main river (the water is cleaner here). Keep a watchful eye on your baggage, as Shintuya also has a sizeable transient population, passing to and from the gold-mining areas downriver. If you're travelling independently, all that remains to do is to seek out a canoe and a reliable boatman/guide, and if you've brought some of your own fuel to bargain with, it should be relatively easy to find a decent deal at the mission; the Moscosa family (especially Cesar, Pepe and Darwin) are reliable guides. Boats from Shintuya cost from around $300 for a week (though it can be double this if it's a busy season); if it's big enough, and most are, this can be shared between as many as seven or eight, and the price of an extra week isn't that much more. Remember that things happen on a different time scale in the Peruvian jungle, so get the boat organized as soon as you arrive, and try to make an early start the next day. If it can be arranged, it's a good idea to take a surplus, small dugout canoe for entering smaller channels and lagoons. Alternatively, you might be able to catch one of the cargo boats prepared to take passengers direct to Boca Colorado (see opposite), for around $25.

Downriver, in a *lancha* with outboard motor, it's half a day down the Alto Madre de Dios to **BOCA MANU**, a mere 300m above sea level and little more than a small settlement of a few families living near the airstrip, though this is likely to change, as oil and gas exploration in the Madre de Dios region has restarted, and Boca Manu may well become utilized by helicopters and service planes, just as it was in the late 1970s when oil companies had a contract for exploration here. There's no hostal (people do **camp** on the other side of the river, these are mostly visiting Indians or tour groups) and while there is a small shop here (prices double those in Cusco, with no guarantee of supply), the population mainly serves the gold-mining settlements downstream towards Puerto Maldonado. Close by is the native Piro community of **Diamante**, responsible for managing the **airstrip**, a major link to Cusco. In 1983, when it was controlled by cocaine smugglers, the airstrip was the scene of Hollywood-style drama when an unmarked Colombian plane was overloaded with cocaine. The plane crashed into the vegetation at the end of the airstrip, and the gang leader had his men torch the plane; its remains are still there in the undergrowth. The Peruvian Army later regained control of the strip, but now the Piro make a little money from each flight that uses it and sell good, cheap, *artesania* at the small hut that serves as the airport.

Organized tours

There are quite a few **organized tours** competing for travellers who want to visit Manu. Many are keen to keep the impact of tourism to a minimum, which means limiting the number of visits per year (it's already running well into the thousands). However, they do vary quite a bit in quality of guiding, level of comfort and price range. If you go with one of the companies listed below, you can generally be confident that you won't be doing anything that might have lasting damage.

Expediciones Vilca, Plateros 363, Cusco (☎ & fax 084/251872, *manuvilca@protelsa.com.pe*, *www.cbc.org.pe/manuvilca*); Amargura 101, Cusco ☎084/681002). Manu specialists, they have a good reputation and their guides are well informed, taking eco-tourism seriously. Their 8-day tour includes camping in Zone B, plus a visit to the macaw lick at Blanquillo. They also offer 5- and 6-day trips, including flights to and/or from Boca Manu. $450–$740.

Inkanatura Travel, Avenida Sol 821, 2nd floor, Cusco (☎084/226392, *inkanatura@chavin. rcp.net.pe*, *www.inkanatura.com*); Avenida Benadvides 3634, Oficina 301, Lima (☎01/271-3735, 271-8156 or 449-1051, fax 271-8156). Inkanatura offer customized travel, from 4 to 5 days, operating from the Manu Wildlife Centre, where one of the nearby highlights is the world's largest tapir saltlick. They also accommodate people at the *Cock of the Rock Lodge*, 6hr by road from Cusco, in one of the best cloud-forest locations for bird-watching. $1050–1150, discounts available to groups of 6 or more.

MANU Aventuras Ecologicas, Plateros 356, Cusco (☎084/261640, fax 225562, *Manuadventures@ computextos.com.pe*, *www.cbc.org.pe/manu/*). Jungle-trip specialists and one of the first operators running trips into Manu, with their own vehicles, boats and multilingual guides. Their camping-based tours are cheaper than most, with the 8-day option going in and out by bus, but they also offer shorter options which go in by bus and out by plane. $550–650.

Manu Expeditions, Avenida Pardo 895, PO Box 606, Cusco (☎084/226671, fax 236706, *Adventure@ManuExpeditions.com*). One of the best and the most responsible companies, run by a British ornithologist. They offer 3- to 9-day camping expeditions into Zone B and to the Manu Wildlife Centre (see p.382), with solar-powered radio communications and a video machine. Thoroughly recommended, the guides and service are top quality, good English is spoken, they offer air and overland transfers to Boca Manu (they have their own overland transport), and food, beds (or riverside campsite) and bird-blinds are all included. $688–1595, discounts available to South American Explorers' Club members.

Manu Nature Tours, Avenida Pardo 1046, Cusco (☎084/252721, fax 234793, *mnt@amauta.rcp. net.pe, www.manuperu.com*); Portal Comercio, 195 Plaza de Armas, Cusco (☎ & fax 084/252526). A highly professional company that operates *Manu Lodge*, one of only two within Zone B, where you can join their 4- to 8-day programmes. They also run 3-day trips to *Manu Cloud Forest Lodge* in their private reserve by the southeast boundary of Zone A, where torrent ducks, *gallos* and even woolly monkeys are often seen. $268–299 for *Manu Cloud Forest Lodge*, $1040–2065 for 4- to 8-day programmes; discounts available to South American Explorers' Club members.

Pantiacolla Tours, Plateros 360, Cusco (☎084/238323 fax 252696, *pantiac@mail.cosapidata. com.pe, www.pantiacolla.com*). A company with a growing reputation for serious eco-adventure tours. Their cheapest option is also the longest, a 9-day tour that takes groups in and out by bus and boat, while the more expensive 5- to 7-day trips go in by road and out by plane from Boca Manu. They have an excellent lodge on the Río Alto Madre de Dios at Itahuania, and their tours into Zone B are based in tents at prepared campsites. $675–$795, discounts available to South American Explorers' Club members.

Onward travel to Puerto Maldonado

It is possible, if adventurous, to follow an unregulated, uninfrastructured overland route from Boca Manu to Puerto Maldonado. Although you're more likely to have already found a boat going downriver from Shintuya, many will also pick up at Boca Manu for the one-day journey downstream ($10) to the sleazy gold-mining frontier town of **BOCA COLORADO** (also known as **Banco Minero**), at the mouth of the Río Colorado. Boca Colorado has a number of very basic hotels, but all have rats running around – they can be heard scampering across wooden-planked floorboards when the town generator goes off and the settlement's televisions fade into silence at 11pm every night. There are also a few simple **restaurants** serving surprisingly tasty food. It's possible to **camp** but, again, don't let your gear out of your sight. From here it's at least one more day ($10–15, depending on the speed of the boat) on to **LABERINTO** – see p.371 – from where it's a two-hour bus ride to Puerto Maldonado.

THE RÍO URUBAMBA

Traditionally the home of the Matsiguenga and Piro Indians, the **Río Urubamba** rolls down from the Inca's Sacred Valley to the humid lower Andean slopes around the town of **Quillabamba**, little more than a pit-stop before moving on and at the end of the rail line from Cusco (though due to a landslide this is likely to be out of operation between Machu Picchu and Quillabamba until around 2003). For the next eighty or so unnavigable kilometres, the Urubamba is trailed by a dirt road to the small settlement of **Kiteni**, where it meets with the tributary Río Kosrentni, then continues to the smaller settlement of Monte Carmelo. From here on, the easily navigable Río Kiteni becomes the main means of transport, a smooth 3500km through the Amazon Basin to the Atlantic, interrupted only by the impressive **Pongo de Mainique** – whitewater rapids, less than a day downstream, which are generally too dangerous to pass in the months of November and December.

Unlike the Manu Biosphere Reserve, most of the Urubamba has been colonized as far as the Pongo, and much of it beyond has suffered more or less permanent exploitation of one sort or another for over a hundred years (rubber, cattle, oil and more recently gas). Consequently, this isn't really the river for experiencing pristine virgin forest, but it is an exciting and remote challenge and a genuine example of what's going on in the Amazon today. Far fewer tour companies operate in the Río Urubamba region than do in Manu or Madre de Dios, but as the political situation continues to improve, and entrepreneurial optimism revives further around Cusco, it seems likely that more adventure tours will become available in the lower Urubamba and that the area will open up further to organized river-rafting and forest-trekking.

Quillabamba

A rapidly expanding market town, growing fat on coffee, tropical fruits, chocolate and to a certain extent perhaps, the proceeds of cocaine production, **QUILLABAMBA** is the only Peruvian jungle town that's easily accessible by road, and the main attraction here for tourists is a quick look at the *selva*. Coming from Cusco, the initial section of road is a narrow gravel track along precipitous cliffs, notoriously dangerous in the rainy season, but after a few hours, having travelled over the magical Abra Malaga – the main pass on this road – the slow descent towards Chaullay starts. From here on, you'll see jungle vegetation beginning to cover the valley sides; the weather gets steadily warmer and the plant life thickens as you gradually descend into the Urubamba Valley.

Your first sight of the town, which tops a high cliff, is of old tin roofs, adobe outskirts and coca leaves drying in the gardens. It's a pleasant enough place to relax, and you can get all the gear you need for going deeper into the jungle; the **market** sells all the necessities like machetes, fish hooks, food and hats. Just ten minutes walk from here, the **Plaza de Armas**, with its shady fountain statue of the town's little-known benefactor, Don Martín Pío Concha, is the other major landmark. Other than that, though about 4km away at **Sambaray**, the once attractive river beach is a bit of a dump these days; much nicer and quite a popular resort is the nearby waterfall area of **Siete Tinjas**.

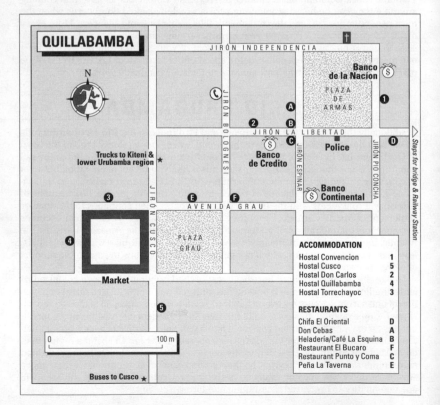

QUILLABAMBA

JIRÓN INDEPENDENCIA

Banco de la Nación

PLAZA DE ARMAS

JIRÓN LA LIBERTAD

Banco de Credito

Police

Banco Continental

Trucks to Kiteni & lower Urubamba region

AVENIDA GRAU

PLAZA GRAU

Market

Steps for bridge & Railway Station

Buses to Cusco

0   100 m

ACCOMMODATION

Hostal Convencion	1
Hostal Cusco	5
Hostal Don Carlos	2
Hostal Quillabamba	4
Hostal Torrechayoc	3

RESTAURANTS

Chifa El Oriental	D
Don Cebas	A
Heladería/Café La Esquina	B
Restaurant El Bucaro	F
Restaurant Punto y Coma	C
Peña La Taverna	E

Practicalities

The main town is a stiff climb from the river and the train station, over a bridge then up a series of steps, though the station is presently defunct due to the landslide. **Buses** from Calle Huascar in Cusco terminate by the market and Plaza Grau side of town; **colectivos** from Calle General Buendio, by the San Pedro railway station in Cusco, or the plaza in Ollantaytambo, terminate near the market in Quillabamba, as do trucks (best picked up from the plaza in Ollantaytambo).

For **accommodation**, the *Hotel Cusco*, Jirón Cusco 233 (☎084/281161; ②), near Plaza Grau and the market square, is somewhat run down at present though it suffices, while the *Hostal Quillabamba*, Avenida Prolongacion Miguel Grau 590 (☎084/281369; ③), very close to the market, offers exceptionally good value given that its modern rooms are comfortable and that it has a car park, swimming pool, hot water and a good restaurant. Just around the corner, the *Hostal Señor de Torrechayoc*, Avenida Grau 548 (☎084/281553; ②), has modern, clean rooms with or without bath. The *Hotel Don Carlos*, Jirón Libertad 546 (☎084/281371; ⑤), is a relatively luxurious newish hotel just up from the Plaza de Armas – cosy, friendly and popular with Peruvians. Rooms are smart and the place has a pleasant garden courtyard; it's also a good place to make connections for organized (though relatively costly) overland trips to Kiteni, and river trips onwards from there. The *Hostal Convecion*, Pio Concha 212 (☎084/281093; ①), is a basic but quaint place with a communal bathroom and no hot water; it's also the base for the Yoyato Club Tourism Adventure run by Sr. Rosas (May–Sept), who takes **tour groups** to Sambaray, the Pongo de Mainique or Espíritu Pampa.

Along the first block of Jirón Cusco are some very inexpensive little **restaurants**, such as the *Restaurant Los Amantes* and the *Restaurant La Estrella*, both of which serve decent set meals. *Don Cebas*, Jirón Espinar 235, on the Plaza de Armas, serves snacks and drinks, and close by the bar-restaurant *Peña La Taverna* offers good cool drinks and usually decent chicken and rice; it's downbeat and pleasant. The *Restaurant El Bucaro*, on the third block of Grau, just off the Plaza de Armas, is a spit-and-sawdust place with a nice and very jungle frontier-like atmosphere with very cheap set meals. The *Heladeria*, Jirón España 207, on the corner of the Plaza de Armas and Libertad, is a popular and cool place to while away an hour or two, with good snacks and wonderful ice creams. On the other side of the Plaza de Armas, the *Chifa El Oriental*, Libertad 375, serves surprisingly good Chinese meals. The *Snack-Restaurant Punto-y-coma*, Libertad 501, over the road from the *Heladeria*, is very popular for its tasty and cheap set lunches.

The Banco de Credito, on Libertad, is your best bet for **changing dollars** and traveller's cheques; failing that, try the Banco Continental, on the first block of Jirón España. Sometimes *cambistas* will change dollars cash on the street outisde these banks, or in the better hotels. **Telephone** calls can be made from Telefonica del Peru, Bolognesi 237–249, or there's a smaller company at Jirón Cusco 242.

Moving on

To get to Kiteni, five to eight hours deeper into the jungle, **buses** (the Alto Urubamba service) and **colectivos** (trucks start at $3; faster estate cars up to $10 per person) leave from Ricardo Palma, close to the Plaza Grau, every day from 8am to 10am. The road does go beyond Kiteni these days, as far as Monte Carmelo (almost to the Pongo de Mainique), though this frontier is constantly moving – trucks sometimes go on to Cumpire and Tinta at the very end of the road, which keeps more or less to the course of the Urubamba, but these little settlements offer nothing much for the independent traveller. Heading back to Cusco, the Hidalgo bus leaves Quillabamba from the market area several times a week, as do the bus companies Turismo Ampay and the less reliable Carhuamayo; trucks (from block 5 of San Martín) are more frequent, but slower, and there are currently no trains.

Kiteni and the Pongo de Mainique

By the time you reach **KITENI**, the Río Urubamba is quite wide and, with the forest all around, the valley is hotter, more exotic and much greener than before. Still a small *poblado*, until 25 years ago Kiteni was a small Matsiguenga Indian village. With its ramshackle cluster of buildings, all wooden except for the schoolhouse and the clinic (where you can get yellow fever shots if you haven't already done so), it is still a one-street town, with more mules than cars.

On **arrival**, trucks and buses stop at a chain across the dirt track. Here you have to register with the *guardia* in their office on the right before walking into the town. About 100m straight down the road, at the other end of town is the basic dormitory-type **hostel**, the *Hotel Kiteni* (①) – a friendly place, attractively situated beside the bubbling Río Kosrentni, and serving good set **meals**; there are no doors for security, but your gear should be safe here. Next to the *Hotel Kiteni* there's an *oroya* (stand-up cable car) for people to pull themselves across the river; a ten-minute stroll on the far bank takes you to an *albergue* that has been officially closed for several years but still occasionally rents out a few rooms for trips organized in advance by agencies or groups from Cusco; it offers seclusion, spoken English, and excellent food for only a few dollars a night. The last transport (mostly combis) from Kiteni to Quillabamba genereally leaves at 3–3.30pm daily (a 6hr trip).

The Pongo de Mainique

Kiteni's main draw – beyond its small jungle-settlement atmosphere – is as a jumping-off point for the awe-inspiring **Pongo de Mainique**, possibly the most dangerous 2km of (barely) navigable river in the entire Amazonian system, made famous by Michael Palin in his travel documentary. Just before you reach the *pongo* there's a community at **San Idriato**. The people here, known as the Israelites, founded their village around a biblical sect; the men leave their hair long and, like Rastas, they twist it up under expandable peaked caps. Not far from San Idriato there's a basic tourist lodge, again now out of general use, right at the mouth of the rapids – a wonderful spot. Across the Urubamba from San Idriato the small community of **Shinguriato**, upstream from the Río Yuyato mouth, is the official entrance to the *pongo* itself.

The rapids and beyond

You'll have heard a lot about the **Pongo de Mainique** before you get there – from the boatmen, the local Matsiguenga Indians, *colonos*, and the Israelites. They are dangerous at any time of year, and virtually impossible to pass during the rainy season (Nov–Jan). As you get nearer, you can see a forested mountain range directly in front of you; the river speeds up, and as you approach closer still it's possible to make out the great cut made through the range over the millennia by the powerful Urubamba. Then, before you realize, the craft is whisked into a long canyon with soaring rocky cliffs on either side: gigantic volcanic boulders look like wet monsters of molten steel; stone faces can be seen shimmering under cascades; and the danger of the *pongo* slips by almost unnoticed, the walls of the canyon absorbing all your attention. The main hazard is actually a drop of about 2m, which is seen and then crossed in a split second. Now and then boats are overturned at this drop, usually those that try the run in the rainy season – although even then natives somehow manage to come upstream in small, non-motorized dugouts.

Beyond the *pongo* the river is much gentler, but on all major curves as far down as the Camisea tributary (about 2 days on a raft) there is **whitewater**. Settlements along this stretch are few and far between – mostly native villages, settlements of *colonos*, or

TOURS TO THE PONGO

Tours down the Urubamba to the *pongo* can sometimes be arranged with one of the Cusco adventure tour operators detailed below. Other people may approach you in Quillabamba or Kiteni for a trip to the *pongo* and perhaps a little camping and fishing; the merits of these are entirely dependent upon the price you have to pay and the confidence you have in the guide. If there are enough of you, though, it might be more economical to **rent a canoe and boatman** (preferably with a powerful outboard motor) for a couple of days; this will cost from around $70 a day. To arrange any of these options you'll do best hanging around the port at Kiteni, on the beach behind the *guardia*'s huts, or asking in one of the few bars and cafés.

To go downriver without renting a boat or taking an organized trip is a matter of being at the dock early every morning and asking every boat that leaves if it's going to the *pongo*: Boats do take goods and people to the lower Urubamba communities, and are often more than willing to take extra passengers for a relatively small fee. Have all your baggage with you in case one is, but check whether it's coming back up. This way a return trip shouldn't cost more than about $40; if you want to go all the way to Sepahua, expect to pay around $55 one-way. You might have to wait a few days until there's one going all the way, but this is much easier than going hungry on a desolate beach somewhere below the *pongo*. Boats tend to arrive from downstream in the afternoon and it's often worth checking with them when they intend to go back. A boat with a powerful motor takes about five to six hours to reach the *pongo*; a *peque-peque* canoe will usually need around ten hours.

Apumayo, Calle Garcilaso 265, Oficina 3, Cusco (☎084/246018, *apumayo@mail. cosapidata.com.pe*). Offering rafting on the Urubamba and Apurimac rivers, they have great expertise and can organize programmes to suit any group's agenda. They usually work with groups pre-booked before arriving in Peru.

Eric Adventures, Plateros 324, Cusco (☎084/232244, fax 239772). A relative newcomer to the business, these specialists have developed a pretty good reputation for whitewater rafting.

Explorandes, Avenida Garcilazo 316A, Wanchaq, Cusco (☎084/238380, fax 233784, *postmast@explorandes.com.pe*, *www.explorandes.com*); or San Fernando 320, Miraflores, Lima (☎01/445-0532 or 445-8683, fax 445-4686, *Postmast@Exploran.com.pe*). A long established company who operate whitewater rafting expeditions mainly on the Apurimac, but they can sometimes be persuaded to work in the Quillabamba or Kiteni *pongo* region.

Instinct, Procuradores 50, Cusco (☎084/238366, *instinct@protelsa.com.pe* or *instinct@chavin.rcp.net.pe*, *www.rcp.net.pe/instinct*). A well-organized river-rafting company who offer rugged trips to tackle some difficult grades and will take groups down the Urubamba.

Mayuc, Portal Confiturias 211, Cusco (☎ & fax 084/232666, *chando@mayuc.com*, *www.mayuc.com*); PO Box 422, Cusco. A highly reliable and experienced company with the knowledge and flair to organize any tour or trek of your choice.

missions. If your boat is going straight back through the *pongo* to Kiteni, you'll have to make a quick choice about whether to try your luck going downstream or return to the relative safety and luxury of town. If it's going further down anyway, the next significant settlement is **SEPAHUA**, between the Pongo and which there are just a few Machiguenga missions and a presently empty, massive oil- and gas-exploration camp near the village of Nuevo Mundo. Sepahua has a **hotel**, a few shops and bars, and a **runway** with fairly regular flights to Satipo (for the road connection with Lima). However, the settlement is a good two or three days downstream by motorized canoe from the Pongo (depending on the type and size of motor), or four to five days on a raft: to be dropped off in between could mean waiting a week on the riverbank for another boat or raft to hitch with. To be on the safe side, you'll need food for at least ten days if you're going to do this.

From Sepahua, it's another couple of days downstream to **ATALAYA**, where the Río Urubamba meets the Río Tambo to form the Ucayali. Run mainly by local Ashaninka Indian leaders (following successful development and land-titling projects), it's a small and relatively isolated jungle town with a reputation for lawlessness. For a **place to stay** here, try the *Hotel Denis* (②) or the cheaper but less pleasant *Hostal d'Souza* (①). For moving on, there are weekly **flights** to Satipo, Pucallpa, and, less frequently, to Lima; information on these can be obtained from the TANS office near the airport. By **boat**, it's another few days from here to Pucallpa, and at least five or six more to Iquitos. To get to Lima, you can catch a boat (generally daily) for a day's travel along the Río Tambo to Puerto Ocopa, after which it's a few hours along a dirt road to Satipo, then ten to twelve hours by a new, surfaced road to Lima, via La Merced and Tarma; several buses daily cover this route, plus there are colectivos between Satipo and La Merced.

PUCALLPA AND LAGO YARINACOCHA

Although an interesting region, the central *selva* around **Pucallpa** doesn't have the strong appeal of the other jungle areas, and it's a tourist destination that suffered greatly during the political violence of the late 1980s and early 1990s. Recovery is slow, yet Pucallpa is still one of Peru's fastest growing cities, and its population of around 300,000 is well over 10 times that of 30 years ago. With its relatively new status as the capital of the independent *departmento* of Ucayali and its oil refineries and massive timber industry, the city represents the modern phase of the jungle's exploitation more than any other.

For travellers here, the big attraction is **Lago Yarinacocha** – a huge, beautiful oxbow lake where you can swim and rest up, watch schools of dolphin and – at a cost – go on wildlife expeditions or visit some nearby native communities. The city is also a main point of departure for trips downstream to the more obvious destination of Iquitos, a thousand-kilometre, week-long journey. Pucallpa is well connected to Lima and elsewhere, and, like Iquitos, is more thoroughly developed than other jungle towns. Similarly, both cities' indigenous Indian life is becoming increasingly Westernized, and as this happens, so tourism in the areas becomes increasingly packaged – or as they say in Peru, *convencional*.

Pucallpa

Long an impenetrable refuge for Cashibo Indians, **PUCALLPA** was developed as a camp for rubber gatherers at the beginning of this century. In 1930 it was connected to Lima by road (850km of it), and since then its expansion has been intense and unstoppable. Saw mills – most of the parquet floors in Lima originated here – surround the city and spread up the main highway towards Tingo María and the mountains, and an impressive floating harbour has been constructed at the new port of **La Hoyada**. Until 1980 it was a province in the vast Loreto *departmento*, controlled from Iquitos, but months of industrial action eventually led to the creation of a separate *departmento* – Ucayali. The end of financial restrictions from Iquitos, which exports down the Amazon to the Atlantic, and the turn of traffic towards the Pacific were significant changes. The new floating dock can service cargo boats of up to 3000 tons, and in 1996, the selling off of contracts for oil exploitation to foreign companies by Fujimori's government gave Pucallpa a further burst of energy and finance (though this particular effect has eased off in recent years).

Although in many ways a lively and vibrant city, there is little here of great interest to travellers, most of whom get straight in a *motokar* or a local bus for **Lago Yarinacocha**. If you stay a while, though, it's difficult not to appreciate Pucallpa's relaxed feel – or the optimism in a city whose red-mud splattered streets are fast giving way to concrete and asphalt.

Arrival, information and city transport

From Lima, Pucallpa is served by several **bus companies**, all of which go via Huánuco (roughly the halfway point); the full journey is supposed to take approximately 24 hours but can take longer; note that it's often difficult to get seats on the buses if you pick them up outside of Lima. If you arrive with Tepsa, you'll get off outside their offices at Jirón Raymondi 649; Ucayali Express offices are by the corner of 7 de Junio with San Martín; while if you travel with León de Huánuco, you disembark close to the Parque San Martín, at the corner of Jirón 9 de Diciembre and Jirón Vargas. Boats arrive at the **floating port** of La Hoyada on the eastern side of town, about 2km from the Plaza de Armas ($1 by *motokar*, $2.50 by taxi). Pucallpa **airport** is only 5km west of town and is served by buses (20min; 35¢), *motokars* (15min; $1.50) and taxis (10min; $4–5). Aero Continente and Lan Peru operate flights between Pucallpa and Lima and Iquitos, and TANS fly here from Tarapoto, Lima and Iquitos once a week. There are also irregular services run by Airtaxis (☎064/575221), based at the airport, from Cruzeiro do Sul just over the Brazilian border.

Tourist information is available the local *consejo*'s office, 2 de Mayo 999 (☎ & fax 064/575110), or from Laser Viajes y Turismo, Avenida 7 de Junio 1043 (☎ & fax 064/573776). **Exchange** is at Banco de Credito, Jirón Tarapaca, two blocks from the Plaza de Armas towards the main market by Parque San Martín, though for good rates on dollars cash try the *cambista* on Calle Tarapaca, where it meets the Plaza de Armas. **Telephones** are available at Telefonica del Peru, Ucayali 357, or on Jirón Independencia; **Internet** services are offered by several places in Pucallpa, but the best is probably the ISTU, Avenida San Martín 383 ($3.50 per hour; *itsu@pol.com.pe*). For snail mail, the **post office** is at San Martín 418.

One of the best ways of **getting around** Pucallpa is as the locals do, by **motorbike**; these can be rented by the hour ($2 approx) from the workshop at Raymondi 654. Otherwise, colectivos leave from near the food market on Avenida 7 de Junio, while **motokars** and **taxis** can be picked up almost anywhere in town.

Accommodation

Pucallpa is full of **hotels**, old and new, and most of the better ones are grouped around the last few blocks of Jirón Tacna and Jirón Ucayali, near the Parque San Martín. At the top end, the *Hotel Sol del Oriente*, Jirón San Martín 552 (☎064/575154, fax 575510; ④), is an attractive old building with a fine pool and excellent service; the *Hotel Inambu*, Federico Basadre 271 (☎064/576822; ③), is almost as good, and has an excellent restaurant, although no pool. Still at the upper end of the scale for Pucallpa, the *Gran Hotel Mercedes*, Raymondi 610 (☎064/571191; ③), is pretty good value and has the added attractions of a popular bar and a fairly nice pool. The *Hostal Confort*, centrally located at Coronel Portillo 381 (☎064/576091; ③), is a good, moderately priced alternative. Slightly cheaper, the *Hotel Amazonas*, Coronel Portillo 729 (☎064/576080; ③), is quite comfortable, and has clean rooms with fans and private bathrooms. Considerably more basic, the *Hotel Europa* (②), at the Parque San Martín end of

Avenida 7 de Junio, and the *Hostel Mori* (②), Jirón Independencia 1114, are reasonably comfortable and quite friendly and clean, though bathrooms are shared.

The Town and around

If you have an hour or so to while away in the town itself, both the downtown **food market** on Independencia and the older central **market** on 2 de Mayo are worth checking out; the latter in particular has interesting and varied stalls full of jungle produce. The port of **La Hoyada** and the older nearby **Puerto Italia** are also interesting places, bustling with activity by day. The only other attractions in town are the **Usko-Ayar Amazonia School of Painting**, at Jirón Sanchez Cerro 467 (Mon–Fri 10am–5pm; free), the home of the School's founding father, the self-taught artist Pablo Amaringo. Once a *vegetalista-curandero*, Dom Amaringo used to use the hallucinogenic *ayahuasca*, as do most Peruvian jungle healers as an aid to divination and curing; his students' works, many of which are displayed at his house, display the same *ayahuasca*-inspired visions of the forest wilderness as his own paintings do.

On Calle Inmaculada, the **Regional Natural History Museum** (Mon–Sat 9am–6pm; $1.50) exhibits dried and stuffed Amazon insects, fish and animals and has good displays of local crafts, including ceramics produced by the Shipibo Indians, plus other material objects such as clothing and jewellery from local Indian tribes. There are also works by the Pucallpa-born wood sculptor Augustin Rivas, who once ran an artists' haven at Lago Yarinacocha, but now runs *ayahuasca* sessions in the Iquitos region.

Some 6km out of town, along the highway towards Lima, there's a small lakeside settlement and zoological park at Barboncocha. Known as the **Parque Natural de Barboncocha** (daily 9am–5.30pm; $1), it consists of almost 200 hectares of lakeside reserve with plenty of alligators, birds and boa constrictors, as well as caged monkeys and a black jaguar. Colectivos to Barboncocha (25min; $0.60) can be caught from near the food market on Avenida 7 de Junio; or hail a motorcycle taxi (20min; $3) from anywhere in town.

Eating

Restaurants are fairly plentiful and include the *Chifa Han Muy*, Jirón Inmaculada 247, which does a wonderful blend of Peruvian Chinese and tropical jungle cuisine. For international dishes, it's hard to beat the restaurant in the *Hostel Inambu*, Federico Basadre 271. Slightly cheaper and very good for fish dishes, like the local speciality *patarashca* (fresh fish cooked in *bijao* leaves), or the delicious *sarapatera* (soup in a turtle shell), there's the *Restaurant El Golf*, at Jirón Huascar 545, or the *Restaurant El Alamo*, on block 26 of Carretera Yarinacocha.

Lago Yarinacocha

Some 9km from Pucallpa, and easily reached by bus or colectivo (20min; 30–50¢) from the food market on the corner of Independencia and Ucayali, **Lago Yarinacocha** is without doubt a more attractive place to stay than the city itself. A contrast to the southern jungle lakes, its waters are excellent for swimming and there is considerable settlement around its banks. River channels lead off towards small villages of Shipibo Indians, luxury tourist lodges, and the slightly bizarre Summer Institute of Linguistics. This last place is the headquarters of an extremely well-equipped, US-funded missionary organization, their aim being to bring God to the natives by translating the New Testament into all Indian languages. At present they're working on over forty, "each as different from each other as Chinese is from Greek".

Puerto Callao and the lake

The lake's main centre, and the place where most travellers stay, is **PUERTO CALLAO**, a town known locally (and slightly ironically) as the "Shangri-la de la Selva", where the bars and wooden shacks are animated by an almost continuous blast of *chicha* music. The settlement boasts one of the best jungle Indian craft workshops in the Amazon, the **Moroti-Shobo Crafts Co-operative** – a project originally organized by Oxfam but now operated by the local Shipibo and Conibo Indians. Located on the main plaza it displays some beautifully moulded ceramics for sale, carved wood and dyed textiles, most of them very reasonably priced.

Various **excursions** to see wildlife, visit Indian villages, or just to cross the lake, are all touted along the waterfront. The standard day-trip goes to the Shipibo village of **San Francisco** ($10 per person), sometimes continuing to the slightly remoter settlements of **Nuevo Destino** and **Santa Clara** (around $15 per person). San Francisco is now almost completely geared towards tourism, so for a more adventurous trip you'll do better to hire a *peque-peque* canoe and boatman on your own (from around $30 a day); these canoes can take up to six or seven people and you can share costs, though if you want to go further afield (say on a 3-day excursion) expect prices to rise to $150 a day.

There's also an interesting botanical garden, the **Jardín Botánico Chullachaqui** (daily 9am–5pm; free) on the far right-hand side of the lake. To reach it you have to take a *peque-peque* canoe, a 45-minute ride ($2) from Callao Port, then walk for almost half an hour down a clearly marked jungle trail. On arrival, you'll find a well-laid-out garden

La Perla Lodge & Community of Nueva Luz de Fatima △   Jardin Botanico Chullachaqui △

La Cabaña Lodge ⊙

San Francisco, Nuevo Destino & Santa Clara

Lake Yarinacocha

FOOTPATH

S.I.L.
(Summer Institute
of Linguistics)

Puerto Callao   FOOTPATH

N

⊙ Restaurant/Hostal
El Pescador

■ Bus Terminal

⊙
Hostal
Los Delfines

Maroti-Shobo
Artesania Co-operative

0   100 m

Pucallpa △

YARINACOCHA

PLAZA

in a beautiful and very exotic location with over 2300 medicinal plants, mostly native to the regions.

Towards the waterfront are most of the liveliest **bars** (try *El Grande Paraiso*); if you fancy something quieter, the lodges around the lake (see below) make a good spot for an evening drink; of the **restaurants**, the best is *El Pescador*. As for **hotels**, *El Pescador* (no tel; ②) also offers good if basic **accommodation**, as does *Hostal Los Delphines* (☎064/571129; ②); and both offer off-season deals in the ① range. You can also **camp** anywhere along the lake, though bear in mind that you'll need to keep a lookout for thieves, but if you fancy something more luxurious, try the **tourist lodges** that surround the lake: they're far more expensive than a basic hotel, but are wonderfully positioned. The well-established *La Cabaña* (④) – possibly the first jungle lodge built in Peru – is an excellent place to stay, though the management request bookings in advance, not least so that they can send their boat to Puerto Callao to meet visitors; they have an office in Pucallpa at Jirón 7 de Junio 1043 (☎064/616679, fax 579242). Another comfortable lodge, *La Perla* (no tel; ③), which has a highly recommended restaurant for patrons, is located more or less next door to *La Cabaña* but is slightly cheaper, with the price including full board; accommodation (in bungalows) is similar to that of *La Cabaña*, though it's a smaller place with a different, perhaps more intimate, atmosphere. Like *La Cabaña*, it can be reached only by boat.

Not a lodge at all, it is sometimes possible to stay in the Medical Centre (①) at the village of **NUEVA LUZ DE FATIMA**, a small settlement a little further down the same bank of Yarinacocha, beyond *La Perla* lodge. Gilber Reategui, an English-speaking neighbour of the Medical Centre, can arrange for meals if required; he is also recommended as a jungle guide – he has a *peque-peque* called *Mi Normita*, which is usually beached at Puerto Callao on the lake when not touring. Write to Sr Gilber Reategui c/o Ruperto Perez, Maynas 350, Yarinacocha, Pucallpa, Ucayali, Peru for advance bookings.

Downriver to Iquitos

Travelling **from Pucallpa to Iquitos** on a boat sounds more agreeable than it actually is. Very few Peruvians, except boatmen, would ever dream of it – over 1000km of water separates the two towns, with very little in between but the endless undulations of the river and verdant forest hemming you in on either side. However, if you are going there, you may want to relax in a hammock for a few days and arrive in the style the rubber barons were accustomed to.

Large **riverboats** generally leave Pucallpa from La Hoyada port, 4km from the Plaza de Armas along Avenida Mariscal, while smaller **launches and canoes** tend to go from Puerto Italia, which is slightly nearer. The cheapest and most effective way of finding a boat is to go down to the ports and ask around. Try to fix a price and a departure date with a reputable-looking outfit; it should cost around $30 per person, including food, but if you want a cabin this can rise to about $50. Few boats on this stretch of water actually have cabins though, and while they're useful for securing your gear in, you'll probably be more comfortable (and certainly cooler) sleeping in a hammock, strung under some mosquito netting. It's quite usual for passengers to string them up several days before departure – which can mean great savings on hotel costs and less risk of the boat leaving without you. If the captain asks for money upfront, don't give the whole bundle to him; you may never see him or his boat again. Additionally, even when everything looks ready for departure, don't be surprised if there is a delay of a day or two – boats leave frequently but unpredictably. Food on board can be very unappetizing, so it's worth taking some extra luxuries, like a few cans of fish, a packet or two of biscuits, and several bottles of water. Depending on how big the boat is and how many stops it makes, the journey to Iquitos normally takes five to seven days. Before you leave there's a certain amount of **paperwork** to go through, since this is a commercial port and one of the main illicit cocaine trails; you'll have to show your documents to the port police (PIP) and get permission from the naval office (your captain should help with all of this).

En route to Iquitos, boats often stop at the settlements of Contamana (10hr; $7) and Requena (a further 4–5 days; $20). In theory it's possible to use these as pit-stops – hopping off one boat for a couple of days while waiting for another – but you may end up stuck here for longer than you bargained. There isn't much at **CONTAMANA**, on the right bank of the Ucayali, but it's ok to **camp**, and **food** can be bought without any problem. A better stopping point is the larger and more pleasant **REQUENA**, developed during the rubber boom on an isolated stretch of the Río Ucayali, a genuine jungle town that is in many ways like Iquitos was just fifty years ago. There are a couple of basic **hostals** here and one quite good one (contact the *Hostal Amazon Garden* in Iquitos; see p.400), or you can also **camp** on the outskirts of town. For those going downstream, it's about a day's journey from Iquitos, with **boats** leaving regularly (around $15 a person). You can also access Pacaya Samiria National Reserve (see p.406) by boat from here, though most people reach it from Lagunas. A few hours to the north, just a few huge bends away, the Río Marañon merges with the Ucayali to form the mighty Amazon.

IQUITOS AND THE AMAZON

At the "island" city of **Iquitos**, by far the largest and most exciting of Peru's jungle towns, there are few sights as magnificent as the **River Amazon**. It's tributaries start well up in the Andes, and when they join together several hours upstream from the town, the river is already several kilometres wide, though a mere 116m above sea level. The town's location, surrounded in all directions by brilliant green forest and hemmed in by the maze of rivers, streams, and lagoons, makes it easy to imagine the awe that Francisco Orellana, the first white man to see it, must have felt only 450 years ago.

Most people visit Iquitos briefly with a view to moving on into the rainforest but, wisely, few travellers actually avoid the place entirely. A busy, cosmopolitan tourist town with a buzzing population of about 300,000, connections to the rest of the world are by river and air only – Yurimaguas, the end of the road from the Pacific coast, is the nearest road to Iquitos. It's the kind of place that lives up to all your expectations of a jungle town, from its elegant reminders of the rubber boom years to the atmospheric shanty-town suburb of **Puerto Belén**, one of Werner Herzog's main film locations for *Fitzcarraldo* and where you can buy almost anything, from fuel to *ayahuasca*.

Tourist facilities here have developed gradually over the last thirty years and the town has a friendly café- and club-life, interesting museums and beautiful buildings, and the surrounding region has some great island and lagoon beaches, a range of easy

---

LINGO FOR GRINGOS

While you're here it might be useful to know a few local **jungle words**: *pakucho* (the local form of "gringo"); *shushupero* ("drunk", from the deadly *shushupe* snake), *La Aguajina* (a refreshing palm-fruit drink), and *siete raices* (a strong medicinal drink, mixed from seven jungle plants and *aguardiente*); *masato* (manioc beer); *remolino* (whirlpool); *pongo* (whitewater rapids); *la bauda* (a curve in the river); and *el monte* (the forest). One mythical figure you might come across is Pishkato, a monster in the form of a white man who steals jungle children and turns them into fuel and grease to power the white man's cargo-producing factories.

excursions into the rainforest, and the possibility of continuing down the Amazon into Colombia or Brazil. The area has also become something of a spiritual focus, particularly for gringos seeking a visionary experience with one of the many local shaman who utilize the sacred and powerful hallucinogenic *ayahuasca* vine in their religious psycho-healing sessions.

When to come

Unlike most of the Peruvian *selva*, the **climate** here is little affected by the Andean topography, so there is no rainy season as such; instead, the year is divided into "high water" (Dec–May) and "low water" (June–Nov) seasons. The upshot is that the weather is always hot and humid, with temperatures averaging 23–30°C and with an annual rainfall of about 2600mm. Most visitors come between May and August, but the high-water months are perhaps the best time for **wildlife**, because the animals are crowded into smaller areas of primary forest and dry land.

As for Iquitos itself, the carnival known as **Omagua** (local dialect for "lowland swamp"), has grown in vigour over recent years and now involves hundreds of Indians, with plenty of chanting and dancing. The main thrust of activities (as always) is on the Friday, Saturday and Sunday before Ash Wednesday, and on the Monday, the town celebrates with the traditional Umisha dance around a sacred tree selected for the purpose. It's similar to Maypole dancing in Britain, though the dancers strike the tree with machetes; when it eventually falls, children dive in to grab their share of the many gifts previously suspended from it. Perhaps the best time to visit Iquitos, however, is at the end of June (supposedly June 23–24, but actually spread over 3 or 4 days), when the main **Fiesta de San Juan** takes place. Focused around the small *artesania* market of San Juan (San Juan being the city's patron saint), some 4km from the city and quite close to the airport, it's the traditional time for partying and for eating *juanes*, delicious little balls of rice and chicken wrapped in jungle leaves; the best place for these is in San Juan itself. June is also the time for **Iquitos Week**, centred around the Fiesta de San Juan though tending to spread right across the month. In October the municipality's tourism directorate organizes an **international rafting competition**, which draws enthusiasts from every continent for a short five-hour, twelve-mile river race, plus a longer six-day race. Jetski racing is being planned, though the environmental issues might well outweigh the tourism benefits of this. At the end of the month there's the **Spirits of the Jungle** festival, which coincides with Halloween and All Souls. For more on this, contact the Iquitos tourist information office (see opposite).

Iquitos

IQUITOS began life in 1739 when Jesuit José Bahamonde established settlements at Santa Barbara de Nanay and Santa Maria de Iquitos on the Río Mazán. It was a particularly daunting task, as the missionaries here faced the task of converting the fierce Iquito Indians, renowned as marksmen with their long poison-dart blowpipes. There are only one or two families of the Iquito tribe left, living way on the upper Río Nanay, and these days the region is better known for the Yaguar, Bora and Witoto tribes, whose handicraft can be seen virtually everywhere you turn in the modern city.

The original town was founded in 1757 under the name of San Pablo de los Napeanos, but the present centre was established in 1864. By the end of the nineteenth century it was, along with Manaus in Brazil, one of *the* great rubber towns. From that era of grandeur a number of structures survive, but during this century Iquitos has vacillated between prosperity – as far back as 1938, the area was explored for oil – and the depths of depression. However, its strategic position on the Amazon, which makes it accessible to large ocean-going ships from the distant Atlantic, has ensured its importance. At present, still buoyed by the export of timber, petroleum, tobacco and Brazil nuts, and dabbling heavily in the trade of wild animals, tropical fish and birds, as well as an insecticide called *barbasco*, long used by natives as a fish poison, Iquitos is in a period of quite wealthy expansion.

One interesting **environmental change** that seems to be happening at Iquitos is that the river is so low that it has receded significantly from the main riverfront, which has necessitated moving the town's downriver port away from its centre. Some locals blame downstream canalization for this shift, others point to a drop in rainfall along the Amazon's headwaters in other parts; or it may be that increasing deforestation of the *ceja de selva* higher up means that, during the rainy season, rainwater simply runs off the surface, leaving none to gradually filter down during the dry season. Whatever the reason, the riverfront now stretches all the way from the old port and market of **Belén**, which the Amazon waters hardly reach anymore, to the newer floating port of **Puerto Masusa**, 3km downriver.

Expeditions around Iquitos are the most developed in the Peruvian jungle, offering a wide and often surprising range of attractions. As usual, anything involving overnight stays is going cost a fair bit, though there are also cheap day-trips. With all organized visits to Indian villages in this area, expect the inhabitants to put on a quick show, with a few traditional dances and some singing, before they try to sell you their handicraft (occasionally over-enthusiastically). Prices range from $1 to $5 for necklaces, feathered items (mostly illegal to take out of the country), bark-cloth drawings, string bags (often excellent value) and blowguns; most people buy something, since the Indians don't actually charge for the visit. While the experience may leave you feeling somewhat ambivalent – the men, and particularly the women, only discard Western clothes for the performances – it's a preferable situation to the times when visits were imposed on communities by unscrupulous tour companies. Visitors are now their major source of income, and it seems that the Bora and Yaguar alike have found a niche they can easily exploit within the local tourist industry.

Arrival, information and getting around

If you've come by boat from Yurimaguas (5 days), Pucallpa (6–7 days), Leticia or Tabatinga (both 3 days), you'll arrive at **Puerto Masusa**, some eleven blocks northeast of the Plaza de Armas. Flights land at Iquitos **airport**, 5km southwest of town and connected by taxis ($4) and cheaper *motokars* ($2). Once you're off the plane, you're likely to be surrounded by a horde of desperate potential jungle guides, all trying to persuade you to take their tours or stay in their lodges; at this stage, the best thing to do is to avoid conversation with any of them, apart perhaps from saying you'll meet them *Ari's Burger* in a couple of hours – which will give you time to get settled in and think about where you want to go and how much you are prepared to pay (see p.402–411 for advice on choosing guides and tours). **Buses** pull in on the Plaza de Armas and on calles *Huallaga* and *La Condamine*.

The local *consejo* run a very helpful **tourist information** kiosk at the airport and an equally friendly office on the Plaza de Armas at Napo 226 (☎094/235621, *turismo.mpm@tvs.com.pe*), which also sells CDs of the region's music and videos of local attractions. They have brochures and maps, plus they can advise on hotels, they keep a list of registered tour operators and guides, and they can help book accommodation.

For **getting around** Iquitos you'll probably want to make use of the rattling **motokars** again; alternatively, **motorbikes** can also be rented – try the shop near the Ferreteria Union (block 2 of Raymondi), or one at Yavari 702. Expect to pay around $2 an hour or $10 for twelve hours (you'll need to show your passport and licence), and remember to check the brakes before leaving. For getting around town by **car**, try the office at Tute Pinglo 431 (☎094/235857). If you want to get onto the river itself, **canoes** can be rented very cheaply from the port at Bellavista (see p.405).

Accommodation

Like every other jungle town, Iquitos is a little expensive, but the standard of its **hotels** is very good and the range allows for different budgets. Even a room in an average sort of place will include a shower and fan, and many others offer cable TV and minibars.

El Dorado Hotel, Napo 362 (☎094/232574, fax 221985, *dorado@tvs.com.pe*). A good hotel with a small pool, less than a block from the Plaza de Armas. ⑥.

El Dorado Plaza, Napo 258, Plaza de Armas (☎094/222555, fax 224304, *dorplaza@tvs.com.pe*). A fine and flashy hotel, the first ever 5-star in Iquitos. There's a very nice pool, a *maloca*-style bar, and a quality restaurant. The vast air-conditioned lobby features a glass lift rising to all 6 floors. ⑧.

Hostal Amazonas Plaza, Plaza de Armas, corner of Napo and Fitzcarrald (☎ & fax 094/242431). A smart, if uninspiring, modern hotel, with pleasant, plain rooms that have cable TV, mini-bars, and hot water. ⑥.

Hostal Amazon Garden, C. Pantago 417, by the Parque Zonal, just off Yavari (☎094/236140, *amazonas@amazongardenhotel.com.pe*); or contact through Amazon Tours and Cruises (see p.410). A new hotel with comfortable air-conditioned rooms, excellent hot showers, probably the nicest outdoor pool in the city, good service, and a restaurant and bar. ⑥.

Hostal Fortaleza, Prospero 311 (no tel). Very basic, but very central. ②.

Hostal la Libertad, Arica 361 (☎ & fax 094/235763). A fine backpackers' place, rooms have private bathrooms, hot water and cable TV, plus there's a restaurant. It's also home to a good tour company (see p.410). ②–③.

Hostal Lima, Prospero 549 (☎094/235152). Rooms have private bath and fans; it also possesses a certain jungle flavour, with parrots on the patio. Good value. ②.

Hostal Monterrico, Arica 633 (☎ & fax 094/235395). Dark rooms and somewhat basic, but it is clean, has a nice enough atmosphere and is safe. ②.

Hostal La Pascana, Pevas 133 (☎094/231418, fax 233466, *hs_pascana@lima.business.com.p*e). Appealing doubles based around a small courtyard close to the river, less than two blocks from the Plaza de Armas. Clean, friendly and popular with travellers, it offers a ventilated, quiet haven from Iquitos's sometimes hectic street life. ③.

Hostal Peru, Prospero 318 (☎094/234961). Good value, if rather down at heel, though still popular with locals and travellers alike, perhaps because of its old-fashioned architecture and fittings. It has shared bathrooms, fans in all rooms and for $2 extra you can have cable TV. ②.

Hostal Safari, Napo 118 (☎094/233828). Less than a block from the plaza, with clean and comfortable rooms, if a little dark. It can be noisy on weekend evenings. ④.

Hotel Acosta, Huallaga corner with Calvo (☎ & fax 094/231761). Clean and quite smart, though not all that friendly. Same owners as the plusher *Hotel Victoria Regia*. ⑤.

Hotel Amazon Suites, Napo 274, on the Plaza de Armas (☎094/243088) A rather odd place, offering rooms and suites, a small pool and Jacuzzi. ⑤–⑦.

Hotel Eunice, Arica 780 (☎094/233405, fax 243607). Some amazingly large rooms, some with TV and stereos, TV and mini-bar. Very friendly and good value. ⑤.

Hotel Europa, Prospero 494 (☎094/231123, fax 235483, *heuropa@telematic.com.pe*). Central and pleasant, with a restaurant and bar. All rooms have cable TV and good private bathrooms. ⑤.

Hotel Maria Antonia, Prospero 616 (☎094/234761, fax 234264). Friendly staff and a pleasant enough place, though nothing special. Cable TV and a laundry service are offered. ④.

Hotel Victoria Regia, Ricardo Palma 252 (☎094/231983, fax 232499, *chasa@meganet.com.pe*). A luxurious place with a small pool, good security and excellent service. ⑧.

Real Hotel, Malecón Tarapaca (☎094/231011). The former *Gran Hotel Iquitos*, this really doesn't look so grand today, despite its location right on the front between El Boulevard and the Malecón Tarapaca. Nevertheless it seems to do good conference trade, offering 76 rooms with commanding views towards the Amazon, and it's comfortable. ⑥.

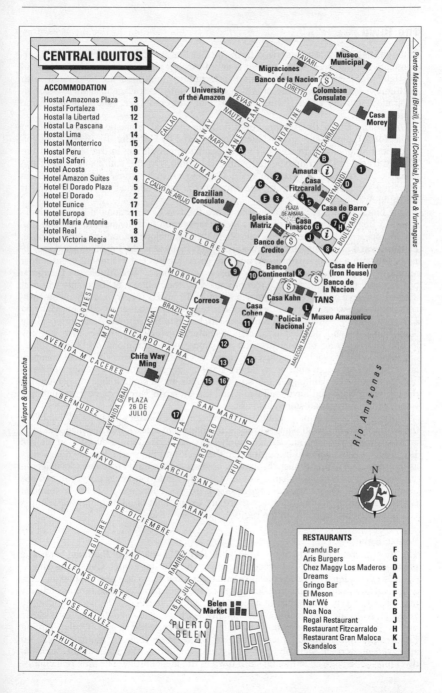

CENTRAL IQUITOS

ACCOMMODATION

Hostal Amazonas Plaza	3
Hostal Fortaleza	10
Hostal la Libertad	12
Hostal La Pascana	1
Hostal Lima	14
Hostal Monterrico	15
Hostal Peru	9
Hostal Safari	7
Hotel Acosta	6
Hotel Amazon Suites	4
Hotel El Dorado Plaza	5
Hotel El Dorado	2
Hotel Eunice	17
Hotel Europa	11
Hotel Maria Antonia	16
Hotel Real	8
Hotel Victoria Regia	13

RESTAURANTS

Arandu Bar	F
Aris Burgers	G
Chez Maggy Los Maderos	D
Dreams	A
Gringo Bar	E
El Meson	F
Nar Wé	C
Noa Noa	B
Regal Restaurant	J
Restaurant Fitzcarraldo	H
Restaurant Gran Maloca	K
Skandalos	L

The Town

Much of Iquitos's appeal is derived from the fact that it's the starting point for excursions into the rainforest, but the town is an interesting place in its own right. Many of the late eighteenth- and early nineteenth-century buildings are decorated with Portuguese *azulejo* tiles, some of which are brilliantly extravagant in their Moorish inspiration, and the **Casa Kahn**, on block 1 of Sargento Lore, is a particularly fine example.

On the the **Plaza de Armas**, you'll find the unusual, majestic **Casa de Fierro** (Iron House), now home to a restaurant but created by Eiffel for the 1898 Paris exhibition and shipped out by one of the rubber barons; outside, in the shadow of the Mamey trees, lurks an unexpected statue by Rodin. On the southwest side of the plaza is the **Iglesía Matriz**, the main Catholic church, whose interior paintings depicting biblical scenes are by the Loretano artists Americo Pinasco and Cesar Calvo de Araujo.

One block southeast of Plaza de Armas are the two best sections of the **old riverfront**, El Boulevard and Malecón Tarapaca. The section that divides the two is gradually disappearing through erosion, and there's some major restoration going on here. **El Boulevard** is the busiest of the two areas, especially at night, full of bars and restaurants and with a small **amphitheatre** where some kind of entertainment occurs most nights, from mini-circuses to mime, comedy and music. The **Malecón Tarapaca** boasts some fine old mansions, presently used by the military, at the points where it meets Putumayo and Sargento Lores; another, at Tarapaca 262, with lovely nineteenth-century *azulejo* work, is presently one of the town's better bakeries. Also on Malecón Tarapaca is the Prefectura de Loreto mansion, home to the **Museo Amazonico** (daily 9am–1pm & 4–7pm), devoted to the region's natural history and tribal culture. The collection includes some unusual life-sized human figures in traditional dress from different Amazon tribes; each fibreglass sculpture was made from a cast that had encapsulated the subject for an hour or so. There's also a gallery devoted to previous *prefectos* of Loreto, some oil paintings, a few stuffed animals and a small military museum. On the corner of Napo and Raymondi you'll find the **Casa de Barro**, made from mud and wood, where Fitzcarrald stored his rubber.

In the Punchana sector of Iquitos, the **Amazon Art Gallery**, Trujillo 438, exhibits the work of the Peruvian painter Francisco Grippa and a few other national and local artists. Grippa, who lives and works mainly in Pevas, arrived in the Amazon in the late 1970s after being educated in Europe and the USA, and his work, described variously as figurative and expressionist, displays an obsession with light and colour, focusing on subjects such as Shipibo Indians, jungle birds and rainforest landscapes; you can see examples on the Web at *www.art-and-soul.com/grippa*. There's more art to be found at **Galeria Amauta**, Nauta 248, where there are exhibitions of oil paintings, caricatures and photographs, mainly from the region.

Puerto Belén

The most memorable part of town, **Puerto Belén** looms out of the main town at a point where the Amazon, until recently, joined the Río Itaya inlet. Consisting almost entirely of wooden huts raised on stilts, and until a few years ago also floating on rafts, it has earned fame among travellers as the Venice of the Peruvian Jungle. Actually more Far Eastern than Italian in appearance, it has changed little over its hundred years or so of life, remaining a poor shanty settlement and continuing to trade in basics like bananas, manioc, fish, turtle and crocodile meat. Whilst filming *Fitzcarraldo* here, Herzog merely had to make sure that no motorized canoes appeared on screen: virtually everything else, including the style of the *barriada* dwellings, looks like an authentic slum town of the last century. The only real change is that the Río Amazonas rarely comes in this far anymore, even in high water; what was once the riverbed is now a mass of river grasses and newly cultivated plots, interspersed with wooden buildings, many of them still on wooden stilts, though they rarely seem to need them any more. These days, even in high water season, boats have to divert just under half a kilometre out into the Río Amazonas before turning back into Belén itself.

Eating and drinking

Food in Iquitos is exceptionally good for a jungle town, specializing in fish dishes but catering these days pretty well for any taste, and eating out is something of a popular pastime in the lively, even energetic evenings, which go on well until after midnight, particularly at weekends. We've given telephone numbers where reservations are advised.

Anita Bar, Fitzcarrald 232. A cool and dark bar, with even cooler beer, close to the plaza.

Arandu Bar, El Boulevard. A pleasant atmosphere and very popular for drinks early in the evening.

Aris Burgers, Prospero 127. Actually serving more than burgers (though these are good value), including plates with a variety of river fish and even caiman meat, plus the best french fries in town. It's the most popular meeting spot in Iquitos and a bit of a landmark for taxi and *motokar* drivers.

Chez Maggy Los Maderos, Raymondi 218. Good pasta and pizzas, though the latter aren't quite as good as those at its sister restaurant in Cusco.

Cold Beer Blues Bar, corner of Requena with Pablo Possell. Run by a US journalist who, as well as being an occasional tour guide, is an expert on local medicines and *ayahuasca*. He's also an excellent cook and serves up some of the best grub in Iquitos, both for lunch and during the evenings. Good beer and great music too.

Restaurant Gran Maloca, Flores 170 (☎094/233126). One of the finest restaurants in town, stylish and with lavish decor, with jungle paintings adorning the walls and a tall, cool interior.

Gringo Bar, Arica 108. A popular meeting point, though with little character, serving drinks virtually in the lobby of the *Hotel Amazonas Plaza*.

Heladeria la Favorita, Prospero 413. A spacious café specializing in juices and delicious jungle-produce flavoured ice creams.

Jugeria Paladar, Prospero 245. A small café serving excellent juices and local snacks.

Nar Wé, Napo 385 (☎094/221181). An art gallery and café in one. The food is good, and it offers excellent value fixed-menu lunches, but the displays of art and antiquities on the walls of its many different rooms are exceptional – from erotic ceramics and Ticuna Indian barkcloth paintings to what the owner claims is the first ever map of the Amazon.

El Meson, El Boulevard (☎094/231857). A popular restaurant serving a good range of local dishes – try the *tacacho* (plantains and pork), or *pescado a la Loretano* (fish). It's not cheap, though a good meal can be had for well under $10, and the location is great, right at the heart of El Boulevard and with tables out front.

El Pollon, Prospero 151. A spacious restaurant and café fronting the Plaza de Armas. Popular with locals, especially at lunchtime, it serves a wide range of tasty meals, cool juices and ice creams.

Red Lion Pub, Putumayo 168. As much a restaurant as it is an English pub, serving decent meals, with tables inside and out on the street. The owners also run the *Regal Restaurant*.

Regal Restaurant, Putumayo 282 (☎094/222732). Upstairs in the Casa de Fierra, this is a busy place with a very pleasant, almost colonial ambience, run by the British Consul and his wife. The food, mainly traditional local dishes, is great, plus there are ceiling fans, fine views over the Plaza de Armas from Eiffel's iron balcony, and a large pool table inside. *Paiche* fish is a speciality.

Restaurant Fitzcarraldo, Napo 100 (☎094/243434). A great new place, close to the nightly action. It isn't cheap but serves some of the best salads in town plus good pastas, fish and *comida criolla*.

Royal Coffee "Me Paiche", Putumayo 133 (☎094/231304). Decent pizzas, pastas and sandwiches, plus a range of other meals, snacks and drinks. Reasonably priced and usually fairly quiet. If you phone in an order, they can also deliver to your hotel.

Nightlife

Whilst mainly an extension of eating out and meeting friends in the main streets, the **nightlife** in Iquitos is pretty good, and there are a number of highly charged discos, clubs and bars worth knowing about. They're quite easy to locate, especially if you are up and about after 11pm in the downtown areas, particularly around the Plaza de Armas and nearby Malecón Tarapaca.

Iquitos has an unusually active gay scene for a Peruvian jungle town, mainly due to many gays fleeing here during the terrorist years (the mid-1980s to the early 1990s), when they suffered persecution, and there are now four dedicated **gay clubs** here: *Discoteca 2003*, on block 25 of Putumayo; *Tragoteca La Jarra*, on Avenida Quinones, near the Pamachicha restaurant; *Las Castañitas*, in front of the electricity power plant in the suburb of Punchana; and *Bar La 4.40*, opposite the Hospital Regional, also in Punchana.

Amauta Café Teatro, Nauta 250. Different music – from jazzy jungle creole to folklore and female romantic – varying from day to day. It also serves drinks and snacks, and there are tables outside. Mon–Sat 10pm–2am.

Arfil Mañoso, Urbino Sargento Lores S-2. Essentially a pick-up joint with girls that you're expected to pay for, though it does play some reasonable music sometimes. It's also about 14 blocks northwest from the centre of town. Mon–Sat 10pm–late; $6 entrance.

Calipso, Putumayo 1670. Kind of slinky, with a strong love theme in the decor displayed in neon flashing lights. Worth checking out if you want a quiet dance with your partner, but rather a long way from the centre of town. Mon–Sat 10pm–late; $5 entrance.

Dreams, Samanez Ocampo 102. More of a dance-pub than a club, with laid-back interior design and a groovy young crowd. Good music, and generally heaving at weekends. $5 entrance.

Noa Noa, Fitzcarrald 298. Easily identified after 11.30pm by the huge number of flashy motorbikes lined up outside, this is the most popular and lively of Iquitos' clubs, attracting young and old, gringo and Iquiteño alike. It has three bars and plays lots of Latino music, including the latest technocumbia. Mon–Sat 10pm–late; $6 entrance.

Skandalos, Tarapaca 328. A popular and centrally located club, renowned for its showgirls and lively performances music and dance. Mon–Sat 10pm–late; $5 entrance.

Listings

Airlines AeroContinente, Propsero 232 (☎094/235990), fly daily to Lima, with connections for Cusco and other main Peruvian destinations; TANS, Sargento Lores 127 (☎094/234632), sell very reasonably priced flights to Requena, Angamos, and Santa Rosa, while the TANS office at Prospero 215 (094/☎221071 or 221086) specializes in flights to Lima, Tarapoto and Pucallpa.

Banks and exchange Banco de Credito, Putumayo 201; Banco Wiese, Prospero 282, for Mastercard; Banco de la Nacion; Banco Continental, block 3 of Prospero, which has a 24hr ATM taking Visa, plus another branch on block 1 of Sargento Lores; Banco Latino, Propsero 332; and the Banco del Trabajo, block 1 of Prospero, has an ATM taking Visa. *Cambistas* gather on the corners where Prospero meets Sargento Lores and Morona.

Cameras and film equipment Foto Aspinar, Prospero 271; Foto Digital, Prospero 467; Tema Color, Prospero 283.

Consulates Brazil, Morona 238 (☎094/232081); Colombia, corner of Nauta with Calloa (☎094/231461); UK, Putumayo 182 (☎094/222732).

Courier services A DHL service is available at Prospero 648 (☎094/232131).

Internet facilities *Cybercafé*, Fitzcarrald 120 (☎094/233608), is the best in town, and the owner speaks good English; also try *Internet Manguaré*, Prospero 249 (☎094/242148), or the relatively cheap *Internet Cabins*, Sargento Lores 180 (upstairs).

Laundry Lavanderia Imperial, Putumayo 150; Lavanderia Popular, Calle Loreto 640.

Migraciones, Yavari 441. Mon–Fri 8am–1pm & 1.30–4.30pm.

Pharmacies Botica Amazonicas, Prospero 699 (☎094/231832); Botica Virgen de Chapi, Prospero 461.

Police Policia de Turismo, Sargento Lores 834 (☎094/242801).

Post office SERPOST, Arica 482 (Mon–Sat 8am–7.30pm).

Shopping Artesanias La Jungla, Prospero 483 (baskets, mats, hammocks, gourds, postcards and souvenirs); Artesanias Sudanmerica, Casa de Fierro, Plaza de Armas, Prospero 175 (hammocks and alpaca goods); Artesanias Todo Peru, Prospero 685 (hammocks, hats, jewellery, musical instruments and souvenirs); Bazar Daniela, 9 de Diciembre 234 (useful trade items for visiting local villages, such as cloth, beads and coloured threads); Comercial Cardinal, Prospero 300 (fishing tackle, compasses, knives); Taller de Arte, Prospero 593/595 (carved wooden sculptures and household artefacts).

Telephones Sargento Flores 321 (daily 7am–11pm).

Short trips and tours from Iquitos

The closest place you can get to without a guide or long river trip is **Padre Isla**, an island opposite town in the midst of the Amazon, over 14km long and with beautiful beaches during the dry season. It's easily reached by canoe from Belén or the main waterfront. Alternatively, some 4km northeast of the centre of Iquitos, just fifteen minutes by bus, is the suburb of **Bellavista**. Now the main access point for smaller boats to all the rivers, there's a rather small (and smelly) market selling jungle products, plus some bars and shops clustered around a port, where you can rent canoes for short trips at around $5 an hour. Like Iquitos, Bellavista has recently been experiencing its highest and lowest recorded water levels, with all of the associated flooding and drying up; the bars sit on their stilts high above dried mud during the dry season, and the boats are moored some forty metres further out than they used to be. From Bellavista you can set out by canoe ferry for **Playa Nanay**, the best beach around Iquitos, where bars and cafés are springing up to cater for the weekend crowds. Be aware that currents here are pretty strong, and although there are lifeguards, drownings have occurred.

From Avenida José Galvez in Puerto Belén, buses and colectivos go to the lagoon at **Quistococha** (a 30min journey; $1 entry), though if you like, you could also try the hot, three-hour walk (13.5km) there; head along the airport road, turning left at the last fork before the airport. One-kilometre long and up to 8m deep, the waters have been taken over by the Ministry of Fishing for the breeding of giant *paiche*, and there's an interesting **zoo** and a small site **museum** of jungle natural history.

On the western edge of Iquitos, an affluent of the Nanay forms a long lake called **Moronacocha**, a popular resort for swimming and waterskiing; some 5km further out (just before the airport) another lake, **Rumococha**, has facilities on the Río Nanay for fishing and hunting. Beyond this, still on the Nanay, is the popular weekend beach of **Santa Clara**. The village of **Santo Tomas** is only 16km from here; a worthwhile trip and well connected by local buses, this agricultural and fishing village is renowned for its jungle *artesania*, and has another beach, on the **Lago Mapacocha**, where you can swim and canoe. If you get the chance, try to make your visit coincide with Santo Tomas's **fiesta** (Sept 23–25), a huge party with dancing and *chicha* music.

Short tours in the area include a boat trip that sets out from Bellista and travels up the Río Momón to visit a community of Yaguar or Bora Indians at **San Andres**, just beyond *Amazon Camp* (see p.409), then goes downriver to visit **Serpentario las Boas**, an anaconda farm near the mouth of the Momón. Here you can see and touch anacondas and more (boas, sloths and monkeys to name a few), slithering around in what is essentially someone's backyard. The whole trip lasts around two hours and costs about $5–10 per person (including a $2 tip at Serpentario las Boas), depending on the size of group. A longer tour, lasting around four hours and costing $10–20, includes the above but also takes you onto the Río Amazonas to visit an alligator farm at **Barrio Florida** and to watch dolphins playing in the river.

Moving on

From Puerto Masusa, **speedboats** go downstream to Santa Rosa, Tabatinga and Leticia (all on the three-way frontier) several times a week, taking up to ten hours there and twelve hours back, for around $40. The main companies have their offices on Raymondi, just a few blocks from the Plaza de Armas: Expreso Loreto, Raymondi 384 (☎094/238021); Transporte Itaya, Loreto 141 (☎094/238690); Transtur, Raymondi 328 (☎094/242367); and Transportes Rapido, Raymondi 346 (☎094/22147).

Larger **riverboats** go upstream from Puerto Masusa to Lagunas (3 days) Yurimaguas (5 days), Pucallpa (6–7 days), or downstream to Pevas (about 1 day), Leticia and Tabatinga (both 3 days). Check with the commercial river transporters for a rough idea of departure dates and times, and keep an eye out for the highly recommended *Jhuiliana* (used by Herzog in his film) and the *Oro Negro*, which costs $40 to the border, including food but not drink. Take along a good book, plenty of extra food and drink, a hammock, a sweater and one or two blankets; it's usually possible to sling your hammock up and sleep free of charge on the larger boats in the days leading up to the unpredictable departure. It's also advisable to secure your baggage with a chain to a permanent fixture on the deck and also keep bags locked, as **theft** is quite common.

Around Iquitos

The massive river system around Iquitos offers some of the best access to Indian villages, lodges and primary rainforest in the entire Amazon. If you want to go it alone, colectivo boats run more or less daily up and down the Río Amazonas, and although you won't get deep into the forest without a guide or the facilities offered by the lodge and tour companies, you can visit some of the larger riverine settlements.

A long day's ride (130km) **upstream from Iquitos** lies **Nauta**, at the mouth of the Río Marañon; from here, **Bagazan** is another couple of hours (40km) further up the Río Amazonas, after which it's slightly longer again (50km) to **Requena** (see p.397), at the mouth of the Río Tapiche. A road from Iquitos to Nauta, due for completion in late 2000, should considerably shorten the journey and open up tourism on the Río Tigre and even into the Pacaya Samiria National Reserve (see below), though this is accessed mainly from Lagunas. The upper Río Tigre is also excellent for its access to wildlife, but it's at least three days away by boat. There are excellent organized tours to be had from **LAGUNAS**, three days upstream ($10–25 depending on whether you take hammock space or a shared cabin). The first day takes you to the "start" of the Río Amazonas, where the Ucayali and the Marañon rivers merge; the second day carries you along the Marañon towards Lagunas, where you arrive on the third day. It's also some twelve hours downstream from Yurimaguas and accessible from there by boat colectivo ($5). There are a couple of **hostals** in Lagunas: the *Hostal Montalban* (②), on the Plaza de Armas, is basic and small but suffices, as does the slightly cheaper *Hostal La Sombra* (①) at Jirón Vasquez 1121. Lagunas is the main starting-point for trips into the huge **Pacaya Samiria National Reserve**, comprising around 2,080,000 hectares of virgin rainforest leading up to the confluence between the Marañon and the Huallaga rivers, two of the largest Amazon headwaters. The reserve is a swampland during the rainy season (Dec–March), when the streams and rivers all rise, arguably comparable to the Pantanal Swamps of southwestern Brazil in the density of astonishingly visible wildlife. It's possible to arrange the **guides** here (about $10 a day per person, less if you're in a group) and to spend as long as you like in the national reserve. You should of course be well prepared with mosquito nets, hammocks, insect repellent and all the necessary food and medicines (see p.364). Officially you should obtain permission from the

AROUND IQUITOS

Explornapo Lodge, Aceer & Tambos

Amazon Rainforest Lodge

Sinchicuy Lodge

Indiana

Explorama Lodge

Mazán

Amazon Camp

Explorama Inn

Río Amazonas

Río Momón

Iquitos

Cumaceba Lodge

Zungaroc6cha Resort

Quisto Cocha

Santa María

Río Tamshiyacu

Río Itaya

Río Tahuayo

Río Yanayacu

Loving Light Lodge

Nauta

Libertad

Río Yarapa

Clavero

Yacumama Lodge

Bagazan

Cumaceba Creek

Majo Creek

Lago Cumaceba

Requena

PACAYA SAMIRIA NATIONAL PARK

BRAZIL

Angamos

Río Ucayali

Río Tapiche

//// Best areas for spotting wildlife & adventure expeditions

0 ————— 50 km

Pucallpa

Lagunas & Yurimaguas

Pevas, Santa Rosa, Brazil & Colombia

Río Napo

Río Nanay

Río Tigre

Río Marañon

Río Yanayacu

Río Pucate

national parks authority, INRENA (see p.366) to get into the Reserve, but not everyone does.

Downstream from Iquitos lies **PEVAS**, some 190km to the east and reached in a day by riverboat colectivo or in a few hours by speedboat. The oldest town in the Peruvian Amazon, it's an attractive, largely palm-thatched town and still a frontier place. The economy here is based primarily on fishing (visit the *mercado*, where produce is brought in by boat every day), and dugout canoes are the main form of transport, propelled by characteristically ovoid-bladed and beautifully carved paddles, which are often sold as souvenirs, sometimes painted with designs. The Witoto and Bora Indians, largely concentrated around Pevas, actually arrived here in the 1930s after being relocated from the Colombian Amazon. They are now virtually in everyday contact with the riverine society of Pevas, producing quality artefacts for sale to passers-by yet retaining much of their traditional knowledge of songs, dances, and legends, plus significant ethno-pharmacological practice in rainforest medicine. The nearby Bora village of Puca Urquillo is a good example, a large settlement based around a Baptist church and school, whose founders moved here from the Colombian side of the Río Putamayou during the hardships of the rubber era rather than be enslaved.

Artist Francisco Grippa also lives in Pevas, though his work is actually exhibited in Iquitos at the Amazon Art Gallery (see p.402), while the surrounding flood forest is home to hundreds of caimans and significant bird-life, not least several types of parrots, eagles and kingfishers. For a good **place to stay**, try the *Casa de la Loma* (write to PO Box 555, Iquitos; fax ☎094/221184, *greentracks@back2u.com (GreenTracks)*, *www. greentracks.com*), also contactable in the US (write to 10 Town Plaza 231, Suite 231, Durango, CO 81301; ☎1-800-9-Monkey, fax 970-247-8378). Set on a small hill close to Pevas, the lodge was set up by two nurses from Oregon who operate a free clinic here for the two thousand or so local inhabitants. They have five large bedrooms with shared bathrooms, and there's electricity, a refrigerator and a kitchen. Visits can be customized, and the head guide speaks good English and has an extensive knowledge of the wildlife and tribes of the region. The area is good for bird- and butterfly-watching, and November, in particular, is a great time to study orchids and bromeliads in bloom; it's also noted for its fishing – piranha being one of the easiest kinds to catch. A number of local Indian groups can be visited, including the Bora, the Witoto and the less-visited Ocainas. Costs are from $60 per person per day, extra for their speedboat transport from Iquitos.

Lodges, cruises and guides

If you're planning on an expedition beyond the limited network of roads around Iquitos, you'll have to take an organized trip with a **lodge operator**, a **river cruise** or hire a **freelance guide**. The larger local entrepreneurs have quite a grip on the market, and even the few guides who remain more or less independent are hard to bargain with since so much of their work comes through the larger agents. That said, they mostly have well worked-out itineraries, though you should always deal with an established office – check out which companies are registered at the tourist office in Iquitos – and insist on a written contract and receipt. Be aware that there's no shortage of con-artists among the many **touts** around town, some of whom brandish brochures that have nothing to do with them. Under no circumstances should you hand them any money.

Before approaching anyone it's a good idea to know more or less what you want in terms of time in the forest, total costs, personal needs and comforts, and things you expect to see. A general rule of thumb to consider is that any expedition of fewer than about five days is unlikely to offer more wildlife than a few birds, some monkeys, and maybe a crocodile if you're lucky; any serious attempt to visit virgin forest and see wildlife in its natural habitat really requires a week or more. That said, if Iquitos is your main contact with the Amazon and you're unlikely to return here, you can rent a boat for an overnight trip from upwards of $40–50 per person. A group in low season may well be able to negotiate a three-day trip for as little as $25–30 per person per day, though there will be little guarantee of quality at this price. One or two of the smaller camps sometimes offer deals from as little as $25, but make sure they provide all the facilities you require.

LODGES

Guided tours require some kind of camp set-up or tourist **lodge** facilities. There are two main types of jungle experience available from Iquitos – what Peruvian tour operators describe as "conventional" (focusing on lodge stays) and what they describe as "adventure trips" (going deeper into the jungle). Prices given are per person.

THE TOURIST PROTECTION SERVICE

If your jungle trip really doesn't match what the agency led you to believe when selling you the tickets, it would help future visitors if you report this to the local tourist office and/or the 24-hour hot line of the **Tourist Protection Service** in Iquitos (☎094/233409, *postmaster@indecopi.gob.pe*).

ACEER Lodge, Explorama, Avenida la Marina 340, Iquitos (☎094/252530 or 252526 or 253301, fax 252533, *amazon@explorama.com*, *www.explorama.com*), or Box 445, Iquitos; toll-free in the US ☎1-800-707-5275. Explorama are the top operator in the region, with over 35 years' experience; they aren't cheap, but they offer great quality. An hour's walk from the company's *Explornapo Lodge*, this particualar establishment owns some 750 hectares of primary forest and was designed for research though it's available for short visits and is quite comfortable, with separate rooms and good shared dining and bathroom facilities. There's an interpreted medicinal plant trail, but the really special feature is the well-maintained canopy walkway (the Amazon's longest), whose top-most platform is 116ft high. Can be visited in conjuction with other Explorama lodges; $100–400 per day, depending on size of group, length of trip and the number of lodges visited.

Amazon Camp, contact through Amazon Tours and Cruises (see overleaf). A pleasant conventional lodge on the Río Momón between the Yaguar and Bora Indian villages. This place can be visited in a day-trip, though it's more fun and better value to stay longer. Around $100 per night.

Amazon Paradise Lodge, Putumayo 132, Iquitos. A quite comfortable and conventional lodge, downriver from Iquitos and close to the town of Indiana. Around $35 for a day trip, $50 for overnighting.

Amazon Rainforest Lodge, Putumayo 159, Iquitos (☎094/233100 or 241628, fax 242231, *schneide@amauta.rcp.net.pe*; in Lima ☎01/445-5620, fax 447-2651). Up the Río Momon (1–3hr, depending on water levels), the heart of this large lodge, run by an English resident, is a vast, thatched native-style *maloca* dining room and bar. Accommodation is in bungalows with bathrooms and the lesser-spotted flush toilet, with hammock spaces out front for relaxing. There's also a pool, though it's not always functioning. There are conventional trips to local Indians, fishing, jungle walks, bird-watching, plus *ayahuasca* sessions ($20) with local healers, one of whom has built a temple space at the back of the lodge. This isn't the best lodge for wildlife (though monkeys do often pass through), but you can walk to the Río Napo (8hr), or go further up the Momón to one of the two main headwaters, the Juano and Agua Planea creeks (both 3hr), the former noted for its marmosets. From $30 to $60 a day, the more expensive options including airport transfers, river travel, guides and food.

Cumaceba Lodge, Putumayo 184 (☎ & fax 094/232229 or 610656, *cumaceba.lodge@mailcity.com*). A highly recommended budget option on the Río Yanayacu, some 40km downriver from Iquitos (45min by speedboat), with accommodation in private rustic bungalows with individual bathrooms. They have the usual communal dining area and hammock lounge, while lighting is by kerosene lamps. They take visitors to the local Yagua village and on jungle walks; bird- and dolphin-watching also form part of their programmes. Optional extras include trips to the Pacaya Samiria National Reserve, waterskiing (June–Nov) and *ayahuasca* sessions. They also run an explorer camp downriver. Around $120 for three days.

Explorama Inn, contact Explorama (see *ACEER Lodge* above). Some 40km from Iquitos, this is the most luxurious Amazon lodge of all, with pools, bars and dining areas, surrounded by 40 hectares of primary forest and 160 hectares of *chacra* and secondary growth. Accommodation is in concrete bungalows with a/c and flushing toilets, or in simpler bungalow-huts. Can be visited in conjuction with other Explorama lodges; $100–400 per day, depending on size of group, length of trip and the number of lodges visited.

Explorama Lodge, contact Explorama (see *ACEER Lodge* above). In a 195-hectare reserve and 90km from Iquitos, this was Explorama's first lodge. Well equipped, it retains its rustic charm and acts as base-camp for long-range programmes. Bora Indian talking drums (*manguare*) announce meal times in the dining room and guides often play Peruvian music in the bar during the evenings. Bedrooms have no locks and are simple but attractive, with individual mosquito-nets; toilets are latrine-style but well maintained, and showers are cold. A few animals – including a tapir, an otter and several macaws – come and go around the place, and you can swim with dolphins in the Amazon, plus there are night walks and visits to the nearby Yaguar Indians. Can be visited in conjuction with other Explorama lodges; $100–400 per day, depending on size of group, length of trip and the number of lodges visited.

Explornapo Lodge, contact Explorama (see *ACEER Lodge* above). Over ninety miles from Iquitos, on the Río Sucusari (Orejon Indian for "way in and out"). The palm-roofed buildings, hammock areas and dining room/bar are linked by thatch-covered walkways. The lodge owns 1785 hectares of surrounding forest, and during full moons you can sometimes hear Tropical Screech Owls and the Common Potoos (related to owls). Can be visited in conjunction with other Explorama lodges; $100–400 per day, depending on size of group, length of trip and the number of lodges visited.

Heliconia Amazon River Lodge, Prospero 574, Iquitos (☎094/235132), or contact via the *Hotel Victoria Regia* (see p.400): or Las Camelias 491, Oficina 503, San Isidro, Lima (☎01/421-9195, fax 442-4338, *chasali@telematic.edu.pe*). A pleasant lodge, 80km downriver from Iquitos, with accommodation in twin rooms with private bathrooms. They offer a basic 3-day programme at around $100 per day.

Loving Light Amazon Lodge, Putumayo 128, Iquitos (☎094/243180, *info@junglelodge.com*, *www.junglelodge.com*): or 7016 248th Avenue NE, Redmond, WA 98053, USA (☎425-836-9431). A range of adventurous tours, from jungle walks and piranha fishing to wildlife observation and camping, plus *ayahuasca* sessions with local *curanderos* ($20). The lodge itself is about 120km upriver from Iquitos, and is only a few years old. From $50 a day if booking locally, up to S100 if booking through the US (though this includes help with transport in Peru, plus the support of a US-registered office).

Napo Camp, contact Explorama (see *ACEER Lodge* on previous page). Two hours' walk from *Explornapo Lodge* deep into primary forest, this is in many ways the ultimate jungle experience. A small collection of open-sided tambo-style huts, it's only for the truly brave and adventurous, offering a night or so close to the earth, the elements and, of course, the animals. Can be visited in conjuction with other Explorama lodges; $100–400 per day, depending on size of group, length of trip, the level of quality and number of lodges visited.

Sinchicuy Lodge, Pevas 246, Iquitos (☎094/231618). Reasonably priced, though a little too near a native village for there to be much wildlife in the immediate vicinity. From $35 per day.

Yacumama Lodge, Sargento Lores 149 (☎094/235510, *yacumama@meganet.com.pe*). A quality operator, providing a good balance between wilderness experience and personal comfort, their well-maintained lodge on the Río Rarapa is about 185km upriver from Iquitos. The 9-level canopy tower here is slightly higher than Explorma's *ACEER* canopy walkway, but it's more limited in its flora and bird-life; the surrounding forest is pristine (dolphins and hoatzin birds are always seen here) and the site operates with solar power, non-polluting flush toilets, composting and an organic garden. The 4- and 6-day programmes cost from $70 a day.

Zungarococha, Prospero 574, Iquitos (☎094/235132). The kind of comfortable rooms and bar associated with upmarket conventional lodges, but only 14km from Iquitos by road. From $60 to $70 a day.

CRUISE OPERATORS

Amazon Tours and Cruises, Requena 336, Iquitos (☎094/233931 or 231611, fax 231265, *amazoncruz@aol.com*, *www.amazontours.com*): in the US; 8700 W Flaglet Street S/190, Miami, Florida 33174 (fax 305-227-1880). Five luxury boats, running up the Río Amazonas to Requena, Pacaya Samiria National Reserve and down to Pevas, Leticia and Manaus, not quite as smart as those operated by Junglex, but better value and still of a high standard. The company is planning to speed up access to the rainforest with flights to places such as Requena and Leticia.

Junglex, Pevas 199, Iquitos (☎094/231870; in the US ☎205-428-1700, fax 205-428-1714, *intlexp@aol.com.net*). Five luxury boats of varying sizes, possibly the fanciest on the Amazon. A variety of expensive trips go to areas such as Requena, up the Río Ucayali on to the Río Tapiche, and even up into the wilder reaches of the Río Yanayacu to visit Lago Umaral, a great area for wildlife. They also go to the Pacaya Samiria National Reserve.

FREELANCE GUIDES

There are some good independent contacts who can help you find the right trip. The Iquitos tourist office (see p.399) has a list of registered **freelance guides**, and the following are all recommended. Juan Nicholas Maldonado, (Pasaje Porvenir H-36, block 19 of Putumayo, Iquitos; ☎094/222350), or contactable through *Aris Burgers* (see p.403), speaks excellent English and is one of the most reliable sources of general information in the whole Loreto *departmento*. He also runs day outings, river trips and guides longer expeditions, plus he can put you in touch with a couple of other people such as the highly experienced Don Moises Torres Viena, and Carlos Grandes, who speaks some English and runs very good trips, usually over 200km upriver from Iquitos using colectivo riverboats to keep costs down (from $25 per person per day). Silvia Grandez, contactable through the *Hostal la Libertad* (see p.400, or *silvia_grandez@origimail.com.ar*) offers expeditions from $30 per person depending on the size of the group, which can last up to 25 days; although she doesn't speak English, some of her assistant guides do. She operates mainly from a base camp at Veagali (250km from Iquitos) and around the bountiful wildlife area of Lago Curahuate. Other recommendations include Richard Fowler (☎094/672098, *manguare@hotmail. com*), based in Iquitos though from the US, a popular naturalist guide who offers customized survival and wilderness trips and is bringing some jet-skis into the area; and David Rios, who speaks English and runs trips down to Río Mazan and nearby lakes (though this area isn't brilliant for wildlife, being too close to Iquitos), and Pepe Lopez, who speaks limited English, is highly responsible and operates excellent tours, both contactable through the tourist office.

For something a little out of the ordinary, Alan Shoemaker based close to Iquitos at Chinchilejo, Santa Clara (☎094/260499, *chinchilejo@hotmail.com*) is a great guide to the sacred and mystical depths of the *ayahuasca* experience; he runs shamanic programmes in the Iquitos region and has a great botanic garden full of exotic and tradional medicinal plants. Another good *ayahuasca* guide is Francisco Montes (Sachamama, 18km from Iquitos on the road to Nauta).

The three-way frontier

Leaving or entering Peru via the Amazon River is often an intriguing adventure. The **three-way-frontier** is eight to ten hours away from Iquitos by speedboat or about three days in a standard larger riverboat (see p.406 for details). Some services go all the way to Leticia (Colombia) or Tabatinga (Brazil), but many stop at one of the two small Peruvian frontier settlements of Santa Rosa or Islandia; at Chimbote, a few hours before

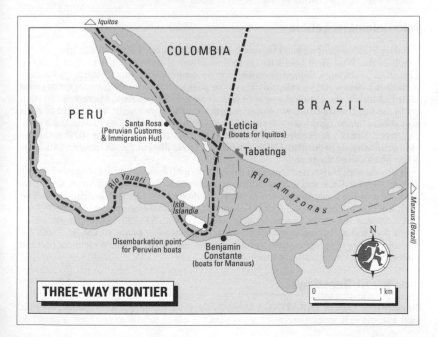

you get to Santa Rosa and on the right as you head towards the frontier, is a small police post, the main **customs checkpoint** (*guarda costa*) for river traffic. The region is interesting in its own right as the home of the Tikuna Indians, once large in numbers but today down to a poulation of around 10,000 that's in permanent contact with the societies of Peru, Colombia and Brazil. It's possible to arrange visits to some native communities from Leticia, and you can buy some of their excellent craftwork – mainly string bags and hammocks – from stores in that town.

SANTA ROSA is your last chance to complete formalities with Migraciones if you haven't already done so at the Iquitos office (see p.404) – essentially obtaining an **exit stamp** from Peru, if you're leaving, or getting an **entry stamp and tourist card** if arriving., which can take up to an hour. On larger boats, you often don't have to disembark here, as the Migraciones official may board the vessel and do the paperwork there and then. There's only one small **hostal**, *La Brisa del Amazonas* (③), which is also a **restaurant** whose owner is a useful contact for local **information**, but there are several cafés, and ferry boats connect the town with Tabatinga and Leticia. **Islandia** is in the middle of the river, on the Peruvian side of the border, and has no hotels; from here you have to take the ferry to Tabatinga or Leticia across the river to enter Brazil or Colombia; most boats prefer to use Tabatinga, especially in low-water season – it's a long, muddy hike from the quay to the surfaced streets of Leticia, whereas at Tabatinga's two ports, the road goes right to the water's edge.

The only other way of crossing these three borders is by **flying** – a much less interesting approach, though not necessarily a more expensive one (though there's an airport departure tax of $2). Flights from Iquitos to Santa Rosa are operated by TANS, and both Varig and Rico fly to Manaus via Tabatinga at least three times a week. TANS tickets can be bought from Señor Teddy, who operates out of one of the restaurants in this tiny town – just ask anywhere for him. From Leticia, Avianca fly to a few major Colombian cities, including Bogota, several times a week.

Into Colombia: Leticia

Growing rich on tourism and contraband (mostly cocaine), **LETICIA** has more than a touch of the Wild West about it. There's no physical border at the port or between Leticia and Tabatinga, though disembarking passengers sometimes have to go through a **customs check** and you should carry your passport at all times. If you want to go on **into Colombia**, the cheapest way is to take a canoe to Puerto Asis, where you can latch on to the bus transport system, but to do this, or to stay overnight, you'll need to get a Colombian tourist card from the consulate at Iquitos (see p.404), or at Manaus if coming from Brazil. Alternatively, head straight for the DAS office (Departmento Administrative de Seguridad, Calle 9, 9–62, ☎098/592-7189 or 592-4878; open 24hr) just a few blocks from the port.

If you do stay, be warned that it's a lively town, with *cumbia* and *salsa* music blasting out all over the place, and that by Peruvian (and even Colombian) standards, it's expensive. Best of the basic **hotels** are *Residencial Monserrate* (③) and *Residencial Leticia* (②), but much nicer are the *Colonial*, near the port square on Carrera 10 (☎098/005-7919; ⑥), and the swish *Anaconda* on Carrera 11 (☎098/592-7891, 592-7119; ⑧), which has a pool and an attractive *maloca*-style bar. The cheapest **place to eat**, and with the greatest variety of food, is at the riverside market, though the *Bucaneer* and *La Taguara* **cafés**, both on Carrera 10, are much better.

Into Brazil: Tabatinga

Smaller than Leticia, **TABATINGA** is hardly the most exciting place in South America, and many people stuck here waiting for a boat or plane to Manaus or Iquitos prefer to hop over the border to Leticia for the duration of their stay, even if they don't plan on going any further into Colombia. There are two docks here; at the smaller of the two, where lesser boats and canoes come and go with local produce and passengers, you'll encounter **customs checks**; Port Bras, the larger dock, is where you find the big *recreo* boats heading for Manaus. Brazilian **entry and exit formalities** are processed at the Policia Federal office (☎092/412-2180; 10am–8pm, though 24hr for emergencies) if you're entering Brazil you'll usually be asked to show an exit ticket or prove that you have $500. There are a few **places to stay**. Try the *Hotel Paje*, Rue Pedro Teixeira (☎092/412-2558; ②), or the much nicer and friendly *Hotel Te Contei*, Avenida da Amizade 1813 (☎092/412-2377 or 413-2566; ④), which is entered via the rickety spiral stairway over a pizzeria of the same name. There are a handful of other **restaurants** dotted about, mainly by the smaller dock.

Continuing on downstream **into Brazil**, boats to Manaus, a four- to seven-day journey that is often very crowded, cost $40 to $80 depending on their size, condition and whether or not you require a cabin. They leave from both Tabatinga and **Benjamin Constante**, on the other side of the Amazon, usually starting from the former in the early afternoons (frequently on Wednesdays, but also less regularly on most other days of the week) and calling at the latter an hour or so later. If there are no boats in Tabatinga, however, it may be worth taking a speedboat ferry ($7; a 30min trip) to Benjamin Constante to see if there are any departing just from there. If you've arrived from Iquitos on a boat that's continuing all the way to Manaus, it's important to let the captain know whether or not you need to go into Tabatinga to sort your visa business quickly (use a taxi) and then meet the boat at Benjamin Constante. Bear in mind that it's virtually impossible to get from Islandia to the federal police in Tabatinga and then back to Benjamin Constante in less than an hour and a half.

travel details

Buses and Trucks

Cusco to: Puerto Maldonado (several weekly; 3–10 days); Shintuya (1–2 every Mon, Wed, Fri & Sat; 18–24hr); Quillabamba via Ollantaytambo (2–3 most days; 12hr), or via Calca Lares (2–3 weekly; 24hr).

La Merced to: Pucallpa, via Puerto Bermudez (weekly, 24hr).

Lima to: Pucallpa (daily; 14hr, or 24hr via Huanuco).

Boats

Iquitos to: Leticia (several weekly; 8hr–3 days, depending on boat); Pucallpa (several weekly;

5–7 days); Tabatinga (several weekly; 8hr–3 days, depending on boat).

Pucallpa to: Iquitos (several weekly; 4–6hr).

Shintuya to: Manu (irregular, 1 daily on average; 6hr); Puerto Maldonado (irregular; 2–4 days).

Flights

Iquitos to: Lima (several daily; 2hr)

Pucallpa to: Lima (1 daily; 1hr 30min)

Puerto Maldonado to: Cusco (several daily; 1hr), Iberia (2–3 weekly; 30min) Lima (daily; 2hr); Trujillo (daily; 2hr)

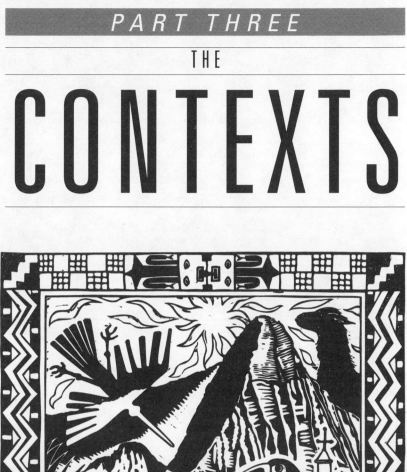

THE HISTORICAL FRAMEWORK

The first Peruvians were descendants of the nomadic tribes which had crossed into the Americas during the last Ice Age (40,000–15,000 BC), when a combination of ice packs and low sea levels exposed a neck of solid "land" to span what's now the Bering Strait. Following herds of game animals from Siberia into what must have been a relative paradise of fertile coast, wild forest, mountain and savannah, successive generations continued south through Central America. Some made their way down along the Andes, into the Amazon, and out onto the more fertile areas of the Peruvian and Ecuadorian coast, while others found their niches en route.

In a number of tribes there seem to be cultural memories of these long migrations, encapsulated in their traditional mythologies – though these aren't really transcribable into written histories. There is, however, archeological evidence of human occupation in Peru dating back to around 15,000–20,000 BC, concentrated in the **Ayacucho Valley**, where these early Peruvians lived in caves or out in the open. Around 12,000 BC, slightly to the north in the **Chillon Valley** (just above modern Lima), comes the first evidence of significant craft skills – stone blades and knives for hunting. At this time there were probably similar groups of hunter tribes in the

mountains and jungle too, but the climatic conditions of these zones make it unlikely that any significant remains will ever be found.

The difficulties of traversing the rugged terrain between the highlands and coast evidently proved little problem for the early Peruvians. From 8000 to 2000 BC, **migratory bands** of hunters and gatherers alternated between camps in the lowlands during the harsh mountain winters and highland summer "resorts", their actual movements well synchronized with those of wild animal herds. One important mountain encampment from this **Incipient Era** has been discovered at **Lauricocha**, near Huanuco, at an altitude of over 4000m. Here the art of working stone – eventually producing very fine blades and arrow points – seems to have been sophisticated, while at the same time a growing cultural imagination found expression in cave paintings depicting animals, hunting scenes and even dances. Down on the coast at this time other groups were living on the greener *lomas* belts of the desert in places like **Chilca** to the south, and in the mangrove swamps around **Tumbes** to the north.

An awareness of the potential uses of plants began to emerge around **5000 BC** with the **cultivation** of seeds and tubers (the potato being one of the most important "discoveries" later taken to Europe); to be followed over the next two millennia by the introduction, presumably from the Amazon, of gourds, Lima beans, then squashes, peanuts, and eventually cotton. Towards the end of this period a climatic shift turned the coast into a much more arid belt and forced those living there to try their hand at **agriculture** in the fertile river beds, a process to some extent paralleled in the mountains.

With a stable agricultural base, permanent settlements sprang up all along the coast, notably at **Chicama**, **Asia** and **Paracas**, and in the sierra at **Kotosh**. The population began to mushroom, and with it came a new consciousness, perhaps influenced by cultural developments within the Amazon Basin to the east: **cultism** – the burial of the dead in mummy form, the capturing of trophy heads, and the building of grand religious structures – made its first appearance. At the same time there were also overwhelming technological advances in the spheres of weaving, tool-making and ornamental design.

THE CHAVÍN CULT

From around 1200 BC to 200 AD – the **Formative Era** – agriculture and village life became established. Ceramics were invented, and a slow disintegration of regional isolation began. This last factor was due mainly to the widespread dispersal of a religious movement, the **Chavín Cult**. Remarkable in that it seems to have spread without the use of military force, the cult was based on a conceptualization of nature spirits, and an all-powerful feline creator god. This widespread feline image rapidly exerted its influence over the northern half of Peru and initiated a period of inter-relations between fertile basins in the Andes and some of the coastal valleys. How and where the cult originated is uncertain, though it seems probable that it began in the eastern jungles, possibly spreading to the Andes (and eventually the coast) along the upper Río Marañon. There may well have been a significant movement of people and trade goods between these areas and the rainforest regions, too, as evidenced by the many jungle-bird feathers incorporated into capes and headdresses found on the coast. More recent theories, however, suggest that the flow may have been in the oppsite direction and that it started on the coast. The stone and adobe temples, for instance, in the Sechin area, pre-date the Chavín era yet seem to be culturally linked.

The Chavín Cult was responsible for excellent progress in the work of **stone carving** and **metallurgy** (copper, gold and silver) and, significantly, for a ubiquity of temples and pyramids which grew up as cultural centres where the gods could be worshipped. The most important known centre was the temple complex at **Chavín de Huantar** in Ancash, though a similar one was built at **Kotosh** near Huánuco; its influence seems to have spread over the northern highlands and coast from Chiclayo down as far as the Paracas Peninsula (where it had a particularly strong impact). There were immense local variations in the expressions of the Chavín Cult: elaborate metallurgy in the far north; adobe buildings on stone platforms in the river valleys; excellent ceramics from **Chicama**; and the extravagant stone engravings from Chavín itself. In the mountains life must have been very hard, based on subsistence agriculture and pilgrimages to the sacred shrines – most of which

probably originated around ideas formulated by an emergent caste of powerful priest-chiefs. On the coast there was an extra resource – seafood – to augment the meagre agricultural yields.

Towards the **end of the Chavín phase**, an experimental period saw new centres attempting to establish themselves as independent powers with their own personalities. This gave birth to **Gallinazo** settlements in the Viru Valley; the **Paracas culture** on the south coast (with its beautiful and highly advanced textile technology based around a cult of the dead); and the early years of **Tiahuanaco** development in the Lake Titicaca region. These three cultural upsurges laid the necessary foundations for the flourishing civilizations of the subsequent Classical Era.

THE CLASSICAL ERA

A diverse period – and one marked by intense development in almost every field – the **Classical Era (200–1100 AD)** saw the emergence of numerous distinct cultures, both on the coast and in the *sierra*. The best documented, though not necessarily the most powerful, are the **Moche** and **Nasca** cultures (both probably descendants of the coastal Paracas culture) and the **Tiahuanuco**, all forebears of the better-known Incas. In recent years, though, archeological discoveries in the Lambayeque Valley on the north coast have revealed important ceremonial centres – particularly the **Sicán** culture's massive sacred complex of truncated pyramids at **Batan Grande**. Contemporaneous with the Moche, to the south, there is also strong evidence that the Sicán revered the same demonic spirit or god, named **Ai-Apaec** in the Moche language, the "Winged Decapitator" who kept the world of human life and death in order. Ai-Apaec is also associated with the veritable treasure-trove found in the royal tombs at **Sipán**, just south of Lambayeque, and those of the Vicus culture, to the north, near Piura. This appears to have been the god that kept the human world and reality of life and death in order.

The **Moche culture** has left the fullest evidence of its social and domestic life, all aspects of which, including its work and religion, are vividly represented in highly realistic pottery. The first real urban culture in Peru, its members maintained a firm hierarchy, an elite group combining both secular and sacred power. Ordinary people cultivated land around clusters of dwelling sites, dominated by sacred pyramids – man-made *huacas* dedicated to the gods. The key to the elite's position was probably their organization of large irrigation projects, essential to the survival of these relatively large population centres in the arid desert of the north coast. In the Moche region, nature and the world of the ancestors seem the dominant elements; occasional human sacrifices were offered and trophy heads were captured in battle. The peak of their influence came around 500 to 600 AD, with cultural and military control of the coast from Piura in the north to the Nepena Valley in the south.

More or less contemporaneous with the Moche, the **Nazca culture** bloomed for several hundred years on the south coast. The Nazca are thought to be responsible for the astonishing lines and drawings etched into the Pampa de San José, though little is known for certain about their society or general way of life. The Nazca did, however, build an impressive temple complex in the desert at **Cahuachi**, and their burial sites have turned up thousands of beautiful ceramics whose abstract designs can be compared only to the quality and content of earlier Paracas textiles.

Named after its sacred centre on the shore of Lake Titicaca, the **Tiahuanuco culture** developed at much the same time as the Moche – with which, initially at least, it peacefully coexisted. Tiahuanuco textiles and pottery spread along the desert, modifying both Mochica and Nazca styles and bending them into more sophisticated shapes and abstract patterns. The main emphasis in Tiahuanuco pottery and stonework was on symbolic elements featuring condors, pumas and snakes – more than likely the culture's main gods, representing their respective spheres of the sky, earth and underworld. In this there seem obvious echoes of the deified natural phenomena of the earlier Chavín cult.

Although initially peaceable, the Tiahuanuco influence is associated in its decadent phase with **militarism**. Originating either at Huari, in the *sierra* near Ayacucho, or on the central coast, this forceful tendency extended from 650 to 1100 AD and was dominated by what today is called the **Huari-Tiahuanuco culture**. The ruins at Huari cover some eight square kilometres and include high-walled enclosures of field

stones laid and plastered with mud, decorated only by a few stone statues along Tiahuanuco lines. Whether or not this was the actual inspirational centre, by around 1000 AD Huari-Tiahuanuco features were dominant in the art forms over virtually all of Peru.

In the north the Valley of the Pyramids, or **Túcume**, was another major ceremonial centre, covering more than 200 hectares. Initially begun by the Sicán culture, who started building here around 1100 AD after abandoning their earlier centre at Batan Grande, it reached its peak in the thirteenth and early fourteenth centuries, during the power vacuum in the Moche valley, between the decline of the Moche and the rise of the Chimu. Archeologists believe that this must have been a time of abundance and population growth for this desert region, with optimum weather conditions for agriculture, the improvement of irrigation techniques, and plentiful seafood.

An increasing prevalence of **intertribal warfare** characterized the ultimate centuries of this era, culminating in the erection of defensive forts, a multiplication of ceremonial sites (including over 60 large pyramids in the Lima area), and, eventually, the uprooting of Huari-Tiahuanuco influence on the coast by the emergence of three youthful mini-empires – the **Chimu**, the **Cuismancu** and the **Chincha**. In the mountains its influence mysteriously disappeared to pave the way for the separate growth of relatively large tribal units such as the **Colla** (around Titicaca), the **Inca** (around Cusco) and the **Chanca** (near Ayacucho).

Partly for defensive reasons, this period of isolated development sparked off a city-building urge which became almost compulsive by the Imperial Era in the twelfth century. The most spectacular urban complex was **Chan Chan** (near modern Trujillo), built by the **Chimu** on the side of the river opposite to earlier Mochica temples but indicating a much greater sophistication in social control, the internal structure of the culture's clan-based society reflected in the complex's intricate layout. By now, with a working knowledge of bronze manufacture, the Chimu spread their domain from Chan Chan to Tumbes in the north and Paramonga in the south – dominating nearly half the Peruvian coastline. To the south they were bounded by the **Cuismancu**, less powerful, though capable of building similar citadels (such as Cajamarquilla near Lima) and of comparable attainment in craft industries. Further down the coastline, the **Chincha** – known also as the **Ica culture** – produced fine monuments and administrative centres in the Chincha and Pisco valleys, too. The lower rainfall on the southern coast, however, didn't permit the Chincha State – or (to an extent) the Cuismancu – to create urban complexes anything near the size of Chan Chan.

THE INCAS

With the **Inca Empire** (1200–1532) came the culmination of the city-building phase and the beginnings of a kind of Peruvian unity, with the Incas, although originally no more than a tribe of around forty thousand, gradually taking over each of the separate coastal empires. One of the last to go – almost bloodlessly, and just sixty years before the Spanish Conquest – were the Chimu, who for much of this "Imperial Period" were a powerful rival.

Based in the valleys around Cusco, the Incas were for the first two centuries of their existence much like any other of the larger mountain tribes. Fiercely protective of their independence, they maintained a somewhat feudal society, tightly controlled by rigid religious tenets, though often disrupted by intertribal conflict. The founder of the dynasty – around 1200 – was **Manco Capac**, who passed into Inca mythology as a cultural hero. Historically, however, little definite is known about Inca developments or achievements until the accession in 1438 of Pachacuti, and the onset of their great era of expansion.

Pachacuti, most innovative of all the Inca emperors, was the first to expand their traditional tribal territory. The beginnings of this were in fact not of his making but the response to a threatened invasion by the powerful, neighbouring Chanca Indians during the reign of his father, **Viracocha**. Viracocha, feeling the odds

to be overwhelming, left Cusco in Pachacuti's control, withdrawing to the refuge of Calca along the Río Urubamba. Pachacuti, however, won a legendary victory – Inca chronicles record that the very stones of the battlefield rose up in his defence – and, having vanquished the most powerful force in the region, shortly took the Inca crown for himself.

Within three decades Pachacuti had consolidated his power over the entire *sierra* region from Cajamarca to Titicaca, defeating in the process all main imperial rivals except for the Chimu. At the same time the capital at **Cusco** was spectacularly developed, with the evacuation and destruction of all villages within a ten-kilometre radius, a massive programme of agricultural terracing (watched over by a skyline of agro-calendrical towers), and the construction of unrivalled palaces and temples. Shrewdly, Pachacuti turned his forcible evacuation of the Cusco villages into a positive plan, relocating the Incas in newly colonized areas. He extended this practice too, towards his subjugated allies, conscripting them into the Inca armies while their chiefs remained as hostages and honoured guests at Cusco.

Inca territory expanded north into Ecuador, almost reaching Quito, under the next emperor – **Topac Yupanqui** – who also took his troops down the coast, overwhelming the Chimu and capturing the holy shrine of Pachacamac. Not surprisingly the coastal cultures influenced the Incas perhaps as much as the Incas influenced them, particularly in the sphere of craft industries. With Pachacuti before him, Topac Yupanqui was nevertheless an outstandingly imaginative and able ruler. During the 22 years of his reign (1471–93) he pushed Inca control southwards as far as the Río Maule in Chile; instigated the first proper census of the empire and set up the decimal-based administrative system; introduced the division of labour and

THE INCA EMPERORS

MANCO CAPAC (cultural hero ca. 1200)	VIRACOCHA INCA
SINCHI ROCA	PACHACUTI (1438–71)
LLOQUE YUPANQUI	TOPAC YUPANQUI (1471–93)
MAYTA CAPAC	HUAYNA CAPAC (1493–1525)
CAPAC YUPANQUI	HUASCAR (1525–32)
INCA ROCA	ATAHUALPA (1532–33)
YAHUAR HUACA	

land between the state, the gods and the local *allyus*; invented the concept of Chosen Women (Mamaconas); and inaugurated a new class of respected individuals (the Yanaconas). An empire had been unified not just physically but also administratively and ideologically.

At the end of the fifteenth century the Inca Empire was thriving, vital as any civilization before or since. Its politico-religious authority was finely tuned, extracting what it needed from its millions of subjects and giving what was necessary to maintain the status quo – be it brute force, protection or food. The only obvious problem inherent in the Inca system of unification and domination was one of over-extension. When **Huayna Capac** continued Topac Yupanqui's expansion to the north he created a new Inca city at **Quito**, one which he personally preferred to Cusco and which laid the seed for a division of loyalties within Inca society. At this point in history, the Inca Empire was probably the largest in the world even though it had neither horse nor wheel technology. The empire was over 5500km long stretching from southern Colombia right down to northern Chile, with Inca highways covering distances of around 30,000km in all.

Almost as a natural progression from overextending the empire in this way, the divisions in Inca society came to a head even before Huayna Capac's death. Ruling the empire from Quito, along with his favourite son **Atahualpa**, Huayna Capac installed another son, **Huascar**, at Cusco. In the last year of his life he tried to formalize the division – ensuring an inheritance at Quito for Atahualpa – but this was totally resisted by Huascar, legitimate heir to the tittle of Lord Inca and the empire, and by many of the influential Cusco priests and nobles. In 1527, when Huayna Capac died of the white man's disease smallpox, which had swept down overland from Mexico in the previous seven years killing over thirty percent of the indigenous population, civil war broke out. Atahualpa, backed by his father's army, was by far the stronger and immediately won a major victory at the Río Bamba – a battle which, it was said, left the plain littered with human bones for over a hundred years. A still bloodier battle, however, took place along the Río Apurimac at Cotabamba in 1532. This was the decisive victory for Atahualpa, and with his army he retired to relax at the hot baths near Cajamarca. Here, informed

of a strange-looking, alien band, successors of the bearded adventurers whose presence had been noted during the reign of Huayna Capac, they waited.

THE SPANISH CONQUEST

Francisco Pizarro, along with two dozen soldiers, stumbled upon and named the Pacific Ocean in 1513 while on an exploratory expedition in Panama. From that moment his determination, fired by native tales of a fabulously rich land to the south, was set. Within eleven years he had found himself financial sponsors and set sail down the Pacific coast with the priest Hernando de Luque and Diego Almagro.

With remarkable determination, having survived several disastrous attempts, the three explorers eventually landed at **Tumbes** in 1532. A few months later a small band of Spaniards, totalling less than 170 men, arrived at the Inca city of **Cajamarca** to meet the leader of what they were rapidly realizing was a mighty empire. En route to Cajamarca, Pizarro had learned of the Inca civil wars and of Atahualpa's recent victory over his brother Huascar. This rift within the empire provided the key to success that Pizarro was looking for.

The day after their arrival, in what at first appeared to be a lunatic endeavour, Pizarro and his men massacred thousands of Inca warriors and captured Atahualpa. Although ridiculously outnumbered, the Spaniards had the advantages of surprise, steel, cannons and, above all, mounted cavalry. The **decisive battle** was over in a matter of hours: with Atahualpa prisoner, Pizarro was effectively in control of the Inca Empire. Atahualpa was promised his freedom if he could fill the famous ransom room at Cajamarca with gold. Caravans overladen with the precious metal arrived from all over the land and within six months the room was filled: a treasure worth over one and a half million pesos, which was already enough to make each of the conquerors extremely wealthy. Pizarro, however, chose to keep the Inca leader as a hostage in case of Indian revolt, amid growing suspicions that Atahualpa was inciting his generals to attack the Spanish. Atahualpa almost certainly did send messages to his chiefs in Cusco, including orders to execute his brother Huascar who was already in captivity there. Under pressure from his worried captains, Pizarro brought Atahualpa to trial in July 1533, a mockery of justice in which he was given a free choice: to be burned alive as a pagan or strangled as a Christian. They baptized him and then killed him.

With nothing left to keep him in Cajamarca, Pizarro made his way through the Andes to Cusco where he crowned a puppet emperor, **Manco Inca**, of royal Indian blood. After all the practice that the Spaniards had had in imposing their culture on both the Moors in Spain and the Aztecs in Mexico, it took them only a few years to replace the Inca Empire with a working colonial mechanism. Now that the Inca civil wars were over, the natives seemed happy to retire quietly into the hills and get back to the land. However, more than wars, **disease** was responsible for the almost total lack of initial reaction to the new conquerors. The native population had dropped from some 32 million in 1520 to only five million by 1548 – a decline due mainly to new European ailments such as smallpox, measles, bubonic plague, whooping cough and influenza.

COLONIAL PERU

Queen Isabella of Spain indirectly laid the original foundations for the political administration of Peru in 1503 when she authorized the initiation of an **encomienda system**, which meant that successful Spanish conquerors could extract tribute for the Crown and personal service in return for converting the natives to Christianity. They were not, however, given title to the land itself. As governor of Peru, Pizarro used the *encomienda* system to grant large groups of Indians to his favourite soldier-companions. In this way the basic colonial land-tenure structure was created in everything but name. "Personal service" rapidly came to mean subservient serfdom for the native population, many of whom were now expected to raise animals introduced from the Old World (cattle, hens, etc) on behalf of their new overlords. Many Inca cities were rebuilt as Spanish towns, although some, like Cusco, retained native masonry for their foundations and even walls. Other Inca sites, like Huanuco Viejo, were abandoned in favour of cities in more hospitable lower altitudes. The Spanish were drawn to the coast for strategic as well as climatic reasons – above all to maintain constant oceanic links with the homeland via Panama.

The **foundation of Lima** in 1535 began a multilayered process of satellite dependency which continues even today. The fat of the land (originally mostly gold and other treasures) was sucked in from regions all over Peru, processed in Lima, and sent on from there to Spain. Lima survived on the backs of Peru's municipal capitals which, in turn, extracted tribute from the scattered *encomenderos*. The *encomenderos* depended on local chieftains (*curacas*) to rake in service and goods from even the most remote villages and hamlets. At the lowest level there was little difference between Inca imperial exploitation and the economic network of Spanish colonialism. Where they really varied was that under the Incas the surplus produce circulated among the elite within the country, while the Spaniards sent much of it to a distant monarch on the other side of the world.

In 1541 Pizarro was assassinated by a disgruntled faction among the conquistadores who looked to Diego Almagro as their leader, and for the next seven years the nascent colonial society was rent by civil war. In response, the first **viceroy** – Blasco Nuñez de Vela – was sent from Spain in 1544. His task was to act as royal commissioner and to secure the colony's loyalty to Spain; his fate was to be killed by Gonzalo Pizarro, brother of Francisco. But Royalist forces, now under Pedro de la Gasca, eventually prevailed – Gonzalo was captured and executed, and Crown control firmly established.

COLONIAL SOCIETY

Meanwhile **Peruvian society** was being transformed by the growth of new generations: Creoles, descendants of Spaniards born in Peru, and *mestizos*, of mixed Spanish and native blood, created a new class structure. In the coastal valleys where populations had been decimated by European diseases, slaves were imported from Africa. There were over 1500 black slaves in Lima alone by 1554. At the same time, as a result of the civil wars and periodic Indian revolts, over a third of the original conquerors had lost their lives by 1550. Nevertheless effective power remained in the hands of the independent *encomenderos*.

In an attempt to dilute the influence of the *encomienda* system, the Royalists divided the existing twenty or so municipalities into **corregimentos**, smaller units headed by a *corregidor*, or royal administrator. They were given the power to control the activities of the *encomenderos* and exact tribute for the Crown – soon becoming the vital links in provincial government. The pattern of constant friction between *encomenderos* and *corregidores* was to continue for centuries, with only the priests to act as local mediators.

Despite the evangelistic zeal of the Spanish, **religion** changed little for the majority of the native population. Although Inca ceremonies, pilgrimages and public rituals were outlawed, their mystical and magical base endured. Each region quickly reverted to the pre-Inca cults deep-rooted in their culture and cosmology. Over the centuries the people learned to absorb symbolic elements of the Catholic faith into their beliefs and rituals – allowing them, once again, to worship relatively freely. Magic, herbalism and divination have continued strongly at the village level and have successfully pervaded modern Peruvian thought, language, and practice. (The Peruvian World Cup soccer squad in 1982 enlisted – in vain – the magical aid of a *curandero*.) At the elite level, the Spanish continued their fervent attempts to convert the entire population to their own ritualistic religion. They were, however, more successful with the rapidly growing *mestizo* population, who shared the same cultural aspirations.

Miraculous occurrences became a conspicuous feature in the popular Peruvian Catholic Church, the greatest example being Our Lord of Miracles, a cult which originated among the black population of colonial Lima. In the devastating earthquake of 1665, an anonymous mural of the Crucifixion on the wall of a chapel in the poorest quarter was supposedly the only structure left standing. This direct sign from God took hold among the local population, and Our Lord of Miracles remains the most revered image in Peru. Thousands of devotees process through the streets of Lima and other Peruvian towns every October, and even today many women dress in purple throughout the month to honour Our Lord of Miracles.

In return for the salvation of their souls the native population were expected to surrender their bodies to the Spanish. Some forms of service (*mita*) were simply continuations of Inca tradition – from keeping the streets clean to working in textile mills. But the most feared was a new introduction, the *mita de minas* – **forced work in the mines**. With the discov-

ery of the "mountain of silver" at Potosi (now Bolivia) in 1545, and of mercury deposits at Huancavelica in 1563, it reached new heights. Forced off their smallholdings, few Indians who left to work in the mines ever returned. Indeed the mercury mines at Huancavelica were so dangerous that the quality of their toxic ore could be measured by the number of weekly deaths. Those who were taken to Potosi had to be chained together to stop them from escaping: if they were injured, their bodies were cut from the shackles by sword to save precious time. Around three million Indians worked in Potosi and Huancavelica alone; some had to walk over 1000km from Cusco to Potosi for the privilege of working themselves to death.

In 1569, **Francisco Toledo** arrived in Peru to become viceroy. His aim was to reform the colonial system so as to increase royal revenue while at the same time improving the lot of the native population. Before he could get on with that, however, he had to quash a rapidly developing threat to the colony – the appearance of a **neo-Inca State**. After an unsuccessful uprising in 1536, Manco Inca, Pizarro's puppet emperor, had disappeared with a few thousand loyal subjects into the remote mountainous regions of **Vilcabamba**, northwest of Cusco. With the full regalia of high priests, virgins of the sun, and the golden idol punchau, he maintained a rebel Inca state and built himself impressive new palaces and fortresses between Vitcos and Espiritu Pampa – well beyond the reach of colonial power. Although not a substantial threat to the colony, Manco's forces repeatedly raided nearby settlements and robbed travellers on the roads between Cusco and Lima.

Manco himself died at the hands of a Spanish outlaw, a guest at Vilcabamba who hoped to win himself a pardon from the Crown. But the neo-Inca State continued under the leadership of Manco's son, Sairi Tupac, who assumed the imperial fringe at the age of ten. Tempted out of Vilcabamba in 1557, Sairi Tupac was offered a palace and a wealthy life in return for giving up his refuge and subversive aims. He died a young man, only three years after turning to Christianity and laying aside his father's cause. Meanwhile Titu Cusi, one of Manco's illegitimate sons, declared himself emperor and took control in Vilcabamba.

Eventually, Titu Cusi began to open his doors. First he allowed two Spanish friars to enter his camp, and then, in 1571, negotiations were opened for a return to Cusco when an emissary arrived from Viceroy Toledo. The talks broke down before the year was out and Toledo decided to send an army into Vilcabamba to rout the Incas. They arrived to find that Titu Cusi was already dead and his brother, **Tupac Amaru**, was the new emperor. After fierce fighting and a near escape, Tupac Amaru was captured and brought to trial in Cusco. Accused of plotting to overthrow the Spanish and of inciting his followers to raid towns, Tupac Amaru was beheaded as soon as possible – an act by Toledo that was disavowed by the Spanish Crown and which caused much distress in Peru.

Toledo's next task was to firmly establish the viceregal position – something that outlasted him by some two centuries. He toured highland Peru seeking ways to improve Crown control, starting with an attempt to curb the excesses of the *encomenderos* and their tax-collecting *curacas* (hereditary native leaders) by implementing a programme of **reducciones** – the physical resettlement of Indians in new towns and villages. Hundreds of thousands of peasants, perhaps millions, were forced to move from remote hamlets into large conglomerations, or *reducciones,* in convenient locations. Priests, or *corregidores*, were placed in charge of them, undercutting the power of the *encomenderos*. Toledo also established a new elected position – the local mayor (or *varayoc*) – in an attempt to displace the *curacas* (hereditary native leaders). The *varayoc*, however, was not necessarily a good colonial tool in that, even more than the *curacas*, his interests were rooted firmly in the *allyu* and in his own neighbours, rather than in the wealth of some distant kingdom.

REBELLION

When the Hapsburg monarchy gave way to the Bourbon kings in Spain at the beginning of the eighteenth century, shivers of protest seemed to reverberate deep in the Peruvian hinterland. There were a number of serious **native rebellions** against colonial rule during the next hundred years. One of the most important, though least known, was that led by **Juan Santos Atahualpa**, a *mestizo* from Cusco. Juan Santos had travelled to Spain, Africa and, some say, to England as a young man in the service of a

wealthy Jesuit priest. Returning to Peru in 1740 he was imbued with revolutionary fervour and moved into the high jungle region between Tarma and the Río Ucayali where he roused the forest Indians to rebellion. Throwing out the whites, he established a millenarian cult and, with an Indian army recruited from several tribes, successfully repelled all attacks by the authorities. Although never extending his powers beyond Tarma, he lived a free man until his death in 1756.

Twenty years later there were further violent native protests throughout the country against the enforcement of *repartiementos*. Under this new system the peasants were obliged to buy most of their essential goods from the *corregidor*, who, as monopoly supplier, sold poor quality produce at grossly inflated prices.

In 1780, another *mestizo*, José Gabriel Condorcanqui, led a rebellion, calling himself **Tupac Amaru II**. Whipping up the already inflamed peasant opinion around Cusco into a revolutionary frenzy, he imprisoned a local *corregidor* before going on to massacre a troop of nearly six hundred Royalist soldiers. Within a year Tupac Amaru II had been captured and executed but his rebellion had demonstrated both a definite weakness in colonial control and a high degree of popular unrest. Over the next decade several administrative reforms were to alter the situation, at least superficially: the *repartimiento* and the *corregimento* systems were abolished. In 1784, Charles III appointed a French nobleman – Teodoro de Croix – as the new viceroy to Peru and divided the country into seven *intendencias* containing 52 provinces. This created tighter direct royal control, but also unwittingly provided the pattern for the Republican state of federated *departmentos*.

The end of the eighteenth century saw profound changes throughout the world. The North American colonies had gained their independence from Britain; France had been rocked by a people's revolution; and liberal ideas were spreading everywhere. Inflammatory newspapers and periodicals began to appear on the streets of Lima, and discontent was expressed at all levels of society. A strong sense of **Peruvian nationalism** emerged in the pages of *Mercurio Peruano* (first printed in the 1790s), a concept which was vital to the coming changes. Even the architecture of Lima had changed in the mid-eighteenth century, as if to welcome the new era. Wide avenues suddenly appeared, public parks were opened, and palatial salons became the focus for the discourse of gentlemen. The philosophy of the Enlightenment was slowly but surely pervading attitudes even in remote Peru.

When, in 1808, Napoleon took control of Spain, the authorities and elites in all the Spanish colonies found themselves in a new and unprecedented position. Was their loyalty to Spain or to its rightful king? And just who was the rightful king now?

Initially, there were a few unsuccessful, locally based protests in response both to this ambiguous situation and to the age-old agrarian problem, but it was only with the intervention of outside forces that independence was to become a serious issue in Peru. The American War of Independence, the French Revolution, and Napoleon's invasion of Spain all pointed towards the opportunity of throwing off the shackles of colonialism, and by the time Ferdinand returned to the Spanish throne in 1814, Royalist troops were struggling to maintain order throughout South America. Venezuela and Argentina had already declared their independence, and in 1817 San Martín liberated Chile by force. It was only a matter of time before one of the great liberators – **San Martín** in the south or **Bolívar** in the north – reached Peru.

San Martín was the first to do so. Having already liberated Argentina and Chile, he contracted an English naval officer, Lord Cochrane, to attack Lima. By September 1819 the first rebel invaders had landed at Paracas. Ica, Huanuco and then the north of Peru soon opted for independence, and the Royalists, cut off in Lima, retreated into the mountains. Entering the capital without a struggle, San Martín proclaimed Peruvian **independence** on July 28, 1821.

THE REPUBLIC

San Martín immediately assumed political control of the fledgling nation. Under the title Protector of Peru he set about devising a workable **constitution** for the new nation – at one point even considering importing European royalty to establish a new monarchy. A libertarian as well as a liberator, San Martín declared freedom for slaves' children, abolished Indian service, and even outlawed the term "Indian". But

in practice, with Royalist troops still controlling large sectors of the *sierra*, his approach did more to frighten the establishment than it did to help the slaves and peasants whose problems remain, even now, deeply rooted in their social and territorial inheritance.

The development of a relatively stable political system took virtually the rest of the nineteenth century, although Spanish resistance to independence was finally extinguished at the battles of Junin and Ayacucho in 1824. By this time, San Martín had given up the political power game, handing it over to **Simón Bolívar**, a man of enormous force with definite tendencies towards megalomania. Between them, Bolívar and his right-hand man, Sucre, divided Peru in half, with Sucre first president of the upper sector, renamed Bolivia. Bolívar himself remained dictator of a vast Andean Confederation – encompassing Colombia, Venezuela, Ecuador, Peru and Bolivia – until 1826. Within a year of his withdrawal, however, the Peruvians had torn up his controversial constitution and voted the liberal **General La Mar** as president.

On La Mar's heels raced a generation of *caudillos*, military men, often *mestizos* of middle-class origins who had achieved recognition (on either side) in the battles for independence. The history of the early republic consists almost entirely of internal disputes between the Creole aristocracy and dictatorial *caudillos*. Peru plunged deep into a period of domestic and foreign plot and counterplot, while the economy and some of the nation's finest natural resources withered away.

Generals **Santa Cruz** and **Gamarra** stand out as two of the most ruthless players in this high-stakes power game: overthrowing La Mar in 1829, Santa Cruz became president of Bolivia and Gamarra of Peru. Four years later the liberal Creoles fought back with the election of General Orbegoso to the presidency. Gamarra, attempting to oust Orbegoso in a quiet palace coup, was overwhelmed and exiled. But the liberal constitution of 1834, despite its severe limitations on presidential power, still proved too much for the army – Orbegoso was overthrown within six months.

Unable to sit on the sidelines and watch the increasing pandemonium of Peruvian politics, Santa Cruz invaded Peru from Bolivia and installed himself as "Protector" in 1837. Very few South Americans were happy with this situation, least of all Gamarra, who joined with other exiles in Chile to plot revenge. After fierce fighting, Gamarra defeated Santa Cruz at Yungay, restored himself as president of Peru for two years, then died in 1841. During the next four years Peru had six more presidents, none of notable ability.

Ramon Castilla was the first president to bring any real strength to his office. On his assumption of power in 1845 the country began to develop more positively on the rising wave of a booming export in guano (birdshit) fertilizer. In 1856, a new moderate constitution was approved and Castilla began his second term of office in an atmosphere of growth and hope – there were rail lines to be built and the Amazon waterways to be opened up. Sugar and cotton became important exports from coastal plantations and the guano deposits alone yielded a revenue of $15 million in 1860. Castilla abolished Indian tribute and managed to emancipate slaves without social-economic disruption by buying them from their "owners"; guano income proved useful for this compensation.

His successors fared less happily. **President Balta** (1868–72) oversaw the construction of most of the rail lines, but overspent so freely on these and a variety of other public and engineering works that it left the country on the brink of economic collapse. In the 1872 elections an attempted military coup was spontaneously crushed by a civilian mob, and Peru's first civilian president – the laissez-faire capitalist **Manuel Pardo** – assumed power.

THE WAR OF THE PACIFIC

By the late nineteenth century Peru's foreign debt, particularly to England, had grown enormously. Even though interest could be paid in guano, there simply wasn't enough. To make matters considerably worse, Peru went to war with Chile in 1879.

Lasting over four years, this **"War of the Pacific"** was basically a battle for the rich nitrate deposits located in Bolivian territory. Peru had pressured its ally Bolivia into imposing an export tax on nitrates mined by the Chilean-British corporation. Chile's answer was to occupy the area and declare war on Peru and Bolivia. Victorious on land and at sea, Chilean forces had occupied Lima by the beginning of 1881 and the Peruvian president had fled to Europe. By

1883 Peru "lay helpless under the boots of its conquerors", and only a diplomatic rescue seemed possible. The **Treaty of Anco**, possibly Peru's greatest national humiliation, brought the war to a close in October 1883.

Peru was forced to accept the cloistering of an independent Bolivia high up in the Andes, with no land link to the Pacific, and the even harder loss of the nitrate fields to Chile. The country seemed in ruins: the guano virtually exhausted and the nitrates lost to Chile, the nation's coffers were empty and a new generation of *caudillos* prepared to resume the power struggle all over again.

THE TWENTIETH CENTURY

Modern Peru is generally considered to have been born in 1895 with the forced resignation of General Caceres. However, the seeds of industrial development had been laid under his rule, albeit by foreigners. In 1890 an international plan was formulated to bail Peru out of its bankruptcy. The **Peruvian Corporation** was formed in London and assumed the $50 million national debt in return for "control of the national economy". Foreign companies took over the rail lines, navigation of Lake Titicaca, vast quantities of guano, and were given free use of seven Peruvian ports for 66 years as well as the opportunity to start exploiting the rubber resources of the Amazon Basin. Under Nicolas de Pierola, some sort of stability had begun to return by the end of the nineteenth century.

In the early years of the twentieth century, Peru was run by an oligarchical clan of big businessmen and great landowners. Fortunes were made in a wide range of exploitative enterprises, above all sugar along the coast, minerals from the mountains, and rubber from the jungle. Meanwhile, the lot of the ordinary peasant worsened dramatically.

One of the most powerful oligarchs, **Augusto Leguia** rose to power through his possession of franchises for the New York Insurance Company and the British Sugar Company. He became a prominent figure, representing the rising bourgeoisie in the early 1900s, and in 1908 he was the first of their kind to be elected president. Under his rule the influence of foreign investment increased rapidly, with North American money taking ascendancy over British. It was with this capital that Lima was modernized – parks, plazas, the Avenida

Arequipa and the Presidential Palace all date from this period. But for the majority of Peruvians, Leguia did nothing. The lives of the mountain peasants became more difficult, and the jungle Indians lived like slaves on the rubber plantations. Not surprisingly, Leguia's time in power coincided with a large number of Indian rebellions, general discontent and the rise of the first labour movement in Peru. Elected for a second term, Leguia became still more dictatorial, changing the constitution so that he could be re-elected on another two occasions. A year after the beginning of his fourth term, in 1930, he was ousted by a military coup – more as a result of the stock market crash and Peru's close links with US finance than as a consequence of his other political failings.

During Leguia's long dictatorship, the **labour movement** began to flex its muscles. A general strike in 1919 had established an eight-hour day, and ten years later the unions formed the first National Labour Centre. The worldwide Depression of the early 1930s hit Peru particularly badly; demand for its main exports (oil, silver, sugar, cotton and coffee) fell off drastically. Finally, in 1932, the Trujillo middle class led a violent uprising against the sugar barons and the primitive conditions of work on the plantations. Suppressed by the army, nearly five thousand lives are thought to have been lost, many of the rebels being taken out in trucks and shot among the ruins of Chan Chan.

The rise of **APRA** – the American Popular Revolutionary Alliance – which had instigated the Trujillo uprising, and the growing popularity of its leader, **Haya de la Torre**, kept the nation occupied during World War II. Allowed to participate for the first time in the 1945 elections, APRA chose a neutral candidate – **Dr Bustamante** – in place of Haya de la Torre whose fervent radicalism was considered a vote loser. Bustamante won the elections, with APRA controlling 18 out of 29 seats in the Senate and 53 out of 04 in the Chamber of Deputies.

Post-war euphoria was short-lived, however. Inflation was totally out of hand and apparently unaffected by Bustamante's exchange controls; during the 1940s the cost of living in Peru rose by 262 percent. With anti-APRA feeling on the rise, the president leaned more and more heavily on support from the army, until General Odria led a coup d'état from Arequipa in 1948 and

formed a military junta. By the time Odria left office, in 1956, a new political element threatened oligarchical control – the young **Fernando Belaunde** and his **National Youth Front** (later Acción Popular) demanding "radical" reform. Even with the support of APRA and the army, Manuel Prado barely defeated Belaunde in the next elections: the unholy alliance between the monied establishment and APRA has been known as the "marriage of convenience" ever since.

The economy remained in dire straits. Domestic prices continued to soar and in 1952 alone there were some two hundred strikes and several serious riots. Meanwhile much more radical feeling was aroused in the provinces by **Hugo Blanco**, a charismatic *mestizo* from Cusco who had joined a Trotskyist group – the Workers Revolutionary Party – which was later to merge with the FIR – the Revolutionary Left's Front. In La Convencion, within the Department of Cusco, Blanco created nearly 150 syndicates, whose peasant members began to work their own individual plots while refusing to work for the hacienda owners. Many landowners went bankrupt or opted to bribe workers back with offers of cash wages. The second phase of Blanco's "reform" was to take physical control of the haciendas, mostly in areas so isolated that the authorities were powerless to intervene. Blanco was finally arrested in 1963 but the effects of his peasant revolt outlived him: in future, Peruvian governments were to take agrarian reform far more seriously.

Back in Lima, the elections of 1962 had resulted in an interesting deadlock, with Haya de la Torre getting 33 percent of the votes, Belaunde 32 percent, and Odria 28.5 percent. Almost inevitably, the army took control, annulled the elections, and denied Haya de la Torre and Belaunde the opportunity of power for another year. By 1963, though, neither Acción Popular nor APRA were sufficiently radical to pose a serious threat to the establishment. Elected president for the first time, Belaunde quickly got to work on a severely diluted programme of agrarian reform, a compromise never forgiven by his left-wing supporters. More successfully, though, he began to draw in quantities of foreign capital. President de Gaulle of France visited Peru in 1964 and the first British foreign secretary ever to set foot in South America arrived in Lima two years later. Foreign investors were clamouring to get in on Belaunde's ambitious development plans and obtain a rake-off from Peru's oil fields. But by 1965 domestic inflation had so severely damaged the balance of payments that confidence was beginning to slip away from Belaunde's international stance.

LAND REFORM AND THE MILITARY REGIME

By now, many intellectuals and government officials saw the agrarian situation as an urgent economic problem as well as a matter of social justice. Even the army believed that **land reform** was a prerequisite for the development of a larger market, without which any genuine industrial development would prove impossible. On October 3, 1968, tanks smashed through the gates into the courtyard of the Presidential Palace. General Velasco and the army seized power, deporting Belaunde and ensuring that Haya de la Torre could not even participate in the forthcoming elections.

The new government, revolutionary for a **military regime**, gave the land back to the workers in 1969. The great plantations were turned virtually overnight into producer's co-operatives, in an attempt to create a genuinely self-determining peasant class. At the same time guerrilla leaders were brought to trial, political activity was banned in the universities, indigenous banks were controlled, foreign banks nationalized, and diplomatic relations established with East European countries. By the end of military rule, in 1980, the land reform programme had done much to abolish the large capitalist landholding system.

Even now, though, a shortage of good land in the *sierra* and the lack of decent irrigation on the coast mean that less than twenty percent of the landless workers have been integrated into the co-operative system – the majority remain in seasonal work and/or the small farm sector. One of the major problems for the military regime, and one which still plagues the economy, was the **fishing crisis** in the 1970s. An overestimation of the fishing potential led to the build up of a highly capital-intensive fish-canning and fish-meal industry, in its time one of the world's most modern. Unfortunately, the fish began to disappear because of a combina-tion of ecological changes and over-fishing – leaving vast quantities of capital equipment inactive and thousands of people unemployed.

Although undeniably an important step forward, the 1968 military coup was always an essentially bourgeois revolution, imposed from above to speed up the transformation from a land-based oligarchy to a capitalist society. Paternalistic, even dictatorial, it did little to satisfy the demands of the more extreme peasant reformers, and the military leaders eventually handed back power voluntarily in democratic elections.

THE 1970S AND 1980S

After twelve years of military government the 1980 elections resulted in a centre-right alliance between Acción Popular and the Popular Christian Party. **Belaunde** resumed the presidency having become an established celebrity during his years of exile and having built up, too, an impressive array of international contacts. The policy of his government was to increase the pace of development still further, and in particular to emulate the Brazilian success in opening up the Amazon – building new roads and exploiting the untold wealth in oil, minerals, timber and agriculture. But inflation continued as an apparently insuperable problem, and Belaunde fared little better in coming to terms with either the parliamentary Marxists of the United Left or the escalating guerrilla movement led by Sendero Luminoso.

Sendero Luminoso (the Shining Path), founded in 1970, persistently discounted the possibility of change through the ballot box. In 1976 it adopted armed struggle as the only means to achieve its "anti-feudal, anti-imperial" revolution in Peru. Following the line of the Chinese Gang of Four, Sendero was led by **Abimael Guzman** (aka **Comrade Gonzalo**), whose ideas it claims to be in the direct lineage of Marx, Lenin and Chairman Mao. Originally a brilliant philosophy lecturer from Ayacucho (specializing in the Kantian theory of space), before his capture by the authorities in the early 1990s Gonzalo lived mainly underground, rarely seen even by Senderistas themselves.

Sendero was very active during the late 1980s and early 1990s, when it had some ten- to fifteen-thousand secret members. Rejecting

Belaunde's style of technological development as imperialist and the United Left as "parliamentary cretins", they carried out attacks on business interests, local officials, police posts, and anything regarded as outside interference with the self-determination of the peasantry. On the whole, members were recruited from the poorest areas of the country and from the Quechua-speaking population, coming together only for their paramilitary operations and melting back afterwards into the obscurity of their communities.

Although strategic points in Lima were frequently attacked – police stations, petrochemical plants and power lines – Sendero's main centre of activity was in the *sierra* around **Ayacucho** and **Huanta**, more recently spreading into the remote regions around the central *selva* and a little further south in **Vilcabamba**: site of the last Inca resistance, a traditional hide-out for rebels, and the centre of Hugo Blanco's activities in the 1960s. By remaining small and unpredictable, Sendero managed to wage its war on the Peruvian establishment with the minimum of risk of major confrontations with government forces.

Belaunde's response was to tie up enormous amounts of manpower in counter-insurgency operations whose main effect seemed to be to increase popular sympathy for the guerrillas. In 1984 more than six thousand troops, marines and anti-terrorist police were deployed against Sendero, and at least three thousand people, mostly peasants, are said to have been killed. "Disappearances", especially around Ayacucho, are still an occurrence, and most people blame the security forces for the bulk of them. In August 1984 even the chief of command of the counter-insurgency forces joined the criticism of the government's failure to provide promised development aid to Ayacucho. He was promptly dismissed for his claims that the problems were "the harvest of 160 years of neglect" and that the solution was "not a military one".

By 1985, new urban-based terrorist groups like the Movimiento Revolutionario Tupac Amaru (**MRTA**) began to make their presence felt in the shanty towns around Lima. Belaunde lost office in the April **1985 elections**, with APRA taking power for the first time and the United Left also getting a large percentage of the votes.

Led by a young, highly popular new president, **Alan Garcia**, the APRA government took office riding a massive wave of hope. Sendero Luminoso, however, continued to step up its tactics of anti-democratic terrorism at the Andean grass roots, and the isolation of Lima and the coast from much of the *sierra* and jungle regions became a very real threat. With Sendero proclaiming their revolution by "teaching" and terrorizing peasant communities on the one hand, and the military evidently liquidating the inhabitants of villages suspected of "collaboration" on the other, these years were a sad and bloody time for a large number of Peruvians.

Sendero's usual tactics were for an armed group to arrive at a peasant community and call a meeting. During the meeting it was not uncommon for them publicly to execute an "appropriate" local functionary – like a Ministry of Agriculture official or, in some cases, foreign aid workers – as a statement of persuasive terror. In May 1989 a British traveller found himself caught in the middle of this conflict and was shot in the head after a mock trial by Senderistas in the plaza of Olleros, a community near Huaraz in Ancash, which had offered him a bed for the night in its municipal building. Before leaving a village, Sendero always selected and left "intelligence officers", to liaise with the terrorists, and "production officers", to ensure that there was no trade between the village and the outside world – particularly with Lima and the international market economy.

Much of Sendero's funding came from the **cocaine trade**. Vast quantities of coca leaves are grown and partially processed all along the margins of the Peruvian jungle. Much of this is flown clandestinely into Colombia where the processing is completed and the finished product exported to North America and Europe for consumption. The thousands of peasants who came down from the Andes to make a new life in the tropical forest throughout the 1980s found that coca was by far the most lucrative cash crop. The cocaine barons paid peasants more than they could earn elsewhere and at the same time bought protection from Sendero (some say at a rate of up to $10,000 per clandestine plane load).

The 1980s, then, saw the growth of two major attacks on the political and moral backbone of the nation – one through terrorism, the other through cocaine. With these two forces working hand in hand the problems facing Garcia proved insurmountable. To make things worse, a right-wing death squad – the **Rodrigo Franco Commando** – appeared on the scene in 1988, evidently made up of disaffected police officers, army personnel and even one or two Apristas. Their most prominent victim so far has been Saul Cantoral, general secretary of the Mineworkers' Federation. RFC has also been sending death threats to a wide range of left-wing militants, union leaders, women's group co-ordinators and the press.

The appointment of **Agustin Mantilla** as minister of the interior in May 1989 suggested knowledge and approval of RFC at the very highest level. Mantilla was widely condemned as the man behind the emergence of the death squads and their supply of arms. He was known to want to take back by force large areas of the central Andes simply by supplying anti-Senderista peasants with machine guns. Opposition to the arming of the peasantry was one topic on which the military and human rights organizations seemed to agree. Many of the arms would probably have gone straight to Sendero, and such action could easily have set in motion a spiral of bloody civil war beyond anyone's control.

Guzman's success had lain partly with his use of Inca millennial mythology and partly in the power vacuum left after the implementation of the agrarian reform and the resulting unrest and instability, and Sendero's power, and even its popular appeal, advanced throughout the 1980s. In terms of territorial influence, it had spread its wings over most of central Peru, much of the jungle and to a certain extent into many of the northern and southern provincial towns.

The **MRTA** had less success, losing several of their leaders to Lima's prison cells. Their military confidence and capacity were also devastated when a contingent of some 62 MRTA militants was caught in an army ambush in April 1988; only eight survived from among two truckloads.

Meanwhile, the once young and popular President Alan Garcia got himself into a financial mess and was chased by the Peruvian judiciary from Colombia to Peru, having been accused of high-level corruption and stealing possibly millions of dollars from the people of Peru. His bad governance probably put an end to APRA's chances of ever getting political control of Peru again.

THE 1990S

Elections in 1990 proved to be a turning point for Peru. In the run-up to them there were four main candidates: the popular and internationally renowned author Mario Vargas Llosa, with his new right-wing coalition, Fredemo; Luís Alvacastro, general secretary of APRA (and minister in charge of the economy under Garcia); Alfonso Barrantes in control of a new left-wing grouping, Acuerdo Socialista; and Henry Peace of the United Left.

Vargas Llosa was the easy favourite as the poll approached, although he had blotted his copybook somewhat during 1989, when he had briefly bowed out of the electoral process, accusing his fellow leaders within Fredemo (which is essentially an alliance between Acción Popular and the Popular Christian Party) of making it impossible for him to carry on as a candidate. Still, by the time of the election he was back, and firmly in charge. APRA, having had five pretty disastrous years in power, were given virtually no chance of getting Alvacastro elected, and the left were severely split. Barrantes was by far the most popular candidate on that side. However, in creating Acuerdo Socialista, and thereby taking away half of the United Left's vote, he effectively spoilt both their chances.

In the event, the real surprise came with lightning speed from a totally unexpected quarter in the guise of an entirely new party – Cambio 90 (Change 90), formed only months before the election – led by a young college professor of Japanese descent, **Alberto Fujimori**. Fujimori came a very close second to Vargas Llosa in the March election, with 31 percent of the total against Llosa's 35 percent. Since a successful candidate must gain half the votes to become president, a second round was scheduled for June.

Once the inital shock of the result had been absorbed, Fujimori rapidly became favourite to win the **second poll**, on the grounds that electors who had voted for left-wing parties would switch their allegiance to him. While Vargas Llosa offered a Thatcherite, monetarist economic shock for Peru, Fujimori recommended protecting all public industries of strategic importance – the oil industry being one of the most important. Llosa was for selling such companies off to the private sector and exposing them to the full power of world market forces. However, ordinary Peruvians were clearly worried that such policies would bring them the kind of hardships that had beset Brazilians or Argentinians, and Fujimori swept into power in the second round of voting, almost immediately adopting many of Vargas Llosa's policies – overnight the price of many basics such as flour and fuel trebled. Fujimori did, however, manage to turn the nation around and gain an international confidence in Peru reflected in a stock exchange that was one of the fastest growing and most active in the Americas.

However, the real turning point, economically and politically, was the capture of Sendero's leader **Abimael Guzman** in September 1992. Captured at his Lima hideout, (a dance school) by General Vidal's secret anti-terrorist police DINCOTE, even Fujimori had not known about the raid until it had been successfully completed. With Guzman in jail, and presented very publically on TV as the defeated man, the political tide shifted. The international press no longer described Peru as a country where terrorists looked poised to take over, and Fujimori went from strength to strength while Sendero's activities were reduced to little more than the occasional car bomb in Lima as they were hounded by the military in their remote hideouts along the eastern edges of the Peruvian Andes. A massive boost to Fujimori's popularity, in the elections of 1995 he gained over sixty percent of the vote. Perhaps it was a recognition too, that his tough policies had paid off as far as the economy was concerned – inflation dipped from a record rate of 2777 percent in 1989 to ten percent in 1996.

The mid-1990s also became the time for the **MRTA** terrorists to battle with Fujimori and his government. First, in 1995, there was the capture of a major Lima cell after a 24-hour siege in the suburb of La Molina Vieja. A 26-year-old North American woman, Lori Helen Berenson Mejia, was arrested with the MRTA in the house and is now serving a life sentence in a women's prison in Peru. Then, on December 17 1996, the MRTA really hit the headlines when they infiltrated the Japanese Ambassor's residence, which they held siege for 126 days, with over 300 hostages. Some of these were released after negotiation, but Fujimori refused to give in to their demands for the freedom of hundreds of jailed MRTA comrades, and in March 1997, the affair ended in the storming of the building by Peruvian forces as the terrorists were playing football inside the residence. All the terrorists, many of them teenagers, were massacred, with only one hostage perishing in the skirmish. Fujimori's reputation as a hard man and a successful leader shot to new heights.

He continued to grow in popularity, despite Peru going to **war with Ecuador** briefly in January 1995, May 1997 and more seriously in 1998. The Ecuadorian army, which was accused of starting the skirmish, imposed significant losses on the Peruvian forces. This dispute has been inflamed by the presence of large oil fields in the region, currently on what the Peruvians claim is their side of the border, a claim the Ecudorians bitterly dispute: Ecuadorian maps continue to show the border much further south than Peruvian maps. The war is not over yet, although the fighting has stopped and at the start of 2000, relations between the two countries appeared better than they had been for decades. But with an upcoming election in 2000, war was perhaps not what Fujimori wanted.

In economic terms, Fujimori also seemed to be just about holding his own. Despite many aid organizations confirming widespread poverty and unemployment in Peru, and despite the nation being hit hard by the El Niño of 1998, the economy has stayed buoyant. Helped to a large extent by a growth in fishing output and a firm hand on inflation, which looked set to drop from its 1999 rate of seven percent to the projected two percent between 2000 and 2002, economic growth has remained steady at around three percent, and in the late 1990s Spain, the US and the UK were the biggest foreign investors in Peruvian communications, energy and mining.

Politically, too, Fujimori gained substantially in July 1999, when he appeared on TV, live from Huancayo, announcing the imminent capture of **Oscar Ramirez Durand**, alias Comrade

Feliciano, Guzman's number two and the then relatively new leader of Sendero Luminoso. An army battalion had already been sent to the Huancayo region in 1997 to destroy Sendero's stronghold; it took them two years, but they managed to achieve a result just in time for the start of the electoral campaign. At the end of the twentieth century, Sendero were left with only a few scattered remnants in one or two parts of the *sierra* and *ceja de selva*, and just one active cell in the cocaine-producing region of the Huallaga valley.

At the close of the twentieth century, apart from the rise and fall of Sendero Luminoso, the most impressive social phenomenon of the last hundred years had been the massive movement from rural to **urban living**. This was particularly true of Lima, which had, for several hundred

---

CULTURAL CHRONOLOGY OF PERU

20,000–10,000 BC
First evidence of human settlement in Peru. **Cave dwellings** in the Ayacucho Valley; stone artefacts in the Chillon Valley.

8000–5000 BC
Nomadic tribes, and more **permanent settlement** in fertile coastal areas. Cave paintings and fine stone tools.

5000–2000 BC
Introduction of cultivation and stable settlements. Early **agricultural sites** include Huaca Prieta in the Chicama Valley, Paracas and Kotosh.

1200 BC–200 AD
Formative Era and emergence of the **Chavín Cult**, with great progress in ceramics and metallurgy. Temple complex at Chavín de Huantar, important sites too at Kotosh and Sechin.

300 AD
Technological advance marked above all in the Viru Valley – the **Gallinazo culture** – and at Paracas.
Sites in the Viru Valley, at Paracas, and the growth of **Tiahuanuco culture** around Lake Titicaca.

200–1100 AD
Classical Cultures emergent throughout the land. Mochica culture and Temples of the Sun and Moon near Trujillo; further Tiahuanuco development; Nazca lines and Cahuachi complex on the coast; Wilkawain temple; Huari complex; and Tantamayo ruins.

1200
The age of the great **city builders**. Well-preserved adobe settlements survive at Chan Chan (near Trujillo) and Cajamarquilla (Lima).

1438–1532
Expansion of the **Inca Empire** from its bases around Cusco, north into Ecuador and south into Chile. Inca sites survive throughout Peru, but the greatest are still around Cusco – Sacsayhuaman and Machu Picchu above all. Inca Highway constructed from Columbia to Chile; parts still in existence.

1535
Foundation of Lima. **Colonial architecture** draws heavily on Spanish influences, though native craftsmen also leave their mark. Church building above all – at Arequipa (Santa Catalina Convent) and around Cusco. The Spanish city of Cusco incorporates much Inca stonework. Meanwhile, the rebel Incas build new cities around Vilcabamba. Throughout colonial rule building follows European fashions, especially into Baroque; churches, mansions and a few public buildings.

1870s
Construction of the high-altitude **rail lines** and other engineering projects. First exploitation of **Amazonian rubber**.

1890–1930
Much **modernization** in Lima (Presidential Palace etc), grandiose public buildings elsewhere. Massive urban growth in Lima from the 1930s onwards.

1963
Organized **shanty towns** begin to grow around Lima.

1980
Development of the jungle – timber trade, oil companies and settlers threaten traditional **tribal life and ecology**; construction of "Marginal Highway" into central Amazon resumed.

PERUVIAN POLITICAL UPDATES

For regular **news** on Peruvian politics and other matters, subscribe to the **Peru Support Group**, 37–39 Great Guildford Street, London SE1 OES, UK (☎020/7620-1103, fax 7261-9291, *perusupport@ gn.apc.org*). Established in 1983, the Peru Support Group aims to promote the rights and interests of the people of Peru, in particular the poorest sectors. Apart from the bi-monthly newsletter, it also produces briefings and educational materials, and organizes workshops and conferences.

years, grown fat on the back of the rich hinterlands of the Andes and, to a lesser extent, the Amazon regions. From the 1960s onwards the migration to Lima from the Andes was heavy and incessant, with people seeking a better living under its bright lights, and it grew in a rapid and disorganized fashion, doubling in size and population between 1976 and 1999. In 1940 just 35 percent of Peruvians lived in cities; by 1993 this had risen to over 70 percent. Conversely, so much of the jungle had been destroyed to make way for coca production that the environmental aspects of the situation became at least as critical as the associated law-and-order problems, though in the late 1990s, US airmen were patrolling the skies between Colombia and Peru, shooting down planes which did not respond to their calls for identification. Whether this helped or not is unsure, but by the end of 1999, cocaine production in Peru was on the decline.

THE ELECTIONS OF 2000

The run-up to the **elections** of April 9, 2000, was marked by Fujimori's controversial decision to stand for a third term of office, despite the Peruvian Constitution only allowing for two continuous terms. His rationale was that since the Constitution was introduced during his second term, he was entitled to stand for one more. However, even with his firm control of the media (especially TV), the election campaign saw strong opposition emerging in the person of Alejandro Toledo, a *serrano* Perú Posible candidate representing in particular the interests of Andean cities and communities. Such was Toledo's popularity that a smear campaign surfaced a few weeks before the voting, accusing him of shunning an illegitimate daughter and organizing a disastrous financial pyramid scheme in the early 1990s.

In the event, the results, which were unusually slow to come out, were announced amid accusations of ballot-rigging by Fujimori's supporters, leading the US to express official concern about the electoral process and to call for a second round of elections. Even though the true figures may never be known, Fujimori technically faced a second round of voting in any case, having failed to gain the fifty percent of the vote necessary to avoid such a run-off – though it had been close, with Fujimori with approximately forty-eight percent against Toledo with around forty percent. The second-round was slated for May or early June 2000.

INCA LIFE AND ACHIEVEMENT

In less than a century, the Incas developed and knitted together a vast empire peopled by something like twenty million Indians. They established an imperial religion in some harmony with those of their subject tribes; erected monolithic fortresses, salubrious palaces and temples; and, astonishingly, evolved a viable economy – strong enough to maintain a top-heavy elite in almost godlike grandeur. To understand these achievements and get some idea of what they must have meant in Peru five or six hundred years ago, you really have to see for yourself their surviving heritage: the stones of Inca ruins and roads; the cultural objects in the museums of Lima and Cusco; and their living descendants who still work the soil and speak Quechua – the language used by the Incas to unify their empire. What follows is but the briefest of introductions to their history, society and achievements.

INCA SOCIETY

The Inca Empire rapidly developed a **hierarchical structure**. At the highest level it was governed by the **Sapa Inca**, son of the sun and direct descendant of the god Viracocha. Under him were the priest-nobles – the royal **allyu** or kin-group which filled most of the important administrative and religious posts – and, working for them, regional *allyu* chiefs, **curacas** or *orejones*, responsible for controlling tribute from the peasant base. One third of the land belonged to the emperor and the state; another to the high priests, gods, and the sun; the last was for the *allyu* themselves. Work on the land, then, was devoted to maintaining the empire rather than mere subsistence, though in times of famine storehouses were evidently opened to feed the commoners.

Life for **the elite** wasn't, perhaps, quite as easy as it may appear; their fringe benefits were matched by the strain and worry of governing an empire, sending armies everywhere, and keeping the gods happy. The Inca nobles were nevertheless fond of relaxing in thermal baths, of hunting holidays, and of conspicuous eating and drinking whenever the religious calendar permitted. *Allyu* chiefs were often unrelated to the royal Inca lineage, but their position was normally hereditary. As lesser nobles (*curacas*) they were allowed to wear earplugs and special ornate headbands; their task was both to protect and exploit the commoners, and they themselves were free of labour service.

The hierarchical network swept down the ranks from important chiefs in a decimalized system. One of the *curacas* might be responsible for ten thousand men; under him two lower chiefs were each responsible for five thousand, and so on until in the smallest hamlets there was one man responsible for ten others. Women weren't counted in the census. For the Incas, a household was represented by the man and only he was obliged to fulfil tribute duties on behalf of the *allyu*. Within the family the woman's role was dependent on her relationship with the dominant man – be he father, brother, husband, or eldest son.

In their conquests the Incas absorbed **craftsmen** from every corner of the empire. Goldsmiths, potters, carpenters, sculptors, masons and *quipumayocs* (accountants) were frequently removed from their homes to work directly for the emperor in Cusco. These skilled men lost no time in developing into a new and entirely separate class of citizens. The work of even the lowest servant in the palace was highly regulated by a rigid division of labour. If a man was employed to be a woodcutter he wouldn't be expected to gather wood from the forests; that was the task of another employee.

Throughout the empire young girls, usually about nine or ten years old, were constantly selected for their beauty and serene intelligence. Those deemed perfect enough were taken to an *acclahuasi* – a special sanctuary for the **"chosen women"** – where they were trained in specific tasks, including the spinning and weaving of fine cloth, and the higher culinary arts. Most chosen women were destined ultimately to become *mamaconas* (Virgins of the Sun) or the concubines of either nobles or the Sapa Inca himself. Occasionally some of them were sacrificed by strangulation in order to appease the gods.

For most Inca **women** the allotted role was simply that of peasant/domestic work and rearing children. After giving birth a mother would wash her baby in a nearby stream to cleanse and purify it and return virtually immediately to normal daily activities, carrying the child in a cradle tied on her back with a shawl. As they still are today, most babies were breast-fed for years before leaving their mothers to take the place in the domestic life-cycle. As adults their particular role in society was dependent first on sex, then on hierarchical status.

Special regulations affected both the **old** and **disabled**. Around the age of fifty, a man was likely to pass into the category of "old". He was no longer capable of undertaking a normal workload, he wasn't expected to pay taxes, and he could always depend on support from the official storehouses. Nevertheless, the community still made small demands by using him to collect firewood and other such tasks; in much the same way the kids were expected to help out around the house and in the fields. In fact children and old people often worked together, the young learning directly from the old. Disabled people were obliged to work within their potential – the blind, for instance, might de-husk maize or clean cotton. Inca law also bound the deformed or disabled to marry people with similar disadvantages: dwarfs to dwarfs, blind to blind, legless to legless.

The **Inca diet** was essentially vegetarian, based on the staple potato but encompassing a range of other foods like quinoa, beans, squash, sweet potatoes, avocados, tomatoes and manioc. In the highlands emphasis was on root crops like potatoes which have been known to survive down to -15°C at over 5000m. On the valley floors and lower slopes of the Andes maize cultivation predominated.

The importance of **maize** both as a food crop and for making *chicha* increased dramatically under the Incas; previously it had been grown for ceremony and ritual exchange, as a status rather than a staple crop. The use of **coca** was restricted to the priests amd Inca elite. Coca is a mild narcotic stimulant which effectively dulls the body against cold, hunger and tiredness when the leaves are chewed in the mouth with a catalyst such as lime or calcium. Its leaves possessed magical properties for the Incas; they could be cast to divine future events, offered as a gift to the wind, the earth, or the mountain *apu*, and they could be used in witchcraft. Today it's difficult to envisage the Incas success in restricting coca-growing and use; even with helicopters and machine guns the present-day authorities are unable to control its production. But the original Inca system of control was frighteningly effective.

EXPANSION AND CONTROL

In Inca eyes the known world was their empire, and **expansion** therefore limitless. They divided their territories into four basic regions, or **suyos**, each radiating from the central plaza in Cusco: Chincha Suyo (northwest), Anit Suyo (northeast), Cunti Suyo (southwest) and Colla Suyo (southeast). Each *suyo* naturally had its own particular problems and characteristics but all were approached in the same way – initially being demoralized or forced into submission by the Inca army, later absorbed as allies for further conquests. In this way the Incas never seemed to overextend their lines to the fighting front.

The most impressive feature of an **Inca army** must in fact have been its sheer numbers – a relatively minor force would have included five thousand men. Their armour usually consisted of quilted cotton shirts and a small shield painted with designs or decorated with magnificent plumes. The common warriors – using slingshots, spears, axes and maces – were often supported by archers drafted from the "savages" living in the eastern forests. When the Spanish arrived on horseback the Incas were quick to invent new weapons: large two-handed hardwood swords and bolas (wooden balls connected by a string), good for tangling up the horses' legs. The only prisoners of war traditionally taken by a conquering Inca army were chieftains, who lived comfortably in Cusco as hostages against the good behaviour of their respective tribes. Along with the chiefs, the most important portable idols and *huacas* of conquered peoples were held in Cusco as sacred hostages. Often the children of the ruling chieftains were also taken to Cusco to be indoctrinated in Inca ways.

This pragmatic approach toward their subjects is exemplified again in the Inca policy of **forced resettlement**. Whole villages were sometimes sent into entirely new regions, ostensibly to increase the crop yield of plants like coca or corn and to vary their diet by importing manioc and chillis – though it was often criminals and rebellious citizens who ended up in the hottest, most humid regions. Large groups of people might also be sent from relatively suspect tribes into areas where mostly loyal subjects lived, or into the newly colonized outer fringes of the empire; many trustworthy subjects were also moved into zones where restlessness might have been expected. It seems likely that the whole colonization project was as much a political manoeuvre as a device to diversify the Inca economic or dietary base. As new regions came under imperial influence, the threat from rebellious elements was minimized by their geographical dispersion.

ECONOMY, AGRICULTURE AND BUILDING

The main **resources** available to the Inca Empire were agricultural land and labour, mines (producing precious and prestigious metals such as gold, silver or copper), and fresh water, abundant everywhere except along the desert coast. With careful manipulation of these resources, the Incas managed to keep things moving the way they wanted. Tribute in the form of **service** (*mita*) played a crucial role in maintaining the empire and pressurizing its subjects into ambitious building and irrigation projects. Some of these projects were so grand that they would have been impossible without the demanding whip of a totalitarian state.

Although a certain degree of local barter was allowed, the state regulated the distribution of every important product. The astonishing Inca **highways** were one key to this economic success. Some of the tracks were nearly 8km wide and at the time of the Spanish Conquest the main Royal Highway ran some 5000km, from the Río Ancasmayo in Colombia down the backbone of the Andes to the coast at a point south of the present-day Santiago in Chile. The Incas never used the wheel, but gigantic llama caravans were a common sight tramping along the roads, each animal carrying up to 50kg of cargo.

Every corner of the Inca domain was easily accessible via branch roads, all designed or taken over and unified with one intention – to dominate and administer an enormous empire. **Runners** were posted at *chasqui* stations and *tambo* rest-houses which punctuated the road at intervals of between 2 and 15km. Fresh fish was relayed on foot from the coast and messages were sent with runners from Quito to Cusco (2000km) in less than six days. The more

difficult mountain canyons were crossed on bridges suspended from cables braided out of jungle lianas (creeping vines) and high passes were – and still are – frequently reached by incredible stairways cut into solid rock cliffs.

The primary sector in the economy was inevitably **agriculture** and in this the Incas made two major advances: large terracing projects created the opportunity for agricultural specialists to experiment with new crops and methods of cultivation, and the transportation system allowed a revolution in distribution. Massive agricultural **terracing projects** were going on continuously in Inca-dominated mountain regions. The best examples of these are in the Cusco area at Tipón, Moray, Ollantaytambo, Pisac and Cusichaca. Beyond the aesthetic beauty of Inca stone terraces, they have distinct practical advantages. Stepping hillsides minimizes erosion from landslides, and using well-engineered stone channels gives complete control over irrigation. Natural springs emerging on the hillsides became the focus of an intricate network of canals and aqueducts extending over the surrounding slopes which had themselves been converted into elegant stone terraces. An extra incentive to the Inca mind must surely have been their reverence of water, one of the major earthly spirits. The Inca terraces are often so elaborately designed around springs that they seem to be worshipping as much as utilizing water.

Today, however, it is Inca construction which forms their lasting heritage: vast **building projects** masterminded by high-ranking nobles and architects, and supervised by expert masons with an almost limitless pool of peasant labour. Without paper, the architects resorted to imposing their imagination onto clay or stone, making miniature models of the more important constructions – good examples of these can be seen in Cusco museums. More importantly, Inca masonry survives throughout Peru, most spectacularly at the fortress of Sascayhuaman above Cusco, and on the coast in the Achirana aqueduct, which even today still brings water down to the Ica Valley from high up in the Andes. In the mountains, Inca stonework gave a permanence to edifices which would otherwise have needed constant renovation. The damp climate and mould quickly destroy anything but solid rock; Spanish and modern buildings have often collapsed around well-built Inca walls.

ARTS AND CRAFTS

Surprisingly, perhaps, Inca masonry was very rarely carved or adorned in any way. Smaller stone items, however, were frequently ornate and beautiful. High technical standards were achieved, too, in **pottery**. Around Cusco especially, the art of creating and glazing ceramics was highly developed. They were not so advanced artistically, however; Inca designs generally lack imagination and variety, tending to have been mass-produced from models evolved by previous cultures. The most common pottery object was the *aryballus*, a large jar with a conical base and a wide neck thought to have been used chiefly for storing *chicha*. Its decoration was usually geometric, often associated with the backbone of a fish; the central spine of the pattern was adorned with rows of spikes radiating from either side. Fine plates were made with anthropomorphic handles, and large numbers of cylindrically tapering goblets — *keros* — were manufactured, though these were often of cedar wood rather than pottery.

The refinements in **metallurgy**, like the ceramics industry, were mostly developed by craftsmen absorbed from different corners of the empire. The Chimu were particularly respected by the Incas for their superb metalwork. Within the empire, bronze and copper were used for axe-blades and tumi knives; gold and silver were restricted to ritual use and for nobles. The Incas smelted their metal ores in cylindrical terracotta and adobe furnaces which made good use of prevailing breezes to fire large lumps of charcoal. Molten ores were pulled out from the base of the furnace. Although the majority of surviving metal artefacts — those you see in museums — have been made from beaten sheets, there were plenty of cast or cut solid gold and silver pieces, too. Most of these were melted down by the conquistadores, who weren't especially interested in precious objects for their artistic merit.

RELIGION

The Inca **religion** was easily capable of incorporating the religious features of most subjugated regions. The setting for beliefs, idols and oracles, more or less throughout the entire empire, had been preordained over the previous two thousand years: a general recognition of certain creator deities and a whole pantheon of nature-related spirits, minor deities and demons. The customary form of worship varied a little according to the locality, but everywhere they went the Incas (and later the Spanish) found the creator god among other animistic spirits and concepts of power related to lightning, thunder and rainbows. The Incas merely superimposed their variety of mystical, yet inherently practical, elements onto those that they came across.

The main religious novelty introduced with Inca domination was their demand to be recognized as direct descendants of the creator-god **Viracocha**. A claim to divine ancestry was, to the Incas, a valid excuse for military and cultural expansion. There was no need to destroy the *huacas* and oracles of subjugated peoples; on the contrary, certain sacred sites were recognized as intrinsically holy, as powerful places for communication with the spirit world. When ancient shrines like Pachacamac, near Lima, were absorbed into the empire they were simply turned over to worship on imperial terms.

The sun is the most obvious symbol of Inca belief, a chief deity and the visible head of the state religion; Viracocha was a less direct, more ethereal, force. The sun's role was overt, as lifegiver to an agriculturally based empire, and its cycle was intricately related to agrarian practice and annual ritual patterns. To think of the Inca religion as essentially sun worship, though, would be far too simplistic. There were distinct layers in **Inca cosmology**: the level of creation, the astral level and the earthly dimension.

The first, highest level corresponds to Viracocha as the creator-god who brought life to the world and society to mankind. Below this, on the astral level, are the celestial gods: the sun itself, the moon and certain stars (particularly the Pleiades, patrons of fertility). The earthly dimension, although that of man, was no less magical, endowed with important *huacas* and shrines which might take the form of unusual rocks or peaks, caves, tombs, mummies and natural springs.

The astral level and earthly dimension were widespread bases of worship in Peru before the Incas rose to power. The favour of the creator was the critical factor in their claims to divine right of imperial government, and the hierarchical structure of religious ranking also reflects the division of the religious spheres into those that were around before, during, and after the empire and those that only stayed as long as Inca domination lasted. At the very top of this **religio-social hierarchy** was the Villac Uma, the high priest of Cusco, usually a brother of the Sapa Inca himself. Under him were perhaps hundreds of high priests, all nobles of royal blood who were responsible for ceremony, temples, shrines, divination, curing and sacrifice within the realm, and below them were the ordinary priests and chosen women. At the base of the hierarchy, and probably the most numerous of all religious personalities, were the **curanderos**, local curers practising herbal medicine and magic, and making sacrifices to small regional *huacas*.

Most **religious festivals** were calendrically based and marked by processions, sacrifices and dances. The Incas were aware of lunar time and the solar year, although they generally used the blooming of a special cactus to gauge the correct time to begin planting. Sacrifices to the gods normally consisted of llamas, cuys or *chicha* – only occasionally were chosen women and other adults killed. Once every year, however, young children were apparently sacrificed in the most important sacred centres.

Divination was a vital role played by priests and *curanderos* at all levels of the religious hierarchy. Soothsayers were expected to talk with the spirits and often used a hallucinogenic snuff from the vilca plant to achieve a trance-like state and communion with the other world. Everything from a crackling fire to the glance of a lizard was seen as a potential omen, and treated as such by making a little offering of coca leaves, coca spittle, or *chicha*. There were specific problems which divination was considered particularly accurate in solving: retrieving lost things; predicting the outcome of certain events (the oracles were always consulted prior to important military escapades); receiving a vision of contemporaneous yet distant happenings; and the diagnosis of illness.

ANCIENT WIZARDRY IN MODERN PERU

Bearing in mind the country's poverty and the fact that almost half the population is still pure Amerindian, it isn't altogether surprising to discover that the ancient shamanic healing arts are still flourishing in Peru. Evidence for this type of magical health therapy stretches back over three thousand years on the Peruvian coast. Today, curanderos (Spanish for "curers") can be found in every large community, practising healing based on knowledge which has been passed down from master to apprentice over millennia.

Curanderos offer an alternative to the expensive, sporadic and often unreliable service provided by scientific medics in a developing country like Peru. But as well as being a cheaper, more widely available option, *curanderismo* is also closer to the hearts and understanding of the average Peruvian.

With the resurgence of herbalism, aromatherapy, exotic healing massages and other aspects of New Age "holistic" health, it should be easier for us in the West to understand *curanderismo* than it might have been a decade or so ago. Combine "holistic" health with psychotherapy, and add an underlying cultural vision of spiritual and magical influences, and you are some way toward getting a clearer picture of how healing wizards operate.

There are two other important characteristics of modern-day Peruvian *curanderismo*. Firstly, the last four hundred years of Spanish domination have added a veneer of Catholic imagery and nomenclature. Demons have become saints, ancient mountain spirits and their associated annual festivals continue disguised as Christian ceremonies. Equally important for any real understanding of Peruvian shamanism is the fact that most, if not all, *curanderos* use hallucinogens. The tribal peoples in the Peruvian Amazon who have managed, to a large extent, to hang on to their culture in the face of the oncoming industrial civilization, have also maintained their spiritual traditions. In almost every Peruvian tribe these traditions include the regular use of hallucinogenic brews to give a visionary ecstatic experience. Sometimes just the shaman partakes, but more often the shaman and his patients, or entire communities, will indulge together, singing traditional spirit-songs which help control the visions. The hallucinogenic experience, like the world of dreams, is the Peruvian forest Indian's way of getting in touch with the **ancestral world** or the world of spirit matter.

THE ORIGINS OF SHAMANISM

The history of healing wizards in Peru matches that of the ritual use of hallucinogens and appears to have emerged alongside the first major temple-building culture – **Chavín** (1200 BC–200 AD). Agriculture, ceramics and other technical processes including some metallurgy had already been developed by 1200 BC, but Chavín demonstrates the first unified and widespread cultural movement in terms of sacred architectural style, and the forms and symbolic imagery used in pottery throughout much of Andean and coastal Peru during this era. Chavín was a religious cult which seems to have spread from the central mountains, quite possibly from the large temple complex at Chavín de Huantar near Huaraz. Taking hold along the coast, the image of the central Chavín deity was woven, moulded, and carved onto the finest funerary cloths, ceramics and stones. Generally represented as a complex and demonic-looking feline deity, the Chavín god always has fangs and a stern face. Many of the idols also show serpents radiating from the deity's head.

As far as the central temple at Chavín de Huantar is concerned, it was almost certainly a centre of sacred pilgrimage built up over a period of centuries into a large ceremonial complex used at appropriate calendrical intervals to focus the spiritual, political, and economic energies of a vast area (at least large enough to include a range of produce for local consumption from tropical forest, high Andean and desert coast regions). The magnificent stone temple kept growing in size until, by around 300 BC, it would have been one of the largest religious centres anywhere in the world, with some three thousand local attendants. Among the fascinating finds at Chavín there have been bone snuff-tubes, beads, pendants, needles, ceremonial spondylus shells (imported from Ecuador) and some **quartz crystals** associated with ritual sites. One quartz crystal, covered in red pigment, was found in a grave, placed after death in the mouth of the deceased. Contemporary anthropological evidence shows us that quartz crystals still play an important role in shamanic ceremonies in Peru, the Americas, Australia and Asia. The well-documented Desana Indians of Colombia still see crystals as a "means of communication between the visible and invisible worlds, a crystallization of solar energy, or the Sun Father's semen which can be used in esoteric undertakings".

In one stone relief on the main temple at Chavín the feline deity is depicted holding a large **San Pedro cactus** in his hand. A Chavín ceramic bottle has been discovered with a San Pedro cactus "growing" on it; and, on another pot, a feline sits surrounded by several San Pedros. Similar motifs and designs appear on the later Paracas and Mochica craft work, but there is no real evidence for the ritual use of hallucinogens prior to Chavín. One impressive ceramic from the Mochica culture (500 AD) depicts an owl-woman – still symbolic of the female shaman in contemporary Peru – with a slice of San Pedro cactus in her hand. Another ceramic from the later Chimu culture (around 1100 AD) shows a woman healer holding a San Pedro.

As well as coca, their "divine plant", the **Incas** had their own special hallucinogen: vilca (meaning "sacred" in Quechua). The vilca tree (probably *Anadenanthera colubrina*) grows in the cloud-forest zones on the eastern slopes of the Peruvian Andes. The Incas used a snuff made from the seeds which was generally blown up the nostrils of the participant by a helper. Evidently the Inca priests used vilca to bring on visions and make contact with the gods and spirit world.

SHAMANISM TODAY

Still commonly used by *curanderos* on the coast and in the mountains of Peru, the San Pedro cactus (*Trichocereus panchanoi*) is a potent hallucinogen based on active mescaline. The *curandero* administers the hallucinogenic brew to his or her clients to bring about a period of revelation when questions are asked of the intoxicated person, who might also be asked to choose some object from among a range of magical curios which all have different meanings to the healer. Sometimes a *curandero* might imbibe San Pedro (or one of the many other indigenous hallucinogens) to see into the future, retrieve lost souls, divine causes of illness, or discover the whereabouts of lost objects.

On **the coast**, healing wizards usually live near the sea on the fringes of a settlement. Most have their own San Pedro plant which is said to protect or guard their homes against unwanted intruders by letting out a high-pitched whistle if somebody approaches. The most famous *curandero* of all lives just outside Trujillo on the north coast of Peru. Eduardo Calderon – better known in Peru as **El Tuno** – is a shaman and a healer. His work consists of treating sick and worried people who come to him from hundreds of miles around. His job is to create harmony where tensions, fears, jealousies, and sickness exist. Essentially a combination of herbalism, magical divination and a kind of psychic shock therapy involving the use of San Pedro, his shamanic craft has been handed down by word of mouth through generations of men and women. El Tuno's knowledge makes him a specialist in healing through inner visions – contact with the "spirit world". He is a master of the unconscious realms and regularly enters non-ordinary reality to combat the evil influences which he sees as making his patients sick. His knowledge is being passed on to the next generation, and, rather than losing its influence in Peru, appears to be gaining in popularity, reputation and healing power.

Describing the effects of San Pedro, El Tuno once said that at first there is "a slight dizziness that one hardly notices. And then a great 'vision,' a clearing of all the faculties of the individual. It produces a light numbness in the body and afterward a tranquillity. And then comes a detachment, a type of visual force in the individual inclusive of all the senses, including the sixth sense, the telepathic sense of transmitting oneself across time and matter . . . It develops the power of perception . . . in the sense that when one wants to see something far away . . . he can distinguish powers or problems at great distance." (Quoted in *Wizard of the Four Winds* by Douglas Sharon (The Free Press, 1978.)

El Tuno and many other coastal wizards get their most potent magic and powerful plants from a small zone in the northern Andes. The mountain area around Las Huaringas and **Huancabamba**, to the north of Chiclayo and east of Piura, is where a large number of the "great masters" are believed to live and work. But it is in the **Amazon Basin** of Peru that shamanism continues in its least changed form.

Even on the edges of most jungle towns there are *curanderos* healing local people by using a mixture of jungle Indian shamanism and the more Catholicized coastal form. These wizards generally use the most common tropical forest hallucinogen, **ayahuasca** (from the liana *Banisteriopsis caapi*). Away from the towns, among the more remote tribal people, *ayahuasca* is the key to understanding the native consciousness and perception of the world – which for them is the natural world of the elements and the forest plus their own social, economic and political setup within that dominant environment. It has been argued by some anthropologists, notably Reichmal Dolmatoff from his work among the Desana Indians of the Colombian rainforest (who also use *ayahuasca*), that the shaman controls his community's ecological balance through his use of mythological tales, ceremony, rituals and a long-established code of avoiding killing and eating certain creatures over complex temporal cycles. Dolmatoff appears to be suggesting that the Desana culture's ritual food taboo cycles are, in fact, a valid system or blueprint for the survival of the tribe and their natural eco-niche – a system worked out and regulated over millennia by the shaman, who listens to the spirits of nature through visions and inner voices.

The Shipibo tribe from the central Peruvian Amazon are famous for their excellent ceramic and weaving designs: extremely complex geometric patterns usually in black on white or beige, though sometimes reds or yellows too. It's not generally known, however, that these designs were traditionally given to a shaman (male or female) by the spirits while they were under the influence of *ayahuasca*. The shaman imbibes the hallucinogen, whose effect is described as "the spirits coming down". The spirits teach the shaman songs, or chants, the vibration of which helps determine the shaman's visions. The geometric designs used on pots and textiles are his or her material manifestation of these visions. The vision and its material manifestations are in turn highly valued as healing agents in themselves. They make something look beautiful; beauty means health. Traditionally the Shipibo painted their houses and their bodies with geometric designs to maintain health, beauty and harmony in their communities. Similarly, painting a sick person from head to toe in the designs given, say, by a hummingbird spirit, was seen as an important part of the healing process.

Throughout the Peruvian Amazon **native shaman** are the only real specialists within indigenous tribal life. In terms of their roles within traditional society – as healers, masters of ritual and mythology, interpreters of dreams, visions and omens, controllers of fish, game and the weather – the forest Indian shaman commands respect from his group. But it is precisely his group and the nonmaterialist, nonaccumulative tendencies of their semi-nomadic lifestyles (which it is the shaman's role to promote and preserve) which keeps them on an economic par with their fellows. Consequently the tribes have retained their organic anarchy on a political and day-to-day level. The size of communities has generally remained low. There is no cultural impetus for the shaman to turn high priest or king, just as there is no cultural incentive to accumulate surplus material objects or surplus forest produce. The shaman in traditional tribal societies is often a major conservative force – preserving his or her culture and conserving the environment, particularly in the face of encroaching development and consumerism.

It is clearly hard to generalize with any accuracy across the spectrum of healing wizards still found in modern Peru, yet there are definite threads connecting them all. On a practical level even the most isolated jungle shaman may well have trading links with several coastal *curanderos* – there are many magical cures imported via a web of ongoing trans-Andean trading partners to be found on the *curanderos'* street market stalls in Lima, Trujillo, Arequipa and Chimbote. It has been argued by some of the most eminent Peruvianists that the initial ideas and spark for the Chavín culture came up the Marañon Valley from the Amazon. If it did, then it could well have brought with it – some three thousand years ago – the first shamanic teachings to the rest of ancient Peru, possibly even the use of power plants and other tropical forest hallucinogens, since these are so critical to understanding even modern-day Peruvian Amazon Indian religion. One thing which can certainly be said about ancient healing wizards in modern Peru is that they question the very foundations of our rational scientific perception of the world. With recent developments in understanding the human mind and the holistic nature of living organisms the scientific establishment may come to learn something about both the inner cosmos as well as healing from these Peruvian masters of *curanderismo*.

PERUVIAN MUSIC

Latin America's oldest musical traditions are those of the Amerindians of the Andes. Their music is best known outside these countries through the characteristic pan-pipes of poncho-clad folklore groups. However, there's a multitude of rhythms and popular musics found here deserve a lot more recognition, incuding huayno and chicha, still relatively unknown abroad, as well as the distinct coastal tradition of Afro-Peruvian music, rooted in black slaves brought to work in the mines.

For most people outside Latin America the sound of the Andes is that of bamboo panpipes and *quena* flutes. What is most remarkable is that these instruments have been used to create music in various parts of this large area of mountains – which stretch 4500 miles from Venezula down to southernmost Chile – since before the time of the Incas. Pre-Conquest Andean instruments – conch shell trumpets, shakers which used nuts for rattles, ocarinas, wind instruments and drums – are ever present in museum collections. And the influence of the Inca empire means that the Andean region and its music spreads far beyond the mountains themselves. It can be defined partly through ethnicity, partly through language – **Quechna** (currently spoken by over six million people) and **Aymara**, both of which are spoken alongside Spanish and other Amerindian languages.

The dominant areas of Andean culture are **Peru**, Ecuador and Bolivia, the countries with the largest indigenous Amerindian populations in South America. Here, in rural areas, highly traditional Andean music, probably little different from pre-Inca times, still thrives today at every kind of celebration and ritual. But beyond this is a huge diversity of music, differing widely not only between countries but between individual communities. Andean people tend to identify themselves by the specific place they come from: in music, the villages have different ways of making and tuning instruments and composing tunes, in the same way as they have distinctive weaving designs, ways of dressing or wearing their hats. Use of different scales involving four, five, six and seven notes and different singing styles are also found from place to place, tied to specific ritual occasions and the music which goes with them.

Andean music can be divided roughly into three types. Firstly, that which is of **indigenous origin**, found mostly amongst rural Amerindian peoples still living very much by the seasons with root Amerindian beliefs; secondly music of **European origin**, and thirdly **mestizo music**, which continues to fuse the indigenous with European in a whole host of ways. In general, Quechna people have more vocal music than the Aymara.

TRADITIONAL MUSIC

Panpipes, known by the Aymara as *siku*, by the Quechna as *antara* and by the Spanish as *zampoña*, are ancient instruments and archeologists have unearthed panpipes tuned to a variety of scales. While modern panpipes – played in the city or in groups with other instruments – may offer a complete scale allowing solo performance, traditional models are played in pairs, as described by sixteenth-century chroniclers. The pipes share the melody, each with alternate notes of a whole scale so that two or more players are needed to pick out a single tune using a hocket technique. Usually one player leads and the other follows. While symbolically this demonstrates reciprocity within the community, practically it enables players to play for a long time without getting too "high" from dizziness caused by over-breathing.

Played by blowing (or breathing out hard) across the top of a tube, panpipes come in various sizes, those with a deep bass having very long tubes. Several tubes made of bamboo reed of different length are bound together to produce a sound that can be jaunty, but also has a melancholic edge depending on tune and playing style. Many tunes have a minor, descending shape to them. Playing is often described as "breathy" as overblowing is popular to produce harmonics. In general those who play panpipes love dense overlapping textures and often syncopated rhythms.

Simple **notched-end flutes**, or **quenas**, are another independent innovation of the Andean highlands found in both rural and urban areas. The most important pre-Hispanic instrument, they were traditionally made of fragile bamboo (though often these days from plumbers' PVC water pipes) and played in the dry season, with **tarkas** (vertical flutes – like a shrill recorder) taking over in the wet. *Quenas* are played solo or in ritual groups and remain tremendously popular today, with many virtuoso techniques.

Large **marching bands of drums and panpipes**, playing in the co-operative "back-and-forth" leader/follower style captivated the Spanish in the 1500s can still be seen and heard today. The drums are deep-sounding, double-headed instruments known as *bombos* or *wankaras*. These bands exist for parades at lifecycle *fiestas*, weddings and dances in the regions surrounding the Peruvian–Bolivian frontier and around Lake Titicaca. Apart from their use at *fiestas*, panpipes are played mainly in the dry season, from April to October.

There is something quite amazing about the sound of a fifty-man panpipe band approaching, especially after they've been playing for a few hours and have had a few well-earned drinks. It is perfectly normal for a whole village to come together to play as an orchestra for important events and *fiestas*. Andean villages are usually composed of *ayllus* (extended families) whose land is often divided up so that everyone gets a share of various pastures, but with everyone working together at key times such as harvest and when caring for communal areas. Music is an integral part of all communal celebrations and symbolically represents that sharing and inter-dependence: drinks are drunk from communal glasses which everyone will empty in turn. The organisation and values of each community are reflected in the very instrument an individual plays, down to the position of players within circles and groups.

Folk music festivals to attract and entertain the tourist trade are a quite different experience to music in the village context. While positively disseminating the music, they have introduced the notion of judging and the concept of "best" musicianship – ideas totally at odds with rural community values of diversity in musical repertoire, style and dress.

CHARANGOS AND MERMAIDS

The **charango** is another key Andean instrument whose bright, zingy sounds are familiar worldwide. This small guitar – with five pairs of strings – was created in imitation of early guitars and lutes brought by the Spanish colonizers, which indigenous musicians were taught to play in the churches. Its small size is due to its traditional manufacture from armadillo shells – though most today are made of wood – while its sound quality comes from the indigenous aesthetic which has favoured high pitches from the pre-Columbian period through to the present.

In rural areas in southern Peru, particularly in the Titicaca region and province of Canas, the *charango* is the key instrument – used by young, single men to woo and court the female of their choice. In this area the tradition often involves the figure of a **mermaid**, *la sirena*, who offers supernatural aid to the young men embarking on a musical pursuit of their chosen one. The ethnomusicologist Tom Turino records that most towns and villages around Titicaca claim a *sirena* lives in a nearby spring, river, lake or waterfall, and notes that new *charangos* are often left overnight in such places – wrapped in a piece of woven cloth, along with gifts – to be tuned and played overnight by the *sirena*. Some villagers construct the sound box in the shape of a mermaid including her head and fish tail to invest their *charango* with supernatural power.

When young men go courting at the weekly markets in larger villages they will not only dress in their finest clothes, but get up their *charangos* in elaborate coloured ribbons. These represent the number of women their *charango* has supposedly conquered, thus demonstrating their manliness and the power of their instrument. At times a group of young people will get together for the ancient **circle dance** called the *Punchay Kashwa* where the men form a half circle playing their *charangos*, facing a half circle of young women. Both groups dance and sing in bantering "song duelling" fashion, participants using a set syllabic and rhyming pattern so that they can quickly improvise. "Let's go walking" one might call, to a riposte such as "A devil like you makes me suspicious", or an insult like "In the back of your house there are three rotten eggs".

In Peru, the *charango* was until the 1960s regarded as an "Indian" instrument of the rural, lower classes. Brought to towns and cities by rural migrants, it crossed over when Spanish-speaking middle-class musicians – who until then had only played European instruments such as guitars and mandolins – began to play it – and as a result of the cultural evaluation following the 1969 Revolution. The Peruvian ideological movement known as **Indigenismo**, active between 1910 and 1940, was also influential in the *charango*'s re-appraisal. Indigenismo was a regionalistic and nationalistic movement that lauded indigenous culture as true Peruvian, rejecting *criolla* and Hispanic values. The movement was particularly strong in Cusco, where *charango* performance by *mestizos* became part of its identity.

CHARANGO STYLES

Charangos were originally made from the shell of an armadillo but as the animal has become rare and protected, today's instruments are made of wood. There are many sizes and varieties: from those capable of deeper, richer, bass sounds with large round backs to flat backed instruments with more strident metal strings.

Tunings vary from place to place and from musician to musician with some preferring metal strings, others nylon, to suit a variety of strumming and plucking techniques. Nylon strings are often thought to produce "deeper" "clearer", "'sweeter" sounds. In certain areas of Peru, for instance at the time of potato planting, a *charango* may play potato-planting songs and dances strictly in strumming style with a single line melody vibrating amongst open sounding strings. In contrast **mestizo styles** – used when playing creole musical forms such as *waynos*, *marineras*, *yaravís* and *vals criollo* – may favour plucked melodic playing styles which can be very complex.

SONG AND BRASS

Most **singing** in the Andes is done by women and the preferred style is very high-pitched –

almost falsetto to European ears. There are songs for potato growing, reaping barley, threshing wheat, marking cattle, sheep and goats, for building houses, for traditional dances and funerals and many other ceremonies.

The astonishing diversity of music, ensembles and occasions can be heard clearly on the superb *Smithsonian Folkways Traditional Music of Peru* series, documented and compiled by music ethnologist Raúl Romero. These recordings are mainly from the Mantaro valley, an area known for its saxophone and clarinet ensembles, and include women singing accompanied by the ancient *tinya* drum and violin and also the harp as well as clarinets and brass bands. There are so many festivities with music that the music profession is considered profitable and there are a great number of **brass bands** (first introduced in the 1920s as part of mandatory military service) as well as **orchestras** (*tipicas*) composed of saxophones, clarinets, violins and diatonic harp.

Romero notes that urbanization, modernization and migration, rather than undermining the need for traditional music, has led to its successful adaptation of new forms, and revival. He also notes the importance of *mestizo* and bilingual Spanish-Quechna culture in this process.

The context of the musical performance is still the determining factor in its style. Music which continues pre-Hispanic models is to be found within the context of closed community and ritual. Music which is *mestizo*, re-creating regional traditions, is dynamically driven by the *fiesta* system. New musical styles have evolved through migration to the capital Lima, with radio and record as their main vehicles of communication.

MUSIC IN CUSCO

Music explodes from every direction in the once Inca lands, but nowhere more so than in **Cusco**, a good first base for getting to grips with Andean music. Stay a week or two and you will hear just about every variety of Andean folk music that is still performed.

The streets are the best place to start. Most street musicians are highly talented performers and will play for hours on end. Around noon, you might see **Leandro Apaza** making his way down the great hill of Avenida Tullumayo. Carrying an Andean harp on his shoulder, he is

THE ANDEAN HARP: DON ANTONIO SULCA

In blind musician **Don Antonio Sulca**, of Ayacucho, Peru is one of the great masters of the Andean harp – one of the mountains' most characteristic instruments. This huge harp has a soundbox built like a boat and a mermaid's head decoration (like many *charangos*). Its form is thought to have evolved from the harp brought from Spain in the sixteenth century and the Celtic harp brought by the Jesuits to the Missions. It has 36 strings spanning five octaves and including resonant bass notes. In processions in the Andes, harpists often sling their instruments upside down across their shoulders, plucking with a remarkable backhanded technique.

Sulca plays solo or, more often, with his group **Ayllu Sulca**, composed of members of his *ayllu* (his extended family), on fiddles and mandolins. Their songs are mostly *huaynos* sung in Quechna. The most familiar of them, *Huerfano pajarillo* (*Little Orphan Bird*), about a bird that has strayed too far from home, is an allegory of the plight of

the Amerindians forced to migrate to earn a living. His stately style of playing *yaravis* – slow sad tunes – is unmatched. A pre-Hispanic form, they probably acquired thier doleful, introspective character during the early colonial period, when at least eighty percent of the Amerindian population perished. The *yaravi* composed at the death of the last member of the Inca royal family, Tupac Amaru, in 1781, became the best-known of all Peruvian tunes – **El Condor Pasa (Flight of the Condor)**.

Don Antonio Sulca also plays **dance music** from the early twentieth century, when forms like the foxtrot, waltz and tango were given the Inca touch to produce hybrid forms like the sublime waltz **incaico** *Nube Gris* (*Grey Cloud*). His version of his city's unofficial hymn, *Adíos pueblo Ayacucho* (*Farewell, People of Ayacucho*), celebrates emotional ties to the place where the Amerindians beat back the Spanish at the time of the Conquest.

led down the street by a small boy because, like many accomplished regional musicians, he is blind. He will turn right onto Hatun Rumiyoq, the narrow alley that every visitor to Cusco visits at some time to see the large stone perfectly fitted into place in the side wall of Inca Roca's palace. Leandro sets up his harp directly across from the great stone. **Benjamin Clara**, who sometimes accompanies him on mandolin, may already be there waiting. Benjamin cannot always meet Leandro downtown as he is lame as well as sightless and needs to be carried (see discography, *Blind Street Musicians of Cusco*, p.450).

The two are there to earn their living by playing the traditional music of the Quechna people. Their repertoire includes a host of styles, the most recognizable being the *huayno*, an unmistakable dance rhythm reminiscent of a hopped-up waltz, which once heard is not easily forgotten. It is musically cheerful, though the lyrics can be sorrowful, and sometimes full of double meaning, occasionally sexually explicit – a fact often not realized by those who cannot understand Quechna.

Very few such musicians achieve any kind of media fame. If they do, it usually means the chance to perform in small clubs or restaurants for a meagre guaranteed wage plus whatever

they receive in tips. One such individual is **Gabriel Aragón**. Another blind musician, he is a huge man, obviously *mestizo*, and possessed of a gentle voice and a soft touch on his harp. His fame means that he will often travel for an engagement, which may be a club date, a wedding or a traditional festival. At his restaurant gigs, he serves up some of the finest traditional folk melodies, ballads and dance tunes – a nostalgic repertoire greatly appreciated by older members of the community.

CONJUNTOS AND CONCERTS

Cusco's tavern scene, like that of any urban region, also plays host to young **cholo** and **mestizo groups**. They are constantly on the move throughout the evening, playing one set in each of the available venues in town during the tourist season. You can pick the club with your favourite ambience and settle in – most of the groups will pass through in the course of an evening, so you are almost bound to hear each of them at some point as the entertainment goes on all night long.

This kind of "one-night tour" is limited only by the size of a city. In Lima, for example, a group of this type might confine itself to a specific area of town. The smaller mountain villages, by contrast, might have only one night spot – and if they are lucky a local band. In regions of heavy tourism, such as Cusco or Ollantaytambo, there is usually a proliferation of groups. If you end up at one of these mini-*fiestas*, you may be egged on to dance, especially if you are a woman, and definitely be forced to join in a drink. Follow along, do your best, and don't mind being the butt of the odd joke. It will be worth it.

The ensembles typically consist of five to seven members. Their **instrumentation** includes one or two guitars, a *charango*, *quenas*, other flutes, panpipes and simple percussion. Harps, considered something of a dying art due to their size, weight, fragility and cost, are rarer these days. Most of the musicians are adept at more than one instrument and are likely to switch roles during their set. Their performing is a social event; their tour a rolling party as they are usually accompanied on their rounds by friends (you are welcome to join them).

As these musicians grow older many of them end up in the backup band of a veteran professional, rather than in a group of traditional musicians. This type of **conjunto** is most likely to be made up of urban middle-class musicians, usually serious students of music since early in life. They often have some type of classical training, may be able to compose and arrange, and, although emotionally tied to ancestral heritage, the bulk of their repertoire is newly composed using traditional idioms played on both modern and traditional instruments. They will also be able to play a variety of standards – classic pieces of traditional highland folk. These ensembles are usually quite well paid and do not normally move about throughout the evening. They play at the more elite nightclubs, hotel lounges and arts centres and sometimes if lucky tour abroad.

Although by the very nature of their own background and that of their audience these bands are not staunch traditionalists, they are promoted as such by those in charge of international cultural exchange. On tour abroad, they usually play well-known traditional pieces, and often accompany **folkloric dance groups**, while another part of their repertoire may be what is marketed as **Andean New Age** music, a blend of traditionalism with modern sounds. The vocal presentation of these groups is generally more accessible to foreign ears than the piercing falsetto tones of a traditional vocalist..

HUAYNOS AND ORQUESTAS TÍPICAS

Europe may know the Andes through the sound of bamboo panpipes and *quenas*, but visit the Peruvian central *sierra* and you find a music as lively and energetic as the busy market towns it comes from – a music largely unknown outside the country. These songs and dances are **huaynos**, one of the few musical forms that reaches back to pre-Conquest times, although the **orquestas típicas** that play them, from *sierra* towns like Huancayo, Ayacucho and Pucara, include saxophones, clarinets and trumpets alongside traditional instruments like violins, *charangos* and the large Amerindian harp.

The music is spirited and infectious, the focus gradually shifting from Inca past and a pan-Andean image to the contemporary cultures of regional departments. Because of the larger size of the *provinciano* colonies from Ancash, Junin and Ayacucho in Lima, the urban-country style primarily grew up around performers from these departments including Pastorita Huancarina (Ancash), Hermanos Zevallos (Junin), Flor de Huancayo (Junin), Princesita de Yungay (Ancash), Paisanita Ancashina (Ancash). Names such as Paisanita Ancashina (Little Fellow Countrywoman from Ancash) clearly evoke nostalgia of place and *paisano* loyalty helping to ensure commercial success and bolster regional group unity and pride.

While some voices maintain the high-pitched dense quality of Andean singing, many major stars incorporate Western vibrato (absent in traditional Andean singing) and a clear – from the diaphragm – vocal style. As musicians have become more professional, specializing in certain styles, technical performance on instruments has become cleaner and instrumental breaks hotter. Arrangements too have become tighter and follow other urban popular forms with vocal verses and instrumental solos.

The names of the singers express the passion of the people for the flora and fauna of their homeland – **Flor Pucarina** (The Flower of Pucará) and **Picaflor de los Andes** (Hummingbird of the Andes) are two of those singing in the 1960s represented on GlobeStyle's *huayno* compilation. Another CD of this music, on the Arhoolie label, features the most celebrated *huayno* singer of all time – **El Jilguero de Huascarán**. When he died in 1988, thousands of people packed the streets of Lima to attend his funeral, and recordings he made over thirty years ago are still sold on the streets today.

The buoyant, swinging rhythms of *huayno* songs are deceptive, for the lyrics fuse joy and sorrow. The musical style is regionally marked with typical *mestizo* instrumental ensembles of the region represented and musical features, such as specific guitar runs, identifying musicians with, for example, Ayacucho or Ancash. Sung in a mixture of Spanish and Quechna, they tell of unhappy love and betrayal, celebrate passion, and often deliver home-spun philosophy. As Picaflor sings in "Un pasajero en tu camino": "On the road of romance, I'm only a passenger without a destination". At the same time, texts often allude to region of-origin or specific towns, important hooks for local audiences.

As well as in their *sierra* home, *huaynos* can be heard in Lima and other coastal towns, where they were brought by Andean migrants in the 1950s. Before then the music of the coastal towns and cities was **musica criolla**, heavily influenced by music from other parts of Latin America, Spain and Europe – a bourgeois music including everything from foxtrot to tango, which filtered down to the working class, often as hybrids called, for example, Inca-Fox. Migrants often found themselves living in desperate poverty in the shantytowns, scraping a living as maids, labourers or street-traders, but in the 1950s and 1960s would meet up at the Lima *coliseo* (a form of stadium) on a Sunday to dance to their music and assert identity and pride.

Between 1946 and 1949 there were thirty such centres for *espectaculos folkloricos* in Lima, but only two remained by the mid 1970s and there are none left today. A blend of resources from the two worlds, this music served as an aid to *provincianos* in the process of forging a new identity for themselves. But the *coliseos* began to lose their public as people began to demand more traditional performances of highland music and dance. In the 1960s and 1970s regional-migrant clubs began to take control over the commercial entrepreneurs who had failed to reward the musicians well. Sunday performances switched to these new clubs which gave a share of the fee to the musicians and featured traditions specifically from their home regions.

Urban *huaynos* are performed and recorded by **orquestas típicas** and enjoy enormous popularity. In the rural areas the style is more rustic. Andean highland settlements are isolated by deep river valleys, making communication difficult in the past. Because of this, students of Quechna are tormented by the extreme variation in language sometimes found between two relatively close villages. One would expect a similar variation between song styles; this is sometimes the case, but the *huayno* beat is pan-Andean. Each district does add its own peculiar flavour, but as the saying goes, a *huayno* is a *huayno*, at least until you listen closely. During daylight hours, some forty Lima radio stations broadcast nothing but *huaynos*. Shortwave radio fans, or visitors to Peru, can tune in for a quick education.

AFRO-PERUVIAN MUSIC

Afro-Peruvian music has its roots in the communities of black slaves brought to work in the mines along the Peruvian coast. As such, it's a fair way from the Andes, culturally and geographically. However, as it developed, particularly in this century, it drew on Andean and Spanish, as well as African traditions, while its modern exponents also have affinities with Andean *nueva canción*. The music was little known even in Peru until the 1950s, when it was popularized by the seminal performer Nicomedes Santa Cruz, whose body of work was taken a step further in the 1970s by the group Peru Negro. Internationally, it has had a recent airing through David Byrne's Luaka Bop label, issuing the compilation, *Peru-Negro*, and a solo album by Susana Baca.

Nicomedes Santa Cruz is the towering figure in the development of Afro-Peruvian music. A poet, musician and journalist, he was the first true musicologist to assert an Afro-Peruvian cultural identity through black music and dance, producing books and recordings of contemporary black music and culture in Peru. In 1959, with his group **Conjunto Cumanana**, he recorded the album *Kumanana*, followed in 1960 by *Ingá* and *Décimas y poemas Afroperuanos*. In 1964 he recorded a four-album set *Cumanana*, now regarded as the bible of Afro-Peruvian music. Santa Cruz himself followed in the footsteps of **Porfirio**

SUSANA BACA

The singer who looks like bringing the Afro-Peruvian scene to international acclaim beyond Latin America is **Susana Baca**, who grew up in the black coastal neighbourhood of Chorrillos outside Lima. Interviewed at WOMAD 1998, she recalled family traditions of getting together for a Sunday meal, and then making music with her father playing guitar, her mother, aunts, uncles and friends singing and dancing. By the time she was a teenager and first heard the recordings of Nicomedes Santa Cruz, she realised she had absorbed quite a repertoire of the traditional songs black people had carried with them to Peru as slaves.

Susana Baca runs her own Instituto Negrocontinuo, with her husband Ricardo Pereira; its aim is to promote and increase the diffusion of Afro-Peruvian music, and to link together old and young musicians through a series of workshops on all aspects of the music and its culture. Her passion for this project first emerged at school and has increased steadily over the years. "We studied the culture of the Spanish and of the Incas which made the Andean girls proud, but we black girls didn't find our people in the history of Peru at all," recalls Baca. "Blacks came to Peru as servants of Spanish and Portuguese, as slaves to be bought and sold. As a child I was aware that we had our way of cooking, our music, dances, even our own traditional medicines – but it was only in the 1960s that this was first really asserted in public. A lot of people until then had been silenced, some ashamed of the whole history of slavery, of the sufferings of their great grandparents, rejecting their past. But then it began to take on a positive hue and people began to understand what it meant to be black."

One of the essential instruments of Afro-Peruvian music is the *cajón* – a box which the percussionist sits astride, leaning down to play. This is the same *cajón* that eventually made its way into Spanish flamenco – through Paco de Lucía who, according to an apocryphal story, played in Lima in 1978 and first heard the *cajón* played at a party. Susana remembers, "It's true, I was there, I even sang and there was a great group of Peruvian musicians playing and of *cajóneros*, and Paco de Lucía liked it all so much they gave him a *cajón*. The instrument is so important because it carries the rhythm and the voice sings within that dialogue between guitar and *cajón*. My mother always said that it was the box of the people who carried fruit and worked in the ports. When they had a free moment they used them to play and sing and dance. Later they had a more special construction, different woods with a hole in one side that gives a more sophisticated sound, more reverberation. Cuba and Brazil also have similar traditions which also emerged amongst black musicians in ports."

Baca's own performing style is intimate and rooted in close contact with her band "Nothing is written down, the musicians improvise and invent, so we need to be able to see each other's eyes to make a good performance, to share and enjoy and release the power of the music. You can hear it in *La Canción para el Señor de los Milagros* (*The Song for the Lord of Miracles*). It's a song of adoration for a Christ who is celebrated for two days in October in Lima. It's now one of the most important popular festivals – people follow the Christ figure in such numbers through the streets the city comes to a halt. It's wonderful. They asked me to sing that sacred song and I do."

Vasquez, who came to Lima in 1920 and was an early pioneer of the movement to regain the lost cultural identity of Afro-Peruvians. A composer of *décimas*, singer, guitarist, *cajonero* (box player) and *zapateador* (dancer) he founded the Academia Folklorica in Lima in 1949. Through Santa Cruz's work and that of the group **Peru Negro** and the singer and composer **Chabuca Granda**, Latin America came to know Afro-Peruvian dances, the names of which were given to their songs such as *Toro mata*, *Samba-malató*, *El Alcatraz* and *Festejo*.

CHICHA

Chicha, the fermented maize beer, has given its name to a new and hugely popular brew of Andean tropical music – a fusion of urban *cumbia* (local versions of the original Colombian dance), traditional highland *huayno*, and rock.

The music's origins lie in the massive migration of Amerindians from the inner mountain areas to the shantytowns around cities such as Arequipa and Lima. Chicha emerged in Lima in the early 1960s and by the mid-1980s had become the most widespread urban music in

Peru. Most bands have lead and rhythm guitars, electric bass, electric organ, a timbales and conga player, one or more vocalists (who may play percussion) and, if they can, a synthesizer.

The first *chicha* hit, and the song from which the movement has taken its name, was *La Chichera* (*The Chicha Seller*) by **Los Demonios de Mantaro** (The Devils of Mantaro), who hailed from the central highlands of Junin. Another famous band are **Los Shapis**, another provincial group established by their 1981 hit *El Aguajal* (*The Swamp*), a version of a traditional

DISCOGRAPHY

COMPILATIONS

Afro-Peruvian Classics: The Soul of Black Peru (Luaka Bop, US). Music of the Black slaves brought to work in the mines of the coastal areas, which began to gain recognition in Peru in the 1940s. Popularized in the last twenty-five years, first by seminal musicologist and performer, Nicomedes Santa Cruz, then by Peru Negro, the group who got the music going in the 1970s; and the great Chabuca Granda; later Susana Baca and Cecilia Barraza continued the style. A unique blend of Spanish, Andean and African traditions, this is different to Caribbean and other Latin black cultures. This compilation includes the definitive dance song *Toro Mata*, the first Afro-Peruvian success outside Peru covered by Queen of Salsa, Celia Cruz. A fine collection intended to introduce the music to a wider audience outside Peru, it does a great job.

The Blind Street Musicians of Cusco: Peruvian Harp and Mandolin (Music of the World, US). Stirringly played *marineras*, *huaynos*, traditional tunes and instrumental solos exactly as heard on the streets of Cusco in 1984–85 from Leandro Apaza on a thirty-three stringed harp; Benjamin Clara Quispé and Carmen Apaza Roca on armadillo-shelled mandolins (not *charangos*); Fidel Villacorte Tejada on *quena*. Excellent ambience recorded in musicians' homes and *chichería* bars.

Flutes and Strings of the Andes (Music of the World, US). The superbly atmospheric recordings of amateur musicians from Peru: harpists, charanguistas, fiddlers, flautists and percussionists, recorded in 1983–84 on the streets and at festivals, bring you as close to being there as you can get without strapping on your pack and striding uphill.

From The Mountains to the Sea: Music of Peru, The 1960s (Arhoolie, US). Brilliant window into the mix of indigenous, *criolla*, *mestizo*, Latin, tropical and European styles to be found in the capital including Peruvian rock, *cumbias*, *valses*, *boleros*, *sanjuanitos*, *huaynos*, tangos. Captures the spirit of many diferent groups, combinations of instruments and atmospheres.

Huaynos and Huaylas: The Real Music of Peru (GlobeStyle, UK). A tremendous selection of urban *orquestas típicas*, who replace traditional instruments with saxophones, clarinets and violins, this is a real eye- and ear-opener. The performers include the late Picaflor de los Andes, Flor Pucarina, with a host of songs expressing loss and love rooted in the Peruvian countryside.

Huayno Music of Peru Vols 1 and 2 (Arhoolie, US). These excellent collections of *huayno* music from the 1950s to the 1980s focus on a slightly more local style than the GlobeStyle disc. Vol 1 includes songs from the master, Jilguero del Huascarn, while Vol 2 is drawn from the recordings of Discos Smith, a small label that released *huayno* and *criolla* music in the late 1950s and 1960s.

Kingdom of the Sun (Nonesuch Explorer, US). An atmospheric mix of Peru's Inca heritage and religious festivals recorded in Ayacucho, Chuschi and Paucartambo.

Mountain Music of Peru (Smithsonian Folkways, US). John Cohen's selection, including a song that went up in the Voyager spacecraft, brings together music from remote corners of the mountains where music is integral to daily life, and urban songs telling of tragedies at football matches. Good sleeve notes, too.

Peru and Bolivia. The Sounds of Evolving Traditions. Central Andean Music and Festivals (Multicultural Media, US). Lively, accessible introduction to today's sounds from both Peru and Bolivia, from Japanese aficionado Norio Yamamoto's brilliant and diverse selection of recordings. Each piece in its natural context from people's homes to clubs to *fiestas* to streets with live local audiences. Harps, violins, drums, panpipes, and much more. Moving from Cusco to Ayacucho, La Paz to Lima, Lake Titicaca and back to Marcapata village near Cusco. Good notes.

huayno. **Pastorita Huaracina** is one of the more well-known female singers. Another good band – and the first to get a Western CD release – are **Belem**, based in Lima.

While most lyrics are about love in all its aspects, nearly all songs actually reveal an aspect of the harshness of the Amerindian experience – displacement, hardship, loneliness and exploitation. Many songs relate to the great majority of people who have to make a living selling their labour and goods in the unofficial "informal economy", ever threatened by the

---

The Rough Guide to Music of the Andes (World Music Network). A vigorous and broad range of Andean music from contemporary urban based groups – including key 1960s musicians Los Kjarkas and Ernesto Cavou, and their 1980s European travelling bretheren Awatinas and Rumillajta; soloists Emma Junaro, Jenny Cardenas and Susana Baca; seminal Chilean group Inti Illimani and new song singer Victor Jara. Plus saxes and clarinets from Picaflor de los Andes.

Traditional Music of Peru: Vol 1 Festivals of Cusco; Vol 2 The Mantaro Valley; Vol 3 Cajamarca and the Colca Valley; Vol 4 Lambayeque (Smithsonian Folkways). A definitive series of field recordings from the 1980s and 1990s of music from specific areas. Includes the whole spectrum of music to be heard if you travelled around the whole of Peru. Excellent CD booklets. too.

ARTISTS AND ALBUMS

Susana Baca

Susana Baca, one of the few Afro-Peruvian artists touring worldwide, grew up in the coastal barrio of Chorillos and learned traditional Afro-Peruvian songs from her family (see box, p.419). Dedicated to recuperating and strengthening this past and making it relevant to the present she runs the Instituto Negrocontinuo (Black Continuum) in Lima and is as involved with the integral dance and other aspects of Afro-Peruvian culture as the music.

Susana Baca (Luaka Bop/Warner Bros). Taking up the mantle of Chabuca Granda and Nicomedes Santa Cruz these are fine version of Afro-Peruvian and *criolla* classics sung with conscious emotion and passion.

Belem

Belem are one of the bands which has made *chicha* a force to be reckoned with in urban Peru.

Chicha (Tumi, UK). A pioneering release of Peru's hot fusion music. Belem's mix of *huayno*, salsa, *cumbia*, and a touch of rock, deserves a listening. Andean pipe music, it ain't.

Arturo "Zambo" Cavero & Oscar Aviles

Arturo "Zambo" Cavero is one of the great male voices of black Peruvian music, as well as being an accomplished cajón player. During the 1980s he teamed up with Oscar Aviles to become a celebrated partnership, their music seen as reflecting the suffering, patriotism and passion of the black people of Peru. As a key member of the group Los Morochucos, Oscar Aviles gained the reputation of being "*La Primera Guitarra del Perú*" – Peru's leading Creole guitarist.

Y siguen festejando juntos (IEMPSA, Peru). Classic Afro-Peruvian music with the most representative voice and guitar musicians on the scene.

On the Wings of the Condor (Tumi, UK). One of the most popular Andean albums ever, but none the worse for that: the engaging sound of the panpipes and *charangos*, smoothly and beautifully arranged.

Hermanos Santa Cruz

Hermanos Santa Cruz are family members of Nicomedes Santa Cruz.

Afro Peru (Discos Hispanos, Peru). Carrying on the tradition and heritage laid down by their forefathers, the Santa Cruz brothers present a 1990s version of Afro-Peruvian traditions.

Nicomedes Santa Cruz

The first true musicologist to assert Afro-Peruvian cultural identity through black music and dance.

Kumanana (Philips, Peru), *Socabon* (Virrey, Peru). Two albums showcasing Santa Cruz's majestic musicological studies of Afro-Peruvian music and culture.

Ayllu Sulca

Blind harpist Ayllu Sulca encapsulates everything that is *mestizo* music – the emergence of a hybrid blend between Amerindian and Spanish cultures. A virtuoso since early childhood, he plays as a soloist but mostly as part of his band – his *ayllu* – which includes three of his sons.

Music of the Incas (Lyrichord, US). Accompanied by violin, mandolin and *quenas*, Sulca plays ancient Inca melodies and more recent waltzes with a pace and swing including rustic versions of salon music.

police. Los Shapis' *El Ambulante* (*The Street Seller*) opens with a reference to the rainbow colours of the Inca flag and the colour of the ponchos the people use to keep warm and transport their wares. "My flag is of the colours and the stamp of the rainbow/For Peru and America/Watch out or the police will take your bundle off you!/Ay, ay, ay, how sad it is to live/How sad it is to dream/I'm a street seller, I'm a proletarian/Selling shoes, selling food, selling jackets/I support my home."

Chicha has effectively become a youth movement, an expression of social frustration for the mass of people suffering racial discrimination in Peruvian society.

PERU'S PERFORMERS

Many performers have achieved mass appeal and recording contracts in Peru and can support themselves solely by their work as musicians. Nationally celebrated performers include **Florcita de Pisaq** (a *huayno* vocalist), **Pastorita Huaracina** (a singer of both *cholo* and *mestizo* varieties) and **Jaime Guardía** (a virtuoso of the *charango*).

These performers take pride in being bearers of tradition, play at most traditional festivals and hire themselves out to wealthier villages to provide music for those festive events that require it. Although they may hold little attraction for the wealthy urban population (who tend to deny their roots), they often appear at large venues in major urban areas. They appeal to the displaced campesinos and city migrants who live in the *pueblos jóvenes*, or squatter settlements, which have sprung up on the outskirts of the large coastal cities. These artists travel a circuit of major urban centres, including Cusco, on local concert tours.

Recordings of these artists are generally only available locally, but they can sometimes be found in shops catering for Latin American immigrants. Occasionally, an artist of this type will end up on an album collection.

FRONT ROOMS AND FESTIVALS

There is a large contingent of non-professional musicians, and, in Peruvian cities, the middle class often perform in impromptu ensembles **at home** in their living rooms. They tend to play *huaynos* or *chicha*, styles accompanied by falsetto singing in Spanish or Quechna, and often a mixture of both.

The only way to hear a performance in someone's living room is, of course, to get yourself invited. Fortunately, this isn't difficult to do in the Andes, where only a committed sociopath could avoid making friends. To speed the process, bring alcohol with you, accept every drink offered, be sure to encourage others to drink from your bottle, eat everything served to you, and ask to learn the words and sing along. You'll quickly pick up the dance steps.

For the less gregarious, **festivals** are an equally rewarding source of traditional music. One of the best takes place in January on the **Isla Amantaní** in Lake Titicaca, its exact date, as is often the case in the Andean highlands, determined by astronomical events. This particular festival occurs during a period often called the "time of protection" when the rainy season has finally begun. It is related to the cleansing of the pasturage and water sources; stone fences are repaired, walking paths repaved, and the stone effigies and crosses that guard the planting fields replaced or repaired. A single-file "parade" of individuals covers the entire island, stopping to appease the deities and provide necessary maintenance at each site. At the front are local non-professional musicians, all male, playing drums and flutes of various types.

There are, too, festivals that are celebrated on a larger scale. On the day of the June solstice (midwinter in the Andes) the Inca would ceremonially tie the sun to a stone and coax it to return south, bringing warmer weather and the new planting season. **Inti Raymi**, the Festival of the Sun, is still observed in every nook and cranny in the Andean republics, from the capital city to the most isolated hamlet. The celebration, following a solemn ritual that may include a llama sacrifice, is more of a carnival than anything else. Parades of musicians, both professional bands and thrown-together collages of amateurs, fill the streets. You will be expected to drink and dance until you drop, or hide in your room. This kind of party can run several days, so be prepared. Anyone spending more than two weeks in the Andes is almost bound to witness a festival of some sort.

Written by Jan Fairley, with thanks to Thomas Turino and Raúl Romero, Gilka Wara Céspedes, Martin Morales and Margaret Bullen. Adapted from the Rough Guide to World Music, *Vol 2.*

WILDLIFE AND ECOLOGY

Peru boasts what is probably the most diverse array of wildlife of any country on earth; its varied ecological niches span an incredible range of climate and terrain. And although mankind has occupied the area for perhaps twenty thousand years, there has been less disturbance there, until relatively recently, than in most other parts of our planet. For the sake of organization this piece follows the country's usual regional divisions – coastal desert, Andes mountains and tropical jungle – though a more accurate picture would be that of a continuous intergradation, encompassing literally dozens of unique habitats. From desert the land climbs rapidly to the tundra of mountain peaks, then down again into tropical rainforest, moving gradually through a whole series of environments in which many of the species detailed below overlap.

THE COAST

The **coastal desert** is characterized by an abundant sea life and by the contrasting scarcity of terrestrial plants and animals. The Humboldt Current runs virtually the length of Peru, bringing cold water up from the depths of the Pacific Ocean and causing any moisture to condense out over the sea, depriving the mainland coastal strip and lower western mountain slopes of rainfall. Along with this cold water, large quantities of nutrients are carried up to

the surface, helping to sustain a rich planktonic community able to support vast numbers of fish, preyed upon in their turn by a variety of coastal birds: **gulls, terns, pelicans, boobies, cormorants** and wading birds are always present along the beaches. One beautiful specimen, the **Inca tern**, although usually well camouflaged as it sits high up on inaccessible sea cliffs, is nevertheless very common in the Lima area. The **Humboldt penguin**, with grey rather than black features, is a rarer sight – shyer than its more southerly cousins, it is normally found in isolated rocky coves or on off-shore islands. Competing with the birds for fish are schools of **dolphins, sea lion** colonies and the occasional coastal **otter**. Dolphins and sea lions are often spotted off even the most crowded of beaches or scavenging around the fishermen's jetty at Chorrillos, near Lima.

One of the most fascinating features of Peruvian bird life is the vast, high-density colonies: although the number of species is quite small, their total population is enormous. Many thousands of birds can be seen nesting on islands like the Ballestas, off the **Paracas Peninsula**, or simply covering the ocean with a flapping, diving carpet of energetic feathers. This huge bird population, and the **Guanay cormorant** in particular, is responsible for depositing mountains of guano (bird droppings), which form a traditional and potent source of natural fertilizer.

In contrast to the rich coastal waters the **desert** lies stark and barren. Here you find only a few trees and shrubs; you'll need endless patience to find wild animals other than birds. The most common animals are feral **goats**, once domesticated but now living wild, and **burros** (or donkeys) introduced by the Spanish. A more exciting sight is the attractively coloured **coral snake** – shy but deadly and covered with black-and-orange hoops. Most animals are more active after sunset; when out in the desert you can hear the eerily plaintive call of the Huerequeque (or **Peruvian thick-knee** bird), and the barking of the little **desert fox** – alarmingly similar to the sound of car tyres screeching to a halt. By day there are several species of small birds, a favourite being the vermilion-headed **Peruvian fly-catcher**. Near water – rivers, estuaries, and lagoons – desert wildlife is at its most populous. In addition to residents such as **flamingos, herons** and

egrets, many migrant birds pause in these havens between October and March on their journeys south and then back north.

In order to understand the coastal desert you have to bear in mind the phenomenon of **El Niño**, a periodic climatic shift caused by the displacement of the cold Humboldt Current by warmer equatorial waters; it last occurred in 1998. This causes the plankton and fish communities either to disperse to other locations or to collapse entirely. At such a period the shore rapidly becomes littered with carrion since many of the sea mammals and birds are unable to survive in the much tighter environment. Scavenging condors and vultures, on the other hand, thrive, as does the desert where rain falls in deluges along the coast, with a consequent bloom of vegetation and rapid growth in animal populations. When the Humboldt Current returns, the desert dries up, its animal populations decline to normal sizes (another temporary feast for the scavengers), and at least ten years usually pass before the cycle is repeated. Generally considered a freak phenomenon, El Niño is probably better understood as an integral part of coastal ecology; without it the desert would be a far more barren and static environment, virtually incapable of supporting life.

THE MOUNTAINS

In the **Peruvian Andes** there is an incredible variety of habitats. That this is a mountain area of true extremes, immediately obvious if you fly across, or along, the Andes towards Lima – the land below shifting from high puna to cloud forest to riparian valleys and eucalyptus tracts (introduced from Australia in the 1880s). The complexity of the whole makes it incredibly difficult to formulate any overall description that isn't essentially misleading: climate and vegetation vary according to altitude, latitude and local characteristics.

The Andes divides vertically into three main regions, identified by the Incas from top to bottom as the Puna, the Qeswa and the Yunka. The **Puna,** roughly 3800–4300m above sea level, has an average temperature of 3–6°C, and annual rainfall of 500–1000mm. Typical animals here include the main Peruvian cameloids – llamas, alpacas, guanacos and vicuñas – while crops that grow well here include the potato and quinoa grain. At 2500–3500m, the **Qeswa**

has average temperatures of around 13°C, and a similar level of rainfall at 500–1200mm. The traditional forest here, including Andean pines, is not abundant and has been largely displaced by the imported Australian Eucalyptus trees; the main cultivated crops include maize, potatoes and the nutritious kiwicha grain. The *ceja de selva* (cloud forest) to high forest on the eastern side of the Andes in the relatively low-lying **Yunka**, at 1200–2500m, has at least twice as much rain as the other two regions and abundant wildlife, including Peru's national bird, the red-crested Gallito de las Rocas (Cock-of-the-Rocks). Plant life, too, is prolific, not least of all its orchids. On the western side of the Andes there is much less rainfall and it's not technically known as the Yunca, but it does share some characteristics: both sides have wild river canes (*caña brava*), and both are suitable for cultivating bananas, pineapples, yuca and coca.

Much of the Andes has been settled for over two thousand years – and hunter tribes go back another eight thousand years before this – so larger predators are rare, though still present in small numbers in the more remote regions. Among the most exciting you might actually see are the **mountain cats**, especially the **puma**, which lives at most altitudes and in a surprising number of habitats. Other more remote predators include the shaggy-looking **maned wolf** and the likeable **spectacled bear**, which inhabits the moister forested areas of the Andes and actually prefers eating vegetation to people.

The most visible animals in the mountains, besides sheep and cattle, are the cameloids – the wild **vicuña** and **guanaco**, and the domesticated **llama** and **alpaca**. Although these species are clearly related, zoologists disagree on whether or not the alpaca and llama are domesticated forms of their wild relatives. Domesticated they are, however, and have been so for thousands of years; studies reveal that cameloids appeared in North America some 40–50 million years ago, crossing the Bering Straits long before any humans did. From these early forms the present species has evolved in Peru, Bolivia, Chile, Argentina and Ecuador, and there are now over three million llamas today – 33 percent in Peru and a further 63 percent over the border in Bolivia. The alpaca population is bubbling under four million, with 87 percent in Peru and only 11 percent in Bolivia.

Of the two wild cameloids, the vicuña is the smaller and rarer, living only at the highest altitudes (up to 4500m) and with a population of just over 100,000, although its numbers are stronger in Peru than the guanaco, of which there are around 4000 here (there are over 500,000 in Argentina alone).

Andean deer are quite common in the higher valley and with luck you might even come across the rare **mountain tapir**. Smaller animals tend to be confined to particular habitats – rabbit-like **viscachas**, for example, to rocky outcrops; **squirrels** to wooded valleys; and **chinchillas** (Peruvian chipmunks) to higher altitudes

Most birds also tend to restrict themselves to specific habitats. The **Andean goose** and **duck** are quite common in marshy areas, along with many species of waders and migratory waterfowl. A particular favourite is the elegant, very pink, **Andean flamingo**, which can usually be spotted from the road between Arequipa and Puno where they turn Lake Salinas into one great red mass. In addition, many species of passarines can be found alongside small streams. Perhaps the most striking of them is the **dipper**, which hunts underwater for larval insects along the stream bed, popping up to a rock every so often for air and a rest. At lower elevations, especially in and around cultivated areas, the **ovenbird** (or Horneo) constructs its nest from mud and grasses in the shape of an old-fashioned oven; while in open spaces many birds of prey can be spotted, the comical **caracaras, buzzard-eagles** and the magical **red-backed hawks** among them. The **Andean Condor** (see "Birds", p.460) is actually quite difficult to see up close to hand as, although not especially rare, they tend to soar at tremendous heights for most of the day, landing only on high, inaccessible cliffs, or at carcasses after making sure that no one is around to disturb them. A glimpse of this magnificent bird soaring overhead will come only through frequent searching with binoculars, perhaps in relatively unpopulated areas, or at one of the better-known sites such as the Curz del Condor viewing platform in the Colca Canyon (see p.220).

TROPICAL RAINFOREST

Descending the eastern edge of the Andes, you pass through the distinct habitats of the Puna, Qeswa and Yunka before reaching the lowland jungle or rainforest. In spite of its rich and luxuriant appearance, the **rainforest** is in fact extremely fragile. Almost all the nutrients are recycled by rapid decomposition, with the aid of the damp climate and a prodigious supply of insect labour, back into the vegetation – thereby creating a nutrient-poor soil that is highly susceptible to large-scale disturbance. When the forest is cleared, for example, usually in an attempt to colonize the area and turn it into viable farmland, there is not only heavy soil erosion to contend with but also a limited amount of nutrients in the earth, only enough for five years of good harvests and twenty years' poorer farming at the most. Natives of the rainforest have evolved cultural mechanisms by which, on the whole, these problems are avoided: they tend to live in small, dispersed groups, move their gardens every few years and obey sophisticated social controls to limit the chances of overhunting any one zone or any particular species.

Around eighty percent of the Amazon rainforest was still intact at the start of the twenty first century, but for every hardwood logged in this forest, an average of 120 other trees are detroyed and left unused or simply burnt. Over an acre per second of this magnificent forest is burned or bulldozed, equating to an area the size of Great Britain, every year, even though this doesn't make ecomomic sense. According to the late rainforest specialist Dr Alwyn Gentry, just one hectare of primary rainforest could yield up to $9000 a year from sustainable harvesting of wild fruits, saps, resins and timber – yet the average income per hecatre from ranching or plantations in the Amazon is a meagre $30 a year.

AMAZON FLORA AND FAUNA

The most distinctive attribute of the Amazon Basin is its overwhelming abundance of plant and animal species. Over six thousand species of plant have been reported from one small 250-acre tract of forest, and there are at least a thousand species of birds and dozens of types of monkeys and bats spread about the Peruvian Amazon. There are several reasons for this marvellous natural diversity of flora and fauna. Most obviously, it is warm, there is abundant sunlight, and large quantities of mineral nutrients are washed down from the Andes – all of which help to produce the ideal conditions for forest growth. Secondly, the rainforest has enormous structural diversity, with layers of vegetation from the forest floor to the canopy 30m above providing a vast number of niches to fill. Thirdly, since there is such a variety of habitat as you descend the Andes, the changes in altitude mean a great diversity of localized ecosystems.

The great diversity of flora has assisted the evolution of equally varied wildlife in the Amazon. With the rainforest being stable over longer periods of time than temperate areas (there was no Ice Age here, nor any prolonged period of drought), the fauna has had freedom to evolve, and to adapt to often very specialized local conditions. But if the Amazon Basin is where most of the plant and animal species are in Peru, it is not easy to see them. Movement through the vegetation is limited to narrow trails and along the rivers from a boat. The river banks and flood plains are richly diverse areas: here you are likely to see **caimans, macaws, toucans, oropendulas, terns, horned screamers** and the primitive **hoatzins** – birds whose young are born with claws at the wrist to enable them to climb up from the water into the branches of overhanging trees. You should catch sight, too, of one of a variety of **hawks** and at least two or three species of **monkeys** (perhaps the **spider monkey**, the **howler**, or the **capuchin**). And with a lot of luck and more determined observation you may spot a rare **giant river otter, river dolphin, capybara**, or maybe even one of the **jungle cats**.

In the jungle proper you're more likely to find mammals such as the **pecary** (wild pig), **tapir, tamandua tree sloth** and the second largest cat in the world, the incredibly powerful **spotted jaguar**. Characteristic of the deeper forest zones too are many species of birds, including **hummingbirds** (more common in the forested Andean foothills), **manakins** and **trogons**, though the effects of widespread hunting make it difficult to see these around any of the larger settlements. Logging is proving to be another major problem for the forest wildlife since with the valuable trees dispersed among vast areas of other species in the rainforest, a very large area must be disturbed to yield a relatively small amount of timber. Deeper into the forest, however, and the further you are from human habitation, a glimpse of any of these animals is

quite possible. Most of the bird activity occurs in the canopy, 30–40m above the ground, but with such platforms as the ACEER Canopy Walkway (see p.409), things are a little easier.

AMAZON FLORA

Aguaje Palm (*Mauritia flexuosa*). A tropical swamp plant, commonly growing up to 15m tall, with fan-shaped leaves that can be be over 2m long and barrel-shaped 6–7cm-long fruit with a purple, plastic-like skin. Beneath this, the thin layer of yellow pulp is consumed raw, made into a drink, or used to flavour ice cream. The leaves can be used for roof-thatch or, more commonly, floor-matting. Younger leafs are utilised to make ropes, hammocks, net bags and sometimes baskets.

Ayahuasca (*Banisteriopsis caapi*). Interpreted from Quechna as "Vine of the Soul" or "Vine of the Dead", this is is found exclusively in northwest Amazonia and is also called *yage* and *caap*. These names also refer to the hallucinogenioc brew, in which ayahuasca is the main ingredient, used widely in the Peruvian Amazon and by *curanderos*.

Brazil nut trees (*Bertholletia excelsa*). Up to 30m tall, these take over ten years to reach nut-bearing maturity, when a single specimen can produce over 450kg every year during the rainy season.

Breadfruits (*Artocarpus altilis*). The tree known locally *as Pan del Arbol*, related to the rubber tree, is cut open and dried so that the large brown beans can be taken and boiled for eating. Only in central America are the whole fruits eaten and even in Peru, people only bother with these when they are out of bananas and *yuca* (manioc). The sap is a good medicine for hernias.

Caimetillo Some spots in the primary forest are devoid of ground growth apart from this one species of small tree. Many Indians see these glades as *supay chacras* ("demons' gardens") and they keep away from them at night. The scientific explanation is the azteca ant that lives on them has such acidic faeces that nothing else can grow where they live.

Capirona Related to the eucalyptus, this tree protects itself from insects by shedding its bark every 2–3 months. A fast grower, achieving 12m in just 5 years, it burns long and well and is consequently sold as firewood. Its sap can be applied to the throat for laryngitis, or mixed with lime and used as a gargle.

Catahua (*Eurocrypitan*). A large, hard-wood emergent tree reaching nearly 50m, this tree depends on the Saki monkey for reproduction and seed dispersal. It's fruits are poisonous to most other animals.

Charapilla A gigantic tree, characterized by its 6m base and a trunk over 1m in diameter. One of the hardest trees in the Iquitos region, it is rarely cut for timber because of its light yellowy colour. Young Conibo warriors were once tested for their strength and ability by how long they took to cut through the wood of ones that had already fallen. The fruit is eaten roasted, although the Achual of the Río Tigre prefer to eat them raw. The leaves are small and used for birth control by the Conibo.

Coca Cocaine is just one of the alkaloids in coca leaves, which are traditionally sacred to Andeans. A vital aid in withstanding the altitude, climate and rigours of the region, they help withstand low temperatures and act as a hunger depressant. Research also shows that they have an nutritional value, containing more calcium than any other edible plant, which is important in the Andes, an area with few dairy foods.

Epiphytes Often shrub-like plants, epiphytes live in the crowns or branching elbows of trees but are functionally independent of them. In the higher jungle areas, they are extremely common and diverse, encompassing various species of orchids, cacti, bromeliads and aroids. There are over 500 varieties of orchids recorded in the Amazon, many of these are to be found in the *ceja de selva*.

Genipap (*Genipa americana*). Also called *Huito*, this is related to coffee but is quite different. Growing up to 20m, this has small creamy flowers and fruit that's eaten ripe or used to make an alcoholic drink that alleviates arthritic pains and bronchial ailments. Unripe juice is taken for stomach ulcers. The sap turns from transparent to blue-black after exposure to the air and is used as a dye, or body and face paint.

Inga (*Inga edulis*). Belonging to the mimosa family and growing to over 35m, there are over 350 species in the Inga genus. Its most distinc-

tive feature is its long bean pods containing sweet white pulp and large seeds, which some Indian groups use to treat dysentry.

Manioc The most important of cultivated plants in the Peruvian Amazon, and known in Peru as *yuca*, it's most useful parts are the large, phallic-shaped tuber roots, the brunt of many indigenous jokes. High in carbohydrates and enzynmes, which assist disgestion of other foods, it is roasted (to get rid of the cyanide it contains) or brewed to make *masato* beer. It is also the basis of tapioca. As far as its medicinal functions go, the juice from these tubers is applied as a head wash for scabies or can be mixed with water to ease diarrhoea.

Monkey-ladder vine (*Leguminosae casalpinioideae*). Also known as the Turtle-ladder vine, this unusual looking vine spirals high up to blossom in the canopy of primary forests.

Peach Palm Also known as the Pihuayao, and common in most areas of the Peruvian rainforest, its new shoots are the source for the Yaguar and Witoto Indians' "grass" skirts and headdresses. The bark of the stems is used for interior wall partitions in native houses. The cork-like insides of the stems are made into sleeping mats, a particularly important symbol of marriage among the Achual trine along the Río Tigre. From its fallen trunks, the larvae of beetles are gathered as a delicacy by many indigenous groups.

Quinilla This yellow flowering tree is easy to spot, not so much by its tall, straight 40m trunk, but by the sweetly scented carpet of flowers beneath it, or the yellow, cauliform patterns of its canopy, seen when flying over the forest.

Rubber trees (*Hevea brasiliensis*). Known as *jebe* in Peru and *seringuera* closer to the Brazilian border, as a valuable export these trees were the key to the Amazon's initial exploitation.

Sabre Pentana (*Lupuna*). A soft-wood tree, mainly used as ply and now in danger of extinction, this is still one of the most impressive plants in the Peruvian Amazon at nearly 50m tall and home to Harpy Eagles, which nest in the same tree for life (if the tree is felled, the bird dies with it by refusing to eat again). The trees are scattered across the forest and are sometimes used by Indians as landmarks when travelling along the rivers.

Stilt Palm (*Socratea exorrhiza*). Also abundant in the Amazon, reaching heights of up to 15m, with a thin trunk and very thorny stilt roots that grow like a tipi above the ground. Its long thin leaves are used by some indigenous groups as a treatment for hepatitis. The most utilised part is the hard bark, which can be taken off in one piece for use as flooring or wall slats.

Thatch Palm (*Lepidocaryum tenue*). A relatively thin plant growing to around 4m and with a noticeably ringed trunk. Its leaves are used as roof thatch throughout the Peruvian Amazon.

Ungurahui Palm (*Oenocarpus bataua*). The rotting trunks of this palm are home to the suri larvae of the Rhinoceros beetle, a favoured food of local Indians. Its green fruits can also be squeezed for their oil, which is used to treat vomiting, diarrhoea and even malaria. The trunk and leaves are often used in house construction.

Walking Palm (*Socratea exercisia*). The wood is often used for parqué flooring. Tradition has it that it developed spikes to protect itself against the now extinct Giant Sloth, which used to push them over.

Wild mango (*Grias neuberthii*). The wild mango tree is frequently seen as an ornamental plant around rainforest lodges. A member of the Brazil nut family, it's actually unrelated to the true mango (*Mangifera indica*), but can grow up to 20m, with thin, spindly trunks and branches. Their delicate yellow flowers are odorous, but the fruit can be eaten raw, boiled or roasted and has a medicinal function as a purgative; the seed is grated to treat veneral tumours and associated fevers, as well as being used as an enema to cure dysentery. The bark can be used to induce vomiting.

AMAZON FAUNA

Anteaters. There are four main types of anteater in Peru; all have powerful curved front claws but no teeth, instead using their long tongues to catch insects in holes and rotting vegetation, and share long, tube-like snouts. They only have one baby at a time which clings to the mother's back when they move through the forest. Giant Anteaters (*Myrmecophaga tridactyla*), which can be 2m long with hairy non-prehensile tails, are black, orange-brown and whiteish, with a a diagonal black-and-white shoulder stripe. Solitary creatures, they can be seen day or night, and, while normally passive, can defend themselves easily with their powerful front legs. Collared Anteaters, or Southern Tamandua (*Tamandua tetradactlya*), are smaller, at less than 1m long. Arboreal and terrestrial, they too are nocturnal and diurnal, though they move slowly as they have poor eyesight. Northern Tamandua (*Tamandua mexicana*) are restricted to the northern jungles in Peru. The Silky or Pygmy Anteater (*Cyclopes didactylus*) is quite small, rarely exceeding 25cm in length. It's a smoky grey to golden colour on the upper parts, sometimes with dark brown stripes from its shoulders to its rear. It's also distinguished by the soft whistling noise it makes.

Armadillos. Of the Giant Armadillos and Nine-banded Long-nosed Armadillos, the former are up to 1m long, the latter usually half this. Both are covered in bony armour and have small heads with wide set ears and have grey to yellow colouring. Mostly nocturnal, they tend to feed on ants and termites, some fruit and even small prey. Giant Armadillos are good diggers and live in burrows.

Bats. Bat species comprise almost 40 percent of all mammals in the Amazon, and all North, Central and South American bats belong to the suborder *Microchiroptera*. Vampire bats, which feed on the blood of mammals, are known to transmit rabies and are commonest in cattle-ranching areas rather than remote forest zones.

Brazilian tapir (*Tapirus terrestris*). Known as *sachavaca* ("forest cow" in Quechua) in Peru, this is the largest forest land mammal at around 2m long, brown to dark grey in colour and with a large upper lip. Their tails are stumpy, their feet three-toed and their backs noticeably convex. Largely nocturnal, they browse swampy forests for fruit and grasses.

Capaybara (*Hydrochaeris hydrochaeris*). The world's largest (but friendly) rodent, the tan or grey capaybara can be over 1m and will give warning yelps to its family when scared. They eat aquatic vegetaion and grasses, but are also known to fish and eat lizards when they come across them.

Dolphins. The Pink River Dolphin (*Inia geoffrensis*) is about 2m long and has a noticeable dorsal fin. They feed exclusively on fish and will swim with or within a few metres of people. The smaller Grey Dolphin or Tucuxi (*Sotalia fluviatilis*) achieves a maximum length of 1.5m and has a more prominent dorsal fin, and usually jumps further and is more acrobatic than the Pink Dolphin.

Giant otter (*Pteronura brasiliensis*). Just over 1m long, ending in a thickish tail with a flattened tip. Their alarm call is a snort and they are very aggressive when in danger. They eat fish and move in extended family groups, with the males doing the least fishing but the most eating.

Manatee (*Trichechus inunguis*). Almost 3m in length, with a large tubular body, a flat tail, short front flippers and a whiskery face, this aqautic mammal is relatively common in the Iquitos area. They feed on water hyacinths and other aquatic vegetation, taking advantage in high water season to graze on the flooded riverside floor.

Paca (*Agouti paca*). Chestnut brown and white-striped, this large, fat rat- and pig-like creature has plenty of flesh but a tiny tail, hardly visible beneath the rump hair. It's primarily nocturnal and feeds on roots and fallen fruit.

Peccaries (*Tayassuidae*). Peccaries, or wild boar, are stocky with relatively spindly legs and biggish heads. The White-lipped peccary (*Tayassu pecari*) is up to 1m long and moves quickly in dangerous herds of fifty to a few hundred. Their diet is of fruit and palm nuts, which they scour vast tracts of forest to find. The Collared peccary (*Tayassu tajacu*) is smaller and moves in groups of five to twenty.

Red brocket deer (*Mazama americana*). Rarely much over 1m in length, these are mostly brown to grey, with large eyes and the males have unbranched antlers which slope back. They are found in the forest or at waterholes, feeding on fruit and fungi.

Sloths. The most common sloth in Peru is the Brown-throated Three-toed Sloth (*Bradypus variegatus*). Up to 1m in length, they have small, round heads and whitish or brown faces with a short tail and long limbs. Their claws help them cling to branches, where they spend most of their time sleeping, but their slow movement makes them hard to spot (though you may see them around jungle lodges, where they are often kept as pets).

CATS

Large cats in Peru include the black, elongated **Jaguarundi** (*Felis yagouaroundi*) and the slender, spotty **Margay** (*Felis wieldii*). But better known are the **Ocelots** (*Felis pardalis*), smallish with black spots and thin stripes on their torso, with short tails and long slender legs. Operating by day and night, they hunt rodents, lizards and birds, mostly in the rainforest.

Jaguar (*Pantera onca*). Powerfully built, jaguars are almost 2m long, with black spots on silvery to tan fur, they hunt large mammals, though they do fish too. Mainly rainforest dwellers, they are most frequently spotted sunning themselves on fallen trees. If you meet one, the best way to react is to make lots of noise.

Pumas (*Felis concolor*). Brown to tan in colour, pumas hunt by day and night, preferring large mammals, but stooping to snakes, lizards and rats. They're most likely to be encountered in the Andes, and although wary of humans, can be dangerous. Guides advise waving one's arms around and shouting in these situations.

PRIMATES

All South American primates are monkeys, which form a group of their own – **Platyrrhini** – subdividing into three main families: Marmosets and tamarins (*Callitrichidae*); Monkeys (*Cebidae*); and the Goeldi's Monkey (*Callimiconidae*). Each of these has many types within it.

Capuchin Monkeys (*Cebus apella*). Reddish brown, with a black cap and paler shoulders, this noisy creature moves in groups of up to twenty while searching for fruit, palm nuts, birds' eggs and small lizards.

Dusky Titi Monkey (*Callicebus moloch*). The necks of these reddish brown creatures are hidden by thick fur, giving them a stocky appearance belied by their hairless faces. Eating leaves and fruit, they are found in dense forest near swamps, or bamboo thickets beside rivers.

Pygmy Marmosets (*Cebuella pygmaea*). These rarely achieve more than 15cm in length, and are distinguished by their tawny to golden-grey head and forequarters and mane of hair, plus slender tails. Found in the lower understorey of the trees in flood forests, they feed on tree sap, insects and fruit.

Saddle-backed Tamarin (*Saguinus fuscicollis*). The most widespread species of Tamarin in the forests of Manu and around Iquitos, though there are a further thirteen subspecies of these. Black to reddish brown, they are diurnal and arboreal, living under the tree canopy and eating nectar, fruit and insects.

Spider monkeys (*Ateles paniscus*). These are entirely black, with a small head and long arms, legs and tail, and can be seen swinging through the primary forest in groups of up to twenty. Highly sociable, intelligent and noisy, they feed on fruit, flowers and leaves.

Woolly Monkey (*Lagothrix lagothricha*). Mostly brown, they have a strong tail, which helps them travel through the upper and middle storeys of the forest in groups of up to sixty. They eat fruit, palm nuts, seeds and leaves and are found in primary forest, including wooded flood plains.

BIRDS

Andean Condor (*Vultur Gryphus*). Up to 1.3m long, with a wingspan of 3.5m and mostly black with a white neck ruff and white wing feathers, these are rarely seen in groups of more than two or three. Their habitat is mainly at 2000–5000m, but they are also seen on the coast of Peru, feeding off carrion.

Black-headed Cotingas (*Cotingidae*). Related to flycatchers, they have a symbiotic relationship with a number of fruiting trees. The Scaled Fruiteater (*Ampelioden tschudii*) is frequently seen in the upper canopy, usually alone but sometimes in pairs or, less frequently, in large mixed flocks.

Curassow (*Crax mitu*). Their well-developed crests are mainly black, with a shiny blue mantle and both the bill and legs are red. Their booming song can be heard as they move in small flocks of 2–5 birds.

Fasciated Tiger-Herons (*Tigrisoma fasciatum*). Graceful river birds with short, dusky bills and a black crown, named for the stripy appearance of their rufous and white underparts.

Hawk (*Buteo magnirostris*). Grey to brown in colour, these are not great flyers or hunters, depending mainly on insects, vertebrates and small birds.

Hoatzin (*Opisthocomus hoazin*) Up to 0.5 long, their most distinctive features are long mohican crests and hooks which the young have on their shoulders. Also, they haven't evolved full stomachs and their chromosomes are close to those of chickens. Usually spotted in sizeable and gregarious gangs, they are poor flyers and hide in swampy areas. Indians use Hoatzins' feathers for arrow flights.

Hummingbird (*Trochilidae*). Distinguished by the fastest metabolisms and wing beats of any bird (up to 80 per second) and the ability to rotatae their wings through 180 degrees, some varieties are the smallest birds in the world. Many tribes have a special place for hummingbirds in their belief-system.

Macaws (*Psittacidae*). Noisy, gregarious creatures with strong bills, macaws mate for life (which can be as long as 100 years), and pairs fly among larger flocks. Common macaws in Peru include the Blue-and-yellow Macaw (*Ara ararauna*) which grows to 33" and has a very long pointed tail, the Scarlet Macaw (*Ara macao*); and the Red-and-green Macaw (*Ara cloroptera*).

Nunbirds With slender red bills and mostly black in plumage, Black-fronted nunbirds (*Monasa nigrifrons*) are found in ones or twos at all levels of the rainforest and are noted for their noisy performance in the early evenings. White-fronted Nunbirds (*Monasa morpheous*) are slightly smaller and with a white forehead but are similar in behaviour.

Oropendulas (*Icteridae*). Related to the blackbird family, these like living near human habitations, their vibrant croaking making them unmistakable. One of the commonest varieties is the large Black Oropendula (*Gymnostinaps guatimoziuus*), which has with a long briliant lemon-yellow tail, with two black central tail feathers.

Swainson's Thrush (*Catharus ustulatus*). Small in stature but magnificent in voice, this timid, solitary bird lives mainly in lower primary forest. The Lawrence Thrush is able to imitate other bird calls (over 100 have been noted from one bird alone).

Tinamous (*Tinamidae*). Rather like chickens with long beaks, the many varieties include the rare Black Tinamou (*Tinamus osgoodi*), the Great Tinamou (*Tinamus major*), noted for its tremulous whistling noises, and the Gray Tinamou (*Tinamos tao*), similar in behaviour to the Great Timamou.

Toucans (*Ramphastidae*). Unmistakable for their colourful plumage and large bill, there are many varieties. One of the more common is the White-throated Toucan (*Ramphastos tucanus*), also one of the largest, mainly black but with bursts of orange and red and a white throat and chest. Rarer and smaller is the Yellow-ridged Toucan (*Ramphastos culminatus*), with a distinctive yellow ridge across the top and a yellow and blue band close to the eyes.

Trumpeters (*Psophiidae*). Common, largely terrestrial birds that eat vegetation, small lizards and shiny objects (gold, silver and sometimes diamonds), they are often kept as pets in Indian and colonist settlements. The Grey-winged Trumpeter (*Psophia crepitans*) tends to be recognized by its nocturnal gutteral sounds, which sound like the loud purring of a cat. Grey in the wild, its wings turn white in captivity.

Vultures (*Cathartidae*). Carrion eaters, this family includes the Andean Condor (see opposite) and the stunning King Vulture (*Sarcoramphus papa*), which has mainly white plumage with black rump, tail and flight feathers. It's mostly spotted in solitary flight and sometimes in pairs. Other vultures include the Turkey Vulture (*Cathartes aura*), the Greater Yellow-headed Vulture (*Cathartes melambrotus*), the Lesser Yellow-headed Vulture (*Cathartes burrovianus*), and the Black Vulture (*Coragyps atratus*) seen around every rubbish dump throughout Peru.

REPTILES AND AMPHIBIANS

Amphibians. Frogs grow to surprising sizes in Peru. Most are nocturnal and their chorus is heard along every Amazonian river after sunset. The most commonly spotted is the Cane Toad (*Bufo marinus*), which secretes toxins that protects them. More common still is the Leaf-litter Dweller (*Bufo typhonius*) but it's harder to spot as it imitates the colours and forms of dead leaves.

Caiman (*Alligatoridae*). There are four types of caiman in Peru. The Black caiman (*Melanosuchus niger*) is increasingly rare due to hunting, while the Spectacled caiman (*Caiman crocodilus*) is usually sunbathing along river beaches. The smaller Musky caiman and Smooth-fronted caiman are found in small tributaries and lakes.

Iguanas. Often reaching 2–3ft long and marked by a spiky crest along their backs, these are wholly vegetarian leaf eaters which can be seen sleeping on high branches soaking up the sun. Less often they can be seen swimming in rivers, mainly to get away from predators, such as hawks.

Snakes. Peru has the world's widest variety of snakes, but it's rare to meet these anacondas, rainbow boas (*Epicrates cenchria*), fer-de-lances (*Bothrops atrox*) or bushmasters (*Lachesis muta*) in the Amazon. Anacondas kill mainly by twisting their tails around tree roots in lakes or riverbanks, then floating out from this before attacking. They also stun fish by violently expelling air from their coiled bodies. Smaller snakes tend to be scared of people and you're more likely to see them in retreat than heading for you.

Yellow-footed tortoise (*Geochelone denticulata*). The only land tortoise in the Amazon, it can grow up to around 1m long but is generally half this size. In prehistoric times, however, they reached the proportions of a Volkswagen Beetle.

CONSERVATION ORGANIZATIONS IN PERU

Peruvian Association for the Conservation of Nature, APECO, Parque José Costa 187, Lima 17 (☎01/264-0094, *apeco@datos.limaperu.net*).

Conservation International, Chinchón 858-A, San Isidro, Lima (☎01/440-8967, *CI-PERU@ conservation.org.pe*).

Perú Verde (Green Peru), Manuel Bañón 461, San Isidro, Lima (☎01/440-2022, *postmaster@peruverde.com.pe*).

ProNaturaleza, Jiron Córdova 518, Miraflores, Lima (☎01/440-8205, *fpcn@mail.cosapidata.com.pe*).

Peruvian Society for Environmental Law, Prolongación Arenales 437, Miraflores, Lima (☎01/421-1394, *todos@spda2.org.pe*).

World Wide Foundation – Lima, Avenida San Felipe 720, Lima 11 (☎01/261-5300, *cathy.wwsopp@datos.limaperu.net*).

PREPARATION

As **preparation** for all this, **Lima Zoo**, in the Parque de las Leyerdas, is well worth a visit. It contains a good collection of most of the animals mentioned above, particularly the predators, and since there are few inexpensive or particularly handy field guides, this is the best way to familiarize yourself with what you might see during the rest of your journey. Be prepared, however, to see animals kept in appalling conditions. You might also check out the Natural History Museum in Lima and the Ministry of Agriculture's "Vida Silvestre" section for publications and off-prints on Peruvian flora and fauna. Relevant books are listed in the Books section (pp.473–474).

INDIGENOUS RIGHTS AND THE DESTRUCTION OF THE RAINFOREST

Within the next few decades Peru's jungle tribes may cease to exist as independent cultural and racial entities in the face of persistent and increasing pressure from external colonization. The indigenous people of the Peruvian jungles are being pushed off their land by an endless combination of slash-and-burn colonization, big oil companies, gold miners, timber extractors and coca-growing farmers organized by drug-trafficking barons and, at times, "revolutionary" political groups.

All along the main rivers and jungle roads, settlers are flooding into the area. In their wake, forcing land title agreements to which they have no right, are the main timber companies and multinational oil corporations. In large tracts of the jungle the fragile *selva* ecology has already been destroyed; in others the tribes have been more subtly disrupted by becoming dependent on outside consumer goods and trade or by the imposition of evangelical proselytizing groups, and the Indian way of life is being destroyed

The first **Law of Native Communities**, introduced in 1974, recognized the legal right of indigenous peoples to own lands that were held collectively and registered as such with the Ministry of Agriculture. Despite this recognition, however, the military government of the time wasn't trying to stop colonization. Such land titling as did occur was a two-edged sword – whilst it guaranteed a secure land base to some communities, it implied that land not so titled was unavailable to them, effectively making it available to colonization.

However, as the most significant legal tool they had in the 1970s, land rights legislation was adopted by the indigenous communities to help protect their territory, even if the creation of native communities as legal entities repre-

sented the imposition of a non-indigenous socio-political structure. New self-determination groups sprang up throughout the 1970s and 1980s, such as the Inter-ethnic Association for the Development of the Peruvian Amazon (AIDESEP) and the Coalition of Indigenous Nationalities of the Peruvian Amazon (CONAP). Since then more regional political structures have been established, usually based on natural geographical boundaries such as rivers. These function as intermediaries between the community and the national levels of Amazonian political organization.

In 1999, a new law was drafted claiming to be for the conservation, sustainable development and respect for indigenoius communities. Received with dismay by all the major organizations working in these fields, there were immediate strikes and protests throughout the Amazon region. However, it actually seemed to sidestep these basic issues and appeared to encourage investment in large-scale developments without regard for environmental issues, introducing tax breaks for private investors while failing to give the same benefits to locals. There appeared to have been no consultation with the regions involved, let alone with conservation organizations or the political organs of the indigenous population.

INDIAN RESISTANCE

Since the early 1970s, the indigenous rainforest nations, in particular the **Campa Ashaninka** from the much threatened central jungle area, have been co-ordinating opposition to these threats. Representatives, sometimes working in conjunction with indigenous political umbrella organizations, have gone increasingly regularly to Lima to get publicity and assert Indian claims to land. For the Ashaninka, this territorial struggle has been and continues to be for titles on the **Ene** and **Tambo**, the only regions left to them after four centuries of "civilizing" influence. In publicity terms they have met with some success. The exploitation of the forests has become a political issue, fuelled in the early 1980s within Peru (and outside) by the bizarre events surrounding Werner Herzog's filming of *Fitzcarraldo*, a film *about* exploitation of Indians, yet whose director so angered local commmunities that at one stage a whole production camp was burned down.

ASHANINKA PROJECTS

There are a number of **projects** working with the Ashaninka to rebuild their communities and strengthen their territorial and economic position. Contact the Rainforest Foundation in London (Suite A5, City Cloisters, 196 Old Street, London EC1V 9FR; *www.rainforestfoundationuk.org*) or the ACPC in Lima (*acpc@correo.dnet.com.pe*) for more information. There is also an **Ashaninka web site** at *www.rcp.net.pe/ashaninka*.

With the rise of Sendero Luminoso things got much worse for some indigenous Peruvian Amazon groups. Again, the Ashaninka suffered greatly because of their close proximity to the Sendero heartlands. Sendero are now virtually extinct, due in part to the fierce stand taken by the Ashaninka themselves, and in the last six years, the Ashaninka have regained control of

AN AMARAKAERI INDIAN OF MADRE DE DIOS SPEAKS FOR HIMSELF

Below is an account by a local Amarakaeri Indian from the southeast province of Madre de Dios, a witness to the way of life that colonists and corporations are destroying. Originally given as testimony to a human rights movement in Lima, it is reprinted by permission of Survival International.

"We Indians were born, work, live, and die in the basin of the Madre de Dios River of Peru. It's our land – the only thing we have, with its plants, animals, and small farms: an environment we understand and use well. We are not like those from outside who want to clear everything away, destroying the richness and leaving the forest ruined forever. We respect the forest; we make it produce for us.

Many people ask why we want so much land. They think we do not work all of it. But we work it differently from them, conserving it so that it will continue to produce for our children and grandchildren. Although some people want to take it from us, they then destroy and abandon it, moving on elsewhere. But we can't do that; we were born in our woodlands. Without them we will die.

In contrast to other parts of the Peruvian jungle, Madre de Dios is still relatively sparsely populated. The woodlands are extensive, the soil's poor, so we work differently from those in other areas with greater population, less woodland, and more fertile soils. Our systems do not work without large expanses of land. The people who come from outside do not know how to make the best of natural resources here. Instead they devote themselves to taking away what nature gives and leave little or nothing behind. They take wood, nuts, and above all gold.

The man from the highlands works all day doing the same thing whether it is washing gold, cutting down trees, or something else. Bored, he chews his coca, eats badly, then gets ill and leaves. The engineers just drink their coffee and watch others working.

We also work these things but so as to allow the woodland to replenish itself. We cultivate our farms, hunt, fish and gather woodland fruits, so we do not have to bring in supplies from outside. We also make houses, canoes, educate our children, enjoy ourselves. In short we satisfy almost all our needs with our own work, and without destroying the environment.

In the upper Madre de Dios River wood is more important than gold, and the sawmill of Shintuya is one of the most productive in the region. Wood is also worked in other areas to make canoes and boats to sell, and for building houses for the outsiders. In the lower region of the river we gather nuts – another important part of our economy. Much is said about Madre de Dios being the forgotten Department of Peru. Yet we are not forgotten by people from outside nor by some national and foreign companies who try to seize our land and resources. Because of this we have formed the Federation of Indian Peoples of Madre de Dios to fight for the defence of our lands and resources.

Since 1974 we have been asking for legal property titles to the land we occupy in accordance with the Law of Indian Communities. The authorities always promise them to us, but so far only one of our communities has a title and that is to barely 5000 hectares.

You may ask why we want titles now if we had not had them before. The answer is that we now

much of the territory they had lost to the terrorists. The problem they face now is one of organized land invasions by settlers, many of these recalcitrant terrorists, frequently with the support of regional authorities. In many cases, the political revolutionary fervour of the late 1980s and early 1990s has been replaced by a spreading religious evangelicalism.

While the Indians have certainly undergone a radical growth in political awareness, in real terms they have made little progress. Former President Belaunde, whose promises of human rights in the late 1970s led to many thousands of Ashaninka making their way down to polling stations by raft to vote for him, has merely speeded up the process of colonization, and in the Ene region alone, the Indians face multinational claims to millions of acres of their territory. To make matters worse, President Fujimori changed the law in 1995 to allow colonization of Indian lands if they had been "unoccupied" for two years or more. Obviously, with many of the traditional rainforest Indians having a semi-nomadic existence, depending

---

have to defend our lands from many people who were not threatening us in the past.

In spite of journeys to Puerto Maldonado to demand guarantees from the authorities, they do not support us by removing the people who invade our land. On the contrary when we defend our land, forcing the invaders to retreat, they accuse us of being wild, fierce and savage.

Equally serious are invasions by gold-mining companies. The Peruvian State considers the issue of mining rights to be separate from that of land rights, and there are supposed to be laws giving priority to Indian communities for mining rights on their lands – but the authorities refuse to enforce them. Many people have illegally obtained rights to mine our lands, then they do not allow us to work there. Others, without rights, have simply installed themselves.

There are numerous examples I could give; yet when my community refused entry to a North American adventurer who wanted to install himself on our land, the Lima *Commercio* accused us of being savages, and of attacking him with arrows. Lies! All we did was defend our land against invaders who didn't even have legal mining rights – without using any weapons, although these men all carried their own guns.

We also suffer from forms of economic aggression. The prices of agricultural products we sell to the truck drivers and other traders in the area have recently been fixed by the authorities. For example, 25lb of yucca used to sell for 800 *soles*. Now we can only get 400 *soles*. Such low prices stop us developing our agriculture further, and we are not able to sell our products outside because we cannot cover our costs and minimal needs. On the other hand, the authorities have fixed the prices of wood and transport so that the amount that we can earn is continually diminishing. And the prices we have to pay for things we need from outside are always rising.

There are also problems with the National Park Police. They no longer allow us to fish with *barbasco* (fish poison) in the waters of our communities, although they are outside the National Park. They say that *barbasco* will destroy the fish. But we have fished this way for so long as we can remember, and the fish have not been destroyed. On the contrary: the fish are destroyed when people come from outside and overfish for commercial sale, especially when they use dynamite.

Our main source of food, after agriculture, is fishing – above all the boquichico which we fish with bow and arrow after throwing *barbasco*. We cannot stop eating, and we are not going to let them stop us from fishing with *barbasco* either!

There are so many more problems. If our economic position is bad, our social position is even worse. Traders reach the most remote areas, but medical facilities don't, even now with serious epidemics of malaria, measles, tuberculosis and intestinal parasites in the whole region. Our children go to primary schools in some communities, but often the schools are shut. And there are no secondary schools.

The commercial centres in the gold zone are areas of permanent drunkenness. Outsiders deceive and insult us and now some of our people no longer want to be known as Indians or speak our languages; they go to the large towns to hide from their origins and culture.

We are not opposed to others living and benefiting from the jungle, nor are we opposed to its development. On the contrary, what we want is that this development should benefit us, and not just the companies and colonists who come from outside. And we want the resources of the jungle to be conserved so that they can serve future generations of both colonists and Indians".

on hunting and gathering for survival, colonists can take over an area of forest claiming it as uninhabited, even though it's part of traditional territory. This particular law change particularly affected the Ashaninka, who had already been forced to leave their usual scattered settlements for self-protection against the terrorists. At the close of the twentieth century, they had largely moved back into their original settlements and territories, though closely followed by more waves of colonists. The civil war against Sendero, in which the Ashaninka played a significant role, did much to unite the traditionally scattered Ashaninka nation, but whether or not it has prepared them sufficiently well to hold things together remains to be seen.

POISON GOLD AND BLACK GOLD

At least as serious a threat to the indigenous peoples of the Peruvian rainforest are **oil exploration** and **gold mining**, which are an enormous potential threat to the rainforest in Peru.

As the danger from terrorism faded in the mid-1990s, Fujimori's politico-economic agenda opened the way for **oil and gas exploration**. Initially, the government appeared to be bending over backwards to assist multinationals exploit the reserves discovered, mainly in the Madre de Dios and Camisea areas. Only the Amazonian indigenous organizations and environmental conservationists were in opposition, and the momentum of fossil-fuel exploitation in the Peruvian Amazon has slowed right down for the moment, but this is more likely to be an unforeseen extension of Fujimori's policies than genuine concern, as the government was not prepared to offer the companies as big a monopoly over the Peruvian power-supply industry as they desired. Consequently, the multinationals pulled out of the Camisea project in mid-1998 after investing many millions, and substantially reduced their plans for the Madre de Dios region. The threat is still there, however – in 1999, the Peruvian Energy Minister claimed that there were over sixty companies expressing an interest in the Camisea gas reserves.

Illegal gold mining is at its worst in the south-eastern jungles of Madre de Dios, home to the Amarakaeri Indians, where monster-sized machinery is transforming one of the Amazon's most bio-diverse regions into a huge muddy scar. A number of gold miners have already moved into the unique Tambopata Reserved Zone, a protected jungle area where giant otters, howler monkeys, king vultures, anacondas and jaguars are regularly spotted.

All plant life around each mine is turned into gravel, known in Peru as *cancha*, for just a few ounces of gold a day. Front-loading machines move up to about 30m depth of soil, which is then washed on a wooden sluice where high-pressure hoses to separate the silt and gold from mud and gravel. Mercury, added at this stage to facilitate gold extraction, is later burnt off, causing river and air pollution. The mines are totally unregulated, and the richer, more established mining families tend to run the show, having the money to import large machines upriver from Brazil or by air from Chile.

The indigenous tribes are losing control of their territory to an ever-increasing stream of these miners and settlers coming down from the high Andes. As the mercury pollution and suspended mud from the mines upstream kill the life-giving rivers, they are having to go deeper and deeper into the forest for fish, traditionally their main source of protein. Beatings and death threats from the miners and police are not uncommon.

There is a hope that **improved gold-mining technology** can stem the tide of destruction in these areas. Mercury levels in Amazon rivers and their associated food chains are rising at an alarming rate. However, with raw mercury available for only $13 a kilo there is little obvious economic incentive to find ways of using less hazardous materials. Cleaner gold-mining techniques have, however, been developed in Brazil. Astonishingly simple, the new method utilizes a wooden sluice with a gentler slope (instead of a steeper, ridged slope) to extract the gold from the washed river sediment and gravel. Trials have shown that this increases gold yields by up to forty percent, and the addition of a simple sluice box at the base of the slope has also led to the recovery of some 95 percent of the mercury used in the process. The same project has also developed a procedure of test-boring to estimate quantities

SURVIVAL FOR TRIBAL PEOPLES

Survival for Tribal Peoples is a worldwide organization supporting tribal peoples, standing for their right to decide their own future and helping them protect their lives, lands and rights. Survival have been active in campaigning against the threats to tribal land and way of life posed by oil exploration and exploitation in Peru and have assisted the Ashaninka tribe over the years in their cause. For more information contact them at 11–15 Emerald St, London WC1N 3QL (☎020/ 7242-1441, fax 7242-1771, *survival@gn.apc.org*, *www.survival-international.org.uk*).

of gold in potential gravel deposits, which minimizes unnecessary and uneconomic earth moving in search for gold. If taken on board by gold miners in the Amazon and elsewhere, these techniques should reduce environmental damage. However, the fact remains that pressure by **international environmental groups**, and the publicity that they generate, continues to make a difference.

PERU'S WHITE GOLD

In recent decades, poverty and the promise of a better life has not only led thousands of Peruvian peasants down the road of guerrilla warfare and bloody terror. Many of them, sometimes the same individuals, have also transformed the most sacred plant of the Incas into one of the world's most commercial cash crops. Seen by many peasants as a road to fortune and freedom, for others cocaine is a scourge, bringing violence, the mobsters and deforestation in its wake.

The only people who make decent money engage in "cooking" **cocaine**. Illegal "kitchens", makeshift coke refineries, have become the main means of livelihood for many ordinary peasant families, as the equipment is simple – oil drums, a few chemicals, paraffin and a fire. Bushels of coca leaves are dissolved in paraffin and hydrochloric acid, heated, and stirred, eventually producing the pasta, which is then washed in ether or acetone to yield powdery white cocaine.

Peru's coca industry netted an estimated $3 billion in 1984 – twenty percent of the country's gross national product. By the end of the 1980s this figure was much higher and the problem had become an issue of global dimensions. However, a combination of market saturation and political pressure from the USA, backed up by anti-cocaine money and hardware like police helicopters, seems to have changed the situation substantially. In 1996 the Peruvian price of cocaine had dropped by over fifty percent on the street, down to almost $4 a gram. Colombian drug cartels were buying less from Peru, having been hit hardest by US anti-cocaine policies, and the protection once afforded by Sendero Luminoso terrorists had turned into more of a liability than anything else. By the end of the twentieth century there was also increasing US intervention, including aerial patrols over the northern jungle border between Peru and Colombia firing on unmarked planes that refuse to identify themselves. Production of cocaine in Peru has dropped further while it has started to rise in Colombia, and these lower levels of supply have brought Peru's internal price for

cocaine back up to a street level of $10 a gram. It seems unlikely that cocaine production will be reduced much further, since there are always new export opportunities and a steady home market; but the basic crop – coca plants – no longer offers quite the relatively stable, safe and so much more remunerative option to small-time cash-croppers that it did just a couple of years ago.

Coca, the plant from which cocaine is derived, has travelled a long way since the Incas distributed this "divine plant" across fourteenth-century Andean Peru. Presented as a gift from the gods, coca was used to exploit slave labour under the Spanish rule: without it the Indians would never have worked in the gruelling conditions of colonial mines such as Potosí.

The isolation of the active ingredient in coca, **cocaine**, in 1859, began an era of intense medical experimentation. Its numbing effects have been appreciated by dental patients around the world, and even Pope Leo XIII enjoyed a bottle of the coca wine produced by an Italian physician, who amassed a great fortune from its sale in the nineteenth century. The literary world, too, was soon stimulated by this white powder: in 1885 Robert Louis Stevenson wrote *Dr Jekyll and Mr Hyde* during six speedy days and nights while taking this "wonder drug" as a remedy for his tuberculosis, and Sir Arthur Conan Doyle, writing in the 1890s, used the character of Sherlock Holmes to defend the use of cocaine. On a more popular level, coca was one of the essential ingredients in Coca Cola until 1906. Today, cocaine is the most fashionable – and expensive – of drugs.

From its humble origins cocaine has become very big business. Unofficially, it may well be the biggest export for countries like Peru and Bolivia, where coca grows best in the Andes and along the edge of the jungle. While most mountain peasants always cultivated a little for personal use, many have now become dependent on it for obvious economic reasons: coca is still the most profitable cash crop and is readily bought by middlemen operating for extremely wealthy cocaine barons. A constant flow of semi-refined coca – pasta, the basic paste – leaves Peru aboard Amazon river boats or unmarked light aircraft heading for the big-time laboratories in Colombia. From here the pure stuff is shipped or flown out, mostly to the USA via Miami or Los Angeles. Much of the rest is refined in Peruvian cocaine "kitchens" in the *ceja de selva* or Lima, before finding its way into nostrils of wealthy Limeños, or going over the border into Brazil and further afield.

Few people care to look beyond the wall of illicit intrigue that surrounds this highly saleable contraband. In the same vein as coffee or chocolate, the demand for this product has become another means through which the privileged world controls the lives of those in the developing world, at the same time endangering the delicate environmental balance of the western edge of Amazonia. As Peruvian Indians follow world market trends by turning their hands to the growing and "cooking" of coca, more staple crops like cereals, tubers and beans are cultivated less and less.

It's a change brought about partly by circumstance. Agricultural prices are state controlled, but manufactured goods and transport costs rise almost weekly, preventing the peasants from earning a decent living from their crops. Moreover, the soil is poor and crops grow unwillingly. Coca, on the other hand, grows readily and needs little attention.

PERUVIAN RECIPES

Peruvian cooking – even in small restaurants well away from the big cities – is appealing stuff. The nine recipes below are among the classics, fairly simple to prepare and (with a couple of coastal exceptions) found throughout the country. If you're travelling and camping you'll find all the ingredients listed readily available in local markets; we've suggested alternatives if you want to try them when you get home. All quantities given are sufficient for four people.

Ceviche

A cool, spicy dish, eaten on the Peruvian coast for at least the past thousand years.
1kg soft white fish (lemon sole and halibut are good, or you can mix half fish, half shellfish)
2 large onions, sliced
1 or 2 chillis, chopped
6 limes (or lemons, but these aren't so good)
1 tbsp olive oil
1 tbsp fresh coriander or cilantro leaves
salt and pepper to taste
Wash and cut the fish into bite-sized pieces. Place in a dish with the sliced onions. Add the chopped chilli and coriander. Make a marinade using the lime juice, olive oil, salt and pepper. Pour over the fish and place in a cool spot until the fish is "soft cooked" (from 10 to 60min). Serve with boiled potatoes (preferably sweet) and corn-on-the-cob.

Papas a la Huancaina

An excellent and ubiquitous snack – cold potatoes covered in a mildly *picante* cheese sauce.
1 kg potatoes, boiled
1 or 2 chillis, chopped
2 cloves of garlic, chopped
200g soft goat's cheese (feta is ideal, or cottage cheese will do)
6 saltines or crackers
1 hardboiled egg
1 small can of evaporated milk
Chop very finely or liquidize all the above ingredients except for the potatoes. The mixture should be fairly thin but not too runny. Pour sauce over the thickly sliced potatoes. Arrange on a dish and serve garnished with lettuce and black olives. Best served chilled.

Palta Rellena

Stuffed avocados – another very popular snack.
2 avocados, soft but not ripe
1 onion, chopped
2 tomatoes, chopped
2 hardboiled eggs, chopped
200g cooked chicken or tuna fish, cold and flaked
2 tbsp mayonnaise
Cut the avocados in half and remove the stones. Scoop out a little of the flesh around the hole. Gently combine all other the ingredients before piling into the centre of each avocado half.

Causa

About the easiest Peruvian dish to reproduce outside the country, though there are no real substitutes for Peruvian tuna and creamy Andean potatoes.
1kg potatoes
200g tuna fish
2 avocados, the riper the better
4 tomatoes
salt and black pepper
1 lemon
Boil the potatoes and mash to a firm, smooth consistency. Flake the tuna fish and add a little lemon juice. Mash the avocados to a pulp, add the rest of lemon juice, some salt and black pepper. Slice the tomatoes. Press one quarter of the tuna fish over this, then a quarter of the avocado mixture on top. Add a layer of sliced tomato. Continue the same layering process until you have four layers of each. Cut into rough slices. Serve (ideally chilled) with salad, or on its own as a starter.

Locro de Zapallo

A vegetarian standard found on most set menus in the cheaper, working-class restaurants.
1kg pumpkin
1 large potato
2 cloves of garlic
1 tbsp oregano
1 cup of milk
2 corn-on-the-cobs
1 onion
1 chilli, chopped
salt and pepper
200g cheese (mozzarella works well)

Fry the onion, chilli, garlic and oregano. Add half a cup of water. Mix in the pumpkin as large cut lumps, slices of corn on the cob, and finely chopped potato. Add the milk and cheese. Simmer until a soft, smooth consistency, and add a little more water if necessary. Serve with rice or over fish.

Pescado a la Chorillana

Probably the most popular way of cooking fish on the coast.
4 pieces of fish (cod or any other white fish will do)
2 large onions, chopped
4 large tomatoes, chopped
1 or 2 chillis, chopped into fairly large pieces
1 tbsp oil
Half a cup of water

Grill or fry each portion of fish until done. Keep hot. Fry separately the onions, tomatoes, and chilli. Add the water to form a sauce. Pile the hot sauce over each portion of fish and serve with rice.

Asado

A roast. An expensive meal for Peruvians, though a big favourite for family gatherings. Only available in fancier restaurants.
1kg or less of lean beef
2 cloves of garlic
200g butter
1 tin of tomato puree
salt and pepper
1 tbsp soy sauce
2 tomatoes
1 chilli, chopped

Cover the beef with the premixed garlic and butter. Mix the tomato puree with salt, pepper and soy sauce. Liquidize the tomatoes with the chopped chilli. Spread both mixtures on the beef and cook slowly in a covered casserole dish for four or five hours. Traditionally the asado is served with *pure de papas*, which is simply a runny form of mashed potatoes whipped up with some butter and a lot of garlic. A very tasty combination.

Quinoa Vegetable Soup

Quinoa – known as "mother grain" in the Andes – is "a natural whole grain with remarkable nutritional properties", quite possibly a "super-grain" of the future. It's simple and tasty to add to any soups or stews.
4 cups of water
Quarter of a cup of quinoa
Half a cup of diced carrots
Quarter of a cup of diced celery
2 tbsp finely chopped onions
Quarter of a green pepper
2 mashed cloves of garlic
1 tbsp vegetable oil
Half a cup of chopped tomatoes
Half a cup of finely chopped cabbage
1 tbsp salt
Some chopped parsley

Gently fry the quinoa and all the vegetables (except the cabbage and tomatoes) in oil and garlic until browned. Then add the water, cabbage and tomatoes before bringing to the boil. Season with salt and garnish with parsley.

Aji de Gallina

Literally translated as "Chillied Chicken", this is not as spicy as it sounds, but utilizes a delicious choosy yellow sauce.
1 chicken breast
1 cup of breadcrumbs
2 soupspoons of powdered yellow chilli
50g of parmesan cheese
50g of ground nuts
1 cup of evaporated milk (more if the sauce seems too dry)
1 sliced onion (red or white)

Boil the chicken breast, then strain and fry it for a bit. Mix the hot chicken water with the breadcrumbs. Meanwhile, in a pot, heat 2 tablespoons full of olive oil and brown the onions. Mix in the yellow chilli powder. Mix in the breadcrumbs as liquidized as possible. After a few minutes still on the heat, add in the parmesan cheese, the chicken, salt to taste and finally the ground nuts. boil for another ten minutes. Add the evaporated milk just before serving and stir in well. Decorate the plate with boiled potatoes, preferably of the Peruvian yellow variety, if not white will do, cut into cross-sectional slices about a centimetre or so thick. Add a sliced egg and black olives on top.

Thanks to Señora Delia Arvi Tarazona for this recipe.

BOOKS

There are few books published exclusively about Peru and very few Peruvian writers ever make it into English. Many of the classic works on Peruvian and Inca history are now out of date, though frequently one comes across them in libraries around the world or bookshops in Lima and Cusco. Travel books, coffee-table editions and country guides are also generally available in Lima bookshops. Others can be obtained through the South American Explorers' Club, Avenida Portugal 146, Breña, between avenidas Bolivia and España (Mon–Sat 9.30am–5pm; ☎01/425-0142, www.samexplo.org, explore@samexplo.org), or from their main USA office at 126 Indian Creek Road, Ithaca, NY 14850, USA (☎607/277-0488, fax 277-6122).

INCA AND ANCIENT HISTORY

Elizabeth Benson, *The Mochica: A Culture of Peru* (o/p). Brief sketch of the Mochica civilization through its vast and astonishingly realist ceramic heritage.

Kathleen Berrin, *The Spirit of Ancient Peru: Treasures from the Museo Arqueológico Rafael Larco Herrera* (o/p). Essentially a detailed exhibition catalogue with essays by reputable Andeanists and plenty of quality illustrations and photographs representing one of Peru's finest collection of mainly pre-Inca artefacts.

Hiram Bingham, *Lost City of the Incas* (Greenwood Publishing, US). The classic introduction to Machu Picchu: the exploration accounts are interesting but many of the theories should be taken with a pinch of salt. Widely available in Peru.

Peter T. Bradley, *The Lure of Peru: Maritime Intrusion into the South Sea 1598–1701* (o/p). A historical account of how the worldwide fame of the country's Inca treasures attracted Dutch, French and English would-be settlers, explorers, merchants and even pirates to the seas and shores of Peru. It includes descriptions of naval blockades of Lima and various waves of buccaneers and their adventures in search of Peru.

Richard Burger, *Chavín and the Origins of Andean Civilisation* (Thames and Hudson). A collection of erudite essays, essential reading for anyone seriously interested in Peruvian prehistory.

Geoffrey Hext Sutherland Bushnell, *Peru* (o/p). A classic, consice introduction to the main social and technological developments in Peru from 2500 BC to 1500 AD; well illustrated, if dated in some aspects.

Evan Hadingham, *Lines to the Mountain Gods: Nazca and the Mysteries of Peru* (University of Oklahoma, US). One of the more down-to-earth books on the Nazca Lines, including maps and illustrations – also available through the *South American Explorers' Club* in Lima.

John Hemming, *The Conquest of the Incas* (Papermac). The authoritative narrative tale of the Spanish Conquest, very readably brought to life from a mass of original sources.

Thor Heyerdahl, Daniel Sandweiss and Alfredo Navárez, *Pyramids of Túcume*. A recently published description of the archaeological site at Túcume plus the life and society of the civilisation which created this important ceremonial and political centre around 1000 years ago. Widely available in Peruvian bookshops.

Richard Keatinge (ed), *Peruvian Prehistory* (Cambridge University Press). One of the most up-to-date and reputable books on the ancient civilizations of Peru – a collection of serious academic essays on various cultures and cultural concepts through the millennia prior to the Inca era.

Ann Kendall, *Everyday Life of the Incas* (o/p). Accessible, very general description of Peru under Inca domination.

J. Alden Mason, *Ancient Civilisations of Peru* (Penguin). Reprinted in 1991, an excellent summary of the country's history from the Stone Age through to the Inca Empire.

Michael E. Moseley, *The Incas and their Ancestors* (Thames and Hudson). A fine overview of Peru before the Spanish Conquest, which makes full use of good maps, diagrams, sketches, motifs and photos.

William Hickling Prescott, *History of the Conquest of Peru* (Random House). Hemming's main predecessor – a nineteenth-century classic that remains a good read, if you can find a copy.

Johan Reinhard, *Nazca Lines: A New Perspective on their Origin and Meaning* (Los Pinos, Lima). Original theories about the Lines and ancient mountain gods – available through the *South American Explorers' Club* and the better bookshops in Lima. The same author also wrote – *The Sacred Centre: Machu Picchu* (Nuevas Imagines, Lima), a fascinating book, drawing on anthropology, archeology, geography and astronomy to reach highly probable conclusions about the sacred geology and topography of the Cusco region and how this appears to have been related to Inca architecture, in particular Machu Picchu.

Gene Savoy, *Antisuyo: The Search For the Lost Cities of the Amazon* (o/p). Exciting account of Savoy's important explorations, plus loads of historical detail.

Garcilasco de la Vega, *The Royal Commentaries of the Incas* (2 vols, o/p). Many good libraries have a copy of this, the most readable and fascinating of contemporary historical sources. Written shortly after the Conquest, by a "Spaniard" of essentially Inca blood, this work is the best eyewitness account of life and beliefs among the Incas.

MODERN HISTORY AND SOCIETY

Americas Watch *Peru Under Fire: Human Rights since the Return to Democracy* (Human Rights Watch). A good summary of Peruvian politics of the 1980s.

Eduardo Calderon, *Eduardo El Curandero: The Words of a Peruvian Healer* (North Atlantic Books). Peru's most famous shaman – El Tuno – outlines his teachings and beliefs in his own words.

Carlos Cumes and Romulo Lizarraga Valencia, *Pachamamas Children: Mother Earth and Her Children of the Andes in Peru* (Llewellyn Publications, US). A New Age look at the culture, roots and shamanistic aspects of modern Peru.

F. Bruce Lamb and Manuel Cordova-Rios *The Wizard of the Upper Amazon* (Atlantic Books). Masterful reconstruction of the true story of Manuel Cordoba Rios – "Ino Moxo" – a famous herbal healer and *ayahuascero* from Iquitos who was kidnapped and brought up by Indians in the early twentith century. Offers significant insight into indigenous psychedelic healing traditions.

Nicole Maxwell, *Witch-Doctor's Apprentice* (o/p). A very personal and detailed account of the author's research into the healing plants used by Amazonian Peruvian tribes; a highly informative book on plantlore.

E. Luis Martin, *The Kingdom of the Sun: A Short History of Peru* (o/p). The best general history, concentrating on the post-Conquest period and bringing events up to the 1980s.

Michael Reid, *Peru: Paths to Poverty* (o/p). A succinct analysis tracing Peru's economic and security crisis of the early 1980s back to the military government of General Velasco.

David Scott Palmer (ed), *Shining Path of Peru* (C. Hurst & Co, UK; St Martin's Press, US). A modern history compilation of meticulously detailed essays and articles by Latin American academics and journalists on the early and middle phases of Sendero Luminoso's civil war in Peru.

Starn, Degregori and Kirk (ed), *The Peru Reader: History, Culture, Politics* (Latin American Bureau, UK; Duke University Press, US). One of the best overviews yet of Peruvian history and politics, with writing by characters as diverse as Mario Vargas Llosa and Abimael Guzman (imprisoned ex-leader of Sendero Luminoso).

FLORA AND FAUNA

J.L. Castner, S.L. Timme and J.A. Duke, *A Field Guide to Medicinal and Useful Plants of the Upper Amazon* (Feline Press). A guide to the most common and useful plants of the Upper Amazon, of interest to enthusiasts and scientists alike. Contains handy colour plates.

Checklist of the Birds of Peru (Buteo Books). A useful summary with photos of different habitats.

L.H. Emmons, *Neotropical Rainforest Mammals: a Field Guide* (University. of Chicago Press). An excellent paperback with over 250 pages of authoritative text, 29 colour plates, and other illustrations covering 260 species.

V. de Feo *Medicinal and Magical Plants in the Northern Peruvian Andes*, (Fitoterapia 63: 417-440). A key book for students of ethnobotany or anyone interested in learning the finer details of plant magic in Peru.

Steven L. Hilty and William L. Brown, *A Guide to the Birds of Colombia* (Princeton University Press, US; OUP, UK). One of the few classic ornithology guides covering the fascinating and rich birdlife of Peru and its surrounding countries. It contains 69 colour and black and white plates, is over 800 pages long and has a useful index.

M. Koepke *The Birds of the Department of Lima* (Harrowood Books). A small but classic guide, for many years the only one available that covered many of Peru's species, and still good for its excellent illustrations.

Richard E. Schultes and Robert F. Raffad, *The Healing Forest* (Dioscorides Press). An excellent and erudite large format paperback on many of the Amazon's most interesting plants. It's well illustrated with exquisite photographs and is a relatively easy read.

Richard E. Schultes and Robert F. Raffauf, *Vine of the Soul* (Synergetic Press). One of the the best large format books about the indigenous use and chemical basis of the hallucinogenic plant *ayahuasca*, so commonly used by tribal peoples in Peruvian Amazonia.

Walter Wust *Manu: el ultimo refugio* (Nuevas Imagenes, Lima). This is an excellent coffee-table book on the wildlife and flora of Manu National Park by one of Peru's foremost wildlife photographers. Available in most good bookshops in Lima and Cusco.

TRAVEL

Timothy E. Albright and Jeff Tenlow, *Dancing Bears and the Pilgrims Progress in the Andes: Transformation on the Road to Quolloriti* (University of Texas). A slightly dry report on the Snow Star annual festival of Quolloriti, which is attended by tens of thousands of Andean peasants at the start of every dry season.

Patrick Leigh Fermor, *Three Letters from the Andes* (Penguin). Three long letters written from Peru in 1971 describing the experiences of a rather uppercrust mountaineering expedition.

Christopher Isherwood, *The Condor and the Cows* (o/p). A diary of Isherwood's South American trip after World War II, most of which took place in Peru. Like Theroux, Isherwood

eventually arrives in Buenos Aires, to meet Jorge Luis Borges.

Dervla Murphy, *Eight Feet in the Andes* (Flamingo). An enjoyable account of a rather adventurous journey Dervla Murphy made across the Andes with her young daughter and a mule. It can't compare with her Indian books, though.

Matthew Paris, *Inca Kola, A Travellers Tale of Peru* (Phoenix). Very amusing description of travelling in Peru, with a perspicacious look at Peruvian culture, past and present.

Tom Pow, *In the Palace of Serpents: An Experience of Peru* (Canonate Press). A well-written insight into travelling in Peru, spoilt only by the fact that Tom Pow was ripped off in Cusco and lost his original notes. Consequently he didn't have as wonderful a time as he might have and seemed to miss the beauty of the Peruvian landscapes and the wealth of its history and culture.

Paul Theroux, *The Old Patagonian Express* (Penguin). Theroux didn't much like Peru, nor Peruvians, but for all the self-obsessed pique and disgust for most of humanity, at his best – being sick in trains – he is highly entertaining.

George Woodcock, *Incas and Other Men* (o/p). An enjoyable, light-hearted tour, mixing modern and ancient history and travel anecdotes, that is still a good introduction to Peru over fifty years after the event.

Ronald Wright, *Cut Stones and Crossroads: A Journey in the Two Worlds of Peru* (Penguin). An enlightened travel book and probably the best general travelogue writing on Peru over the last few decades, largely due to the author's depth of knowledge on his subject.

PERUVIAN WRITERS

Martín Adán, *The Cardboard House* (Graywolf Press, Minnesota). A poetic novel based in Lima and written by one of South America's best living poets.

Ciro Alegría, *Broad and Alien is the World* (Merlin Press). Another good book to travel with, this is a distinguished 1970s novel offering persuasive insight into life in the Peruvian highlands.

Jose Maria Arguedas, *Deep Rivers* (Pergamon Press, Spanish-language edition only), *Yawar Fiesta* (Quartet Books). Arguedas is an *indigenista* – writing for and about the native peoples. Yawar Fiesta focusses on one of the most impressive Andean peasant ceremonial cycles involving the annual rite of pitching a live condor against a bull, the condor representing the indigenous Indians and the bull the Spanish conquistadores.

Mario Vargas Llosa, *Death in the Andes* (Faber & Faber), *A Fish in the Water* (Farrar, Straus and Giroux), *Aunt Julia and the Scriptwriter* (Picador), *The Time of the Hero* (Picador), *Captain Pantoja and the Special Service* (Faber), *The Green House* (Picador), *The Real Life of Alejandro Mayta* (Faber), *The War of the End of the World* (Faber), *Who Killed Palomino Molero?* (Faber). The best-known and the most brilliant of contemporary Peruvian writers, Vargas Llosa is essentially a novelist but has also written on Peruvian society, run his own TV current affairs programme in Lima, and even made a (rather average) feature film. *Death in the Andes* deals with Sendero Luminoso and Peruvian politics in a style which goes quite a long way towards illuminating popular Peruvian thinking in the late 1980s and early 90s. His ebullient memoir, *A Fish in the Water*, describes, among other things, Vargas Llosa's experience in his unsuccessful running for Peruvian presidency. *Aunt Julia*, the best known of his novels to be translated into English, is a fabulous book, a grand and comic novel spiralling out from the stories and exploits of a Bolivian scriptwriter who arrives in Lima to work on Peruvian radio soap-operas. In part, too, it is autobiographical, full of insights and goings-on in Miraflores society. Essential reading – and perfect for long Peruvian journeys.

Cesar Vallejo, *Collected Poems of Cesar Vallejo* (Penguin). Peru's one internationally renowned poet – and deservedly so. Romantic but highly innovative in style, it translates beautifully.

NOVELS SET IN PERU

Peter Mathiessen, *At Play in the Fields of the Lord* (Collins Harvill). A celebrated American novel, which catches the energy and magic of the Peruvian *selva*.

James Redfield, *The Celestine Prophecy* (Bantam). A best-selling novel that uses Peru as a backdrop. Despite not having much to say about Peru, it's a popular topic of conversation among travellers these days; some were actually inspired to visit Peru from having read this

intriguing book, which expresses with some clarity many New Age concepts and beliefs. Unfortunately the book's descriptions of the Peruvian people, landscapes, forests and culture, bear so little relationship to the Peruvian reality that it feels like the author has never been anywhere near Peru.

SPECIALIST GUIDES

John Biggar, *The High Andes: A Guide for Climbers* (Andes, 93 Queen Street, Castle Douglas, Kirkcudbrightshire DG7 1EH). The first comprehensive climbing guide to the main peaks of the Andes, with a main focus on Peru but also covering Bolivia, Ecuador, Chile, Argentina, Colombia and Venezuela.

Hilary and George Bradt, *Backpacking and Trekking in Peru and Bolivia* (Bradt). Detailed and excellent coverage of some of Peru's most rewarding hikes – worth taking if you're remotely interested in the idea, and good anyway for background on wildlife and flora.

Charles Brod, *Apus and Incas: A Cultural Walking and Trekking Guide to Cusco* (Bradt). An interesting selection of walks in the Cusco area. Available locally.

Richard Danbury, *The Inca Trail: Cuzco and Machu Picchu*. Good, highly informative and smoothly written guide to this trekking destination, with fine contextual pieces. Also inlcudes practical information for Lima.

Peter Frost, *Exploring Cusco* (Nueva Imagines, Lima). A very practical and stimulating site-by-site guide to the whole Cusco area (where it is widely available in bookstores). Unreservedly recommended if you're spending more than a few days in the region, and also for armchair archeologists back home.

Peter Frost and Jim Bartle, *Machu Picchu Historic Sanctuary* (Nuevo Imagines). A long-awaited, well-written and beautifully photographed coffee-table book on South America's most alluring archaeological site.

David Mazel, *Pure and Perpetual Snow: Two Climbs in the Andes*. Climbing reports on Ausangate and Alpamayo peaks. Available locally or from the South American Explorers' Club.

Lynn Meisch, *A Traveller's Guide to El Dorado and the Incan Empire* (Penguin). Huge paperback full of fascinating detail – well worth reading before visiting Peru.

LANGUAGE

Although Peru is officially a Spanish-speaking nation, a large proportion of its population, possibly more than half, regard Spanish as their second language. When the conquistadores arrived, Quechua, the official language of the Inca Empire, was widely spoken everywhere but the jungle. Originally known as Runasimi (from runa, "person", and simis, "mouth"), it was given the name Quechua – which means "high Andean valleys" – by the Spanish.

Quechua was not, however, the only pre-Columbian tongue. There were, and still are, well over **thirty Indian languages** within the jungle area and, up until the late nineteenth century, **Mochica** had been widely spoken on the north coast for at least 1500 years.

With such a rich linguistic history it is not surprising to find non-European words intruding constantly into any Peruvian conversation. *Cancha*, for instance, the Inca word for courtyard, is still commonly used to refer to most sporting areas – *la cancha de basketball*, for example. Other linguistic survivors have even reached the English language: *llama, condor, puma* and *pampa* among them. Perhaps more interesting is the great wealth of traditional **Creole slang** – utilized with equal vigour at all levels of society. This complex speech, much like Cockney rhyming slang, is difficult to catch without almost complete fluency in Spanish, though one phrase you may find useful for directing a taxi driver is *de fresa alfonso* – literally translatable as "of strawberry, Alfonso" but actually meaning "straight on" (*de frente al fondo*).

Once you get into it, **Spanish** is the easiest language there is – and in Peru people are eager to understand even the most faltering attempt. You'll be further helped by the fact that South Americans speak relatively slowly (at least compared to Spaniards in Spain) and that there's no need to get your tongue round the lisping pronunciation.

Among **dictionaries,** you could try the *Dictionary of Latin American Spanish* (University of Chicago Press).

PRONUNCIATION

The rules of **pronunciation** are pretty straightforward and, once you get to know them, strictly observed. Unless there's an accent, words ending in d, l, r, and z are **stressed** on the last syllable, all others on the second last. All **vowels** are pure and short.

A somewhere between the "A" sound of back and that of father
E as in get
I as in police
O as in hot
U as in rule
C is soft before E and I, hard otherwise: *cerca* is pronounced "serka".
G works the same way, a guttural "H" sound (like the ch in loch) before E or I, a hard G elsewhere – *gigante* becomes "higante".
H is always silent
J is the same sound as a guttural G: *jamon* is pronounced "hamon".
LL sounds like an English Y: *tortilla* is pronounced "torteeya".
N is as in English unless it has a tilde (accent) over it, when it becomes NY: *mañana* sounds like "manyana".
QU is pronounced like an English K.
R is rolled, RR doubly so.
V sounds more like B, *vino* becoming "beano".
X is slightly softer than in English – sometimes almost SH – except between vowels in place names where it has an "H" sound – for example México (Meh-Hee-Ko) or Oaxaca.
Z is the same as a soft C, so *cerveza* becomes "servesa".

On the facing page is a list of a few essential words and phrases, though if you're travelling for any length of time a dictionary or phrase book is obviously a worthwhile investment – some specifically Latin American ones are avail-

BASICS

Yes, No	*Sí, No*	Open, Closed	*Abierto/a, Cerrado/a*
Please, Thank you	*Por favor, Gracias*	With, Without	*Con, Sin*
Where, When	*Dónde, Cuando*	Good, Bad	*Buen(o)/a, Mal(o)/a*
What, How much	*Qué, Cuanto*	Big, Small	*Gran(de), Pequeño/a*
Here, There	*Aquí, Allí*	More, Less	*Más, Menos*
This, That	*Este, Eso*	Today, Tomorrow	*Hoy, Mañana*
Now, Later	*Ahora, Más tarde*	Yesterday	*Ayer*

GREETINGS AND RESPONSES

Hello, Goodbye	*Hola, Adios*	I don't speak Spanish	*(No) Hablo español*
Good morning	*Buenos días*	My name is . . .	*Me llamo . . .*
Good afternoon/night	*Buenas tardes/noches*	What's your name?	*¿Como se llama usted?*
See you later	*Hasta luego*	I am English	*Soyinglés(a)*
Sorry	*Lo siento/disculpeme*	. . . American	*americano(a)*
Excuse me	*Con permiso/perdón*	. . . Australian	*australiano (a)*
How are you?	*¿Como está (usted)?*	. . . Canadian	*canadiense (a)*
I (don't) understand	*(No) Entiendo*	. . . Irish	*irlandés (a)*
Not at all/		. . . Scottish	*escosés (a)*
You're welcome	*De nada*	. . . Welsh	*galés (a)*
Do you speak English?	*¿Habla (usted)inglés?*	. . . New Zealander	*neozelandés (a)*

NEEDS - HOTELS AND TRANSPORT

I want	*Quiero*	How do I get to. . .?	*Por dónde se va a. . .?*
I'd like	*Querría*	Left, right, straight on	*Izquierda, derecha,*
Do you know. . .?	*¿Sabe. . .?*		*derecho*
I don't know	*No sé*	Where is. . .?	*¿Dónde está. . .?*
There is (is there)?	*(¿) Hay (?)*	. . .the bus station	*. . .la estación de*
Give me. . .	*Deme. . .*		*autobuses*
(one like that)	*(uno así)*	. . .the train station	*. . .la estación de*
Do you have. . .?	*¿Tiene . . .?*		*ferrocarriles*
. . .the time	*. . .la hora*	. . .the nearest bank	*. . .el banco más*
. . .a room	*. . .un cuarto*		*cercano*
. . .with two beds/	*. . .con dos camas/*	. . .the post office	*. . .el correo*
double bed . . .	*cama matriomonial*	. . .the toilet	*. . .el baño/sanitario*
It's for one person	*es para una persona*	Where does the bus	*¿De dónde sale el*
(two people)	*(dos personas)*	to. . . leave from?	*camión para. . .?*
. . .for one night	*. . .para una noche*	Is this the train for	*¿Es éste el tren para*
(one week)	*(una semana)*	Lima?	*Lima?*
It's fine, how much is it?	*¿Está bien, cuánto es?*	I'd like a (return)	*Querría un boleto (de ida*
It's too expensive	*Es demasiado caro*	ticket to. . .	*y vuelta) para. . .*
Don't you have	*¿No tiene algo*	What time does it	*¿A qué hora sale*
anything cheaper?	*más barato?*	leave (arrive in. . .)?	*(llega en. . .)?*
Can one. . . ?	*¿Se puede. . ?*	What is there to eat?	*¿Qué hay para comer?*
. . .camp (near) here?	*¿. . .acampar aqui*	What's that?	*¿Qué es eso?*
	(cerca)?	What's this called	*¿Como se llama este*
Is there a hotel nearby?	*¿Hay un hotel aquí cerca?*	in Spanish?	*en Castlllano?*

able (see above). If you're using a **dictionary**, bear in mind that in Spanish CH, LL, and Ñ count as separate letters and are listed after the Cs, Ls, and Ns respectively.

NUMBER AND DAYS

1	un/uno.una	16	dieci séis	1000	mil
2	dos	20	veinte	2000	dos mil
3	tres	21	veitiuno	first	primero/a
4	cuatro	30	trienta	second	segundo/a
5	cinco	40	cuarenta	third	tercero/a
6	seis	50	cincuenta		
7	siete	60	sesenta		
8	ocho	70	setenta	Monday	lunes
9	nueve	80	ochenta	Tuesday	marters
10	diez	90	noventa	Wednesday	miércoles
11	once	100	cien(to)	Thursday	jueves
12	doce	101	ciento uno	Friday	viernes
13	trece	200	doscientos	Saturday	sábado
14	catorce	201	doscientos uno	Sunday	domingo
15	quince	500	quinientos		

GLOSSARY OF PERUVIAN TERMS

ALLYU Kinship group, or clan

APU Mountain god

ARRIERO Muleteer

BARRIO Suburb, or sometimes shanty town

BURRO Donkey

CACIQUE Headman

CALLEJÓN Corridor, or narrow street

CAMPESINO Peasant, country dweller, someone who works in the fields

CEJA DE LA SELVA Edge of the jungle

CHACRA Cultivated garden or plot

CHAQUIRAS Pre-Columbian stone or coral beads

CHICHA Maize beer

COLECTIVO Collective taxi

CORDILLERA Mountain range

CURACA Chief

CURANDERO Healer

EMPRESA Company

ENCOMIENDA Colonial grant of land and native labour

EXTRANJERO/A Foreigner

FARMACIA Chemist

FLACO/A Skinny (common nickname)

GORDO/A Fat (common nickname)

GRINGO/A European or North American

HACIENDA Estate

HUACA Sacred spot or object

HUACO Pre-Columbian artefact

HUAQUERO Someone who digs or looks for *huacos*

JIRÓN Road

LOMAS Place where vegetation grows with moisture from the air rather than from rainfall or irrigation

MAMACONA Inca Sun Virgin

PEÑA Nightclub with live music

PLATA Silver; slang for "cash"

POBLADO Settlement

PUEBLOS JOVENES Shanty towns

PUNA Barren Andean heights

QUEBRADA Stream

SELVA Jungle

SELVATICO/A Jungle dweller

SIERRA Mountains

SERRANO Mountain dweller

SOROCHE Altitude sickness

TAMBO Inca Highway rest-house

TIENDA Shop

TRAMITES Red tape, bureaucracy

UNSU Throne, or platform

INDEX

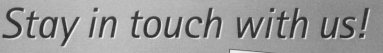

ROUGH GUIDES: Travel

Amsterdam
Andalucia
Australia

Austria
Bali & Lombok
Barcelona
Belgium &
  Luxembourg
Belize
Berlin
Brazil
Britain
Brittany &
  Normandy
Bulgaria
California
Canada
Central America
Chile
China
Corfu & the
  Ionian Islands
Corsica
Costa Rica
Crete
Croatia
Cyprus
Czech & Slovak
  Republics
Dodecanese &
  the East Aegean

Dominican
  Republic
Ecuador
Egypt
England
Europe
Florida
France
French Hotels &
  Restaurants
  1999
Germany
Goa
Greece
Greek Islands
Guatemala
Hawaii
Holland
Hong Kong &
  Macau
Hungary
India
Indonesia
Ireland
Israel & the
  Palestinian
  Territories
Italy
Jamaica
Japan
Jordan

Kenya
Lake District
Laos
London
Los Angeles
Malaysia,
  Singapore &
  Brunei
Mallorca &
  Menorca
Maya World
Mexico
Morocco
Moscow
Nepal
New England
New York
New Zealand
Norway
Pacific
  Northwest
Paris
Peru
Poland
Portugal
Prague
Provence & the
  Côte d'Azur
The Pyrenees
Rhodes & the
  Dodecanese

Romania
St Petersburg
San Francisco
Sardinia
Scandinavia
Scotland
Scottish
  highlands and
  Islands
Sicily
Singapore
South Africa
South India
Southwest USA
Spain
Sweden
Syria

Thailand
Trinidad &
  Tobago
Tunisia
Turkey
Tuscany &
  Umbria
USA
Venice
Vienna
Vietnam
Wales
Washington DC
West Africa
Zimbabwe &
  Botswana

AVAILABLE AT ALL GOOD BOOKSHOPS

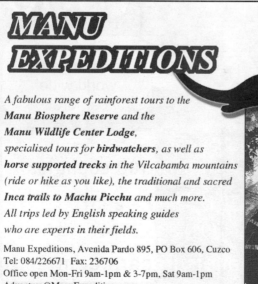